MAKING WAR AND BUILDING PEACE

MAKING WAR AND BUILDING PEACE

UNITED NATIONS PEACE OPERATIONS

Michael W. Doyle and Nicholas Sambanis

PRINCETON UNIVERSITY PRESS   PRINCETON AND OXFORD

Published by Princeton University Press, 41 William Street, Princeton, New Jersey 08540
In the United Kingdom: Princeton University Press, 3 Market Place, Woodstock, Oxfordshire OX20 1SY

Library of Congress Cataloging-in-Publication Data

Doyle, Michael W., 1948–
  Making war and building peace : United Nations peace operations / Michael W. Doyle and Nicholas Sambanis.
     p.   cm.
  Includes bibliographical references and index.
  ISBN-13: *978-0-691-12274-8 (cl : alk. paper)
  ISBN-13: *978-0-691-12275-5 (pb : alk. paper)
  ISBN-10: 0-691-12274-1 (cl : alk. paper)
  ISBN-10: 0-691-12275-X (pb : alk. paper)
     1. United Nations—Peacekeeping forces.   2. Peace-building.   3. Pacific settlement of international disputes.   I. Sambanis, Nicholas, 1967–   II. Title.

JZ6374.D69 2006
341.5'84—dc22   2005055060

British Library Cataloging-in-Publication Data is available

This book has been composed in Sabon

Printed on acid-free paper. ∞

pup.princeton.edu

Printed in the United States of America

10 9 8 7 6 5 4 3 2 1

For Abigail, best of daughters,
in hope that her world will experience more peace than has mine.
—Michael Doyle

To my parents, Panayiotis (Takis) and Elena Sambanis,
for their love and sacrifice.
—Nicholas Sambanis

Contents

List of Figures ix

List of Tables xi

List of Boxes xiii

Acknowledgments xv

Acronyms xvii

One
Introduction: War-Making, Peacebuilding, and the
United Nations 1

The New Interventionism 6
Generations of UN Peace Operations 10
The Challenge of Peacebuilding 18
Plan of the Book 23

Two
Theoretical Perspectives 27

Internal (Civil) War and Peacebuilding 28
Theories of Civil War 31
Implications of Civil War Theory for UN Intervention 49
A Peacebuilding Triangle 63

Three
Testing Peacebuilding Strategies 69

Triangulating Peace 69
The Peacebuilding Dataset 72
Analysis of Peacebuilding Success in the Short Run 86
Policy Hypotheses and Hypothesis Testing 93
Policy Analysis 125
Conclusion 131
Appendix A: Definitions and Coding Rules 132
Appendix B: Summary Statistics for Key Variables 138

Four
Making War 144

Somalia 145
The Former Yugoslavia 161

Congo   172
Clausewitz and Peacekeeping   184

Five
Making Peace: Successes   197

Monitoring and Facilitation in El Salvador   200
Administratively Controlling (but Barely)
    Peace in Cambodia   209
Executive Implementation of Peace in Eastern Slavonia   223
Dayton's Dueling Missions and Brcko—Dayton's
    Supervisory Footnote   230
East Timor   243

Six
Making Peace: Failures   257

Cyprus   257
Rwanda   281

Seven
Transitional Strategies   303

The Four Strategies   304
Transitional Authority   319

Eight
Conclusions   334

The Peacebuilding Record   334
A Seven-Step Plan   337
The Costs of Staying—and Not Staying—the Course   342
Alternatives?   346

Bibliography   353

Index   381

Figures

Figure 2.1 Matching Problem Type and Strategy Type 53
Figure 2.2 The Peacebuilding Triangle 64
Figure 3.1 The Peacebuilding Triangle 70
Figure 3.2 Predictors of Probability of Peacebuilding Success
    a) Effect of Development by Hostility Level 126
    b) Effect of Development by PKO and Treaty 126
    c) Effect of Factions for Low and High
       Local Capacities 126
    d) Effect of Deaths and Displacements by War Type 126
Figure 3.3 International Capacities in "Hard" and
       "Easy" Peacebuilding Ecologies
    a) Effect of Deaths by UN/Treaty in a Hard Case 129
    b) Effect of Development by UN/Treaty in a
       Hard Case 129
    c) Effect of Deaths and Displacements by UN/Treaty in
       an Easy Case 129
    d) Effect of Development by UN/Treaty in an
       Easy Case 129
Figure 4.1 The Peacebuilding Triangle in Somalia 157
Figure 4.2 The Peacebuilding Triangle in Bosnia 171
Figure 4.3 The Peacebuilding Triangle in Congo 181
Figure 5.1 The Peacebuilding Triangle in El Salvador 203
Figure 5.2 The Peacebuilding Triangle in Cambodia 212
Figure 5.3 The Peacebuilding Triangle in Croatia
       (Eastern Slavonia) 227
Figure 5.4 The Peacebuilding Triangle in East Timor 247
Figure 6.1 The Peacebuilding Triangle in Cyprus, 1974 259
Figure 6.2 UNFICYP Troops, 1964–1998 271
Figure 6.3 Shooting Incidents in Cyprus, 1964–1975 274
Figure 6.4 The Peacebuilding Triangle in Rwanda, 1990–1993 281

Tables

Table 3.1 Civil Wars Starting in 1945–1999 and Peacebuilding
Outcomes, Two Years after the "Peace Stimulus"   76
Table 3.2 Issues, War Outcomes, and War Recurrence   87
Table 3.3 Issues, War Outcomes, and Peacebuilding Outcomes   89
Table 3.4 Peacebuilding Outcomes by Type of UN Mandate   90
Table 3.5 Logit Models of Participatory Peacebuilding Success
Two Years after the "Stimulus"   94
Table 3.6 First Differences of the Estimated Probability of
Success in Participatory Peace   116
Table 3.7 Index Models of Peacebuilding Success   124
Table B.1 Summary Statistics   139
Table 4.1 Somalia   159
Table 4.2 Former Yugoslavia   170
Table 4.3 Congo   180
Table 4.4 Total Staff Assigned on a Full-Time Basis to Support
Complex Peacekeeping Operations Established in 1999   190
Table 5.1 El Salvador   204
Table 5.2 Cambodia   210
Table 5.3 Croatia   226
Table 5.4 Indonesia and East Timor   245
Table 6.1 Cyprus   260
Table 6.2 Rwanda   283
Table 7.1 Ecologies of Transitional Politics   322
Table 7.2 Local Capacities and Ecologies of Transitional Politics   323
Table 7.3 Transitional Authority   332

Boxes

Box 4.1 UNOSOM II Mandate   150
Box 4.2 UNPROFOR's Mandate   165
Box 4.3 ONUC's Mandate   176
Box 5.1 ONUSAL's Mandate   207
Box 5.2 UNTAC's Mandate   214
Box 5.3 UNTAES's Mandate   224
Box 5.4 UNMIBH's Mandate   233
Box 5.5 Brcko Arbitration   237
Box 5.6 UNTAET's Mandate   249
Box 5.7 UNMISET's Mandate   254
Box 6.1 UNFICYP's Mandate   268
Box 6.2 UNAMIR's Mandate   290

Acknowledgments

This book addresses three audiences: policy makers/debaters, students, and political scientists. We have learned from each of them as well.

We have worked together on this study for a number of years and published preliminary results in the *American Political Science Review*[1] (which we further develop here) and are pleased to continue this partnership.

Michael Doyle particularly wants to thank the many colleagues in the United Nations from whom he has learned much of what he knows about peacebuilding. He had the great pleasure of serving as Assistant Secretary-General and Special Adviser to Secretary-General Kofi Annan from 2001 to 2003. His research for this book, however, was completed before he joined the Secretary-General's staff and the views expressed in no way reflect an official UN view of the matter. What they do reflect is the information and insights generously shared by local officials, extraordinary citizens, and dedicated military and civilian peacekeepers in Cambodia (1993 and 1996), El Salvador (1994), Eastern Slavonia in Croatia (1998 and 1999) and Brcko in Bosnia (1999 and 2000). He is also grateful for the delightful environment he enjoyed while drafting early versions of the chapters for this book at the Center for Advanced Study in the Behavioral Sciences, where he benefited from the support of a Hewlett Foundation Fellowship, the Center of International Studies and the Woodrow Wilson School of Princeton University, the Christian Johnson Endeavor Foundation, and the World Bank. He thanks students in courses at the Woodrow Wilson School at Princeton and Columbia's School of International and Public Affairs and Law School who stimulated productive rethinking of many of the propositions we include here. Colleagues at Stanford, Duke, Princeton, Brown, Yale, Columbia, the Fletcher School at Tufts, and the University of Wisconsin offered many helpful comments at various seminars. He also wants to express his gratitude for advice and assistance to Michael Barnett, Andrea Craig, Michael Dark, Kate Cronin-Furman, Page Fortna, Amy Gardner, Olena Jennings, Ian Johnstone, Bruce Jones, Shonar Lala, Moza Mfuni, Darren Rosenblum, Jessica Stanton, and Kimberly Marten—none of whom should be held responsible, but all of whom helped.

[1] Michael W. Doyle and Nicholas Sambanis, "International Peacebuilding: A Theoretical and Quantitative Analysis," *American Political Science Review* 94, 4 (December 2000): 778–801.

Nicholas Sambanis thanks Katherine Glassmyer, Annalisa Zinn, Jonah Schulhofer-Wohl, Douglas Woodwell, Daniela Donno, Ana Maria Arjona, and Steven Shewfelt for their help with revising and expanding various parts of the Doyle and Sambanis (2000) dataset. He also thanks seminar participants at Duke, Emory, Georgetown, Oxford, and Brown Universities, the Peace Research Institute in Oslo, Norway, and the Blankensee Workshop of the Free University of Berlin, Germany. Some of Sambanis's research for this project was conducted as part of his Ph.D. dissertation on United Nations peacekeeping, which was written under Michael Doyle's supervision at Princeton's Woodrow Wilson School and was supported by grants from the Mellon Foundation (Sawyer Fellowship) and Princeton's Center for International Studies and Hellenic Studies Program. This project on post–civil war peacebuilding was later integrated in the Project on the Political Economy of Civil Wars at the World Bank's Research Department, where Sambanis worked for two years, prior to joining Yale's Department of Political Science. His research for this book was supported by a grant from the World Bank's Post-Conflict Fund and Yale's Program on Hellenic Studies, and parts of the book were written while he was on academic leave at the Russell Sage Foundation in New York.

Both authors thank colleagues for helpful suggestions, including George Downs, Alan Gerber, Michael Gilligan, Donald Green, Håvard Hegre, Jeffrey Herbst, Robert Keohane, Alan Krueger, John Lapinski, Bruce Russett, Kenneth Scheve, Jack Snyder, Stephen Stedman, and James Sutterlin.

Nicholas Sambanis
New Haven, Connecticut

Michael Doyle
New York, New York
March 2005

Acronyms

ASEAN	Association of Southeast Asian Nations
ECOMOG	Economic Community of West African States Monitoring Group
IFOR	NATO Implementation Force in Bosnia
INTERFET	International Force in East Timor
NATO	North Atlantic Treaty Organization
OAS	Organization of American States
OAU	Organization of African Unity
ONUC	United Nations Operation in Congo
ONUCA	UN Observer Group in Central America
ONUMOZ	UN Operation in Mozambique
ONUSAL	UN Observer Mission in El Salvador
SC	Security Council
SFOR	NATO Stabilization Force (in Bosnia)
SRSG	Special Representative of the Secretary General
UN	United Nations
UNAMIR	UN Assistance Mission for Rwanda
UNAVEM	UN Angola Verification Mission
UNFICYP	United Nations Force in Cyprus
UNHCR	United Nations High Commissioner for Refugees
UNICEF	United Nations Children's Fund
UNITAF	Unified Task Force (in Somalia)
UNMIBH	United Nations Mission in Bosnia and Herzegovina
UNMISET	United Nations Mission of Support in East Timor
UNOSOM I	UN Operation in Somalia I
UNOSOM II	UN Operation in Somalia II
UNPROFOR	UN Protection Force
UNTAC	UN Transitional Authority in Cambodia
UNTAES	United Nations Transitional Authority in Eastern Slavonia, Baranja, and Western Sirmium
UNTAG	UN Transitional Assistance Group (Namibia)

MAKING WAR AND BUILDING PEACE

1

Introduction: War-Making, Peacebuilding, and the United Nations

THE COLLAPSE OF STATE institutions in Somalia, a coup in Haiti, and civil wars in Bosnia, Cambodia, El Salvador, Guatemala, and other countries have marked the distinctive contours of civil strife in the past twenty years. The international community's responses to these emergencies have been, despite sometimes major efforts, mixed at best: occasional successes in restoring a legitimate and effective government are matched by striking failures to do so.

At the end of the Cold War, the member states of the United Nations (UN) expanded its agenda, defining a near revolution in the relation between what is in the legitimate realm of state sovereignty and what is subject to legitimate international intervention. From 1990 through 1993, the UN Security Council adopted a strikingly intrusive interpretation of UN Charter Chapter VII, the enforcement provisions concerning international peace and security. Member states thus endorsed a radical expansion in the scope of collective intervention just as a series of ethnic and civil wars erupted across the globe. Unfulfilled commitments, on the one hand, and escalating use of force, on the other, soon provoked a severe crisis in "peace enforcement." In Bosnia and Somalia "peace enforcement" amounted to "war-making" as the United Nations threatened to impose by force outcomes—ranging from disarmament, to safe havens, "no fly zones," and new state borders—on armed factions that recognized no political authority superior to their own.[1] Elsewhere, as in Rwanda, the UN record was a failure even to attempt to exercise enforcement as peace agreements fell apart. As a consequence, more than 700,000 Tutsis and moderate Hutus fell at the hands of genocidal extremists that had seized the government. The current balance sheet on

---

[1] We realize that, and will explain below how, the UN regarded these activities as "peacekeeping" or "peace enforcement," not war-making. The parties, however, can have reason to see them differently. Imagine, for example, how the U.S. federal government would have viewed a decision of the European Concert in 1864 to establish Washington, Baltimore, Atlanta, Mobile, and New Orleans as "safe havens" and to ban all interference with American commerce in American territorial waters—a "no sail zone"—by either the federal government or the Confederacy. None of this questions whether the UNPROFOR operation in the former Yugoslavia was justified.

UN "war-making" thus suggests that while the UN has served an effective role in legitimizing enforcement coalitions for interstate, armed collective security (as in Korea and against Iraq in Gulf War I), the United Nations has proven to be a very ineffective peace enforcer, or war-maker, in the many intrastate, civil conflicts that emerged in the post–Cold War world.

But that is only half the story. At the same time, evidence from the peace operations in Namibia, El Salvador, Cambodia, Mozambique, Eastern Slavonia (Croatia), and East Timor suggests a seemingly contradictory (but actually complementary) conclusion. Here the UN succeeded in fostering peace through consent, building on an enhancement of Chapter VI–based peace-making negotiations and a creative, multidimensional implementation of the transitional authority that the peace agreements provided.

Clearly, consent does not guarantee success. The wars in Angola refuted each of the many agreements that supposedly settled them, and the Rwanda genocide belied the peace agreement signed at Arusha. Weak implementation undermines even the best of agreements. None, moreover, of the successfully implemented operations lacked challenges. In Cambodia the United Nations undertook a multidimensional peace operation—the United Nations Transitional Authority in Cambodia—but the peace it left behind in 1993 was partial as the Khmer Rouge resumed sporadic armed resistance. Cambodia also suffered a coup in 1997 and then struggled ahead with an elected government that has been accused of numerous election irregularities. In El Salvador, Guatemala, Namibia, Eastern Slavonia (Croatia), and Mozambique peace is firmer. But even there the long run prospects of social integration remain problematic. In Bosnia, the international community struggles to unite what emerged from the Dayton Peace process as a de facto partition. Current stability is a direct function of the coercive glue of NATO (Stabilization Force) peacekeeping. The international community intervened and assumed temporary sovereignty in Kosovo and East Timor. East Timor is now an independent state; the task of assisting the development of a viable polity in Kosovo has barely begun.

Despite overcoming many challenges and achieving many successes, the UN's future as peace-maker has been under challenge in the U.S. Congress and elsewhere from those who fail to understand how successful the UN has been and can continue to be in a "peacebuilding" role.[2]

---

[2] The U.S. Congress, National Security Revitalization Act (H.R. 7) included provisions for charging the UN for a wide range of indirect as well as direct costs of U.S. participation in peacekeeping. If it had been adopted in this form, the legislation (in the eyes of many expert witnesses) would have bankrupted UN peacekeeping as the United States and other states proceeded to charge the UN for what have been extensive voluntary commitments in support of UN peacekeeping efforts. See the testimony of Secretary of State Warren

Obviously, multilateral peacebuilding cannot replace national foreign policy, even in policies directed toward states in crisis. Not only does multilateral peace enforcement regularly fail, but multilateral peace-building, because of its impartial character, will not be the choice that states that seek unilateral advantages will choose. It is not the favored means to impose neo-imperial clients, acquire military bases, or garner economic concessions. Successful multilateral peacebuilding builds func-tioning states that can defend their own interests. But where states seek a sustainable peace to end a festering civil war, multilateral peacebuilding, when well designed and well managed, can produce that peace from which neighbors and the wider international community will benefit, and do so while sharing costs on a fair basis. Clearly, we should avoid "throwing the baby out with the bathwater."

Stopping civil wars has never been more important. Since the end of the Cold War period, almost all new armed conflicts have occurred within the territories of sovereign states.[3] Repeat civil wars in Rwanda and Angola, products of failed peace agreements, alone resulted in several million casualties in the 1990s. Internal (civil or intrastate) war has re-placed interstate war as the paramount concern of organizations charged with maintaining international peace and security. Civil wars have nega-tive security and economic externalities and can destabilize entire re-gions. Beyond the deaths and displacements that are caused directly by the war, civil wars also cause a deterioration of health levels for the en-tire region long after the fighting ends.[4] Civil wars have regional conta-gion or diffusion effects,[5] and they reduce rates of economic growth in both the directly affected countries and their neighbors.[6] Civil wars typi-cally do not occur between standing armies, but rather between a gov-ernment army, or militia, and one or more rebel organizations. Violence

Christopher (Thursday, January 26, 1995) and C. William Maynes (January 19, 1995) be-fore the House International Relations Committee.

[3] There have been few interstate wars, including the war between Ethiopia and Eritrea—which is itself the continuation of an earlier internal war—the Gulf War in 1991, the U.S. invasion of Afghanistan and Iraq in 2001 and 2004, respectively, and the war in the Demo-cratic Republic of the Congo, which involved many neighboring states and had a large civil war component.

[4] Hazem Ghobarah, Paul Huth, and Bruce Russett, "Civil Wars Kill and Maim People, Long after the Fighting Stops," *American Political Science Review* 97 no. 2 (2003): 189–202.

[5] Michael E. Brown, "The Causes and Regional Dimensions of Internal Conflict," in *In-ternational Dimensions of Internal Conflict* (Cambridge: MIT Press, 1996), 571–602; D. A. Lake and D. Rothchild, eds., *The International Spread of Ethnic Conflict: Fear, Diffu-sion, and Escalation* (Princeton: Princeton University Press, 1998); Nicholas Sambanis, "Do Ethnic and Non-ethnic Civil Wars Have the Same Causes? A Theoretical and Empiri-cal Inquiry (part 1)," *Journal of Conflict Resolution* 45, no. 3 (2001): 259–82.

[6] James C. Murdoch and Todd Sandler, "Economic Growth, Civil Wars, and Spatial Spillovers," *Journal of Conflict Resolution* 46 (February 2002): 91–110.

is usually targeted at civilians, and the objectives of civil wars range from secession to control of the state or resource predation. Civilian deaths as a percentage of all war-related deaths increased to 90 percent in 1990 from approximately 50 percent in the eighteenth century. Internal wars have created approximately 13 million refugees and 38 million internally displaced persons.[7]

This book will discuss theories of the origins of and solutions to civil wars, the principles behind and the practices of the United Nations as an institution, and the debate over doctrines and strategies of intervention. But its key purpose is to explain how the international community, and the UN in particular, can assist the reconstruction of peace in civil war–torn lands. We address the policy problem, but we assess it in ways that draw on and apply relevant theories and methods in political science.

We focus on the international role in peacebuilding, even though it is only part of what makes for success or failure. We will argue that "sustainable peace" is the measure of successful peacebuilding. Our central claim is that successful and unsuccessful efforts to resolve civil wars are influenced by three key factors that characterize the environment of the postwar civil peace:

1. the degree of hostility of the factions (measured in terms of human cost—deaths and displacements—the type of war, and the number of factions);

2. the extent of local capacities remaining after the war (measured, for example, in per capita GDP or energy consumption); and

3. the amount of international assistance (measured in terms of economic assistance or the type of mandate given to a UN peace operation and the number of troops committed to the peace effort).

Together, these three constitute the interdependent logic of a "peacebuilding triangle": *the deeper the hostility, the more the destruction of local capacities, the more one needs international assistance to succeed in establishing a stable peace.*[8] We find support for this hypothesis both in our case studies and in our statistical analysis of all civil wars since 1945. Controlling for levels of hostility and local capacities, we find that the international capacities—UN missions with a mandate and resources to build peace—increase the chance for peace after civil war.

[7] United Nations High Commissioner for Refugees, "State of the World's Refugees, 1997–98," cited in Michael W. Doyle and Anne Bayefski, "Sustainable Refugee Return: A Report of a Workshop at Princeton University," Unpublished paper, Princeton University (February 1998).

[8] Michael Doyle and Nicholas Sambanis, "International Peacebuilding: A Theoretical and Quantitative Analysis," *American Political Science Review* 94, no. 4 (2000): 779–801.

We find that peace operations must be designed to fit the case, with the kind and degree of international authority to shape the transition from war to peace. The valuable monitoring that can be sufficient to reinforce trust and serve as a midwife to peace in one case is the idle observer that merely witnesses the collapse of a peace among hostile factions in a second case that would have required robust transitional executive authority for success.

We further find that peace operations supplemented by extensive programs to rebuild economies have a particularly prominent role in promoting long-run peace. Peacebuilding requires the provision of temporary security, the building of new institutions capable of resolving future conflicts peaceably, and an economy capable of offering civilian employment to former soldiers and material progress to future citizens.

Peacebuilding, however, does not require that the United States, or another great power, take the lead. When residual violence is plentiful, such leadership may be necessary. In less violent circumstances, however, multilateralism works well, delivering the legitimacy, staying power, experienced UN peacekeepers, and multiple sources of modest national commitment that it promises.

Lastly, controversially, we find that peacebuilding trumps military victories. Most civil wars since World War Two have been settled by military victory, and these victories can deliver a stable peace by eliminating the organized military opposition that truces leave in place to stir up future trouble. But a comprehensive peace agreement implemented through a peace operation has an even better success rate.

Our policy message is simple: while the UN is very poor at "war," imposing a settlement by force, it can be very good at "peace," mediating and implementing a comprehensively negotiated peace. This will not shock the insiders. What is new in this book is demonstrating this assertion carefully and explaining why and how this is the case. In exploring "why" we argue that the UN, as a multilateral organization, cannot manage force as rationally as is necessary but it is well suited to mediate, mobilize, and manage legitimate international assistance. These institutional capacities reflect wider views on the illegitimacy of colonialism and the growing acceptability of peacekeeping and peacebuilding.[9]

---

[9] That is not to say that multilateral management guarantees either good or selfless management. Peacekeeping operations can be, and have been, exploited for private or national gain, as the "Oil for Food" investigation has alleged (July 2005). Ordinary peacekeeping operations generate opportunities for profit, as Michael Bhatia has illustrated in "Postconflict Profit: The Political Economy of Intervention," *Global Governance* 11 (2005): 205–24. Multilateralism, nonetheless, has value in establishing internationally agreed common ground, mitigating the exploitation of simple national advantage and enhancing transparency. In 2003–4, for example, the importance attached by the United

In explaining "how" we identify the sources of failures in UN war-making and explore the four innovations (enhanced forms of peacemaking, peacekeeping, peacebuilding, and "discrete enforcement") that led to success. And we describe how the authority embedded in peacebuilding operations must be tailored to the circumstances they face.

These conclusions are important, partly because the use of UN authorized peace operations greatly increased in the 1990s, reflecting a new wave of interventionism and redefining a new generation of strategies in peacekeeping designed to fulfill the ambitious expectations unleashed by the new willingness to intervene. The connections between interventionism, new strategies, and successful peacebuilding were intimate and serious: no matter how well intentioned an intervention is, unless the intervenor can also claim that the intervention is likely to produce a sustainable improvement—both peace and human rights—the intervention is unlikely to be either ethically justifiable or politically viable.

The New Interventionism

As Secretary-General Kofi Annan memorably described the new UN role in 1998: "Our job is to intervene: to prevent conflict where we can, to put a stop to it when it has broken out, or—when neither of those things is possible—at least to contain it and prevent it from spreading."[10] He was reflecting the activism of the Security Council, which between 1987 and 1994 had quadrupled the number of resolutions it issued, tripled the peacekeeping operations it authorized, and multiplied by seven the number of economic sanctions it imposed per year. Military forces deployed in peacekeeping operations increased from fewer than 10,000 to more than 70,000. The annual peacekeeping budget skyrocketed correspondingly from $230 million to $3.6 billion in the same period, thus reaching to about three times the UN's regular operating budget of $1.2 billion.[11]

States and its coalition of allies in Iraq in both securing international legitimacy and mobilizing international assistance in peacebuilding there are one measure of this. One frequent critic of the UN, William Safire, even went so far as to acknowledge that the contrast between the successful elections in Afghanistan in October 2004 and the escalating crisis in Iraq could partly be attributed to the multilateral legitimacy the former enjoyed, in William Safire "The Best Political News of 2004," *New York Times*, October 26, 2004.

[10] Kofi Annan, "Reflections on Intervention," Ditchley Park, UK, June 26, 1998, in Kofi Annan, *The Question of Intervention* (New York: United Nations, 1999) p. 4.

[11] Boutros Boutros-Ghali, *Supplement to "An Agenda for Peace": Position Paper of the Secretary-General on the Occasion of the Fiftieth Anniversary of the United Nations*, A/50/60; S/1995/1, January 3, 1995, p. 4.

The activities of the Security Council in preventive diplomacy and sanctions, the Secretariat's role in election monitoring, and above all, the massive growth in peacekeeping and peace enforcement all testified to the newly appreciated role the international community wanted the UN—or somebody—to play.

The international legal prohibitions against intervention were more relevant than ever given the demands for national dignity made by the newly independent states of both the Third World and the former Second World. But the rules as to what constitutes intervention and what constitutes international protection of basic human rights shifted as well. Sovereignty was redefined to incorporate a global interest in human rights protection. The traditional borders between sovereign consent and intervention were blurred. Peacekeeping and peace enforcement almost merged into "robust peacekeeping," which signaled a willingness to use force if needed whether in consent-based peacekeeping or imposed peace enforcement. A newly functioning United Nations, moreover, was seen to be a legitimate agent to decide when sovereignty was and was not violated.

The revival of the UN Security Council led to a reaffirmation after years of Cold War neglect of the UN Charter's Article 2, clause 7 affirming nonintervention, except as mandated by the Security Council under Chapter VII. The UN then claimed a "cleaner hands" monopoly on legitimate intervention. Although the letter of the Charter prohibited UN authorizations of force other than as a response to threats or breaches of "international" peace, the Genocide Convention and the record of condemnation of colonialism and apartheid opened an informally legitimate basis for involvement in domestic conflict. The Security Council's practice thus broadened the traditional reasons for intervention, including aspects of domestic political oppression short of massacre and human suffering associated with economic misfeasance—the so-called failed states and the *droit d'ingerence*.[12] Building on new interpretations advanced during the Cold War that made, for example, apartheid a matter for international sanction, the United Nations addressed the starvation of the Somali people when it became clear that its government was incapable of doing so. (In this case, however, the traditional criteria of "international" threats were also invoked—including Somali refugees spread-

[12] See Lori F. Damrosch, ed., *Enforcing Restraint: Collective Intervention in Internal Conflicts* (New York: Council on Foreign Relations Press, 1993): G. Helman and S. Ratner, "Saving Failed States," *Foreign Policy* 89 (Winter 1992–93): 3–20: but for a more skeptical reading, Edward Mortimer, "Under What Circumstances Should the UN Intervene Militarily in a 'Domestic' Crisis?" in Olara Otunnu and Michael Doyle, eds., *Peacemaking and Peacekeeping for the New Century* (Lanham, MD.: Rowman and Littlefield, 1998), pp 111–44.

ing across international borders—in order to justify forcible intervention under Chapter VII.) The Security Council also demanded international humanitarian access to vulnerable populations, insisting, for example, that humanitarian assistance be allowed to reach the people affected in Yugoslavia and in Iraq.[13]

Regions differed on the meaning of operational sovereignty. The Association of Southeast Asian nations (ASEAN) remained a bastion of strict sovereignty, and nonintervention is the norm. Although Cambodia and Burma's acceptance into ASEAN were delayed by their human rights record and instability, they were both eventually accepted. The Organization of African Unity (OAU), on the other hand has defined standards of (1990) "Good Governance" that included democracy and declared (July 3, 1993) that internal disputes are matters of regional concern. And, more strikingly, the Organization of American States (in Res. 1080 and in the "Santiago Commitment of 1991") has declared coups against democracy illegitimate and has adopted economic sanctions against coups in Haiti and Peru. The European Union makes democracy an element in the criteria it demands for consideration in membership.

It was also important that the "international community" had a newly legitimate means of expressing its collective will on an internationally impartial basis. The Security Council lays claim to being the equivalent of a "global parliament" or "global jury"[14] representing not merely the individual states of which it is composed but also a collective will and voice

[13] In an important recent report, the International Commission on Intervention and State Sovereignty has affirmed and called upon the Security Council to recognize "a responsibility to protect." International Commission on Intervention and State Sovereignty, *The Responsibility to Protect* [Ottawa: International Development Research Centre, 2001]. States of course have the first responsibility to protect the basic rights and welfare of their citizens, but if they should fail to do so through lack of will or capacity, the responsibility should devolve, the commission argues, onto the international community, with the Security Council as its agent. Widely discussed, though not formally endorsed at the United Nations in 2002, the report sets a new benchmark against which future interventions and noninterventions will be judged. The report, however, deals less well with a separate problem: What should happen when the Security Council is deadlocked? Michael Walzer, in "The Politics of Rescue," *Dissent* (Winter 1995), has persuasively argued that the Security Council should not have the last word, when it comes up with the wrong answer. Tom Farer has explored the circumstances under which the responsibility to intervene devolves from a deadlocked Council to regional organizations and national governments. See Tom J. Farer, "Humanitarian Intervention before and after 9/11: Legality and Legitimacy," in J. L. Holzgrefe and Robert Keohane, eds., *Humanitarian Intervention: Ethical, Legal, and Political Dilemmas* (Cambridge: Cambridge University Press, 2003).

[14] Farer 2003; and Thomas Franck, "Interpretation and Change in the Law of Humanitarian Intervention," in J. L. Holzgrefe and Robert Keohane, eds., *Humanitarian Intervention: Ethical, Legal, and Political Dilemmas* (Cambridge: Cambridge University Press, 2003), p. 227.

of the "international community." The Security Council includes five permanent members (United States, Russia, France, the United Kingdom, and China) and ten nonpermanent, elected members, always including members from Asia, Africa, and Latin America. Its authorization for an intervention requires the affirmative vote of nine states, including no negative votes from the five permanent members (the P5) and four positive votes from the ten elected members. Such a vote would have to incorporate representatives of a variety of cultures, races, and religions. It would always include representatives of large and small countries, capitalist and socialist economies, and democratic and nondemocratic polities. If the mandated operation is UN directed and if troops and funding are required, many other troop contributing states will be needed, and they can say no in practice. The combination makes for a genuinely international impartial intervention, and hence "cleaner hands."

Those developments coincided with a temporary conjunction of power and will. Following the collapse of the USSR, the United States experienced a "unipolar moment" when its power eclipsed that of all other states. At the same time the international community, including the United States, adopted a strategy of "assertive multilateralism," which lasted from the Gulf War in January 1991 until the October 3, 1993, disaster in Mogadishu, Somalia. The Five Permanent Members of the Security Council, led by the United States, provided a degree of commitment and resourceful leadership that the UN had rarely seen before. Eschewing the national role of "Globocop" in order to address a pressing domestic agenda, the Clinton administration encouraged then UN Secretary-General Boutros Boutros-Ghali to take an ever more assertive role in international crises. The small dissenting minority in the Security Council—which included China on some occasions and Russia on others—was not prepared to resist the United States on issues that did not affect their paramount national interests. The successful reversal of Saddam Hussein's aggression in the Gulf and the December 1992 U.S.-led rescue of segments of the Somali population from starvation heralded what appeared to be a remarkable partnership. The Security Council decreed, the United States led, and—conveniently, for the while—many other states paid and supported.

But cleaner hands need not mean better hands. The international community still needed to find a way to promote sustainable peace, one that enlisted the support of a substantial majority of the local population and embodied basic principles of human rights. This proved to be a challenge in the 1990s as massive UN interventions, warlike enforcement operations, provoked some of the same sorts of resistance as did colonial interventions in places such as Somalia and Bosnia. But in other cases the UN found a way to cultivate consent and then build a peace with genuine indigenous roots. These peacebuilding operations rested on important innovations in peacemaking, peacekeeping, and institutional reconstruction, as well as discrete residual enforcement, all of which evolved to address particular aspects of these challenges.

Generations of UN Peace Operations

In the early 1990s, with the end of the Cold War, the UN's agenda for peace and security thus rapidly expanded. At the request of the UN Security Council Summit of January 1992, then Secretary-General Boutros Boutros-Ghali prepared the conceptual foundations of an ambitious UN role in peace and security in his seminal report, *An Agenda for Peace* (1992).[15] In addition to preventive diplomacy designed to head off conflicts before they became violent, the Secretary General outlined the four interconnected roles that he hoped the UN would play in the fast changing context of post–Cold War international politics.

- *preventive diplomacy*, undertaken in order "to prevent disputes from arising between parties, to prevent existing disputes from escalating into conflicts and to limit the spread of the latter when they occur." Involving confidence-building measures, fact-finding, early warning and possibly "preventive deployment" of UN authorized forces, preventive diplomacy seeks to reduce the danger of violence and increase the prospects of peaceful settlement.
- *peace enforcement*, authorized to act with or without the consent of the parties in order to ensure compliance with a cease-fire mandated by the Security Council acting under the authority of Chapter VII of the UN Charter, these military forces are composed of heavily armed national forces operating under the direction of the Secretary-General.
- *peacemaking*, designed "to bring hostile parties to agreement" through peaceful means such as those found in Chapter VI of the UN Charter. Drawing upon judicial settlement, mediation, and other forms of negotiation, UN peacemaking initiatives would seek to persuade parties to arrive at a peaceful settlement of their differences.
- *peacekeeping*, established to deploy a "United Nations presence in the field, hitherto with the consent of all the parties concerned," as a confidence-building measure to monitor a truce between the parties while diplomats strive to negotiate a comprehensive peace or officials to implement an agreed peace.

[15] Boutros Boutros-Ghali, *An Agenda for Peace: Report of the Secretary-General*, A/47/277-S/24111 (June 17, 1992), http://www.un.org/Docs/SG/agpeace.html. Quotes that follow are from paragraphs 20–21 and 55–99.

- *postconflict reconstruction,*[16] organized to foster economic and social cooperation with the purpose of building confidence among previously warring parties, developing the social, political, and economic infrastructure to prevent future violence, and laying the foundations for a durable peace.

The Secretary-General's Agenda for Peace is the culmination of an evolution of UN doctrine and an adjustment of the instruments used to maintain the peace since the organization was formed in 1945. It combines in a radical way instruments of warlike enforcement and peacelike negotiation that were once kept separate and that evolved separately. A unique vocabulary separates distinct strategies that fit within the generic UN doctrine of building peace. These strategies, evolving over time, have encompassed three generational paradigms of peacebuilding.[17] They include not only the early activities identified in UN Charter Chapter VI (or so-called 6 and 1/2)[18] *first generation* peacekeeping, which calls for the interposition of a force after a truce has been reached, but also a far more ambitious group of *second generation* operations that rely on the consent of parties and an even more ambitious group of *third generation* operations that operate with Chapter VII mandates and without a comprehensive agreement reflecting the parties' acquiescence. In today's circumstances, these operations involve less interstate conflict and more factions in domestic civil wars, not all of whom are clearly identifiable— and few of whom are stable negotiating parties. Current peace operations thus intrude into aspects of domestic sovereignty once thought to be beyond the purview of UN activity.

Indeed, the post–World War Two UN Charter can be seen as having been designed for interstate wars (e.g., Article 39's threats to "international" peace); appropriately so, since, from 1900 to 1941, 80 percent of all wars were interstate among state armies. But from 1945 to 1976, 85 percent of all wars were on the territory of one state and internally oriented—of course with proxies.[19]

---

[16] The Secretary-General and the UN often refers to this as "post-conflict peacebuilding." To avoid confusion with the wider meaning of peacebuilding we employ, we will call it postconflict reconstruction.

[17] It is worth recalling that the time line of evolution has by no means been chronologically straightforward. One of the most extensive "third generation" operations undertaken by the UN was ONUC in the then-Congo, from 1960 to 1964, which preceded the spate of "second generation" operations that began with UNTAG in Namibia in 1989.

[18] The "6 and 1/2" refers to the fact that peacekeeping per se is nowhere described in the Charter and thus falls between Chapter VI, peacemaking (good offices, etc.), and Chapter VII, peace enforcement.

[19] Ernst B. Haas, *The United Nations and Collective Management of International Conflict* (New York: UNITAR, 1986); and Henry Wiseman, "The United Nations and International Peace," in UNITAR, *The United Nations and the Management of International Peace and Security* (Lancaster: Martinus Nijhof, 1987), 219.

Traditional peace operations, or *first generation peacekeeping*, were designed to respond to interstate crises by stationing unarmed or lightly armed UN forces between hostile parties to monitor a truce, troop withdrawal, or buffer zone while political negotiations went forward.[20] As F. T. Liu, an eminent peacekeeping official of the UN has noted: monitoring, consent, neutrality, nonuse of force, and unarmed peacekeeping—the principles and practices of first generation peacekeeping—constituted a stable and interdependent combination. These key principles were articulated by Secretary-General Dag Hammarskjold and former Canadian prime minister Lester Pearson in conjunction with the creation of the first peacekeeping operation, the UN Emergency Force (UNEF) in the Sinai, which was sent to separate Israel and Egypt following the Franco-British-Israeli intervention in Suez in 1956.[21] The principle of neutrality referred to the national origin of UN troops and precluded the use of troops from the permanent five members of the Council in order to quiet fears of superpower intervention. Impartiality implied that the UN would not take sides in the dispute and was a precondition for achieving the consent of all the parties. Enjoying the consent of all factions in turn made it easier for monitors of peacekeepers not to have to use force except in self-defense.[22] Lastly, the Secretary-General exercised control of the force and the Security Council authorized it (or rarely, the General Assembly under the auspices of the "Uniting for Peace Resolution").[23]

[20] The first peacekeeping operation was the United Nations' Emergency Force (UNEF) in Egypt, deployed in October 1956 to maintain a truce between the Egyptian army and Israel, England, and France during the Suez crisis. UNEF's experience helped define the four principles of traditional peacekeeping: consent, impartiality, neutrality, and use of force only in self-defense. The UN Treaty Supervision Organization (UNTSO) was deployed in 1948 in Palestine, but it was a limited observer mission.

[21] United Nations, *The Blue Helmets*, 2d ed. (New York: United Nations, 1990), 5–7; and Brian Urquhart, *A Life in Peace and War* (London: Weidenfeld and Nicolson, 1987), p. 133.

[22] Traditional peacekeeping is a shorthand term that describes many but by no means all Cold War peacekeeping missions (the most notable exception being the Congo operation and possibly also the Cyprus operation, as we discuss later in the book). For cogent analyses of different types of peacekeeping, see Marrack Goulding, "The Evolution of United Nations Peacekeeping," *International Affairs* 69, no. 3 (1993): 451–64; F. T. Liu, *United Nations Peacekeeping and the Nonuse of Force*, International Peace Academy Occasional Paper Series (Boulder, CO: Lynne Rienner, 1992); Thomas G. Weiss, ed., *Collective Security in a Changing World* (Boulder CO: Lynne Rienner, 1993).

[23] A controversial resolution introduced in the context of the Korean War designed to circumvent the deadlock in the Security Council that resulted from the return of the USSR to the Council, following the boycott that allowed the Council in the USSR's absence to authorize the U.S.-led force in Korea in June 1950. It was applied to authorize the Sinai peace force in 1956.

Impartiality and *neutrality* are frequently used interchangeably. Scholars and practitioners often speak of peacekeepers as "neutral," "disinterested," "impartial," or "unbiased," and they tend to mistake the need for impartiality with a policy of "strict neutrality" and a disposition of passivity. In this book, we define neutrality as a synonym for noninterference with respect to peacekeeping outcomes and impartiality as equal enforcement of unbiased rules. Good cops act impartially but not neutrally when they stop one individual from victimizing another. We argue that it is as important for peacekeepers to be *impartial* concerning, for example, which party in a freely conducted democratic election wins the election as it is for them to be *nonneutral* (i.e., not passive) with respect to violations of the peace and obstructions to their ability to implement their mandate. This is closely related to the interpretation of the fourth principle of peacekeeping—the nonuse of force. Peacekeeping uses soldiers not to win wars, but rather to preserve the peace. But peacekeepers must also protect their right to discharge their functions, in accordance with the spirit of the parties' consent as extended at the outset of the operation. Raising the costs of noncooperation for the parties must, on occasion, allow the use of force in defense of the mandate. The limited use of force to protect a mandate authorized by a peace treaty or to enforce an agreed-upon cease-fire (as happened in Cyprus in 1974 or Namibia in 1989), does not equate peacekeeping with peace enforcement (which attempts to impose an overall settlement), but it does generate concerns with mission creep if the need to use force is extensive.

During the Cold War, the UN record indicated much success in interstate conflicts (while little in intrastate) and much in material and territorial settlement (while little in value or identity conflicts).[24] The success of traditional peacekeeping was also dependent on successful *peacemaking*: a strategy designed "to bring hostile parties to agreement" through peaceful means such as those found in Chapter VI of the UN Charter. Drawing upon judicial settlement, mediation, and other forms of negotiation, UN peacemaking initiatives would seek to persuade parties to arrive at a peaceful settlement of their differences. Traditional peacekeeping operations referred to the deployment of a United Nations presence in the field, with the consent of all the parties concerned, as a confidence building measure to monitor a truce while diplomats negotiated a comprehensive peace. Peacekeeping was therefore designed as an interim arrangement where there was no formal determination of aggression, and was frequently used to monitor a truce, establish and police a buffer

---

[24] Hugh Miall, *The Peacemakers: Peaceful Settlement of Disputes since 1945* (New York: St. Martin's, 1992), p. 185, 112–13; Paul Diehl, *International Peacekeeping* (Baltimore: Johns Hopkins University Press, 1993), p. 171.

zone, and assist the negotiation of a peace. Monitoring or observer missions had several of the same objectives as traditional peacekeeping operations, though they were typically less well armed (or unarmed) and focused on monitoring and reporting to the Security Council and the Secretary-General.

Both monitoring operations and traditional peacekeeping provided transparency—an impartial assurance that the other party was not violating the truce—and were supposed to raise the costs of defecting from an agreement by the threat of exposure and the potential (albeit unlikely) resistance of the peacekeeping force. The international legitimacy of UN mandates increased the parties' benefits of cooperation with the peacekeepers. The price of first generation peacekeeping, as in the long Cyprus operation, was sometimes paid in conflicts delayed rather than resolved. Today these monitoring activities continue to play an important role on the Golan Heights between Israel and Syria and, until recently, on the border between Kuwait and Iraq.

Monitoring and traditional peacekeeping operations were strictly bound by the principle of consent. Consent derives from the parties' "perceptions of the peacekeepers' impartiality and moral authority."[25] It reduces the risk to the peacekeepers and preserves the sovereignty of the host state. Eroding consent can significantly diminish the peacekeepers' ability to discharge their mandate, so the peacekeepers have an incentive to enhance the parties' consent. Since eroding consent could turn PKOs into multibillion-dollar "obsolescing investments" that are easy hostages to insincere parties, it follows that the UN should develop strategies to enhance consent.[26] This flexibility is more easily provided in *second generation, multidimensional operations* that involve the implementation of complex, multidimensional peace agreements designed to build the foundations of a self-sustaining peace and have been utilized primarily in post–civil war situations. In addition to the traditional military functions, the peacekeepers are often engaged in various police and civilian tasks, the goal of which is a long-term settlement of the underlying conflict. These operations are based on the consent of the parties, but the nature of and purposes for which consent is granted are qualitatively different from traditional peacekeeping.

In addition to monitoring and traditional peacekeeping, the key strat-

---

[25] William J. Durch, *The Evolution of UN Peacekeeping: Case Studies and Comparative Analyses* (New York: St. Martin's Press, 1993), p. 12.

[26] Michael W. Doyle, *UN Peacekeeping in Cambodia: UNTAC's Civil Mandate* (Boulder, CO: Lynne Rienner Publishers, 1995), p. 85; Steven R. Ratner, *The New UN Peacekeeping: Building Peace in Lands of Conflict after the Cold War* (New York: St. Martin's Press, 1995), p. 39.

egy was to foster economic and social cooperation with the purpose of building confidence among previously warring parties, developing the social, political, and economic infrastructure to prevent future violence, and laying the foundations for a durable peace. Multidimensional peace-keeping is aimed at capacities expansion (e.g., economic reconstruction) and institutional transformation (e.g., reform of the police, army, and judicial system, elections, civil society rebuilding). In these operations, the UN is typically involved in implementing peace agreements that go to the roots of the conflict, helping to build long-term foundations for stable, legitimate government. As Secretary-General Boutros-Ghali observed in *An Agenda for Peace*, "peace-making and peace-keeping operations, to be truly successful, must come to include comprehensive efforts to identify and support structures which will tend to consolidate peace. . . . [T]hese may include disarming the previously warring parties and the restoration of order, the custody and possible destruction of weapons, repatriating refugees, advisory and training support for security personnel, monitoring elections, advancing efforts to protect human rights, reforming or strengthening governmental institutions, and promoting formal and informal processes of political participation."[27]

The UN has a commendable record of success, ranging from mixed to transformative, in "second generation," multidimensional peace operations as diverse as those in Namibia, El Salvador, Cambodia, Mozambique, and Eastern Slavonia (Croatia).[28] The UN's role in helping settle those conflicts has been fourfold. It served as a peacemaker facilitating a peace treaty among the parties; as a peacekeeper monitoring the cantonment and demobilization of military forces, resettling refugees, and supervising transitional civilian authorities; as a peacebuilder monitoring and in some cases organizing the implementation of human rights, national democratic elections, and economic rehabilitation; and in a very limited way as peace enforcer when the agreements came unstuck.

In Secretary General Boutros-Ghali's lexicon, "peace-enforcing"—effectively war-making—missions are *third generation* operations, which extend from low-level military operations to protect the delivery of humanitarian assistance to the enforcement of cease-fires and, when necessary, authoritative assistance in the rebuilding of so-called failed states. Like Chapter VII UN enforcement action to roll back aggression, as in Korea in 1950 and against Iraq in the Gulf War, the defining characteristic of "third generation" operations is the lack of consent by one or

---

[27] Boutros-Ghali 1992, para. 21.

[28] Success is of course an ambiguous and contested term. We explain later how we define and measure it in our statistical analysis and case studies.

more of the parties to some or all of the UN mandate.[29] These operations have been of three types. In the first, international forces attempt to impose order without significant local consent, in the absence of comprehensive peace agreement, and must in effect conquer the factions (as was attempted in Somalia). In the second, international forces did not have unanimous consent and have chosen to impose distinct arrangements on parties in the midst of an ongoing war (e.g., no-fly zones or humanitarian corridors of relief). In the third, international forces exercise force to implement the terms of comprehensive peace from which one or more of the parties has chosen to defect.

legality of enforcement operations

Enforcement operations draw upon the authority of UN Charter Article 42, which permits the Security Council to "take such action by air, sea, or land forces as may be necessary to maintain or restore international peace and security"; Article 25 under which member states "agree to accept and carry out the decisions of the Security Council"; and Article 43 in which they agree to "make available to the Security Council, on its call, . . . armed forces, assistance and facilities."

Insightful doctrine for these peace-enforcing operations appeared just as Somalia and Bosnia exposed their practical limitations. Recent studies have thoughtfully mapped out the logic of the strategic terrain between traditional UN peacekeeping and traditional UN enforcement action. Militarily, these operations seek to deter, dissuade, and deny.[30] By precluding an outcome based on the use of force by the parties, the UN instead uses collective force (if necessary) to persuade the parties to settle the conflict by negotiation. In the former Yugoslavia, for example, the UN following this strategy could have established strong points to deter attacks on key humanitarian corridors. (It actually did, but the Serbs bypassed them.) Or it could threaten air strikes, as was done successfully around Sarajevo in February 1994, to dissuade a continuation of the Serb shelling of the city. Or it could have denied (but did not) the Serb

---

[29] Other recent categories include "preventive deployments" deployed with the intention of deterring a possible attack, as in the Former Yugoslav Republic of Macedonia. There the credibility of the deterring force must ensure that the potential aggressor knows that there will be no easy victory. In the event of an armed challenge, the result will be an international war that involves costs so grave as to outweigh the temptations of conquest. Enforcement action against aggression (Korea or the Gulf), conversely, is a matter of achieving victory—"the decisive, comprehensive and synchronized application of preponderant military force to shock, disrupt, demoralize and defeat opponents"—the traditional zero-sum terrain of military strategy. See John Mackinlay and Jarat Chopra, "Second-Generation Multinational Operations," *Washington Quarterly* 15 (Summer 1992), pp. 113–31.

[30] See John Ruggie, "The United Nations Stuck in a Fog between Peacekeeping and Peace Enforcement," *McNair Paper* 25 (Washington, DC: National Defense University, 1993), for these distinctions.

forces their attack on Dubrovnik in 1992 by countershelling from the sea or bombing from the air of the batteries in the hills above the city. Forcing a peace depends on achieving a complicated preponderance in which the forces (UN and local) supporting a settlement acceptable to the international community hold both a military predominance and a predominance of popular support, which together permit them to impose a peace on the recalcitrant local military forces and their popular supporters.

Countries provide troops to UN peace operations in various ways. Troop-contributing countries negotiate in detail the terms of the participation of their forces either under UN command and thus with the Secretary-General (as in El Salvador or Cambodia); with a regional organization authorized as delegated in Chapter VIII; or with the leader of a multinational "coalition of the willing" authorized under Chapter VII, as was the case of U.S. leadership of Unified Task Force (UNITAF, sandwiched in between the two UN operations in Somalia). Many operations draw on a combination of authorizations: peace treaties among factions, backed up or supplemented by other measures authorized (such as arms embargoes, no-fly zones) under Chapter VII, as did the various UN Protection Force (UNPROFOR) and NATO Implementation Force (IFOR) operations in the former Yugoslavia.[31] And, as named in honor of its sponsors, "Chinese Chapter Seven" (employed to authorize the use of force for UNTAES) has emerged as a new way to signal firm intent to enforce a Chapter Six operation. In essence, however, it reaffirms the "Katanga Rule" of the ONUC operation in the Congo: the traditional principle that force can be used both in self-defense of peacekeeping troops and of the mission (mobility of the force).

The result of these three "generations" operating together in the post–Cold War world was an unprecedented expansion of the UN's role in the protection of world order and in the promotion of basic human rights in countries, until recently, torn by costly civil wars. Self-determination and sovereignty were enhanced and a modicum of peace, rehabilitation, and self-sustaining self-determination was introduced in Namibia, Cambodia, El Salvador, Mozambique, and Eastern Slavonia. Tens—perhaps, even hundreds—of thousands of lives were saved in Somalia and the former Yugoslavia. But in 1993 and 1994, the more ambitious elements of "third generation" peace enforcement encountered many of the problems interventionist and imperial strategies have faced in the past, and discovered fresh problems peculiar to the UN's global character.

---

[31] For a valuable discussion of the international law on the use of force and its bearing on authority for peace operations see Karen Guttieri's "Symptom of the Moment: A Juridical Gap for US Occupation Forces," *International Insights* 13, special issue (Fall 1997): 131–55.

The debacles in Somalia and Bosnia forced a radical rethinking of when and where the UN should get involved. Disingenuously, President Clinton told the General Assembly that it needed to learn when to say no. Many came to believe that the UN was not well suited to mounting effective peace operations—no more suited to make peace than the lobbyists who represented a trade group of hospitals would be to conduct surgery.[32] Others thought that such operations should be delegated to regional organizations, and NATO preeminently. This last group began calling for a "fourth generation" of delegated peacekeeping.[33]

The Challenge of Peacebuilding

The United Nations, as we will argue, has been and can continue to be effective at peace operations, provided it takes to heart the true meaning of its successes and failures. This is not a straightforward task.

Measuring successful peace is a complicated substantive and methodological issue and much debated in the literature. Many use the Correlates of War (COW) definition of peace (fewer than 1,000 battle deaths per annum).[34] We adopt a similar standard as one measure of peace, which we call "negative" or "sovereign" peace, reflecting that single sovereignty, a Hobbesian Leviathan, has been reestablished and exercises a legitimate monopoly of violence. We add to that standard measure a second definition of peace. The second definition is "positive," or "participatory" peace, which discounts "peaces of the grave" (the former enemy is all dead or in prison) in favor of a peace that includes wider participation.[35] We add data from the Polity project to code a minimal degree of political assent and participation.[36] We add this second definition for

---

[32] Michael Mandelbaum, "The Reluctance to Intervene," *Foreign Policy* 95 (Summer 1994): 3–18.

[33] For an account of the various positions and factors, see Ramesh Thakur, "UN Peace Operations and US Unilateralism and Multilateralism," in David Malone and Yuen F Kong, eds., *Unilateralism and US Foreign Policy* (Boulder, CO: Lynne Rienner, 2003), pp. 153–79.

[34] See, for example, Barbara Walter, *Committing to Peace: The Successful Settlement of Civil Wars* (Princeton: Princeton University Press: 2002).

[35] In our previous work (Doyle and Sambanis 2000) we called "sovereign" peace "lenient" peacebuilding and "participatory" peace "strict" peacebuilding. We now prefer the more descriptive terms that rest on the distinction drawn by Kenneth Boulding between negative and positive peace and followed by many others. See Kenneth Boulding, "Toward a Theory of Peace," in Roger Fisher, ed., *International Conflict and Behavioral Science* (New York: Basic Books, 1964), pp: 70–87.

[36] Monty Marshall and Keith Jaggers, "Polity IV Project," Codebook and Data Files, 2000, www.bsos.umd.edu/cidcm/inscr/polity.

two reasons. One is to tap into the ordinary association of "peace" with a condition of agreement and acceptance. The other is to identify peace with participation as the beginning of what can be a much more lasting and stable peace. The statistical association between peace and democracy may be U-shaped; both tough autocracies and well-established (usually wealthy) democracies maintain civil peace. Semi-democracies (or anocracies) tend to be most prone to civil war.[37] Participatory peace is thus a difficult status, one designed to measure whether the postwar state has entered a path toward democratic civil peace.

We are thus fully aware how challenging peacebuilding can be. Stable participatory polities usually reflect and rely upon a shared national identity, well-functioning state institutions, a wide middle class, and a growing economy. Both in part and often in whole, these are just what are missing in the typical post–civil war environment where there is often more than one ethnic identity, national identity is weak or contested, state institutions have been corrupted or destroyed altogether, the middle class is small (or has fled), and the economy has been geared to military production and the civilian economy (what there was in the first place) has been looted. Successful peacebuilding is the surprise, not the expectation.

Participatory peace is, however, worth striving for (hence measuring) because it offers the prospect of peace as a self-sustaining conflict resolution mechanism—the promise that future disputes will be negotiated, resolved according to constitutionally agreed procedures. Moreover, the likely alternatives seem worse. On the one hand, the destructiveness of civil anarchy is unacceptable both to all who suffer and to much of the international community forced to observe the suffering. Weak as the second sentiment is, it seems to be enough to launch peace operations when the destructiveness becomes overwhelming as it did in Somalia in 1992 and in Rwanda (after the genocide in 1994) or when the parties at last agree upon a peace. On the other hand, the humiliations and costs of international hierarchy make neocolonialism also unacceptable in the

---

[37] Håvard Hegre, Tanja Ellingsen, Scott Gates, and Nils Petter Gleditsch, "Toward a Democratic Civil Peace?" *American Political Science Review* 95, no. 1 (March 2001): 33–48. Both democracy and wealth, which highly correlate in stable democracies, are doing the work, not democracy alone. See James D. Fearon and David D. Laitin, "Ethnicity, Insurgency and Civil War," *American Political Science Review* 97, no. 1 (2003): 75–90. In related, ongoing research, Jennifer Gandhi and James R. Vreeland show that even in autocracies, political institutions can help reduce the risk of civil war. This would be consistent with our theoretical argument, if institutions are seen as ways to devolve some decision-making authority and increase participation, however marginally. See Jennifer Gandhi and James R. Vreeland, "Political Institutions and Civil War: Unpacking Anocracy," Unpublished manuscript, Emory University and Yale University (August 30, 2004).

current age.[38] Too many postcolonial peoples who have been subject to its indignities are determined to rule themselves. None of the potential imperial powers seem prepared to pay the military and economic costs of permanent rule. While we summarize and expand our earlier results on the determinants of peacebuilding, in this book we want a more finely textured discussion that reflects other aspects of success—the quality of public liberties, degrees of social integration, or the rates of economic growth, and these vary among our cases. So we present a systematic comparison based on statistical analysis and then a more nuanced discussion of the quality of the peace in our case studies.[39] (It does make a difference that a former guerrilla commander became the mayor of San Salvador.)

Distinguishing strategies and outcomes is another methodological challenge. In the real world, they are never completely separable: political strategies rely on expectations about expected outcomes. But the analytic separation should be highlighted as much as is feasible.[40] For example, concerning the use of force—a UN-managed strategy of force is usually ineffective when it seeks to impose a peace (e.g., Somalia), but often effective when it is used in discrete bits to implement a comprehensive peace treaty (Cambodia, Eastern Slavonia). The difference here is the context of the comprehensive peace, not the same strategy with different outcomes. Then the complications set in about how much coercion is compatible with "agreement" and so forth, and in the case studies we will discuss this.

We also distinguish between fulfilling a mandate and establishing a peace. Peacebuilding, when comprehensively planned and executed, achieves a sustainable peace. But not all peace operations are well designed; some are stopgaps and others are misconceived. Peace operations can fulfill their specific mandates authorized by the Security Council or NATO or another body, and yet sustainable peace can still be elusive. Lightly armed peacekeepers sent into the middle of raging civil wars

---

[38] For good discussions of the issue see Daniel Philpott, *Revolutions in Sovereignty* (Princeton: Princeton University Press, 2001); William Bain, *Between Anarchy and Society: Trusteeship and the Obligations of Power* (Oxford: Oxford University Press, 2003); and Nicholas Wheeler, *Saving Strangers* (Oxford: Oxford University Press, 2000).

[39] Much of the statistical analysis is included in a supplement that we make available online (see chapter 3 for the web address), but we discuss the main results in chapter 3. This organizational structure of the book allows readers who are not interested in the technical details to follow the argument without having to read through extensive technical discussions of data collection and coding, model estimation, and hypothesis testing.

[40] If strategies are endogenous to expectations about outcomes, and we want to evaluate the effects of strategies on outcomes, this raises several technical issue with selection and endogeneity that we address in our statistical analysis in chapter 3 and in our supplement.

where there is "no peace to keep" do their job, but in circumstances of frustration. Beleaguered peacekeepers and harried UN civil servants naturally want their performance to be measured by whether or not they fulfilled the mandate (to monitor a truce, deliver humanitarian supplies, hold an election, etc.) that they were given by the Security Council.[41] This is reasonable and this we do in the case studies that follow. But we also want to assess in our statistical analysis whether the mandate itself is well designed to achieve a sustainable peace, and thus whether the Security Council itself did its job.[42] This we will measure also when we note how long the peace lasts after the peacekeepers leave. And, sometimes, though rarely, peace operations can fail their mandates and fortunate domestic circumstances can rescue the peace, as happened when Angolan military forces killed opposition leader Jonas Savimbi and the intractable (to the UN) insurgency collapsed.

In our analysis of the UN's role in making war and making peace, we will focus on four cases of failure—Somalia, Bosnia, Rwanda,[43] and Cyprus—and six cases of success—Congo,[44] El Salvador, Cambodia, Eastern Slavonia in Croatia, Brcko in Northern Bosnia, and East Timor. In the conclusion, we will highlight the lessons of these cases for understanding the ongoing challenges of peace operations.

Some of these cases are well known, and we draw on available evidence to develop them in our analysis. Others we have observed in person and, in those cases, we draw on firsthand experience and primary research. Each case represents a particular type of failure or success, chosen to illustrate the key factors that our quantitative study and our theoretical model reveal as important. Other cases will also be addressed in this book, though only in passing.

[41] Many scholars follow them in this preference; see for example Simon Chesterman's thoughtful and informative study of the variety of mandates: *You the People* (Oxford: Oxford University Press, 2004).

[42] The Security Council has welcomed the Secretary-General's Report, "No Exit without Strategy" (S/2001/394, April 20, 2001) in which sustainable peace is recognized as the goal toward which an exit strategy should be designed.

[43] In our dataset, we code two events of civil war in Rwanda in the 1990s. The failure here refers to the peace process that started with the Arusha Accords in 1993 and ended with the genocide of 1994. The postgenocide peace process has been a mixed case: there have been genuine improvements in governance and reconciliation, but also significant violence in border regions.

[44] This is a good example of the difference between success conceived narrowly as the implementation of the mandate and a broader view of success that focuses on levels of violence and participation in the country after the peacekeepers leave. With respect to both sovereign and participatory peace, the Congo was a peacebuilding failure according to criteria that we establish later in the book. But the UN mission in the Congo (ONUC) was successful in implementing its mandate of keeping the country together despite strong secessionist conflict in Katanga and elsewhere.

The book will focus on the 1990s because there was very little of this comprehensive peacebuilding before then.[45] Our two Cold War cases—Congo and Cyprus—were exceptions. This was partly because the Cold War precluded UN involvement (due to Soviet or U.S. vetoes in the Security Council). Consequently, there emerged a backload of addressable civil wars, accounting for the surge in the early 1990s. Although the rate of onset of civil wars may be declining, the challenges of peacebuilding are all too likely to continue to arise.

One of the most important challenges the international community faces is thus the question of how to rebuild stable polities in the aftermath of civil war. How can the international community assist former combatants with a will to peace to prevent renewed hostility and to contain the ambitions of those who seek renewed civil war? What role should the international community play in ensuring that failed states do not relapse into chaos as soon as the international peacekeepers leave? The United Nations and various regional organizations, including NATO, have accepted the responsibility to undertake "postconflict peacebuilding" and commissioned their member states to undertake extensive intrusions into the domestic affairs of other legally sovereign states.[46]

What guidelines should be developed to help steer these ambitious mandates? In current usage in the UN and among private voluntary organizations, peacebuilding is an attempt, after a peace has been negotiated or imposed, to address the sources of present hostility and build local capacities for conflict resolution. Strengthening state institutions, increasing political participation, engaging in land reform, deepening civil society, finding ways to respect ethnic identities: all these are seen as ways to improve the prospects for peaceful governance.[47] In pluralistic

[45] However, in our statistical analysis, we use data from the entire post-1945 period to evaluate the UN's record. We tested for significant differences between the pre–Cold War and post–Cold War periods, but the number of cases becomes too small when we break the postwar period in this way, so we prefer to analyze all years since 1945.

[46] For a discussion of the concept, see Goulding 1993: 451–64; Thomas Franck, "A Holistic Approach to Peace-building," in Olara Otunnu and Michael Doyle, eds., *Peacemaking and Peacekeeping for the New Century* (Lanham, MD: Rowman and Littlefield, 1998); and Elizabeth Cousens, Chetan Kumar, and Karin Wermester, eds., *Peacebuilding as Politics: Cultivating Peace in Fragile Societies* (Boulder, CO: Lynne Rienner 2000). The UN's own views can be found in Boutros-Ghali 1992); and Kofi Annan, *The Causes of Conflict and the Promotion of Durable and Sustainable Peace in Africa: Report of the Secretary-General* (New York: United Nations, 1998).

[47] For a discussion of comprehensive peace, see Boulding 1964; and Arie Kacowicz, *Peaceful Territorial Change* (Columbia: University of South Carolina Press, 1994), chap. 1. For a valuable collection of papers on peacebuilding see Cousens, Kumar, and Wermester 2000; UN Department for Development Support and Management Services and UN Industrial Development Organization (1995); and Gareth Evans, *Cooperating for Peace* (London: Allen and Unwin, 1993).

societies, conflicts are inevitable. The aim of peacebuilding is to build the social, economic, and political institutions and attitudes that will prevent the inevitable conflicts that every society generates from turning into violent conflicts.[48] In effect, peacebuilding is the front line of preventive action.

Plan of the Book

We begin in chapter 2 with the development of a theoretical framework that explains how peacekeeping can help achieve sovereign and participatory peace after civil war. We start with an analytical review of the debate on the causes and cures of civil wars—the primary strategic element in which the UN found itself in the 1990s. Then we develop the logic behind our concept of the *peacebuilding triangle* that explains *how* the international community could become involved effectively. The chapter highlights the ways in which international peacekeeping and peace enforcement assistance can compensate for two key barriers to building peace: on the one hand, the hostility that civil wars generate and, on the other hand, the lack of local capacity that makes political and economic reconstruction so difficult. The argument presented here thus identifies the centrality of an international role in resolving civil war conflicts and the key elements essential for successful peacebuilding.

In chapter 3, we draw on a data set we have constructed that includes all civil wars since 1945 in order to analyze the determinants of successful peacebuilding after civil war. Here, we assess the effectiveness of UN peace operations by comparing peacebuilding outcomes in cases with and without a UN intervention. This macrolevel analysis demonstrates the centrality of the peacebuilding triangle and identifies the kinds of roles that the international community has played when peacebuilding has been successful.

Drawing on examples from Somalia and Bosnia, chapter 4 offers a microlevel case study analysis of how and why the UN tends to fail at making war—imposing by force an overall settlement of civil conflict. Here we also discuss the exceptional case of the Congo in 1960–65, where for special reasons the UN succeeded in imposing an (albeit in many ways inadequate) peace. Chapter 5 explores, also at the microlevel, how the UN has succeeded in making peace in countries as various as El Sal-

---

[48] No peace is perfect. Isaiah prophesied that we shall know peace when we see the lamb lie down with the lion. The American comedian Woody Allen has added a valuable warning for our world: one of the two might not get much sleep. *Isaiah 11:6* and Woody Allen, *Without Feathers* (New York: Warner Books, 1976) p. 28.

vador, Cambodia, Croatia Bosnia (post-Dayton), and East Timor. And chapter 6, focusing on the long drawn out peacekeeping effort in Cyprus and the horrendous tragedy in Rwanda, explains how peacekeeping has sometimes failed. Five and six focus on strategies and management and the key role transitional authority plays in managing the trade-offs of the peacebuilding triangle.

The case studies expand the scope of the statistical analysis by allowing us to explore the distinction between macrolevel and microlevel peacebuilding success that we do not explore in the statistical analysis. In the cases, we focus on microlevel success and on variables that are hard to measure and use in a large-N statistical analysis; while in the statistical analysis, we focus on macrolevel success and analyze the effects of UN operations while controlling for other factors. In the macrolevel statistical analysis we are able to assess the effectiveness of the UN because we can compare civil wars with UN involvement to those civil wars where the UN did not intervene. The case studies complement that analysis by focusing more closely on cases of UN intervention and giving us a better view of the dynamics between the factions and UN missions.

While the statistical analysis includes all peace processes since 1945 and helps us discuss correlations between peacebuilding outcomes and types of UN missions, the case studies help trace the mechanisms through which UN peace operations contribute to successful peacebuilding. Here we focus on the processes of institutional transformation and capacity expansion that increase the costs of noncooperation for the factions and create incentives for them to keep the peace. We focus on the peacekeepers' implementation of their mandate, identifying particular successes and failures in each case, and offering a perspective of the *process* of peacebuilding over time, discussing both the period before and after the UN's involvement.

The case studies also help us identify possible explanations for particular peacebuilding outcomes that are not always captured by our model. These can be idiosyncratic explanations—which do not concern our triangle model of peacebuilding—or they can be more important, generalizable explanations that our model overlooks. To identify explanations that go beyond our model, but also to place our discussion of the UN's missions in context, we begin each case with a brief history of the conflict and introduce the main actors as well as the circumstances that led to the UN's involvement. We present "vital statistics" for each case for all variables that we consider in our statistical analysis so that readers can get an immediate sense of how this case fits with the average case in our dataset. We also discuss explicitly how well (or how poorly) those cases fit the statistical model and explain why. We consider alternative explanations and link our analysis of the success or failure of peacebuilding to the theoretical explanations of civil war onset and recurrence developed in the theory chapter.

In chapter 7, we compare how various strategies to make, keep, build, and enforce peace were implemented and illustrate the role transitional authority plays in managing a transition to peace. Here, we develop the concept of ecologies of peacebuilding and return to our case studies and our data to characterize the particular peacebuilding ecology for each of our cases. This allows us to better evaluate the type of UN involvement that we should have observed in each case if the UN mandated and re-sourced its missions efficiently. Finally, in the conclusion, we consider alternatives to UN peacebuilding and summarize the record of experience from which the organization is still learning today.

If the world does not fall back into another cold war among the permanent members of the Security Council, then the UN is likely to be involved in the new civil and international wars. Anthony Lake, the Clinton administration national security adviser, expressed it well in his 6 Nightmares: "America must also do its part in peacekeeping operations, working whenever possible through the United Nations. If we do not, our interests suffer, our leadership diminishes, and innocent people die."[49] After much initial skepticism about the value of peacebuilding, the Bush administration (following 9/11) launched two extremely ambitious efforts to remake Afghanistan and Iraq, both eventually with UN involvement.

The CIA's Global Trends 2015 study presented a comprehensive summary of the prospective threat and is worth quoting at length:

> Through 2015, internal conflicts will pose the most frequent threat to stability around the world. . . . Many internal conflicts, particularly those arising from communal disputes, will continue to be vicious, long-lasting and difficult to terminate—leaving bitter legacies in their wake. They frequently will spawn internal displacements, refugee flows, humanitarian emergencies, and other regionally destabilizing dislocations. If left to fester, internal conflicts will trigger spillover into inter-state conflicts as neighboring states move to exploit opportunities for gain or to limit the possibilities of damage to their national interests. . . .
>
> The United Nations and several regional organizations will continue to be called upon to manage some internal conflicts because major states—stressed by domestic concerns, perceived risk of failure, lack of political will, or tight resources—will wish to minimize their direct involvement.[50]

---

[49] Anthony Lake, 6 Nightmares: The Real Threats to American Security (Boston: Little, Brown, 2000), p. 284.

[50] http://www.odci.gov/cia/publications/globaltrends2015/index.html#link3, January 5, 2001.

Despite the stresses of the global war on terrorism, the *Global Trends 2015* around the world today. Indeed, a new set of peacebuilding challenges—with or without the UN—are on the horizon, reflecting if nothing else the ambitious agenda of disarmament-through-regime-change embodied in the new U.S. National Security Doctrine of preventive "preemptive defense." Unfortunately, it thus appears, the lessons that this book will be drawing will likely be useful both for the present and the future.

2

Theoretical Perspectives

WHY DO SOME TRANSITIONS from civil war to civil peace succeed and others fail? Part of the answer can be found in theoretical perspectives on the causes, duration, and termination of civil wars. If the root causes of the war are left untreated, and if the opportunities for rebellion are left intact, then the risk of a failure of the peace is significant. In this chapter, we consider what theories of civil war tell us about the risk of civil war and draw out the implications of these theories for the strategic environment within which UN peace operations function in postwar transitions.

In considering the implications of theories of civil war for the design and effectiveness of peacebuilding operations, we distinguish between the success of a peacekeeping or peacebuilding *mission* and the success of a peace *process*. In our theory, peacebuilding is a key part of the international capacities for peace that can compensate for the lack of local capacities and mute the residual hostilities of civil war. Combinations of these three dimensions—local and international capacities and hostilities—create different "ecological spaces" for peace, that is, different opportunity structures within which actors involved in the peace process decide whether to support the peace or return to war. Successful implementation of a narrow peacekeeping mandate is not sufficient for a successful peace process. But we will argue that both peacekeeping and peacemaking are integral parts of peacebuilding as they affect actors' incentives to support or undermine peace implementation. Here, we engage the literature on peace spoilers and utilize basic insights from game theory to explain the conditions under which different types of peacekeeping intervention can help promote peacemaking and peacebuilding. We see peace as the outcome of a dynamic process, which is shaped partially by the peacekeepers' performance and their peacemaking and peacebuilding efforts and by the parties' reactions to those efforts and partially by other factors, such as the level of local capacities and residual hostility after civil war. In this chapter, we propose a model of the interaction between peacemaking, peacekeeping, and peacebuilding that highlights the importance of picking good strategies that develop out of a proper understanding of the conflict at hand. Strategic peacekeeping and peacebuilding, we argue, must match means to ends and fit within the conflict's "ecology."

Internal (Civil) War and Peacebuilding

As discussed in the introduction, the United Nations has evolved generations of peace operations that have shaped its peacebuilding strategy.
The political strategy of a peacebuilding mandate is the concept of operations embodied in its design. Just as civil wars are usually about failures
of legitimate state authority, sustainable civil peace relies on its successful reconstruction. Peacebuilding is about what needs to happen in between. Civil wars arise when individuals, groups, and factions discover
that a policeman, judge, soldier, or politician no longer speaks and acts
for them. Rather than "the local cop on the beat," the cop becomes "the
Croatian, Serb or Muslim cop." When the disaffected mobilize, acquire
the resources needed to risk an armed contest, and judge that they can
win, civil war follows.[1]

Although we can imagine purely cooperative solutions to domestic
peace,[2] the confusion, "noise," violence, and changing identification that
characterize the onslaught and conduct of civil war do not seem to be
promising circumstances for rational cooperation among factions. Instead the establishment of civil peace seems to require addressing directly both the defensive and aggressive incentives that motivate faction
leaders (and sometimes their followers). Defensive incentives arise in the
domestic "security dilemma." Under emerging conditions of anarchy
(the collapse of central authority) each group/faction seeks to arm itself
in order to be protected; but, as in interstate anarchy, each defensive ar-
mament constitutes a threat to other factions.[3] Offensive incentives arise
because factions and their leaders will want to impose their ideology or
culture, to reap the spoils of state power, to seize the property of rivals,
or to exploit public resources for private gain, or all of the above. Estab-

---

[1] The literature is extensive. We have especially benefited from Harry Eckstein, *Internal
War: Problems and Approaches* (Glencoe, IL: Free Press, 1964); Ted Robert Gurr, *Minori-
ties at Risk: A Global View of Ethnopolitical Conflicts* (Washington, DC: United States In-
stitute of Peace, 1993); James DeNardo, *Power in Numbers: The Political Strategy of
Protest and Rebellion* (Princeton: Princeton University Press, 1985); David A. Lake and
Donald Rothchild, "Containing Fear: The Origins and Management of Ethnic Conflict,"
International Security 21 (Fall 1996): 41–75 and Steven R. David, "Internal War: Causes
and Cures," *World Politics* 49 (July 1997): 552–76.

[2] See for example, James D. Fearon and David D. Laitin, "Explaining Interethnic Cooperation," *American Political Science Review* 90 (December 1996): 715–35; but note that
the authors are not, nor do they claim to be, explaining the empirical record of domestic
peace. They acknowledge that state power and domestic authority are alternative explanations (see p. 731).

[3] Barry Posen, "The Security Dilemma and Ethnic Conflict," in Michael E. Brown, ed.,
Ethnic Conflict and International Security (Princeton: Princeton University Press, 1993),
103–25.

lishing peace will thus also require the elimination, management, or control of "spoilers"[4] or war entrepreneurs.[5]

Conquest by one faction can solve the problem (but even in this case political and social reconstruction can be vital for longer-term legitimacy and stability). Peace through agreement can employ the separation of populations and territorial partition to address war-prone incentives,[6] but partition is often not successful in preventing war recurrence.[7] Civil wars can be turned into international wars (as in Eritrea-Ethiopia) or stable and relatively secure international or intercommunal balances of power, as in Cyprus or Somaliland-Somalia:[8] to each spoiler, his or her separate pile of spoils. But in many civil wars the contest is over who or what "ideology" controls a single polity. Moreover, in some ethnic wars the costs of ethnic "cleansing" will seem too high, or a common basis for overarching civic citizenship exists or can be created. Combatants in these circumstances still have continuing disputes over material interests, who or what rules, and safety. They have experienced devastating destruction (though in varying degrees), and both leaders and followers are likely to harbor deep resentment for losses sustained, particularly to family and village members. They also are experiencing the costs of war and may have come to a "hurting stalemate," in which no faction sees that it can win and each is experiencing net costs of continuing strife.[9] In these latter circumstances, sustainable peace needs state authority as a starting point to overcome security concerns. Hobbes's Leviathan—state sovereignty, or authority—fills that role, restoring "legitimate power."[10]

The specific motivations that shape the behavior of combatants are

[4] Stephen John Stedman, "Spoiler Problems in Peace Processes," *International Security* 22 (Fall 1997): 5–53.

[5] Rui De Figueiredo and Barry Weingast, "The Rationality of Fear: Political Opportunism and Ethnic Conflict," in Barbara Walter and Jack Snyder, eds., *Civil Wars, Insecurity, and Intervention* (New York: Columbia University Press, 1999).

[6] Chaim Kaufmann, "Possible and Impossible Solutions to Ethnic Civil Wars," *International Security* 20 (Spring 1996): 136–75.

[7] Nicholas Sambanis, "Partition as a Solution to Ethnic War: An Empirical Critique of the Theoretical Literature," *World Politics* 52, no. 4 (2000): 437–83.

[8] Jeffrey Herbst, "Responding to State Failure in Africa," *International Security* 21(Winter 1996–97): 120–44.

[9] I. William Zartman, *Ripe for Resolution: Conflict and Intervention in Africa* (New York: Oxford University Press, 1985).

[10] *The Oxford English Dictionary* defines authority: "right to command," "power to influence action," "power over the opinions of others." An enlightening essay is "What Is Authority" (Arendt 1961) and an insightful treatment of the Hobbesian problem applied to economic development is the concept of the "stationary bandit" (Olson 1993). See Hannah Arendt, "What is Authority," in *Between Past and Future* (New York: Viking, 1961). 91–141; Mancur Olson, "Dictoratorship, Democracy, and Development," *American Political Science Review* 87, no. 3 (1993): 567–76.

thus complex and varied. The classical Thucydidean and Hobbesian trinity of motives (fear, honor, interest) are present in modern variations—security dilemmas, ethnic identity and/or ideological fervor, and loot seeking—and each of them is complicated by potential differences between leaders and followers, and factions and patrons. Thus, the decision to organize or participate in a rebellion and then attempt to achieve a viable peace is not a straightforward matter and may differ greatly across actors. What each motivated actor shares, however, is a political environment in which success in achieving peace depends on the degree of harm sustained, the resources available for development, and the international assistance to overcome gaps. We map that environment as a function of local capacities, hostility, and international capacities. Low levels of economic development and other deficiencies in local capacities may motivate actors to violence, due to the low opportunity cost of war and the opportunities for private gains from violence.[11] Increased hostility due to the experience of war makes reconciliation more difficult. To achieve peace and reconciliation under these circumstances, I.William Zartman has argued that we need some combination of (1) reconcentrating central power (the powerful must be recognized as legitimate—or the legitimate made powerful); (2) increasing state legitimacy through participation (elections, power sharing); and (3) raising and allocating economic resources in support of peace. Given the devastation of civil war; all three generally require (4) external, international assistance or international authority in a transitional period.[12]

It is this last dimension that is the particular focus of this book. We do not intend to model a specific decision-making framework or to predict where the UN will choose to become involved, but rather explore the determinants of successful and unsuccessful peacebuilding after civil war (while controlling for the factors that might influence the UN's decision to intervene and other factors that determine the likelihood of peacebuilding success). What role does external international assistance play in the peace process? How much and of what kind is required? We will argue that the levels of war-related hostility and the pre- and postwar levels of local capacities interact with present international capacities to

[11] Paul Collier and A. Hoeffler, "Greed and Grievance in Civil War," October 21, 2001 version, http://econ.worldbank.org/programs/conflict/library/doc?id=12205 (accessed July 3, 2002). The published version of this argument is available in Paul Collier and Anke Hoeffler, "Greed and Grievance in Civil War," Oxford Economic Papers 56 no. 4 (2004): 563–95.

[12] I. William Zartman, *The Elusive Peace* (Washington, DC: Brookings, 1995). Not every country, however, would benefit from external mediation or intervention in its civil war. Some wars, we could argue with hindsight, are more likely to promote stable and just government if they are fought to a conclusion and the just side wins. Such an argument might be made for the U.S. civil war.

deliver specific postconflict outcomes. And, for given levels of local capacity and hostility, we will identify the right form of international assistance to maximize the available space for peace. We do this mainly through an analysis of several cases of peacebuilding processes, while our statistical analysis establishes that UN peace operations play a significant role in postwar peacebuilding, even when we control for local capacities and hostility.

Theories of Civil War

The literature on civil war is sizable and rapidly growing. We glean from it several insights on the causes of civil war, and we will later link these to our theory of peacebuilding.[13]

A Definition of Civil War

We must start by defining civil war: Civil war is an armed conflict that pits the government and national army of an internationally recognized state against one or more armed opposition groups able to mount effective resistance against the state; the violence must be significant, causing more than a thousand deaths in relatively continual fighting that takes place within the country's boundaries; and the rebels must recruit mostly locally, controlling some part of the country's territory.[14] By our definition, there have been 151 civil wars in the post–World War II period.[15]

Political-Economic Theories of Civil War Onset

There is an assortment of theories (economic, political, psychological, rational choice, constructivist) that attempt to explain the occurrence, duration, termination, and magnitude of civil war. Important insights can be derived from all of these theories.

---

[13] This section draws on Nicholas Sambanis, "A Review of Recent Advances and Future Directions in the Literature on Civil War," *Defense and Peace Economics* 13, no. 2 (June 2002): 215–43.

[14] Our definition is similar to, but more precise than, several others in the literature. The coding guidelines are presented in the appendix to chapter 3 and coding decisions and sources for each case are discussed in a supplement that we have posted online (see chapter 3 for the URL). In brief, we code a new war if a peace treaty is signed and violence stops for six months or more or if one side achieves victory, leading to regime change. Civil wars can also end if there is a substantial period (at least two to three years) with no armed conflict.

[15] See chapter 3 for a list of all civil wars in our dataset.

To explain the occurrence of these wars, early economic theories focused on the impact of modernization on the political mobilization of ethnic groups or social classes.[16] The argument was that rapid economic change intensified group competition for the distribution of scarce resources, leading people or groups to support rebellion.[17] In ethnically divided societies, economic competition often takes on an ethnic hue,[18] particularly where there is professional specialization of ethnic groups,[19] and competition will increase if the state's commitment to protecting individual and group interests is questioned.

More recent economic theories have focused on the economic dimensions of the opportunity structure for rebellion. The main argument is that for each individual, there exists a trade-off between effort dedicated to productive versus appropriative economic behavior.[20] If property rights are not credibly supported by the state and if economic activity is unprofitable, individuals or groups will have greater incentives to engage in appropriation rather than production, and each individual or group will need to spend more resources to privately provide for its security, challenging the authority of the state.[21] Violent resistance or rebellion is therefore seen as a rational decision, influenced by the economic opportunity costs of violence, which are weighed against the net expected utility of using violence.

Despite its rationality, war is nevertheless inefficient. If the state and

[16] See, e.g., Robert Melson and Howard Wolpe, *Nigeria: Modernization and the Politics of Communalism* (East Lansing: Michigan State University Press, 1976); Susan Olzak and Joane, Nagel, eds., *Competitive Ethnic Relations* (New York: Academic Press, 1986).

[17] For a review of modernization theory of conflict, see Saul Newman, "Does Modernization Breed Ethnic Conflict?" *World Politics* 43, no. 3 (1991): 451–78. A modern variant of the theory is Robert H. Bates, *Prosperity and Violence: The Political Economy of Development* (New York: Norton and Norton, 2001).

[18] Michael Hechter, *Containing Nationalism* (Oxford: Oxford University Press, 2001); Donald L. Horowitz, *Ethnic Groups in Conflict* (Berkeley and Los Angeles: University of California Press, 1985).

[19] For an example with reference to ethnic conflict in India, see Ashutosh Varshney, *Ethnic Conflict and Civic Life: Hindus and Muslims in India* (New Haven: Yale University Press, 2002).

[20] Herschel I. Grossman, "A General Equilibrium Model of Insurrections," *American Economic Review* 81 (September 1991): 912–21; Herschel I. Grossman, "Insurrections," in K. Hartley and T. Sandler eds., *Handbook of Defense Economics* (Amsterdam: Elsevier, 1995), 1:191–212; Jack Hirschleifer, "Theorizing about Conflict," in K. Hartley and T. Sandler, eds., *Handbook of Defense Economics* (Amsterdam: Elsevier, 1995), 1:165–92; Jack Hirschleifer, "Conflict and Settlement," in J. Eatwell, M. Milgate, and P. Newman, eds., *New Palgrave: A Dictionary of Economics* (London: Macmillan Press, 1987); Kai Konrad and Stergios Skaperdas, "The Market for Protection and the Origin of the State." Working paper, CEPR and University of California, Irvine, 1999.

[21] Bates uses this model to explain patterns of state formation in Europe and Africa. See Bates 2001.

its challengers were purely motivated by profit and were fully informed, they would avoid the costs of conflict and peacefully divide the net value of the "rents" that offices and taxation can provide.[22] Thus, the fact that we observe war must either be due to incompatible preferences among key actors or the inability to credibly commit to a peaceful settlement of disputes, or both.[23]

According to these economic theories, ideology and ethnic or religious identity need not explain the onset of civil war, and rebels are essentially indistinguishable from criminals, "bandits," or "pirates."[24] This explanation stands in contrast to the view that ethnic divisions and ideological differences, particularly when met by state repression, create grievances that lead to rebellion; and it also negates earlier explanations of rebellion as the result of relative deprivation.[25] According to modern economic theories of civil war, for a given level of grievance, what determines if there will be a rebellion is the ability to organize and support an insurgency. Insurgency is less likely when the state is strong[26] and more likely when the country has abundant natural resources that can be used to finance rebellion[27] or when external support is available to the rebels.[28] The greater

[22] Stergios Skaperdas, "An Economic Approach to Analyzing Civil Wars," paper presented at the World Bank Conference "Civil Wars and Post-war Transitions," University of California, Irvine, May 18–20, 2001.

[23] For a formal model of this process, see Skaperdas 2001. The credible commitment hypothesis is developed with reference to interstate war by James Fearon, "Rationalist Explanations for War," *International Organization* 49 (Summer 1995): 379–414. For an insightful explanation of the U.S. civil war along these lines, see Gerald Gunderson, "The Origins of the American Civil War," *Journal of Economic History* 34, no. 4 (December 1974): 915–50. Gunderson uses archival sources to estimate the expected utility of secession (for the South) or war over secession (for the North) and provides evidence that such calculations took place at the time and influenced the decision to go to war.

[24] Paul Collier, "Rebellion as a Quasi-Criminal Activity," *Journal of Conflict Resolution* 44 (December 2000a): 838–52; Herschel I. Grossman, "Kleptocracy and Revolutions," *Oxford Economic Papers* 51 (April 1999): 267–83, p. 269.

[25] See especially Gurr 1993; and Ted Robert Gurr, *Peoples versus States: Minorities at Risk in the New Century* (Washington, DC: US Institute of Peace, 2000). For a discussion of shortcomings in economic theories of civil war, see Nicholas Sambanis, "Expanding Economic Theories of Civil War Using Case Studies," *Perspectives on Politics* 2 no. 2 (2004a): 259–80.

[26] This is the main argument in Fearon and Laitin 2003.

[27] Collier and Hoeffler (2001) argue that the relationship between natural resources and risk of civil war should be nonlinear: low levels of resources reduce risk by removing incentives to loot the natural resources; very high levels reduce risk because they provide significant resources to the states to quell the rebellion.

[28] Ibrahim Elbadawi and Nicholas Sambanis, "External Intervention and the Duration of Civil Wars," World Bank Policy Research Working Paper 2433 (September 2000), consider external intervention as a factor that allows even small or relatively weak groups to rebel against a stronger state.

the amount of resources that can be appropriated, the weaker the state, and the lower the economic opportunity cost of rebellion (i.e., the lower the expected gains from productive economic activity), the greater will be the available supply of recruits to a rebel organization.

These economic models therefore pit "greed" (i.e., economic motives) and "grievance" (political motives) as competitive explanations of civil war. Despite the apparent clarity of these models, "greed" and "grievance" are in practice complementary or overlapping explanations of rebellion. In richer countries, the state may be stronger, but the demand for rebellion arising out of conditions of absolute or relative deprivation of groups is also likely to be lower than in poorer countries. High rates of economic growth, which increase the opportunity cost of violence as economic opportunities become more abundant, may also help sustain democratic institutions,[29] which in turn may enhance the power of non-violent forms of conflict resolution. Thus, the relationship between economic and political factors is complicated, and it is hard to sort out empirically the impact of each factor on the risk of civil war occurrence.

Empirical tests of these economic theories of civil war have not yet produced a consensus, though some findings do appear robust. In particular, low levels of per capita income (which most authors interpret as a measure of poverty) significantly exacerbate the risk of civil war.[30] This is the most robust empirical finding in the literature. Other empirical results are more debated. Some authors have found that the technology of insurgency (mountainous terrain, external financing) also enhances the rebels' ability to organize a rebellion, so it makes a civil war more likely.[31]

Others have found support for the hypothesis that heavy reliance on natural resources increases the risk of a civil war, though the precise mechanism that links resources to war is not always clear. The negative effects of natural resources are more difficult to demonstrate empirically and robustly, but certain types of "lootable" resources (oil, some precious stones) have been linked to civil war.[32] Resource predation is especially important for sustaining rebel organizations once the violence has started, though some authors find that natural resource dependence does not influence civil war duration, which contradicts that hypothesis.[33]

---

[29] Adam Przeworski, Michael Alvarez, Fernando Limongi, and Jose Cheibub, *Democracy and Development* (Cambridge: Cambridge University Press, 2000).

[30] Poverty is usually measured in absolute terms (e.g., as income lower than $1 per day). But here, as in the civil war literature, we refer to low per capita income as a measure of poverty.

[31] Collier and Hoeffler 2001; Fearon and Laitin 2003.

[32] Collier and Hoeffler 2001; M. Berdal and D. M. Malone, eds., *Greed and Grievance* (Boulder, CO, and London: Lynne Rienner. 2000).

[33] Paul Collier, A. Hoeffler, and M. Soderbom, "On the Duration of Civil War." *Journal of Peace Research* 41 no. 3 (2004): 253–74.

Elbadawi and Sambanis find no statistically significant difference in the effects of natural resource dependence on war onset and war continuation.[34] However, with respect to war recurrence and postwar peacebuilding, our earlier research suggests that countries with a high dependence on natural resources face greater difficulties in building a stable peace.[35]

In contrast to theories that focus on the role of economic variables, political scientists have generally focused on the association between *political* group incentives, capacities, and opportunities for rebellion.[36] Among *theories* the key factors influencing group capacities and opportunities for rebellion are regime characteristics and political instability.[37] According to authors such as Ted Robert Gurr and Håvard Hegre and his colleagues, rebellion is the product of political grievance, and it becomes more likely when there is greater opportunity for organized political action.[38] Thus, a number of factors that allow groups to overcome the collective action problems associated with rebellion should make war more likely.[39] And the risk of civil war should be greatest in so-called anocracies—regimes that are neither democratic enough to reduce grievances by allowing greater participation nor autocratic enough to be able to suppress opposition during the early stages of rebellion.[40] However, despite much theorizing about the effects of democracy and civil war, the statistical evidence is not robust, perhaps due to the empirical proxies used to test the relationship. When more fine-grained measures of political institu-

[34] Ibrahim Elbadawi and Nicholas Sambanis, "How Much War Will We See? Estimating the Prevalence of Civil War, 1960–1999," *Journal of Conflict Resolution* 46 (June 2002): 307–44.

[35] Doyle and Sambanis 2000; see also Stephen J. Stedman, Donald Rothchild, and Elizabeth M. Cousens, eds., *Ending Civil Wars: The Implementation of Peace Agreements* (Boulder, CO: Lynne Rienner, 2002).

[36] A classic reference is Ted Robert Gurr, *Why Men Rebel* (Princeton: Princeton University Press, 1970); Charles Tilly, *From Mobilization to Revolution* (New York: Random House, 1978).

[37] This idea dates back to Plato, who thought that rebellion would occur only when elites were weakened.

[38] Gurr 2000; Håvard Hegre, Tanja Ellingsen, Scott Gates, and Nils Petter Gleditsch, "Toward a Democratic Civil Peace? Democracy, Political Change, and Civil War, 1816–1992," *American Political Science Review* 95 (March 2001): 33–48.

[39] See Gurr's (2000) model of ethnopolitical rebellion in chapter 3 of his book for a discussion of factors influencing ethnic groups' capacity for rebellion.

[40] For results on the relationship between "anocracy" and rebellion, see Gurr 2000; Hegre et al. 2001; D. C. Esty, J. Goldstone, T. R. Gurr, P. T. Surko, and A. N. Unger, *Working Papers: State Failure Task Force Report* (McLean, VA: Science Applications International Corporation, 1995); D. C. Esty, J. Goldstone, T. R. Gurr, P. T. Surko, A. N. Unger, and R. S. Chen, *The State Failure Task Force Report: Phase II Findings* (McLean, VA: Science Applications International Corporation, 1998); Elbadawi and Sambanis 2002; and Fearon and Laitin 2003. The concept of an "anocracy" is somewhat problematic and studies applying it to civil war have not explained which characteristics of an anocracy increase the risk of a civil war.

tions are used in empirical tests, there is more positive evidence. For example, there is some preliminary evidence linking peace to proportional representation systems[41] and systems with significant executive constraints.[42]

A variable at the core of both economic and political theories of civil war is the salience of ethnic identity and the degree of ethnic fractionalization in the society.[43] There can be several mechanisms through which ethnic identity and fractionalization influence the risk of political conflict and violence. Economists are interested in ethnicity both as a cause of grievances[44] and as a determinant of the ease of organization of rebellion. Ethnic ties can improve social communication;[45] facilitate the coordination of collective action by enhancing group solidarity;[46] and if more trust exists among members of an ethnic group,[47] they can reduce the costs of enforcing social contracts under conditions of uncertainty.[48] Political scientists focus on ethnicity either as a primordial affiliation that can easily generate violence[49] or as an instrument at the hands of elites who capitalize on the existence of ethnic networks to mobilize public support for violence.[50]

[41] Marta Reynal-Querol, "Ethnicity, Political Systems, and Civil Wars," *Journal of Conflict Resolution* 46, no. 1 (2002): 29–54.

[42] Amitabh Dubey, "Domestic Institutions and the Duration of Civil War Settlements." Unpublished paper (2003). Empirically, however, the estimation of the effects of different types of institutions on the likelihood of civil war onset or recurrence is complicated by the fact that the type of system should be endogenous to expectations about its effects on the likelihood of civil war.

[43] For an insightful survey of theories of ethnic conflict, see Donald L. Horowitz, "Structure and Strategy in Ethnic Conflict," Paper presented at the Annual Bank Conference in Development Economics (Washington, DC: World Bank, April 20–21, 1998).

[44] Grievances, for example, can arise from unequal distribution of economic resources and services among ethnic groups (though theories that interpret ethnic fractionalization in this way already presuppose a positive level of conflict among ethnic groups). See, for example, Alberto Alesina, William Easterly, and Reza Baquir, "Public Goods and Ethnic Divisions," Policy Research Working Paper 2108 (Washington, DC: World Bank, 1999).

[45] Karl W. Deutsch, *Nationalism and Social Communication: An Inquiry into the Foundations of Nationality* (Cambridge and New York: Published jointly by the Technology Press of the Massachusetts Institute of Technology and Wiley, 1953).

[46] Hechter 2001.

[47] Anthony D. Smith, *Nationalism* (Cambridge: Polity Press, 2001).

[48] Horowitz 1985; Russell Hardin, *One for All: The Logic of Group Conflict* (Princeton: Princeton University Press, 1995); Ronald Wintrobe, "Some Economics of Ethnic Capital Formation and Conflict," in A. Breton et al., eds., *Nationalism and Rationality* (Cambridge: Cambridge University Press, 1995).

[49] Clifford Geertz, "The Integrative Revolution: Primordial Sentiments and Civil Politics in the New States," in *Old Societies and New States* (New York: Free Press, 1963); Walker Connor, "Beyond Reason: The Nature of the Ethnonational Bond," *Ethnic and Racial Studies* 16 (July 1993): 373–89.

[50] For an excellent review, see Rogers Brubaker and David D. Laitin, "Ethnic and Nationalist Violence," *Annual Review of Sociology* 24, no. 1 (1998): 243–52.

Mirroring the many conflicting theoretical perspectives on the link between ethnicity and violence, there is also substantial disagreement in the empirical literature. Most studies find that high levels of ethnic fractionalization do not increase the risk of civil war onset,[51] though they might make civil war duration longer, and some also argue that they make war recurrence more likely.[52] However, countries with higher levels of ethnic fractionalization are in greater risk of *secessionist* war[53] and of lower-level armed conflict that might escalate to civil war.[54] Moreover, ethnic fractionalization may not be the right measure to use in assessing the risk between ethnicity and violent conflict. Theorists have made this point very clear. Horowitz, for example, describes the differences in conflict risk between societies where ethnic groups are completely hierarchically ranked and societies where there is not a complete overlap between class and ethnic divisions. Other authors have focused more directly on ethnic polarization and dominance rather than fractionalization, and they have found stronger evidence that polarization and dominance increase the risk of civil war occurrence, though there is some ambiguity about how to measure dominance and what types of "ethnic" affiliation are most important (linguistic, religious, tribal, etc.).[55]

Perhaps the most important disjuncture between the theoretical and empirical literature is the fact that standard measures of ethnic fractionalization cannot be used as measures of nationalist ideology, and it is nationalism that is most often seen as increasing the risk of ethnic rebellion.[56] It is difficult to discern (or measure) the conditions under which ethnocultural identity will be more salient than other identities in an individual's identity repertoire or when ethnicity will be used to support violence. The spread of nationalist ideology through education might explain why ethnic identities are so salient in some parts of the world and why they can be used to support violence, whereas in other places ethnic divisions are not as politically charged.[57]

Actual or expected group-level grievances or experience of violence can also increase the proneness of ethnic groups to violence.[58] Such expe-

[51] See, in particular, Collier and Hoeffler 2001; and Fearon and Laitin 2003.

[52] We also find some support for this hypothesis in our analysis in chapter 3.

[53] See Sambanis 2001.

[54] Nicholas Sambanis, "What Is Civil War? Conceptual and Empirical Complexities of an Operational Definition," *Journal of Conflict Resolution* 48, no. 6 (2004b): 814–58.

[55] Collier and Hoeffler 2001. See also Elbadawi and Sambanis 2002.

[56] See, for example, Gurr 2000; and Hechter 2001.

[57] On the role of schooling and the formation of national identities, see Ernest Gellner, *Nations and Nationalism* (Ithaca: Cornell University Press, 1983); Eric Hobsbawn and Terence Ranger, *The Invention of Tradition* (New York: Cambridge University Press, 1993); and Keith Darden, "The Scholastic Revolution: Explaining Nationalism in the USSR," Unpublished manuscript, Yale University (2004).

[58] Gurr 2000.

riences can increase the fear of victimization at the hands of another group, creating motives for preemptive use of violence.[59] Irreconcilable cultural differences[60] and the failure of in-group policing[61] can also exacerbate such tensions. Under those conditions, elites can capitalize on the availability of ethnic networks to induce a coordination process that leads to violence.[62] Such manipulation can take many forms, ranging from the organization of large-scale civil war, as in the case of Yugoslavia,[63] to the tacit support of electoral violence, as in the case of India.[64] These explanations do not view identity as inherently conflictual and focus instead on social interactions and systems and patterns of identity evolution to explain violence.[65] But such instrumentalist accounts ultimately rely on some positive preexisting level of conflict or hostility that they cannot explain and that makes a synthesis between "harder" (i.e., primordialist) and "softer" (instrumentalist) perspectives necessary to explain the occurrence of violent ethnic conflict.[66]

Rebellion can be considered as a public good (or a public bad, depending on one's perspective vis-à-vis the state). As such, it is subject to the usual collective action problems associated with the production of public goods. Ethnicity is a central concept in the literature because if ethnic affiliation increases group cohesion by building trust or by making individuals more interested in group-defined goals rather than only personal gain, then ethnic identity can be a determining factor in the mass mobilization that is necessary to fight a civil war. If large-scale coordination is needed to rebel against the state, then high levels of ethnic fractionalization might reduce the risks of rebellion by increasing the costs of coordinating collective action across several ethnic groups. By contrast, in polarized societies—that is, societies with two or three large

---

[59] See Posen 1993; de Figueiredo and Weingast 1999. Underlying both these models is a positive probability of victimization at the hands of a perceived hostile group.

[60] Samuel P. Huntington, "The Clash of Civilizations?" *Foreign Affairs* 72 (Summer 1993): 22–49.

[61] Fearon and Laitin 1996.

[62] Paul R. Brass, *Theft of an Idol: Text and Context in the Representation of Collective Violence* (Princeton: Princeton University Press, 1997); Paul R. Brass, *Ethnic Groups and the State* (London: Croom-Helm, 1985); Hardin 1995.

[63] Susan Woodward, *Balkan Tragedy: Chaos and Dissolution after the Cold War* (Washington, DC: Brookings Institution, 1995).

[64] Steven I. Wilkinson, *Votes and Violence: Electoral Competition and Ethnic Riots in India* (Cambridge: Cambridge University Press, 2004).

[65] Benedict Anderson, *Imagined Communities: Reflections on the Origins and Spread of Nationalism* (London: Verso, 1983); R. Brubaker, "National Minorities, Nationalizing States, and External National Homelands in the New Europe," *Daedalus* 124 (Spring 1995): 107–32.

[66] This point is made very persuasively by Horowitz (1998).

groups—these coordination costs should be lower and these societies are at higher risk of civil war.[67] In these cases, coordination within each of these large groups is easier, and the distribution of the costs of rebellion is more concentrated among members of the group, which also stand to gain more from the rebellion than the excluded group(s).

Where ethnic groups are territorially concentrated, the risks of civil war should also be greater, and the aims of the war may focus on achieving greater self-determination or even secession. Secessionist civil war will occur with greater probability where institutional collapse at the center creates a power vacuum that leaders at the periphery try to fill; where regional inequality creates unmet demand for greater autonomy in a federal or decentralized state; where the income gains from remaining within the predecessor state are not sufficient to offset the gains from greater self-determination; and where the ethnic makeup of regions is very different, supporting the growth of nationalist ideology.[68] Authors have also suggested that demands for self-determination are more likely to be expressed in countries where ethnic networks exist linking communities that straddle borders;[69] in old empires or postcolonial states with incomplete state-building and nation-building experiences and in regions with high levels of internal migration or "internal colonialism;"[70] in modern states with peripheral *ethnicities* that are subordinated to core *ethnicities*;[71] in countries with a dependence on territorially concentrated natural resources;[72] in authoritarian states that repress minority rights and cultural practices;[73] in countries with high levels of regional disparities in income;[74] and in regions of "backward" countries occupied by the

---

[67] For a conceptual discussion, see Horowitz 1985. For empirical evidence related to ethnic polarization, see Reynal-Querol 2002; Elbadawi and Sambanis 2002; and Robert H. Bates, "Ethnicity, Capital Formation, and Conflict," CID Working Paper no. 27 (Cambridge: Harvard University, 1999).

[68] For such a theory, see Hechter 2001; and Nicholas Sambanis and Branko Milanovic, "Explaining the Demand for Sovereignty," Unpublished manuscript, Yale University (May 2004). Monica Toft, "Indivisibile Territory, Geographic Concentration, and Ethnic War," *Security Studies* 12 no. 2 (2002): 82–119, also makes the argument about greater territorial concentration of groups and civil war.

[69] Horowitz 1985. For an empirical test of the effects of such networks on interstate conflict, see Douglas R. Woodwell, "Unwelcome Neighbors: Shared Ethnicity and International Conflict during the Cold War," *International Studies Quarterly*, 48, no. 1 (2004): 197–223.

[70] Hechter 2001; Michael Hechter, *Internal Colonialism: The Celtic Fringe in British National Development, 1536–1966* (New Brunswick, NJ: Transaction Publishers, 1999); Anthony D. Smith, *National Identity* (Reno: University of Nevada Press, 1991).

[71] A. Smith 1991.

[72] Sambanis and Milanovic 2004.

[73] Gurr, 2000.

[74] Sambanis and Milanovic 2004.

most backward groups of those countries, though secession by "advanced" groups in "backward" states is also possible.[75]

Our review of these economic and political theories of civil war suggests to us that in peace transitions, the risk of war recurrence and peacebuilding failure will be higher in countries with low levels of local capacities—slow economic growth, high levels of poverty, and significant resource dependence—and in politically divided societies with many factions engaged in conflict over issues that are important to the definition of each faction's ethnic or religious identity. Therefore, in assessing the effects of international capacities on peacebuilding later in this book, we control for these theoretically significant factors and estimate the likelihood of peacebuilding success in countries with varying levels of local capacities and ethnopolitical divisions and war-generated hostility.

International Dimensions of Civil War

Civil wars are sometimes linked to bad leaders and sometimes to bad neighborhoods or bad external influences by neighboring states or by the major powers. Our own theory of postwar peacebuilding focuses heavily on international influences as we explore the effectiveness of external intervention by the United Nations in building sustainable peace after civil war. Our theory is therefore relevant to international relations (IR) perspectives on civil war. However, the skeletal theories of IR—neorealism and neoliberalism—offer poor explanations of civil war.[76] Neorealism cannot explain why ethnic, religious, or class-based divisions occur or why they may be important causes of civil war, since it assumes that states are unitary actors and explains policy outcomes and state behavior as a result of structural changes at the level of the international system. State failure, which is frequently associated with civil war, generates conditions of domestic anarchy that parallel the condition of international anarchy. This makes structural realism (neorealism) tangentially relevant to civil war, given the central role of anarchy in neorealism. However, anarchy in civil war emerges endogenously as a result of domestic political competition and is not a preexisting (constant) structural condition. Neorealism therefore cannot explain the causes of domestic anarchy (e.g., elite-based explanations or the implications of ethnic divisions and institutional failure), so it can be of use only in explaining patterns of violence after civil war erupts and once state control collapses.

By contrast, neoliberalism's focus on domestic political institutions

---

[75] Horowitz 1985.
[76] See David 1997 for a useful discussion of this point.

allows that theory to better explain why civil war occurs in the first place.[77] Neoliberalism also takes into consideration nonstate actors (e.g., ethnic networks, crime syndicates, multinational corporations) and can consider their influence on civil war risk. But neoliberalism also has important shortcomings as it cannot explain domestic institutional change or the use of force in ethnic antagonisms, nor can it explain patterns of alliance and conflict among insurgent groups and the government. Thus, the usefulness of mainstream IR theory in analyzing civil war or peacebuilding after civil war is limited.

The macrosystemic dimensions of civil war—for example, the effect of the end of the Cold War—are perhaps less important than the narrower regional dimensions of these wars. IR theory can be useful in explaining "neighborhood" effects as civil wars can have negative externalities that can be transmitted across borders.[78] An important contribution is Lake and Rothchild's exploration of the transmission of civil violence to the neighborhood through diffusion or contagion mechanisms.[79] We still have only limited empirical evidence of these mechanisms. Sambanis's empirical analysis suggests that living in "bad" neighborhoods—that is, next to countries with civil wars or in countries with authoritarian polities—can increase a country's chance of having an ethnic war.[80] There can be several mechanisms through which civil war becomes internationalized. Current evidence suggests that ethnic conflict will spread when ethnic groups straddle borders and an ethnic group involved in a rebellion has coethnics who are in the numerical majority in a neighboring state. Other channels have also been shown to increase the risk of interference and internationalization of civil war.[81] More research is needed to under-

---

[77] The literature on the democratic peace focuses on political, legal, and economic democratic institutions and the norms against the use of force they create vis-à-vis other democratic institutions. See Michael W. Doyle, "Liberalism and World Politics," *American Political Science Review* 80, no. 4. (December 1986): 1151–69.

[78] Michael E. Brown, "The Causes and Regional Dimensions of Internal Conflict," in *International Dimensions of Internal Conflict* (Cambridge: MIT Press, 1996): 571–602; Manus I. Midlarsky, "Identity and International Conflict," in *Handbook of War Studies II* (Ann Arbor: University of Michigan Press, 2000), pp. 25–58; and Lake and Rothchild 1998.

[79] "Diffusion occurs largely through information flows that condition the beliefs of ethnic groups in other societies. Escalation [or contagion] is driven by alliances between transnational kin groups as well as by intentional or unintentional spillovers, . . . or by predatory states that seek to take advantage of the internal weaknesses of others" (Lake and Rothchild 1998, p. 5).

[80] Kristian Gleditsch, "Transnational Dimensions of Civil War," Unpublished paper, University of California, San Diego (January 2003) finds similar results. Others disagree. Fearon and Laitin (2003) find no evidence of diffusion or contagion.

[81] Woodwell 2004.

stand how civil war spreads and to distinguish patterns of contagion from patterns of diffusion.

An important gap in the literature is the lack of analysis of the links between international and internal war. Studies of external intervention in civil war are related to this topic, as intervention is one way in which civil wars become internationalized. However, to date, we do not have an integrated analysis of the regional dimensions of civil war, except in studies that analyze one type of war (i.e., either interstate or intrastate) while controlling for the occurrence of the other type of war.[82] There is some evidence that links external and internal conflict and shows that they have a jointly negative impact on economic activity, which further increases the risk of more violence.[83] Civil wars have negative economic effects that are not limited to the countries in which they occur, but also affect neighboring countries, where they can reduce economic growth (this effect is proportional to the magnitude of the war).[84] This evidence suggests that a "conflict trap" can be created that locks poor countries and neighboring regions in a cycle of economic deterioration and recurrent violence.[85]

This brief discussion of international perspectives on civil war suggests not only that the postwar peacebuilding environment might be different in wars that are highly internationalized, but also that external impartial intervention by a regional or multilateral organization might be necessary to break the conflict trap. Thus, the benefits of peacebuilding intervention would extend far beyond the country (or region within the country) that is most affected by the violence. Moving from this policy perspective back to the scholarly literatures, the theories of neorealism and neoliberalism that we surveyed are relevant to our study as they have offered differing perspectives on the effectiveness of international organizations in promoting cooperation and peace. Our analysis of the effectiveness of UN peacebuilding speaks directly to those literatures as it attempts to evaluate the effectiveness of multilateral institutions on patterns of international security throughout the postwar period and especially after the end of the Cold War.

[82] A. Raknerud and Håvard Hegre, "The Hazard of War: Reassessing the Evidence for the Democratic Peace," *Journal of Peace Research* 34 no. 4 (1997): 385–404; Hegre et al. 2001; Woodwell 2004.

[83] Brock Blomberg and Gregory Hess, "The Temporal Links between Conflict and Economic Activity," *Journal of Conflict Resolution* 46 (February 2002): 74–90.

[84] James C. Murdoch and Todd Sandler, "Economic Growth, Civil Wars, and Spatial Spillovers," *Journal of Conflict Resolution* 46 (February 2002): 91–110.

[85] See the World Bank's policy research report for policy implications of the conflict trap: Paul Collier et al., *Breaking the Conflict Trap: Civil War and Development Policy* (Oxford and Washington, DC: Oxford University Press and World Bank, 2003).

Civil War Duration, Termination, and Recurrence

Once war starts, mistrust and hostility increase, and ending the war through negotiation becomes harder. Long civil wars are sustained through the enmity that violence creates in afflicted populations and by instilling discipline and cohesion in the rebel organization as well as by finding sources of financing that allow continued insurgency. High levels of death and displacement of people can generate hatred and fear that make a negotiated settlement difficult to implement. Rebel cohesion is also affected by the ability of rebel groups to find ways to finance their insurgency, and looting of natural resources can be one way to support a long rebellion. There are several examples of this, ranging from timber trade by the Khmer Rouge in Cambodia or diamond trading by the Union for the Total Independence of Angola (UNITA), a rebel group in Angola. External support of the rebels by an ethnic diaspora is often another key source of rebel financing, as it has been in Northern Ireland, Sri Lanka, or Kosovo. Finally, our review of the literature on ethnicity and violence in the previous section suggests that rebel cohesion may be greater when rebel groups recruit members of their own ethnic, religious, or tribal group, so we might expect ethnic or secessionist wars to be longer lasting, harder to resolve, and easier to restart than other types of civil war.

All these factors influence the strategic environment within which factions decide whether to continue fighting or to make and keep a peace. Simply put, in a rationalist model, we would observe a failure of the peace if the expected utility of a new war is greater than the expected utility of peace. Thus, the logic of war recurrence is similar to the logic of economic models of civil war we have already discussed.[86] As in those models, our theory of peacebuilding also assumes that the warring parties are rational though not infallible; that war generates private and public gains and losses that are unevenly distributed among groups; and that private gains explain why war may be rational for some groups, while being collectively suboptimal. These assumptions allow us (and other analysts) to make a series of hypotheses regarding the likelihood of war onset and recurrence.

A series of additional assumptions might also be necessary to build a decision-making model to explain how and why some wars end and others restart. For example, in divided societies and societies with large

---

[86] See Collier and Hoeffler 2001; Paul Collier and Anke Hoeffler, "On the Economic Causes of Civil War," Oxford Economic Papers 50 (December 1998) pp. 563–73; Jean Paul Azam, "How to Pay for Peace," Public Choice 83 no. 1–2 (1995): 173–84; Hirschleifer 1987; and D. Mason and P. Fett, "How Civil Wars End: A Rational Choice Approach," Journal of Conflict Resolution 40, no. 4 (1996): 546–68.

power disparities between the government and potential insurgent organizations, civil wars will be unlikely, and if they do occur, they will last for only a short time and they can end in a decisive victory. In the case of a military victory by one of the parties, for example, the risk of war recurrence may be lower as the victory resolves any misinformation or miscommunication or other uncertainty that might have created false expectations on the part of the party that lost the war.

But some wars last long, and a quick, decisive victory is not possible. One way in which civil wars can be protracted even in societies with power asymmetries and fractionalized, incoherent parties is through external intervention that levels the playing field. Such interventions are frequent in civil wars. Looking at the period from 1944 to 1999, Patrick Regan finds that unilateral interventions occurred in most civil wars, and the longer the duration of a war, the greater the chance of an outside power intervening to end it.[87] Regan finds that external interventions have the effect of lengthening the expected duration of a conflict, and that this effect holds for all interventions, economic and military, partial and impartial. Elbadawi and Sambanis develop this idea further through an elaboration of the Brito and Intriligator insurgency model.[88] They argue that external interventions provide a mechanism for long insurgencies even in fractionalized societies, where a narrow social basis of support for the insurgency would otherwise reduce its expected length (if support relied exclusively on the size of the ethnic or social group supporting the rebels). For a given level of ethnic/social fractionalization, intervention in favor of the rebels lowers the rebels' expected costs of fighting if it increases the probability of success of the rebellion, thereby attracting more rebel recruits and discouraging defections. Intervention provides a counterweight to the government's superior strength, limiting its ability to repress the rebellion at its early stages.[89]

This discussion reveals that there exist important qualitative differences between the problems of war onset and war continuation or termination. Empirical evidence to date confirms that some of the variables that influence civil war onset do not have equivalent power in explaining war duration. This is not altogether surprising, given that war duration is analyzed (by definition) on a subsample of countries and years that al-

[87] Patrick M. Regan, "Conditions for Successful Third Party Interventions," *Journal of Conflict Resolution* 40, no. 1 (1996): 336–59; Patrick M. Regan, *Civil Wars and Foreign Powers* (Ann Arbor: University of Michigan Press, 2000); Patrick M. Regan, "Third Party Interventions and the Duration of Intrastate Conflicts," *Journal of Conflict Resolution* 46 (February 2002): 55–73.

[88] D. Brito and M. Intriligator, "An Economic Model of Guerrilla Warfare," *International Transaction*, 15, no. 3, 319–29; Elbadawi and Sambanis, 2000.

[89] Collier, Hoeffler, and Soderbom 2004.

ready share certain characteristics (which explains why war occurred in those cases as compared to countries and years with no war). But the most important conceptual difference between the processes of war onset and duration or recurrence is that war duration or recurrence will be affected by conflict dynamics that are absent from the process of initial war onset. The strategy of insurgency and the effects of violence are different in the two processes. This becomes apparent in studies of the magnitude of violence in civil war, which highlight the importance of a host of new factors that are not directly applicable to the question of initial war onset. Stathis Kalyvas has conducted one of a few microlevel studies of violence during civil war, and his research has revealed that macrolevel cleavages (such as political ideology or ethnic affiliation) often do not explain variation in microlevel motives for violence. People commit violent acts often for idiosyncratic reasons that do not necessarily correspond to the macrolevel cleavages that we observe at the national level.[90]

By drawing on these insights about the differences between the processes of war onset, war duration, and termination, we can identify a set of determinants that might explain the risk of postwar failure of peace that are not due entirely to the same factors that caused the war in the first place. Our theory focuses on the role of international peacebuilding operations, which can help provide information that resolves any uncertainty about the parties' commitment to a peace settlement or the likelihood of military victory in a new cycle of hostilities. The effect of a negotiated peace with a UN peacekeeping operation should be able to create the conditions for a lasting peace, and a decisive military victory should not be the only way to achieve an end to civil war. Multilateral peace operations can help shape the parties' incentives to cooperate in peace implementation by increasing the costs of defection from agreement through selective enforcement and by providing financial and other inducements to those who cooperate. And they can support the emergence of new players whose actions can counterbalance the actions of spoilers. We consider those functions of international peacebuilding and peacekeeping operations later in the chapter.

The fact that violence intensifies hostility and fear implies that peacekeepers will face tough challenges in wars that have caused large-scale human suffering. Kalyvas's research on the magnitude of violence in civil war is relevant here because he demonstrates how violence can be self-sustaining by creating deep animosities that make a stable peace hard to negotiate and by providing a context for the opportunistic use of more

[90] Stathis N. Kalyvas, *The Logic of Violence in Civil War* (Cambridge: Cambridge University Press, 2006); Stathis Kalyvas, 2003, "The Ontology of "Political Violence": Action and Identity in Civil Wars," *Perspectives on Politics* 1 no. 3 (2000): 475–94.

violence. Wars that have produced a lot of killing leave deep wounds in societies that need much time to heal. While an arsenal of military strategies and socioeconomic policies have been used to help civil war–ravaged countries transition to peace, we do not yet know how effective each policy (or combination of policies) has been in countries with different levels of war-generated hostility and variable local capacities to rebuild peace.[91] A first positive sign for peace is the signing of a peace treaty by all or most of the factions involved in a civil war. But often such commitment is missing or the parties need constant reassurances. Multilateral peacekeeping can help in these cases, though in the worst environments only forcible external intervention can ensure compliance with the terms of an imposed or forcibly negotiated settlement.

Thus, in hostile environments, ending civil wars may require enforcement, but not just enforcement. In contrast to economic models of civil war, we would argue that addressing underlying grievances and resolving institutional failure is a necessary component in preventing war recurrence and building positive peace. Simply limiting the opportunity to organize insurgency is not sufficient. Negotiated settlements must ultimately rebuild the country's institutional capacity for self-sustaining peace. This is an argument that we develop throughout the book.

Ending the war through negotiated settlement is a function of the parties' relative capabilities, as extreme power imbalances will typically result in military solutions to the war.[92] Impartial external intervention might result in accommodative policies by the state, including some sort of power-sharing arrangement.[93] But there are risks associated with all interventions and civil war solutions. For example, power sharing can backfire if elites do not interact with each other as necessary, and former allies may come into conflict in the new polity.[94] Support for multiparty

---

[91] For a critique of neoliberal economic orthodoxy in designing postconflict transitions, see Roland Paris, "Peacebuilding and the Limits of Liberal Internationalism," *International Security* 22 (Fall 1997): 54–89. For a critique of democratization as a strategy to end civil wars, see Jack Snyder, *From Voting to Violence: Democratization and Nationalist Conflict* (New York: Norton Publishers, 2000).

[92] Roy Licklider, *Stopping the Killing: How Civil Wars End* (New York: New York University Press, 1993); Roy Licklider, "The Consequences of Negotiated Settlement in Civil Wars, 1945–1993," *American Political Science Review* 89 (September 1995): pp. 681–90.

[93] Fen O. Hampson, *Nurturing Peace* (Washington, DC: U.S. Institute of Peace, 1996); Donald Rothchild, "Implementation and Its Effects on Building and Sustaining Peace: The Effects of Changing Structures of Incentives," unpublished paper (Center for International Security and Cooperation, Stanford University and University of California, Davis, 2000).

[94] I. William Zartman, "Putting Humpty-Dumpty Together Again," in D. Lake and D. Rothchild, *The International Spread of Ethnic Conflict: Fear Diffusion, and Escalation* (Princeton: Princeton University Press, 1998), 317–37; Pierre Atlas and Roy Licklider, 1999, "Conflict among Former Allies after Civil War Settlement: Sudan, Zimbabwe, Chad, and Lebanon," *Journal of Peace Research* 36 no. 1 (1989): 35–54.

electoral competition can increase intergroup collaboration (e.g., where minorities form useful electoral constituencies), but it may also mobilize ethnic and nationalist conflict over control of the new polity.[95] Therefore, the design and pace of postwar transitions must be carefully monitored and assisted by experienced peace-makers and peacekeepers. Successful elections must not be rushed and should be the culmination of a peacebuilding process that has successfully transformed political institutions.[96] External intervention that focuses narrowly on rebuilding the military capabilities of the state will fail in that important dimension. Thus, we will argue in this book, external intervention must necessarily address this complex mix of challenges, and only a certain type of multi-dimensional intervention will be successful in difficult peacebuilding ecologies.

We see the problem of rebuilding a war-torn state as one of rebuilding social trust. To increase trust in the new political institutions, power-sharing arrangements may have to take the form of regional autonomy or federalism, as war will typically limit minority groups' trust in the time consistency of cooperation within a unified, centralized state.[97] The problem of creating shared institutions is more difficult to resolve in civil wars that are fought over issues that are thought to be indivisible.[98] However, issue indivisibility is a slippery concept. If utility can be ascribed to each issue over which the war is fought, then trade-offs among different issues can be constructed, and the parties can exchange bundles of concessions that generate equal levels of utility. A secessionist conflict might thus be settled through a combination of increased cultural autonomy and a redistribution of the state's fiscal surplus, leaving the central government undivided while satisfying the insurgents' key concerns without resulting in secession. The possibility for such trade-offs implies that

[95] See Donald Rothchild, "Settlement Terms and Postagreement Stability," in Stephen J. Stedman, Donald Rothchild, and Elizabeth M. Cousens, eds., Ending Civil Wars: The Implementation of Peace Agreements, (Boulder, CO: Lynne Rienner, 2002), pp. 117–40. See, also, E. D. Mansfield and J. Snyder, "Democratization and the Danger of War," International Security 20, no. 1 (Summer 1995): 5–38; Snyder 2000.

[96] Michael W. Doyle, "Authority and Elections in Cambodia," in M. Doyle, Ian Johnstone, and Robert Orr, eds., Keeping the Peace (Cambridge: Cambridge University Press, 1997), pp. 134–64.

[97] Gurr 2000; Rothchild 2000; David Lake and Donald Rothchild, "Political Decentralization and Civil War Settlements," in Miles Kahler and David Lake, eds., Governance in a Global Economy: Political Authority in Transition (Princeton: Princeton University Press, 2003).

[98] Barbara F. Walter, "The Critical Barrier to Civil War Settlement," International Organization 51 (Summer 1997): 335–65; Walter 2002. Elisabeth Jean Wood, Insurgent Collective Action and Civil War in El Salvador, (Cambridge: Cambridge University Press, 2003a, 2003); Monica Toft, The Geography of Ethnic Violence (Princeton: Princeton University Press, 2003).

no good is truly indivisible, but some issues require much more complex solutions that the parties often cannot negotiate among themselves.[99] International peacebuilding intervention can help develop solutions to complex problems, structure trade-offs that support incentives for peace, and assure parties of each other's commitment to a negotiated solution. It can also help create the political and social institutions that are necessary for a participatory process of resolving the underlying political conflicts that led to the civil war.

A critical difficulty in negotiating an end to civil wars is that negotiated agreements are often not credible. By that we mean that an agreement must be either self-enforcing or externally enforced so that violators will be punished.[100] Even without the informational asymmetries that can complicate the negotiation of peace, negotiated settlements are often time inconsistent in the absence of external security guarantees. This is typically because the government can easily renege on its promises after the rebels have demobilized and surrendered their arms.[101]

If the problem of postwar cooperation lies in an inability to make a credible bargain to share power, and if this problem is exacerbated by a perceived power asymmetry between the parties, then solutions that divide the disputed territory among the different groups and permit each group to retain its weapons might increase the likelihood of postwar peace. Thus, territorial partition is in principle consistent with rationalist accounts of how to end civil war, particularly wars between ethnic groups.[102] While in some cases, partition may indeed work, it can also backfire by transforming internal to international war and cause human suffering greater than that caused by the war.[103] Partition can transform

---

[99] Even if truly indivisible goods do exist, we cannot find a way to identify and measure such goods, so we do not pursue this topic further in our analysis.

[100] Walter 1997, 2002.

[101] This is the thrust of Walter's (1997, 2002) theoretical argument, which draws heavily on Fearon 1995. In turn, rationalist theories of war are very similar to economic theories of time-consistent monetary policy, as developed by Finn E. Kydland and Edward Prescott, "Rules Rather than Discretion: The Inconsistency of Optimal Plans," *Journal of Political Economy* 85 (June 1977): 473–92; and Robert Barro and David Gordon, "Rules, Discretion, and Reputation in a Model of Monetary Policy," *Journal of Monetary Economics* 12, no. 1 (1983), 101–21; Jenna Bednar, William N. Eskridge Jr., and John Ferejohn, "A Political Theory of Federalism," in J. Ferejohn, J. Riley, and J. N. Rakove, eds., *Constitutional Culture and Democratic Rule* (New York: Cambridge University Press, 2001), discuss noncredible power-sharing arrangements in federal systems. See Lake and Rothchild 1998 for an application of Fearon's (1995) theory to explain civil war.

[102] Kaufmann 1996; and Chaim Kaufmann, "When All Else Fails," *International Security* 23, no. 2 (Fall 1998): 120–56.

[103] Radha Kumar, "The Troubled History of Partition," *Foreign Affairs* 76, no. 1 (1997): 22–35; R. Schaeffer, *Warpaths: The Politics of Partition* (New York: Hill and Wang, 1990).

a highly diverse society into a polarized one or one that is dominated by a single group. This can create fears among minorities, causing conflict where none existed previously. Moreover, despite its simplicity and plausibility, partition theory does not pass simple empirical tests as it does not outperform other solutions to civil war in terms of its impact on the likelihood of war recurrence.[104] Thus, before we can advocate that the international community support a policy of ethnic partition, we need to conduct more systematic testing to identify the conditions under which partition can provide a lasting and acceptable peace.

We argue in this book that stable peace might also be achieved through the internationally assisted implementation of a peace agreement. International peacebuilding can be a major component of strategies to satisfy people's "basic needs" and create institutions that can support the peace, resolving at least partially the credibility problems associated with peace implementation. Peacebuilding can be an alternative to other, more extreme strategies, such as partition or conquest. An ingredient of that strategy is good peacekeeping, which reduces the opportunity for insurgency and enhances incentives for peace. But peacekeeping can only be as credible as the peacekeepers' mandate and resources, and effective peacekeeping must be able to adapt to the particularities of the civil wars they are sent to resolve. We turn to this question next.

Implications of Civil War Theory for UN Intervention

Peacekeeping was initially designed to respond to threats to international security and relied on truce supervision and monitoring of the behavior of standing armies. It is now being used heavily to respond to internal conflicts. In thinking about how to adapt peacekeeping strategies to respond to internal war, we can learn useful lessons from the theories of civil war that we surveyed in the previous pages. Peacekeeping can help if it reduces the parties' fear of victimization by providing security; improves the flow of information to prevent the political manipulation of fear by elites; facilitates the negotiation and implementation of peace

---

[104] See Sambanis 2000. If partition succeeded in ethnically "cleansing" the disputed territories, and if the new territories with ethnically "pure" populations acquired sovereignty, then by definition, ethnic civil war could not recur. But such manipulations of a country's demography are often more painful than the war itself and can hardly be considered good outcomes. And in practice, partitions fail to relocate entire ethnic groups and usually leave behind residual populations. Moreover, new cleavages can be activated along preexisting fissures within ethnic groups that were previously considered to be homogeneous.

agreements; reassures parties of each other's compliance with the terms of a negotiated settlement; identifies spoilers and increases their costs from violating peace agreements; identifies moderates and offers them inducements to cooperate in building participatory political institutions; permits the emergence of new actors—voters, parties, civil society— committed to a sustainable peace.

Not all types of peacekeeping can achieve those difficult goals. Peacekeeping—particularly first generation operations—has a tendency to favor the status quo.[105] While this need not be an obstacle to effective peacekeeping in interstate conflicts, where recognized boundaries can be the fallback position for both parties, it is more problematic in internal conflicts, where the status quo ante at the time that peacekeepers are deployed is usually not acceptable to one or more of the parties.

Both peacekeeping and peace-making are easier when the conflict is over a small number of well-defined issues and the parties are few and readily identifiable.[106] In internal war, issues are often interrelated, and the aggressor is not easily identifiable. The problem of "issue indivisibility" that we mentioned earlier is exacerbated if factions split during peace negotiations, making it harder to negotiate trade-offs and concessions among several hostile and often incoherent factions.[107] Peacemakers must therefore create trade-offs between issues, and peacekeepers must credibly reduce the expectation that any one of the parties can make its goals "indivisible" by violating the peace agreement and using force. In doing so, different strategies must be used to solve different problems. Peacekeeping will only work where there is a peace to keep, where the parties perceive an incentive to collaborate. Where there is no such agreement on peace, peace must be enforced. Understanding this elemental difference between peacekeeping and peace enforcement is a key to peacebuilding success. But so is the need to use force selectively within the context of a consent-based operation so as to allow peacekeepers to enhance the parties' initial consent and prevent spoilers from undermining the process.

---

[105] Diehl 1993.

[106] Gareth Evans, *Cooperating for Peace* (London: Allen and Unwin, 1993), 62, 77–79. For an insightful application of theory to interstat peacekeeping along these lines see Virginia Page Fortna, *Peace Time*, chap. 1.

[107] Walter (2002) defines indivisible (or hard to divide) conflicts (1) where the stated goals of the rebels are total; (2) where rebels are interested in control of the government; and (3) where it is hard to separate population and resources within the country easily. This definition is useful, though not without problems, as it is not clear why a conflict over "control of the government" is more of a "total" conflict than a conflict over secession. However, the basic idea seems right: it is easier to strike a bargain in some conflicts than others. Even if trade-offs are always theoretically possible, they may be so costly as to make a negotiated settlement unlikely.

Type of Conflict and Optimal Peacebuilding Strategy

The peacekeepers' first concern in designing intervention strategies is to properly identify the type of conflict underlying the civil war. Political scientists have explored a wide range of theories about why and how parties enter into and resolve various kinds of conflicts. At the more abstract level, "neoliberal" theories explore conflicts among rational actors over absolute goods valued for their own sakes. "Neorealists" examine conflicts among rational actors that raise issues of security and relative gains, based on the assumption that relative power (dominance) alone provides security and therefore the gains that truly matter. "Constructivists" relax the assumption that perceived identities and interests are fixed and explore the circumstances in which conflicts and social relations more generally constitute and then reshape identities and interests.[108] We find aspects of each of these three factors in the cases we examine. Factions and their leaders seek absolute advantages as well as relative advantages. Sometimes, international actors assist the peace process by eliminating old actors (war criminals, factional armies) or introducing new actors (domestic voters, political parties, international monitors, NGOs) or fostering changes of identity (reconciliation)—or by all three together. But a more informative analytic lens portrays the peacebuilding process through two classic game situations, coordination and cooperation, each of which incorporates neoliberal, neorealist, ands constructivist dynamics.

Thus, to simplify, conflicts can be over coordination or cooperation, depending on the structure of the parties' preferences over possible outcomes of the negotiations. Each preference structure characterizes a specific type of conflict, and different intervention strategies are optimal for different conflict types. Some conflicts are mixed, reflecting elements of both, and conflicts do change over time, evolving from one to the other and, sometimes, back again.[109] Well-chosen strategies can maximize the available space for peace, whereas strategies that are poorly matched to the conflict at a particular time can reduce the space for peace.

We draw on insights from simple applications of game theory to problems of international cooperation to discuss intervention strategies

[108] The literature expounding the three is vast, but for central differences see Robert Keohane, *After Hegemony* (Princeton: Princeton University Press, 1984); Joseph Grieco, "Anarchy and the Limits of Cooperation: A Realist Critique of the Newest Liberal Institutionalism," *International Organization* 42, no. 3 (1998): 485–507; and Martha Finnemore and Kathryn Sikkink, "Taking Stock: The Constructivist Research Program in International Relations and Comparative Politics," *Annual Review of Political Science* 4 (2001).

[109] For a theoretical discussion of the problem of providing assurance and building trust in conflicts that combine elements of both coordination and cooperation games, see Andrew Kydd, "Trust, Reassurance, and Cooperation," *International Organization* 54, no. 2 (Spring 2000): 325–57.

for coordination and cooperation problems.[110] Coordination problems
have a payoff structure that gives the parties no incentives to unilaterally
move out of equilibrium, once they reach equilibrium.[111] A classic example is driving on the right (or the left, if you are in Great Britain). It is
well established that the best strategy to resolve coordination problems
is information provision and improvement of the level of communication between the parties.[112] Communication gives the parties the ability
to form common conjectures about the likely outcomes of their actions.[113] Without the ability to communicate, they will not choose the
most efficient outcome. By contrast, cooperation problems create incentives to renege on agreements, particularly if the parties discount the
benefits of long-term cooperation in favor of short-run gain. In one-shot
games of cooperation (of which the Prisoner's Dilemma is a well-known
example), the parties will try to trick their adversaries into cooperating
while they renege on their promises. In the Prisoner's Dilemma, for example, two accomplices in police custody are offered a chance to "rat"
on their partner. The first to rat gets off and the "sucker" receives a very
heavy sentence. If neither rats, both receive light sentences (based on cir-
cumstantial evidence); and, if both rat, both receive sentences (but less
than the sucker's penalty). Even though they would be better off trusting
each other by keeping silent, the temptation to get off and the fear of being the sucker make cooperation extremely difficult. These structural differences between cooperation and coordination problems imply that different peacebuilding strategies should be used in each case. In figure 2.1,
we suggest that different strategies are needed to resolve different types
of problems. Transformative intervention strategies, such as multidimensional peacekeeping or enforcement with considerable international authority, are needed to resolve cooperation problems, whereas facilitative
peacekeeping strategies, such as monitoring and traditional peacekeeping, are sufficient to resolve coordination problems. Facilitative peacekeeping has no enforcement or deterrence function. Transformative
peacekeeping through multidimensional operations can increase the costs
of noncooperation for the parties and provide positive inducements by

[110] See Arthur A. Stein, *Why Nations Cooperate: Circumstance and Choice in International Relations* (Ithaca: Cornell University Press, 1992).

[111] For a precise game-theoretic definition of coordination and collaboration games, re-
fer to James Morrow, *Game Theory for Political Scientists* (Princeton: Princeton University
Press, 1994); and David M. Kreps, *Game Theory and Economic Modeling* (Oxford:
Clarendon Press, 1990).

[112] A useful summary of the literature is Robert Axelrod and Robert Keohane, Introduction and Conclusion, to Kenneth Oye, ed., *Cooperation under Anarchy* (Princeton: Princeton University Press, 1986).

[113] Morrow 1994, 222.

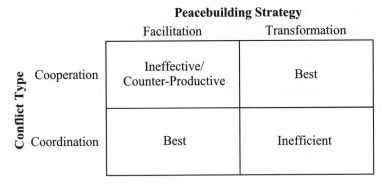

Figure 2.1 Matching Problem Type and Strategy Type

helping rebuild the country and restructure institutions so that they can support the peace. Enforcement may be necessary to resolve the toughest cooperation problems.[114] Not all civil war transitions are plagued by cooperation problems. Some wars resemble coordination problems, whereas frequently we find both types of problems, in which case intervention strategies must be carefully combined or sequenced.

Enhancing Coordination by Improving Communication, Providing Assurance, and Building Capacity

In a game of pure coordination, both parties want to pursue compatible strategies—in the example we gave, to both drive on their right (or left). But if neither knows the rules or what the other party prefers, they will be tempted to experiment, to try one and then the other, and these of course can be costly whether in driving or other activities. Coordination can be readily achieved by credible information on rules, payoffs, and the parties' compliance or stated preferences. Once the rule is known or the other parties' preference is clear, coordination can be achieved. UN monitors or observers can assist such communication and help the parties coordinate to an efficient outcome.

A second formulation of a coordination problem is the "assurance" game. The classic story (as told by the eighteenth-century French philosopher Jean-Jacques Rousseau) is a stag hunt in which catching the stag depends on all the hunters cooperating. But if a rabbit suddenly appears,

---

[114] Transformative peacekeeping is different from peace enforcement, as discussed in the introduction. Transformative peacekeeping can only deter or punish occasional violations. If the violations are systematic and large-scale, a no-consent enforcement operation might be necessary.

some of the hunters may be tempted to defect in order to catch the rabbit which, though less desirable than the hunter's share of the deer, can be caught (in this story) by one hunter on his own. If all chase the rabbit, they divide the rabbit. Here, if players A and B can choose between strategies of cooperation and defection, we get an ordinal payoff structure such as the following: mutual cooperation yields a payoff of (4, 4) for players A and B, respectively, as each gets a share of the deer. When A cooperates and B defects A gets 0 and B gets 3 (the rabbit) and correspondingly when A defects and B cooperates, A gets 3 and B, 0. When both defect, each gets 2 (the share of the rabbit). In this case, peacekeeping needs to be more involved than in the previous coordination game. In both cases communication should be sufficient, but the temptation to defect out of fear that another hunter will do so first (even though this is rational for neither) requires more active facilitation and continual reassurance. Information alone may not be enough; the peacekeepers may need to provide regular reports on each party's compliance, and so reduce the costs of communication between the parties and allow them to coordinate their strategies.[115] The more the peacekeepers need to increase the costs of noncooperation, the more we move from a coordination game to a game of cooperation.

Third, in the more complicated framework of actual peace processes, many parties that have a "will" to coordinate lack the "way." Coordination is promoted when parties receive assistance in capacity building, demobilizing armies, and transforming themselves from military factions to coherent political parties. Parties that want to "drive on the right" will better succeed if they know how to drive and their vehicles are steerable. Such assistance permits them to act rationally according to their preferences, rather than incoherently.

Enhancing Cooperation by Making Noncompliance Costly and Compliance Cheap, or Transforming the Game

Cooperation problems are much more difficult to solve. How can cooperation failure (defection) be avoided? In the classic Prisoner's Dilemma one-shot game, we always end up at double defection (both rat) unless there is some external enforcement mechanism. Conditions of repeated play (iteration) may produce cooperation in infinite-horizon games even without external enforcement, but not if there is a visible end to the

---

[115] Regional powers can play this role, if organized by an impartial party with broad legitimacy. See Michael W. Doyle, Ian Johnstone, and Robert C. Orr, eds., *Keeping the Peace* (1997), pp. 376–77, for a discussion of the role played by the "Friends of the Secretary-General" in the El Salvador negotiations, and Teresa Whitfield's "Friends Indeed" (manuscript, 2005) for a wider study of the topic.

game.[116] Short-term defection from agreements may even be possible from iterated games if one of the parties discounts the future severely. Strong third-party involvement would be necessary to support effective cooperation, unless the parties' agreements are self-enforcing. However, self-enforcement of peace agreements in internal conflicts may be impossible for at least three reasons.

First, many conflicts are characterized by power asymmetry, which implies that the costs of cooperating while other parties are defecting may be extremely large for the weaker party. In internal conflicts, a settlement implies that the rebels would disarm, making themselves vulnerable to an attack by the state, if the state reneges on the agreement. Walter argues that this is the "critical barrier" to negotiated settlement in civil wars.[117] The potential for time-inconsistent behavior by the state makes the settlement noncredible.

Second, internal conflicts—especially of the ethnic variety—can escalate to the point where one or more of the groups are eliminated, forcibly displaced, or weakened to the point of not having any bargaining leverage. This seems to have been the strategy of the *genocidaires* in Rwanda and of the Serbs in the Bosnian war. This also implies that the potential gains from short-term defection for the stronger party could be infinite, if such defection could eliminate the weaker party from future bargaining. Thus, the usual long-term benefits to cooperation in iterated play need not be greater than short-term gains from defection.

Third, in computer-simulated results of iterated Prisoner's Dilemma games (where the solutions from iterated play come from), players have access to strategies that cannot be replicated in real life. For example, tit-for-tat punishment strategies of permanent exclusion of one of the parties may be feasible in a simulated environment, but are not realistic in actual civil wars. Parties that defect from peace agreements cannot be permanently excluded from further negotiation, so reciprocal punishment strategies against defection are implausible.[118] This should increase the discounting of expected future costs of short-term violations by parties who can expect to be included in future negotiations regardless of their previous behavior.

Given these enforcement problems, strong peacekeeping is necessary in internal conflicts resembling cooperation problems to increase the

[116] By contrast, even in finite yet multiple-iteration games, if the timing of the game's end is not known, players can be expected to play as if they were engaged in an infinite horizon game. But if the endgame is visible, then finite game strategies will be used.

[117] Walter 1997.

[118] As an impartial third party, the UN cannot formally exclude parties from negotiations. The inclusion of the Khmer Rouge in the negotiations leading to the Paris Accords over the Cambodian civil war is a case in point. Moreover, exclusion of parties from the terms of the settlement can generate grievances that lead to renewed fighting.

parties' costs from noncooperation, or reduce the costs of exploitation, or increase the benefits from cooperation—and ideally all three at once.

Can peacekeeping have such an impact and how? The literature suggests that peacekeepers can change the costs and benefits of cooperation by virtue of the legitimacy of their UN mandate, which induces the parties to cooperate; by their ability to focus international attention on noncooperative parties and condemn transgressions; by their monitoring of and reporting on the parties' compliance with agreements; and by their function as a trip wire that would force aggressors to go through the UN troops to change the military status quo.

Ultimate success, however, may depend less on changing incentives for existing parties within their preferences and more on transforming preferences—and even the parties themselves—and thus turning a cooperation problem into a coordination problem. Later we will describe the institution-building aspects of peacebuilding as a revolutionary transformation in which voters and politicians replace soldiers and generals; armies become parties; war economies, peace economies. Reconciliation, when achieved, is a label for these changed preferences and capacities. To be sure, the difficulty of a transformative strategy cannot be overestimated. Most societies, postwar, look a great deal like they did prewar. But, for example, if those that have committed the worst war crimes can be prosecuted, locked up, and thus removed from power, the prospects of peace rise. The various factions can begin to individualize rather than collectivize their distrust and hostility and, at the minimum, the worst individuals are no longer in control.[119]

Therefore, even where enforcement is used at the outset, the peace must eventually become self-sustaining, and consent needs to be won if the peace enforcers are ever to exit with their work done. And consensual peace agreements can rapidly erode, forcing all the parties to adjust to the strategies of "spoilers." Their success or lack of success of doing so tends to be decisive in whether a sustainable peace follows.

Strategic Peacebuilding

The first thing peacekeepers must do is identify the nature of the conflict they face. Telling a prisoner in a Prisoner's Dilemma what his or her accomplice plans to do (enhancing communication) ensures defection and exploitation. Enforcing solutions on every driver when most drivers

---

[119] See Gary Bass, *Stay the Hand of Vengeance* (Princeton: Princeton University Press, 2000); and for the difficulties, Jack Snyder and Leslie Vinjamuri, "Trials and Errors: Principle and Pragmatism in Strategies of International Justice," *International Security* 28, no. 3 (2003–4): 5–44; and Chandra Sriram, *Confronting Past Human Rights Violators* (2004).

already want to coordinate is a waste of resources. Peacebuilders there-fore must decide when a peace must be enforced—to save lives, to avoid an escalating conflict. And they must decide when it can be negotiated and an agreement can be implemented. But their decisions, to take this a step further, can rarely be static. Circumstances change and strategic peacebuilding must adjust to "spoilers" and mobilize appropriate incentives.

How can the peacekeepers know which type of conflict they are fac-ing? A first clue is the peace treaty. If a treaty has been signed that out-lines a postwar settlement, then the parties' preferences have been re-vealed to some extent (though the fact that some peace treaties are quickly undermined also means that only by observing the parties' com-pliance with the treaty can we be more certain about their true pref-erences). Patterns of compliance with the treaty can help distinguish moderates from extremists. In other cases, such knowledge cannot be attained until the first (or several) encounters with the parties. Where a treaty is not in place, all parties can be assumed to be spoilers, and strong peacekeeping must be used. Subsequent cooperation or conflict with the peacekeepers can help distinguish those parties who respond to inducements from those who are committed to a strategy of war. This also means that UN missions must be flexible to adjust their mandate given observations of cooperation or conflict on the ground and based on the peacekeepers' changing assessments about the nature of the con-flict.

A treaty is usually the outcome of a "mutually hurting stalemate," which is a necessary, but not sufficient, condition for successful peace-building.[120] Such a stalemate exists when the status quo is not the pre-ferred option for any faction, while overturning the status quo through military action is unlikely to be successful. This condition pushes parties to the negotiating table, and their declared preferences for peace are more credible as a result of their inability to forcibly achieve a better outcome.[121]

However, the parties will not negotiate a settlement unless peace is likely to generate higher rewards than continued fighting. This condition becomes unattainable if "spoilers" are present. Spoilers are leaders or parties whose vital interests are threatened by peace implementation.[122] These parties will undermine the agreement and reduce the expected

[120] The mutually hurting stalemate is part of Zartman's (1985) concept of "ripe" con-flicts. Additional conditions for conflict "ripeness" in Zartman's theory are: a sense of cri-sis; a deadline for negotiations; a reversal in the parties' relative strength; a leveraged exter-nal mediation; and a feasible settlement that can address all the parties' basic needs.

[121] The settlement of El Salvador's civil war is a good example of a hurting stalemate.

[122] Stedman 1997, 7.

utility of a negotiated settlement for all parties. In terms of our previous arguments, the presence of spoilers implies the "payoff structure" of a Prisoner's Dilemma or an assurance game as spoilers will not coordinate their strategies with moderates. Thus, if spoilers are present in a peace process, peacekeepers can keep the peace only if they can exercise some degree of enforcement by targeting the spoilers and preventing them from undermining the negotiations. The dynamics of spoiler problems deserve a closer look.

Spoiler problems were first systematically analyzed by Stephen Stedman, who identified three types—total, greedy, and limited spoiler—according to their strategies and likely impact on the peace implementation process. These are behavioral types, and Stedman defines them in terms of their preferences over the strategies they use to undermine the peace. However, all parties can act as total spoilers if conditions deteriorate markedly. But parties whose ultimate goals over the outcomes of the peace are more moderate will have incentives not to spoil the peace process if they can get a reasonable outcome. The difficulty facing the peacekeepers is to distinguish moderates from extremists, or total spoilers, when conditions are such as to encourage all parties to defect from agreements.

The principal gain of good UN peacekeeping will be to allow moderates—limited spoilers with specific stakes—and greedy opportunists to act like peacemakers in the peace process without fearing reprisals from total spoilers who are unalterably opposed to the peace settlement. Effective strategies must combine consent from those willing to coordinate and cooperate with coercive carrots and sticks directed at those who are not. We will suggest that the record shows that by strategically combining peace-making, peacekeeping, postconflict reconstruction, and peace enforcement, peace can be built from problematic and unpromising foundations.

Our case-study work (which we develop in subsequent chapters) suggests that to manage spoilers effectively, peacekeepers should avoid acquiring a reputation for weakness or inconsistency and they should raise the costs of noncooperation early in the peace process. A combination of threat and weakness will signal to extremists that their projects will succeed and that they should strike soon, as it did in Rwanda. Failure to perform as indicated would lead to peacekeeping failures that may force all parties—including moderates—to defect from the peace process. Several such failures over time may institutionalize the conflict, as the parties will establish a pattern of noncooperative action, and promises of future cooperation will be noncredible (we develop this explanation in some detail with reference to the case of Cyprus).

In other words, unless offset by successes in other parts of the peacekeeping mandate, peacekeeping failure can dynamically reduce the parties' preferences for peacemaking. In these cases, the peacekeepers must discover ways to transform the conflict by, for example, generating new actors, as the Cambodian election created legitimate power through the vote of the electors; transforming preferences for cooperation by offering development assistance to cooperating parties; building new institutions, as was the case with the reformed police and judiciary in El Salvador; or establishing an effective state and even fostering a new nation, as is occurring in East Timor and as peacekeepers are still struggling to do in Bosnia. For all those strategies to succeed, spoilers must be identified and marginalized to the degree possible. Peacekeepers on the ground have the knowledge that is needed to identify the parties who are intent on undermining the peace. Selective use of force in defense of the mandate against the most uncooperative parties must be a viable option for peacekeeping so that they can credibly raise the costs of noncooperation. However, if use of force is required on a regular basis, as was the case in Bosnia and the Congo, then peacekeeping can no longer be effective and peace-enforcement strategies must be used.

Defining Peacekeeping Success in a Dynamic Model of Peacebuilding

Peacekeeping may be partly determined by a number of other variables that may also have a direct effect on the final outcome of a peace process.[123] Thus to measure the added value of peacekeeping on civil war outcomes, we must control for other relevant variables. We must also understand how peacekeeping interacts with other strategies. Peacekeeping, peace-making, postconflict reconstruction, and discrete enforcement *dynamically* and *interactively* influence the outcome of the peace process.

Peacebuilding success is a function of the success of peace operations, and that success can be measured in terms of the degree to which the mandate was implemented and by whether or not a stable peace was attained. We distinguish between these two standards, as the latter standard depends more heavily than the former on factors that are generally outside the peacekeepers' control. In the empirical analysis, we analyze both standards of success. First, we assess the effectiveness of UN mandates on attaining self-sustaining peace in a macrolevel statistical analy-

---

[123] In the empirical section of the book, we control for all observable variables that we would expect to influence the peacebuilding outcome as well as the probability of UN intervention, and we explore the potential endogeneity of peacekeeping intervention as well as other selection effects.

sis (chapter 3). Then, we focus on microlevel success in several case studies that analyze both successful and failed implementations of UN mandates.[124]

Peacekeeping success may be a function of a number of variables: the support of the major powers and interested third parties in the region, a clear and implementable mandate;[125] the parties' continuing consent;[126] the peacekeepers' ability to remain impartial; the likelihood of competing external intervention by a third party; support by nonstate actors;[127] a deadline for troop withdrawal;[128] adequate financial and logistic support;[129] effective command structure[130] and manageable geographic deployment of peacekeeping troops.[131] Some of these variables can be considered exogenous (predetermined) and also influence the outcome of the peace process directly, while others are endogenous, shaped by the outcomes of specific strategies and decisions by the peacekeepers during an ongoing peace process. While peacebuilding strategy is in part determined by those exogenous factors, it is not epiphenomenal and has real consequences for the success of the peace process. Our case studies will show that it is through the shaping of their mandate and its correct implementation that peacekeepers can have an independent effect on the final peacebuilding outcome.

The success of peacekeeping is partly determined by the quality of the peace-making—the peace treaty that the peace negotiators have made. It is also shaped by the resources available and the strategy employed to direct postconflict reconstruction. And lastly, it may be crucially influenced by the enforcement capacities that the peacekeepers can draw upon to deter or coerce potential spoilers. Peacekeeping must exhibit the strategic dynamism to manage all these. While resources can be considered exogenous in the sense that the UN relies on member states to offer resources, strategy is influenced by a dynamic bargaining process that involves the Security Council, the General Assembly, the Secretariat, the

---

[124] Other perspectives on how to evaluate peacekeeping include Diehl 1993; Bruce R. Pirnie and William E. Simons, *Soldiers for Peace: An Operational Typology* (Santa Monica, CA: RAND, for the Office of the Secretary of Defense, 1996); and Duane Bratt "Explaining Peacekeeping Performance: The UN in Internal Conflicts" *International Peacekeeping*, 4 no. 3 (1994): 65–81.

[125] Boutros Boutros-Ghali, *An Agenda for Peace*, 2d edition (New York: United Nations, 1995), p. 59.

[126] Doyle 1997, p. 378; Steven R. Ratner, *The New UN Peacekeeping: Building Peace in Lands of Conflict after the Cold War* (New York: St. Martin's Press, 1995).

[127] Doyle, Johnstone, and Orr 1997.

[128] Evans 1993.

[129] Boutros-Ghali 1995.

[130] Diehl 1993, p. 67.

[131] Evans 1993.

parties to the war, and other interested actors. Once the troops are deployed and begin interacting with the parties, they acquire information on if and how their mandate and operational guidelines must be amended so that they can be effective. This leads to adaptation. Peacekeepers can use judgment and discretion in interpreting their mandate, which almost always is stated in sufficiently vague terms to allow some agency slack in the field. Good peacekeepers can select strategies that preserve their impartiality while enhancing their leverage over the parties. The Secretariat—not just members of the P5 in the Council—has input in adapting peacekeeping strategy. Strategy adjustment is certainly constrained by the exogenous factors (such as superpower interest or troop contributions from member states), but it is also endogenous to the peacekeepers' initiative and creativity, their training and abilities, their proactive use of available resources, and their ability to update their beliefs about the optimal strategy in a changing environment. If these "soft" variables played no role in determining the outcomes of peacekeeping operations, then peacekeeping success or failure would be due entirely to those exogenous factors that determined the initial mandate and resources of the peacekeeping operation, and UN peacekeeping would be entirely epiphenomenal.

The parties also learn throughout this dynamic process, and their strategies change. The whole is best seen as a spiral in which good peacemaking can set the stage for the use of peacekeeping (by helping the parties to negotiate a treaty), which in turn can allow civilian missions to aid the country in postconflict reconstruction. And should peacekeepers be deployed as monitors or peace enforcers sent out to maintain order before a peace is negotiated, their successful management will enhance the prospects for an agreement that establishes a more thoroughgoing process of institutional and economic reconstruction.

This model of the peacekeeping-peacemaking relationship has two major implications. First, the outcome of the peace process cannot be determined ex ante simply on the basis of the level of hostility and local capacities in the country. International capacities for peace do play a role, but only if interventions are well designed. In a few cases, peacekeeping may succeed if initial mandates fail. It may inspire international concern if violence escalates, ultimately improving the likelihood of peacekeeping success (international attention to Bosnia increased after the tragic failure of the UN to protect the inhabitants of the safe areas). At the same time, if peacekeepers are deployed before a peace agreement, a major failure may undermine the parties' political will for a settlement if that failure reverses the political or military status quo, making a negotiated settlement less appealing to one or more of the parties. In subsequent chapters, we evaluate different peacekeeping operations in terms of both a narrow and a broad type of success and failure: the narrow type concerns success in discharging the mandate (which we refer to as the "microlevel"); broad success refers to the peacekeepers' contribution to final outcome of the peace process (the "macrolevel"). While our statistical analysis focuses on "broad" success (success or failure of the peace process), our case studies allow us to focus more closely on the narrow view, explaining specific success or failures of UN missions.

Second, the model suggests that the outcome of a peace process does not depend entirely on peacekeeping efforts, but that we must evaluate the impact of peacekeeping while controlling for variables that might influence the UN's decision to intervene as well as variables that influence the final peacebuilding outcome. The initial peacekeeping mandate, some might argue, is potentially determined by the levels of hostility, local capacities, and other variables. Thus, some might argue that the UN has no independent effect on the peace process.[132] Critics might also argue that the UN selects the easy cases to intervene, so as to avoid the costs of failure. But proving this is difficult, for a number of reasons.

First, the UN is not a unitary actor, and the mandate and resources of each mission are the result of a bargaining process that involves member states of the Security Council, the Secretariat, which represents the interests of the organization, and other interested actors. Even if the Secretariat wanted to pick easy cases to establish a record of success for the UN, the interests of member states are often antithetical to such an approach, as they often use the UN as scapegoat, unloading difficult cases in which they have no strategic interest. Thus, the UN's complex institutional structure makes it difficult to argue that the organization is following a consistent strategy of intervening only in the "easy" cases.

Second, as an empirical matter, the UN seems to intervene in the "hard" cases. Average levels of deaths and displacements are higher, local capacities lower, and numbers of factions higher in cases where the UN has sent peacekeepers as compared to the rest of the cases. Moreover, our model makes clear that once the mission is deployed, both the initial levels of resources and the initial mandate can change in unpredictable ways and as a result of the peacekeepers' actions on the ground. Peacekeepers often have leeway to interpret their man-

---

[132] There are variables that influence the discharge of peacekeeping mandates and are not affected by any of the other variables in our model, which allows us to treat peacekeeping as exogenous in our regression analysis. Such variables are: peacekeeping doctrine; training; institutional constraints to changing the peacekeepers' operational guidelines after they are deployed; and the stickiness of peacekeeping operations, which makes it difficult for peacekeepers to pull out and then redeploy in response to a rapidly changing strategic environment.

date creatively, adjusting their strategy as required by conditions on the ground.

Our statistical analysis considers this problem of endogeneity carefully, and we believe that we can identify an independent contribution of UN operations while taking account of measurable indicators of state interest and other factors that might influence peacebuilding outcomes as well as the UN's decision to intervene.[133] Our case studies put this argument into richer historical context and offer narratives that demonstrate the value added of peacekeepers, by providing before-and-after accounts of several peace processes that highlight the precise contribution of UN missions.

In sum, our model illustrates the channels (mechanisms) through which peace-making, peacekeeping, and postconflict reconstruction can shape peacebuilding outcomes. We argue that the strategic conception that unites these strategies is a peacebuilding triangle.

A Peacebuilding Triangle

International peacebuilding strategies, concepts of operations, therefore should be "strategic" in the ordinary sense of that term, matching means to ends. Although a peacebuilding strategy must be designed to address a particular conflict, broad parameters that fit most conflicts can be identified. These strategies combine peace-making, peacekeeping, postconflict reconstruction, and (where needed) enforcement.

Effective transitional strategy must take into account levels of hostility and factional capacities. Whether it in fact does so depends on strategic design and international commitment. Designs for transitions incorporate a mix of legal and bureaucratic capacities that integrate, in a variety of ways, domestic and international commitments.

Important lessons can already be drawn from efforts to establish effective transitional authority.[134] First, a holistic approach is necessary to deal with the character of factional conflicts and civil wars. Successful exercises of authority require a coordinated approach that draws in elements of "peace-making" (negotiations), peacekeeping, peacebuilding

---

[133] The fact that the UN intervenes in harder cases might mean that if there is a selection effect in the decision to intervene that we have not captured, then the results of our empirical analysis in chapter 3 would underestimate the true effect of UN missions, and the actual impact of UN peacekeeping could be even greater.

[134] See the chapter by Thomas Franck, "A Holistic Approach to Peace-Building," in Olara Otunnu and Michael Doyle, eds, *Peacemaking and Peacekeeping for the New Century* (Lanham, MD Rowman and Littlefield, 1998), pp. 275–95; and Cousens, Kumar, and Wermester 2000.

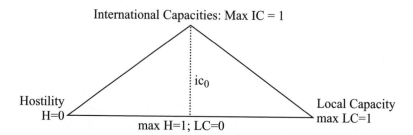

Figure 2.2 The Peacebuilding Triangle. The triangle is a metaphor for the peacebuilding space after civil war. Available space is determined by the interaction of the triangle's three sides: Local Capacities (LC), International Capacities (IC), and Hostility (H) level. The greater local and international capacities and the lower the hostility, the greater will be the space for peace. We assume a strictly positive level of IC, given the support and legitimacy offered sovereign states by international law and norms. This positive level of international support is denoted by the constant ic_0 which ensures that IC cannot be zero. All three variables, LC, IC, and H can be measured as indices, ranging from 0 to 1 (maximum).

reconstruction, and discrete acts of enforcement, when needed, to create a holistic strategy of reconciliation.[135]

Transitional strategies should first address the local causes of continuing conflict and, second, the local capacities for change. Effective transitional authority is the residual dimension that compensates for local deficiencies and the continuing hostility of the factions—the (net) specific degree of international commitment available to assist change.

Local root causes, domestic capacity, and effective transitional authority are three dimensions of a triangle, whose area is the "political space"—or effective capacity—for building peace (see figure 2.2). This metaphor suggests that some quantum of positive support is needed along each dimension, but that the dimensions also substitute for each other—more of one substitutes for less of another, less deeply rooted causes of war substitute for weak local capacity or minor international commitment. In a world where each dimension is finite we can expect, first, that compromises will be necessary in order to achieve peacebuilding; second, that the international role must be designed to fit each case; and, third, that self-sustaining peace is not only the right aim, it is the practically necessary aim of building peace when the international community is not prepared to commit to long-term assistance.

[135] See Alvaro DeSoto and Graciana del Castillo, "Obstacles to Peacebuilding in El Salvador," *Foreign Policy* 94 (Spring 1994): 69–83. This is the coordinating role that Japan for example played in Cambodia in organizing the Tokyo conference and the International Committee on the Reconstruction of Cambodia (ICORC).

For example, in a small community enjoying a deep and broad sense of affinity, considerable social and full political equality, substantial sources of social capital and wealth, and access to even greater resources from its national capital, peacebuilding is easy. The space for effective action is nearly boundless; in an emergency, habits of cooperation, emergency public assistance, and inflows of national relief pour in. The disaster is addressed. The community might even be strengthened as it successfully meets a natural challenge. Imagine now a Cambodian town escaping from the devastation inflicted by the Khmer Rouge, up until recently governed by a force composed largely of Cambodia's historic enemy, Vietnam, and lacking technical skills, medicine, education, infrastructure. Its national capital rather than being a source of assistance is also devastated. National GDP per capita is between $200 and $300 per year. Here the space for peacebuilding is thin and tenuous.

International peace operation mandates must take into account the characteristics of the factions and whether the parties are prepared to coordinate or must be persuaded or coerced into cooperation. These mandates operate not upon stable states but, instead, on unstable factions. These factions (to simplify) come in various dimensions of hostility. Hostility, in turn, is shaped by the number of factions, including the recognized state as one (if there is one). Numerous factions make it difficult for them to cooperate and engender suspicion. Two, few, or many factions complicate both coordination and cooperation. In addition, harm done—casualties and refugees generated—create the resentment that makes jointly beneficial solutions to coordination and cooperation that much more difficult to envisage. The more hostile and numerous the factions, the more difficult the peace process will be and the more international assistance/authority will be needed if peace is to be established.[136]

In less hostile circumstances (with few factions, a hurting stalemate, or less harm done), international monitoring and facilitation might be sufficient to establish transparent trust and self-enforcing peace. Monitoring helps create transparency among partners lacking trust but having com-

[136] By "factions" we refer to actual factions in a civil war. While the peacebuilding triangle measures hostility generated by these factions (e.g., it can measure the number of factions, whether or not they have signed a treaty, and the issues over which they are fighting a war), we cannot measure the factions' local capacities except at the national level, so we use country-level indicators of local capacities in our empirical analysis. This is not inconsistent with our analysis, as national-level capacities are crucially important for economic reconstruction after civil war. In some cases, only a small part of a country is affected by civil war, and local capacities are lower in that part as compared to the rest of the country. But even in those cases, the capacity of the central government to rebuild the war-torn region by redirecting resources to it is critical for the peacebuilding process. Our measure of national-level capacities captures this.

patible incentives favoring peace. Traditional peacekeeping assistance can also reduce trade-offs (helping, for example, to fund and certify the cantonment, demobilization, and reintegration of former combatants). In these circumstances—with few players, some reconciliation, less damage—international coordination and assistance can be sufficient to overcome hostility and solve implementation problems. An international peacekeeping presence itself can deter defections from the peace treaty, because of the possible costs of violating international agreements and triggering further international involvement in an otherwise domestic conflict. International capacity building—such as foreign aid, demobilization of military forces, institutional reform—will assist parties that favor the peace to meet their commitments.

In more hostile circumstances, international enforcement can help solve commitment and cooperation problems by directly implementing or raising the costs of defection from peace agreements. International enforcement and long-term trusteeship will be required to overcome deep sources of distrust and powerful incentives to defect from agreed provisions of the peace. As in other conflictual-cooperative situations such as Prisoner's Dilemma and mixed motive games,[137] the existence of deeply hostile or many factions or factions that lack coherent leadership complicate the problem of achieving self-enforcing cooperative peace. Instead, conscious direction and enforcement by an impartial international agent to guarantee the functions of effective sovereignty becomes necessary, and peacebuilding must include activities such as conducting a free and fair election, arresting war criminals, and policing and administering a collapsed state. The more difficult it is for the factions to cooperate, the greater the international authority and capacity the international peacebuilders must wield. In addition to substantial bodies of troops, extensive budgets for political reconstruction and substantial international authority need to be brought to bear because the parties are so unlikely to trust each other and cooperate. International mandates may need to run from monitoring to administration to executive authority and full sovereign trusteeship-like supervision—if peace is going to be maintained and become eventually self-sustaining.

War-torn countries also vary in economic and social capacity. Some war-torn countries started out with considerable economic development (the former Yugoslavia) and retain levels of social capacity in an educated population. Others began poor and the war impoverished them further (Angola, Sudan, Cambodia). In both cases reconstruction is vital; the more the social and economic devastation, the larger the multidimen-

---

[137] Axelrod and Keohane 1986; Kenneth Oye, "Explaining Cooperation under Anarchy," *World Politics* 38, no. 1 (1985): 1–24.

sional international role must become, whether consent-based multidimensional peacekeeping or nonconsent enforcement followed by and including multidimensional peacekeeping. International economic relief and productive jobs are the first signs of peace that can persuade rival factions to truly disarm and take a chance on peaceful politics. Institutions need to be rebuilt, including a unified army and police force and the even more challenging development of a school system that can assist the reconciliation of future generations.[138] In countries with low levels of local capacities, competition over resources will be intense at the early stages of the peace process, and this can further intensify the coordination and collaboration problems that the peacekeepers will be asked to resolve.

There thus should be a relation between the depth of hostility (harm and factions) and local capacities (institutional and economic collapse), on the one hand, and the extent of international assistance and effective authority, from monitoring to enforcing, needed to build peace, on the other. In a world where each dimension is finite we can expect, first, that compromises will be necessary to achieve peacebuilding success; and second, that the international role will be significant in general and successful when it is designed to fit the case. The extent of transitional authority that needs to be delegated to the international community will be a function of the level of postwar hostility and local capacities.

The relations among the three dimensions of the triangle are complicated. The availability and prospect of international assistance and the existence of extensive local capacities, for example, can, if poorly managed, both raise the gains from victory (spoils of war and rebuilding assistance) and reduce the costs of fighting (as the assistance serves to sustain the fighting). So, too, deep war-related hostilities can have dual effects. They make peace more difficult to make and increase the rational incentives for ending the conflict.

That relationship is loosely reflected in the variable shapes of the "peacebuilding triangles" for the different cases that we analyze in later chapters. The triangular metaphor suggests that the larger the triangle, the greater the chances of success and that smaller "areas," or "political spaces" will not on average tend to be sufficient. But success or failure comes in a variety of forms depending on the local conditions, with more or less hostility, more or less local capacity, and more or less internationally assisted capacity (and thus more or less intrusive foreign presence).

This triangular shape also makes it possible to visualize our key hy-

---

[138] Having observed negotiations in El Salvador, Cambodia, Eastern Slavonia (Croatia), Brcko (Bosnia), and Cyprus, it is our opinion that establishing a unified army or multiethnic police force, though difficult, is easy compared to agreeing on an elementary school curriculum.

potheses since the three sets of variables interact competitively (H vs. IC and LC) and cooperatively (LC and IC) to produce a space for peace. Specifically, this model posits that:[139] (*a*) the larger the international capacities (IC), the higher the probability of peacebuilding success, given hostility (H) and local capacities (LC); (*b*) the greater (deeper) the hostility, the lower the probability of peacebuilding success, given LC and IC; and (*c*) the larger the local capacities, the higher the probability of peacebuilding success, given H and IC.

In the next chapter, we test this model by identifying and measuring proxy variables for Hostility, Local Capacities, and International Capacities and estimating a statistical model that identifies the significance of each of these determinants of peacebuilding success. Our analysis draws upon and extends our earlier work,[140] which presented the first quantitative analysis of the contribution of UN peace operations to peacebuilding outcomes.[141] We then follow the statistical analysis with case studies that explore how each of the dimensions has operated in successful and unsuccessful peacebuilding.

[139] We use the triangle as a metaphor to visualize our three core variables. We do not suggest that the equation that gives the area of the triangle is a precise way in which the variables that produce peacebuilding interact or that we should estimate that equation econometrically. Rather, the triangle should illustrate our broad point that local and international capacities have positive effects on the likelihood of peacebuilding success, while hostility levels have negative effects. In our statistical analysis, we estimate both independent effects for each of these three dimensions and we also explore interactive effects, which we present in a supplementary document available online (see chapter 3).

[140] Doyle and Sambanis 2000.

[141] There are, however, many informative and comparative case studies of peacebuilding. For a valuable critical assessment and bibliography see Cindy Collins and Thomas Weiss, "An Overview and Assessment of 1989–1996 Peace Operations Publications," Thomas J. Watson Institute Occasional Paper no. 28 (Providence: Watson Institute, 1997). Among the many we have found especially helpful are William J. Durch, *The Evolution of UN Peacekeeping: Case Studies and Comparative Analyses* (New York: St. Martin's Press, 1993); William J. Durch, ed., *UN Peacekeeping, America's Policy and the Uncivil Wars of the 1990s* (New York: St. Martin's Press, 1996); Licklider 1993; Brown 1996; Hampson 1996; the case studies in Doyle, Johnstone and Orr 1997; Paris 1997; and Jarat Chopra, *Peace Maintenance* (London: Routledge, 1999). Ernst B. Haas, *The United Nations and Collective Management of International Conflict* (New York: UNITAR, 1986); and Paul F. Diehl, Jennifer Reifschneider, and Paul R. Hensel, "United Nations Intervention and Recurring Conflict," *International Organization* 50 (Autumn 1996), 683–700 analyze the impact of UN missions on conflict recurrence focusing on interstate conflicts of varying intensity. A classic piece is Ernst B. Haas, Lyle Butterworth, and Joseph Nye, *Conflict Management by International Organization*. (Morristown, NJ: General Learning Press, 1972), who argue that the UN works best when elaborate (e.g. multidimensional) peace operations are used.

3

Testing Peacebuilding Strategies

> The most perilous moment for a bad
> government is when it seeks to mend its ways.
> —Tocqueville[1]

JUST AS CIVIL WAR is about failures of legitimate state authority, civil peace is about its successful reconstruction. Peacebuilding strategy is what comes between. Effective strategies must be designed to fit the case if it is going to succeed in building peace. In this chapter, we would like to explain how the triangle of local hostility, local capacities, and international capacities that we previously described favors or disfavors the prospects of sustainable peace.

Triangulating Peace

The probability that peacebuilding will succeed is a function of a country's capacities for peace, the available international assistance, and the depth of war-related hostility.[2] The relations among these dimensions are complicated. The availability and prospect of international economic assistance and the existence of extensive local capacities, for example, can both raise the gains from victory (spoils of war and rebuilding assistance) and reduce the costs of fighting (as the assistance serves to sustain the fighting). But they can also provide incentives for peace. So, too, deep war-related hostilities can have dual effects. The decision to support peacebuilding is enhanced by both local and international capacities for peace; net local capacities are given by the difference between local capacities (LC) or developmental potential minus war-generated hostility (H); and international capacities (IC) can substitute for deficiencies in local capacities to compensate for the depth of hostility.

---

[1] Alexis de Tocqueville, *The Old Regime and the French Revolution* [1856], trans. S. Gilbert (New York: Doubleday, 1955), p. 177.

[2] This section draws on and expands Doyle and Sambanis 2000.

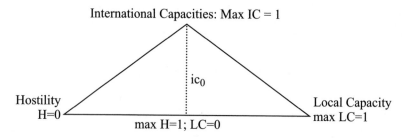

Figure 3.1 The Peacebuilding Triangle

Thus, we theorize that the peacebuilding process is loosely reflected in the shape of a "peacebuilding triangle" (see figure 3.1).[3]

This convenient shape makes it possible to visualize our key hypotheses since the three sets of variables interact competitively (H vs. IC and LC) and cooperatively (LC and IC) to produce a space for peace.[4] Specifically, we hypothesize that: (a) the larger the international capacities (IC), the higher the probability of peacebuilding success, given hostility (H) and local capacities (LC); (b) the greater (deeper) the hostility, the lower the probability of peacebuilding success, given LC and IC; and (c) the larger the local capacities, the higher the probability of peacebuilding success, given H and IC.

We will test our model by using different measures of the three "concept" variables—the dimensions of the peacebuilding triangle—Hostility, Local Capacities, and International Capacities. We are interested both in evaluating the broader "triangle" theory (i.e., to assess if all three

---

[3] H, LC, and IC can be thought of as indices ranging from 0 to 1 (maximum). IC = $ic_0 + IC_1$, where IC_1 is the amount of international assistance after the war and ic_0 is a positive constant ($0 < ic_0 < 1$) representing the lowest level of international aid that is available ex ante to sovereign states, as provided by international laws ensuring that if LC − H does not equal 0, the probability of peacebuilding success can be defined as the area of the triangle.

[4] We use the term "interact" loosely here to mean that each dimension's effect on the peace must be assessed while controlling for the other two dimensions. Each dimension has independent effects on the peace. The triangle is simply a metaphor used to visualize the interaction of our three core variables. Other geometric shapes may also fit (e.g., a pyramid, where each dimension is mapped separately). In our statistical analysis, we assume a linear component in the way each of these variables/dimensions influences peacebuilding success, but the logit model specification that we use for most of our analysis takes into account the interaction of all variables in producing estimates of the effects of each variable on the probability of peacebuilding success. We also consider the interaction between IC and the other two dimensions more formally in supplementary analysis that we post online.

dimensions have significant effects on the probability of peacebuilding success) and in determining the effects of individual measures or proxies for each of the dimensions, or concept variables. Each of the measures or proxies that we use, has a theoretical link to our argument and is related to one or more of the theories of civil war that we reviewed in chapter 2.

Our quantitative analysis of the correlates of successful peacebuilding sets the stage for a more fine-grained case-study analysis of the contribution of UN peace operations to the outcomes of peace processes.[5] The statistical analysis maps the strategic environment within which actors make their decisions to support peace or war, and we explain how best to use UN peace operations to prevent civil wars from recurring. (UN operations are our main measure of international capacities.) The case studies in subsequent chapters delve into greater depth to give readers a better sense of the process through which peacebuilding takes hold.

We analyze a new dataset that we compiled, where we included all civil wars since 1945, both with and without UN operations. The main point of the chapter is to demonstrate that the logic of the peacebuilding triangle is consistent with the empirical record. To convince ourselves and the reader that the inferences we draw from the data are correct, we used several different estimation methods and conducted a number of robustness tests. But we present only key results in this chapter and relegate the bulk of the statistical analysis and most technical details to a supplement that we have posted online.[6] Another document includes "additional results" that we refer to in passing in this chapter. For easy reference, we cite specific pages in the supplement and in the "additional results" document where the reader can find more details. Next, we describe the dataset briefly. Appendix A includes details on our coding rules and appendix B presents variable descriptions and summary statistics for all variables used in the analysis.

---

[5] For a valuable critical assessment and bibliography on peacekeeping see Collins and Weiss 1997. Among the many we have found especially helpful in formulating our hypotheses are Durch 1993, 1997; Licklider 1993; Brown 1996; Hampson 1996; the case studies in Doyle, Johnstone, and Orr 1997; Paris 1997; and Chopra 1999; Haas 1986; and Diehl, Reifschneider, and Hensel 1996 analyze the impact of UN missions on conflict recurrence focusing on interstate conflicts of varying intensity. A classic piece is Ernst B. Haas, L. Butterworth, and J. Nye, *Conflict Management by International Organization* (Morristown, NJ: General Learning Press, 1972), who argue that the UN works best when elaborate (e.g., multidimensional) peace operations are used.

[6] The supplement, data files, computer programs, and coding notes are available here: http://pantheon.yale.edu/~ns237/index/research.html#Peace.

The Peacebuilding Dataset

Our dataset includes all peace processes after civil war from 1945 until the end of 1999.[7] According to our coding rules, there have been 151 civil wars in that period. Appendix A.1 presents our rules for coding the start and end of a civil war, including criteria used to separate civil wars from other forms of political violence and to distinguish episodes of civil war in the same country.[8] Each post–civil war transition is an "observation" for our statistical analysis. We exclude wars that were ongoing at the end of our analysis period (December 31, 1999) and/or cases where there was no significant peace process prior to that point.[9] If a peace process started and failed immediately, we coded a failure of the peace in the first month of the peace process.[10] This leaves 121 cases that are included in the statistical analysis.[11]

The Dependent Variable

Our dependent variable is peacebuilding success. There can be several ways to define and measure this concept. In the introduction, we offered several reasons that we believe justify our decision to use a positive, complex measure of peacebuilding. While we use a few different measures throughout the book and in the supplement to check the robustness of

---

[7] A handful of civil wars in our dataset may have started in 1944, but all peace processes started after 1945.

[8] For a discussion of the conceptual and empirical foundations of the civil war definition we use in our analysis, see Nicholas Sambanis, "What Is a Civil War? Conceptual and Empirical Complexities of an Operational Definition," *Journal of Conflict Resolution* 48, no. 6 (2004b): 814–58. We have also performed our analysis using the list of civil wars from our earlier work (2000); and by dropping or recoding all ambiguous cases in this new dataset (both cases that might not meet one or more of the criteria for civil war and cases for which the coding of peacebuilding outcomes may be ambiguous). We report results from these analyses in the supplement. We also explain all coding decisions for the civil war list and for all other variables used in this book in our coding notes, which we have posted online along with the supplement.

[9] In a few cases, a war was ongoing in 1999, but a serious peace effort had taken place earlier (and obviously failed). We included those cases, but we have also conducted the analysis without them.

[10] These are cases where a military victory fails to end the war (e.g., Afghanistan in 1992). Or, there are cases where the UN intervenes to end the fighting, but fails (e.g., Angola, Sierra Leone, Somalia). These cases are included. We do not include any peace processes that started after December 31, 1999, and this causes us to lose a few civil wars with UN missions (e.g. UNAMA in Afghanistan; MONUC in the Democratic Republic of the Congo; UNAMSIL in Sierra Leone).

[11] Two observations are dropped due to missing data.

our results, our main dependent variable for the statistical analysis in this chapter is a short-run measure of peacebuilding success. We code short-run outcomes two years after the end of the civil war as a binary variable: 1 signifies "success" and 0 signifies "failure." We use both a lenient definition of peace, which we call "negative" or *sovereign* peace, and a strict or "positive" definition, which we call *participatory* peace.[12] *Sovereign peace* requires an end to the civil war, undivided sovereignty, no residual violence (i.e., no minor or intermediate-level organized violence that challenges the state in its territory) and no mass-level human rights abuses by the state (e.g., politicides, population expulsions). This is a negative standard of peace, focusing on the absence of large-scale violence. *Participatory peace* requires sovereign peace plus a minimum level of political openness, which we code based on the well-known Polity index.[13] We do not require that the country be a democracy, but rather only exclude the most authoritarian of regimes, as higher-order peace cannot be based on the complete exclusion or repression of a group of citizens. We require a very low level of political openness, as most countries would fail to attain a higher standard two years after the war.[14] At the same time, avoiding totalitarianism is a reasonable goal of societies emerging from civil war, and our low polity threshold allows us to exclude the peaces of the grave—that is, those cases where most of the challengers of the state are either dead or in prison. Appendix A.2 explains our coding rule for the dependent variable in more detail.

Most of our discussion in this chapter will focus on explaining successes

[12] Throughout the chapter, italicized variable names refer to the names of variables used in the statistical analysis. Abbreviated labels of variables are used in the actual analysis and we have included a list of variable names and corresponding labels in our supplement.

[13] Marshall and Jaggers 2000, www.bsos.umd.edu/cidcm/inscr/polity.

[14] We require a Polity score of 3 out of 20 (with 20 indicating a perfect democracy). In some cases, democracy scores are missing due to war or regime transition. In those cases, we use democracy scores interpolated by the coders of the Polity project. In Doyle and Sambanis 2000 (hereafter DS2000), we used several thresholds and found that as we increased the threshold of democracy, the number of peacebuilding successes declined rapidly. Two years after a civil war, most countries are not democracies; thus expectations for them should be modest. There are several possible combinations of authority characteristics of a regime that can produce the same Polity score. Thus, our threshold cannot say much about which aspects of a polity are especially relevant for peacebuilding (we discuss this question much more in our case studies). If the goal of supporting political openness is to avoid a future civil war (in our view, political openness is important for a wider set of political and economic goals and should not be pursued simply as a way to reduce the risk of another civil war), then one could focus on particular aspects of regimes, for example, on whether or not there are political parties and a legislature. In this way, one could distinguish autocracies with political institutions from those without institutions. For such an analysis, which finds that autocracies with institutions are less likely to experience a civil war than are autocracies without institutions, see Gandhi and Vreeland 2004.

or failures in achieving participatory peace two years after the civil war. We have also conducted an analysis of the effects of UN operations in the longer term and present results in our supplement, summarizing the main findings at the end of this chapter. In our supplement, we also present results based on a decomposition of our complex measure of peacebuilding success into its four components.[15] Some important differences emerge that help us better understand when and how UN missions can be effective. By decomposing the peacebuilding success measure, we are able to analyze the effectiveness of UN missions with respect to preventing the recurrence of war, both in the short and long term, and assess the effects of UN missions on postwar democratization while controlling for levels of violence. We leave most technical details as well as the analysis of the individual components of peacebuilding success for the supplement, and summarize the main substantive results in this chapter.

In our theoretical discussion in chapter 2, we argued that self-sustaining peace is the standard that we should use to evaluate the success or failure of a peace process. While the UN is still present, the peace process is still ongoing, so we cannot speak of self-sustaining peace. Thus, we code peacebuilding outcomes two years after what we call the peace "stimulus"—that is, a settlement, military victory, or long-lasting truce, or the completion of a UN operation.[16] In some cases, war resumes while a UN peace operation is present. In those cases, we code a peacebuilding failure, even though the UN mission may remain deployed throughout the new war. But we cannot code a peacebuilding success while the UN is still present. In those cases, we can speak of peace*keeping*, not peace*building* success. This coding rule implies that cases where the UN has not departed for at least two years before the end of December 1999 must be excluded from the analysis.[17] We have coded peacebuilding outcomes for 119 cases with available data for any of the explanatory variables.

[15] See supplement, pages 24–31 and table 6.

[16] This is an important conceptual difference with DS2000, where peacebuilding outcomes were coded two years after the end of the war, regardless of whether or not the peacekeepers were still present. Our results are robust to using the "old" definition from DS2000 (see table 2 and discussion on pages 6–7 in the supplement). But the old definition measures peace*keeping* success rather than peace*building* success understood as self-sustaining peace. In the new definition, the peace can fail, but not succeed while the UN is still present. In the supplement (pages 9–11) we also discuss our "fix" for a problem with left-censoring that arises with our new definition—i.e., the problem that for those cases where the UN was present for several months after the end of the war, but departed before the end of our analysis period, our two-year evaluation point comes later than that corresponding to the other cases with no UN intervention or with failed UN intervention. This, however, does not influence our conclusions about the effectiveness of UN operations.

[17] These are all cases where the UN has not yet failed, but neither has there been a new war. So dropping these cases should make it harder for us to find significant effects for UN missions.

Out of these, 84 were *participatory peace* failures (69.42 percent) and 37 successes (30.58 percent). Achieving *sovereign peace* is easier: there are 68 failures and 53 successes.[18] Table 3.1 presents our list of civil wars and peacebuilding outcomes for each case and also identifies those cases with a UN intervention.

Explanatory Variables

The three sides of the peacebuilding triangle represent "concept" variables—hostility, local capacity, and international capacity—in our theory and they are not easily measured. To test our model empirically, we relied on measurable proxies for them. The proxies were selected because they follow directly from some of the theories of civil war that we considered in chapter 2, and some have obvious policy significance. We used available indicators from the literature and also coded several new variables.

One could think of several proxies for the level of hostility. The *number of deaths and displacements* is a key variable, as a larger human cost for the war should result in greater levels of postwar hostility among the factions.[19]

The type of war may also be an important indicator of hostility. There is some debate in the literature on whether or not ethnoreligious wars are harder to resolve than revolutions or other types of civil war. Hatred or resentment may be more intense among ethnic groups than among income groups; adversaries from different ethnic or racial groups may be more easily identifiable than adversaries from class-based groups and hence targeting for violence may be easier in ethnic wars; and ethnic wars may be more often about conflict over nondivisible goods, making conflict resolution harder. There is no consensus on these hypotheses in the literature, and some authors argue that the very concept of an ethnic

[18] If we used a five-year cutoff point to evaluate peacebuilding success, there would be 74 participatory peace failures and 35 successes; and 58 sovereign failures and 51 successes. In the supplement (table 7) we present results using the five-year period. We have also coded an alternative version of peacebuilding success, where all ambiguous cases are either dropped (if the criteria for coding a civil war may not all be met) or recoded as the opposite outcome (if the initial coding of peacebuilding outcome was questionable). For participatory peace two years after the war, the alternative version has 78 failures and 25 successes (for a total of 103 observations). See the supplement (table 3) for results using this version of the peacebuilding variable (discussion on pages 12–14 of the supplement).

[19] We take the natural log of this variable as the range of *deaths and displacements* that has a large variance. We combine numbers of deaths and displacements, but also use the *natural log of deaths* alone in the regressions and code a *per capita measure of deaths and displacements* as well. Estimates of people killed and displaced in civil war are uncertain, so we have used two versions of this variable to check the robustness of our results. Comments and sources for the coding of each case are provided in the document labeled "Civil War Coding" in our Web site (comments are also inserted in the dataset).

TABLE 3.1
Civil Wars Starting in 1945–1999 and Peacebuilding Outcomes, Two Years after the "Peace Stimulus"

Country	War Start	War End	Sovereign Peace	Participatory Peace	Type of UN Operation
Afghanistan	1978	1992	Failure	Failure	None
Afghanistan	1992	1996	Failure	Failure	None
Afghanistan	1996	2001	—	—	None
Algeria	1962	1963	Success	Failure	None
Algeria	1992	—	—	—	None
Angola	1975	1991	Failure	Failure	Observer mission
Angola	1992	1994	Failure	Failure	Traditional PKO
Angola	1997	2002	Failure	Failure	Traditional PKO
Angola	1994	1999	—	—	None
Argentina	1955	1955	Success	Success	None
Argentina	1975	1977	Failure	Failure	None
Azerbaijan	1991	1994	Failure	Failure	None
Bangladesh	1974	1997	Success	Success	None
Bolivia	1952	1952	Success	Success	None
Bosnia	1992	1995	—	—	Enforcement
Burundi	1965	1969	Failure	Failure	None
Burundi	1972	1972	Success	Failure	None
Burundi	1988	1988	Failure	Failure	None
Burundi	1991	—	—	—	None
Cambodia	1970	1975	Failure	Failure	None
Cambodia	1975	1991	Success	Success	None
Central African Republic	1996	1997	—	—	Multidimensional PKO
Chad	1965	1979	Failure	Failure	Multidimensional PKO
Chad	1980	1994	Failure	Failure	None
Chad	1994	1997	Success	Success	None
China	1946	1949	Failure	Failure	None

Country					
China	1947	1947	Success	Failure	None
China	1950	1951	Success	Failure	None
China	1956	1959	Success	Failure	None
China	1967	1968	Success	Failure	None
Colombia	1948	1948	Failure	Failure	None
Colombia	1978	—	Failure	Failure	None
Congo (Brazzaville)	1993	1997	Failure	Failure	None
Congo (Brazzaville)	1998	1999	—	—	None
Congo-Zaire	1960	1965	Failure	Failure	Enforcement
Congo-Zaire	1967	1967	Success	Failure	None
Congo-Zaire	1977	1978	Failure	Failure	None
Congo-Zaire	1996	1997	Failure	Failure	None
Congo-Zaire	1998	2001	—	—	Observer mission
Costa Rica	1948	1948	Success	Success	None
Croatia	1992	1995	Success	Success	Enforcement
Cuba	1958	1959	Failure	Failure	None
Cyprus	1963	1967	Failure	Failure	Traditional PKO
Cyprus	1974	1974	Failure	Failure	Traditional PKO
Djibouti	1991	1994	Success	Success	None
Dominican Republic	1965	1965	Success	Success	Observer mission
El Salvador	1979	1992	Success	Success	Multidimensional PKO
Egypt	1994	1997	Success	Success	None
Ethiopia	1974	1991	Success	Success	None
Ethiopia	1978	1991	Success	Success	None
Ethiopia	1976	1988	Failure	Failure	None
Georgia	1991	1992	Failure	Failure	None
Georgia	1992	1994	Failure	Failure	Observer mission
Greece	1944	1949	Success	Success	Observer mission

(continued)

TABLE 3.1 (*continued*)

Country	War Start	War End	Sovereign Peace	Participatory Peace	Type of UN Operation
Guatemala	1966	1972	Failure	Failure	None
Guatemala	1978	1994	Success	Success	Multidimensional PKO
Guinea-Bissau	1998	1999	—	—	None
Haiti	1991	1995	—	—	Multidimensional PKO
India	1989	—	Failure	Failure	None
India	1984	1993	Success	Success	None
India	1989	—	—	—	None
India	1990	—	—	—	None
India	1946	1948	Success	Success	None
Indonesia	1950	1950	Failure	Failure	None
Indonesia	1953	1953	Failure	Failure	None
Indonesia	1956	1960	Failure	Failure	None
Indonesia	1976	1978	Failure	Failure	None
Indonesia	1975	1999	—	—	Enforcement
Indonesia	1990	1991	Failure	Failure	None
Indonesia	1999	2002	—	—	None
Iran	1978	1979	Failure	Failure	None
Iran	1979	1984	Failure	Failure	None
Iraq	1959	1959	Failure	Failure	None
Iraq	1961	1970	Success	Success	None
Iraq	1974	1975	Failure	Failure	None
Iraq	1985	1996	Failure	Failure	None
Iraq	1991	1993	Failure	Failure	None
Israel	1987	1997	Success	Success	None
Israel	2000	—	—	—	None

Jordan	1970	1971	Success	Failure	None
Kenya	1963	1967	Success	Failure	None
Kenya	1991	1993	Failure	Failure	None
Korea	1948	1949	Success	Success	None
Laos	1960	1973	Failure	Failure	Observer mission
Lebanon	1958	1958	Success	Success	Traditional PKO
Lebanon	1975	1991	Failure	Failure	None
Liberia	1989	1990	Failure	Failure	Observer mission
Liberia	1992	1997	Failure	Failure	None
Liberia	1999	—	—	—	None
Mali	1990	1995	Success	Success	None
Moldova	1991	1992	Failure	Failure	None
Morocco/Western Sahara	1975	1991	Failure	Failure	Observer mission
Mozambique	1976	1992	Success	Success	Multidimensional PKO
Myanmar/Burma	1948	1951	Failure	Failure	None
Myanmar/Burma	1948	1988	Failure	Failure	None
Myanmar/Burma	1960	1995	Failure	Failure	None
Namibia	1973	1989	Success	Success	Multidimensional PKO
Nepal	1996	—	—	—	None
Nicaragua	1978	1979	Failure	Failure	None
Nicaragua	1981	1990	Success	Success	Observer mission
Nigeria	1967	1970	Success	Failure	None
Nigeria	1980	1985	Failure	Failure	None
Oman	1971	1975	Success	Failure	None
Pakistan	1971	1971	Success	Success	None
Pakistan	1973	1977	Failure	Failure	None
Pakistan	1994	1999	—	—	None
Papua New Guinea	1988	1998	—	—	None

(continued)

TABLE 3.1 (*continued*)

Country	War Start	War End	Sovereign Peace	Participatory Peace	Type of UN Operation
Paraguay	1947	1947	Success	Success	None
Peru	1980	1996	Failure	Failure	None
Philippines	1950	1952	Success	Success	None
Philippines	1972	1992	Failure	Failure	None
Philippines	1971	—	Failure	Failure	None
Russia	1994	1996	Failure	Failure	None
Russia	1999	—	—	—	None
Rwanda	1963	1964	Failure	Failure	None
Rwanda	1990	1993	Failure	Failure	Traditional PKO
Rwanda	1994	1994	Success	Success	Observer mission
Senegal	1989	1999	—	—	None
Sierra Leone	1991	1996	Failure	Failure	None
Sierra Leone	1997	2001	Failure	Failure	Traditional PKO
Somalia	1988	1991	Failure	Failure	None
Somalia	1991	—	Failure	Failure	Enforcement
South Africa	1976	1994	Success	Success	Observer mission
Sri Lanka	1971	1971	Success	Success	None
Sri Lanka	1983	2002	Failure	Failure	None
Sri Lanka	1987	1989	Success	Success	None
Sudan	1963	1972	Success	Failure	None
Sudan	1983	2002	Failure	Failure	None
Syria	1979	1982	Success	Failure	None
Tajikistan	1992	1997	—	—	Observer mission
Thailand	1966	1982	Success	Success	None
Turkey	1984	1999	—	—	None

Country	Year	Year			PKO
Uganda	1966	1966	Success	Success	None
Uganda	1978	1979	Failure	Failure	None
Uganda	1981	1987	Failure	Failure	None
Uganda	1990	1992	Failure	Failure	None
Uganda	1995	—	—	—	None
United Kingdom	1971	1998	—	—	None
USSR	1944	1948	—	—	None
USSR	1944	1947	—	—	None
USSR	1944	1950	—	—	None
USSR	1944	1948	—	—	None
Vietnam	1960	1975	Success	Failure	None
Yemen Arab Republic	1948	1948	Success	Success	None
Yemen	1994	1994	Success	Success	None
Yemen Arab Republic	1962	1970	Success	Success	Observer mission
Yemen Peoples Rep.	1986	1986	Success	Failure	None
Yugoslavia	1991	1991	Failure	Failure	Traditional PKO
Yugoslavia	1998	1999	—	—	Enforcement
Zimbabwe	1972	1979	Failure	Failure	None
Zimbabwe	1983	1987	Success	Success	None

Note: This list includes some cases that are not included in the analysis. See text for dropped cases and reasons for exclusion. Ongoing wars, for example, are excluded. The USSR wars are excluded due to missing data in several of our variables and because they started before the start of our analysis period. There are some differences between our civil war list and some others in the literature. See appendix A1 for a detailed description of our coding rules and our supplement for results using different civil war lists and corresponding peacebuilding outcomes.

war is questionable. But given that these hypotheses are plausible, we include the type of war in our model as a measure of hostility. We have three versions of the *war type* variable, each reflecting a slight difference in the coding rules. The variable that we use in most of our models is *war type*, a binary variable based on other authors' research and coding of ethnoreligious wars. Two variations of that variable (*ethnic war 1* and *ethnic war 2*), are also used to check robustness, based on our own coding of the cases, drawing on a close reading of case histories for all civil wars in our dataset. We code as "ethnic" those wars where patterns of rebel recruitment and alliance for all major factions (including the government for *ethnic war 2*) follow ethnic lines.[20]

Another indicator of hostility is the *number of factions*, including international actors directly involved in the fighting. Our theory suggests that the peacebuilding "ecology" is a function of the number of factions involved in the peace process. As outlined in chapter 2, more hostile factions imply a greater difficulty in reaching an agreement to end the war.

A related measure is the country's level of *ethnic fractionalization*. We use the well-known ethnolinguistic fractionalization index (*elf*) to control for it,[21] as well as Fearon's index of ethnic and cultural fractionalization (*ef*).[22] These two indices are highly correlated and serve as proxies for the difficulty of achieving national reconciliation, particularly after ethnoreligious wars.

Another indicator of hostility is the outcome of the war. We coded the following outcomes: *negotiated settlement, truce/stalemate*, and *military victory by the rebels or the government*. *Negotiated settlement* indicates some degree of reconciliation, or at least the potential for reconciliation. It is not the same as simply signing a peace treaty, since *negotiated settlement* implies that treaties are at least partially implemented and the fighting stops for at least six months.[23] By researching the histories of all the wars in our dataset, we were able to code whether or not a peace *treaty* was ever signed by the majority of the parties.[24] The signing of a peace

[20] See Sambanis 2002. For results using these alternative measures of war type, see "additional results," section 1.

[21] S. I. Bruk, and V. S. Apenchenko, eds., *Atlas Narodov Mira* (Moscow: Glavnoe Upravlenie Geodezii I Kartografii Gosudarstvennogo Geologischeskogo komiteta SSSR and Institut etnografii im H. H. Miklukho-Maklaia, Akademia nauk SSSR, 1964).

[22] James D. Fearon, 2003, "Ethnic and Cultural Diversity by Country," *Journal of Economic Growth* 8 (2): 195–222.

[23] In DS2000, the variable "treaty" was closer to what we now code as a negotiated settlement. Since a treaty can facilitate the dispatching of a UN mission even if the treaty fails shortly after signing, the new coding rule is more appropriate.

[24] We have posted online our notes comparing our coding of *treaty* with that in other datasets. Where our coding differs from others, we provide an explanation, including a description of the case and excerpts from the actual text of the treaty.

treaty signals at least a modest desire for conflict resolution and indicates that the parties have the ability to reach an agreement on the basic character of the postwar political system. But a *treaty* need not mean that the war ends and indeed, in many cases it does not. A *treaty* is distinguished from a cease-fire by the requirement that at least half of all major parties sign an agreement that addresses in some way the postwar political realities that the parties will have to deal with. Simply agreeing to a cease-fire does not qualify as a treaty, and cease-fires, which deal only with the military aspects of the conflict, are far too commonly used as ways for the parties to simply stall and regroup for a new round of fighting.

Our proxies for local capacities include several country-level indicators of socioeconomic development. We mainly use *electricity consumption per capita*[25] and the annual *rate of change in real per capita income*.[26] *Real per capita income* (or gross domestic product, GDP) is another indicator that we can use, measured at the start of the war.[27]

Other key measures of local capacities are two indicators of the country's dependence on natural resources. *Primary commodity exports as a percentage of GDP* and *oil export-dependence* are two variables used extensively in the literature.[28] Many authors in the literature have explored the hypothesis that high levels of resource dependence increase the risk of civil war. The resource dependence measures, as well as income level and growth, serve both as purely economic measures of a society's capacity to rebuild itself after civil war and as measures of the economic opportunity cost of returning to war, as we discussed in chapter 2.

[25] This measure is highly correlated with income: 77.67 percent with Fearon and Laitin's (2003) income series and 79.78 percent with the income series from Przeworski et al. (2000).

[26] We computed income growth using the Fearon and Laitin (2003) real income series.

[27] We collected several versions of GDP, including Purchasing Power parity-adjusted figures, as well as figures from various other datasets. We use Fearon and Laitin's (2003) data because it is the most complete. Their GDP series correlates 98.37 percent with the ACLP data and 95.65 percent with the Penn World Tables series 6.1 data (Alan Heston, Robert Summers, and Bettina Aten, Penn World Table Version 6.1, Center for International Comparisons at the University of Pennsylvania (CICUP), October 2002). We use prewar GDP to avoid the endogeneity of the variable to the intensity of the war, which we measure by other variables in the model. We use data for the year immediately preceding the start of the war, except where those are not available (where the war started during the first year of independence), in which case we use GDP data for the year the war started.

[28] We use Collier and Hoeffler's (2001) *primary commodity exports* variable with missing values imputed using data from other relevant variables, such as total exports as percentage of GDP, and fuel and merchandise exports as percentage of total merchandise exports. Two versions of this variable are imputed, using different combinations of variables to ensure that the imputation process does not influence the results of the analysis. Second, we use Fearon and Laitin's (2003) binary variable denoting *oil export dependence*, coding 1 if a country's fuel exports make up more than 33 percent of its total merchandise exports and 0 otherwise.

The greater the opportunities for productive economic activity, the higher the opportunity cost of the war and the lower should be the factions' motives to return to war.

Some of the indicators of local capacities are also good proxies of institutional quality. For example, oil dependence and other forms of natural-resource dependence have been associated with underdeveloped political institutions and high levels of corruption, which could explain societies' inability to build peace after civil war.[29] Other indicators of local capacities, which are correlated with income but are less obviously related with the incentives to fight, such as life expectancy, infant mortality, and literacy level, are used to construct indices of relative local capacities for all countries. We use those indices to test the "triangle" theory later in this chapter.

Our key measure of international capacities is the presence and mandate of UN peace operations. This is the variable of greatest interest to us. The mandate is a proxy for the mission's strength, its technical and military capabilities, and the level of international commitment.[30] Coded *UN mandates* reflect the types of missions that we discussed in earlier chapters:[31] *observer missions*; *traditional peacekeeping*; *multidimensional peacekeeping*; and *enforcement missions* with or without transitional administration.[32] A binary indicator identifies all cases of *UN intervention* while the categorical variable *UN operations* lumps together monitoring missions (*observer* and *traditional peacekeeping operations*) and the more intrusive missions (*multidimensional* and *enforcement*). We have combined multidimensional and enforcement missions into a variable labeled *Transformational UN* missions because our theoretical discussion makes a distinction between weak and strong peacekeeping, and we argue that more extensive mandates should be more effective controlling for local challenges. The variable *peacekeeping operations* combines *traditional peacekeeping* and *multidimensional peacekeeping* and, finally, the variable *Chapter 6* identifies all missions authorized under Chapter VI of the UN Charter (i.e., it includes all but *enforcement* missions). These

---

[29] See Collier and Hoeffler 2004.

[30] Mandates should be correlated with numbers of troops and budgets for UN missions. Sometimes they are not, however, which indicates planning failure at the level of the Security Council. We discuss this point later.

[31] We have also coded ten cases of UN mediation or peacemaking without, however, a follow-up peacekeeping mission. Mediation cases are not considered "peace operations" and are excluded from the analysis of the effects of UN peace operations.

[32] Our results on the effectiveness of UN missions are not driven by arbitrary decisions on the coding of UN mandates. Our coding notes offer a detailed explanation of each case. In "additional results," section 2, we discuss cases where the coding might be ambiguous, tracing out the substantive effects of small coding changes in the UN mandate variable.

different measures of the UN's involvement will allow us to develop a nuanced argument about the conditions under which the UN is likely to help build self-sustaining peace. Mandates must be matched to local challenges. We return to this point in our case studies.

We have coded UN mandates based on a close reading of each mission's operational guidelines, status of forces agreements (where those were available), and a review of UN documents that described the main functions of the peace operation.[33] We focus on UN operations because they are the predominant form of multilateral peace operation in the entire post-1945 period and because peacekeeping is the main function of the United Nations since the end of the Cold War, and we are interested more broadly in the uses of international organizations in promoting international security and cooperation. The conclusions we draw here might apply to other multilateral peace operations, including some regional ones such as the NATO operation in Bosnia. We have therefore researched *non-UN peace operations* and coded their mandates as well, adding them as controls to some of our models. In some cases, non-UN involvement was encouraged by the UN's participation in a peace process. If significant bilateral or regional involvement took place only in the context of a UN mission, we code a UN peace operation only. In some cases, both a UN mission and a separate third-party peace operation took place simultaneously, and this is reflected in our coding.[34]

Another obvious measure of international capacities is foreign economic assistance. We have tried to measure the amount of economic assistance available to the country, though it was not possible to obtain measures of international aid from all sources (bilateral, NGO, multilateral) for all cases in our dataset. Thus, we use as our key measure the amount of *net current transfers per capita* to the balance of payments of the country.[35] And we have also collected data on the amount of *effective development assistance* as a percentage of the country's GDP, though

[33] Differences with DS2000 with respect to this variable are small. See our coding notes online for summaries of the mandate, list of functions actually performed by each mission, and information on changes in mission mandate over time.

[34] The list of all *non-UN peace operations* and information on these missions (names, deployment dates, departure dates, and mandates) are given in our coding notes online.

[35] This variable is sometimes measured several years away from the war's start or end. We used data from the IMF's *International Financial Statistics* to code this variable. See IMF, *Financial Statistics* (Washington, DC: International Monetary Fund 1949–98). The economic assistance proxies are the two variables for which we have the least accurate information. To make sure that measurement error in these variables does not affect the results of our analysis, we checked that dropping *net current transfers per capita* did not affect the results on UN peace missions or any of the other key explanatory variables.

this variable is available for only about half of our cases, so we do not use it extensively in our analysis.[36]

In various specification tests, we added other control variables to test the robustness of our results. We controlled for the government's capacity to deter any external intervention by the *per capita size of its military*;[37] we controlled for systemic constraints by adding a binary variable denoting *Cold War conflicts*; we controlled for region-specific effects by adding *regional dummy variables*;[38] and for time trends in local capacities and other variables by adding a variable denoting the *decade during which the war started*.[39] Appendix B includes summary statistics for all variables that appear in the statistical analysis, including variables that are used in analyses reported in our supplement.

Analysis of Peacebuilding Success in the Short Run

Peacebuilding is a process that sometimes lasts for years after the end of a civil war. To assess peacebuilding outcomes in the short run, we imposed an arbitrary cutoff point at two years after the end of the civil war. Within two years, several peace transitions will fail. The outcome and type of the war can influence the probability of war recurrence (see table 3.2). Most civil wars end in a decisive *military victory*, as table 3.2 clearly shows. *Military victory* tends to decrease the risk of a new war in the short term as compared to *negotiated settlement* in both ethnic and nonethnic wars, though settlements also have a weak positive effect. Settlements in cases where there was a UN mission are significantly more likely to support the peace than settlements without a UN mission.

This empirical observation has given rise to arguments that civil wars are better solved in the battlefield and that intervening need not produce

---

[36] *Effective development assistance (EDA)* is more accurately measured than *net current transfers per capita*, and we have data for the year immediately after the end of the war. But there are too many missing values, and we would lose nearly half of our cases if we included *EDA* in the model.

[37] Countries with stronger militaries may also make it less likely that the UN would intervene, particularly in Chapter VII missions. We also computed a per capita measure of the size of the military and interacted it with *negotiated settlement*.

[38] We code five regions: Europe and North America, Latin and Central America and the Caribbean, Middle East, Asia, and Africa. The UN is less likely to intervene in Asia and more in Europe or Africa, other things equal. We used geographic region as an instrumental variable in models where we endogenize UN intervention (see supplement, pages 45–49; and "additional results," section 10).

[39] The decade dummies are not intended to explain peacebuilding outcomes, but rather to control for trends in right-hand-side variables, especially local capacity proxies such as per capita GDP, that tend to increase over time.

TABLE 3.2
Issues, War Outcomes, and War Recurrence

	No War 2 years After Termination	New War 2 years After Termination	Total Number of Cases	Pearson $\chi^2(1)$
Military Victory				
All wars				
Military victory	55	15	70	5.50 (p = 0.019)
No victory				
(truce/settlement)	30	21	51	—
Total number of cases	85	36	121	—
Ethnoreligious wars				
Military victory	34	9	43	4.35 (p = 0.037)
No victory				
(truce/settlement)	20	15	35	—
Total number of cases	54	24	78	—
Nonethnic wars				
Military victory	21	6	27	1.17 (p = 0.280)
No victory				
(truce/settlement)	10	6	16	—
Total number of cases	31	12	43	—
Negotiated Settlement				
All wars				
Negotiated settlement	19	3	22	3.34 (p = 0.068)
No settlement				
(truce/victory)	66	33	99	—
Total number of cases	85	36	121	—
Ethnoreligious wars				
Negotiated settlement	11	2	13	1.73 (p = 0.188)
No settlement				
(truce/victory)	43	22	65	—
Total number of cases	54	24	78	—
Nonethnic wars				
Negotiated settlement	8	1	9	1.60 (p = 0.206)
No settlement				
(truce/victory)	23	11	34	—
Total number of cases	31	12	43	—
Wars with no UN peace operations				
Negotiated settlement	7	1	8	1.12 (p = 0.289)
No settlement				
(truce/victory)	60	26	86	—
Total number of cases	67	27	94	—
Wars with a UN peace operation				
Negotiated settlement	12	2	14	4.75 (p = 0.029)
No settlement				
(truce/victory)	6	7	13	—
Total number of cases	18	9	27	—

a better outcome. However, once we control for other determinants of war recurrence, we find that *negotiated settlements* are also more likely to reduce the risk of war recurrence relative to less clear outcomes, such as cease-fires or truces, even when we control for decisive *military victory*.[40] Moreover, the "positive" effects of *military victory* do not carry over to a broader concept of peacebuilding, such as the concept we use in our analysis (see table 3.3). If we do not limit our focus on war recurrence, but rather consider the achievement of participatory peace as the goal of the peace process, the data (table 3.3) show no significant statistical association between *military victory* and peacebuilding success, whereas they show a strong association between peace and *negotiated settlement*, particularly those settlements that are negotiated and are implemented through a UN operation.

Our main concern in this book is to analyze how UN peace operations influence the probability of peacebuilding success. The statistics in tables 3.2 and 3.3 are merely descriptive, and we delve much deeper in the data to analyze the effects of UN missions. Among the 121 cases that are included in our analysis, we have 11 *observer missions*, 8 *traditional peacekeeping* missions, 5 *multidimensional peacekeeping* missions, and 3 cases of *enforcement* or transitional administration. In all other cases, there was no UN involvement.[41] Table 3.4 shows peacebuilding outcomes by the type of UN mandate. It is easy to see that achieving participatory peace is harder than achieving sovereign peace, and UN involvement is much more useful with respect to participatory peace.

In some cases, a UN operation was ongoing past the two-year cutoff point that we use to evaluate peacebuilding success or failure. An ongoing

[40] These results are included in table 6, model 3 in the supplement. Negotiated settlements are coded when treaties that address the political terms of a settlement are negotiated and implemented, at least partially, by the parties and the fighting stops for at least a short period of a few months. Victories are also coded when there is at least a short period of war termination, this time as the result of one side's ability to forcibly achieve its goals or as the result of a forcible regime change, where the rebels take over the government. The only case in our data where the fighting did not stop despite a victory, yet we code a new war onset is Afghanistan, but the emergence of new parties and new issues lead us to code new war onsets in 1992 and 1996. In several cases, the government changes hands frequently during the fighting (e.g., this happened four times in Sierra Leone's civil war in the late 1990s). If we coded a new war onset in all these cases, the stabilizing effects of military victories would almost certainly disappear. Note also that "treaties" are coded differently from "negotiated settlements" and "treaties" can be signed even while fighting is ongoing or when the outcome to the war is a victory. See our coding rules for more details.

[41] We lose two cases with *observer* missions, two with *multidimensional* PKOs, and three with *enforcement* missions due to our coding rules, which require that we observe peacebuilding outcomes for at least two years after the end of the war before the end of our analysis time in December 1999. These cases are incorporated in the long-run analysis of the duration of the peace (see supplement).

TABLE 3.3
Issues, War Outcomes, and Peacebuilding Outcomes

	PB Success 2 years After War	PB Failure 2 years After War	Total Number of Cases	Pearson $\chi^2(1)$
Military Victory				
All wars				
Military victory	20	50	70	0.32 (p = 0.575)
No victory				
(truce/settlement)	17	34	51	—
Total number of cases	37	84	121	—
Ethnoreligious wars				
Military victory	9	34	43	0.25 (p = 0.618)
No victory				
(truce/settlement)	9	26	35	—
Total number of cases	18	60	78	—
Nonethnic wars				
Military victory	11	16	27	0.35 (p = 0.555)
No victory				
(truce/settlement)	8	8	16	—
Total number of cases	19	27	43	—
Negotiated Settlement				
All wars				
Negotiated settlement	15	7	22	17.91 (p = 0.000)
No settlement				
(truce/victory)	22	77	99	—
Total number of cases	37	84	121	—
Ethnoreligious wars				—
Negotiated settlement	8	5	13	13.00 (p = 0.000)
No settlement				
(truce/victory)	10	55	65	—
Total number of cases	18	60	78	—
Nonethnic wars				
Negotiated Settlement	7	2	9	5.21 (p = 0.022)
No settlement				
(truce/victory)	12	22	34	—
Total number of cases	19	24	43	—
Negotiated Settlement with a UN Peace Operation				
All wars				
Settlement plus UN mission	11	3	14	17.18 (p = 0.000)
All other cases	26	81	107	—
Total number of cases	37	84	121	—
Ethnoreligious wars				
Settlement plus UN mission	5	2	7	10.13 (p = 0.001)
All other cases	13	58	71	—
Total number of cases	18	60	78	—
Nonethnic wars				
Settlement plus UN mission	6	1	7	5.85 (p = 0.016)
All other cases	13	23	36	—
Total number of cases	19	24	43	—

TABLE 3.4
Peacebuilding Outcomes by Type of UN Mandate

	No UN Mission	Observer Mission	Traditional PKO	Multidimensional PKO	Enforcement (Chapter VII)	Total
Sovereign peace, two years after war ended						
Failure	54	4	8	0	2	68
Success	40	7	0	5	1	53
Total	94	11	8	5	3	121
Participatory peace, two years after war ended						
Failure	70	4	8	0	2	84
Success	24	7	0	5	1	37
Total	94	11	8	5	3	121

Note: Sovereign peacebuilding success implies no war recurrence, no divided sovereignty, and no large-scale violence short of war. Participatory peace also requires a minimum level of political openness (i.e., the regime must not be completely authoritarian). Short-term outcomes (two years after the end of the civil war) are given here. See appendix A2 for more details on the coding of peacebuilding outcomes. An explanation of the coding of each case is available in our supplement online.

UN operation does not mean that the peace cannot fail; but it also does not mean that the peace must necessarily succeed. Oftentimes, a UN mission is dispatched with narrow objectives and few resources that cannot determine the outcome of the entire peace process. In this view, it is important to keep separate the success or failure of the UN peace operation and the success or failure of the peace process. In the statistical analysis that follows, we focus on the outcomes of the *peace process* and control for the presence or absence of a UN operation, trying to identify their effects while controlling for other factors. In the case studies in later chapters, we shift our focus to the success or failure of the UN *peace operation*, offering a microlevel analysis as compared to the macrolevel analysis that the statistics give us. Thus, in the case studies, we analyze only cases with UN involvement, whereas in the statistical analysis, we are able to evaluate the effectiveness of UN missions because we analyze the universe of civil war transitions, including cases with no UN involvement.

Our concept of self-sustaining peace implies that we cannot code peacebuilding success if the peacekeepers have not left. This reflects an ordinary understanding of conflict resolution: if the cop must be continuously present, the underlying conflict has not been resolved. It also corresponds with extensive discussions in the United Nations Security Council in which "sustainable peace" was proposed as the ultimate purpose of all peace operations, and sustainability was defined as the capacity for a sovereign state to resolve the natural conflicts to which all societies are prone by means other than war.[42] "Peace-building," the report noted, "is an attempt, after a peace has been negotiated or imposed, to address the sources of present hostility and build local capacities for conflict resolution." Thus, for example, few observers think that peace has been successfully built in Kosovo today, even though Kosovo is not at war. NATO forces militarily separate the resident Kosovars and Serbs and deter both a potential attack from Belgrade to reunify the breakaway province and a potential declaration of formal independence by the Kosovars.[43] Consistent with this theoretical perspective, we code peacebuilding success only after the UN has departed for at least two years.

We evaluate peacebuilding outcomes while taking into consideration the fact that peaces that last without external assistance are more "true" than those that require the UN or another party to hold the country together. A complication is that not all civil wars have had a UN peace operation, and among those that did, the UN sometimes departed soon

---

[42] UN Doc S/2001/394.

[43] Anthony Lloyd, "AVery Dirty Little War," Timesonline, May 14, 2002, http://www. timesonline.co.uk/article/0,7-295526,00.html (accessed March 30, 2005).

after the end of the war and other times stayed on for several years to manage a fragile peace process. This leads to a difficult determination of just when the peace operation "ended," as sometimes UN reconstruction and peacebuilding mandates require a UN presence several years beyond the end of the war. Thus, not all peace processes can be evaluated at the same two-year mark if we want to ensure that no UN operation is still ongoing.

We considered various approaches to resolving these problems. We determined that the best way was to evaluate peacebuilding outcomes two years after the peace "stimulus." Earlier we mentioned that we consider a negotiated settlement (a peace treaty that ends the violence for at least six months), military victory, or the completion of a UN operation each to be stimuli, part of an ongoing peacebuilding process.[44] It is not clear if different war outcomes imply peace processes of different lengths. Different outcomes might be associated with longer war durations, which in turn might prepare the country differentially for a postwar transition: victory might have taken much longer than a truce, and a peace treaty could take much longer to negotiate than a simple end to hostilities. UN peace operations also differ in their length, but the duration of a peace mission by itself should not have a clear relationship to the probability of peacebuilding success. Both long and short UN missions could potentially be successful, depending on underlying conditions and the type of mandate.[45] But in all cases we seek to evaluate the effect of the "therapy" on the eventual health of the "patient" country, two years after the therapy is complete. Treaties and victories have relatively obvious dates; we consider a UN peace operation as having ended when the military forces are withdrawn (forces that might have been artificially holding together the peace).[46] Thus, our dependent variable measures peacebuilding success two years after the end of the "stimulus." If war resumes before the UN departs or if there is residual violence or divided sovereignty while the UN is present two years after the end of the civil

---

[44] In the supplement (pages 9–11) we discuss some complications that arise from this coding and the fact that in those cases where there was a UN mission and it stayed beyond the two-year mark, we evaluate peacebuilding outcomes at a different time than in other cases. This only happens in a few cases and it does not affect our results.

[45] We look into the impact of mission duration in the "additional results" document (section 3) and find that only *multidimensional PKOs* become more successful if they last longer.

[46] If the UN stays long after the war ends, this suggests a need for more peacebuilding; hence we cannot consider the peace as having started with the war's end. The "therapy" in such a case requires a UN presence. In another case, where a peace settlement is implemented, the UN might not need to be part of the "therapy." The time that the UN departs would be equivalent to the time the peace agreement is signed and implemented in terms of when the peace actually starts in these two cases.

war, we code a peacebuilding failure; but the UN must withdraw before we can code a success.[47]

The results from the statistical analysis presented next are based on logistic regression. We have also utilized other estimation methods, including bootstrapping, instrumental variables and selection models, propensity score matching, random effects models using time-series cross-sectional data, and survival analysis with time-varying covariates. Although we do not present the results of all these additional methods here, the main conclusions that we emphasize in this chapter are robust to changes in estimation method. We summarize the main conclusions from these analyses at various parts throughout this chapter. A more technical discussion and full presentation of these analyses can be found in our supplement.

Policy Hypotheses and Hypothesis Testing

The results from the logistic regressions strongly support the logic of the peacebuilding triangle (see table 3.5).[48] We find that international capacities, local capacities, and hostility proxies are all significant determinants of participatory peace. Our core model (model A, table 3.5) shows that all our explanatory variables are statistically significant and have the expected relationship with peacebuilding success.[49] (In model J, we present standardized coefficients for all variables included in our core model for easier comparisons of the magnitude of their effects on the probability of peacebuilding success.)[50]

[47] This coding rule sets a high bar for success for UN missions. If we only coded peacebuilding failure if war resumed while the UN was still present (and dropped the divided sovereignty and residual violence criteria), then we would have treated cases such as Cyprus, Georgia, Lebanon, and Western Sahara as ongoing, and they would have been excluded from the analysis. Given that these are coded as failures with our current coding rules, the results would be stronger for UN missions if we dropped these cases.

[48] In all models, we cluster same-country observations, considering that peace processes in the same country may share common characteristics. We clustered all former Soviet Republics together and all former Yugoslav Republics together for this reason. In the supplement, we also present results without clustering, yet with robust standard errors, as well as results with bootstrapped standard errors and no clustering.

[49] As a robustness test, we reran the model, dropping all cases that might not meet one or more criteria for civil war, and some of the coefficient estimates became nonsignificant as we were left with only ninety nine observations. But there is at least one proxy variable for each of the three concept variables that is significant, and the estimates of the effects of UN missions are not affected qualitatively. As another robustness test, we identified cases where there might be ambiguity in the coding of peacebuilding outcomes, we dropped all those cases, and the model's fit to the data improved (see supplement).

[50] We standardized the coefficients by subtracting the mean from each variable and then dividing it by its standard deviation before estimating the model.

TABLE 3.5
Logit Models of Participatory Peacebuilding Success Two Years
after the "Stimulus"

	Model A	Model B	Model C	Model D
Ethnic War	−1.5885	−1.6392	−1.6075	−1.6517
	(0.5110)	(0.4977)	(0.4952)	(0.5043)
Log Deaths & Displaced	−0.3179	−0.3396	−0.3392	—
	(0.1370)	(0.1439)	(0.1391)	—
Log of Deaths	—	—	—	−0.3251
	—	—	—	(0.2138)
Number of Factions	−0.6074	−0.5712	−0.5686	−0.6601
	(0.2291)	(0.2509)	(0.2699)	(0.2296)
Net Transfers per Capita	0.0388	0.0318	0.0275	0.0317
	(0.0118)	(0.0108)	(0.0118)	(0.0114)
MultiPKO & Enforcement	3.1039	—	—	3.4239
	(1.0290)	—	—	(1.1711)
UN Mandate	—	0.5684	—	—
	—	(0.2009)	—	—
Any UN Intervention	—	—	1.9247	—
	—	—	(0.6118)	—
Signed Peace Treaty	1.5799	1.5329	1.6153	1.2181
	(0.6654)	(0.6653)	(0.6643)	(0.5837)
Electricity Consumption per Capita	0.0562	0.0456	0.0422	0.0528
	(0.0281)	(0.0274)	(0.0282)	(0.0317)
Primary Commodity Exports/GDP	−7.7346	−7.7445	−7.8967	−8.5415
	(2.1829)	(2.1411)	(2.2121)	(2.1400)
GDP Growth (annual change)	—	—	—	—
	—	—	—	—
Log of War Duration	—	—	—	—
	—	—	—	—
Ethnic Fractionalization	—	—	—	—
	—	—	—	—
Oil Export Dependence	—	—	—	—
	—	—	—	—
Non-UN peace operations	—	—	—	—
	—	—	—	—
Constant	5.3226	5.4365	5.4447	5.3756
	(1.5400)	(1.5988)	(1.5529)	(2.2048)
Observations	119	119	119	119
Pseudo-R^2	33.54%	32.16%	32.22%	32.32%
Log-Likelihood:	−49.02	−50.04	−49.99	−49.92
% Correctly Classified	80.67%	79.83%	81.51%	83.19%

Note: Reported: coefficients and robust standard errors (in parentheses); estimates in bold are significant at least at the 0.05 level; estimates in italics are significant at the 0.05 level with one-tailed test. The variable *UN Mandate* includes ten cases of mediation (i.e., active peacemaking diplomacy by the UN, but not qualifying as on observer mission or peacekeeping). We have coded another ordinal variable (*UN Operations*) that excludes these ten cases. See the supplement for results using *UN Operations*. Our binary indicator of *UN Intervention* also excludes those cases.

In the supplement, we also present estimates without clustering as well as estimates with robust, yet not clustered standard errors. All our measures of UN intervention are significant without clustering, as are all our variables from our core models A–C in this table, except electricity consumption per capita, which loses significance in most cases. Clustering produces lower standard errors in some (but not all)

Model E	Model F	Model G	Model H	Model I	Model J
−1.3475	−1.5703	−1.3030	−1.4273	−1.6525	−0.7551
(0.4806)	(0.5182)	(0.4840)	(0.5060)	(0.5065)	(0.2429)
—	−0.2835	−0.3443	−0.3741	−0.3455	−0.7796
—	(0.1484)	(0.1477)	(0.1493)	(0.1474)	(0.3359)
−0.3406	—	—	—	—	—
(0.1781)	—	—	—	—	—
−0.4758	−0.5808	−0.5473	−0.5701	−0.7200	−0.9002
(0.2566)	(0.2308)	(0.2336)	(0.2198)	(0.2808)	(0.3395)
0.0117	0.0331	0.0365	0.0405	0.0359	0.5452
(0.0128)	(0.0130)	(0.0116)	(0.0113)	(0.0111)	(0.1651)
—	3.1000	3.1297	3.0485	—	0.8735
—	(1.0630)	(1.0026)	(0.9823)	—	(0.2896)
—	—	—	—	1.7152	—
—	—	—	—	(0.5348)	—
1.6300	—	—	—	—	—
(0.5699)	—	—	—	—	—
1.4406	1.7740	1.6938	1.4310	1.5524	0.7306
(0.5795)	(0.7354)	(0.7086)	(0.6635)	(0.7492)	(0.3077)
—	0.0619	0.0486	0.0690	0.0502	0.5525
—	(0.0309)	(0.0243)	(0.0304)	(0.0292)	(0.2766)
−9.3184	−8.3364	−7.4147	—	−7.8017	−1.4280
(2.3121)	(2.6568)	(2.3661)	—	(2.1433)	(0.4030)
0.0624	—	—	—	—	—
(0.0306)	—	—	—	—	—
—	−0.1812	—	—	—	—
—	(0.2748)	—	—	—	—
—	—	−1.2440	—	—	—
—	—	(1.0966)	—	—	—
—	—	—	−2.3129	—	—
—	—	—	(0.5754)	—	—
—	—	—	—	−0.1559	—
—	—	—	—	(.3731)	—
4.9336	5.4816	5.8628	5.1536	5.8803	−1.3520
(1.8488)	(1.5727)	(1.7614)	(1.6624)	(1.7498)	(0.2992)
120	119	119	119	119	119
31.74%	34.00%	34.52%	34.30%	34.91%	33.54%
−50.60	−48.68	−48.30	−48.46	−48.01	−49.02
85%	82.35%	84.87%	83.19%	81.51%	80.67%

of our models most likely because there is some negative within-cluster correlation in some clusters that offsets some of the positive within-cluster correlation in other clusters, so the robust variance estimates is smaller within clusters as compared to individual observations. We can always check the standard errors by bootstrapping, as we have done in the supplement, where we bootstrapped both individual observations and clusters. Bias-corrected bootstrapped confidence intervals for all our measures of UN intervention (*Transformational UN*, *UN intervention*, and *UN operations*) all exclude zero. Some of our other variables are less robust, especially electricity consumption per capita. We present these results in the supplement and, where bootstrapped estimates are significantly different from the estimates presented in this Table, we mention this in the text or in a footnote.

In what follows, we mainly discuss the short-term (two-year) participatory peace model, focusing on the effects of UN missions and conducting sensitivity analysis by making small specification changes to the model.[51] Multivariate regressions show that international capacity and hostility variables are very robust and local capacity variables less so due to their competitive interaction with other explanatory variables. Below, we discuss results with respect to each variable after first explaining our rationale for including those variables in the model.

Hostility Indicators

Ethnoreligious Wars

The probability of peacebuilding success should be lower after ethnic and religious wars. Hostility is easily channeled across ethnic lines, and several scholars have identified the ease with which ethnic passions can be mobilized into support for ethnic war.[52] Further, the ease of ethnic identification makes it harder to reconcile differences among combatants after civil war,[53] particularly because many of the "goods" over which there is ethnic conflict are considered to be nondivisible by the combatants (e.g., access to religious sites, control of territory).[54]

We find support for that hypothesis in our data (model A, table 3.5). Our indicator of ethnoreligious wars (*war type*) is highly significant and negatively correlated with peacebuilding success in most specifications that we tried, though it seems less significant for sovereign peace than for participatory peace.[55] This indicates that ethnoreligious wars create more problems in constructing stable participatory polities than in establishing peace narrowly defined as the absence of large-scale fighting.

---

[51] The short-term focus of the analysis is justified. International peacebuilding is time sensitive in many ways. Most countries and organizations have tight deadlines and limited horizons when extending military and economic aid to other war-torn states. After two to five years, moreover, accidents (hurricanes, droughts) and other factors enter into the determinants of the stability of a country that have little to do with either the success or failure of peacebuilding strategies. We do present results of a longer-term analysis in the supplement (pages 70–112).

[52] See Lake and Rothschild 1998; De Figuereido and Weingast 1999.

[53] That argument underlies Kaufmann's (1996) theory of ethnic partition.

[54] On issue indivisibility and civil war, see Elisabeth Jean Wood, "Modeling Robust Settlements to Civil War: Indivisible Stakes and Distributional Compromises," Santa Fe Institute Working Paper no. 03-10-056 (2003); and Ron Hassner, "To Halve and to Hold: Conflicts over Sacred Space and the Problem of Indivisibility," *Security Studies* 12, no. 4 (Summer 2003): 1–33.

[55] For results on sovereign peace, see supplement, table 5 and pages 20–21.

A complication is that it is often difficult to distinguish those wars that are truly ethnoreligious as opposed to revolutionary or some other type.[56] Thus, while we use *war type* in most of our analysis, we also tried two different versions of the variable that we coded ourselves (*ethnic war 1* and *ethnic war 2*). We coded wars as ethnic if the majority of the parties recruit members and form alliances strictly within ethnic or religious lines.[57] Regardless of which measure we use, the results on ethnoreligious wars are consistent with our hypothesis.[58]

Deaths and Displacements

According to our theory, the probability of peacebuilding success should be lower the greater the human cost of the war, as it increases postwar levels of hostility.[59] We measure total deaths including civilian casualties and displacements (refugees and internally displaced persons) that resulted from the war. We take the log of this variable (the sum of *deaths and displacements*), which proxies hostility levels. This variable may also have a "local capacity" interpretation: the greater the human cost of the war, the lower a society's social and human capital and the lower its capacity to rebound after civil war.

Before we discuss results for *deaths and displacements*, we must note the difficulty of getting accurate data on people killed and, in particular, data on the number of displaced persons. We had to resort to a number of fixes to handle data problems.[60] Some of the figures on deaths that we found differ dramatically from figures used by other scholars, so we coded a second version of *deaths and displacements* that is based on

[56] For such an argument, see Kalyvas 2003 and Fearon and Laitin 2003.

[57] See Sambanis 2002. *Ethnic war 1* focuses only on rebel groups. If recruitment or alliance patterns cross group lines, we only code wars as ethnic if major cleavage lines are not crossed (e.g., parties may recruit across linguistic lines, but not across religious lines). *Ethnic war 2* does the same but also codes the government's recruitment practices (except in countries where there is mandatory military conscription).

[58] For results with *ethnic war 1* and *ethnic war 2*, see "additional results," section 1.

[59] Both absolute and per capita measures should be important. A million casualties in Cambodia amount to 10 percent of the population; and in the United States, 0.4 percent of the population. But with modern communications and threshold effects the political/psychological shock of a million casualties in the United States is likely to be much more than 1/25th the effect that it would have in Cambodia.

[60] So as not to lose cases due to listwise deletion because of missing data on refugees and internally displaced persons, we assumed that if we could not find any mention of displacements in the literature despite our considerable research efforts across a wide range of sources, this would indicate that there were no significant numbers of displaced persons and we coded *displacements* = 0 in those cases. Our assumption is likely to be correct in cases of low-intensity conflicts (indeed, most of the cases with missing *displacements* data have very low deaths), particularly in nonethnic conflicts or coups that developed into

other scholars' data whenever there was significant disagreement between our data and theirs. We then reran our entire analysis using that
second version of the *deaths and displacements* variable.[61] We also estimated the model using the *log of total deaths* alone, dropping the potentially more problematic *displacements* variable.

We find that the human misery created by the war is negatively and
significantly associated with peacebuilding success (see model A, table
3.5). This result does not hold as well with respect to *total deaths* alone,
without accounting for *displacements* (see model D, table 3.5), except if
we make another small specification change and replace *per capita electricity consumption* with the *rate of growth of real income* as our key
measure of local capacities (model E, table 3.5). Our hypothesis also
does not seem to hold with respect to the *per capita human cost*. The
problem here is that there are a few extreme outliers in the data—in particular the Rwandan civil war and genocide of 1994 and the Bangladeshi
war of secession in West Pakistan in 1971 are both cases with huge numbers of deaths where there was nonetheless a peacebuilding success.
Dropping the Pakistan case brings the *log of total deaths* variable within

---

short revolutionary civil wars. However, this assumption will also be wrong in a few cases
(in some conflicts—perhaps ethnic conflicts in densely populated areas—it may be the case
that large numbers of displacements will substitute for low numbers of deaths as people
flee the violence). An alternative approach is to use mean replacement for the *log of deaths
and displacements* variable for those missing cases. The mean value of *log of deaths and
displacements* is 11.55, and replacing it for cases where we have no data on displacements
alone does not affect the results of the other variables in the model and *log of deaths and
displacements* is weakly significant with a p-value of 0.056 (see "additional results," section 1). Another approach that we used is to compute the ratio between deaths over displacements for those cases where we have data on displacements and then use the average
of that ratio to impute missing values of displacements using data on deaths where displacements data are missing. The average ratio is 38.29, excluding Israel, which is an outlier and has a ratio of 2,333 because we count all displaced persons since the start of the
conflict in 1947 (see "additional results," section 1). The adjusted version of the *log of
deaths and displacements* is now significant at the 0.05 level (see "additional results," section 1), but only if we do not apply this adjustment method to the displacement figures for
the 1971 war in Pakistan, since the imputed figure of displacements in that case would ex-
ceed 81 million, making Pakistan an even more extreme outlier than it already is. There
were actually up to 10 million refugees as a result of the Bangladesh war, but these were
Bengali Hindus who moved to India and were neither internally displaced nor West Pakistani refugees to Pakistan, who would be the refugee population of interest to our theory.
If we dropped the *log of deaths and displacements* entirely from the regression to avoid potentially biasing the estimates by our treatment of missing values of *displacements*, the results on the other variables would not be affected, but the risk of omitted variable bias now
increases as we lose a key measure of hostility. Finally, we tried a multiple imputation program that produced mixed results for the *log of deaths and displacements*, but results for
all other variables were entirely unaffected.

[61] See "additional results," section 1 and section 12.

reasonable significance levels (p-value = 0.057) using our original model.[62] The Rwanda case presents a problem because *per capita deaths and displacements* are more than two standard deviations above the average for all the other cases. Since in our dataset post-genocide Rwanda is coded as a peacebuilding success, this observation is influencing heavily the estimates of the relationship between peacebuilding success and *per capita deaths and displacements*.[63]

The effects of *deaths and displacements* and *war type* are both substantial (see the standardized coefficients in model J), but ethnic wars are much more robust to alternative estimation methods and specification tests. With respect to sovereign peace, both *ethnic wars* and *deaths and displacements* are weakly significant.[64]

War Duration

We do not have a clear sense of how *war duration* might be influencing the probability of peacebuilding success. In our earlier work, partly in contradiction to our hypotheses about the effects of hostility as measured by *deaths and displacements*, we had expected the probability of peacebuilding success to be higher after longer wars.[65] This seemed counterintuitive as one might reasonably argue that longer wars increase hostility by creating more casualties. However, long wars also induce war fatigue and resolve any prewar uncertainty about the probability of military victory or the parties' relative resolve.[66] Thus, longer wars might create chances for peace by allowing the parties to learn and update their beliefs about the likelihood of victory in a new war. *War duration* (in logs) is not statistically significant when added as an explanatory variable

---

[62] More than 2 million people were killed in that war, yet we code a peacebuilding success in Pakistan after Bangladesh's secession in 1971. See "additional results," section 1. An extensive set of diagnostic tests identifying influential observations can be found in "additional results," section 8.

[63] In our data the mean value and standard deviation for *per capita deaths and displacements* is 81.74 and 148.99, respectively. The value for Rwanda is 449.44. This is an ambiguous case that we recode as a failure in some of our robustness tests because of persistent insurgency in border regions of the country (see "additional results," section 1 for the results and for an explanation of our coding of peacebuilding success in this case).

[64] See results in the supplement, table 5.

[65] In DS2000, we had included a measure of the war's duration in our analysis, but had not found strong results for it. We do not control for it here, since *deaths and displacements* and *war duration* should be consequences of one another and *deaths and displacements* is a better measure for our theory. *War duration* is significant in some specifications, but it generally does not reduce the significance of *deaths and displacements*, and it is very fragile.

[66] See Geoffrey Blainey, *The Causes of War* (New York: Free Press, 1973); and Fearon 1995 for a similar argument that explains war occurrence at least partially as the result of uncertainty about relative capabilities and resolve.

to our core model (see model F, table 3.5). However, adding war duration to the regression makes *deaths and displacements* nonsignificant, and we find that *deaths and displacements* and *war duration* are jointly significant.[67] Indeed, a regression of the log of *deaths and displacements* on the log of *war duration* reveals a strong and significant correlation as longer wars should also produce greater casualties, other things held constant.[68] Since *war duration* can either cause high deaths or be caused by them (if violence begets more violence), and since we think there is a clearer relationship between hostility and *deaths and displacements*, we drop *war duration* from the model to avoid controlling for two theoretically and perhaps causally related measures of hostility.

We explore further in the "additional results" document the theoretical ambiguity of the effects of war duration. We argue (and find evidence) that long wars may be more likely to bring the parties to the negotiation table to sign a treaty because of reduced uncertainty about the prospects of a military victory, but that due to their effects of raising hostility levels, the implementation of the peace treaty is harder after long wars.[69]

Factions

The probability of peacebuilding success should be lower if more factions are involved in the peace process. More factions imply a larger pool of potentially divergent preferences, which makes it harder to negotiate and implement a settlement.[70] A proliferation of factions and splinter groups also implies incoherence in the peace process (we return to the effects of the number, coherence, and reconciliation of factions in chapter 7). For these reasons, we consider a large number of factions as an indicator of greater hostility. But this clearly does not capture cases of intense hatred in polarized societies. We could hypothesize, therefore, that the relationship between the number of factions and peacebuilding outcomes is nonmonotonic and that it peaks when factions are few and large. This idea can be found in theories of the international balance of power and is consistent with results in game theory. While the initial impact of increasing numbers of factions is negative, at very large numbers of factions, the probability of peacebuilding success may rise, as crosscutting coalitions might emerge. Intermediate levels of factions could make peace bargaining

---

[67] A joint significance test for (*log of*) *deaths and displacements* and (*log of*) *war duration* yields a χ^2 statistic of 6.64 (p-value = 0.036).

[68] See "additional results," section 1. War duration has a positive and very significant coefficient (t-statistic = 3.14).

[69] See "additional results," section 1.

[70] See Keohane and Axelrod 1986.

harder because it is easier to forge crosscutting coalitions among larger groups of factions than among a few polarized groups.[71]

We find that the *number of factions* is significant and negatively associated with peacebuilding in most models that we estimated (see, for example, model A, table 3.5) as well as for sovereign peace. Factions, however, become significant only when we control for other variables in multivariate regression. The quadratic term of the *number of factions* is positively associated with peacebuilding and significant, as hypothesized above indicating a potentially nonlinear effect, and this result holds both for sovereign peace and participatory peace.[72] Nevertheless, we do not include the *squared number of factions* in the models used in the rest of our analysis, because it introduces multicolinearity that may artificially raise the standard errors of other parameter estimates.[73]

Ethnicity

The probability of peacebuilding success should be lower in countries with higher levels of *ethnic fractionalization*. Although ethnic groups in heterogeneous societies need not be hostile toward one another, each group could have different preferences over the terms of a settlement or other distributive issues. Thus, coordination over mutually acceptable peacebuilding solutions should be harder with a high degree of *ethnic fractionalization*. This argument echoes Collier and Hoeffler's result that ethnic dominance significantly increases the risk of civil war.

The relationship between *ethnic fractionalization* and civil war is heavily debated in the literature, as we discussed in chapter 2. Reynal-Querol has argued that religious polarization increases the risk of civil war,[74] while Sambanis has found that *ethnic fractionalization* increases

---

[71] This hypothesis reflects similar lines of reasoning in the literature on international alliances. There are many sources; three classics are Deutsch and Singer (1964) for multipolar stability, Waltz (1964) bipolar stability, and Selten (1973) for nonmonotonic factors. See Karl Deutsch and J. David Singer, "Multipolar Systems and International Stability," *World Politics* 16 (April 1964): 390–406; Reinhard Selten, "A Simple Model of Imperfect Competition: Where 4 are Few and 6 are Many," *International Journal of Game Theory* 2, no. 3 (1973), 141–201; Kenneth Waltz, "The Stability of a Bipolar World," *Daedalus* 93 (Summer 1964): 881–909.

[72] See "additional results," section 1.

[73] The small number of countries with many factions may be driving the significance of the *squared number of factions*. Adding this term to the regression introduces multicolinearity. The mean Variance Inflation Factor for the model increases to 3.86 (12.47 for *squared number of factions* and 13.67 for *number of factions*). If we drop the square term, *number of factions* has an inflation factor of 1.26 and the mean VIF for the model is 1.21. (We estimated the regression as a linear probability model to implement these tests.)

[74] Reynal-Querol 2002.

the risk of lower-level political violence, insurgency, and separatist war, but not necessarily other types of civil war.[75] However, it is possible that both ethnic homogeneity and high levels of fractionalization can reduce the risk of civil war relative to midlevels of fractionalization.[76] Thus, we could also expect a similar effect in peacebuilding processes for the same reasons: ethnically polarized societies should be less able to cooperate in a peace process than ethnically homogeneous or very heterogeneous societies.

As a measure of *ethnic fractionalization* we used Fearon's index of *ethnic fractionalization* (*Ef*) and added it to the regression (model G, table 3.5). We also used the better-known index of *ethnolinguistic fractionalization* (*Elf*).[77] Neither measure is statistically significant nor does it influence the results on other variables.[78] The mean value of *ethnic fractionalization* is only slightly lower in peacebuilding successes (0.45) than in failures (0.57). One might argue that countries with high levels of fractionalization may also have more ethnoreligious wars, and more factions will be involved in those wars. Thus, the fact that we already control for these variables in the model may explain the nonsignificance of *ethnic fractionalization*. To check this further, we dropped *war type* and *number of factions* from the model and found that while *Elf* was still nonsignificant, Fearon's measure of *ethnic fractionalization* became statistically significant and was negative, reducing the probability of peacebuilding.[79]

Thus, the channels through which *ethnic fractionalization* may make peacebuilding success harder seem to be the higher number of factions that become involved when civil wars are fought along ethnic lines, making agreement over the peace settlement and implementation of the settlement more difficult. Moreover, the nonsignificance of the *ethnic fractionalization* measures may be due to differences in the ways in which fractionalization affects the different components of our complex PB variable. In a regression of our model on war recurrence alone, *ethnic fractionalization* is highly significant and increases the risk of a return to war, and this is true both in the short-term and the longer-term.[80] This is an important result, as several authors have identified *ethnic fractionalization* as a key variable in

[75] Sambanis 2004b, 2001.

[76] See Bates 1999 and Elbadawi and Sambanis 2000 for such an argument in the context of African conflicts.

[77] See section 1 in "additional results."

[78] Adding the quadratic term for *Elf* to check for a parabolic relationship to peacebuilding does not make a difference to the results, and the squared term is nonsignificant.

[79] See "additional results," section 1.

[80] See supplement, table 6.

models of civil war onset and duration, but there are few empirical results with respect to war recurrence.[81] Our results also suggest the need for better measures of ethnic diversity so we can sort out the differences between available measures (including the two that we have used here).

Treaty

The probability of peacebuilding success should be higher if the parties sign a peace treaty that outlines a political solution or at least points to an acceptable compromise.[82] Wars that have ended in a negotiated settlement should be more likely to support participatory peacebuilding. Treaties are indicators of postwar levels of hostility since, at the moment of signing, they typically reflect the parties' will to end the violent phase of their conflict. Further, treaties enable international involvement, in the form of lending, foreign aid programs, transfers of goods and services, and the deployment of UN peace operations. Thus, treaties should be significant for peacebuilding, while controlling for these related variables.

The hypothesis that treaties are positively correlated with peacebuilding success cannot be rejected for participatory peace (model A, table 3.5), but it is not convincing with respect to sovereign peace.[83] Treaties alone seem unable to stop war recurrence, but if the violence stops, countries that have signed a treaty are more likely to develop the bases for political participation. This might indicate the importance of having worked out a political compromise among the majority of the parties before attempting to reform or rebuild political institutions.

In the supplement, we consider the selection issue that might arise due to the fact that UN missions are more likely to be used in cases where the parties have signed a treaty.[84] We found a very large positive joint effect of treaties and UN operations (by adding to the model an interaction of the two variables). We also estimated the effects of UN missions on

[81] On war onset and duration, Collier and Hoeffler 2001; and Collier, Hoeffler, and Soderbom 2004. On war recurrence, see Barbara Walter, "Does Conflict Beget Conflict?: Explaining Recurring Civil War" *Journal of Peace Research* 41, no. 3 (2004): 371–88. Several authors have focused on the effects of ethnolinguistic fractionalization on economic growth. See Easterly and Levine 1997; Mauro 1995; Alesina, Easterly, and Baquir 1997. This may be a channel through which ethnic divisions influence the risk of war recurrence.

[82] Our results concerning peace treaties here (and in 2000) thus complement for civil wars the important results that Virginia Page Fortna found for international wars. See V. Page Fortna, *Peace Time: Cease-Fire Agreements and the Durability of Peace* (Princeton: Princeton University Press, 2004).

[83] See supplement, table 5 (models 1 and 2).

[84] In the supplement, see the discussion on pages 36–37 and 50–51 and results from selection models in table 10. See, also, "additional results," section 9.

participatory peace while selecting on the signing of a *treaty* using a Heckman model.[85] We added the *log of war duration* and the *size of the government army* (in logs) as determinants of *treaties* in the selection equation. The effects of *UN intervention* are still significant in that model. A new result is that *deaths and displacements* have a dual, contradictory effect on the peace process. On the one hand, high levels of *deaths and displacements* may push the parties to sign an agreement, presumably because they suggest that victory will simply be too costly or because they serve as an additional indicator of a mutually hurting stalemate. On the other hand and consistent with our hypothesis, more *deaths and displacements* also increase postwar hostility and make the implementation of the peace harder.[86]

Other war outcomes are not significant determinants of peacebuilding. For example, *military victory* is completely nonsignificant, and this finding does not change if we discriminate between government and rebel victory.[87] Wars that end in informal *truces* or stalemates are not significantly associated with success in participatory peace.[88] By contrast, *negotiated settlements* double the chance of success.[89] Thus, if the parties are able to reach *and* implement a political and military agreement that stops the violence for at least six months, this is a good omen for short-run peacebuilding success. UN missions, or other third-party intervention, might be needed less in such cases. The effect of UN missions may also be amplified in cases where a treaty is in place, so we will explore the interactive effects between those two variables when we look closely at the effects of UN missions.

Local Capacities Indicators

Development Level

The probability of peacebuilding success should be higher the higher the country's overall economic development level. More developed economies with lower levels of poverty and better infrastructure should be both better able to rebuild after civil war and less susceptible to war recurrence due to economic grievances and lack of economic opportunity. As we mentioned in chapter 2, economic underdevelopment has been shown by

[85] James Heckman, "Sample Selection Bias as a Specification Error," *Econometrica* 47 no. 1 (1979): 153–61. See results in the supplement, table 10.

[86] See supplement (table 10) for statistical results that support these conclusions.

[87] See "additional results," section 1.

[88] See "additional results," section 1.

[89] See "additional results," section 1. We dropped *treaty* from the regression since there are no cases of negotiated settlement without a treaty.

many studies to motivate or facilitate large-scale violent conflict. After a civil war, higher levels of economic development should be able to compensate for war-generated hostility.

We find support for this hypothesis, controlling for the overall level of economic development by the *per capita electricity consumption*, which is positively and significantly correlated with peacebuilding success (models A–D, F–J in table 3.5).[90] But this result is not very robust.[91] *Electricity consumption* is mostly significant in logit regressions on participatory peace success, but it is not very robust to specification changes and to alternative estimation methods, as we discuss further in the supplement.[92]

Alternative measures of local capacities are *real per capita income* or the *annual rate of growth of real per capita income (economic growth)*.[93] A fast-growing economy may offer more important incentives for people to avoid another war than a high level of development. In model E (table 3.5), we replace *electricity consumption per capita* with *economic growth* and find it significant (just at the 0.05 significance level). But *economic growth* is only weakly correlated with participatory peace, and it becomes

[90] Data on electricity consumption were not always available for the desired year, so they had to be supplemented with data for nearby years. The correlation between per capita electricity consumption and real income is 75 percent. In a few cases, data are missing for this variable and were imputed using regression. We use three observations with imputed values in the analysis. Imputations used data on energy consumption, drawing on Singer and Small's National Material Capabilities dataset (J. David Singer and Melvin Small, "National Material Capabilities Data, 1816–1985," Computer file [Ann Arbor, MI: ICPSR, 1993]), electricity consumption in 1980 and five-year averages in electricity consumption (drawing on data from the World Bank's World Development Indicators, 1999, 2000, 2001, 2003). We also used real income to impute different versions of the *per capita electricity consumption* variable and ran the regression with at least three different versions of the imputed variable to check robustness (the three versions are highly correlated). The results were robust to these alternative versions. Estimating the model without imputed values for local capacity proxies (*electricity consumption* and *primary commodity exports as a percentage of* GDP) does not change qualitatively the results on any variable in the model except for *net current transfers*, which become nonsignificant (we lose nineteen observations).

[91] *Electricity consumption per capita* is nonsignificant if we bootstrap the standard errors from model A. Some observations for this variable have imputed values, and this may increase the uncertainty surrounding the estimates, from bootstrapping.

[92] See bootstrap results in pages 40–44 in the supplement. See, also, results from other estimators in the supplement.

[93] We used prewar measures of local capacity variables to avoid endogeneity problems and to forge a link with previous literature on civil wars, which has identified several local capacity variables as a deterrent to civil war initiation. In some cases, however, the analytical argument requires that we measure the variable at the end of the war. We do so when we measure the rate of growth of income, for example. Growth rates refer to the year the war ended or the following year, to give us a sense of local capacities at the start of the peacebuilding processes.

nonsignificant if we control for *transformational UN* interventions, though it is much more important with a larger coefficient with respect to sovereign peace.[94] By contrast, the significance of UN missions declines and only *transformational UN mandates* are marginally significant with respect to sovereign peace.[95] We therefore see a trade-off here between rapid economic growth and international capacities: rapid growth may substitute for the effects of strong UN missions with respect to reducing the risk of a recurrence of violence. But for higher-order peace, faster growth is not sufficient.

The results on local capacities seem more sensitive than other variables to region-specific and country-specific characteristics, but they are not affected significantly by time trends. One unexpected result is that *per capita GDP* is not significantly correlated with participatory peace.[96] Adding a variable that controls for Middle Eastern countries, where we had several peacebuilding failures in relatively high-income countries, improves the results somewhat, but income is still far from significant.[97] *Per capita income* does not have a significant relationship to our complex definition of peacebuilding success, but we will see later that it is strongly significant with respect to more limited definitions, especially war recurrence.[98] Overall, local capacity variables measure a country's economic development and are not very robust correlates of participatory peace. This picture changes once we unpack our concept of peacebuilding success. Local capacities are crucial predictors of negative or sovereign peace.

Resource Dependency

Another measure of local capacities is the country's dependence on natural resources. The risk of new war—hence the probability of peacebuilding failure—should be higher in highly resource-dependent countries. These countries have generally lower levels of local capacities as indicated by the fact that their economies are less diversified. The abundance of natural resources in those countries may also create predatory incentives that can lead to violence, or it can make it easier for rebel groups to finance a resumption of violence if they gain control of some of those

---

[94] See supplement, table 5, models 7 and 9.

[95] See supplement, table 5.

[96] See "additional documents," section 1. Using logs did not change the results.

[97] Dropping some Middle Eastern countries (e.g., Iraq, Iran) also does not improve the results. We tried dropping the two Yemens, where all development indicators are very low yet we observe peacebuilding success. The range of *per capita income* in our data is 0.05 to 11.366. Income during the first Yemen war has the lowest value among all our cases (0.05), and during the third war in Yemen it comes close to last (0.151).

[98] See supplement, table 6; see, also the analysis of war duration in the supplement and results in tables 15 and 16.

resources. Examples of the use of mineral riches as both a motive and a means to support rebellion are the civil wars in Angola, Sierra Leone, and Liberia, where the rebels have financed their activities by diamond looting and the wars themselves could have been loot driven.[99] Oil-rich countries usually have considerable corruption and underdeveloped state institutions and are correspondingly less able to rebuild their polities after civil war.[100] Natural resource dependence further implies an undiversified economy that is more vulnerable to commodity price shocks and less able to develop manufactures and services that develop human capital and facilitate economic growth.

Two proxies for natural resource dependence that are extensively used in the literature are the share of *primary commodity exports in GDP*,[101] or the country's *oil export dependence*.[102] Both variables are highly significant and negatively associated with peacebuilding success, both with respect to sovereign and participatory peace (see models A–G and I–J for *primary commodity exports*; and Model H for *oil export dependence*).[103] This finding confirms the basic argument that peace implementation is difficult in countries with high levels of lootable resources.[104] The coefficient of *oil export dependence* more

[99] For a discussion of various mechanisms through which natural resources can lead to war, see Macartan Humphreys, "Natural Resources, Conflict, and Conflict Resolution: Uncovering the Mechanisms," *Journal of Conflict Resolution* (2005); 49(4): 508–37 and Michael J. Ross, "How Do Natural Resources Influence the Risk of Civil War: Evidence from 13 Case Studies," *International Organization* 58, no. 1 (Winter 2004): 35–67. Both studies refer to civil war onset, but the analysis should also apply to war recurrence.

[100] See Michael L. Ross, "Does Oil Hinder Democracy?" *World Politics* 53 (April 2001), 325–61.

[101] There is a debate in the civil war literature on what *primary commodity exports* really measure and if they can be used as a proxy for the resource-looting hypotheses (cf. Collier and Hoeffler 2001). In our work, we use it primarily as a measure of an undiversified and relatively less-developed economy. This variable has seventeen missing observations, which we imputed using regression with three different specifications to ensure that the variable combinations used in the imputations were not driving the results. See the "additional results," section 1, for results using all three versions of this variable.

[102] See Przeworski et al. 2000; and Fearon and Laitin (2003).

[103] In a couple of cases, the coding of *oil export dependence* is ambiguous in the Fearon and Laitin (2003) dataset, which is our source for this variable. Indonesia before 1963 is not coded as dependent on oil exports. Nigeria (Biafra war) is coded as not dependent on oil exports on the basis of data for 1967 (the year the war started), but by the time the war ended Nigeria was much more dependent on oil exports. Even after tinkering with the coding of *oil export dependence* in such cases, it is robustly negative (see "additional results," section 1).

[104] This is one of the conclusions of a sixteen-country case study analysis by Stedman, Rothchild, and M. Cousens 2002. The very high coefficient is partly a function of scaling. See model J (table 3.5) for results with normalized coefficients.

than triples in the sovereign peace model, consistent with the economic literature on the causes of civil wars.[105] These results support our hypothesis about the positive association between local capacities and peacebuilding success and link our arguments about war recurrence and postwar peacebuilding with recent findings in the literature on civil war onset.

International Capacities Indicators

Economic Transfers

Economic assistance is a significant part of peacebuilding efforts. Higher levels of *net current transfers per capita*, which include unilateral transfers, food aid, and the like, should substantially increase the probability of peacebuilding success. The coefficient of *net current transfers per capita* is statistically significant and positive as hypothesized (table 3.5). However, the measurement of this variable is imprecise, and the results are sometimes sensitive to the loss of some observations. Given measurement problems with this variable, we confirmed that dropping *net current transfers per capita* from the model did not affect any of the other results.[106]

We also collected data on a different measure of international economic aid. *Effective development assistance (EDA)* is both a more accurate measure of economic assistance than *net current transfers per capita*, and it is measured with less error for the years that the war ended.[107] Unfortunately, these data are available only starting in 1970, and all other data series that we found that could be used as indicators of international economic assistance were similarly incomplete. *EDA as a percentage of GDP* used in place of *net current transfers per capita* is highly significant in our model, although we lose about half our observations due to missing data.[108]

---

[105] See supplement, table 5.

[106] See "additional results," section 1.

[107] *Effective development assistance* (EDA) measures the part of official development aid that countries do not have to repay. Thus, it is a good measure of the contribution of international economic assistance to a country's economic growth. Our source was Charles C. Chang, Eduardo Fernandez-Arias, and Luis Serven, "Measuring Aid Flows, A New Approach," World Bank, Working Paper (1998).

[108] See "additional results," section 1. Cases of successful peacebuilding have more than twice the amount of EDA as a percentage of GDP than do cases of peacebuilding failure. The loss of so many observations makes the coefficients in three other variables nonsignificant (*electricity consumption per capita*, the *log of deaths and displacements*, and *primary commodity exports as a percentage of GDP*).

UN Peace Operations

Turning next to peacekeeping, our hypothesis is that United Nations peace operations should have a positive and significant effect on the probability of peacebuilding, but not all types of UN missions need have the same strong and positive effect. We expect those missions that combine nonpassivity in the implementation of the mandate with high levels of resources and technical capacity needed to rebuild political institutions to have a strong effect. Those missions that simply utilize force or act as buffers to separate combatants need not have a significant effect on peacebuilding outcomes.

To test our hypotheses, we coded the mandates of all UN missions since 1945 according to the classification of mandate types that we introduced earlier in the book: *observer* missions; *traditional peacekeeping*; *multidimensional peacekeeping*; and *enforcement and transitional administration*. These mandates can be ordered in a single variable (*UN mandate*) according to degree of intrusiveness on state sovereignty. In chapter 2, we referred to peacemaking and monitoring, including traditional peacekeeping, as *weak* peace operations and to multidimensional peacekeeping, enforcement, and transitional administration as transformational peacekeeping. We use an ordered variable (*UN operations*) that reflects this distinction between facilitative and transformational peacekeeping, classifying all UN missions into one of these two categories.[109]

We find very strong support in the data for our hypotheses about UN missions.[110] All the models that we estimated point to the positive influence of *transformative UN peacekeeping*, which combines *multidimensional* and *enforcement* missions.[111] *Traditional peacekeeping*, by contrast, predicts failure perfectly so it, also, cannot be used in the regression. Thus, the facilitative/transformational peacekeeping variable (*UN operations*) gives us a better handle with which to study the differences between these types of mandates. We find that *UN operations* is highly significant

[109] The *UN operations* variable is coded 0 if there were no UN missions, 1 for weak mandates, and 2 for transformational UN peacekeeping.

[110] All three variables that we use to control for UN missions are significant in bias-corrected bootstrapped estimates standard errors of the coefficients from model 4.3 (see supplement, table 8).

[111] There are no peacebuilding failures among *multidimensional PKOs*, so that variable would predict success perfectly if added to the model. There are some cases of multidimensional operations that are dropped from the analysis because the UN had not departed for at least two years by the end of our period. In two cases, the peacebuilding outcome is ambiguous. We recode them as failures and still we find *multidimensional PKOs* to be highly significant. However, the number of cases is still very small: five successes and two failures.

(results not shown) as is a categorical variable coding all *UN mandates* (see model B, table 3.5). If we control for both *monitoring* and *transformational UN* peacekeeping in the regression, comparing them to the excluded category of no UN involvement, we find that the effects of each of these UN variables is very large and significant.[112]

Given that we expect the effects of different mandates to be different, we focus most of our discussion on *transformational UN* mandates. But we also expect to find significant results for all UN operations taken together, as compared to those cases where no UN mission had been used. UN operations signal international interest in ending the conflict and offer needed assistance to the parties. They also imply the transfer of much needed international assistance and technical expertise that compensates for war-related hostility and low-levels of domestic capacities, as outlined in our model. To test this hypothesis, we used a binary variable indicating any type of UN involvement (*UN intervention*) and found it highly significant (see model C, table 3.5). The presence of the UN increases the chance of peacebuilding success, but this is not also true for sovereign peace.[113]

A complex picture emerges if we contrast the effects of UN missions with respect to sovereign peace and participatory peace.[114] While *multidimensional peacekeeping* works well with respect to both measures, UN missions in general seem to have their greatest effect in preventing lower-level violence and enabling countries to democratize and rebuild institutions after civil war rather than prevent the resumption of full-scale war. In the short run, whether the parties resume warfare is not significantly affected by the presence of a UN mission. This is not altogether surprising, since most UN missions do not have sufficiently strong policing capacities as to deter large armies from resuming armed conflict if they are determined to do so. War recurrence is much more strongly influenced by the level of economic opportunity—income growth, level of income, and overall development. Some hostility variables are also significant with respect to both participatory and sovereign peace.[115]

However, as we show in our supplement, the UN's effects on preventing war recurrence increase in the longer term, most likely because it takes some time for its positive contribution through institutional reconstruction to influence the parties' preferences for war and peace. First, in our supplement we show that our results from the two-year analysis of participatory and sovereign peace are qualitatively unchanged (with

---

[112] See "additional results," section 1.

[113] See supplement, table 5.

[114] See supplement, pages 20–24.

[115] See supplement, table 6 and discussion on pages 24–26.

minor exceptions) if we use a five-year cutoff for the evaluation of peace-building outcomes after the end of the civil-war.[116] Second, in an analysis of the duration of the peace measured in months from the end of the war until the war resumes, we find that UN missions do have a significant positive influence, but their effect is overshadowed by the effect of a strong economy. We give an overview of this analysis in the section on robustness later in this chapter and discuss the analysis of peace duration in detail in the supplement.[117]

Earlier, we noted that there is a positive (though not a large) correlation between UN *mandates* and the signing of a peace *treaty*, since treaties are necessary for certain UN operations (those authorized under Chapter VI of the UN Charter). Thus, we considered the interactive effects of those variables and found that they work in concert.[118] Their combination enhances the chances for peace, so in simulations of the effect of UN missions later in this chapter, we will co-vary the use of a transformational UN mission and the signing of a treaty, to estimate their combined effect on participatory peace. In the supplement, we examine in detail several other interactive effects.[119]

We reestimated our model controlling for different types of UN missions individually and saw that *enforcement* alone cannot achieve participatory peace.[120] And the fact that in all cases of *traditional PKOs* we get peacebuilding failure is neither surprising nor an artifact of our coding rules for participatory peace. Even if we decompose the definition into its components, we find that *traditional peacekeeping* does not work well, and may even have negative effects, particularly as compared to multidimensional peacekeeping. In most cases, those operations tend to

---

[116] See supplement, table 7 and page 34.

[117] See pages 70–112 of the supplement.

[118] See "additional results," section 9.

[119] See pages 36–39 in the supplement. We examine several possible selection effects. For example, a reasonable argument is that the UN was less likely to intervene during the Cold War. However, our model combines pre–Cold War and post–Cold War conflicts. We therefore included a variable identifying those wars that started during the Cold War, but it was not significant and did not affect the results on the UN or other covariates. We also used the Cold War as a variable explaining UN involvement in propensity score matching models (see additional results, section 12), and again it did not alter the results on UN missions. Another variable that might enter into the UN's decision to intervene is the military strength of the host country. Intervention in countries with large armies may make intervention less likely as the costs of a confrontation would be large. We therefore added that variable, too, as a control, but it was not significant and did not affect our results.

[120] However, if enforcement is followed by more diversified missions, the results may be different. We only have four cases of enforcement in our data, so these results should be interpreted with caution. See "additional results," section 1.

remain in place for long periods of time and may be able to keep such peace as exists, but they cannot *build* self-sustaining peace.[121] Consistent with our theory, we would expect weak mandates to be unsuccessful in resolving cooperation dilemmas. UN *observer missions* and even *traditional PKOs*, will tend to be unsuccessful if they are used in difficult conflicts. By contrast, *observer missions*, or even just mediation, may be successful in resolving coordination-type problems, with low levels of hostility and high local capacities.

Our case studies are better suited to analyze the fit between the mandate and the type of conflict, and we leave much of that analysis for later. But we do find some evidence in the statistical analysis that suggest that *observer missions* have been more successful both with respect to participatory and sovereign peace largely because they are used in situations that present less difficult peacebuilding ecologies (e.g., coordination dilemmas). We discuss this point further in the supplement, focusing on differences in the results of *observer missions* and *traditional PKOs* with respect to the various components of sovereign peace.[122]

Another consistent result is that the *number of peacekeeping troops* alone is not a good predictor of peacebuilding success and that we must consider the effect of UN troops in relation to the mission's mandate.[123] We have coded the maximum number of troops that served in a peacekeeping mission, including military and civilian police. First, there is no statistically significant difference in the *number of peacekeeping troops per square kilometer* in transformational peacekeeping as compared to weak missions. Thus, it is not the case that transformational peacekeeping works better than weak peacekeeping because there is more concentrated force in transformational peacekeeping. Second, the effects of *peacekeeping troops per square kilometer* on the probability of participatory peace success are negative. Foreign aid, reconstruction assistance, and other policy interventions designed to increase local capacities might make both peace and war more likely in the short run. Thus, such policies must be combined with interventions that increase the costs of noncompliance for potential spoilers. A large concentration of peacekeepers without a strong mandate cannot increase the costs of noncompliance sufficiently. The negative correlation of troops per square kilometer and peacebuilding success might seem jarring. But, the result is actually

---

[121] Another possibility, if we do not treat UN missions as exogenous, is that the actual effect of *Traditional PKOs* may be underestimated in our model. If *Traditional PKOs* are used in cases with difficult peacebuilding ecologies (high hostility and low capacities) *and* where the international community's interest in a resolution is weak, then the cards will be stacked against finding a positive effect for those types of missions, and the statistical estimates may be biased downward.

[122] See supplement, table 6 and pages 27–31.

[123] See "additional results," section 4.

consistent with our theory.[124] A large troop deployment with a weak mandate is a sure sign of lack of commitment by the Security Council and creates an impediment for effective intervention by the peacekeepers. We find that large numbers of troops per capita in monitoring missions (*observer missions* and *traditional PKOs*) actually *reduce* the chance of peacebuilding success (examples are Cyprus, Lebanon, Rwanda).[125] Our model from chapter 2 would say that such deployments are inefficient and potentially counterproductive since the peacebuilding ecology in most cases where traditional peacekeeping was used is very similar to the ecology of cases where strong peace missions were used, but the mandate is insufficient to respond effectively to the demands of peacebuilding. The fact that large numbers of troops are nonetheless deployed with a narrow mandate in monitoring missions indicates, on the one hand, the realization by the Security Council of the severity of the conflict (more troops per capita are used when the peacebuilding ecology is more hostile) and, on the other hand, an inability or lack of will to give those troops the mandate they need to be successful. This suggests a mismatch between the nature of the problem and the treatment assigned by the UN. Thus, large troop concentrations with a monitoring mandate mean a low ex ante chance of peacebuilding success, though paradoxically, it might also imply a high chance of what we have called microlevel success if the larger deployments facilitate the discharge of a limited peacekeeping mandate with no effect, however, on the broader peace process.

Returning to the discussion of the effectiveness of different types of mandates, we find that *multidimensional peacekeeping* and, to a lesser extent, *observer* missions are highly significant. The positive effects of UN missions are not reduced if we control for *non-UN peace operations* by regional organizations or other third parties. *Non-UN peace operations* do not have a statistically significant effect on participatory peace (model I, table 3.5).[126] In some cases, third parties were participating in a peace process while the UN was also present. The coefficient for *UN*

---

[124] It is also heavily influenced by one case—the third Rwandan observation. *Peacekeeping troops per square kilometer* is negative, but not statistically significant in the participatory peace model unless we drop that case, which was a peacebuilding success with one of the highest troop concentrations. In the sovereign peace model, *troops per capita* is negative and significant even with this case, and adding it to the model makes *UN intervention* significant.

[125] See "additional results," section 4.

[126] This is also true for sovereign peace (see "additional results," section 5). Our main source in coding the presence and mandate of *non-UN peace missions* was Birger Heldt, "Peacekeeping Operations by Regional Actors, 1948–2000" (version November 18, 2002, unpublished paper, Swedish National Defense College). We supplemented Heldt's coding with additional sources. In this regression, we use the *UN operations* variable rather than the *UN mandate* variable, which explains the difference in the coefficients as compared to, say, model B.

mandate nearly triples when we control for *non-UN peace missions* in model I, which suggests that, while *non-UN peace missions* on their own may not employ the right strategies for self-sustaining peace, they may be useful in boosting the effects of *UN mandates.*

In principle, our theory should apply to those missions, as well, if they use the right treatment for the right problem. We looked closer, given the large difference between the results for UN intervention and non-UN intervention and estimated our model on the various components of participatory peace, adding *non-UN peace missions* to the model. We did not find support for the work of *non-UN peace missions*, but did find some weak evidence to suggest that the presence of the UN enhances the effects of *non-UN peace missions.*[127] The sharp difference in the results for UN and non-UN missions is instructive and worth further study. It may be the case that the implementation of peacekeeping or peacebuilding mandates is much more often ineffective when regional actors or other third parties are the primary agents, because they are not perceived as impartial, hence they do not have the UN's greater legitimacy that is needed to reassure the parties at critical junctures of the peace process. The UN also possesses greater technical capacities than most regional organizations. While we do not understand well why non-UN peace operations are generally not effective, our results suggest that a conservative strategy for third parties interested in engaging in peacebuilding initiatives is to do so in coordination with the UN.

In sum, we found that UN operations—especially those with a transformational mandate—contribute to a reduction in violence and to higher-order peace—the participatory peace standard that involves institutional and political reform and democratization. In the supplement, we estimate selection models that delve deeper into the relationship of UN missions and postwar democratization, controlling for war termination or sovereign peacebuilding success.[128] We also estimate models that account for the potential endogeneity of UN missions, though we have provided a theoretical argument why such endogeneity is unlikely to be a problem. Given the small number of cases in each of the categories of UN mandates, we do not want to push too hard the statistical results on

---

[127] See "additional results," section 5.

[128] Estimates from a model of democratization, while selecting on war termination are presented in the supplement, table 11 (see discussion on pages 53–57). See also OLS estimates from a regression of postwar democracy on UN operations and other covariates (supplement, table 12). Postwar democracy is positively and significantly associated to the use of UN multidimensional operations and negatively and significantly associated to the use of enforcement operations. The strongest predictor of postwar democracy is the prewar five-year average level of democracy: countries with a tradition of democracy have much more success in building democratic institutions after the war than countries with little or no recent experience in democratic governance.

the effects of different missions as these results may be sensitive to a few influential observations. We conducted a variety of robustness tests in the supplement to identify such influential cases and to explore other dimensions of sensitivity of our estimates.[129] Overall, our confidence in the significant contributions of UN peace operations increased as a result of these additional tests. We explore further the differences among types of UN mandates in several case studies later in the book, where we focus more closely on mechanisms through which the UN can help build peace in the aftermath of civil war.

Measuring the Effects of UN Missions on the Probability of PB Success

To better see the substantive effects of the explanatory variables, we estimated the participatory peace model and simulated changes in the estimated probability of peacebuilding success as a result of small changes to the explanatory variables.[130] Table 3.6 presents those results. We simulated probabilities based on mean values of continuous explanatory variables and median values of binary or categorical variables, except for *UN operations*, which we set at 1 (weak mandates). The average probability of success two years after the end of the war (or after the peace stimulus) is 0.26 with a standard error of 0.10. We computed the change in the estimated probability of success by successively varying each covariate. We changed *war type* from nonethnic to ethnic; the *number of factions* from 3 to 4; *UN operations* from facilitative to transformational; *treaty* from 0 to 1; and the level of *electricity consumption per capita, net per capita current transfers, primary commodity exports as a percent of GDP*, and the *log of deaths and displacements* by about one standard deviation (from the 40th to 60th percentile). Most changes in the probability estimates are statistically significant, but the 95 percent confidence intervals for the point estimates are sometimes quite large. We can see, for example, that going from a facilitative peacekeeping mission

---

[129] See pages 16–19 in the supplement. The model is generally robust to dropping each observation sequentially or to dropping entire subsets of the data (such as geographical regions, all coups, all monarchies, highly internationalized civil wars, wars with low death count, etc.). In a few cases, the results with respect to *per capita electricity consumption* and to a lesser extent the *log of deaths and displacements* changed appreciably, but the results on UN missions are not affected (see also "additional results," section 7).

[130] We used software by Michael Tomz, Jason Wittenberg, and Gary King, "CLARIFY: Software for Interpreting and Presenting Statistical Results," Version 2.1. Stanford University, University of Wisconsin, and Harvard University (January 5, 2003). Available at http://gking.harvard.edu/. Gary King, Michael Tomz, and Jason Wittenberg, "Making the Most of Statistical Analyses: Improving Interpretation and Presentation," *American Journal of Political Science* 44, no. 2 (April 2000): 347–61.

TABLE 3.6
First Differences of the Estimated Probability of Success in Participatory Peace

Mean Change in the Probability of PBS	95% Confidence Interval		As a Result of the Following Change:
−.364	−.563	−.157	*War type* from nonethnic to ethnic
−.074	−.151	−.013	*Deaths and displacements* from 40th to 60th percentile
−.103	−.212	−.024	*Number of factions* from 3 to 4
.0066	.0023	.0121	*Net current transfers* from 40th to 60th percentile
.359	.093	.554	UN *mandate* from facilitative to transformational
.324	.03	.61	*Treaty* from 0 to 1
.012	−.002	.028	*Development level* from 40th to 60th percentile
−.05	−.083	−.018	*Primary commodities* from 40th to 60th percentile

to a transformational one increases the probability of success on average by 36 percent, and the confidence interval ranges from 9 percent to 55 percent.

The simulated effects in table 3.6 assume that we can keep other variables constant while varying the values of a single independent variable. Of course, in the example we gave above, a *transformational UN* mission would be less likely without a peace *treaty*. Looking at our data, we can see that UN interventions are more likely when the factions are many, when they have signed a treaty, and when levels of hostility are high. Given these associations between UN *intervention* and some of the other explanatory variables in the model, we should consider only how the probability of peacebuilding success changes as a result of small changes in each covariate while holding the others constant. For larger changes in one covariate, we might have to consider also how other variables that are correlated with it would have to change. In the supplement, we explore such interaction effects among the explanatory variables and discuss the implications of nonlinearities in the data.[131]

Robustness Tests

Throughout this chapter, we have been referencing in the text or in footnotes results from our supplement that point to the robustness of our

[131] See supplement, pages 36–39 and "additional results," section 9.

findings. Some of these results are based on different estimation methods, and our conclusions still hold even if we use three different versions of the civil war list (each list reflecting slight differences in the definition of civil war).

The model is also robust to small coding changes in the independent variables. There are a few cases where the coding of peacebuilding success may be questionable. Those are usually "mixed" outcome cases, that is, cases where some elements of the peace held (e.g., there was no war, but in other aspects there was peacebuilding failure). So, we recoded all ambiguous cases as the opposite (coding a peacebuilding failure where we had previously coded a success and vice versa). Moreover, in some cases it is hard to classify the armed conflict as a civil war as opposed to a coup or genocide and it is not always clear if all the criteria for coding a civil war are satisfied. So, we dropped all those cases. After those two types of coding changes, we are left with 103 observations: 78 participatory peace failures and 25 successes (and 64 sovereign peace failures and 39 successes). When we reestimated our model with the new data, we found that one or two variables were affected by the coding changes, but not the UN variables, which continued to be significant.[132]

An alternative way to handle potentially ambiguous cases is to code peacebuilding success as an ordinal variable, where 0 indicates a clear failure, 1 indicates "mixed" outcomes, and 2 indicates a clear success. We recoded our cases in this way.[133] There are 78 failures, 16 "mixed" outcomes, and 26 successes in our data and now two influential cases with high-profile UN operations (Cambodia after the 1975–91 war and Rwanda after the 1994 genocide) are coded as "mixed" outcomes. The model, estimated via ordered logit regression, fits the data very well, and UN missions are highly significant.

We mentioned earlier that the model does not fit sovereign peace as well as it does participatory peace, and only multidimensional peace missions are significant in helping to achieve sovereign peace. We do find support for the triangle model with respect to sovereign peace, but the results on several individual variables are sensitive to small specification changes.[134] The analysis of sovereign peace reveals that income growth and the presence of a transformational UN mission seem to be substitutes with respect to sovereign peace, whereas transformational UN

[132] For results, see table 3 and the discussion on pages 12–13 in the supplement. See, also, section 6 in "additional results."

[133] Explanations of the coding for each case are included in our notes online. See pages 14–15 and table 4 in the supplement for a discussion of the results from the ordered logit model.

[134] See table 5 in the supplement. Even the results on *Transformational UN* are not very robust for sovereign peace.

peace missions are more important than income growth for postwar democratization.

In light of these differences between the results of the participatory peace and sovereign peace models, we decomposed the participatory peace variable to study how the model fits each of its components individually.[135] We found that parts of the model are better at explaining different components of positive peacebuilding. Our model does not work well with respect to war resumption alone (in the short run).[136] But local capacity variables have a large and statistically significant effect with respect to war recurrence. Higher income reduces the risk of a new war, and higher dependence on natural resources and a highly fractionalized society increase that risk.

However, a more developed and rapidly growing economy with lower dependence on natural resources is not less likely to experience divided sovereignty after civil war. Ethnic wars, by contrast, are much more likely to have peacebuilding failure due to persisting claims over sovereignty. High levels of hostility are particularly damaging with respect to higher-order, positive peace and are also more likely to lead to persistent divisions in state sovereignty. Treaties are also more important for the design of positive peace and are generally less useful in either ensuring that sovereignty will be undivided or that war and other large-scale violence will recur. UN missions are not very effective in preventing a resumption of full-scale war in the short run, but they are helpful in preventing peace failures that result from persistent divisions in sovereignty, minor armed conflict, or a failure of political institutions.

Returning to participatory peace—our main dependent variable—we found that our conclusions about the positive effects of UN operations still hold even if we treat UN operations as endogenous and use instrumental variables estimation.[137] We cannot reject the exogeneity assumption for most specifications of the model and, even when we do and estimate instrumental variables models, the results on UN missions do not change qualitatively. And we checked that the results were robust to various possible selection issues.[138]

[135] See our discussion on pages 24–31 in the supplement.

[136] Results for war recurrence are presented in table 6 in the supplement.

[137] A discussion of estimation of the model using instrumental variables can be found in pages 45–49 in the supplement, and statistical results are presented in section 11 of the "additional results" document.

[138] One selection effect with serious implications for our analysis would be if the prospect of a UN intervention somehow determined the parties' decision to start a civil war in the first place. We do not think this is plausible. Not only is UN decision making highly unpredictable, but we have also argued that UN missions are frequently given the wrong mandate and insufficient resources for the job, and the most common form of UN intervention is consent based; hence it is unlikely to affect outcomes decidedly in favor of

We explored the possibility that the small number of observations might influence the logit estimates and reestimated our core model via bootstrapping. Most of our estimates (including all the results on UN operations) continue to be statistically significant when we compute bias-corrected bootstrapped standard errors for our parameter estimates.[139]

Finally, we show that a model with interaction effects does not outperform the core model from table 3.5. We explored interaction effects with UN operations because there are statistically significant differences between the means of some variables in cases with UN mission as compared to cases with no UN mission. But we found that adding interaction terms to the model introduces severe multicolinearity, which prevents us from estimating a highly interactive model and considering the conditional effects of UN missions. Moreover, standard goodness-of-fit tests reject the model with interactions in favor of the model we used in table 3.5.[140]

SELECTION ON OBSERVABLES

The fact that cases with a UN mission look different from cases without a UN mission might create a "selection" problem that can affect our estimates of the effects of UN missions. We mentioned earlier that our results are robust to the use of Heckman selection models. In those models, we estimated the effects of UN missions and other explanatory variables on participatory peace or democratization while first estimating the selection equation, which explained why some civil wars resulted in a treaty or how the war ended.[141] These models might capture the effect of some variable that explains both the signing of the treaty and participatory peace and is not explicitly included among the variables in the peacebuilding model. Another sort of selection problem arises if the "treatment" (UN intervention) does not occur randomly across ranges

---

one side. Thus, both theoretically and empirically, we find it improbable that the prospect of UN intervention would encourage civil war. Yet some of the determinants of civil war onset may also influence the likelihood of war recurrence and may be correlated with UN intervention. We did explore this possibility. Using a time-series cross-section version of our dataset, we estimated a seemingly unrelated bivariate probit model of war recurrence, and as the dependent variable in the selection equation we used the initial onset of the civil war (the war that ended and resulted in the peace process that we study). We used Fearon and Laitin's (2003) civil war onset model in the selection equation. UN intervention still had a significant positive effect on peace duration in such a model.

[139] See tables 8 and 9 and the related discussion on pages 40–42 in the supplement.

[140] See pages 38–39 in the supplement and "additional results," section 9.

[141] See supplement, table 11 and pages 53–57.

of the other variables that are included in the model (the "observables"). If the UN is more likely to intervene in certain types of cases, this makes it difficult for us to consider how changes in patterns of UN intervention would affect the probability of peacebuilding success without also considering changes to the other covariates.

An approach that attempts to correct for this problem is estimation of the average effects of UN intervention via propensity score matching. The propensity score is an estimate of the probability that the UN will intervene in a peace process. When UN interventions are not randomly assigned, their causal effects on peacebuilding can be estimated by conditioning either on the set of variables that influence the outcome variables *and* the assignment of the treatment (this is the approach that we have followed in the logistic regressions in chapter 3) or by conditioning on the propensity score.[142]

The propensity score is estimated by regressing the treatment variable on all the covariates from the outcome equation (in our case, the explanatory variables in our peacebuilding model). We used a logit model, and the covariates can be used in any interaction with each other. Squaring or interacting the covariates should be done only if they are needed to satisfy the balancing hypothesis.[143] The propensity score is divided in blocks, subject to the conditional mean independence assumption (i.e., the means of the covariates must be roughly equal for the treated and control group observations in each block).

A variety of "balancing" hypotheses have been developed to test that this assumption applies. Once a balanced propensity score has been estimated, it can be used to match observations with similar chances to receive the treatment (a UN mission). Matches will then be made between cases with and without a treatment within what is called the area of "common support"—that is, the range of the propensity score that includes both treatment and control group observations. In our dataset, this condition eliminates a large number of observations, but matches outside the area of common support effectively imply that there is a very large distance between the counterfactual and the observed data. The average treatment effect on the treated is then estimated by simply comparing the means of

---

[142] Paul R. Rosenbaum and Donald B. Rubin, "The Central Role of the Propensity Score in Observational Studies for Causal Effects," *Biometrika* 70, no. 1 (1983): 41–55. In the logit models we condition on observables that influence the outcome and the assignment of a treatment. We have not been able to think of omitted variables that might cause bias. We also estimate selection and instrumental variables models that address the same problems that might call for matching.

[143] The propensity score must be balanced, allowing for matches in each bin, or block. The more parsimonious the specification of the model used to estimate the propensity score, the better, as the multidimensionality problem is reduced. See Sasha O. Becker and Andrea Ichino, "Estimation of Average Treatment Effects Based on Propensity Scores," *Stata Journal* 2, no. 4 (2002): 358–77.

the outcome variable (participatory peace) in the two groups in each balanced block. This approach addresses the nonlinearities we spoke of earlier, since the propensity score enters as a control in matching selection.

We use four commonly used matching methods—Stratification, Kernel, Radius-Caliper, and Nearest Neighbor—to estimate the causal effects of UN operations on the probability of participatory peace success.[144] We find strong, positive, and stable average treatment effects for both *transformational UN* missions and for all *UN intervention*. These results are also robust to using two other matching estimators, one by Leuven and Sianesi[145] and another by Abadie and Imbens.[146] Our supplement includes those matching estimates and a discussion.[147] In a separate paper, we detail the advantages and disadvantages of applying matching methods to our data. Based on our own analysis and on a close reading of the econometrics literature on matching, we argue that matching is not necessarily a good method to apply to our data.[148] Matching is more appropriate if the data are of high quality, with many observations and many variables related to both participation and outcomes.[149] We demonstrate how

[144] These methods differ in the way they match observations and compute average effects. The treatment effects could be a weighted (by the number of treated) average of the block-specific treatment effects (as in stratified matching) or an average of unit-level treatment effects of the treated where control(s) are matched to treated observations within a specified radius (as in radius matching). See Becker and Ichino 2002.

[145] Edwin Leuven and Barbara Sianesi, 2003, "PSMATCH2: Stata Module to Perform Full Mahalanobis and Propensity Score Matching, Common Support Graphing, and Covariate Imbalance Testing," http://ideas.repec.org/c/boc/bocode/s432001.html, version 1.1.3 (September 2003).

[146] Alberto Abadie, David Drukker, Jane Leber Herr, and Guido W. Imbens, "Implementing Matching Estimators for Average Treatment Effects in STATA," *Stata Journal* 4 no. 3 (2004): 290–312; Alberto Abadie and Guido W. Imbens, "Simple and Bias-Corrected Matching Estimators," Technical Report, Department of Economics, University of California, Berkeley (2002). http://emlab.berkeley.edu/users/imbens/.

[147] See pages 59–69 and table 13 in the supplement.

[148] On matching, see, especially: Guido W. Imbens, "Nonparametric Estimation of Average Treatment Effects under Exogeneity: A Review," Unpublished paper, University of California, Berkeley (September 2003); Guido W. Imbens, "Simple and Bias-Corrected Matching Estimators for Average Treatment Effects," NBER Technical Working Paper no. 283 (October 2002); James J. Heckman, Hidehiko Ichimura, and Petra Todd, "Matching as an Econometric Evaluation Estimator," *Review of Economic Studies* 64 no. 4 (1998): 605–54; R. H. Dehejia and S. Wahba, "Causal Effects in Nonexperimental Studies: Reevaluation of the Evaluation of Training Programs," *Journal of the American Statistical Association* 94 (1999): 1053–62; R. H. Dehejia and S. Wahba, "Propensity Score Matching Methods for Non-experimental Causal Studies," Columbia University, Department of Economics, Discussion Paper 0102–14 (2002); Jeffrey A. Smith and Petra E. Todd, "Reconciling Conflicting Evidence on the Performance of Propensity-Score Matching Methods," *American Economic Review* 91 no. 2 (2001): 112–18.

[149] On this point, see Jeffrey A. Smith and Petra E. Todd, "Does Matching Overcome LaLonde's Critique of Nonexperimental Estimators? (Comments on R. J. Lalonde and R. Dehejia and S. Wahba)," *Journal of Econometrics* 125, no. 1–2 (2005): 305–53.

sensitive matching estimates are to small changes to model specification that affect the number and quality of the matches if the dataset is small. Other estimators (such as logistic regression) are not as sensitive to those changes. Nevertheless, we present these matching results in response to growing interest in the literature on matching estimation and we find that even if we abandon the linearity assumption underlying our logit models, our results are still robust. Moreover, given the small number of observations in our data and the sparse data on UN intervention, linearity is an assumption that gives us useful leverage in analyzing the data and making extrapolations based on our results.

LONG-TERM ANALYSIS OF PEACE DURATION

A shortcoming of the short-run analysis we have presented so far in this chapter is that we have artificially chosen a cutoff point (two years after the war) at which to code peacebuilding outcomes. In some cases, the peace might fail soon after the two-year cutoff point. We can instead measure the duration of the peace without choosing an arbitrary cutoff point and use a different estimation method—survival analysis—to analyze why some peaces fail while others last until a censoring point, which in our case is the end of our analysis period at the end of December 1999. Survival analysis produces estimates of the risk (or "hazard") of peace failure at time t given that the peace has not failed up to that point.

We conducted such an analysis using first a single-record, single-failure duration dataset, which is a slightly modified version of the dataset that we used in the logistic regressions; and second, using a time-series cross-section (TSCS) version of the dataset that allows us to add time-varying covariates to the model. We focused on the most fundamental form of peacebuilding failure—war recurrence—particularly since our logistic regressions had shown that UN missions did not have a significant effect on preventing war recurrence in the very short run. We wanted to see if this is also the case in the longer term.

In the single-record, single-failure dataset, out of 138 "subjects" (peace processes), we have 73 failures with mean peace duration of 53 months, and the longest peace duration in the dataset is 634 months.[150] Contrary to the results of the very short-term models of war recurrence, we find that UN intervention is significant in reducing the risk of a new war in survival models of peace duration. A plausible explanation for

---

[150] We can now use more than the 121 observations that were included in the logistic regression analysis because we do not require that the peace process has lasted for at least two years before the end of 1999. For results and discussion of the survival analysis using the single-record, single-failure version of the dataset, see supplement, pages 70–86.

the nonsignificance of UN interventions in the very short run is that while UN missions are almost always too weak to prevent determined parties to return to war if the peace seems to be failing soon after it is signed, in the longer term the UN may influence the parties' proneness to return to war through its assistance in rebuilding institutions.

There is also a difference between the positive effects of *multidimensional PKOs* on peace duration and the negative effects of *enforcement* missions, which are more likely to result in a return to war. Consent-based peacekeeping does make a difference, and some of its effects last beyond the time that UN missions are present.[151] But the strongest result that we found in the survival analysis is that local capacities are critical determinants of the likelihood of war recurrence. Thus, a war-prevention strategy for the UN in countries that are emerging from civil war should help build institutions that resist the corrupting pressures of resource-dependent economies and allow for fast economic growth. The UN's impact in rebuilding institutions will be particularly important in ethnically divided societies, which we find to be at higher risk of war recurrence.[152] Moreover, the effects of UN missions decline over time. They are strongest in the first one to three years of the peace process, when the risks of war recurrence are also the highest.[153] Thus, it is important for UN missions to become involved early in the peace process.

Index Models of Peacebuilding Success

Having completed the tests of our policy-relevant hypotheses, we now return to a final test of our core peacebuilding triangle model. We aggregated our proxies for Hostility (H), Local Capacities (LC), and International Capacities (IC) in three indices, each of which gives each country's relative position vis-à-vis all others.[154] We estimated logistic models, regressing both participatory and sovereign peace on different combinations of the indices (table 3.7).

---

[151] See our analysis of peace duration using the TSCS dataset (and time-varying covariates) in our supplement, pages 87–112.

[152] See the results on ethnic fractionalization in the survival analysis in the supplement, tables 15 and 16.

[153] See our analysis of peace duration using the TSCS dataset (table 16) in the supplement.

[154] Each variable included is indexed to the highest value of that variable's range. So, for example, the country with the highest per capita GDP would get a GDP index component of 1. Each index is an additive combination of several component variables and ranges from 0 to 1. Some variables might be relevant to more than one index, but we only include each variable in a single index so as not to double-count variables in the regression analysis.

TABLE 3.7
Index Models of Peacebuilding Success

	Participatory Peace (1st index combination)	Sovereign Peace (1st index combination)	Participatory Peace (2d index combination)	Sovereign Peace (2d index combination)	Participatory Peace (3d index combination)	Sovereign Peace (3d index combination)
Hostility Index	-4.02	-3.12	-5.38	-4.30	-3.18	-2.49
	(1.32)	(1.07)	(1.69)	(1.31)	(1.18)	(1.11)
Local Capacity Index	3.14	1.65	7.09	11.38	5.89	11.01
	(1.42)	(1.40)	(2.36)	(3.48)	(2.24)	(3.13)
Int'l Capacity Index	2.91	1.66	5.08	3.52	3.56	1.39
	(0.97)	(0.86)	(1.61)	(1.55)	(1.36)	(1.44)
Constant	0.60	1.03	1.09	1.38	0.38	0.84
	(0.57)	(0.58)	(0.70)	(0.63)	(0.56)	(0.64)
Observations	116	116	111	111	120	120
Pseudo-R^2	0.15	0.07	0.23	0.26	0.16	0.22
Wald Statistic	15.41	12.98	20.86	25.79	19.19	20.50
Log-likelihood	-61.89	-73.82	-53.61	-56.61	-62.52	-64.13

Reported: coefficients and robust standard errors (in parentheses); bold indicates significance at least at the 0.05 level; italics indicate significance with one-tailed test at the 0.05 level. The indices are based on different combinations of variables for each concept variable. For the first combination, the hostility index includes war type, the log of deaths and displacements, and war duration; the local capacity index includes only electricity consumption per capita; and the international capacity index includes an interaction between the type of UN mandate and signed peace treaty. For the second combination, the hostility index includes war type, the log of deaths and displacements, war duration, and number of factions; the local capacity index includes per capita GDP, rate of growth of per capita GDP, and primary commodity exports as a percent of GDP; and the international capacity index includes the interaction between the type of UN mandate and signed peace treaty plus net current transfers to the balance of payments. For the third combination, the hostility index is the same as the first combination; the local capacity index is the same as the second combination, but now we use a different imputation of missing values for the primary commodity exports variable; and the international capacity index includes everything that is included in the second combination plus an index of the troops strength of the UN mission.

All three indices are highly significant, and their coefficient signs are those predicted by our theory.[155] Higher levels of *International Capacities* and *Local Capacities* compensate for increasing levels of *Hostility*. However, in varying the composition of the indices, we found more combinations of the *Hostility* and *International Capacities* indices that were statistically significant for participatory peace than was the case for the *Local Capacities* index. Thus, as was the case for the individual proxies, the index models also explain sovereign peace less well than they do participatory peace. As with the individual proxies, *international capacities* are sometimes nonsignificant with respect to sovereign peace (see results for the third combination of indices). *Local capacities* are also less robust with respect to sovereign peace (see results for the first combination of indices in table 3.7). Thus, the results of the index models are in line with the previous discussion and indicate that the precise proxy used for *local capacities* is important in testing the broader theory and that, because our dataset is small, a few observations may be influential, pulling the results on *local capacities* in the opposite direction from that predicted by the model.[156]

Policy Analysis

Armed with these findings, we can use the core model to analyze how the interactions between key explanatory variables influence the probability of peacebuilding success using conditional effects plots. The four panels of figure 3.2 graph the estimated probability of participatory peace success when we allow a key variable to vary from the 75th to the 25th percentile of its range while allowing another key explanatory variable to vary throughout its range. Other variables are set at their median level.

Figure 3.2a maps the probability of peacebuilding success across all levels of economic development (proxied by *per capita electricity consumption*) for the 75th and 25th percentile of the range of the *log of deaths and displacements*, which proxies high and low levels of hostility

---

[155] All three indices are also significant in bootstrap models with bias-corrected standard errors (see supplement, table 9).

[156] Israel, for example, is one of the countries with the highest level of *local capacities*, yet the Oslo peace process failed within a few years of the agreement. At the other end of the spectrum is Yemen, one of the least developed countries in the world, which has had several civil wars that resulted in decisive military victories that sustained the peace in the short run (though the recurrence of war in Yemen in the longer term is more consistent with our model).

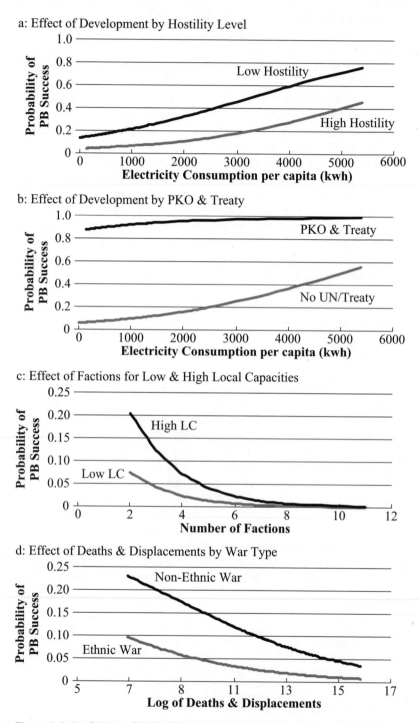

Figure 3.2 Predictors of Probability of Peacebuilding Success

respectively. We see clearly that peacebuilding success is much more likely if hostility is low across all levels of economic development. Local capacity does appear to make a reconciled peace easier, especially if the two sides have avoided the worst forms of mutual violence.

Figure 3.2b maps the probability of peacebuilding success across variable local capacities (*per capita electricity consumption* is allowed to vary throughout its range) with and without a *transformational UN peacekeeping operation* and a *treaty* (we look at the combined or interactive effect of these two variables given that consent-based PKOs typically require a treaty). The probability of peacebuilding success is remarkably higher if a *transformational PKO* with a *treaty* is used. Even at high levels of local capacity, a *transformational PKO* and *treaty* make a positive difference, but their greatest effect can be seen at low levels of local capacity: a *treaty* and UN mission substitute for the lack of local capacities (contrast the gap between two lines at low and high levels of *electricity consumption per capita*).

Figure 3.2c maps the probability of peacebuilding success for variable *numbers of factions* and for low and high levels of local capacities. Low local capacities imply values at the 25th percentile of the range of *electricity consumption per capita* and the 75th percentile of the range of *primary exports as percent of GDP*. High local capacities would imply the opposite (values that define the 75th percentile of *electricity consumption per capita* and the 25th percentile of *primary commodity exports as a percentage of GDP*). The *number of factions* has a clearly negative effect on the likelihood of peacebuilding success. Overall, we see that there is not much interaction between the *number of factions* and local capacity levels, except in those cases where the *number of factions* is small (under four).

Figure 3.2d maps the probability of peacebuilding success for variable levels of *deaths and displacements* (a key measure of hostility) for *ethnoreligious* and *nonethnic* (revolutionary and other) wars. There is a huge difference between the two types of wars at low levels of hostility, and even at the highest levels of *deaths and displacements, nonethnic* wars are more likely to result in a success. While *ethnoreligious* wars are four times harder to resolve at extremely low levels of *deaths and displacements*, at extremely high levels of hostility, *war type* matters less and both *war types* are unlikely to result in successful peacebuilding. This suggests that *war type* is overwhelmed by the hostile effects of human misery, whatever their source. Cambodia, an ideological war with a nonethnic massacre of close to 2 million people, and Rwanda, an ethnic war with genocide, are similarly challenging cases in terms of achieving peacebuilding success. This plot emphasizes as well the importance of early intervention, before the parties have done extensive killings and especially in a nonethnic or religious war. That is when the probability of success is greatest.

Using model A of table 3.5, we can compute the probability of participatory peace success for conflicts that have just ended.[157] We do so by computing in-sample probabilities for all the cases that we consider in later chapters. We will use these probability estimates in our case studies to discuss the fit of the model to each case. The model helps us identify broad guidelines for peacebuilding strategies after civil war, given different levels of local capacities and hostility. Some broad guidelines for UN involvement can be suggested with the help of figure 3.3.

For simplicity, imagine that peacebuilding processes can be divided into difficult and easy cases. In a hypothetical difficult case all the variables with a negative coefficient in our model would have high values (we set them at their 75th percentile) and all the variables with positive coefficients would have low values (we set them at their 25th percentile).[158] In figure 3.3, we create hypothetical difficult and easy cases and explore the impact of international capacities on the probability of peacebuilding success under different combinations of local capacities and hostility levels. Figures 3.3a and 3.3b represent two hypothetical difficult cases, whereas figures 3.3c and 3.3d represent two hypothetical easy cases.

Figure 3.3a maps the probability of peacebuilding success in a difficult case across all levels of hostility (measured by the *log of deaths and displacements*) with and without a *transformational UN operation* and a *treaty*. This figure represents a hypothetical difficult case. The results are striking: a difficult case without a *treaty* or *UN mission*, even at the lowest level of hostility, has a very low likelihood of success, several times lower than with a UN mission and a *treaty*. Peacekeeping does make a positive difference, and early intervention pays. But at very high levels of

---

[157] For example, plugging into the model the values for the war that just ended in Afghanistan (coding an enforcement mission, no treaty, four major factions, an ethnic war, and the values for local capacity variables and net transfers pertaining to the start of the war) we find that the probability of Success two years after the war ends and the UN withdraws is 34 percent (with a wide confidence interval from 0.07 to 0.76). The probability of success in the DRC, with traditional PKO, a treaty, high hostility due to the 3 million dead and displaced in the war, and the other variables coded at prewar levels, is very low (2 percent with a confidence interval from 0.0014 to 0.06). For Liberia, the estimate is 9 percent with a confidence interval from 2 percent to 28 percent.

[158] Easy cases imply a nonethnic war, two factions, 75th percentile in net transfers per capita and electricity consumption per capita, and 25th percentile in primary exports as percentage of GDP and deaths and displacements. Hard cases imply an ethnic war with four factions, electricity consumption and net current transfers at the 25th percentile of their ranges and deaths and displacements, and primary commodity exports at the 75th percentile of their ranges.

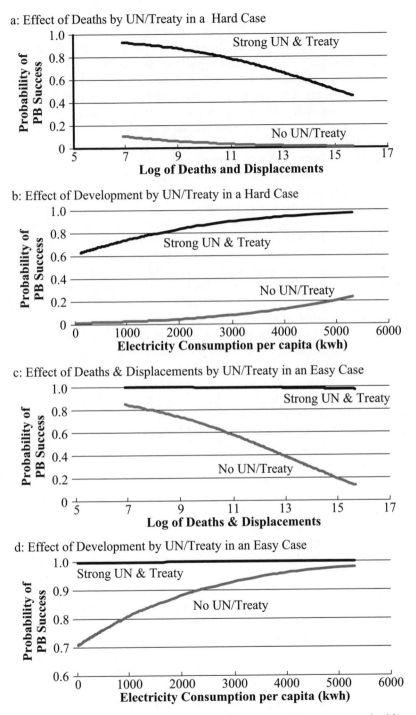

Figure 3.3 International Capacities in "Hard" and "Easy" Peacebuilding Ecologies

hostility, after massive civilian slaughter, the two probabilities decline and the probability declines more rapidly in the case with a UN mission and a treaty, although there is still a greater chance of success with a PKO and treaty. For example, a substantial *multidimensional PKO* made a positive difference in Cambodia, despite the massive killings and displacements that took place there; an equivalent effort might have been useful in Rwanda.

These results are almost the opposite of those for an easy case (figure 3.3c). Here, the probability of success is quite high at low levels of hostility, even though it is still slightly higher if a *transformational UN* mission is deployed on the basis of a *treaty* among the parties. But the major effect of the *treaty* and the UN occurs at high levels of hostility, where they are crucial in maintaining the probability of success. This appears, for example, to map the situation in Bosnia today, one of the more developed countries among those that have had a civil war and one that has suffered many casualties. It is held together in peace by the agreements reached at Dayton and the continuing presence of NATO, and a plethora of other international organizations. Without a *treaty* and transformational *UN* mission, the likelihood of success drops substantially from an initial value of about 80 percent to less than 5 percent at extreme values of hostility.

Figure 3.3b maps the probability of peacebuilding success for a difficult case across all levels of *electricity consumption per capita* with and without *UN mission* and peace *treaty*. This figure represents a hypothetically difficult case because we have set hostility variables at their 75th percentile. We see that a *treaty* and *UN mission* are even more important for success since the slope of the curve with a *transformational UN* mission gets much steeper much sooner than the slope of the curve without a UN mission or *treaty*, and the resulting probability of success without a *treaty* and UN mission is very low even at extremely high levels of economic development.

By contrast, figure 3.3d maps the probability of peacebuilding success across levels of local capacities (*electricity consumption per capita*) for a hypothetical easy case with and without a *transformational UN* mission and peace *treaty*. This figure represents a hypothetically easy case because we have set hostility variables at their 25th percentile. The effect of a UN mission and a *treaty* is highest at very low levels of development, whereas neither a *treaty* nor a strong international presence seems necessary for peacebuilding success at very high levels of development. Developed countries that experience minor civil violence can put themselves back together. The UN is most needed elsewhere, in the less developed countries that have suffered extensive violence.

In sum, our analysis identifies the critical determinants of peacebuilding success. We find that higher order, or democratic, peacebuilding is more successful after nonethnic wars, in countries with relatively high development levels and when UN peace operations and substantial financial assistance are available. Lower-order peacebuilding—an end to the violence—is more dependent on muscular third-party intervention and on low hostility levels rather than on the breadth of local capacities (although here, too, a rapidly improving economic situation will help create disincentives for renewed violence).

Peacemaking aimed at facilitating a negotiated settlement is potentially life saving, since we find that treaties that stick and result in an end to the violence are highly correlated with peacebuilding success, at least in the short term. Moreover, strategically designed peacekeeping combined with peace enforcement does make a difference. International capacities can foster peace by substituting for limited local capacities and alleviating factors that feed deep hostility. Such intervention improves the prospects for peace, but only if the peace operation is appropriately designed. Enforcement operations alone cannot create the conditions for a self-sustaining democratic peace. Consent-based peacekeeping operations with civilian functions (multidimensional PKOs) are, by contrast, good not only in ending the violence, but also in assisting with the institutional and political reform that helps secure longer-term peace. Truly intractable conflicts, such as those in Bosnia, Kosovo, and East Timor, probably will require both enforcement and peacebuilding operations, coordinated and in the right order.

Conclusion

Our analysis confirms the basic insight of the peacebuilding triangle and thus points to a positive contribution of UN peace operations in post–civil war transitions. The greater the hostility, measured in terms of casualties and refugees and the less the local capacity, measured by an underdeveloped and undiversified economy, the greater must international capacities be to increase the probability of peacebuilding success.

It also provides us with an empirical basis to support the conceptual distinction between peacebuilding understood narrowly as the absence of war and more demanding standards of peacebuilding. UN missions—particularly transformational PKOs—have a lasting positive contribution to the peace that expands beyond the short term. This is particularly true for higher-order peace. The benefits that UN peace missions have on the prevention of war recurrence seem to occur via the institutional development that UN missions foster in the immediate postwar period. The effects of UN missions are felt beyond the initial two-year period, but they are stronger in the early postwar phase. Peace interventions must happen quickly, if they are to be successful, as our models perform better in the short run than in the long run, and peace duration becomes more stable over time, making early interventions pay more than late ones. This also makes the results of the short-term analysis of the effects of UN operations more reassuring, since they make a positive difference early in the peace process. Longer UN missions or more troops are not necessarily the solution. These resources must be matched with an appropriate mandate and, if this is done, then the UN can have a positive influence.

A shortcoming of UN interventions is that they have not focused adequately on the link between economic reconstruction and development and peace. We found that local capacities are more important in achieving negative peace both in the short run and in the long run. Good as UN peacebuilding is in expanding political participation, it has not served to jump-start self-sustaining economic growth. Economic growth is critical in supporting incentives for peace (particularly negative peace) and helps achieve war avoidance even in the absence of extensive international capacities. In addition to being a significant determinant of sustainable peace, growth and a reduction in poverty levels are determinants of sustainable democracy.[159] Thus, narrowing the policy gap between peacekeeping, with its humanitarian assistance, and development assistance, with its emphasis on structural transformation, is a good peacebuilding strategy. UN peacebuilding would clearly benefit from an evolution that made economic reform the additional element that plugged this decisive gap.

Appendix A: Definitions and Coding Rules

The dataset used in this book is a revised version of the dataset we used in our earlier work on peacebuilding.[160] In this appendix, we discuss in more detail the coding rules we used to identify civil wars and code their onset and termination. We also explain our coding of the dependent variable used in the analysis. Extensive coding notes for all variables and all cases in our data are available online.

[159] Collier and Hoeffler 2001; Przeworski et al. 2000.
[160] DS 2000.

A.1: Definition and Coding of Civil War

Our definition of civil war is similar to others found in the literature, but our coding rules are more detailed and allow us to be more precise in coding the war's start and end. We have tried to apply as closely as possible the detailed coding rule presented below, and we discuss our coding of each case in detail in notes we have posted online.

An armed conflict is classified as a civil war if:

    a. the war takes place within the territory of a state that is a member of the international system[161] with a population of 500,000 or greater.[162]

    b. the parties are politically and militarily organized and they have publicly stated political objectives.[163]

    c. the government (through its military or militias) is a principal combatant. If there is no functioning government, then the party representing the government internationally and/or claiming the state domestically must be involved as a combatant.[164]

    d. the main insurgent organization(s) is locally represented and must recruit locally. Additional external involvement and recruitment need not imply that

[161] This includes states that are occupying foreign territories that are claiming independence (e.g., West Bank and Gaza in Israel and Western Sahara in Morocco). A strict application of this coding rule could drop those cases if the international community (through the UN) rejects the state's claims of sovereignty on the occupied territories.

[162] We could include countries after their population reaches the 500,000 mark, or from the start of the period if population exceeds the 500,000 mark at some point in the country series. If a civil war occurs in a country with population below the threshold, we could include it and flag it as a marginal case. Cases of civil war close to the 500,000 mark are Cyprus in 1963 (578,000 population) and Djibouti in 1991 (450,000 population). With a per capita death threshold, we could relax the population threshold.

[163] This should apply to the majority of the parties in the conflict. This criterion distinguishes insurgent groups and political parties from criminal gangs and riotous mobs. But the distinction between criminal and political violence may fade in some countries (e.g., Colombia after 1993). "Terrorist" organizations would qualify as insurgent groups according to this coding rule if they caused violence at the required levels for war (see other criteria). Noncombatant populations that are often victimized in civil wars are not considered a "party" to the war if they are not organized in a militia or other such form, able to apply violence in pursuit of their political objectives.

[164] Extensive indirect support (monetary, organizational, or military) by the government to militias might also satisfy this criterion (e.g., Kenya during the ethnic clashes in the Rift Valley). However, in such cases it is harder to distinguish civil war from communal violence. In other cases, where the state has collapsed, it may not be possible to identify parties representing the state as all parties may be claiming the state, and these conflicts will also be hard to distinguish from intercommunal violence (e.g., Somalia after 1991).

the war is not intrastate.[165] Insurgent groups may operate from neighboring countries, but they must also have some territorial control (bases) in the civil war country and/or the rebels must reside in the civil war country.[166]

e. the start year of the war is the first year that the conflict causes at least 500–1,000 deaths.[167] If the conflict has not caused 500 deaths or more in the first year, the war is coded as having started in that year only if cumulative deaths in the next three years reach 1,000.[168]

f. throughout its duration, the conflict is characterized by sustained violence at least at the minor or intermediate level. There should be no three-year period during which the conflict causes fewer than 500 deaths.[169]

g. throughout the war, the weaker party is able to mount effective resistance. Effective resistance is measured by at least 100 deaths inflicted on the stronger party. A substantial number of these deaths must occur in the first year of the war.[170] But if the violence becomes effectively one-sided, even if the

[165] Intrastate war can be taking place at the same time as interstate war.

[166] This rule weeds out entirely interstate conflicts with no local participation. The Bay of Pigs, for example, would be excluded as a civil war because the rebels did not have a base in Cuba prior to the invasion. Some cases stretch the limits of this definitional criterion: e.g., Rwanda in the late 1990s, where former FAR recruits with bases in the DRC engaged in incursions and border clashes against government army and civilians. But if we code this is a civil war, then we should also code conflicts such as the one between Lebanon-based Hezbollah and Israel as a civil war (assuming the other criteria are met).

[167] This rule can be relaxed to a range of 100 to 1,000 since fighting might start late in the year (cf. Senegal or Peru). Given the lack of high-quality data to accurately code civil war onset, if we do not have a good estimate of deaths for the first year, we can code the onset at the first year of reported large-scale armed conflict provided that violence continues or escalates in the following years. Note that in the dataset, we also code the start/end month, where possible. In some cases, our coding rules can be used to identify the start month (e.g., in cases where the war causes 1,000 deaths in the first month of armed conflict). But in most cases, the month indicates only the start of major armed conflict or the signing of a peace agreement, which can give us a point of reference for the start/end of the war, respectively.

[168] This rule also suggests when to code war termination if the three-year average does not add up to 500. In such a case, we can code the end of the war on the last year with more than 100 deaths unless one of the other rules applies (e.g., if there is a peace treaty that is followed by more than six months of peace).

[169] This criterion makes coding very difficult, as data on deaths throughout the duration of a conflict are hard to find. However, such a coding rule is necessary to prevent one from coding too many war starts in the same conflict or coding an ongoing civil war for years after the violence has ended. Three years is an arbitrary cutoff point, but is consistent with other thresholds found in the literature. The data notes give several examples of cases where the coding of war termination has been determined by this criterion. A more lenient version would be a five-year threshold with fewer than 500 deaths.

[170] This criterion must be applied proportionally to the war's intensity in the first years of the war. If we code the war's onset on the first year with 100 deaths (as often happens in low-intensity conflicts), then we would not be able to observe effective resistance in the first year of the war if we defined effective resistance as 100 deaths suffered by the state.

aggregate effective resistance threshold of 100 deaths has already been met, the civil war must be coded as having ended and a politicide or other form of one-sided violence must be coded as having started.[171]

h. a peace treaty that produces at least six months of peace marks an end to the war.[172]

i. a decisive military victory by the rebels that produces a new regime marks the end of the war.[173] Since civil war is understood as an armed conflict against the government, continuing armed conflict against a new government implies a new civil war.[174] If the government wins the war, a period of peace longer than six months must persist before we code a new war (see also criterion k).

j. a cease-fire, truce, or end to the fighting results in at least two years of peace.[175] The period of peace must be longer than what is required in the case of a peace agreement, as we do not have clear signals of the parties' intent to negotiate an agreement in the case of a truce/ceasefire.[176]

[171] This criterion distinguishes cases in which insurgent violence was limited to the outbreak of the war and, for the remainder of the conflict, the government engaged in one-sided violence. A hypothetical example is a case where insurgents inflicted 100 deaths on the government during the first week of fighting, and then the government defeated the insurgents and engaged in pogroms and politicide for several years with no or few deaths on the government's side. If we cannot apply this rule consistently to all cases (due to data limitations), then periods of politicide at the start or end of the war should be combined with war periods. But this implies that civil wars will often be observationally equivalent to coups that are followed by politicide, or other such sequences and combinations of different forms of political violence.

[172] Treaties that do not stop the fighting are not considered (e.g., the Islamabad Accords of 1993 in Afghanistan's war; the December 1997 agreement among Somali clan leaders). If several insurgent groups are engaged in the war, the majority of groups must sign. This criterion is useful for the study of peace transitions, but may not be as important if researchers are interested in studying, e.g., civil war duration.

[173] Thus, in secessionist wars that are won by the rebels who establish a new state, if a war erupts immediately in the new state, we would code a new war onset in the new state (an example is Croatia in 1992–95), even if the violence is closely related to the preceding war. A continuation of the old conflict between the old parties could now count as an interstate war, as in the case of Ethiopia and Eritrea, who fought a war in 1998–2000, after Eritrea's successful secession from Ethiopia in 1993.

[174] This criterion allows researchers to study the stability of military victories. Analysis of the stability of civil war outcomes would be biased if we coded an end to civil war through military victory only when the victory was followed by a prolonged period of peace. This would bias the results in favor of finding a positive correlation between military outcomes and peace duration. Yet, if new parties or issues do not emerge, the war must stop for at least a few months to determine that the victory is "decisive." This criterion is important to analyze war recurrence, but not necessarily war prevalence.

[175] Peace implies no battle-related deaths, or, in a lenient version of this criterion, fewer deaths than the lowest threshold of deaths used to code war onset—i.e., fewer than 100 deaths per year.

[176] These situations are different from those where there is no violence as a result of armies standing down without a cease-fire agreement, which would fall under criterion (f).

k. new parties enter the war over new issues, a new war onset should be coded, subject to the same operational criteria.[177] If the same parties return to war over the same issues we generally code the continuation of the old war, unless any of the above criteria for coding a war end apply for the period before the resurgence of fighting.

Using these coding rules, we have coded 151 civil war starts from 1944 to 1999. Without coding new war onsets in countries with already ongoing civil wars, the number of civil wars is 119. Out of all the cases in our dataset, 20 might be called "ambiguous"—that is, in those one or more of the coding rules might not be satisfied, though we have considered them as sufficiently close to our concept of civil war so as to include them in our analysis. In the supplement, we report on the robustness of our results if we drop or recode some of these ambiguous cases.[178]

A.2: Coding of the Dependent Variable

Our main dependent variable is *participatory peace* two years after the end of the war. We also code *sovereign peace* two years after the end of the war. *Sovereign* peace is a prerequisite for *participatory* peace. *Participatory peace* is coded as a combination of four intermediate variables.

First, we code if civil war has resumed in the country (*war end*) within two years of the end of the war or the end of the "therapy" (i.e., victory, truce, settlement, or departure of a UN mission). *War end* is coded 1 if civil war has not restarted and 0 otherwise. Details on the coding of each case are given in our coding notes online.

Second, we code lower-level, or *residual*, violence after the war. Lower-level violence refers to what other datasets call intermediate armed conflict (about 200 deaths per year).[179] It also refers to mass violations of human rights, such as politicide, genocide, widespread extrajudicial killings, torture, and mass-level imprisonments of the political opposi-

[177] These incompatibilities must be significantly different or the wars must be fought by different groups in different regions of the country. For example, we would code three partially overlapping wars in Ethiopia (Tigrean, Eritrean, Oromo) from the 1970s to the 1990s. New issues alone should not be sufficient to code a new war, as "issues" are not typically used to define civil war. We could apply such a rule if we classified civil wars into categories—e.g., secessionist wars vs. revolutions over control of the state. In addition to having new issues, most parties must also be new before we can code a new war onset.

[178] See pages 12–15 and tables 3 and 4 in the supplement.

[179] See, e.g., Nils Petter Gleditsch, Peter Wallensteen, Mikael Eriksson, Margareta Sollenberg and Håvard Strand, "Armed Conflict 1945–1999: A New Dataset," *Journal of Peace Research* 39 no. 5 (2001): 615–37.

tion. If we do not find evidence of these types of events within two years after the end of the war, we code *no residual violence* = 1; otherwise, *no residual violence* is coded 0. A number of sources were used to code this variable.[180] We have included a table with more detailed information on how we code *no residual violence* in our notes online.

Third, we establish if claims against the government's sovereignty persist after the end of the war. If state authority can be exercised in the entire territory of the state, then our requirement that sovereignty be undivided is satisfied and we code *undivided sovereignty* = 1. If there is de facto or de jure partition or regional autonomy that obstructs government control of an area of the country, then this criterion is not satisfied and *undivided sovereignty* = 0.

Our measure of sovereign peace is composed of these three variables: *sovereign* peace requires *no war recurrence, no residual violence,* and *undivided sovereignty* two years after the end of the war or the end of the "therapy."

To define *participatory* peace, we add a fourth component to *sovereign* peace, based on the country's polity score two years after the end of the war (*pol2*). This is the difference of the regime's democratic and autocratic characteristics.[181] The variable ranges from 0 (extreme autocracy) to 20 (maximum democracy). Our cutoff point is a low score of 3 on that scale. Regimes that fall below this cutoff point are coded as *participatory peace* failures.[182] Others are coded as successes if they also satisfy the sovereign peace criteria. Thus, *participatory peace* two years after the war is coded 1 (success) if *sovereign peace* is coded 1 (success) and *pol2* > 3.

---

[180] Esty et al. 1995. Regan 1996; Peter Wallensteen and Margareta Sollenberg, "Armed Conflicts, Conflict Termination, and Peace Agreements, 1989–1996," *Journal of Peace Research* 34 (1997): 3; Gleditsch et al 2001; Barbara Harff and Ted Robert Gurr. "Research Note: Toward Empirical Theory of Genocides and Politicides: Identification and Measurement of Cases since 1945," *International Studies Quarterly* 32 (1998): 359–71; Roy Licklider, "The Consequences of Negotiated Settlements in Civil Wars, 1945–1993," *American Political Science Review* 89 (September): 681–90; Barbara Harff, "No Lessons Learned from the Holocaust? Assessing Risks of Genocide and Political Mass Murder since 1955," *American Political Science Review* 97 no. 1 (2003): 57–73; and research in Keesings Archives and Lexis-Nexis.

[181] We use data from the Polity dataset as our source. For years in which Polity scores are missing (i.e., if they indicate regime transition or war in the country), we use interpolated scores. The "Polity2" series of the 2002 version of the database is already interpolated by the Polity database coders. We have also used that series to perform comparisons with our own interpolations. If the Polity score is "66" indicating that the country is under foreign occupation and this is due to the UN presence (e.g., Bosnia), we do not consider this as a case of divided sovereignty.

[182] We also confirmed that using a slightly lower threshold (pol2 > 2) did not affect any of our results.

Appendix B: Summary Statistics for Key Variables

In table B.1, we present summary statistics and sources used to code all variables that are included in our statistical analysis. We group them under the concept variable category (hostility, local capacities, and international capacities) within which they primarily belong. We also summarize control variables used in our analysis.

---

[183] In the regression results presented in table 3.5, we have rescaled the imputed electricity consumption per capita variable by dividing it by 100 and have rescaled the current transfers per capita variable by dividing it by 10,000 so that we can present easily readable coefficient estimates and standard errors in four decimal points for all variables. We have used the original ranges for these variables in the supplement.

TABLE B.1
Summary Statistics

Variable	N	Mean	S.D.	Min	Max	Source
Hostility Proxies						
War Type (Ethnic/Religious War?)	147	0.659	0.475	0	1	Harff and Gurr 1998; Licklider 1995; various secondary sources (see country notes)
Ethnic War 1 (Ethnic/Religious War?)	147	0.497	0.501	0	1	Sambanis 2002
Ethnic War 2 (Ethnic/Religious War?)	147	0.653	0.477	0	1	Sambanis 2002
Log of Deaths and Displacements	145	11.55	2.45	6.908	15.672	Various sources (see comments on each case in our coding notes)
Deaths and Displacements per Capita	145	81.74	148.99	0.006	854.17	As above
Log of Total Deaths	145	9.84	2.02	6.21	14.57	As above (see comments on each case in our coding notes)
Log of War Duration (in months)	147	3.54	1.42	0	6.17	Various sources (see coding notes for each country)
Number of Factions	147	3.23	1.48	2	11	Various secondary sources (see bibliography and online supporting documents)
Ethnic Fractionalization (Ef)	151	0.558	0.264	0.003	1	Fearon 2003
Ethnolinguistic Fractionalization Index (Elf)	151	52.07	29.17	0	90	Original source: Bruk and Apenchenko 1964, translated and compiled into an index by Collier and Hoeffler 2001
Signed Treaty	147	0.306	0.462	0	1	Walter 1997, 2003; Licklider 1995; Wallensteen and Sollenberg 1997; see "Treaty Summaries" document in our coding notes

(continued)

TABLE B.1 (*continued*)

Variable	N	Mean	S.D.	Min	Max	Source
Implemented Treaty	147	0.190	0.394	0	1	As above
Military Victory	151	0.503	0.502	0	1	As above
Rebel Victory	151	0.219	0.414	0	1	As above
Government Victory	151	0.285	0.452	0	1	As above
Truce or Cease-fire	151	0.139	0.347	0	1	As above
Negotiated Settlement	151	0.178	0.384	0	1	As above
Outcome of the War	147	1.86	1.29	0	4	As above
International Capacity Proxies						
Net Transfers per Capita	146	44741	140475	−479480	943036	IMF Financial Statistics, 1949–98; World Bank, World Development Indicators 1999. See dataset notes for country details
Effective Development Assistance, % GDP	83	386.28	550.59	−9.13	2943.3	Chang, Fernandez-Arias, Serven, 1998; World Bank 1988;
Any UN intervention	151	0.225	0.419	0	1	United Nations 1996; Web site of UN Department of Peacekeeping Operations
UN Operations (distinguishing facilitative from transformational PKOs)	151	0.311	0.623	0	2	United Nations 1996; Web site of UN Department of Peacekeeping Operations; see UN mandate document in online supporting documentation
UN mandate type	151	0.781	1.42	0	5	United Nations 1996; Web site of UN Department of Peace-keeping Operations; see UN mandate document in online supporting documentation

	N	Mean	SD	Min	Max	Source
(Multidimensional and Enforcement Operations) *Transformational UN Peacekeeping*	151	0.086	0.281	0	1	United Nations 1996; Web site of UN Department of Peacekeeping Operations; see UN mandate document in online supplement
UN Monitoring	151	0.086	0.281	0	1	United Nations 1996; Web site of UN Department of Peacekeeping Operations; see UN mandate document in online supporting documentation
Traditional Peacekeeping Mission	151	0.053	0.225	0	1	United Nations 1996; Web site of UN Department of Peacekeeping Operations; see UN mandate document in online supporting documentation
Multidimensional Peacekeeping	151	0.046	0.211	0	1	United Nations 1996; Web site of UN Department of Peacekeeping Operations; see UN mandate document in online supporting documentation
UN Enforcement	151	0.039	0.196	0	1	United Nations 1996; Web site of UN Department of Peacekeeping Operations; see UN mandate document in online supporting documentation
Non-UN Peace Operations	151	0.596	1.04	0	1	Heldt 2002 and other sources (see online supporting documentation)
Local Capacity Proxies						
Electricity Consumption (kwh) per Capita	135	502.28	819.20	10	5387	World Bank World Development Indicators (WDI) 2002; see dataset notes for country-specific notes

(continued)

TABLE B.1 (*continued*)

Variable	N	Mean	S.D.	Min	Max	Source
Electricity Consumption (kwh) per Capita (with Imputed Missing Values)	146	606.93	982.77	10	5387	Sources as above; 11 observations imputed using data on oil consumption (Singer and Small National Material Capabilities dataset), electricity consumption in 1980, and five-year averages in electricity consumption (WDI data)
Primary Commodity Exports as % of GDP (w/Imputed Missing Values)	141	0.164	0.188	0.007	1.018	World Bank WDI 2002; Collier and Hoeffler 2001. Missing observations imputed using regression and data on fuel exports as % of merchandise exports and total exports as % of GDP (WDI 2000, 2003 is source for these data)
Primary Commodity Exports as % of GDP (w/Imputed Missing Values— Version 2 of Imputation)	151	0.162	0.185	−0.013	1.018	World Bank WDI 2002; Collier and Hoeffler 2001. Missing observations imputed using regression and data on oil dependence, total manufacturing exports as % of merchandise GDP. exports and total exports as % of WDI 2000, 2003 are source for these data
Oil Exports Greater than 30% of GDP	151	0.205	0.405	0	1	Fearon and Laitin 2003; with revisions from Sambanis 2004a
Real per Capita GDP	151	1.79	1.83	.05	11.37	Fearon and Laitin 2003, mostly drawing on Penn World Tables 5.6

Variable	N	Mean	SD	Min	Max	Description
Annual Rate of Growth of Real per Capita GDP (at End of War)	134	0.24	11.47	−40.19	37.91	Computed from the GDP series for those cases where there are data both for the start and end of the war. If the war is ongoing but a peace operation had started, we use year the peace operation started to compute the rate of change in income from the war's start
Control Variables						
Decade War Started	151	3.72	1.57	1	6	Dummy variables representing the decade the war started, from 1945 to 1954, 1955 to 1964, etc.
Cold War Conflict	151	0.689	0.464	0	1	Dummy variable coded 1 for cases with year of war onset before 1990 and 0 if war started in 1990 or afterwards
Geographic Region	151	3.62	1.33	0	1	Five regions: North America & Europe; Latin America & Caribbean; Middle East & North Africa; Asia; Sub-Saharan Africa
Military Personnel (in Thousands, at the End of the War or Closest Year)	138	254.09	633.06	1	3360	World Bank, World Development Indicators 2000

Note: In the regression results presented in table 3.5, we have rescaled the imputed electricity consumption per capita variable by dividing it by 100 and have rescaled the current transfers per capita variable by dividing it by 10,000 so that we can present easily readable coefficient estimates and standard errors in four decimal points for all variables. We have used the original ranges for these variables in the supplement.

4

Making War

A CLOSE READING OF Secretary-General Boutros Boutros-Ghali's June 1992 report, the *Agenda for Peace,* revealed what would soon become telling phrases. Slipped in among the innocuous bureaucratic prose of the landmark document were references to "peacekeeping, *heretofore* [emphasis supplied] with the consent of the parties,"[1] a "wider mission" including "nations torn by civil war and strife" and the passing of "absolute and exclusive sovereignty,"[2] and arguments favoring the establishing of "peace enforcement units . . . *available on call* [emphasis supplied]."[3] Read carefully, this was a revolutionary manifesto. Peacekeeping had long been defined as essentially consent-based monitoring of forces, operations limited to international disputes, and what Sir Brian Urquhart, the eminent chief of the UN's peacekeeping department in the 1970s and 1980s, had dubbed the "sheriff's posse" model of ad hoc voluntary troop provision. All three traditions had insured that the UN role in conflict was limited and that member states kept a very close rein on field activities.

During the Cold War, interstate peacekeeping had been the UN activity; interstate peace enforcement had been delegated to member states (as in Korea). Peacekeeping rested on consent of the parties, and their cooperation was the precondition of the effectiveness of the UN's lightly armed troops who were volunteered for each mission by member countries. Now, consent was becoming "heretofore," the Secretary-General was looking for "peace enforcement units," and peace was domestic, not interstate.

Secretary-General Boutros Boutros-Ghali's doctrinal test balloons were fully supported by some of the key member states, the United States most prominently. The Clinton administration's U.S. ambassador to the UN, Madeleine Albright, declared the opening of an era of "assertive multilateralism" in U.S. foreign policy. But President George H. Bush had prefigured a similar commitment when he offered (the about to be closed) Fort Dix in New Jersey as a training base for the UN forces that he thought were needed to help sustain the "New World Order"

[1] Boutros Boutros-Ghali, *An Agenda for Peace* (New York: United Nations, 1992), p. 11. Henceforth BBG.

[2] BBG 1992, pp. 8–9.

[3] BBG 1992, p. 26.

of international law and U.S. leadership that he had proclaimed in the wake of the Gulf War victory.[4]

These "assertive" ambitions, however, clashed with deeply held UN doctrines of traditional peacekeeping relearned in the painful aftermath of the Congo crisis of the 1960s. There the UN had ventured into both a civil war and peace enforcement and muddled through to a success of a sort—the Congo was reunified and the colonialists were out, but a corrupt dictatorship was left behind. In the aftermath of the Congo, the UN had found itself both bereft of its widely revered Secretary-General, Dag Hammarskjold, a victim of the tortuous politics of the Congo civil war, and both isolated and bankrupt when France and the USSR refused to pay the assessments for the mission they no longer supported.[5]

Peace enforcement was thus a dangerous turn in UN doctrine and strategy.[6] In the 1990s ambitious plans for peace enforcement again eroded painfully as the UN tried to cope with a series of conflicts beyond its means in Somalia and the former Yugoslavia. It discovered that making peace without the consent of the parties was something very close to war, and war was something it did not do well.

In this chapter, we will offer an account of what went wrong in Somalia and Bosnia, contrast these failures in enforcement to the semisuccess the UN experienced earlier in the Congo, and then explain why war fighting is beyond current UN capabilities.

Somalia

> This is unacceptable; this means war.
> —Colonel Abdi Qaybiid, June 4, 1993
> (Aidid adviser, when told that UNOSOM
> planned to inspect a weapons cantonment
> site at General Aidid's radio station)

---

[4] *New York Times*, September 1, 1992.

[5] BBG, Goulding, and Jonah were very reluctant to endorse a smooth transition between the U.S. and UN forces in Somalia, regarding the U.S. plan as too committed to coercive force and too controlled by the United States, both violating traditional UN principles for peacekeeping operations; see p. 45 of John L. Hirsh and Robert B. Oakley, *Somalia and Operation Restore Hope* (Washington, DC: United States Institute of Peace, 1995). Apparently, however, the Secretary-General's objection was not to the Chapter VII enforcement authority, but to its delegation to the United States outside UN control (Boutros-Ghali, *Unvanquished* [New York: Random House, 1999], p. 59).

[6] For an insightful survey of the challenges of peace enforcement that draws on the experience of colonial occupations see Kimberly Zisk Marten, *Enforcing the Peace* (New York: Columbia University Press, 2004), esp. chap. 6.

There are plenty of people in the United States
who still don't know that this was, is a war.
   —Major General Montgomery (deputy force
      commander, commander U.S. Forces,
      December 1993, *Washington Post*)[7]

For most of its history, Somalia was a loosely defined area occupied by
pastoralists and nomads who shared a common ethnic, linguistic, and
religious background. Kinship served as the basis of political and social
life, and there was no tradition of centralized government or clearly de-
marcated territorial boundaries.[8] In 1960, the union of Italian-held Somalia and British-held Somaliland combined six major clans: the Darood, Issaq, Hawiye, Dir, Digil, and Rahanwein. Each of these clans is
further divided into subclans and each subclan is divided into families.[9]
In 1960, the population in the north was about 70 percent Issaq, 15 percent Dir, and 15 percent Darood. In the south, the Hawiye constituted
38 percent of the population, with the Digil, Rahanwein Darood, and
the Dir having smaller percentages. The Hawiye and Darood dominated,
and competition between them and the Issaq shaped much of the postindependence politics of Somalia.

A short-lived parliamentary democracy from 1960 to 1969 suffered
from clientelism, clan favoritism, and factional politics, giving way to a
coup led by Mohamed Siad Barre and a Supreme Revolutionary Council
(SRC) led by his own Marehan subclan and excluding other important
subclans. For financial and military support, Barre turned to the USSR,
but when the Soviets began supporting Ethiopia in 1977, Somalia turned
to the United States.[10] Long-standing Somali claims on the Ogaden region in neighboring Ethiopia led to a failed war of conquest in which
Ethiopian forces were victorious. A large influx of Ogaden refugees in
1978 threatened the status of the Isaaq and other disadvantaged clans,[11]

[7] Both quoted by John Drysdale, *Whatever Happened to Somalia: A Tale of Tragic
Blunders* (London: Haan Associates, 1994), p. 181.

[8] William J. Durch, ed., *UN Peacekeeping, America's Policy, and the Uncivil Wars of the
1990s* (New York: St. Martin's Press, 1996); Walter Clarke, "Failed Visions and Uncertain
Mandates in Somalia," in Walter Clarke and Jeffrey Herbst, eds., *Learning from Somalia*
(Boulder, CO: Westview Press, 1997), pp. 3–19.

[9] As the major source of identity differentiation in Somalia is the clan, measures of ethnic difference that rely mainly on linguistic differences (e.g., the *Elf* index) characterize Somalia as ethnically homogeneous. Broader conceptions of ethnic difference (e.g., Horowitz
1985) include clan differences, and Somalia would be heavily heterogeneous by that standard.

[10] Durch 1996.

[11] I. M. Lewis, *A Modern History of Somalia* (Boulder, CO: Westview Press, 1988),
p. 248.

leading some of them to join in a (failed) coup against Barre in 1978. With a declining economy, a seemingly directionless state, and clan favoritism, militias that would eventually recruit thousands of members began to be formed. Two major insurgent organizations, the Somali National Movement (SNM) and the Somali Salvation Democratic Front (SSDF), both engaged in border raids from their bases in Ethiopia as early as 1981.

A peace agreement between Ethiopia and Somalia in 1988 limited the ability of SNM rebels to operate from Ethiopian territory and gave them an incentive to step up their efforts and launch attacks into northern Somalia so as to gain a territorial base.[12] The SNM—rooted in the Isaaq—moved into the Isaaq-homeland areas of northern Somalia in May 1988. Border wars fought between the government and a loose coalition of rebel organizations (including the SNM and SSDF) escalated until the Somali army was eventually defeated and the balance among the clans tipped against the Barre-favored Darood.[13] The government collapsed as Somali clans formed rival political organizations, including the United Somali Congress (USC) formed by the Hawiye, which occupied large parts of Central Somalia and Mogadishu, and the "Manifesto Group" formed by Mogadishu elites.[14]

As rebels were closing in on Mogadishu in January 1991, Siad Barre fled the country. Central government collapsed entirely and factional conflict grew as Ali Mahdi was declared interim leader by the Manifesto Group and declared himself president following the reconciliation conference held in Djibouti in July 1991.[15] But the conference had excluded Mohammed Aidid and his Habr Gedir forces, who had participated actively in the war against Barre. Mutual resentment and political ambition combined to spur a clash between Aidid's and Ali Mahdi's forces, causing between 30,000 and 50,000 deaths from November 1991 until March 1992 and turning Mogadishu into a war zone.[16] Amid escalating factional conflict in the south, Somaliland in the north declared independence in the summer of 1991. In the rest of the country, especially in rural areas, clan warfare destroyed what limited infrastructure existed, and that contributed to the collapse of the agricultural sector that in turn led to the onset of famine.

The famine of 1991–92 was unlike past famines in Somalia in that it affected both rural and urban areas and in that drought was not the single

[12] Durch 1996, 314.

[13] Mark Bradbury, *The Somali Conflict: Prospects for Peace* (Oxford: Oxfam, 1994), p. 68; David D. Laitin and Said S. Samatar, *Somalia: Nation in Search of a State* (Boulder, CO: Westview Press, 1987).

[14] Durch 1996, 314.

[15] Durch 1996, 315.

[16] Clarke 1997, 5.

most important cause of this disaster. Starvation soon gave way to disease and, with 2 million people in danger of dying, the country faced a short-fall that was driving food prices up by 800–1,200 percent.[17] International assistance began supplying some of that food, and some of that assistance got through, lowering the death rate. But ongoing clan warfare meant that much of the aid was looted upon arrival by armed gangs, merchants, and militias. The UN and the Red Cross had to resort to hiring armed guards and security personnel to assist them in the delivery of aid.[18]

Within this climate of state failure, the first UN operation in Somalia (UNOSOM I) was created in April 1992, with a mandate to provide humanitarian relief. The main threat that it was sent to address was the famine and the difficulties associated with delivery of relief by NGO workers who were impeded by the ongoing clan warfare.[19] UNOSOM, however, was not equipped with the mandate or resources necessary to protect relief workers and assist in the delivery of food aid. As the situation worsened in the fall of 1992, a change in U.S. policy on Somalia—largely precipitated by media coverage of the famine—led to the adoption of UN Security Council Resolution 794, which gave the U.S. military the command and control of the UN operation.[20] The United States launched Operation Restore Hope, also known as the United Task Force (UNITAF), in December 1992 with a mandate to establish "a secure environment for the delivery of relief supplies and the consolidation of the security framework so that it could be handed over to the regular UN forces."

President George H. W. Bush took care to limit UNITAF's commitment with a public statement to the U.S. public. According to that statement, UNITAF was seen as a very limited, apolitical mission that would help deliver aid and hand over the completion of that task to the UN.[21] As a result, the U.S. public was never informed of the dangers associated with that operation, and this would later haunt the mission, as the public could not understand how a humanitarian mission would bring U.S. soldiers into direct combat with the population that they had been sent to assist.[22]

[17] Andrew Natsios, "Humanitarian Relief Intervention in Somalia: The Economics of Chaos," in Walter Clarke and Jeffrey Herbst *Learning from Somalia* (Boulder, CO: Westview Press, 1997) p. 79.

[18] Durch 1996, 319.

[19] Hirsch and Oakley 1995.

[20] Robert B. Oakley, "Humanitarian Response: The Consequences of Intervention" Paper given at the Carnegie Forum, Geneva, Switzerland (February 16–17, 1997), p. 7

[21] Durch 1996, 321.

[22] Walter Clarke and Jeffrey Herbst, "Somalia and the Future of Humanitarian Intervention," in Walter Clarke and Jeffrey Herbst, eds., *Learning from Somalia* (Boulder, CO: Westview Press, 1997), pp. 239–53.

Operation Restore Hope's political guidance was given to Central Command (CENTCOM) in Florida, where plans for an extensive component with civil affairs officers and military police training were quickly removed from the package.[23] CENTCOM's primary concern was not to accept any tasks that might require it to remain in Somalia beyond its planned stay.[24] UNITAF's limited mandate soon became a point of contention between Secretary-General Boutros Ghali and the U.S. administration, as Boutros Ghali wanted to expand the mandate to include the disarmament of the factions. Soon after deployment, it was clear that UNITAF's mandate had to be expanded, and UNITAF began seizing heavy weapons around Mogadishu and enforcing the cease-fire agreed upon by the factions in Addis Ababa. But it did not reinforce the peace initiatives that Special Representative of the Secretary-general (SRSG) Sahnoun had launched, involving local leaders and elders in discussion and a locally supported conflict resolution process.[25]

In sharp contrast to UNITAF, which had ample resources and a narrow mandate, its successor, United Nations Operation in Somalia (UNOSOM II) in May 1993, was given fewer resources and a more expanded mandate.[26] In addition to providing humanitarian assistance and maintaining a secure environment, UNOSOM II's mandate also included economic and social reconstruction, repatriation of refugees, and disarmament.[27] Security Council Resolution 814 (1993) gave UNOSOM II a mandate for national reconciliation in Somalia, including the reestablishment of regional institutions and civil administration in the entire country and the support of a process of political reconciliation.[28] U.S. ambassador to the UN, Madeleine Albright, one of its key authors, described 814 as "an unprecedented enterprise aimed at nothing less than

---

[23] Clarke 1997, 9.

[24] Clarke 1997, 9.

[25] Elders meetings known as *shir* were later applied with some success in Somaliland in March–May 1993 and Kismayu throughout 1993 (Clarke 1997, 14) and might have been useful in providing a framework within which to build a political system to replace the collapsed Barre regime. Of course, the urgency in 1992 was to stop the famine, and, supporting gradual peacemaking through grassroots organizations might not have been an effective way to achieve this goal (Ken Menkhaus, "International Peacebuilding and the Dynamics of Local and National Reconciliation in Somalia," in Walter Clarke and Jeffrey Herbst, eds., *Learning from Somalia* [Boulder, CO: Westview Press, 1997], pp. 42–63, 54).

[26] Lessons Learned Unit, Department of Peacekeeping Operations et al., *Comprehensive Report on Lessons Learned from United Nations Operation in Somalia, April 1992–March 1995* (Sweden: Life and Peace Institute, December 1995).

[27] See Security Council Resolution 814 (March 26, 1993), and Security Council Resolution 837 (June 6, 1993).

[28] Menkhaus 1997, 42–43.

Box 4.1 UNOSOM II Mandate

ESTABLISHMENT: Following the recommendations in the Secretary-General's 3/3/93 Report, the Security Council, by Resolution 814 (March 26, 1993), established UNOSOM II to take over from UNITAF. The mission was mandated to fulfill the following responsibilities: "monitoring that all factions continued to respect the cessation of hostilities and other agreements to which they had consented; preventing any resumption of violence and, if necessary, taking appropriate action; maintaining control of the heavy weapons of the organized factions which would have been brought under international control; seizing the small arms of all unauthorized armed elements; securing all ports, airports and lines of communications required for the delivery of humanitarian assistance; protecting the personnel, installations and equipment of the United Nations and its agencies, ICRC as well as NGOs; continuing mine-clearing; and assisting in repatriation of refugees and displaced persons in Somalia."[1] After attacks on mission personnel on June 5, 1993, the Security Council passed Resolution 837 (June 6, 1993) which "Reaffirm[ed] that the Secretary-General is authorized under resolution 814 (1993) to take all necessary measures against all those responsible for the armed attacks."

CHANGES TO MANDATE: In Resolution 897 (February 4, 1994), the Security Council changed the mandate to specifically exclude the use of coercive measures. As revised, the mandate included: "assisting the Somali parties in implementing the "Addis Ababa Agreements," particularly in their cooperative disarmament and ceasefire efforts; protecting major ports, airports and essential infrastructure; providing humanitarian relief to all in need throughout the country; assisting in the reorganization of the Somali police and judicial system; helping repatriate and resettle refugees and displaced persons; assisting the political process in Somalia; and protecting the personnel, installations and equipment of the United Nations and its agencies as well as of NGOs providing humanitarian and reconstruction assistance."[2]

TERMINATION: The Security Council, in Resolution 954 (November 4, 1994), recognized that UNOSOM II was initially envisioned to terminate at the end of March 1995 and decided that, given

continued

Box 4.1 continued

the lack of progress in the peace process, there was no reason to extend the mandate beyond that point. Consequently, UNOSOM II left Somalia in March 1995.

[1] http://www.un.org/Depts/dpko/dpko/co_mission/unosom2mandate.html
[2] http://www.un.org/Depts/dpko/dpko/co_mission/unosom2mandate.html

the restoration of an entire country."[29] Unfortunately, UNOSOM II was not given sufficient resources for the task and lacked good training and a clear strategy to implement its mandate.[30] In addition to these serious external constraints, UNOSOM II also had to deal with Somali parties that were generally less cooperative than they had been with UNITAF. In particular, General Aidid believed the UN to be biased against him, partly due to his earlier exchanges with Boutros-Ghali.[31] Warlords had been emboldened by UNITAF's unwillingness to disarm them, and the substantial reduction in fire power that followed UNITAF's withdrawal made it impossible for UNOSOM to implement its Chapter VII mandate.

Yet in early 1993, the UN peace enforcement effort in the large part of southern Somalia outside of General Aidid's stronghold in Mogadishu was making a positive difference in the lives of ordinary Somalis. By mid-1993, starvation was not an issue in the areas within the reach of UN protection. In contrast, 300,000 Somalis died in 1991–92 in a famine induced by the depredations of roving armed militia and the devastating competition of the Somali warlords. In 1993, with the protection of UNOSOM II, UNICEF was assisting forty thousand pupils. Thirty-two hospitals and 103 mobile vaccination teams were active (75 percent of the children under five received measles vaccine). Seventy thousand refugees returned from Kenya. Thirty-nine district councils and

[29] Hirsch and Oakley 1995, p. 111; and for an informative discussion of the politics of U.S. planning for this peace operation see David Halberstam, *War in a Time of Peace: Bush, Clinton, and the Generals* (New York: Scribner, 2001).

[30] The expansion of the mandate should not be seen as a UN initiative that was unsupported by the United States. As Clarke and Herbst (1997, 241) point out, the United States was involved in the drafting of Resolution 814.

[31] Hirsch and Oakley 1995. Aidid had negotiated with SRSG Sahnoun and agreed to the deployment of a small UN force but while that force was on its way, Boutros-Ghali requested and received authorization from the Security Council for the deployment of a 3,000-strong force. While this was favored by Ali Mahdi and smaller factions, Aidid and his Somali National Alliance opposed the larger external presence. See Durch 1996, 316–17.

six regional councils were formed. UNOSOM had begun to recruit 5,000 former Somali policemen to perform basic police functions.

The fundamental flaws in UNOSOM II's strategy became evident on June 5, 1993, when twenty-four Pakistani peacekeepers were killed after they fired on a Somali crowd while trying to inspect a weapons site. Security Council Resolution 837 then authorized the use of "all necessary measures" to be taken against those responsible for the attack, authorizing the arrest and trial of individuals. General Aidid had been singled out for arrest, and several clashes followed, culminating in a disastrous incident on October 3, 1993, which involved the killing of 18 U.S. soldiers and more than 300 Somalis.[32]

The fruitless effort to capture General Mohammed Aidid exposed what had become a politically bankrupt attempt to enforce law and order on an increasingly resistant population. The entire UN operation relied too much on the military and logistic backbone of the U.S. contingent, which was poorly coordinated with the overall UNOSOM II force. UNOSOM II survived casualties inflicted on the Pakistanis in June, but when Aidid attacked the Americans in October he struck UNOSOM II's Achilles' heel.[33]

With the advantage of hindsight, we can identify policy mistakes, without which Somalia might look very different today.[34] A more thorough partnership with Somalia's regional neighbors in a mediation effort in 1991,[35] a more extensive mandate for the U.S.-led Unified Task Force (UNITAF) in December 1992 (when controlling the heavy and light weapons of the clans would have been easier), and above all a smoother political transition from UNITAF's partial successes in negotiating with the warlords to UNOSOM's more ambitious state-building agenda might have made a difference.

The fundamental problem, of course, was a famine induced by drought and greatly exacerbated by the ravages of the civil war that followed on the collapse of Siad Barre's dictatorship and by the rapacious extortion of

[32] United States Senate, Committee on Armed Services, "US Military Operations in Somalia," May 12, 1994.

[33] Terrence Lyons and Ahmed I. Samatar, *Somalia: State Collapse, Multilateral Intervention, and Strategies for Political Reconstruction* (Washington, DC: Brookings Institution, 1995).

[34] See Jonathan Stevenson, "Hope Restored in Somalia," *Foreign Policy* (Summer 1993): 138–54; Jeffrey Clark, "Debacle in Somalia: The Failure of Collective Response," in Lori Damrosch, ed., *Enforcing Restraint* (New York: Council on Foreign Relations, 1993); Samuel Makinda, *Seeking Peace from Chaos: Humanitarian Intervention in Somalia* (Boulder, CO: Lynne Rienner, 1993); and Jane Perlez, "Somalia Self-Destructs and the World Looks On," *New York Times*, December 29, 1991.

[35] For this argument see Mohammed Sahnoun, *Somalia: The Missed Opportunities* (Washington, DC: United States Institute of Peace, 1994).

the Somali warlords who taxed relief convoys in order to fund their competition for power. Only a Somali "Leviathan" with a monopoly of violence or a "Super Warlord" capable of playing warlord against warlord could restore order and end the famine throughout Somalia. UNOSOM I (with 500 Pakistani troops holed up in the port of Mogadishu) could do very little, not even prevent grain ships from being shelled from shore. The UN Special Representative Mohammed Sahnoun valiantly tried to negotiate a peace, appealing to the humanity of the very warlords who ran the famine. In December 1992 the U.S.-led UNITAF temporarily became the Somali Leviathan, and the roads were opened and the famine broken.[36] UNITAF met almost no opposition because the mass of the people welcomed the relief, and the warlords knew it was temporary— no threat to their power.

But stopping the war and ensuring it would not recur could not have been achieved through a military operation alone. The international community would have had also to be prepared to undertake a broad, trustee-like transitional authority, an almost colonial role, although one geared toward its rapid self-transcendence into self-determination. It seemed a poor fit to Somalia's intense political problems to provide a UN mission with a clear lack of well-defined political objectives and strategies through which to achieve those objectives. UNOSOM II had a vague, albeit extensive, mandate and lacked a set of coherent, mutually reinforcing strategies that would allow it to implement the various components of the mission.

A common, expert critique raised at the time was that UN peace initiatives revealed a poor understanding of Somali political culture and did not utilize conflict resolution mechanisms that could have sustained a locally supported peace.[37] With a collapsed state and no legitimate political institutions, the UN had no footholds into developing a peacebuilding mission. The UN mission could either devolve authority to the local level (and abandon the idea of a central Somalia) or help build a Somali state that could control the warlords. UNOSOM II never quite settled on its role. Humanitarian assistance and the provision of a temporarily secure environment were stopgap measures. Disarmament is not a feasible strategy when there is no viable and lasting alternative to the status quo. Lack of civil affairs officers and a police component meant that UNITAF could not restore public order and could not even begin rebuilding the collapsed justice system.

UNITAF left these tasks to the less well-equipped UNOSOM II. UNITAF's provision of inducements to warlords to gain their cooperation

[36] For President Bush's rationale, see Michael Wines, "Bush Outlines Somalia Mission to Save Thousands," *New York Times*, Dec. 5, 1992.

[37] I. M. Lewis, *Understanding Somalia: Guide to Culture, History, and Social Institutions* (London: Haan Associates, 1993).

for the distribution of food may even have influenced the balance of power among rival warlords and intensified their competition after UNITAF's departure. In Mogadishu, for example, the major obstacle for the implementation of the UN mandate was the ongoing conflict between Ali Mahdi and Mohammed Farah Aidid, both members of the dominant Hawiye clan. By their acts of omission (failure to disarm warlords) and commission (cooperating with warlords), UNITAF stayed formally neutral but enhanced the power of warlords.[38]

In May 1993, UNOSOM II came face to face with the fundamental problems. Its mandate included the authority to disarm the factions—a disarmament to which, we should note, the faction leaders had, on paper, agreed at the Addis Ababa Conference in March 1993.[39] This mandate, unlike UNITAF's, threatened the political existence of the warlords. It proposed the establishment of a Somali national authority that would be elected by the people and sustained by a police force trained by the UN. UNOSOM II, however, lacked a vision of how it would achieve its ambitious objectives and was unprepared for the opposition the warlords would soon mount. UNOSOM inherited UNITAF's plan that proposed that the warlords keep their weapons in special cantonment areas in and around Mogadishu, but this also meant that these weapons could easily be reseized by the factions.[40] The bulk of UNOSOM II's troops were lightly armed, vulnerable to the weapons the warlords withdrew from the temporary UNITAF cantonment. UNOSOM II's logistics were immobile, dependent on Mogadishu port facilities, which made the UN too dependent on Aidid to threaten a credible withdrawal from his zone. The rank-and-file faction fighters were required to disarm in May 1993, but UNOSOM II established an alternative employment program only in January 1994.

More than thirty-five local, regional, and international initiatives to foster a negotiated peace from 1991 to 1995 failed to produce effective peace.[41] Mostly as a result of the lack of a legitimate central authority, strong interests in favor of war existed among local warlords who sought to maximize their control over their regions. Moreover, international efforts to support local and regional governance in Somalia may have

---

[38] Clarke and Herbst 1997.

[39] *Further Report of the Secretary General Submitted in Pursuance of Para.19 Res. 814 (1993) and para. 5 (Res. 865) of 1993*, S/26738, November 12, 1993. For excellent accounts of UNOSOM I see Hirsch and Oakley 1995; and for UNOSOM II see Walter Clarke and Jeffrey Herbst, eds., *Learning from Somalia* (Boulder, CO: Westview 1997); and Jarat Chopra, *Peace-Maintenance* (New York and London: Routledge, 1999), chap. 6.

[40] This was known as the "Oakley-Johnstone" demobilization strategy. Boutros-Ghali wanted a permanent domobilization of heavy weapons and the disarmament of irregular forces and roving gangs.

[41] Menkhaus 1997, p. 43.

exacerbated this problem.[42] Accepting local warlords as the de facto rulers of Somali regions gave warlords incentives to fight harder to maintain their control so as to benefit from the legitimacy imputed from their interaction with the UN and from the international economic assistance given to their region.

UNOSOM II and the Security Council were frustrated and did little to foster peacebuilding activities, partly due to lack of funds and partly due to staffing shortages.[43] UNOSOM tried desperately to support local initiatives for peace and, with the appointment of Ambassador Oakley as U.S. special envoy to Somalia, in the aftermath of the October 3 disaster, UNOSOM brought General Aidid back into the political process, while the Security Council reversed its previous policy on pursuing Aidid for the killing of the Pakistani peacekeepers. This development served to underscore the lack of direction in UNOSOM's strategy, as in the absence of a Somali authority with which to negotiate, the UN was forced to deal with factions that they considered responsible for undermining the peace.

Another error at the design phase of both UN operations was the failure to consider the tension that exists between a military enforcement operation on the one hand and a humanitarian assistance program on the other hand. The goals of the enforcement mission can be counterproductive to the humanitarian mission, and better integration of planning for various mission components is required. The humanitarian providers resisted integration of their mission to the military missions and viewed the military component with suspicion.[44] The involvement of troops in opening up food supply routes and in securing eight cities for the distribution of food had the ironic result of increasing violence against relief workers. Within the first three months of UNITAF's food relief operation, more relief workers were killed than in the previous two years combined.[45] The tension between the military and humanitarian components also created poor communication in UNOSOM II and an inability to coordinate the activities of the humanitarian, military, and civil mandates of the mission.

Added to this problem was a general weakness in command and control that resulted from frequent changes to the chief of the mission as five SRSGs were appointed to UNOSOM I and II within a three-year period. With each change of SRSG came also a change in leadership style and peacemaking strategy.[46]

[42] Menkhaus 1997.

[43] Lessons Learned Unit 1995, p. 12.

[44] Lessons Learned Unit 1995, pp. 7–8.

[45] See Hirsch and Oakley 1995.

[46] Durch (1996, 317) notes that Ismat Kittani's replacement of SRSG Sahnoun meant the abandonment of Sahnoun's initiatives to engage clan elders in the peacemaking process.

U.S. Admiral Jonathan Howe, the UN special representative, diagnosed well the shortfalls in military and humanitarian capacities that afflicted UNOSOM II:[47]

> Further strengthening of the U.S. military contribution, however, did not appear to be politically viable. By September 1993 both the United States and the UN were beginning to lose patience with protracted guerrilla assaults on their forces. . . . Even as the guerrilla campaign became more intense, with remote-controlled mines and much larger ambushes, requests from the field for heavier equipment for the lightly armored [U.S.] Quick Reaction Force were rejected in Washington. . . . Gradual loss of military momentum and initiative during the hostilities, however, was not the result of some single shortfall, such as the withholding of specific assets. Rather, it was caused by a combination of factors associated with operation of the UN multinational force. . . . The uneven advance of political, humanitarian, justice, and media programs also decreased the overall impact of the strategy. Even though the drive toward Somali self-governance made progress, UNOSOM suffered from insufficient resources and personnel to push forward and follow up effectively on initiatives throughout the country. Humanitarian efforts decreased in effectiveness because of limited success in bypassing South Mogadishu, where NGO and UN agency operations had been centered before organized hostilities began.

The Somali civil war was simply beyond what even the United States was prepared to invest in a UN operation it had adopted, at least for awhile, as its own. U.S. commitment had been marginal from the beginning. President Bush chose to intervene in Somalia due to a combination of media pressure and a desire to avoid the pressure to intervene in (what was thought to be) the much more difficult civil war in the former Yugoslavia.[48] When U.S. Secretary of Defense Les Aspin gave a speech in Washington recognizing the need for disarmament of the factions, UNITAF was already withdrawing, leaving only 1,200 troops behind. The U.S. thus passed on the responsibility to disarm hostile Somali factions to a much less well-trained, well-funded, and smaller UN force.[49] Yet, for the United Nations, UNOSOM I and II were major commitments, costing the international community somewhere near $1.6 billion from May 1992 to February 1995.[50]

According to our model, the "space" for peacebuilding in Somalia was very narrow: low local capacities combined with very high hostility to create a narrow base for peace (see figure 4.1). The presence of a large

---

[47] T. Jonathan Howe, "The United States and United Nations in Somalia: The Limits of Involvement," *Washington Quarterly* 18 no. 3 (1995): 47.

[48] Halberstam, 2001, p. 251.

[49] Clarke and Herbst 1997, p. 244.

[50] UNA-USA, *Global Agenda 1997–1998* (Lanham, MD: Rowman and Littlefield, 1997).

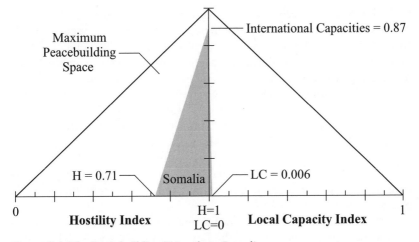

Figure 4.1 The Peacebuilding Triangle in Somalia

UN mission with an enforcement mandate might at first appear to have increased the space for peace, but our analysis here suggests that it did not. Indeed, the model fails in its prediction of a high probability of peacebuilding success in Somalia.[51] Hostility factors were worse in Somalia than in the average case in our dataset (there were more factions, they were more unreconciled, and deaths and displacements were higher) and local capacities were lower (Somalia was at the lowest 10th percentile of our development measure). As figure 4.1 suggests, what is driving this high prediction is the presence of a strong UN mission and the signing of a treaty. It is not clear that the treaty was seriously negotiated and, in any case, it was never implemented. There were too many opposing views at the Addis Ababa Conference over how to resolve the conflict.[52] The UN mandate was also not well designed or well implemented.

What was needed was a peace enforcement mission to force the peace, combined with a multidimensional mission to rebuild political institutions and a peacekeeping mission to keep the peace throughout the transition process. The UN missions ultimately sent to Somalia did not match the problems at hand. UNOSOM I and UNITAF operated on the inadequate

[51] The predicted probability is 0.63, whereas we code a peacebuilding failure in Somalia.

[52] In the cross-section version of our dataset, which we use to obtain these predictions, it is not entirely clear when to code a peacebuilding failure in Somalia, since the UN mission was ongoing for several years while the war continued. We code it at the point of transition to UNOSOM II, given the failure of UNITAF and UNOSOM I to end the war. By that date, there was no treaty (that came later, in 1997). The model's prediction with no treaty coded for Somalia is half our original estimate at 0.30, which is only narrowly above the average for all cases.

basis that Somalia's crisis was humanitarian and could be addressed by material assistance. This strategy merely exacerbated the security problem, while not addressing the question of a political settlement. UNOSOM II was given an ambitious peacebuilding mandate (which was better suited to the problem at hand) but without the resources needed to succeed. While an evaluation of the peacekeeping operation according to the standards of peacekeeping success suggests that UNOSOM I and UNITAF were partially successful in implementing most aspects of their mandate (they were partial successes at the microlevel), but their mandate was narrow and ineffective, contributing to an overall peacebuilding failure. This is an example where weak peacekeeping strategies were used under cover of a "strong" mandate and in a context where strong peacekeeping was needed.

With the limited scope of the peace operation, the likelihood of a successful transition to peace after the Barre regime collapsed and again in 1995 when the UN withdrew from Somalia was minimal. The country had virtually no local capacities and heightening levels of hostility (see table 4.1). Factions were unreconciled and numerous; and the war—even if it was being fought among members of the Somali "nation"—had the distinct flavor of an "ethnic" conflict.[53] And a large number of deaths due to famine and suppression by Barre and a large number of refugees and internally displaced persons increased levels of hostility. High levels of militarization of the society and a proliferation of small arms cultivated a culture of impunity in a country with a history of low levels of central government control and severe violations of human rights. These conditions spell out a difficult peacebuilding ecology that can be fully addressed only with a transitional administration with enforcement capacity and extensive resources to help rebuild the country. The fact that such a mission was never in the cards in Somalia implies that there was a macrolevel peacekeeping failure (i.e., at the level of the Security Council), coupled with the various microlevel failures (i.e., failures of strategy, interpretation, implementation, and leadership at the field, as we discussed above).

In collapsed states such as Somalia, there usually exist "conflict constituencies with a vested interest in continued instability, communal tension and an economy of plunder."[54] As a complement to firm enforcement of an agreed peace, an incremental approach should be used, aimed at transforming the interests of noncooperative parties by

[53] As we noted above, even though Somalis claim a common ethnic origin, the clan divisions that governed social relations in Somalia and that served as the basis for the organization of the rebellion and subsequent interclan warfare constituted the equivalent of an ethnic conflict. These divisions made a power-sharing agreement and the design of post-Barre political institutions more difficult.

[54] Lessons Learned Unit 1995, 13.

TABLE 4.1
Somalia

	Somalia (1988–91)	Somalia (1991–) UNOSOM I (1992–93) UNOSOM II (1993–95)
Sovereign peace	Failure	Failure
Participatory peace	Failure	Failure
War type	"Ethnic"	"Ethnic"
Factions	5	5 (up to 20, counting small clans)
UN mandate	No UN operation	Enforcement
Duration of UN mission (months)	n/a	38
Was UN present during the war? If so, for how long?	n/a	Yes; 33 months
Maximum troop strength of UN mission, if any	n/a	29,545
War duration (in months)	32	105
Real per capita GDP (year before war start; constant $)	801	703
Real per capita GDP (at end of the war; constant $)	670	n/a
GDP growth at end of the war (% annual change)	–4.69	–4.69
People killed during the war	25,000	400,000
People displaced during the war	800,000	1,000,000
Outcome of the war	Rebel victory	War ongoing
Was a treaty signed by most parties?	No	Yes
Date of the treaty, if any was signed	n/a	December 1997
Was the treaty implemented?	n/a	No
Primary commodity exports as % of GDP	10.2	6.5
Is the country a major oil exporter?	No	No
Ethnolinguistic fractionalization (100 = highest)	8	8
Ethnic heterogeneity index (1 = highly diverse)	0.812	0.812
Population at start of war (in thousands)	6,962.36	8,146.24
Area (square kilometers)	637,660	637,660
Effective development assistance as % of GDP	222.687	222.687

committing sufficient resources to fund demobilization, training, and growth-generating activities. One of UNITAF's "microlevel" or "endogenous" failures was its cooperation with local warlords, which was a convenient way to achieve the goal of distributing humanitarian assistance, but which legitimized their claims on their respective territories, as did their participation in peace conferences organized by the United Nations.[55] These conferences were seen by the UN as events that could produce a peace agreement and reconciliation, but experts on Somali culture suggest that such an outcome is only viewed possible by locals as the result of a long and piecemeal process of negotiation by clan elders.[56] The UN's legitimization of warlords and factions participating in the conferences made it harder both to promote peace initiatives by elders and groups excluded from those conferences and to identify legitimate authority in Somalia. This, however, might be an unavoidable problem in peacemaking efforts in countries where the state has collapsed or has no legitimacy and where several groups claim the state. Under such conditions, a transitional administration might be necessary that would take over civilian government until local institutional mechanisms can help identify groups with local bases of support that can be included in deliberations to form a new state. (This seems to be the approach currently being taken in Iraq by the U.S.-led transitional authority.)

Ultimately, the example of Somalia demonstrated that in the face of complex humanitarian emergencies, state failure, and civil war, Chapter VII operations cannot be simply military operations. Enforcement operations must be followed or complemented by a civilian mission that is able to rebuild the basis for locally sustainable peace. The U.S. military operation designed to deliver food to vulnerable populations in 1992 disrupted Somalia's political economy that revolved around the looting of food.[57] The famine was largely the result of Somali politics, so its consequences could not have been mitigated simply with a "humanitarian" intervention. But the type of intervention that might have had a chance of working in Somalia was much beyond what the world was willing to provide. Given the complete collapse of the state and the devastation of the economy due to the drought and the civil war, UNOSOM I's and UNITAF's mandates were clearly inadequate to support a lasting peace. UNOSOM II's capacities (and strategy) failed to match its extensive mandate. The level of international capacities that was necessary to rebuild basic political structures and restore some economic activity was that of an international trusteelike transitional administration. That would have

[55] Clarke 1997, pp. 12–13; Menkhaus 1997, p. 43.
[56] Menkhaus 1997; Lewis 1988.
[57] Clarke and Hebrst 1997, 242–43.

required a much greater and much longer commitment by the international community than what was available. The peacekeeping and peacebuilding failures that we discussed above were the direct result of this lack of international capacities—that is, of the external constraints within which the peacekeepers operated in Somalia.

Within the confines of their external constraints, and with a few notable exceptions of violent abuse and corrupt activity, the peacekeepers implemented their mandate efficiently, but that success was not enough to restore peace in Somalia. In the early stages of the conflict, the peacekeepers of UNOSOM I were generally successful in saving the lives of many people who might have died as a result of the famine, but they did not establish the conditions for peace. Sadly, while some semblance of order had been achieved in Mogadishu around the time of withdrawal of the UN forces, the countryside remained largely in civil war, a condition continuing until today.

The Former Yugoslavia

The opposite problem to UNOSOM's unguided aggressiveness emerged in the United Nations Protection Force (UNPROFOR) operation in the former Yugoslavia. There, the UN was not doing what it had been criticized for doing in Somalia. The UN was committed to protecting the humanitarian convoys and the safe areas as well as maintaining an arms embargo over the entire area and an economic embargo against Serbia. But a narrow and very cautious reading of the mandate resulted in a failure to protect the Bosnian Muslims (but also the Croats and Serbs) and the relief convoys; even the peacekeepers themselves were vulnerable and under attack. In Bosnia alone, after the establishment of UNPROFOR, 140,000 Muslims, 90,000 Serbs, and 20,000 Croats died according to official estimates,[58] and more than 2 million (considerably more than half were Muslims) had to flee their homes. Industrial production fell to 5 percent of prewar levels, and 80 percent of the population had become entirely dependent on foreign aid.[59]

The protection dilemma was real. With more than half the population in the UN-designated Bosnian "safe areas" directly dependent on UN

---

[58] Other estimates of total deaths are lower and a figure of 70,000 seems more accurate according to our sources. See our dataset notes.

[59] According to the estimates of Lord Robertson, NATO Secretary-General, and Thorvald Stoltenberg, the UN mediator. See Lord Robertson "The Work Ahead in Bosnia," *New York Times*, Op-Ed, November 25, 2000. The figures are controversial. For the debate and Stoltenberg citations, see David Rieff, *Slaughterhouse: Bosnia and the Failure of the West* (New York: Simon and Schuster, 1995); and George Kenney, "Bloody Bosnia," *Washington*

convoys for food and medicine, military action against the predominantly Serb aggressors would have been met by a complete cutoff of humanitarian assistance by those same Serbian forces, which controlled the access roads.[60]

None of UNPROFOR's military forces were prepared to undertake a massive military campaign designed to defeat the Bosnian Serb forces. The United States limited its contribution to air forces. The United States' once preferred strategy—"lift [the 1991 UN arms embargo] and strike [by air, against Serb gunners]"—was designed to level the playing field between Serb forces and the poorly equipped Bosnian forces.[61] But the United States was never prepared to invest its own soldiers on the ground in a peace enforcement operation. It did covertly ship quantities of light weapons to Bosnia (by air), but it did not provide heavy weapons.[62] Radical Muslim forces from Iran and the Palestine Liberation Organization were ready to come to Bosnia's aide but they were rejected by Russia and would, it seemed to many observers, merely widen the fighting to Kosovo, Macedonia, and even beyond. The resulting UNPROFOR strategy—"constrict (the level of violence) and contain"—was not without costs to its European proponents. UNPROFOR, with large contingents of British, French, and Canadian troops, sustained more than 160 fatalities. But the strategy had two great advantages: it was tolerated by the Russians and the killing was contained within Croatia and Bosnia.

There are several rival (but in reality complementary) explanations for the origin of the wars in Croatia and Bosnia. Some authors emphasize the security dilemma created by the emerging anarchy after the collapse

---

Monthly (March 1995): 49–52. One widely publicized estimate is "at least 200,000" deaths or disappearances in Bosnia, more than 2 million displaced persons of Bosnia's prewar population of 4.3 million, 1.1 million of whom now live abroad; "Bosnia Enters 4th Year of War," *New York Times*, April 6, 1995. For latest estimates of deaths cited R. Jeffrey Smith, "Proofs of Atrocities Divide Bosnians," *Washington Post*, December 28, 2000.

[60] Rosalynn Higgins, "The New United Nations and the Former Yugoslavia," *International Affairs* 69, no. 3 (1993): 468–70; James B. Steinberg, "International Involvement in the Yugoslav Conflict," in Damrosch 1993; Sabrina Ramet, "War in the Balkans," *Foreign Affairs* 71 no. 4 (Fall 1992): 79–98; and Misha Glenny, "Yugoslavia: The Great Fall," *New York Review of Books*, March 23, 1995.

[61] We should note, however, that leveling the playing field would have likely extended the duration of the civil war. On the relationship between different types of external intervention and civil war duration, see Regan 2002.

[62] Michael Gordon, "Pentagon Is Wary of Role in Bosnia," *New York Times*, March 13, 1994. The United States did assist the covert acquisition of light weapons for the Bosniac forces in cooperation with Croatian forces.

of central authority in Yugoslavia.[63] The secession of Slovenia and Croatia led quickly to the disintegration of this weakly held together ethnofederal Republic, creating fears of ethnic dominance among Bosnian Serbs and Muslims and fueling irredentist nationalism in Serbia. The collapse of the Yugoslav state was triggered by economic crisis, which in turn was due to austerity programs pushed by the International Monetary Fund (IMF) exacerbating the country's debt crisis and creating a huge stress of economic liberalization.[64] Real income declined markedly in the late 1980s and unemployment skyrocketed. Yugoslav states experienced a dramatic decline in economic growth from 1989 to 1991, going from a rate of approximately 1–2 percent to negative 15 percent, whereas the decade previous to that was relatively stable with rates between 0–5 percent.[65] Crime rates were increasing in all Republics and interregional inequality was growing. Memories of the last major conflict during and after World War II between the Chetniks and Ustasha remained alive and shaped much of the nationalist historiography of each region.[66] Under these dangerous social conditions, opportunistic leaders mobilized public opinion and gambled with ethnic fears and hatred.[67] Yugoslavia did not have the democratic institutions that might have been able to peacefully address growing conflict, and the state was weak, inheriting ethnic fault lines that Tito's regime had not tried to bridge, but simply blanketed temporarily largely through the use of fiscal transfers to the poorest members of the Federation and through the use of political repression.[68]

Rather than carefully design policies that might have dampened growing ethnic conflict, international actors acted irresponsibly and incoherently, looking the other way, sending mixed signals, and recognizing Croatia and Slovenia before deciding on how to handle demands for self-determination in Bosnia. The UN's initial response was to try peacemaking, extending the Secretary-General's good offices and mediation efforts to prevent a war in Slovenia. Early efforts by the UN and EU mediators Vance and Owen and Owen and Stoltenberg were noticeably unsuccessful.

---

[63] See, for example, Posen 1993. The "loot" explanation of civil war does not seem to fit the Yugoslav case well, as there were few previous natural resources worth fighting over and the country was generally more economically developed than most other civil war states.

[64] Susan Woodward, Balkan Tragedy: Chaos and Dissolution after the Cold War (Washington, DC: Brookings Institution, 1995).

[65] Woodward 1995, p. 55.

[66] Glenny 2000.

[67] See Laura Silber and Allan Little, The Death of Yugoslavia (London: Penguin-BBC, 1995); De Figueiredo and Weingast 1999.

[68] Glenny 2000.

The problem was that methods were being used that were appropriate to solve an easy coordination problem, whereas the parties confronted each other in a much harder competition.

Again, with the advantage of hindsight, we can see what appear to be mistakes, most of them occasioned by the Security Council's foisting mandates (without the means to implement them) on the UN forces in the field. Resolutions were issued that bore upon the Bosnian Serbs; yet the international community was not prepared to exert effective pressure. What pressure there was came from the indirect effects of the misery that the international economic embargo inflicted on the Serbian public. In retrospect, we can see that the UN Protected Areas in Croatia lacked adequate buffer zones and sufficient peacekeepers, providing the Serbs with excuses not to disarm and the Croats with opportunity to engage in incursions.[69] In Bosnia, the declared Safe Havens were never adequately provided with UN forces. They were too small, militarily vulnerable, economically nonviable, and they lacked wide enough connecting corridors.[70]

It is important to distinguish between what the Security Council mandated and equipped UNPROFOR to do and what some parts of the media and the public would have liked UNPROFOR to have done. UNPROFOR was very specifically not sent to help one side in the conflict or to declare war on one side, but to mitigate the sufferings of war and to help promote peace. If it was to function properly, and given its existing military capacities, the force needed the cooperation of all parties. With the forces then available to it, were it to have declared war on one of the parties in the conflict, the peacekeeping force in Bosnia would inevitably have become part of the problem it was sent to solve, as happened in Somalia.[71]

The Security Council sent UNPROFOR, a peacekeeping force, into a war situation because the not-so-united nations that made up the Council were unwilling to contemplate any one of four drastic alternatives: allowing the Serbs a free hand to "ethnically cleanse" Bosnia, partitioning Bosnia in order to conduct a UN transfer of populations ("benign cleansing?"), actually going to war to create a unified Bosnian state, or

[69] Andrew Bair, "Yugoslav Lessons for Future Peacekeepers," *European Security* 3, no. 2 (Summer 1994): 340–49, p. 345.

[70] The UN's Srebenica Report: Kofi Annan, 1999, Report of the Secretary General pursuant to General Assembly resolution 53/35. (The situation in Bosnia and Herzegovina). The Srebrenica Report Presented to the General Assembly. A/54/549. New York: United Nations, November 15, 1999, David Rohde's *Endgame* (New York: Farrar, Straus and Giroux, 1997); and Jan Willem Honig and Norbert Both, *Srebenica* (New York: Penguin, 1996) offer eloquent testimony to all these factors.

[71] These paragraphs draw on Brian Urquhart and Michael Doyle, "Peacekeeping Up to Now: Under Fire from Friend and Foe," *International Herald Tribune*, OpEd, December 16, 1995.

Box 4.2 UNPROFOR's Mandate

ESTABLISHMENT: By Resolution 743, the Security Council established a United Nations Protection force for an initial period of twelve months, as an "interim arrangement to create the conditions of peace and security required for the negotiation of an overall settlement of the Yugoslav crisis."[1] Six weeks later, UNPROFOR's deployment was authorized by resolution 749.[2]

CHANGES TO MANDATE: UNPROFOR's mandate was enlarged by resolution 758 to include supervision of the withdrawal of antiaircraft weapons from Sarajevo toward the goal of securing the Sarajevo airport for the delivery of humanitarian aid.

In resolution 762, the Security Council authorized (as requested in Secretary-General's 6/26/92 report) the addition of up to 120 civilian police and 60 military observers to carry out monitoring in the specific areas of Croatia controlled by the Jugoslav National Army (the "pink zones") and the creation of a Joint Commission to monitor the restoration of authority in the pink zones.[3]

By resolution 769,[4] the Council accepted the recommendations of the Secretary-General's 7/27/92 plan to enlarge UNPROFOR's strength and mandate to "enable the Force to control the entry of civilians into the UNPAs and to perform immigration and customs functions at the UNPA borders at international frontiers."[5]

By resolution 776, the Council expanded the mandate to support the delivery of humanitarian relief to Bosnia and Herzegovina, leading to the establishment of a separate Bosnia and Herzegovina Command.[6]

Resolution 779 authorized UNPROFOR to "assume responsibility for monitoring the arrangements agreed for the complete withdrawal of the Yugoslav Army from Croatia, the demilitarization of the Prevlaka peninsula and the removal of heavy weapons from neighboring areas of Croatia and Montenegro" and additionally approved the Secretary-General's actions taken "to ensure [UNPROFOR's] control of the Peruca dam."[7]

The mandate was further enlarged by resolution 795, which established UNPROFOR's presence in Macedonia.[8] By resolution 836 the Security Council expanded UNPROFOR's mandate to protecting safe areas in Bosnia-Herzegovina and authorized the use of self-defensive force to deter attacks against them.[9]

continued

Box 4.2 continued

TERMINATION: UNPROFOR's mandate was extended several times until 1995 and was additionally expanded to include monitoring the cease-fire agreement signed by the Bosnian Government and the Bosnian Croats on 2/23/94 and the agreement between the Bosnian Government and the Bosnian Serbs which entered into force on 1/1/95.[10] On 3/31/95, by resolutions 981–83, the Security Council restructured UNPROFOR, putting in place three related peacekeeping missions.[11]

[1] S/RES/743 (1992) available at http://ods-dds-ny.un.org/doc/RESOLUTION/GEN/NR0/011/02/IMG/NR001102.pdf
[2] S/RES/749 (1992) available at http://ods-dds-ny.un.org/doc/RESOLUTION/GEN/NR0/011/08/IMG/NR001108.pdf
[3] S/RES/762 (1992) available at http://ods-dds-ny.un.org/doc/RESOLUTION/GEN/NR0/011/21/IMG/NR001121.pdf
[4] S/RES/769(1992) available at http://ods-dds-ny.un.org/doc/UNDOC/GEN/N92/368/91/IMG/N9236891.pdf
[5] http://www.un.org/Depts/dpko/dpko/co_mission/unprof_b.htm
[6] S/RES/776 (1992) available at http://ods-dds-ny.un.org/doc/UNDOC/GEN/N92/438/40/IMG/N9243840.pdf
[7] S/RES/779 (1992) available at http://ods-dds-ny.un.org/doc/UNDOC/GEN/N92/484/28/IMG/N9248428.pdf
[8] S/RES/795 (1992) official link broken, but available at: http://www.nato.int/ifor/un/u921211a.htm
[9] S/RES/836 (1993) available at http://ods-dds-ny.un.org/doc/UNDOC/GEN/N93/330/21/IMG/N9333021.pdf
[10] http://www.un.org/Depts/dpko/dpko/co_mission/unprof_p.htm
[11] http://www.un.org/Docs/scres/1995/scres95.htm

applying sufficient military pressure to force the parties to negotiate a condominium (the eventual outcome at Dayton). Only the Bosnian Serbs wanted the first; only the Bosnian government the last; and nobody was prepared to do the second or the fourth (until late 1995). Regrettably, the Security Council was also unwilling to provide the forces that UNPROFOR required to meet the mandate it had been given.

The successive mandates that the Security Council gave UNPROFOR dictated a dispersal of its lightly armed forces and thus precluded more forceful action even if this had been authorized. When the Security Council set up the "safe areas," it did not ask UNPROFOR to defend or protect these areas, only to "deter attacks" on them and, in extremis, to call in air strikes in self-defense. The Secretary-General asked for 34,000 soldiers to provide "deterrence through strength" in the so-called safe areas. When the Security Council chose to authorize only 7,600 troops, which then took a year to arrive, it initiated a dangerous bluff. Representations by UNPROFOR commanders about the nonviability of this mandate seem to have fallen on deaf ears in the Security Council. The meager UN forces in the safe areas thus became dependent on the cooperation of the surrounding Serbs for their lines of communication and daily survival.

Resolutions 819 (April 16, 1993, for Srebenica), 824 (May 6, adding five more "safe areas"), and 836 (June 4, emphasizing Chapter VII authority) established a dangerously confusing mandate for military planners on the ground.[72] Shashi Tharoor, then the special assistant to UN peacekeeping chief Kofi Annan, pinpointed the confusion: "[The resolutions] required the parties to treat [the safe areas] as 'safe,' imposed no obligations on their inhabitants and defenders, deployed United Nations troops in them but expected their mere presence to 'deter' attacks, carefully avoided asking the peacekeepers to 'defend' or 'protect' these areas, but authorized them to call in air power 'in self-defence'—a masterpiece of diplomatic drafting, but largely unimplementable as operational directive."[73]

The wording and consequent frustrations reflected real differences on the Security Council. The Europeans were most concerned that Muslim forces would use the safe areas as havens from which to launch attacks (as they did from Bihac especially). The United States was concerned that air power would not be requested in time to defend and deter attacks (but the United States had no intention of putting its own forces at risk on the ground). Muslims refused to disarm because they disbelieved (quite rightly, given their experience in 1992 and 1993) the willingness of UNPROFOR to defend civilians against even unprovoked attacks; and so the circle of mistrust was complete. Outraged by the pastiche of paper promises, the original sponsor of the first resolution, the charismatic Venezuelan ambassador Diego Arria, abstained from the resolutions.[74] The UN prevailed upon the one NATO country with a commitment to the policy, the Netherlands, to garrison Srebenica, with tragic results in the summer of 1995 when, following the surrender of the Dutch battalion, the safe area was overrun and 6,000 to 7,000 of its men were slaughtered by the forces of Serb General Ratko Mladic.

UNPROFOR responded to the general demand to do something about Bosnia, but it was not authorized or equipped to create by force the results that much of the media and many politicians were clamoring for. In

[72] General Lars-Eric Wahlgren, UNPROFOR force commander in 1993, is particularly informative on the confusions surrounding safer areas policy. He was strongly opposed to having UNPROFOR forces codeployed with Muslim armed units still waging war on the Serbs. But he acknowledged that the existing level of UNPROFOR forces was not sufficient to defend the safe areas. Hence the dilemma: how could the UN ask the Muslims to disarm units in the safe areas? See Lars-Eric Wahlgren, "Start and End of Srebenica," in Biermann and Vadset 1998, pp. 168–85.

[73] Shashi Tharoor, "Should UN Peackeeping 'Go Back to Basics'?" *Survival* 37 no. 4 (1995–96): p. 60.

[74] See Ambassador Arria's statement on Safe Areas, Security Council Meeting 3228, June 4, 1993 and discussions with Ambassador Diego Arria.

practice, its very limited objective was to contain the situation and to do what it could for the victims of war while a fourth alternative was pursued—political negotiations to achieve a solution acceptable to all the parties.

What did UNPROFOR, within the constraints of mandate and resources, actually achieve? Certainly a decline in deaths in direct proportion to its deployment—from tens of thousands in 1992 to fewer than 3,000 in 1994—bad enough, but still a notable improvement before the big push campaigns of 1995 raised the number back up to 55,000 casualties (deaths and injuries).[75] The presence of the peacekeepers, along with the arms embargo and the constant mediation efforts, undoubtedly kept down the level of fighting and moderated the conflict. The humanitarian relief effort that the peacekeeping force made possible, including the largest airlift in history and a huge operation by road, delivered an average two thousand metric tons of humanitarian supplies, saving many lives and easing the suffering of millions. The force repaired and rebuilt housing, roads, bridges, pipelines, and the electrical grid. It restored and maintained basic services as well as keeping the aid flowing where extreme war conditions did not make this impossible. UNPROFOR also provided an accurate picture of events for the international community.

On a wider level, UNPROFOR and the UN preventive force in Macedonia contained a war that, especially in its early stages, could well have spelled the end of the new state of Bosnia and Herzegovina. International intervention, even if limited, meant the survival of the state of Bosnia and gave it time to improve its capacity for self-defense.

The Security Council, speaking for the governments of the world, was not willing to intervene militarily in Bosnia. It may, indeed, have believed that such an intervention would have risked a wider and deeper war. The international community was thus committed firmly to a negotiated, not a military, solution. Only after a solution had been negotiated would a much more heavily armed NATO force be committed, albeit with much anxiety and apprehension.

The taproot of error was identified in Cyrus Vance's warnings in December 1991 not to recognize the independence of Croatia and Bosnia outside of the framework of an overall settlement of Yugoslavia.[76] The only separable parts of Yugoslavia immediately recognizable as independent, sovereign nation states were Slovenia and (arguably) Macedonia. For Serbs, the federal unity of "Yugoslavia" was what made "small" Ser-

reasons for not letting go.

[75] General Sir Michael Rose, "Military Aspects of Peacekeeping," in Biermann and Vadset 1998, pp. 153–68, p. 156.

[76] Thorough histories of the political origins of the conflicts can be found in Woodward 1995; and Steven Burg and Paul Shoup, _The War in Bosnia-Herzegovina_ (Armonk, NY: M. E. Sharpe, 1999).

bia tolerable and the non-Serb governments of Croatia and Bosnia safe for their Serbs. For Croats, the inclusion of Bosnia in Yugoslavia was what made Bosnia safe for its Croats. For Bosnian Muslims, the inclusion of Croatia in Yugoslavia was what made the Bosnian republic safe in Yugoslavia, which otherwise would have been dominated by the Serbs. Croatia, some suggest, might have been partitioned between Croats and Serbs, but the ethnic mix was too intimate in Bosnia to allow a peaceable partition.

In terms of the model we have presented, Bosnia presented a difficult peacebuilding ecology with high levels of hostility: an ethnic war with high numbers of deaths and displacements. Local capacities were also declining (see table 4.2). But, like Somalia, this is primarily a failure of international capacities. This is not obvious simply by glancing at the peacebuilding triangle, as Bosnia received the lion's share of the UN's peacekeeping resources, particularly when UNPROFOR's mandate turned into enforcement (see figure 4.2). Bosnia had the highest level of international capacities (in terms of mandate and troop numbers) than all our other cases.[77] It also received large amounts of reconstruction assistance. Given the extensive local hostility engendered by the horrendous destruction of civilian life and the economic devastation the wars quickly wrought, a considerable international presence would have been required to establish the beginnings of sustainable peace. But UNPROFOR lacked the mandate to impose peace and the will and capacity to do so.[78]

In addition to these failures in understanding, design, and resources, there were failures in the management of peacekeeping. Akashi's reluctance to use close air support in defense of the safe areas was a prime example of such a failure—a conservative interpretation of the mandate and a proclivity toward passivity rather than impartiality. But overall, our assessment is that most of the failures occurred at the level of planning and resource provision. The Security Council assigned the wrong treatment to the problem at hand.

In the summer and fall of 1995, the wars came to a halt. UNPROFOR and NATO had at last been provoked by the Bosnian Serbs to mount a full-scale bombing campaign. As importantly, Croatia "solved" its Krajina problem the old-fashioned way—with "blood and iron," ethnically

[handwritten margin note: War end]

[77] This refers to the period of enforcement in Bosnia. In our cross-section dataset, we code only the highest mandate given to a UN force throughout its duration. In the time-series cross-section version of our dataset, we code the switch from a traditional peacekeeping mandate to enforcement in Bosnia.

[78] Bosnia is excluded from our analysis because there UN was present throughout our analysis time and there was no peace failure after the war's end in 1995. Our discussion in this section of peacekeeping failures refers mostly to microlevel failures and to failures in ending the war before the Dayton Accords of 1995. The probability estimate that our model generates for Bosnia is high (0.63) and refers to the post-Dayton period.

TABLE 4.2
Former Yugoslavia

	Yugoslavia/ Croatia (1991) UNPROFOR/ UNCRO (1992–95)	Bosnia (1992–95) UNPROFOR (1992–95) OHR/UNMIBH (1995–ongoing)
Sovereign peace	Failure	—
Participatory peace	Failure	—
War type	"Ethnic"	"Ethnic"
Factions	3	5
UN mandate	Traditional PKO	Enforcement (with Multidimensional PKO Components after 1995)
Duration of UN mission (months)	45	93
Was UN present during the war? If so, for how long?	No	Yes, 93
Maximum troop strength of UN mission, if any	39,922	39,922
War duration (in months)	7	44
Real per capita GDP (year before war start; constant $)	4,548	3,098
Real per capita GDP (at end of the war; constant $)	2,740	—
GDP growth at end of the war (% annual change)	−39.754	18.75
People killed during the war	2,000	70,000
People displaced during the war	320,000	2,500,000
Outcome of the war	Rebel Victory	Negotiated Settlement
Was a treaty signed by most parties?	No	Yes
Date of the treaty, if any was signed	n/a	November 1995
Was the treaty implemented?	n/a	Yes
Primary commodity exports as % of GDP	—	11.4 (imputed)
Is the country a major oil exporter?	No	No
Ethnolinguistic fractionalization (100 = highest)	75	69
Ethnic heterogeneity index (1 = highly diverse)	0.8	0.681
Population at start of war (in thousands)	23,928	3,837.71
Area (square kilometers)	230,090	51,233
Effective Development Assistance as % of GDP	—	—

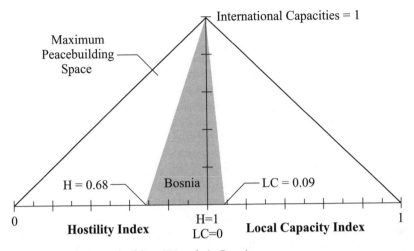

Figure 4.2 The Peacebuilding Triangle in Bosnia

cleansing the entire region of its Serb inhabitants. (The one exception was Eastern Slavonia, about which more in chapter 5, which was peacefully reintegrated by the UN Transitional Administration in Eastern Slavonia (UNTAES) from January 1996 to January 1998.) The Bosnian Serbs had done the same to Srebenica and Zepa, leaving Gorazde as the only safe area, apart from Sarajevo in the eastern region of the former Bosnia. Slowly and painfully, thus borders and ethnicities had begun to correspond in the former Yugoslavia. Peace efforts culminated in the Dayton Agreement. But the fighting in the region was also far from over. President Milosevic soon faced another insurgency in Kosovo, the overwhelmingly Albanian zone of Serbia, and he proceeded to try to resolve it the same way he had the movements for independence in Croatia and Bosnia.

Bosnia today, five years after Dayton, is one country, and there are pockets of integrated peace (as in Brcko, about which more in chapter 5), but in many ways it is a de facto partition. The international community has spent $5.2 billion, excluding military costs. It is a Western protectorate of NATO and European Union, with unemployment ranging approximately at 45 percent and 20 percent of the population living in poverty.[79]

[79] Dusko Doder, "Letter from Bosnia," *The Nation*, 272, no. 6 (February 12, 2001): 14–18. World Bank data, 2002, http://devdata.worldbank.org/external/CPProfile.asp?SelectedCountry=BIH&CCODE=BIH&CNAME=Bosnia+and+Herzegovina&PTYPE=CP (accessed October 28, 2004).

Congo

One has to go back more than forty years to find a successful UN effort to impose a peace on recalcitrant parties who lacked a peace treaty or framework of agreement. Even so, that success produced one of the most corrupt and tyrannical regimes in postindependence Africa, and the peace crumbled in renewed fighting soon after the UN departed. The key question turned out to be not so much how to design and implement deeper peacebuilding (including a degree of democratization) but rather how to uphold other UN principles, such as political independence and territorial integrity. The Congo was freed from Belgium and, largely as a result of the UN's intervention, secessionist Katanga was kept within the nascent nation. But the costs were so severe for the UN and the Congo, that the Operation des Nations Unies en Congo (ONUC) became the "success" that was never to be repeated.[80]

After a long history of brutal colonial rule, Belgium was pressured, in January 1960, to grant independence to the Congo. A rapid schedule for decolonization was decided, though it was unclear how Congo was supposed to transition to self-rule. Out of a population of 14 million, there were virtually no trained Congolese administrators, scientists, or university graduates. Belgians manned the senior civil service and military. The Congo, an area as large as Western Europe, contained more than seventy ethnic groups, speaking more than two hundred different languages, with significant regional divisions among the five major regions of Leopoldville, Equateur, Orientale, Kivu, Kasai, and Katanga. Historically, the most important ethnic group was the Bakongo, an agglomeration of tribal groups sharing a common language and dominating Leopoldville. Katanga included two big groups, the Lunda in the south and the Baluba in the north. The Luba and Lulua kingdoms made up Kasai.[81] At the time of independence, the Congo had no local capacities, little social cohesion, and no national identity.

With the exception of Patrice Lumumba's Mouvement National Congolais (Congolese National Movement, MNC), political groups were mostly organized along ethnic lines.[82] Among the first political parties to be formed was Alliance des Ba-Kongo, led by Joseph Kasavubu. In the

[80] Here, we refer to success with respect to the mandate. At the macrolevel, there was pecebuilding failure in the Congo both in terms of "negative" peace (a new round of fighting took place in Kisangani in 1967), and with respect to "positive" peace (Mobutu's autocracy took hold at least partly due to the UN's efforts to support a unitary state solution in the Congo).

[81] D. K. Orwa, *The Congo Betrayal: The UN-US and Lumumba* (Nairobi: Kenya Literature, 1985), pp. 13–14; Edgar O' Ballance, *The Congo-Zaire experience, 1960–1998* (New York: Macmillan & St. Martin's Press, 2000), 5–7.

[82] Crawford Young, *Politics in the Congo* (Princeton: Princeton University Press, 1965).

mineral-rich Katanga province, the most powerful party was Moise Tshombe's Confédération des Associations Tribales du Katanga, created in 1958 to defend the interests of the Lunda, Baluba of Katanga, and Bayeke against "strangers," mostly from Kasai (Lulua and Baluba from Kasai), who were recruited by the Union Minière du Haut Katanga to work in the mines. Conflict among those parties intensified as independence neared.

Drawing from this pool of local elites, an "Executive College" of six Congolese leaders was formed to assist the governor-general of the colony to draft a transitional constitution. Belgium counted on maintaining its influence and economic interests in the Congo after independence, but it had underestimated the strength of nationalist sentiment among some Congolese. Lumumba, whose party formed the first government, was a nationalist whose vision for a unified, independent Congo quickly brought him into conflict with foreign powers as well as provincial leaders, neither of whom wished to see a centralized Congolese state. That conflict would soon lead to the splintering of the MNC.

In early 1960, violent clashes broke out between "Lumumbists," breakaway MNC factions, other factions in Katanga, and ninety thousand displaced Balubas and Luluas. Elections to provincial and national assemblies were held in May 1960, shortly before the scheduled date for independence. The MNC won majorities in both the senate and the central assembly, and Lumumba formed a government whose parliament selected Kasavubu as president, which was meant to be a largely ceremonial position. Tshombe won a narrow majority of seats in the Katangan provincial assembly and was elected president of that body.

The Republic of the Congo became independent on July 1, 1960, with conflict brewing in every corner.[83] The relationship of independent Congo with Belgium was at the core of political disputes among Congolese parties, as was the question of the new constitution. The Loi Fondamentale (the transitional constitution), established a parliamentary democracy with substantial autonomy for the provinces, but did not establish a clear division of power between the central and provincial governments or the president and the prime minister. Lumumba favored a unitary, centralized Congo. His opponents, led by Katangese strongman Tshombe, wanted decentralization or secession. At the heart of the matter was Tshombe's desire to keep a close grip on Katanga's mineral resources.[84] President Kasavubu and head of the ABAKO party also favored a federal structure for the Congo.

[83] O'Balance 2000, p. 15.

[84] Tshombe stated it as follows: "We want a relation between development and people, a share on the basis of the contribution to the development and to the needs created by it" cited in Leonce Ndikumana and Kisangani Emizet, "The Economics of Civil War: The Case of the Democratic Republic of the Congo," Paper prepared for the World Bank Project on Civil Wars (2003), p. 5.

Seeing Belgium as a thorn on his side, Lumumba decided to undercut Belgian control on the 25,000-strong armed forces, known as the Armee Nationale Congolaise (ANC), by appointing Victor Lundula (from Kasai) as commander in chief and Colonel Joseph Désiré Mobutu as chief of staff. The 1,000 Belgian officers left behind lost effective control when the ANC mutinied. However, at the heels of the mutiny, violence against Belgian civilians triggered military action by Belgium, which sent 3,000 paratroopers to major Congolese cities to secure the European quarters. Fighting between the ANC and Belgian troops intensified, and to prevent a large conflagration, the Congolese leadership turned to the UN for assistance. In the meantime, Tshombe had taken advantage of the turmoil to declare Katanga's secession on July 11.

Katanga had a history of autonomy. Under the Congo Free State, it was administered by the privately owned Comité Spécial du Katanga and was brought under central colonial rule only in 1933.[85] Most of the population of Katanga consisted of Congolese migrants from outside the province, who had been attracted by the province's mineral wealth.[86] At the time of independence, Katanga provided 75 percent of Congo's mineral output and 50 percent of total national resources.[87]

Katanga's attempted secession started a wave of secessionist rebellions. By late July, demonstrations seeking independence had been mounted in Leopoldville, in Kasai, and in Equator. On November 9, in Stanleyville, Orientale, refugees from the violence in Katanga joined with Lumumbaist MNC members to declare a new province in Katanga that would be part of the Congo. This was, in effect, secession from secession. The province was to be led from Orientale, Lumumba's home region, by Antoine Gizenga, Lumumba's deputy prime minister.

As of the beginning of 1961, the Congo was divided into four sections. In the capital of Leopoldville, Kasavubu and Mobutu led the government and 7,000 strong ANC, claiming jurisdiction over all of the Congo (the ANC had been divided between supporters of the main parties). In Stanleyville, Lumumba's supporters, led by Gizenga and supported by 5,500 troops, also claimed rightful leadership of all of the Congo. Tshombe was based in Elisabethville with between 5,000 and 7,000 troops, including many holdover European irregulars, and alternated between demanding complete independence and accepting membership in a loose confederation.

[85] Ndikumana and Emizet 2003, 2.

[86] Rene Lemarchand, *Political Awakening in the Congo* (Berkeley and Los Angeles: University of California Press, 1994), pp. 233–34.

[87] Ndikumana and Emizet 2003, p. 3.

In this confusion, Lumumba turned to the Soviets for help. The ANC entered Kasai in the end of August, but the poorly led Congolese forces disintegrated and the fighting resulted in a massacre of hundreds of Balubas. On September 5, Kasavubu dismissed the prime minister.[88] Lumumba, in turn, dismissed Kasavubu and attempted to run the government while under a semi–house arrest. Meanwhile, Kasavubu and Joseph Ileo suspended the Chamber of Representatives and promoted Mobutu to the position of commander in chief of the army.

Amidst this political turmoil, ONUC, which had been authorized by the Security Council on July 14, 1960, was deployed to help restore order and evacuate Belgian troops and nationals. UN troops were very quickly deployed. By July 18, 3,500 troops were on the ground and a total of 14,500 had arrived within a month. ONUC was the UN's largest mission to date (and for years to come), with up to 20,000 troops deployed by March 1963.[89] But ONUC soon found itself enmeshed in an explosive situation.

From the outset, there was disagreement between Lumumba and ONUC over what role the UN should play in the ongoing conflict. Lumumba thought that the UN should assist him, since he represented the first elected government. His initial request for UN assistance emphasized the need to restore order, train the ANC, and prevent an all-out war between the ANC and Belgian troops.[90] But ONUC's initial mandate was limited to overseeing the withdrawal of Belgian troops and serving as an impartial force in preserving public order. Lumumba interpreted this as evidence that the UN was working against him in collaboration with the United States, so he turned to the Soviets for help.[91] Other parties were also unhappy with the UN's work in the Congo. Tshombe, in particular, insisted that he did not need ONUC to preserve order, as he had Belgian support and objected to the demands for withdrawal of Belgian troops (some Belgian officers and mercenaries stayed behind despite the UN Resolutions).[92]

[88] Gibbs reports that there is reason to believe Kasavubu would not have taken the action he did without significant encouragement from the United States and Hammarskjold.

[89] All troop count figures from William J. Durch, "The UN Operation in the Congo," in *The Evolution of UN Peacekeeping: Case Studies and Comparative Analyses* (New York: St. Martin's Press, 1993), pp. 315–52, 335–36.

[90] Ernest W. Lefever, *Crisis in the Congo: a United Nations Force in Action; Studies of U.S. policy and the U.N.* (Washington, DC: Brookings Institution, 1965).

[91] D. N. Gibbs, 2000, "The United Nations, International Peacekeeping and the Question of 'Impartiality': Revisiting the Congo Operation of 1960," *Journal of Modern African Studies* 38 no. 3 (2000): 359–82, p. 364; C. C. O'Brien, *To Katanga and Back.* (New York: Universal Library, 1966), p. 56.

[92] Gibbs 2000, p. 366.

Box 4.3 ONUC's Mandate

ESTABLISHMENT: By its resolution 143 of July 14, 1960, the Security Council created ONUC by authorizing "the Secretary-General to take the necessary steps, in consultation with the Government of the Republic of the Congo, to provide the Government with such military assistance as may be necessary, until, through the efforts of the Congolese Government with the technical assistance of the United Nations, the national security forces may be able, in the opinion of the Government, to meet fully their tasks."

CHANGES TO MANDATE: The Security Council clarified ONUC's objectives by its resolutions during the operation:

- Resolution 145 of July 22 made withdrawal of Belgian troops part of ONUC's mandate;

- Resolution 146 of August 9 ordered ONUC into Katanga to facilitate Belgian withdrawal from that province;

- Resolution 161 of February 21, 1961 added to ONUC's mandate preventing civil war within the Congo and securing the withdrawal of Belgian forces and "other foreign military and paramilitary personnel and political advisers not under the United Nations Command, and mercenaries";

- Resolution 169 of November 24, 1961 "demande[d]" that Katanga's secessionist activities cease and "declare[d]" its intention, implicitly through ONUC, to assist the Congolese government in the maintenance of "law and order and national integrity."

TERMINATION: ONUC withdrew in June 1964.

Given the vagueness of Resolution S/4387, which described ONUC's authority to "provide the Government with such military assistance as may be necessary," Secretary-General Dag Hammarskjold played a crucial role in defining ONUC's operational guidelines. In response to his reports of growing lawlessness, the Security Council passed Resolution 146 on August 9, authorizing ONUC to enter Katanga and remove the Belgian troops. The resolution also, however, stated that ONUC would "not be a party to or in any way intervene in or be used to influence the outcome of any internal conflict, constitutional or otherwise." Hammarskjold took this mandate to heart, explicitly articulating a policy of equidistance from all the factions. He also personally escorted the first ONUC troops into Katanga on August 12. After the Belgians had withdrawn, Hammarskjold insisted that ONUC not take part in Lumumba's efforts to put down the Katangan secession. Lumumba thought that Hammarskjold's policy of equidistance legitimized the secessionists. He turned to the Soviets, who helped him transport ANC troops to Kasai to put down the rebellion there. When that intervention degenerated into massacres of local Baluba in Kasai and Kasavubu took the opportunity to dismiss Lumumba, Hammarskjold responded favorably to news of the dismissal.[93] ONUC was ordered by Hammarskjold to close the country's airports and the Leopoldville radio station, to prevent Lumumba from getting support to move back to the capital and fight Kasavubu in an all-out civil war and, in November, the General Assembly seated Kasavubu's delegation as the official representatives of the Congo regime.

By the time that the fourth Council Resolution 161 concerning the Congo was adopted on February 21, 1961, Lumumba had been murdered (most likely by Tshombe's forces) and four armed factions were engaged in open warfare. ONUC was not only criticized by each faction for failing to assist them, but it also became the target of violent attacks. Hammarskjold then urged the Council to approve a stronger mandate for ONUC. Resolution 161 stated that ONUC troops could employ "force, if necessary in the last resort" to prevent civil war and defend their mandate.[94] The resolution was not vetoed by the British only because Hammarskjold reassured the Council that the new authority did not extend to any objective other than the prevention of civil war. ONUC would not impose a political solution.[95] This of course was a distinction difficult to maintain in the field, where every military action had political repercussions.

ONUC tried to protect national leaders, maintain local order, and provide relief services for displaced civilians as well as resettle refugees. It also continued providing the government with technical assistance in running essential social services that had collapsed with the fighting.[96]

[93] Gibbs (2000) argues that Kasavubu would not have dismissed Lumumba without external ONUC encouragement.

[94] UN website: http://www.un.org/Depts/DPKO/Missions/onucM.htm (accessed July 4, 2003)

[95] Lefever 1965, p. 55.

[96] UN Web site: http://www.un.org/Depts/DPKO/Missions/onucB.htm (accessed July 4, 2003)

When, on April 3, an Indian ONUC brigade seized the Elisabethville airport to transport troops to the capital, Tshombe encouraged the Katangese to attack ONUC troops, leading, on April 8, to the use of force by ONUC.[97] After two failed peace conferences, ONUC's peace-making initiatives eventually helped the parties agree, on August 2, 1961, to declare Cyrille Adoula as prime minister and head of a new government that included representatives of most of the factions. Parliament was reconvened in August 1961 under United Nations auspices and most constitutional issues had been resolved.[98] Katanga now remained the most pressing concern.[99]

By now, both the Soviets and the United States wanted ONUC to end Katanga's secession, but they were opposed by the British, French, and Belgians, along with several African states, which supported Tshombe and did not want ONUC to use force. ONUC undertook a series of operations in Katanga aimed at arresting European mercenaries and disarming the gendarmerie. One of these, operation "Morthor," authorized by Conor Cruise O'Brien, the UN representative on the spot in Katanga, turned violent.[100] Significant clashes occurred between ONUC and Tshombe's forces in Katanga in September. Tragically, while flying to the Congo to arrange a cease-fire, Hammarskjold was killed in an air crash.

On November 24, 1961, the Security Council adopted its fifth and final resolution 169 on the Congo, demanding that foreign troops be removed by all "requisite measures of force, if necessary." By early December, fighting escalated and thousands of troops were involved. Tshombe met with Adoula at Kitona, agreeing to a cease-fire and initiating intermittent negotiations that would last for a year. During the cease-fire, both the Katangan gendarmerie and the ANC built up their forces. Adoula successfully put down a simmering rebellion by Gizenga in Stanleyville with ONUC's help, and ONUC continued to assist refugees, working toward the repatriation of Baluba in Katanga.

At the end of 1962, pressure to resolve the Katanga problem was mounting. In December, the United States dispatched a mission to determine what additional support it could give to the peace talks, and Secretary-General U Thant imposed sanctions against Tshombe. Belgium severed its relations with Katanga and announced that it considered Tshombe a rebel. The UN needed to solve the problem quickly. India was preparing to withdraw its large brigade in 1963, due to China's attack of

---

[97] Lefever 1965, p. 65.

[98] UN Web site: http://www.un.org/Depts/DPKO/Missions/onucB.htm (accessed July 4, 2003).

[99] Lefever 1965, p. 72.

[100] Lefever 1965, p. 83.

India's northern border.[101] And the Cuban Missile Crisis gave the United States and USSR new incentives to resolve outstanding disputes in remote Africa.[102] All these conditions combined to support the UN's "Operation Grand Slam," which began on Christmas Eve 1962, during which ONUC reunified Katanga with the Congo with a concerted attack against the Katangese gendarmerie. Grand Slam, completed by January 21, 1963, put Katanga under control of the UN and the central government.

The UN had hoped that resolving the Katangan issue would help promote law and order in the rest of the Congo. But ONUC was not as successful in achieving that part of its mandate. Over the next year and a half, ONUC drew down its forces and began withdrawing from sectors of the country that it turned over to ANC officials. The ANC, however, was still undisciplined and, for the next eighteen months, rebellions and tribal clashes cropped up in various provinces.[103] Lawlessness, undisciplined ANC troops, political infighting, and regional rebellion reigned. But in 1965 General Mobutu deposed President Kasavubu and assumed the presidency, slowly building an authoritarian kleptocracy that would rule for more than three decades.

Several other minor rebellions erupted in the mid-1960s.[104] Katanga was also engulfed in another bout of violence in 1977 and 1978 (the Shaba wars), representing the first organized challenge to Mobutu's attempt to create a strong, unitary state. In that instance, violence was largely the result of the economic crisis due to Mobutu's disastrous "zairianization" and "radicalization" programs.[105] Real per capita GDP declined at an annual rate of 1.2 percent from 1978 to 1988, and inflation hovered at around 56 percent as Mobutu took Zaire's already low levels of local capacities to even lower levels (see table 4.3).

In terms of our model, the Congo in 1960 presented a peacebuilding ecology nightmare: a new, poor state with uncertain grip on a vast territory, with almost no local capacities and multiple rebellions being fought by many hostile factions (see figure 4.3). Most of the local factions had only limited support among their tribes, but did not represent interests outside their regions.

[101] Lefever 1965, p. 107.

[102] Durch 1993. *The Evolution of UN Peacekeeping: Case Studies and Comparative Analysis.*(New York: St. Martin's Press), p. 328; and see Brian Urquhart, *Hammarskjold* (New York: Knopf, 1972) for the view from New York.

[103] Lefever 1965, p. 133.

[104] A third rebellion occurred in Kwilu, on January 22, 1964, lasting until end of December 1965, and a fourth rebellion in the Eastern region took place from April 15, 1964, until July 1, 1966. We do not focus on these rebellions, since ONUC had departed by then.

[105] Crawford Young and Thomas Turner, *The Rise and Decline of the Zairian State* (Madison: University of Wisconsin Press, 1985).

TABLE 4.3
Congo

	Congo-Zaire (1960–65) ONUC (1960–64)
Sovereign peace	Failure
Participatory peace	Failure
War type	"Ethnic"
Factions	4
UN mandate	Enforcement
Duration of UN mission (months)	47
Was UN present during the war? If so, for how long?	Yes; 47 months
Maximum troop strength of UN mission, if any	19,828
War duration (in months)	64
Real per capita GDP (at start of the war; constant $)	489
Real per capita GDP (at end of the war; constant $)	548
GDP growth at end of the war (% annual change)	2.62
People killed during the war	100,000
People displaced during the war	—
Outcome of the war	Government victory
Was a treaty signed by most parties?	No
Date of the treaty, if any was signed	n/a
Was the treaty implemented?	n/a
Primary commodity exports as % of GDP	9.1%
Is the country a major oil exporter?	No
Ethnolinguistic fractionalization (100 = highest)	90
Ethnic heterogeneity index (1 = highly diverse)	0.933
Population at start of war (in thousands)	15,986
Area (square kilometers)	2,344,860
Effective Development Assistance as % of GDP	—

The combination of challenges was daunting. First, a military mutiny led to sporadic violence soon after independence, ending in more than 100,000 people being killed in fighting and eliminating the legitimate government that had provided the basis for consent to the UN operation. Second, a Belgian military intervention, initially welcomed by Lumumba, soon committed its own excesses and demonstrated a determination to reestablish control. And, third, Katanga, the Congo's richest province, seceded (with Belgian support).

A weak peacekeeping mission could not have succeeded in the Congo. Use of force was necessary to keep the country together and help restore order. Hence, the "mission creep" from traditional peacekeeping to en-

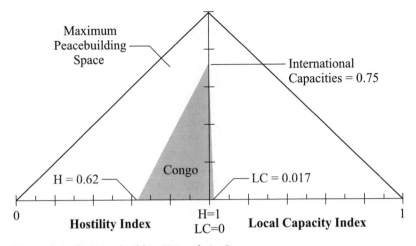

Figure 4.3 The Peacebuilding Triangle in Congo

forcement was justified. If the goal was to keep the country together, then the decision to step up the enforcement role of the UN in the Congo increased the available space for peace (see figure 4.3). Indeed, even without a peace treaty and despite the high levels of hostility and non-existent local capacities, our model predicted a significant probability of peacebuilding success for the Congo.[106] On this occasion, enforcement was successful (if success is understood narrowly to refer to mandate implementation) because, at the beginning, it enjoyed the support of both the United States and the USSR, and much of the Third World. Groping in new strategic territory, Hammarskjold's insistence on his policy of equidistance was a direct application of the doctrine of international peacekeeping and reflected an uncertainty over how one should deal with the problem of illegitimate government. When President Kasavubu and Premier Lumumba split, Lumumba, judging the UN and the West insufficiently committed, turned to the Soviets for assistance in expelling the Belgians and reunifying Tshombe's Katanga. Kasavubu and later General Mobutu turned to the West. No pristine neutrality was open to Hammarsjkold. Hammarskjold, siding with the West, supported Kasavubu

[106] The point estimate is .53. The estimate would have been lower if the primary commodity exports variable measured correctly the country's high degree of dependence on natural resources. The value for this variable in our dataset is 9 percent, far lower than the average 16 percent for all cases. This low figure must be more due to a low level of trade in the Congo so soon after independence and does not reflect the importance of natural resources in shaping much of the country's history.

and Mobutu, but rejecting Belgian interests in Katanga, demanded Belgian withdrawal and refused to recognize Tshombe's secession. This difficult problem of impartial enforcement continued to plague UN missions, as we also saw in the case of Somalia.[107]

ONUC also exemplifies the difficulty of evaluating peacekeeping or peacebuilding success: On the one hand, the mission was a success, despite facing great challenges; on the other hand, its success did not contribute to self-sustaining peace in the Congo. Moreover, ONUC's success in keeping the country together came at a high cost to the UN. The military component of ONUC cost the UN $402 million (around $2 billion at 1991 prices), of which the United States provided slightly less than 42 percent through assessed and voluntary contributions.[108] At its peak, ONUC cost the UN $120 million per year (at a time when the basic UN budget was $75 million per year).[109] The General Assembly's budgetary and administrative body proposed in December 1960 that ONUC's expenses should be considered expenses "of the organization" and thus subject to mandatory assessments. This was opposed by the USSR, claiming that the UN General Assembly had usurped the Council's authority by voting funds for a military operation. France, claiming ONUC was biased, joined the Eastern bloc countries in refusing to pay their assessments, leading to a huge financial crisis at the UN.

Accusations of bias (against Lumumba) leveled against Hammarskjold and the UN hurt the organization's legitimacy in Africa.[110] The Congolese parties were ambivalent about the usefulness of the UN, and their initial consent had been extended in hopes that the UN would help them establish their political authority. UN peacekeeping was a new instrument in the management of internal conflict, so it was easy for the parties to develop misconceptions about the meaning of UN impartiality. But ONUC's actions were all consistent with the spirit of its impartial mandate. After the military component of ONUC's mission had been completed in 1963, the civilian assistance program continued and was the most ambitious such program in the UN's history up to that point, employing two thousand experts at the program's peak in 1963–64. UN peacemaking was instrumental in promoting a political solution that led

---

[107] In Cyprus, too, the Greek Cypriot government often complained that the UN's policy of equidistance implicitly bestowed legitimacy on the Turkish Cypriot leadership.

[108] Lefever 1965, p. 15.

[109] Durch "The UN Operation in the Congo," 1993.

[110] As noted above, there are indications that Hammarskjold coordinated UN policy much more closely with the United States and other Western powers than he did with the Soviet Bloc; though he also opposed the United States on occasion. See Gibbs 2000, pp. 359–82, 377 particularly.

to the appointment of Adoula's government, but because the UN lacked a commitment to democratization, they also played a part in Mobutu's ascent to power with all that this meant for Congo's subsequent history. Moreover, ONUC's leadership demonstrated a keen understanding of conflict dynamics and adjusted ONUC's mandate and operational guidelines to match the escalation of the conflict.[111] This all suggests that ONUC was a peacekeeping (or, rather, peace-enforcement) success in the sense of endogenous, microlevel success.

However, ONUC had no peacebuilding vision in the Congo.[112] The mission began phasing out as soon as Katanga had been reintegrated in the country, before any of the peacebuilding challenges could be addressed. Perhaps as a result of this peace*building* failure, several episodes of large-scale violence, including civil war, took place in the 1960s and 1970s, after which Mobutu was able to secure his autocracy. War resumed in Katanga in 1977 and 1979, when Katangese exiles entered the province from Angola and tried once more, but failed, to regain control of their province. The UN's intervention in the Congo had the distinct flavor of a Cold War conflict. The Council's main concern was to prevent the conflict from escalating and from encouraging ethnic partitions elsewhere in the continent. As a result, ONUC's peace-enforcement mandate was restrictive, and even though it was successfully discharged, peace had to be imposed through more violence after the UN departed.

Overall, the combination of limited local support, ongoing conflict among several factions, and limited international support implied that ONUC could only restore unity and centralization in the Congo. Without inculcating deeper peacebuilding roots in an effective and participatory state, centralization proved a shallow benefit. In the 1960s, the UN's model for multidimensional peace operations had not yet been developed and international powers were willing to contribute money and troops to impose a Cold War solution to the Congo. They were not interested in helping the UN to build a healthy Congolese state where peace was coupled with political participation. While ONUC might be considered a success in the narrow sense of achieving its goal of holding the country together, the "peace process" in the Congo would later fail even according to a lenient peacebuilding standard, since several violent rebellions took place in the years following ONUC's presence, and Mobutu was able to keep control only by violently repressing political dissent.

---

[111] In this, ONUC's leadership was aided by the Council, which, authorized the use of force, if necessary to implement the mandate, by Resolution 161 of November 24, 1961.

[112] There was a substantial civilian mission focused on training the civil service and the army, but this did not stand in the way of Mobutu's kleptocracy.

Clausewitz and Peacekeeping

The operations in Somalia and Bosnia may have saved hundreds of thousands of lives. UNITAF and UNOSOM II made a positive contribution; without intervention, the starvation probably would have continued in Somalia, resulting in the loss of 110,000 to perhaps 250,000 more lives.[113] Only UNPROFOR prevented the complete ethnic cleansing of Muslims from Bosnia by the Serbs and the Croats. But the political costs of strategic failure and the humanitarian consequences of inadequate action in both operations were high.

The Congo operation was different, a limited success. The UN helped to preserve its territorial integrity and political independence. Unfortunately, due to its limited mandate and the intractability of the problem, Mobutu was the end result. The only outcome likely to have been worse would have been a continuation of civil war.

Although the bloody-mindedness of the parties to the conflicts warrants the largest share of the blame, the international community, the United Nations, and the peace operations themselves warrant a significant share, as the Srebenica report has acknowledged.

The failures in Somalia and Bosnia soon claimed victims elsewhere. Following the October 3 crisis in Somalia, U.S. senators clamored for immediate withdrawal of all U.S. forces from UNOSOM. The Clinton administration barely succeeded in holding out for a March 31, 1994, withdrawal date. Emboldened by the prospective U.S. withdrawal from Somalia, associates of the attaché's terrorizing Haiti chased U.S.-UN advisers from the harbor of Port-au-Prince, wrecking the Governor's Island peace plan and eventually forcing the administration to pursue the very risky decision (from the standpoint of domestic U.S. politics) to invade Haiti. Learning to say no, the United States led the Security Council's rejection of the request to protect thousands of displaced persons in Burundi who were fleeing the coup and slaughter of the government in October 1993. It also sought to limit the scope of the UN's engagement in massacre-torn Rwanda in April 1994, which resulted in the slaughter of hundreds of thousands and the displacement of even more into Tanzania and Zaire.

---

[113] Eric Schmitt, "Somalia's First Lesson for Military Is Caution," *New York Times*, March 5, 1995. The Refugee Policy Group suggested less dramatic figures, estimating that 220,000–238,000 died during the famine, 100,000 were saved, and because casualty rates were declining in the fall of 1992, only 10,000 of the 100,000 were saved after UNITAF landed. Casualty rates fell because some aid was getting through and people can die only once. The larger estimates of casualties averted seem to assume the famine would have spread as factional fighting spread beyond the "triangle of death." These issues are discussed in Michael Maren, *The Road to Hell* (New York: Free Press, 1997), chap. 12 and pp. 214–15.

In both cases the triangulation of peacebuilding came up short. Relative to the level of local hostility and local capacity, the international community invested too little international capacity. A varying combination of resources, mandate, and, something harder to pin down—strategic authority—was insufficient.

A Fantastic Gap

Time and again, UN "warmaking" (general peace enforcement) provoked what General Francois Briquemont, the former commander of UNPROFOR, denounced as "the fantastic gap between the resolutions of the Security Council, the will to execute those resolutions and the means available to commanders in the field."[114] The "fantastic gap" signals to some that borders are up for grabs and that massacres and ethnic cleansing will go unpunished. The UN thus showed itself to be ineffective in imposing order by force, whether to disarm factions in Somalia or provide humanitarian protection in Bosnia. Instead it became complicit in a record of inadequate protection, mission creep, seemingly unnecessary casualties, Vietnam-like escalation, on the one hand, and 1930s-style appeasement, on the other. It is difficult to disagree with the conclusion that the UN is remarkably ill suited to war-making.

As SG Boutros Boutros-Ghali has himself remarked, this boils down to the fact that "[t]he United Nations cannot keep peace where there is no peace to keep."[115] The UN is particularly poorly suited to interventionist strategies involving the strategic employment of coercive force. Indeed, Clausewitz's famous principles, ranging from the tactical to the political, seem to have been consistently honored in the breech.[116] Again, this leads us to pay attention to what made the Congo somewhat different.

Tactics

Tactically, even at the high point of the violence associated with UNOSOM, UN forces lacked the heavy equipment, including in particular the armored personnel carriers and tanks that would have been needed to ensure the safety of UN forces and domination of the urban battlefield. Well-protected troops, in hard battle vehicles, need to use less force than those exposed to fire in soft vehicles. General Thomas Montgomery, the

---

[114] Reuters, "UN Commander in Bosnia assails Security Council," *The Montreal Gazette* December 31, 1993.

[115] BBG 1992, Introduction, p. 7; United Nations, *The Blue Helmets*, 3d ed. (New York: United Nations, 1996) p. 7.

[116] Carl von Clausewitz, *On War*, edited and translated by Peter Paret (Princeton: Princeton University Press, 1976). See especially book 8, "War Plans." For a discussion of strategic categories applied to the Cambodian operation see Lieutenant General John Sanderson, "Dabbling in War" in Otunnu and Doyle 1998, pp. 145–68.

senior U.S. officer in UNOSOM II, requested armored vehicles but had been turned down, and the consequences were suffered in the summer of 1993 (although, in any case, casualties were likely given the mandate to hunt down Aidid in the midst of a hostile city).[117]

Gary Anderson, a U.S. Marine Corps officer who studied the UNO-SOM II operation, judged that

> the vast majority of the contingents that remained after May 4, 1993, the start date for UNOSOM II, were better suited for peacekeeping than peace enforcement. Peace-enforcement requires troops who are prepared for combat as well as situations short of combat (such as crowd control) which can re-quire even more training and discipline than combat itself. Ironically, at the very moment when they were creating an environment [by challenging Aidid] which virtually ensured that they would become a party to the conflict, the UNOSOM II leadership was losing the US combat troops that might have given it a chance to stabilize the situation in the face of armed resistance.[118]

UNPROFOR suffered from a lack of operationally relevant military information. Despite the escalating levels of violence, the missions in So-malia and Bosnia remained defined as peacekeeping, not war fighting. The war that did occur was supposed to occur in the midst of a civilian population whose protection was the first purpose of the operation. All this gave rise to what has become known as the Force Commander's Complaint: "If you order me to fight a war, I will; but not in vehicles painted white!" The Congo differed here in that weak as they were, ONUC forces in Katanga clearly dominated the indigenous forces avail-able to Tshombe, and European mercenaries were restrained from taking on the UN forces by their European patrons.

Strategy

Strategically, force commanders lacked command and control, the clas-sic requirement of unity of command. The first act of every peacekeeping battalion was to establish a communications and command link with its national command authority. Any proposed action involving the threat of violence would be referred to national authorities for approval.[119] Force commanders, by consequence, negotiated rather than directed their

---

[117] See Howe 1995; and Michael O'Hanlon, *Saving Lives with Force* (Washington, DC: Brookings, 1997) p. 75.

[118] Gary Anderson, "UNOSOM II: Not Failure, Not Success," in Donald Daniel and Bradd Hayes, eds. *Beyond Traditional Peacekeeping* (New York: St. Martin's, 1995) p. 273.

[119] William Doll and Steven Metz, *The Army and Multinational Peace Operations: Problems and Solutions* (Carlisle Barracks, PA: U.S. Army War College, 1993), p. 14. The problem of field command and control was less severe in first generation peacekeeping be-cause it did not usually involve the use of force.

forces, which was part of the reason for the lack of support on both June 24, when the Pakistani's took twenty-four casualties, and October 3, when the U.S. Rangers (who operated independently of the UNOSOM command) experienced disaster.[120] In a famous case in Bosnia, Force Commander General Bertrand De Lapresle directed French troops to escort a British contingent reinforcing Gorazde only to be overruled by Paris as the troop column was about to set off from the Sarajevo airport.[121] Force commanders generally lack what any NATO commander would consider to be minimal battlefield intelligence. UN battalions usually operate without key operational information. In Croatia in October 1993 the inability to be forewarned of an impending Croatian attack on Serb forces prevented what might have been successful efforts to deter the attack and maintain a crucial cease-fire line.[122] Multinational units raise other and obvious problems of coordination: In Sarajevo in September 1992, the lower ranking officers and men in Ukrainian, Egyptian, and French units naturally experienced difficulty finding a common language for joint operations. Here, too, ONUC had advantages in the quality of the battalions, their Indian leadership, and the remoteness of the country and the weaker 1960s quality communications between the field and headquarters. ONUC was inherently more independent that any 1990s operation could be. ONUC also, under the cover of technical assistance, developed a remarkably competent political capacity on site.

Another strategic gap yawns between the military and the civilian leadership in the field. In Bosnia, the diplomacy was in the hands of the International Conference on the Former Yugoslavia (a joint UN-EU diplomatic team); peacekeeping, in the hands of UNPROFOR. Coordination was weak—notoriously so when the Dutch battalion in Srebenica was refused air support because of the delicate state of negotiations between ICFY and Serbia.[123] In Somalia, the opposite prevailed when humanitarian assistance and peacemaking disappeared from the UNOSOMII agenda as the hunt to capture Aidid dominated the agenda.[124] In the Congo, Dag Hammarskjold set the strategy and offered relatively clear strategic guidance. Where that was inadequate, an excellent partnership between the UN's political leaders (Bunche, Cordier, Urquhart)

---

[120] See Mark Bowden, *Blackhawk Down* (New York: Atlantic Monthly Press, 1999), pp. 90–96.

[121] Michael C. Williams, *Civil-Military Relations and Peacekeeping*, Adelphi Paper 321 (London: Oxford University Press, 1998), p. 26.

[122] Andrew Bair, "Yugoslav Lessons for Future Peacekeepers," *European Security* 3, no. 2 (Summer 1994), 340–49.

[123] Bair 1994, p. 29.

[124] Drysdale (1994) describes in gripping (and somewhat partisan) detail the hunkering down and militarization of UNOSOM II.

and the force commander McKeown and the strikingly independent judgment of the UN representative in Katanga, Conor Cruise O'Brien, who
exceeded his instructions creatively, made the difference.[125]

Grand Strategy

At the grand strategic, or political command, level, the UN suffers from
a troubling divorce between the Security Council and the UN operation
in the field. At its worst, the Security Council appears, by issuing resolution after resolution, to be seeking rhetorical solutions to strategic
problems and satisfying CNN and the domestic publics of the member
countries, making those more important than providing well-designed
missions with sufficient forces. If Clausewitz's dictum about war as the
continuation of politics is applied to UN peace enforcement, enforcement appears to be the continuation of Security Council politics: a committee passing the buck, both seeking to appear to do something and actually doing very little at the same time.

At times, the Security Council issued mandates—for example, for Bosnian safe areas—without providing the forces that military experts had argued were necessary to implement the mandates.[126] Delays also erode the
effectiveness of UN peace operations, and delays in deployment of up to a
year are not uncommon. At the political policy level that shapes all strategic implementation, UN warmaking suffers from severe disabilities: some
a product of the incapacity of the organization; others due to the competing interests and limited support offered by member countries (particularly the permanent 5); and others a product of the first two in combination with the kind of civil wars the UN has tried to address.

First, the UN Secretariat, despite the lead role of the Department
of Peacekeeping Operations (DPKO), lacked for much of the 1990s an
overall focal point for coordination with peacekeeping operations in the
field, which need the assistance of development and the humanitarian
agencies. The provisions for rapid deployment were minimal, and the organization did not have a corps of peacekeepers whose careers could
be developed in a coherent way, unlike, for example, the well-planned
career available in UNHCR or many national bureaucracies (see the
Brahimi Report). The UN Secretariat, moreover, having been sanctioned
numerous times before, was disinclined to actively reinterpret Security
Council resolutions to make them more effective in the field because they
saw themselves as lacking the authority to do so.[127] But most significantly,

[125] Urquhart 1972 pp. 556–59; and, earlier, Cordier described his unusually creative impartiality: "we have not chose sides, but the constitutional party has chose to follow the
UN line" (p. 44).

[126] The safe havens were said to require 34,000 troops; the Security Council authorized
7,600.

[127] Honig and Both 1996, p. 146.

as the Brahimi Report documented in much detail, the Secretariat was woefully underresourced to fulfill the mandates assigned to it. Where in national militaries "teeth-to-tail" (front-line soldiers to logistic and head-quarters staff) ratios were typically of the order of one to three, the UN by 2000 was spending less than 2 percent of the peacekeeping budget in headquarters planning and logistics.[128] The UN, of course, does not need to provide a complete support, logistics, or a training package to its peacekeeping battalions (most of the functions are provided by the home governments of troop contributing countries); still, the numbers in table 4.4 below are illustrative of how thin the UN planning staff is.

The UN Secretariat lacks thus the skills and the number of personnel needed to manage (that is, coordinate) a large-scale armed enforcement operation. The Secretariat's traditional ideology (despite recent practice) is highly protective of national sovereignty and (to its credit) lacks the psychological distance required to order coercive punishment on political movements with even the smallest of popular support.[129] Having had the repeated experience of having been used as a scapegoat by its leading member states, it also tends to be extremely risk adverse and self-protective of the organization even when risk taking might be justified.

Adam Roberts summarized the problem of waging war with UN forces well:[130] "Military actions require extremely close coordination between intelligence-gathering and operations; a smoothly functioning decision-making machine and forces with some experience of working together to perform dangerous and complex tasks. These things are more likely to be achieved through existing national armed forces, alliances, and military relationships, than they are within the structure of a UN command."

Second, the international political roots of the UN's "command and control" over grand strategy are deep-seated in the nature of multilateral organization. On the one hand, countries with battalions in UN peace operations are reluctant to see their (often lightly armed) troops engaged in combat under UN direction, distrusting that a UN force commander of any nationality other than their own will take due care to minimize risks. Countries with seats on the Security Council, on the other hand, pressured to achieve a response to civil war crises and unwilling to confront the UN's ongoing resource crisis, assign missions to UN peace

---

[128] Brahimi Report, table 4.1.

[129] See the account of the UN decision process concerning Rwanda in Michael Barnett, "The UN Security Council, Indifference, and Genocide in Rwanda," *Cultural Anthropology* 12 no. 4 (1997): 551–78. An added problem is that the use of force in civil wars frequently causes casualties among civilians, opening the UN and its members to accusations of neocolonialism and brutality. Adam Roberts, *The Crisis in Peacekeeping*, (Institutt for Forsvarsstudier, 1994) p. 24.

[130] Adam Roberts, "The United Nations and International Security," *Survival* 35 no. 2 (1993): 3–31 15.

TABLE 4.4
Total Staff Assigned on a Full-Time Basis to Support Complex Peacekeeping Operations Established in 1999

	UNMIK (Kosovo)	UNAMSIL (Sierra Leone)	UNTAET (East Timor)	MONUC (Democratic Republic of the Congo)
Budget (estimated) July 2000–June 2001	$410 million	$465 million	$540 million	$535 million
Current authorized strength of key components	4,718 police 1,000-plus international civilians	13,000 military	8,950 military 1,640 police 1,185 international civilians	5,537 military 500 military observers
Professional staff at headquarters assigned full-time to support the operation	1 political officer 2 civilian police 1 logistics coord. 1 civilian recruitment specialist 1 finance specialist	1 political officer 2 military 1 logistics coord. 1 finance specialist	1 political officer 2 military 1 civilian police 1 logistics coord. 1 civilian recruitment specialist 1 finance specialist	1 political officer 3 military 1 civilian police 1 logistics coord. 1 civilian recruitment specialist 1 finance specialist
Total Headquarters support Staff	6	5	7	8

Source: Brahimi Report, p. 32.

operations without providing adequate means to achieve those missions, unless those missions reflect their own more narrow national interest.

Thus President Clinton announced in a speech to the General Assembly on September 27, 1993: "In recent weeks, in the Security Council, our nation has begun asking harder questions about proposals for new peace-keeping missions: is there a real threat to international peace? Does the proposed mission have clear objectives? Can an end point be identified for those who will be asked to participate? How much will the mission cost? . . . The United Nations cannot be engaged in every one of the world's conflicts. If the American people are to say yes to UN peacekeeping, the United Nations must know when to say no."[131]

The statement was both sensible and, indeed, reflected long-standing and traditional UN doctrine. But it was also chock full of ironies. First, the "UN" could never take action without the concurrence of the United States and the four other permanent members in the Security Council. Second, within months of this statement the United States said no to an operation that both was a threat to international peace and that involved genocide, where intervention was required by international treaties to which the United States was a party. And then it spent more than double the cost on a humanitarian assistance mission to contain the refugee consequences of having failed to intervene. Within the same few months, the United States persuaded the other members of the Security Council to intervene in another crisis that involved no threat to international peace, whose humanitarian consequences were severe but in no way comparable to those in the first, and whose mission, although worthwhile from a humanitarian point of view, was both unclear and open-ended. The first, of course, was Rwanda; the second, Haiti. However worthwhile, proximate national interests made all the difference as the Clinton administration sought to contain a refugee exodus from Haiti to Florida provoked by the oppressive Cedras regime and economic devastation (itself partly inflicted by the UN's own embargo). Russia engaged in a similarly national operation with UN endorsement at the same time in Georgia as it sought to police its near-abroad, and indeed, the votes in the Security Council for Georgia were the political cost of the support for Haiti.[132] And similar operations followed as Nigeria led interventions in Liberia and Sierra Leone and Australia in East Timor.

The disaster at Srebenica illustrated how these factors can interact to produce strategic irresponsibility. On May 24, 1995, General Bernard Janvier, UNPROFOR force commander, briefed the Security Council on

[131] http://www.findarticles.com/p/articles/M9584/is/_N39_v4/ai_1429 (August 5, 2005).

[132] David Malone, *Decision-Making in the Security Council: The Case of Haiti, 1990–1997* (Oxford: Clarendon Press, 1998); Thomas G. Weiss, *Military-Civilian Interactions* (Lanham, MD: Rowman and Littlefield, 1999).

UNPROFOR's inability to fulfill its mandate.[133] The safe areas were not safe, food and medicine convoys could not get through, and 173 peacekeepers had lost their lives. Secretary-General Boutros Boutros-Ghali then presented the Council will three options: increase the size and capabilities of the contingent and use force to implement the mandate; keep UNPROFOR as it was and reduce its responsibilities; or stay the course. The United States and the Netherlands favored the first. Both were experiencing public pressure to do something. But with no U.S. troops on the line, U.S. arguments were unpersuasive to France and the United Kingdom, who bore the brunt of the burden in Bosnia. With the UN's credibility very much on the line, Boutros-Ghali and Janvier favored the second. They urged a withdrawal from the exposed safe areas. But, they suggested, Bosnian security could actually be improved in this fashion. Without UNPROFOR troops as hostages and given the improvements over the past year in Bosniac military capabilities, NATO forward air controllers could call in close air support and wider air strikes to back up the Bosnians, should the Bosnians be attacked. But this proposal (one that eventually, when implemented much too late, saved Gorazde and Sarajevo) put NATO and the UN on the front lines and in potential warlike confrontation with the Serbs. Neither the Americans nor the Germans (it looked weak) nor the Russians (the Serbs' political support) found this attractive. And, so, the third, the irresponsible option that so obviously failed to match mandate to means, prevailed.

Third, the civil wars that have ensnared the UN in the 1990s are strategically challenging. Civil wars are difficult strategic environments, fought for deep purposes and involving civilians as closely as uniformed fighters. External attempts to impose order can easily turn into the addition of just another faction to the ongoing conflict, as the UN and the United States became in Somalia, unless the international intervention is well planned and equipped. Interventions clearly can work, as Britain demonstrated in its repression of the Malayan insurgency in the 1950s and 1960s. With forces superior in size and equipment to the largest potential opposition and public security ratios of one to five interveners per thousand inhabitants, interventions can establish law and order even when local cooperation is minimal.[134] A successful "exit" (self-sustaining peace), however, requires both eliciting local cooperation in public secu-

---

[133] Boutros Boutros-Ghali 1999, pp. 233–34; Rohde 1997, pp. 72–74; Honig and Both 1996, pp. 152–54.

[134] See Michael O'Hanlon, *Saving Lives with Force: Military Criteria for Humanitarian Intervention* (Washington, DC: Brookings, 1997), esp. pp. 40–41. But, significantly, in the face of serious opposition, as in Malaya, the British required a public security ration of 20 per 1,000 inhabitants. For additional analysis of occupations and nation building see, James Dobbins et al., *America's Role in Nation-Building: From Germany to Iraq* (Santa Monica, CA: RAND 2003).

rity and a well-planned transfer of political responsibility to locally legitimate forces.

Some have argued that effective intervention requires choosing sides. If the intervener is not prepared to deploy massive impartial force to impose law and order, Richard Betts has argued that effective intervention tends to require nonimpartial and nonneutral use of force in order to economize on the characteristically limited availability of force or, alternatively, massive impartial intervention. The most economical intervention thus assists the strongest party to achieve effective sovereignty or assists the party whose interests are closest to those of the intervener. Otherwise, the international actor finds itself caught in the middle, providing material support to each of the factions without the support of any of the factions. Picking the winner makes considerable sense for unilateral interventions with national objectives. (Although we know that the task is still challenging enough, as the United States and Soviet quagmires in Vietnam and Afghanistan showed.)

UN intervention, however, is a special problem. The Security Council faces difficulties in directing any form a strategic military campaign; but choosing sides would be even more difficult in any campaign short of one directed against international aggression or genocide because of the variety of national objectives that enter into the multilateral intervention. Each permanent member of the Security Council can use its veto to prevent a UN-endorsed intervention that would disadvantage its perceived client. Minimally equipped and with a mandate produced by a delicately negotiated least common denominator in the Security Council, neutrality too often tends to be the limit of UN peace operations. If the UN had at its disposal substantial forces, impartial intervention would become more feasible but only in the service of genuinely multilateral goals.

Impartial but massive interventions are most unlikely, for "peace-forcing fatigue" afflicts the UN's contributing countries, whether new or old. States are rarely willing to invest their resources or the lives of their soldiers in war other than for a vital interest (such as oil in the Persian Gulf). But if states have a vital national interest in a dispute, they are not likely to exercise the impartiality a UN peace operation requires. Nor are they likely to cede decision-making control over or command of their forces to the UN.

The very act of intervention, even by the UN, can mobilize nationalist opposition against the foreign forces. In Somalia, it contributed to a significant growth of support for Aidid's Somali National Alliance. Aidid's supporters soon roundly condemned the UN's "colonialism."[135] The

---

[135] Mr. Abdi Hassan Awale, an Aidid adviser in Mogadishu, complained, "[r] the UN wants to rule this country. They do not want a Somali government to be established. The UN wants to stay and colonize us." New York Times, March 2, 1994.

strategic balance is not static. Military intervention tilts two local balances, improving the military correlation of forces but often at the cost of undermining the more important political balance.

Coercively intervening for eventual self-determination is very often a self-contradictory enterprise.[136] If the local forces of freedom, self-determination, and human rights cannot achieve sovereignty without a foreign military intervention, then they are very unlikely to be able to hold on to power after the intervention force leaves. Either the installed forces of freedom will collapse or they themselves will employ those very coercive methods that provoked and justified the initial intervention.[137] Successful intervention is thus rare, requiring a large commitment of resources, determined leadership, a genuine commitment to self-determination, and favorable local circumstances: the sort of conditions that made the allied occupations of Germany and Japan produce what eventually became vibrant democracies.

The Congo was exceptional on all of these dimensions. The Security Council was temporarily united as the United States and USSR both rejected the colonial flavor of Belgium's manipulative exit from the country. With that international support, quality battalions from Africa, India, and Europe were quickly mobilized and flown by the United States to the area. The purpose of the intervention was limited to reunifying the country and assisting the existing government, eschewing deeper programs of peacebuilding reform, but retaining the support of Congo's African neighbors as it served the purpose of centralizing Congo's government. ONUC also enjoyed the advantages of going early, before faction leaders learned the weakness of the UN and while outsiders retained confidence in its impartiality. In short, despite all its challenges of poverty, tribalism, and outside intervention, the Congo benefited from a combination of multilateral legitimacy and national (particularly U.S.) commitment.

[136] For a classic discussion of these problems see J. S. Mill, "A Few Words on Nonintervention" (1859) in Gertrude Himmelfarb, ed. *Essays on Politics and Culture* (Gloucester: P. Smith, 1973). And see Edward Mortimer, "Under What Circumstances Should the UN Intervene Militarily in a Crisis," in Otunnu and Doyle 1998, pp 111–44.

[137] The Kurds, for example, won widespread sympathy for their resistance to Saddam Hussein and benefited from an UN-endorsed U.S.-French-British intervention in the aftermath of the war against Iraq. But until the 2003 invasion, the Kurdish factions were so divided that they appeared incapable of establishing law and order in their territory. Instead, three factions divided the region. None appeared capable of sustaining itself against whatever attempts to reincorporate Kurdistan that Saddam Hussein might have made. The international community had thus placed itself in the awkward position of either adopting Kurdistan as a long-term ward or returning it to the not-so-tender mercies of Saddam Hussein. Chris Hedges, "Quarrels of Kurdish Leaders Sour Dreams of a Homeland," *New York Times*, June 18,1994.

Indeed, neither multilateralism nor great power commitment alone appear to be sufficient for success. Great power interventions stir up anticolonial resistance and are often corrupted by local exploitations, as was Nigeria's thinly veiled ECOMOG intervention in Liberia. Nor is the success record even for U.S.-led operations remarkable. In one recent study of a limited set of sixteen cases, while eleven out of sixteen operations achieved a degree of peace, seven of the eight UN-led ones were successful and only four of the eight U.S.-led ones were (and of the four successful ones, two relied on the continuing presence of international forces).[138]

Multilateralism in general and United Nations in particular present almost textbook cases of multiple strategic incapacity produced both by institutional incapacity and lack of support from its member countries. In Somalia, there was dominant great power commitment. This was a U.S. operation top to bottom. But it lacked coordination (in that U.S. forces operated independently of UN forces) and a comprehensive strategy of civilian reconstruction. In Bosnia, many powers—France and the United Kingdom and NATO more variously—made substantial military commitments, but again coordination among them was weak and none were committed to finding a solution.

The failings of the UN as a warmaker appear deeply structured in its multilateral character, which serves as an invitation to buck passing and rhetorical solutions to substantive problems. Multilateral cooperation is far from impossible. It has been achieved numerous times, even under trying circumstances. The Combined Chiefs of Staff managed the World War II Grand Alliance. The IMF, the World Bank, the WTO and numerous multilateral regimes work, though often with smaller coalitions of like-minded states in charge or through imaginative schemes of delegation.[139] But the UN Security Council is a special problem. It lacks the forced commonality of interests against the Axis that shaped the World War II Grand Alliance (its immediate ancestor). It usually lacks the cultural consensus or charismatic leadership that can bind other multilateral institutions. Yet its global security role is more strategically demanding—facing uncertainties absent a clear regime of norms or procedures, required to adjust flexibly means to fluid ends—than that of the typical successful multilateral organizations. The fifteen-member Security Council,

---

[138] See the valuable, if limited, comparison of sixteen cases in James Dobbins, et al., *The UN's Role in Nation-Building: From the Congo to Iraq* (Santa Monica: Rand, 2005) pp. xxv–xxix, and their earlier volume, Dobbins et al. 2003.

[139] For valuable analytic surveys of multilateralism and how it can work see John Ruggie, "Multilateralism: The Anatomy of an Institution," *International Organization* 46, no. 3 (Summer 1992): 561–98; and Miles Kahler, "Multilateralism with Small and Large Numbers," *International Organization* 46, no. 3 (Summer 1992): 681–708.

subject to the veto of the permanent five, looks much like the storied, eighteenth-century Polish Diet subject to its debilitating vetoes. Neither was/is suited for rational strategic action.

Nonetheless, encountering strategic problems while intervening in ethnic and civil wars is not unique to the United Nations. The Multinational Force in Lebanon created even larger catastrophes of misdirected, overly violent, and intrusive intervention in 1983. Even with national-quality command and control, the United States failed to impose peace in Vietnam in the 1960s; the Soviets failed in Afghanistan. Moreover, the United Nations is nothing more than the collective agent of its member states. Some of the UN's organizational incapacities could be cured by additional resources from its member states, which devote but a tiny fraction of the resources they spend on national security to collective action under the United Nations. And, lastly, the UN can delegate general warmaking (peace-enforcement) functions to a member state and then step in to assist with the peacebuilding, as occurred in Haiti, an option to which we return in the conclusion. But short of major increase in UN capacity, doing it on its own is a most risky proposition.

The UN's strengths as an organization lie elsewhere. The very multilateralism that is so debilitating as a structure from which to wage war and enforce law and order over resisting factions is remarkably conducive to making, keeping, building, and strategically enforcing a comprehensively negotiated peace—the innovative UN strategies of the 1990s to which we next turn.

5

Making Peace: Successes

> If men were angels, no government would be
> necessary. If angels were to govern men,
> neither external nor internal controls on
> government would be necessary. In framing a
> government which is to be administered by
> men over men, the great difficulty is this: You
> must first enable the government to control the
> governed; and in the next place, oblige it to
> control itself.
>   —James Madison, Federalist no. 51,
>   February 6, 1788

MAKING A SUSTAINABLE PEACE is not unlike making a constitution. Fortunately, the UN has done relatively well in assisting civil-war-torn populations in discovering terms—the "constitutional" external and internal
controls—that make a peace agreement sustainable. Like a good consti-
tutionalist, the UN has helped embed external controls, such as democracy and the rule of law, and internal controls, such as power sharing
and judicial reform, into effective peace settlements.

Indeed, the UN's deficiencies as a war-maker are by and large offset by
its often-unappreciated successes as a peace-maker and peacebuilder.
The UN has succeeded when it has negotiated and then implemented a
consensual basis for a restoration of law and order and human rights.
Taking a substantial step beyond "first generation" operations in which
the UN monitors a truce and keeping a significant step short of the third
generation "Peace Enforcing" operations in which the UN uses force to
impose a peace, second generation multidimensional operations have
been based on consent of the parties. In significant ways, all these successes embody solutions to coordination problems in that there is
some basis of consent among the factions that the UN can then facilitate and expand. But the nature of and purposes for which consent has
been granted are qualitatively different from traditional peacekeeping.
In these operations, the UN is typically involved in exercising transitional authority in the implementation of peace agreements that go
to the roots of the conflict, helping to transform the conflict and build

a long-term foundation for stable, legitimate government. As Secretary-General Boutros-Ghali observed in *An Agenda for Peace*, "peace-making and peace-keeping operations, to be truly successful, must come to include comprehensive efforts to identify and support structures which will tend to consolidate peace. . . . [T]hese may include disarming the previously warring parties and the restoration of order, the custody and possible destruction of weapons, repatriating refugees, advisory and training support for security personnel, monitoring elections, advancing efforts to protect human rights, reforming or strengthening governmental institutions and promoting formal and informal processes of political participation."

One might imagine that successful operations are special because the conflicts are different, coordination as opposed to collaboration games, where consent is easy and stable and all that is needed is facilitation. Or, one could imagine that although the conflicts are just as challenging as collaboration games, the UN is a successful enforcer that eliminates credible commitment problems. But neither simple outcome reflects the facts on the ground.

Though consent-based, these operations are far from harmonious. Consent is not a simple "bright line" demarcating the safe and acceptable from the dangerous and illegitimate. Each function requires an enhanced form of consent if the UN is to help make a peace in the contentious environment of civil strife. We need, therefore, to focus on new ways to design peace operations if the UN, in the face of likely resistance, is to avoid having to choose between either comprehensive enforcement or complete withdrawal.[1]

The key is usually finding a way to combine consent with coercion. Consent is necessary because otherwise costly resistance (as illustrated in the previous chapter) will arise and overwhelm the resources an international organization can deploy and because few great powers today are prepared to bear the costs of imperial conquest (for humanity's sake). But given the unstable character of civil war factions and powerful incentives (fear, looting, prestige) fostering conflict, coercion will also be needed to manage the spoilers likely to defect from the peace agreement. We must, therefore, both avoid the danger that seeking consent will weaken the capacity to coerce and that exercising coercion will discredit the act of consent. Needless to add, succeeding at both simultaneously is a considerable challenge.

The UN has a commendable record of success in these Second Generation, multidimensional peacekeeping operations as diverse as those

---

[1] On the need to "enhance" the parties' consent so as to increase the likelihood of peacekeeping and peacebuilding success, see Doyle 1995; and Ratner 1995.

in Namibia (UNTAG), El Salvador (ONUSAL), Cambodia (UNTAC),[2] Mozambique (ONUMOZ), and Eastern Slavonia, Croatia (UNTAES), and most recently, East Timor (UNTAET). As we discussed in chapter 2, the UN's role in helping settle those conflicts has been fourfold. It served as a *peacemaker* facilitating a peace treaty among the parties; as a *peacekeeper* monitoring the cantonment and demobilization of military forces, resettling refugees, and supervising transitional civilian authorities; as a *peacebuilder* monitoring and in some cases organizing the implementation of human rights, national democratic elections, and economic rehabilitation; and in the last resort and in a discrete, carefully constrained, and impartial manner as a *peace enforcer*. Together these roles create new dimensions of transitional authority for the international community, ranging from "monitoring and facilitating" to "administrative controlling," to "executing" to quasi-sovereign "supervision." Matching the right authority to the right situation and exercising those authorities well makes all the difference.

Every peacekeeping operation is different, even if they combine similar parts. In this chapter, we survey five successes, noting their similarities and differences. We pay particular attention to the mixed character of most successes; for, even when successful, rarely are all parts of a mandate fulfilled. What accounts for which parts of the mandate were met; what for those that were not? With these issues in mind, we look at El Salvador, Cambodia, and Eastern Slavonia, trying to account for their considerable success is establishing a sustainable peace. We also examine Brcko in northern Bosnia. Bosnia, as a whole, is still far from a sustainable peace, despite the substantial accomplishments under the Dayton Agreement, except in one small and quite special district, Brcko.[3] We conclude with an account of the UN's recent successful effort to establish an independent and (so far) durable peace in East Timor. We look at these five successes before turning in chapter 6 to an examination of how, despite some consent, an agreement can stagnate, failing to move from a truce to sustainable peace, as has occurred so far (2004) in Cyprus; or collapse altogether into (in this case) genocide, as occurred in Rwanda. We then compare lessons among all the cases in chapter 7 to identify determinants of how to successfully design and manage peacebuilding.

---

[2] Before the UN became involved, during the Cold War when action by the Security Council was stymied by the lack of consensus among its five permanent members, the international community allowed Cambodia to suffer an autogenocide and El Salvador a brutal civil war. Indeed the great powers were involved in supporting factions who inflicted some of the worst aspects of the violence the two countries suffered. We should keep this in mind when we consider the UN's difficulties in Somalia and Bosnia.

[3] Bertrand de Lapresle, " Principles to be Observed," in Biermann and Vadset 1998, pp. 137–52, p. 149.

Monitoring and Facilitation in El Salvador

The roots of the eleven-year civil war in the Central American nation date back at least to the last century.[4] A program of state intervention in the economy at that time led to substantial economic growth, based mainly on the production and export of coffee. In the mid-1800s the government decreed that an ever-increasing proportion of land should be devoted to coffee, and by the end of the century the best land was concentrated in the hands of the wealthiest "fourteen families." Most of the presidents of the country during the period—who were generals prior to their elections—came from that oligarchy. By 1931, the social cost of this concentration of wealth and power had precipitated a series of peasant and worker uprisings, culminating in an attempted insurrection led by Augustín Farubundo Martí. The uprisings were brought to a bloody end in December 1931 by a number of young military officers who seized power in a coup d'état.

By the end of 1932, the military was firmly in control. It ruled to preserve its own position and to serve the interests of the oligarchy—goals that were often, but not always, compatible. The years 1932 to 1979 were characterized by cycles of repression and reform, dominated by the army and the oligarchy, although after 1960 the Church and popular organizations began to make their presence felt.[5] These new actors wielded more influence after the election of 1972, which by all accounts was stolen from the Christian Democrat José Napoleon Duarte.[6] The period of repression that ensued throughout most of the 1970s was fertile ground for the growth of so-called political-military organizations, which came increasingly to believe in the necessity of armed revolution. Four of these organizations were formed in the 1970s and, joined by the Communist Party of El Salvador, united in 1980 to become the FMLN. By this point, full-scale civil war had already erupted.

---

[4] This section draws on Doyle, Johnsone, and Orr 1997, introduction and conclusion. For thorough discussions of the background of conflict in El Salvador, see Charles Call, "Assessing El Salvador's Transition from Civil War to Peace," in Stedman, Rothschild, and Cousens 2002, pp. 383–420; Tommie Sue Montgomery, *Revolution in El Salvador: From Civil Strife to Civil Peace*, 2d ed. (Boulder, CO: Westview Press, 1994); Christopher C. Coleman, *The Salvadoran Peace Process: A Preliminary Inquiry*, Norwegian Institute of International Affairs, Research Report no. 173 (December 1993); Terry Lynn Karl, "El Salvador's Negotiated Revolution," *Foreign Affairs* 71, no. 2 (Spring 1992): 147; William Stanley, *The Protection Racket State: Elite Politics, Military Extortion, and Civil War in El Salvador* (Philadelphia: Temple University Press, 1996); and Elizabeth Jean Wood, *Forging Democracy from Below: Insurgent Transitions in South Africa and El Salvador* (Cambridge: Cambridge University Press, 2000).

[5] Montgomery 1994, p. 79.

[6] Montgomery 1994, pp. 62–65; Coleman 1993, p. 11.

Throughout the 1980s, a number of presidential, legislative, and mayoral elections were held, but political developments were determined more by what happened on the battlefield than at the ballot box. Salvadoran society was militarized, with civilian rule constrained and undermined by widespread right-wing violence, military will, and active U.S. government involvement. Acts of political violence by right-wing "death squads" increased dramatically, and untold human rights abuses were committed.[7] In the end, over 75,000 lives were lost and more than 1 million people—almost one-quarter of the population—had been displaced.

Regional peace efforts in Central America began in 1983, when the members of the Contadora Group (Columbia, Mexico, Panama, and Venezuela) initiated a series of consultations with five governments of the region. What has been called the "official birth" of the Central American peace process did not come until August 1987, however, when the presidents of the five nations signed the Esquipulas II Agreement.[8] In it, they requested all governments concerned to terminate support for irregular forces and insurrectional movements in Central America, and reiterated their commitment to prevent the use of their own territory to destabilize their neighbors. The Security Council endorsed the agreement in July 1989 and lent its full support to the Secretary-General's good offices efforts.

The first UN operation to be deployed in the region was ONUCA, in November 1989, with a mandate to monitor compliance with Esquipulas II by patrolling the borders of the five countries. Meanwhile, in September 1989, the government of El Salvador and the FMLN agreed to a dialogue to end the armed conflict. Given the rapprochement that was taking place between the United States and the USSR, it seemed that real progress was possible. However, following the murder of a key trade union leader at the end of October 1989, the FMLN launched a major offensive, which for the first time brought the war to the capital of the country.

The parties fought to a stalemate, until both were convinced that a military victory was impossible.[9] With the backing of the five Central American presidents, they separately requested the diplomatic intervention by the Secretary-General. His personal representative, Alvaro de Soto, spent the next three years helping to hammer out a series of six

[7] See United Nations, *Report of the Commission on the Truth for El Salvador*, "From Madness to Hope: The 12-Year War in El Salvador," S/25500 (April 1, 1993), p. 27.

[8] *The United Nations and El Salvador, 1990–1995*, UN Dept. of Public Information, (1995), p.9. For a recent and insightful account by an insider see Blanca Antonini, "El Salvador," in David Malone, ed., *The UN Security Council* (Boulder, CO: Lynne Rienner, 2004), pp. 423–36.

[9] UN Dept. of Public Information 1995, p. 12.

accords between the parties, culminating in the Chapultepec Agreement signed in Mexico City on January 16, 1992.

The cumulative effect of the six agreements was a triumph of mediated peacemaking and a profound transformation of Salvadoran society, what the new Secretary-General, Boutros Boutros-Ghali, called "a revolution achieved by negotiation." In a nutshell, the accords brought an end to the war by drawing the FMLN into the political process in exchange for extensive institutional and legal reforms designed to "demilitarize" Salvadoran society. The overarching objectives of the negotiations were set out in the framework agreement reached in Geneva in April 1990: to end the armed conflict by political means; promote the democratization of the country; guarantee respect for human rights; and reunify Salvadoran society. One month later, an agenda and timetable for the negotiations were agreed upon in Caracas, identifying seven substantive topics for negotiation.

The San José Agreement on Human Rights was the first substantive agreement reached by the parties, in July 1990. It set out a number of rights both sides had to respect and, most importantly, provided for the establishment of a UN human rights verification mission, intended to take up its responsibilities *after* a cease-fire was achieved. For various reasons, however, the parties subsequently requested the deployment of the verification mission in mid-1991, before negotiations on other issues were completed and the cease-fire was in place.

Meanwhile, almost a year after the San José Agreement was signed, the parties agreed in Mexico to a set of constitutional reforms relating to the armed forces, the justice system, and the electoral system. The reforms were approved by the outgoing National Assembly, whose term ended on April 30, 1991, and ratified by the new Assembly shortly thereafter. The Mexico Agreement also provided for the establishment of a Truth Commission to investigate "serious acts of violence that have occurred since 1980 and whose impact on society urgently requires that the public should know the truth."

The fifth accord, the New York Agreement, was signed in September 1991. Its key elements were the creation of the National Commission for the Consolidation of Peace (COPAZ) and agreements in principle to the reduction, doctrinal reform, and "purification" of the armed forces. Because the FMLN was represented on COPAZ, the insurgent group had a channel to participate in overseeing implementation of the agreements even before it became a political party. The agreement on reform of the armed forces—the most difficult issue in the negotiations—did not cover all details, but the principle of "purification" pointed the way to a final settlement. Finally at midnight, December 31, 1991—the last hour of

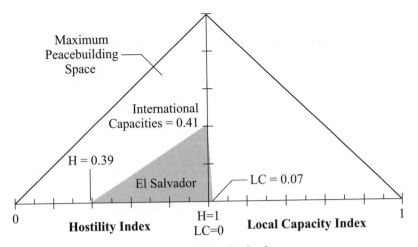

Figure 5.1 The Peacebuilding Triangle in El Salvador

Secretary-General Pérez de Cuellar's term—the parties reached agreement on all outstanding issues, including the cessation of armed conflict. The final peace agreement was signed in Chapultepec two weeks later.

Our model predicts the case of El Salvador quite well. Relative to other cases, the available peacebuilding space after the end of the civil war in 1992 was substantial (see figure 5.1). The predicted probability of peacebuilding success (0.69) is more than double the average for all other cases. Although local capacities in El Salvador were low and hostility levels were high in terms of the numbers of people killed and displaced, this was not an ethnic or religious war, which would have made peace implementation harder, and more importantly, the parties were reconciled to their inability to achieve a military victory.

The signing of peace agreements since 1983 outlined the framework of a workable settlement. The UN, in turn, responded with the appropriate mandate and resources: it dispatched a multidimensional peacebuilding mission that was designed to facilitate, not enforce a peace (ONUSAL's maximum troop strength was under 1,000). ONUSAL served a critical function in verifying the parties' compliance with the terms of the treaty, helping to resolve the assurance problem that each party faced and that might have led them to return to war. Thus, there was a good match between the mandate and resources on the one hand and the peacebuilding ecology on the other hand. In addition, the peacekeepers implemented their mandate well, and they were assisted in doing so by a group of Friends of the Secretary-General. This regional

TABLE 5.1
El Salvador

	El Salvador (1979–92) ONUSAL/ONUCA (1989–95)
Sovereign peace	Success
Participatory peace	Success
War type	"Nonethnic"
Factions	2 (7 minor)
UN mandate	Multidimensional PKO
Duration of UN mission (months)	64
Was UN present during the war? If so, for how long	Yes; 25 months
Maximum troop strength of UN mission, if any	683
War duration (in months)	147
Real per capita GDP (year before war start; constant $)	2,330
Real per capita GDP (at end of the war; constant $)	1,876
GDP growth at end of the war (% annual change)	1.241
People killed during the war	75,000
People displaced during the war	600,000
Outcome of the war	Treaty/Settlement
Was a treaty signed by most parties?	Yes
Date of the treaty, if any was signed	January 1992
Was the treaty implemented?	Yes
Primary commodity exports as % of GDP	1.32
Is the country a major oil exporter?	No
Ethnolinguistic fractionalization (100 = highest)	16
Ethnic heterogeneity index (1 = highly diverse)	0.197
Population at start of war (in thousands)	4,457
Area (square kilometers)	21,040
Effective Development Assistance as % of GDP	139.073

diplomatic assistance was critical in leveraging the UN's efforts and is a factor that is not fully captured by our model (though we do control for non-UN peace efforts in some specifications of the model). Moreover, El Salvador received significant foreign economic assistance: effective development assistance was 139 percent of GDP in 1992 (see table 5.1).

ONUSAL's success rate was, as we shall see, higher than UNTAC's, although not surprisingly so, given the less ambitious mandate and the greater willingness of the parties to make peace and cooperate with the UN. The human rights situation in El Salvador has vastly improved, a new police force has been created, a large portion of the senior military establishment has been removed, and the FMLN won the second largest number of legislative seats in elections that, though flawed, were fair enough to have been deemed acceptable. On the other hand, the reform of the judiciary and the police were not completed. In particular, the new civilian police force manifested a host of serious problems, including alleged assassination plots and membership in illegal armed groups within the ranks. In addition, the ongoing crime wave—especially the increase in drug trafficking, organized crime, and the proliferation of street gangs and illegal armed vigilante groups—has prompted the government to use the military to patrol rural areas in contravention of the constitutional procedures established under the peace accords.

Similarly, the Salvadoran peace process has done little to meet the economic and social grievances of the people at large.[10] Although never intended to directly redress El Salvador's deep social inequities—for example, patterns of land ownership—it was expected that through institutional and political reforms disadvantaged groups would gain a greater say in decisions that affected their lives. Indicative of the frustration felt by many who did not benefit from the peace process, in late 1995 peasants took part in at least seventeen different land occupations in the western region of the country, demanding the government investigate landowners who continue to own lands in excess of the 245-hectare constitutional limit. Even providing former combatants and "squatters" with the land and wherewithal to reintegrate into civilian life has proven to be very difficult. As late as January 1996, only 36 percent of the potential recipients eligible for land under the peace accords had received their registration and fully completed the land transfer process, though 87 percent of the land had been transferred.

Despite these problems and others, the Security Council terminated the ONUSAL mission in April 1995, confident that the peace process in El Salvador was irreversible. On the Secretary-General's recommendation, a small political office, MINUSAL, was left behind to provide good offices and follow through on implementation of the outstanding obligations, in cooperation with UN agencies and other donors.

ONUSAL achieved many significant successes despite a few striking failures. Perhaps the most important factor in determining ONUSAL's greater success rate was the fact that the Salvadoran parties were more prepared to make peace than the Cambodian parties. Because the parties

---

[10] On the economic and social challenges facing El Salvador, see James K. Boyce et al., *Adjustment Toward Peace: Economic Policy and Post-war Reconstruction in El Salvador* (San Salvador: UNDP, 1995); and Graciana del Castillo, "The Arms for Land Deal in El Salvador," in Doyle, Johnstone, and Orr, 1997, pp. 342–66.

still mistrusted one another deeply and had trouble agreeing on the precise terms of their peace, they still needed the UN, but on the whole ONUSAL was asked to do relatively less than UNTAC. Thus ONUSAL became one of the most successful post–Cold War UN peace operations. While not all aspects of the peace accords have been fully implemented and problems of violence, weak institutions, and social and economic tensions remain, the UN was instrumental in bringing an end to the longest civil war in Latin America in the twentieth century.

The key to ONUSAL's success was that monitoring and facilitation (expert assistance) was sufficient because the parties had arrived at a hurting stalemate that favored genuine negotiation. In terms of our discussion of peacebuilding theory, the conflict generated problems of coordination or assurance, so monitoring and information provision was the optimal peacekeeping strategy. Combined with strategic peacebuilding— institutional transformation and technical assistance—ONUSAL's monitoring and facilitation was sufficient to promote cooperation.

Successes

In contrast, as we shall see, to Cambodia, the military element of the UN mission in El Salvador was a significant success. The armed conflict was brought to an end, the FMLN was fully demobilized and disarmed (if with some difficulty), and government forces were dramatically reduced, restructured, and, after great resistance, purged at senior levels. Although structural changes were not as deep as originally envisioned, unregistered military weapons remained in the hands of civilians, and the military still participated in internal security affairs (despite the new constitution's clear restrictions on such action); Salvadoran society was significantly demilitarized.

The human rights dimension of ONUSAL also stands out as an important success story. While human rights violations persist in El Salvador, the level of tolerated impunity has reduced dramatically. Together, the Truth Commission, Ad Hoc Commission, and the Joint Group (appointed to look into a resumption of political killings in 1994) achieved a credible threat of transparent exposure that would be backed by formal and informal sanctions. When the Ad Hoc Commission and the Truth lustrated (sacked) senior military officers and civilians both in the government and the FMLN and then forced the resignation of the Supreme Court a message was sent.[11] Though a significant step short of criminal accountability (due to the amnesties that accompanied the release of the Truth Commission report) and less effective than might have been hoped in generating

[11] See Ian Johnstone, "Rights and Reconciliation in El Salvador," in Doyle, Johnstone and Orr 1997.

Box 5.1 ONUSAL's Mandate

ESTABLISHMENT: ONUSAL was established by Security Council resolution 693 (May 20, 1991) to "monitor all agreements between the two parties . . . [ONUSAL's] initial mandate in its first phase as an integrated peacekeeping operation will be to verify the compliance by the parties with the Agreement on Human Rights signed at San Jose on 26 July 1990."[1] Initially, the mission consisted only of the Human Rights Division.

CHANGES TO MANDATE: Security Council resolution 729 (October 13, 1992) expanded the mandate, in line with the Secretary-General's recommendation to include verification and monitoring of "all the agreements once these are signed at Mexico City between the Government of El Salvador and [FMLN], in particular the Agreement on the Cessation of the Armed Conflict and the Agreement on the Establishment of a National Civil Police."[2] At this time, the Military and Police Divisions were established.

Security Council Resolution 832 (May 27, 1993) extended the mandate until November 30, 1993, and established the Electoral Division, mandated to monitor the election process.[3] By his report of August 30, 1993, the Secretary-General announced that the verification and destruction of FMLN weapons had been completed on August 18, as contemplated in the Peace Agreements.

TERMINATION: Security Council Resolution 920 (May 26, 1994) dissolved the electoral division and extended the mandate until November 30, 1994 as recommended by the Secretary-General's postelection report of May 11, 1994.[4] On November 11, 1994, the Council, in resolution 961, followed the Secretary-General's recommendation of extending the mandate until April 30, 1995, at which point the Secretary-General expected that the military and police personnel would no longer be necessary.[5] On April 28, 1995, the Council confirmed in resolution 991 that ONUSAL's mandate would terminate on April 30, 1995.[6]

[1] S/RES/693 (1991) *available at* http://ods-dds-ny.un.org/doc/RESOLUTION/GEN/NR0/596/29/IMG/NR059629.pdf
[2] S/RES/729 (1992) *available at* http://ods-dds-ny.un.org/doc/RESOLUTION/GEN/NR0/010/88/IMG/NR001088.pdf

continued

Box 5.1 continued

[3] S/RES/832 (1993) *available at* http://ods-dds-ny.un.org/doc/UNDOC/GEN/N93/313/32/IMG/N9331332.pdf

[4] S/RES/920 (1994) *available at* http://ods-dds-ny.un.org/doc/UNDOC/GEN/N94/230/11/PDF/N9423011.pdf

[5] S/RES/961 (1994) *available at* http://ods-dds-ny.un.org/doc/UNDOC/GEN/N94/464/53/PDF/N9446453.pdf

[6] S/RES/991 (1995) available at http://ods-dds-ny.un.org/doc/UNDOC/GEN/N95/128/67/PDF/N9512867.pdf

a "catharsis" in which Salvadoran society would come to terms with its past, they sent an important signal that impunity would no longer be tolerated, neither in El Salvador nor the international community.

A third area of success—though mixed—is that of promoting institutional reform. The peace process generated a range of constitutional and legal reforms that have opened the possibility of a new political framework for El Salvador. Of primary importance is the conversion of the FMLN into a legal political party, enabling El Salvador's first inclusive, democratic—if somewhat flawed—elections in 1994. A new National Civilian Police (PNC) and civilian police academy were created from scratch and have done relatively well despite attempts to politicize the force, problems with some internal abuses, and a serious postwar crime wave. The National Counsel for the Defense of Human Rights has established itself as a viable and trusted institution. The election of a new Supreme Court, albeit after great partisan wrangling, has created the opportunity for real change in a previously farcical judicial system. Moreover, these changes might stimulate progress in other areas of judicial reform and help create a truly independent and professional justice system.

Failures

The most striking setback of the Salvadoran peace process thus far has been the inability to bring the initial stages of the reintegration process to a satisfactory close. The first major problem has been that of land distribution. Long after the program was scheduled to be over, only 36 percent of the potential beneficiaries have received land and completed the titling and registry process. Even those beneficiaries that received land were saddled with debt and not given necessary credit and technical support, raising serious questions about their ability to pay off these debts and hold on to the land. A second major problem, in part because it has detracted attention from the critical land issue, was the violent protest of demobilized members of the Armed Forces and the subsequent decision to grant these forces more favorable terms.

A second area of difficulty has been that of public security. Not only has the new PNC been unable to cope with the crime wave in postwar El Salvador (including renewed death squad activity); there are numerous indications that criminality has taken root in the PNC itself, including such serious offenses as assassination, participation in illegal armed vigilante groups, and dramatic rises in the excessive use of force and other violations of due process. Equally serious has been the increasing use and institutionalization of the use of the military to address internal security concerns. On one hand, there appear to be few options to deal with pronounced lawlessness in parts of the country, especially given the insufficient numbers of PNC, their inexperience, and lack of specialized training. On the other hand, this precedent seriously challenges one of the most critical aspects of the constitutional reforms resulting from the entire peace process—that of permanently removing the military from internal security functions. Efforts to address this problem continue, both by the UN and bilaterally by the United States and others. However, lawlessness and use of the military for internal security functions remain a problem with little hope of any significant change in sight.

A third failure of the Salvadoran process was in the area of social and economic development. The parties not only attempted very little in the social and economic arena, but they failed on the few measures they undertook. Even if the highly problematic land transfer program were successful, the scope of the program would do little to affect the fundamental inequities in land distribution in the country. The Forum for Economic and Social Consultation was designed in part to make up for the lack of attention to such issues in the peace accords, but it made little progress other than in the area of labor rights, and this only after the United States threatened to revoke special trade privileges.

To sum up, ONUSAL provided the right treatment for the right problem: monitoring and facilitation, along with technical assistance for institution-building. In discharging most of its functions effectively, ONUSAL achieved what in chapter 2 we called "microlevel success," which in turn contributed positively to "macrolevel" peacebuilding success.

Administratively Controlling (but Barely) Peace in Cambodia

After more than twenty years of civil war and a genocidal campaign that killed more than 2 million people, Cambodia transitioned into a precarious peace in 1991. A long ideological struggle between the Khmer Rouge and several other factions had left the country with deep scars and very low levels of local capacities (see table 5.2). With low levels of income,

TABLE 5.2
Cambodia

	Cambodia (1970–75)	Cambodia (1975–91) UNTAC (1991–93)
Sovereign peace	Failure	Success
Participatory peace	Failure	Success
War type	"Nonethnic"	"Nonethnic"
Factions	2	4 (3 major)
UN mandate	None	Multidimensional PKO
Duration of UN mission (months)	n/a	22
Was UN present during the war? If so, for how long?	n/a	No
Troop strength of UN mission, if any	n/a	19,350
War duration (in months)	58	197
Real per capita GDP (year before war start; constant $)	915	391
Real per capita GDP (at end of the war; constant $)	399	1,014
GDP growth at end of the war (% annual change)	2.046	2.115
People killed during the war	156,000	2,000,000
People displaced during the war	360,000	500,000
Outcome of the war	Rebel victory	Treaty/Settlement
Was a treaty signed by most parties?	No	Yes
Date of the treaty, if any was signed	n/a	October 1991
Was the treaty implemented?	n/a	Yes
Primary commodity exports as % of GDP	5.2	1.9
Is the country a major oil exporter?	No	No
Ethnolinguistic fractionalization (100 = highest)	30	30
Ethnic heterogeneity index (1 = highly diverse)	0.186	0.186
Population at start of war (in thousands)	6,897	7,098
Area (square kilometers)	181,040	181,040
Effective Development Assistance as % of GDP	109.524	98.028

most of its educated citizens dead or in exile, and a modest rate of economic growth, Cambodia's prospects for a durable peace were dim. The successful transition to peace in Cambodia is a classic example of significant international capacities filling the gap for almost nonexistent local capacities to help offset high levels of hostility.

Our model of peacebuilding success works very well in this case—perhaps a little too well, since it predicts a probability of peacebuilding success of 0.97 percent. Cambodia is widely considered a case of successful peacebuilding, particularly when one compares the post-1993 period to the country's previous two decades' history. However, there were some failures both in the implementation of the mandate (which we discuss below) and at the "macrolevel," as low levels of violence persisted after the departure of the United Nations Transitional Authority in Cambodia (UNTAC) in 1993. The main influences on our high estimate of peacebuilding success in this case are the facts that the parties managed to overcome their hostility and sign a peace treaty that placed the UN at the top of key administrative tasks during the peace process; and that the UN was given the resources it needed to field a large multidimensional peacekeeping operation with both technical expertise to discharge civilian administrative tasks and a large military presence required to signal the commitment of the international community.

According to our model from chapter 3, the high levels of deaths and displacements in Cambodia (among the highest for all civil wars) should have increased the risk of failure in the peace process. Indeed, there were failures: halfway through, the Khmer Rouge abandoned the peace process altogether and Hun Sen's State of Cambodia launched not-so-covert attacks on its major rival within the peace process, Prince Ranariddh's FUNCINPEC party (more below). But the overall hostility index in our model was not as high in this case as for some other cases due to the fact that the war was not over ethnic and religious issues, and lasted a long time. Both factors pushed the parties to sign a treaty. Thus, the fact that we combine deaths and displacements with war type and war duration to create the hostility indices that we use in graphing the available space for peace (see the PB triangle for Cambodia in figure 5.2) might not be a good reflection of the depth of hostility in Cambodia. After all, this was the only civil war with a nonethnic genocide. And there may also be instances of poor fit between some of the proxy variables used in our model and the theoretically significant variables that should drive our predictions. For example, the primary commodity exports variable, which is very low for Cambodia (see table 5.2), would indicate no significant resource dependence, hence a higher probability of peacebuilding success. But in this case, our proxy does not pick up the illegal timber trade that was a major way that the Khmer Rouge were able to finance the war. Had the

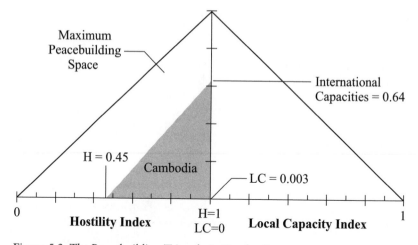

Figure 5.2 The Peacebuilding Triangle in Cambodia

resource-dependence proxy been better measured in this case, our estimate of peacebuilding success for Cambodia would have been lower.

But the main reason for the high estimate of peacebuilding success is that a coalition of UN-endorsed international mediators was able to help the parties to overcome their hostility to find common ground in a postwar settlement, which was mapped out in the Paris agreements of 1991. Here, too, our model could have been better, if it shed some light on how and why a treaty was signed. We delve into these questions in the rest of this case study, since our statistical analysis does not account for the positive influence of UN peacemaking prior to the deployment of UNTAC nor does it account for the bilateral pressures that were applied to each Cambodian faction by their principal supporters during the war. The UN's peacemaking was successful partly because the factions were deprived of external assistance and because they had grown tired from two decades of fighting. Thus, as in El Salvador, so in Cambodia, there was an important role for non-UN third-party mediation in leveraging the UN's peacebuilding efforts.

The path to peace in Cambodia was rocky. By some accounts, civil war or something close to that resumed around the elections of 1993, and a coup a few years later undermined the stability of the postwar political structure. In this regard, Cambodia might best be considered as a mixed-outcome case.[12] Such a high level of war-related devastation

[12] In the statistical analysis, we ran our model while coding this case both as a success and a failure to see how this change would affect the results. We also estimated an ordered logit, and coded this case as a mixed outcome (the dependent variable is ordered from failure, to "mixed" outcome, to success). See our online supplement for the results.

could not be fully corrected by a short UN mission, however well designed, and more extensive support was needed. Building an open political system after a civil war can be greatly assisted by a multidimensional
peacekeeping mission such as UNTAC, but the country's level of local
capacities and its democratic traditions are even more important. Two
decades of civil war in Cambodia and a relatively short horizon for the
UN's involvement meant that there was a large chance that the level of
political openness that UNTAC tried to build in Cambodia would decline soon after the peacekeepers left.

The key feature of managing the peace in Cambodia was that the UN
had a significant degree of administrative control over key elements of
the peace process. The UN was "at the helm" in the UNTAC between
1992 and 1993.[13] UNTAC was a classic case of a unified and integrated
mission, with an effective division of labor. Indeed, if there is one lesson
that should be drawn from the UNTAC operation, it is that an integrated and unified mission, with one organization at the helm, is essential both for establishing the unity of purpose that is needed to move toward peace and for succeeding overall in the face of many failures of its
components. Flexibility and organizational coherence were decisive in the
success that UNTAC achieved. That success did not preclude, however,
significant conflicts inside the mission or between the mission and other
actors and organizations.

The objectives of the security arrangements during the transitional period were the traditional ones: to stabilize the military situation, build
confidence among parties to the conflict, and prevent the risks of a return to warfare. The signatories of the Paris Agreements agreed to the
withdrawal and nonreturn of foreign forces, advisers, and military personnel; the implementation of a cease-fire; the termination of external
military assistance to all factions; the regroupment, cantonment, and demobilization of armed forces; and the release of all prisoners of war and
civilian internees. UNTAC, in short, was required to supervise a military stand-down including verification of the withdrawal of Vietnamese
troops and the cessation of external arms supply. It also undertook to supervise demining and to canton the forces of the four parties, which then
would be followed by the demobilization of 70 percent of the factions'
troops. But the true complexities of the security mission arose later,
when the military component had to step in to support a faltering civilian effort to organize the national elections. UNTAC also was required
to add two key new civilian duties.

---

[13] This section draws on Peou 2000; Findlay 1995; Ratner 1993, 1996; Doyle 1995 and
1999; Doyle, Johnstone, and Orr 1997; Brown and Zasloff 1998; Heder and Ledgerwood
1996; and Ashley 1998.

Box 5.2 UNTAC's Mandate

ESTABLISHMENT: The Paris Agreements granted extraordinary power to the UN during the transition period. UNTAC was required to assume traditional peacekeeping responsibilities:[1]

- To monitor the cease-fire and the withdrawal of all foreign forces and to supervise the cantonment and demobilization of Cambodian military forces;

- To control and supervise crucial aspects of civil administration;

- To organize and monitor the elections as a first step toward a system of liberal democracy, on the basis of pluralism; and, furthermore:

- To coordinate with the UN High Commissioner for Refugees (UNHCR) the repatriation of more than 370,000 refugees living in camps on the Thai side of the border;

- To foster an environment ensuring respect for human rights and fundamental freedoms, and;

- To help plan and raise funds for the social and economic rehabilitation of Cambodia.

CHANGES TO MANDATE: Regroupment to Secure Election (S/24800, 9/15/92)

TERMINATION: UNTAC withdrew in September 1993

[1] A/46/608-S/23177; S/23613 (2/19/92)

On the civilian side, the Paris Agreements focused on two key issues. First, they specified five areas of UNTAC control in the sphere of civil administration necessary to achieve the "neutral political environment" that would be conducive to the holding of "free and fair" elections. The areas specified for the strictest level of scrutiny and control over each of the four factions were defense, public security, finance, information, and foreign affairs. Lesser degrees of scrutiny were required over other governmental functions, such as education, public health, agriculture, fisheries, energy, transportation, and communications. These levels of scrutiny and control were considered necessary to ensure a politically neutral environment in which no faction (especially the State of Cambodia) would be able to employ state resources to tilt the electoral contest in its favor. The Secretary-General's special representative also had the apparent authority to appoint UNTAC officials within the factional administrations and to remove officials who did not respond to his directives.

Second, one of the Paris accord's most striking civilian features was that the international community and all four factions agreed to "a system of liberal democracy, on the basis of pluralism," as the foundation for the Cambodian constitution. Although it remains to be seen whether the Cambodians will embrace the principles and practice of constitutional democracy, the parties to the negotiation process (with the encouragement of the international community in general) explicitly agreed to a peace plan that required them to establish constitutional democracy in Cambodia. What was unique about this process was the UN's role in guaranteeing democracy. The agreements specified all the elements necessary for a constitutional democracy: periodic and genuine elections; freedom of assembly and association for all, including political parties; due process and equality before the law; and an independent judiciary. Indeed the Cambodian people's right of self-determination through free and fair elections became the hallmark and linchpin of the Paris Agreements.

For the first time, a UN operation (unlike those in Namibia, Nicaragua, Haiti, and Angola), was in charge of the entire organization and supervision of elections. UNTAC's responsibilities included establishing electoral laws and procedures, invalidating existing laws that would not further the settlement, setting up the polling, responding to complaints, arranging for foreign observation, and certifying the elections as free and fair. The creation of laws and procedures regarding elections was a critical function granted to UNTAC. The authority to draft legislation was not provided to UNTAC in other areas of civilian administration and signified an innovative and intrusive role for the UN in the internal affairs of a member state.

The Secretary-General divided UNTAC into seven "components," each with a role in the multidimensional mandate. Yashushi Akashi served as the special representative in overall command. The official budget came to $1.5 billion; unofficially, with the inclusion of pledged rehabilitation and repatriation assistance and off-budget costs, the amount would come to $2.5–$2.8 billion.

The Military Component had four functions: verifying the withdrawal of all foreign (Vietnamese) forces; supervising the cease-fire, cantonment, and demobilization of the military forces of the four factions; confiscating the caches of weapons and monitoring the cessation of all outside military assistance; and training in mine clearance. Commanded by Australian Lieutenant General John Sanderson, the force included twelve infantry battalions on peacekeeping duty from eleven countries, as well as engineering and unarmed military observers and other units, for a total of about 16,000 military personnel. Originally deployed to supervise the cantonment and demobilization of the factional armies, the Military Component redeployed in support of the election in November 1992.

The Civilian Police Component (CIVPOL) was mandated to monitor and control local officers in order to ensure that law and order were implemented fairly and that basic human rights were protected. With twenty-one provincial and two hundred district-level units and a total of thirty-six hundred, UNTAC managed eventually to field one monitor for each fifteen local civil police.

The Repatriation Component, led by the UN High Commissioner for Refugees (UNHCR), was to facilitate the return of more than 370,000 persons from Thailand and other areas. It was charged with verifying that individuals chose repatriation voluntarily, overseeing their transportation from the refugee camps to the desired location and providing immediate food and reintegration assistance. The work of the Rehabilitation Component was eventually assumed by the economic adviser to the special representative. He focused on the assessment and coordination of rehabilitation efforts in food security, health, training, housing, and education as well as on raising funds for Cambodian development. In Tokyo in June 1992, the Ministerial Conference on Rehabilitation and Reconstruction of Cambodia pledged $880 million and established the International Committee on the Reconstruction of Cambodia. But only $200 million had been disbursed by the end of August 1993, and the bulk of that was not issued until after the May election.

The Human Rights Component had the responsibility to foster an environment in which human rights would be respected and in which a free and fair election could take place. It attempted to meet this responsibility by instituting an education campaign, overseeing general human rights conditions, and investigating alleged human rights abuses. With a minuscule staff (one officer in each of Cambodia's provinces), this component faced an enormous challenge.

The Information/Education Division (Info/Ed) played a crucial role in apprising Cambodians of the content of the Paris Agreements, human rights conditions, UNTAC's role, and their own right to a free and fair election. Having established Radio UNTAC, the division promulgated this information throughout the country and supplemented its broadcasts with a variety of videos, billboards, and posters. It sought to educate

Cambodians about the voting process and the parties seeking their votes and to encourage the active participation of the electorate.

Although the UN had gained experience in some of these areas through past peacekeeping operations, the combination of these tasks made UN-TAC larger than any previous UN peacekeeping operation.

Important lessons emerge from the Cambodian peace operation, each of which is valuable for future operations. First, the peace agreement was comprehensive and multidimensional and fit the conflict. There were four Cambodian parties: The National United Front for an Independent, Neutral, Peaceful, and Co-operative Cambodia (FUNCINPEC), represented by King Sihanouk and his son Prince Ranariddh that led the independence of Cambodia from 1954 until the coup in 1970. King Sihanouk was the embodiment of Cambodian legitimacy. The second faction was the KPNLF, a republican and military group who staged a coup in 1970 with strong evidence of U.S. backing and a rather unfortunate outcome for Cambodia in the years 1970–75 as the government proceeded to collapse. Then there was the notorious Khmer Rouge, who took power in 1975 and inflicted an "auto-genocide" of about 1.5 million deaths out of a population of 9 million—a truly horrendous impact on the country and its future. Their opposition to any form of modern, pluralistic life is demonstrated by their opposition even to literacy. The best way they could identify literacy was by anyone who wore glasses, which was reason enough to be executed on the spot between 1975 and 1979! The last group, a splinter group from the Khmer Rouge, was eventually led by Hun Sen (the Cambodian People's Party [CPP] and State of Cambodia), following Vietnam's invasion—and rescue—of the Cambodians in December 1978. Vietnam established CPP as a puppet regime for the next decade that ruled with a very heavy hand, but also slowly began the recovery of the country.

Each of these partners had international patrons and each had differing degrees of legitimacy and effectiveness. The CPP had effectiveness; in the 1980s it ruled over 80 percent of the country. The coalition of FUNCINPEC, the Khmer Rouge, and KPNLF had international legitimacy, as reflected in their recognized seat at the UN. Then prince, now king, Sihanouk enjoyed wide and deep traditional legitimacy.

The challenge of peace, law, and order was joining effective government (the CPP) to legitimate government (the coalition of opposition forces in refugee camps on the Thai border, led by Prince Sihanouk). A stable government had to be both legitimate and effective. This was complicated, since each of the factions had an international patron that had a stake in the peace and a stake in resolving their conflicts in Cambodia for the broader purpose of ending the cold war. The CPP was backed by Vietnam and Russia; FUNCINPEC relied on the West, most clearly the

218

United States and France; the Khmer Rouge had residual, but marginal backing from the PRC; and the KPNLF, the smallest and declining faction, had U.S. support. Then there were regional leaders, all of whom had a stake. For some the stake was a special interest, but the broader stake was that of regional peace. Indonesia, Australia, Malaysia, and Thailand all had that interest and sought to transform Southeast Asia from a "war place" to a "marketplace." None of these actors could be excluded; each of them was tied together, and therefore an inclusive, comprehensive peace was necessary.[14]

The first effort at peace resolution relied on Australia and Indonesia, who brokered negotiations designed to create a power-sharing arrangement. These negotiations collapsed in 1989 at the first Paris Peace Conference. Unable to agree on sharing power, the parties then turned to the UN looking for an impartial outside body that could effect a transition to a new regime in which they could all coexist. They hoped that the people of Cambodia would solve their problem of deciding who should be the legitimate ruler of Cambodia, hoping as well that they could create an effective government on that basis. That was the underlying strategy of the next attempt at peace in Cambodia.

The 1991 Paris Peace Agreement was comprehensive and inclusive. It mandated a cease-fire and the return of 370,000 refugees from the Thai border. It attempted to foster human rights; but because the Khmer Rouge was a part of the Paris Peace Agreement, the only reference to the "auto-genocide" in the agreement was "avoiding a return to the unfortunate practices of the recent past." That is one price of an inclusive peace agreement. Then, more strikingly, it established a transitional authority to control civil administration in order to create a neutral political environment under which the parties could fairly compete for the national election. And lastly and most importantly, it mandated the UN to organize and direct, not merely to monitor or supervise, from the ground up a national election for Cambodia. This was a key provision: none of the parties trusted each other sufficiently to permit organization by the Cambodian parties.

To find a legitimate government when the parties could not agree on who should rule, the UN needed to step in as the unified temporary "transitional authority" at the helm. The Paris Agreement devised a solution in a temporary sovereign entity of all the factions, a Supreme National Council (SNC). If the SNC agreed, their agreement would constitute a

---

[14] For thorough accounts of the negotiations see Jin Song, "The Political Dynamics of the Peacemaking Process in Cambodia," in Doyle, Johnstone, and Orr 1997 and especially the participant interpretation of Solomon 1999.

transitional sovereign decision for Cambodia. If they failed to agree, Prince Sihanouk was authorized to make a decision in the name of the council. But, if he failed to act, then Special Representative Yasushi Akashi was authorized to act. Here was a lawyerly way of combining recognition of Cambodia's sovereign status—in a "Chapter 6 and 1/2," consent-based operation—with the need for transitional effective authority.

Turning to a second lesson—the management of the division of labor, task sharing, and command and control—UNTAC is an important example of success in trying circumstances. Akashi was at the helm of a unified, integrated international operation. He had formal legal command and control over the entire operation, civilian and military. The component organizations, such as UNHCR reported through him to the Security Council. It was a complex operation: 23,000 total personnel, including 15,000 military, commanded by General John Sanderson, an Australian. The very effective electoral component was run by Reginald Austin, who had successfully run the transitional election in Zimbabwe and the UN election in Namibia. His success reflected his prior experience. There was a CIVPOL of 1,800, but unfortunately this was one of the least effective CIVPOL operations. The Information and Education also played a key role in informing and persuading the Cambodian people of the significance of the election.

One important example of effective coordination at work was how the military very effectively supported the return of refugees and provided security for the refugee flow back into Cambodia. UNHCR also cooperated by accelerating the return of refugees, even though it knew that many of the regions of the country were not as safe as they ideally should have been. UNHCR realized that it was important to secure their return in time to be registered to vote, because voting was going to be the decisive outcome of this peace process.

The crucial payoff, however, of unified command and control was a very striking midcourse adjustment in the mandate. The Khmer Rouge defected from the peace when they refused to canton and demobilize their military forces. When they balked, Hun Sen's "State of Cambodia" withdrew its military forces from cantonment and refused to allow its administration to be controlled by the UN, creating circles of bureaucratic red tape that confused and stymied the UN officials. At this stage, with demobilization and the cease-fire collapsing around them, UNTAC decided to focus on the election. The UN would help to create a legitimate government that then could go on and tackle the other problems. The UNTAC military had lost its central mandate. But rather than going home and declaring the mission a failure, the UNTAC team met together and restructured the entire operation, turning the military component from a cantonment and demobilization mandate into an electoral security mandate. They repositioned all the battalions and took on a risky task, providing security for an election about to be held in the middle of a conflict threatening to escalate to civil war. This was a job that none of the national contingents had signed up to do, making this revision a remarkable achievement. This kind of unity is not impossible in coalition organizations with multiple chains of authority; it is just much more difficult without the formal unity that can create a sense of mutual responsibility and that can ensure that the components of the operation are judged together, rather than separately.

There were also some coordination problems. Among these were the normal institutional tensions present in a "Chapter 6 and 1/2" military operation. General Sanderson said that he was never in operational control of more than two-thirds of the forces. One battalion repeatedly abused Cambodian civilians; two military units refused to follow orders directly. There were also some ideological and political differences within the components, including a serious difference between the French military contingent and the overall force command, such that one French deputy force commander had to be sent home. Moreover, trying to get APRONUC (l'Autorité Provisoire des Nations Unies en Cambodge—the French translation of UNTAC) and UNTAC to cooperate was difficult. The civil administration operated in French; the rest of UNTAC operated in English. Some jealousies and numerous coordination problems arose.

The most important operational gap was the lack of an effective development component.[15] There was an economic component on the books, but it collapsed very quickly. UNTAC was incapable of mobilizing the World Bank, the Asian Development Bank, the International Monetary Fund, and others into playing an effective role to try to rebuild Cambodia, despite Cambodia's immense need. UNTAC focused on its mandate, the short run. And those organizations partly refused to cooperate because they refused to recognize the SNC as a sovereign entity to which one could lend money. The United States limited its bilateral aid because it regarded the "State of Cambodia" as a communist regime. These and other coordination failures among donor governments severely hampered what should have been a key function of UNTAC, which was to begin the rehabilitation of this devastated country.[16]

As a third lesson, the UNTAC experience also teaches that even the most effective division of labor is not sufficient to ensure success. UNTAC

---

[15] For a study of the gaps in the development effort and the post-UNTAC efforts by NGOs and aid-providers see, Grant Curtis, *Cambodia Reborn: The Transition to Democracy and Development* (Geneva: UNRISD, 1998) and Shawcross 1994.

[16] Curtis 1998, pp. 71–74.

would not have achieved its successes without the support of key nations and NGOs. Here there was no single lead nation, differing from some other missions in this respect. UNTAC was a truly multilateral, multinational, cooperative affair.

The "Extended P5," which were the permanent Security Council members joined by Japan, Australia, Indonesia, and others, met regularly to support Akashi and to solve some of these difficulties. Japan took a particular role in organizing financing for Cambodia. Overcoming initial UN resistance, the United States funded the radio and television station, which allowed the UNTAC operation to speak directly to the Cambodians and persuade them that the elections would be free and fair. (Ninety percent of the potential voters were registered and 90 percent of the registered voters then went on to vote in the election.) There were also some less than cooperative neighboring states. Thai military generals on the border cooperated with the Khmer Rouge in the illegal sale of gems and timber, and despite the efforts of the Thai government, this could not be stopped, until in 1996 and 1997, cut off from their sources of funds and riven by internal splits, the Khmer Rouge collapsed.

International NGOs played a key implementing role as usual, assisting refugees and supporting humanitarian assistance. Because of the devastation of Cambodia, there were virtually no Cambodian NGOs. UNTAC here was significantly innovative. They helped establish Cambodian NGOs in human rights, democracy, development, and women's rights, offering them start-up funding and advice. Those NGOs continue today to represent Cambodian civil society.

UNTAC thus succeeded, despite the many separate failures in the mandate, in establishing a government that is both legitimate and sovereign. The coalition government of FUNCINPEC and CPP was elected by the Cambodian people, and it had sovereign control over law and order and a monopoly of legitimate force in the 80 percent of Cambodia not subject to the Khmer Rouge. This was a striking success despite the defection of the Khmer Rouge, despite the bureaucratic resistance of Hun Sen's forces, despite the continuation of the civil war from 1991 through the elections in June 1993 and afterward, and despite the Khmer Rouge's decision to attack UNTAC with mines, ambushes, and other forms of aggression. Without the ability to adjust the mandate and redeploy its components—both of which should be credited to UNTAC's integrated division of labor—UNTAC would have had to close down. Instead, it persisted and organized a free and fair election, even in the face of the Khmer Rouge's violent opposition and considerable efforts at intimidation by Hun Sen's forces. The election led to a coalition government composed of the CPP and FUNCINPEC. That is, the faction that had bureaucratic and military power (CPP) and the faction that had traditional popular legitimacy (FUNCINPEC) together, after serious squabbling and threats, established a nationally legitimate and internationally recognized government.

There were however two important and abiding failures. One was the failure to start the desperately needed peacebuilding—the rehabilitation and development of Cambodia. With 85 percent of the population in the countryside, assisting the development of the countryside was (and is) essential to a sustainable peace in Cambodia. Although industry and services are likely to lead Cambodia's integration into the ASEAN region, rural development can support national development or be a drag on it.[17] But UNTAC introduced into Cambodia a group of twenty-three thousand very well paid (by Cambodian standards) foreigners. (The daily subsistence allowance in Cambodia of UNTAC civilians was $140 a day and the GDP per capita of Cambodians was $240 per year.) UNTAC spending had a very severe inflationary impact on the Cambodian economy. This, plus urban bias, rapid urbanization, and the introduction of AIDS to an unprotected population left severe problems that now needed to be addressed.[18]

The second and equally important failure was the absence of a training mandate—a mandate to train and assist the improvement of the police, judiciary, and army. Cambodian bureaucrats, soldiers, and police continued to identify themselves as FUNCINPEC or CPP, rather than Cambodian. UNTAC thus left Cambodia extremely short of trained civil service and military personnel and split by continuing factional governance, rather than unified with national governance. This was a legacy that made stable governance so difficult from 1993 onward and eventually contributed to the 1997 coup. It continues today to make the effective government of Cambodia a severe challenge, especially given the developmental needs of the country.

To sum up: UNTAC and Cambodia experienced great success, significantly because of the unification of command and control, which allowed those key adjustments in the mandate to produce overall success despite the many separate failures. But at the same time, the centralization of authority with the UN at the helm may have stymied larger, long-term peacebuilding adjustments of the mandate. UNTAC was a single organization that was going in and getting out together, looking for an

---

[17] Caroline Hughes, *The Political Economy of Cambodia's Transition, 1991–2001* (New York: Routledge Curzon, 2003), pp. 30–33; Judy Ledgerwood, "Rural Development in Cambodia," in Frederick Brown and David Timberman, eds., *Cambodia and the International Community* (New York: Asia Society, 1998); and Michael Doyle, *Peacebuilding in Cambodia*, IPA Policy Briefing Series (New York: IPA, December, 1996).

[18] Uphoff-Kato, in Doyle, Johnstone, and Orr 1997; see Pouligny 2004, esp. chap. 6; and Marks 1994.

electoral exit to justify withdrawal (especially given the UN's many responsibilities in 1993). UNTAC's unity made adding new functions to the overall mandate difficult (establishing UN TV, a training function) and may have precluded the recruitment of new organizations that could have begun the longer-term peacebuilding process, before the peacekeeping was over. This may be the hidden cost of having one organization at the helm.

Executive Implementation of Peace in Eastern Slavonia

In the face of much skepticism about the UN's effectiveness in peacebuilding, it is worth recalling that in the shadow of the Dayton Agreement and hardly noticed by international public opinion, the UN achieved a success under very trying circumstances in the Croatian region of Eastern Slavonia.[19] While it obviously does not hold all the answers to the tough questions of enforcing and building a viable peace in Kosovo, the experience in Eastern Slavonia provides more than a few hints of how the UN could facilitate the return of traumatized refugees and help the transition from a war-torn society to a peaceful and civil one.

Eastern Slavonia was under the "executive authority" of the UN from 1996 to 1998.[20] When the Croatian army overran the Serb Republics in 1995, Eastern Slavonia was temporarily spared and became a refuge for Serbs from all over Croatia. It was then that the UN, with Croatian acquiescence and largely at the insistence of the Americans, took over, to recreate a multiethnic area with Serb minority rights, but under Croatian sovereignty.

What they found seemed to set the stage for yet another round of UN frustration and failure. Thousands of Serbs occupied houses owned by Croatians before the war, while Croatian refugees waited impatiently in

---

[19] This section draws on Doyle's "Anatomie eines Erfolgs: Die UN-Mission in Ostslawonien (Anatomy of a success: The UN mission in Eastern Slavonia)," written with Jan Mueller, *Internationale Politik* 53, no. 6 (June 1998), pp. 34–38; Derek Boothby, "The Political Challenges of Administering Eastern Slavonia," *Global Governance* 10 (2004): 37–51; and see for its economic component, Jana Smoljan, "Socio-Economic Aspects of Peacebuilidng: UNTAES and the Organization of Employment in Eastern Slavonia," *International Peacekeeping* 10, no. 2 (Summer 2003).

[20] Ambassador Jacques Klein, the UNTAES Special Representative, and numerous officials of UNTAES shared their insights during interviews in July, 1997, and July, 1998, in Vukovar. Particularly helpful were: Philip Arnold (head of public affairs), Gary Collins (legal adviser), Didier Fau (reconstruction adviser), Commissioner Fallmann (CIVPOL chief), Jaque Grinberg (head of political affairs), Jeannie Peterson and Erica Johnson (reconciliation unit), Alister Livingstone (chief of border monitors), Fedor Klimtchouk (adviser on Council of Municipalities), and Mak Peterson (political affairs).

Box 5.3 UNTAES's Mandate

ESTABLISHMENT: UNTAES was established by Security Council resolution 1037 (January 15, 1996) to assist with the implementation of the November 12, 1995, "Basic Agreement" between the Croatian government and the local Serb Authorities.[1] It grew out of the May 21, 1995, signing of the Dayton Peace Agreement. The Secretary-General's December 13, 1995, report identified the purpose of the transitional administration as the peaceful reintegration of Eastern Slavonia into Croatia. Its end goal was to be a demilitarized region with a multiethnic government in Croatia after free and fair elections and the right of return for all displaced persons.

According to the Department of Peacekeeping Operations, UNTAES was mandated to do the following: "supervise and help in the demilitarization of the region as provided for in the Basic Agreement, which was carried out by the parties within 30 days after the full deployment of UNTAES; oversee the return of refugees and displaced persons to their homes; establish and train a temporary police force to build professionalism among the police and confidence among all ethnic communities; monitor treatment of offenders and the prison system; organize elections for all local government bodies; maintain international monitors along the international borders of the region to facilitate the free movement of persons across existing borders; restore the normal functioning of all public services in the region without delay; monitor the parties' commitment to respect human rights and fundamental freedoms; cooperate with the International Tribunal for the former Yugoslavia in its task of investigating and prosecuting war crimes; promote the realization of the commitments made in the Basic Agreement between Croatia and local Serb authorities and contribute to the overall maintenance of peace and security."[2]

CHANGES TO MANDATE: By his report of May 20, 1996, the Secretary-General reported that the mission was fully deployed. Demilitarization began on May 21, 1996, as envisioned in the Basic Agreement and was completed on June 20, 1996. In Resolution 1079 (November 15, 1996), the Security Council extended the mandate through July 15, 1997, and asked that after the "successful holding of elections and no later than 1 July 1997 Secretary-General provide recommendations for a further UN presence for the six month period starting on July 16, 1997."[3] Resolution 1120 (July 14, 1997) further extended the mandate until January 18, 1998. The resolution

continued

Box 5.3 continued

"endorse[d] the plan for the gradual devolution of the executive responsibility for civil administration in the region by the Transitional Administrator" and approved the "drawdown of the UNTAES military component by 15 October 1997," both proposed by the Security Council in his June 23, 1997, report.[4]

TERMINATION: In Resolution 1145 (December 18, 1997) the Security Council confirmed that the mandate would terminate on January 15, 1998.[5]

[1] S/RES/1037 (1996) *available at* http://ods-dds-ny.un.org/doc/UNDOC/GEN/N96/007/55/PDF/N9600755.pdf
[2] http://www.un.org/Depts/DPKO/Missions/untaes_b.htm#MANDATE
[3] S/RES/1079 (1996) *available at* http://ods-dds-ny.un.org/doc/UNDOC/GEN/N96/322/26/PDF/N9632226.pdf
[4] S/RES/1120 (1997) *available at* http://ods-dds-ny.un.org/doc/UNDOC/GEN/N97/195/04/PDF/N9719504.pdf
[5] S/RES/1145 (1997) *available at* http://ods-dds-ny.un.org/doc/UNDOC/GEN/N97/375/35/PDF/N9737535.pdf

camps just outside the UN-controlled zone; paramilitaries like the notorious Arkan freely roamed the country and dominated the political scene; the main city of Vukovar (which holds enormous symbolic importance for the Croats as their "Stalingrad") and the economy were utterly devastated, and what little economic activity there was consisted of smuggling timber, cigarettes, and stolen cars. Moreover, atrocities like the Ovcara massacre, in which the Serbs killed dozens of Croatians, had left memories that seemed to make any dialogue, let alone reconciliation, impossible. Close to a million mines and countless weapons left over from the war made the region a powder keg, ready to blow up any minute that the Serbs realized that their struggle for autonomy had been lost for good and felt that they had no future in an independent Croatia.

In the face of these extreme challenges, the UN avoided another failure and achieved a successful UN-led transition. How? Our model offers helpful cues. Despite high levels of postwar hostility, Croatia had high levels of local capacities relative to other civil war countries (see table 5.3). Its local capacities, combined with a muscular transitional administration, were able to restore effective governance and isolate spoilers like Arkan. Croatia was one of the richest countries to have had a civil war in the post-1945 period (its per capita GDP given in table 5.3 is that corresponding to the period that Croatia was still a Yugoslav

TABLE 5.3
Croatia

	Yugoslavia (Croatia, 1991) UNPROFOR/UNCRO (1992–95)	Croatia (1992–95) UNTAES (1996–99)
Sovereign peace	Failure	Success
Participatory peace	Failure	Success
War type	"Ethnic"	"Ethnic"
Factions	3 (Serbia and Serb secessionists in Croatia counted separately)	3 (including Serbia)
UN mandate	Traditional PKO	Enforcement and Transitional Admin.
Duration of UN mission (months)	45	93
Was UN present during the war? If so, for how long?	No	Yes; 46 months
Troop strength of UN mission, if any	39,922	15,522
War duration (in months)	7	46
Real per capita GDP (year before war start; constant $)	4,548 (Yugoslavia)	5,808
Real per capita GDP (at end of the war; constant $)	2,740	—
GDP growth at end of the war (% annual change)	–39.75	4.3
People killed during the war	2,000	1,000–8,000
People displaced during the war	320,000	386,000
Outcome of the War	Rebel victory	Treaty/Settlement
Was a treaty signed by most parties?	No	Yes
Date of the treaty, if any was signed	n/a	November 1995
Was the treaty implemented?	n/a	Yes
Primary commodity exports as % of GDP	—	11.35 (imputed)
Is the country a major oil exporter?	No	No
Ethnolinguistic fractionalization (100 = highest)	75	33
Ethnic heterogeneity index (1 = highly diverse)	0.8	0.375
Population at start of war (in thousands)	23,928	4,782.3
Area (square kilometers)	230,090	56,540
Effective development assistance as % of GDP	—	—

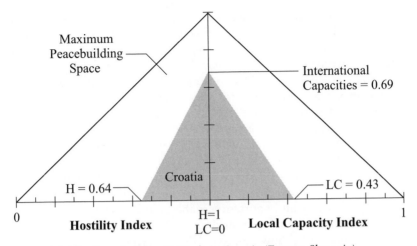

Figure 5.3 The Peacebuilding Triangle in Croatia (Eastern Slavonia)

Republic, before the start of the war). The combination of international and local capacities significantly expanded the space for peace in Croatia in 1995 (see figure 5.3).

As a result, our model predicts a high (0.97) probability of peacebuilding success after the second Croatian war. This prediction is sharply contrasted to the low prediction of peacebuilding success after the first Croatian war in 1991 (0.20). Why are the two cases so different? Both were ethnoreligious wars, fought between roughly the same factions, with similar motives (secession), and they generated relatively similar levels of deaths and displacements (see table 5.3). One important difference was that local capacities were greater in Croatia than in the former Yugoslavia as a whole, and this influences the model's predictions, since it is the prewar levels of national-level capacities that we measure and use in our model, so in the first Croatian war local capacities refer to Yugoslavia as a whole, whereas in the second, they refer to Croatia only. Moreover, rapidly deteriorating economic conditions in the areas of the former Yugoslavia in 1991, where by some accounts economic growth declined by as much as 40 percent, significantly increased the risk of new violence. According to theories of civil war onset that we reviewed in chapter 2, the decline in economic opportunity would have resulted in an abundance of rebel supply among young unemployed men. By contrast, economic growth was rising in post-1995 Croatia, reducing the available supply of rebels.[21]

---

[21] The pool of potential rebels was also smaller in the second Croatian war, as they were limited to enclaves of Serbs in the new Croatian state.

Another important difference is that after the end of the second war, the UN could work from an extensive agreement between the Croatian government and the local Serb leaders, which envisaged a clear political outcome toward which all sides could work. And the role of political elites was very different in the two periods. While nationalist elites were engaged in mass mobilization for war in 1991, they were much more conciliatory after the Dayton Accord was signed in 1995. This agreement also had the backstage support of the great Balkans political opportunist Slobodan Milosevic, who wanted to avoid an influx of Serbian refugees into Serbia proper, and the Croatian nationalist theologian Franjo Tudjman, who wanted a reintegrated Croatia under terms acceptable to the international community. The role of elites is not captured by our model, but it is an important variable in this case as in most other civil war transitions that we studied.

Most importantly, however, the UN mandate envisaged unprecedented executive authority for the transitional administrator in the region, enabling the UN to "govern" and to practically become a colonial administrator, or even a benevolent dictator. While the UN had deployed more than 30,000 troops in response to the first Croatian war, most of these troops were quickly occupied by the surge of violence in the Bosnian war. The mandate and resources, moreover, given to those troops were poorly conceived, as we explain in chapter 4, and a traditional peacekeeping mandate was authorized where there was no peace to keep.[22] By contrast, the UN's resolve in Eastern Slavonia was firmer. The UN mission was supported by American firepower and had the mandate needed for the job.

Commitments on paper were not enough, though: it took the forceful American general/diplomat Jacques Klein and a team of exceptionally tough negotiators to bring Serbs and Croats together time and time again, persuade them to focus on the future rather than history, and make them live up to the painfully reached agreements. Klein, usually chewing on a cigar and wearing an air force bomber jacket on his trips around the region, ceaselessly shuttled between Zagreb, Belgrade, New York, Washington, Vukovar, and the capitals of the countries providing peacekeeping troops, in order to keep vital international support for the peacebuilding process. Importantly, the mission also succeeded because various capitals left Klein alone (or let him get away with not asking permission). Klein also had to tread a thin line between using and thereby possibly losing his

---

[22] Our statistical analysis suggested that large troop deployments with narrow (weak) mandates are ineffective and may actually increase the risk of peacebuilding failure if they are sent into countries where the parties are still committed to war.

extensive authority and appearing as yet another UN pushover in the eyes of local leaders. More than once, he had to make impromptu speeches to Serbian crowds or storm into local meetings to get agreements hammered out.

But talking and international threats can go only so far. Ultimately, this proactive, forceful leadership was made possible because Klein had 5,000 soldiers, a tank unit, attack helicopters, and NATO air power to back him up. From the very start, the UN demonstrated that it was willing to flex its—for UN missions unprecedented—military muscle, but also to work with local Serb leaders and authorities. With this combination of authority and cooperation, the UN oversaw the demilitarization of the region and arrested one Serb war criminal. It also gave an ultimatum to the Serb paramilitaries plundering the profitable oilfields in the southern part of the region, whereupon a convoy of Mercedes and Audis left for Serbia proper. Finally, a not-too-corrupt multiethnic police force was established, and elections were held in April 1997. The elections in particular, despite being chaotic and delayed, made the Serbs switch out of their state of denial that reintegration would actually happen. The UN also established a market at the border between Eastern Slavonia and Croatia proper, enabling friends and relatives to meet and starting reconciliation at a grassroots level. All these steps toward reintegration not only made the Serbs increasingly trust the UN, but also slowly gave them a feeling that they had a stake in the Croatian political system.

One cannot forget that these successes had their paternalist underside: the UN practically had to handpick moderate Serb leaders, shield them from their more extremist competitors, and suggest policies (and even appropriate speeches) to them. While some of these leaders matured into politicians trusted by the local population, others still lack basic political skills and have become heavily dependent on the UN at a time when they should stake their own political claims in Zagreb and try to become players on the national political scene.

Moreover, and acknowledging UNTAES's success in reestablishing the rule of law, genuine reconciliation and rehabilitation were as remote at the end of the mission as they were at its beginning. Very few Croatian refugees chose to return. And many Serbs still trembled and suffered shock when they crossed into the rest of Croatia, especially when they felt they might run into prewar friends. Vukovar itself remained a ghost town, in which only fancy boutiques, a carwash, and cafés, all run by the local gangsters, have been reconstructed. And there was an air of resignation in the region, although many Serbs were aware that, as one man in a village café said, "our stupid leaders are to blame." The only certainty was that at least the old people would not pack up and go to Serbia, since, as one young Serb woman explained, "they have lived here all their lives and they want to die here." Younger Serbs harbored deep suspicions about what was going to happen in a fully sovereign Croatia. A young Serb woman, who wanted to be a high school teacher before the war, told a rueful joke to illustrate the subtle or not so subtle discrimination that the Serbs expected to take place in the public services and schools: A Croatian teacher asks a Croatian pupil: "What was the name of the big ship that sank in 1912?" "Titanic," answers the pupil. "Full marks!" the teacher responds. Then the next Croatian student is asked how many people died: "Fifteen hundred," he says proudly. "Brilliant!" the teacher replies. "So, Jelena," the teacher finally asks the Serb pupil, "what were their names?"[23]

UN peacebuilding set up a stable political framework and gave the Serb minority both a stake in the system and a guarantee of basic securities, opening up a window of opportunity for genuine peacebuilding. But, as one veteran peacekeeper said, while peacebuilding offers the opportunity for once-warring sides to live together, it does not make them like each other. If the UN were to do as much in Kosovo to restore the Kosovars to their homes and protect any Serbs who chose to remain, it would have accomplished a great deal indeed.

Dayton's Dueling Missions and Brcko—Dayton's Supervisory Footnote

The management of the peace under the Dayton Agreement was a different and much less coherent example of multidimensional peacekeeping.[24] To begin with, the Dayton Agreement may look like one settlement but it actually contained two distinct plans for peace, ironically mirroring its formula for "one Bosnia-Herzegovina, two 'Entities.'" (The "entities" are the Muslim-Croat federation and the Bosnian Serb republic.) The Clinton administration adopted the first plan: essentially, a combination of a military assistance effort and a traditional peacekeeping

---

[23] Doyle benefited from many interviews with officials and residents of the area and officials in Zagreb, some of whom preferred to remain anonymous. Particularly helpful were: Tanya Mihailovic, Andrija Matic (deputy prefect, Vukovarsko-Srijemska Zupania), M Stanimirovic (president Vukovar Council), Branka Kaselv (head, Center for Peace) and the residents of the Displaced Persons camp, Osijek.

[24] This section draws on Cousens and Doyle 1995 and Holbrooke 1998, chap. 19, "Slow Start") and Elizabeth Cousens and Chetan Kumar, eds., *Peacebuilding as Politics: Cultivating Peace in Fragile Societies* (Boulder, CO: Lynne Rienner, 2001).

operation. The U.S.-led multilateral forces would serve as a buffer to help Bosnian Serbs and Bosnian Muslims stay put on their respective sides of a "Zone of Separation." At the same time, the force would stabilize the balance of military power on the ground—building up the Bosnians and building down the Serbs—so that U.S. troops could leave in one year with the expectation that each party had defensible and sustainable borders.

There was, however, another peace plan in the 130 pages of the Dayton Agreement. This second plan was one of peacebuilding—arguably the most ambitious multidimensional peace operation ever undertaken. It was comprehensive, addressing issues from a new Bosnian constitution (the full text was there!), resettlement of refugees, human rights abuses, civilian policing, negotiation of property claims, preservation of national monuments, and reconstruction of highways and civilian infrastructure. In its details, it demonstrated how much has been learned from both successes and mistakes of past peace operations in Cambodia, El Salvador, Haiti, and Somalia. This second, civilian plan recognized that sustainable peace depended on rebuilding "civil society"; it also afforded room for nongovernmental actors to play a crucial role in that task.

The peacekeeping management trouble resided in the gap between the U.S. focus on selling the first, narrowly military plan and the need to build political support for the second, ambitiously political plan that was, arguably, the only plan that mattered if peace in Bosnia-Herzegovina was to be lasting or genuine. Ideally, the first plan should have been seen as a necessary condition for the second: establishing the secure context in which the residents of the former Yugoslavia, with aid from various nonmilitary agencies, could build their own peace.

But the two plans could also collide. Most importantly, the military plan assumes that the ethnically intermixed Muslim-Croat Federation was viable. Much peacebuilding would be needed to make it so, and this is progressing slowly at best. Slowing down progress was administrative collision. Strikingly, Dayton made almost no provision for linking command and control between military and civilian authorities. In its strictly military provisions, the details of command and control were impeccably clear. The proposed Implementation Force (IFOR) would operate under the authority and direction of the North Atlantic Council and according to the well-defined NATO chain of command. Yet substantial operations by new and existing civilian agencies were authorized under the Dayton Accord. These activities would have to be protected. All of these spilled over into arenas of military activity, but none of them were clearly integrated with military command and control. The surprise was that this bugbear of American political debate was not addressed in a document that was substantially a Washington creation.

A simple list makes the point. The UNHCR was charged with managing the repatriation of refugees and displaced persons. A special commission under the supervision of the European Court of Human Rights was to adjudicate property disputes. The Organization of Security and Cooperation for Europe (OSCE) set up a Provisional Election Commission to oversee elections. The UN set up and directed an International Police Task Force to train and supervise local police. The Council of Europe and the OSCE together handled human rights. UNESCO was assigned the development of a commission to deal with the preservation of "National Monuments." And all civilian implementation was to be supervised by a soon-to-be-designated "High Representative."

Which was the full extent of Dayton's treatment of military-civilian command and control? That the High Representative must "exchange information and maintain liaison" with IFOR. The trouble here was that IFOR was expected to protect all of these activities that together encompassed the meat of the agreement. Yet, it was asking the impossible—or depending on extreme good luck—to expect IFOR to adequately protect activities over which it had no formal control or to support adequately activities that it did not wish to protect. Uncertain chains of command have bedeviled far less ambitious operations than the one proposed in Bosnia and Herzegovina. The UN's specific role was defined clearly but in narrow terms.

Under these circumstances, failure to coordinate military and civilian efforts has plagued peace missions in the past. As we saw in Cambodia, polling sites had to be closed where the UN force could not offer adequate protection from Khmer Rouge violence. In El Salvador, the schedule of the entire mission had to be adjusted to accommodate the differing rates of progress of the various aspects of the peace accord. Who would make those decisions for Bosnia?

Beyond command and control, the Dayton plan needed to speak more explicitly about the role of information. Particularly when the task envisaged is complex and multidimensional, information that is adequate, reliable, and timely is crucial. In Cambodia it was crucial that the UN could directly inform the Cambodians about the purposes and plans of the peace operation. By doing so, it helped win their trust in a secret ballot, which allowed the make-or-break election run by the UN to succeed, despite efforts by some of the parties to disrupt it. Access to reliable information at the grassroots level is especially crucial in a context like Bosnia, where basic trust has been destroyed between former neighbors and communities. Absence of information and its manipulation fanned the fear and insecurity among residents of Bosnia and Herzegovina that allowed the war to escalate. In Cambodia a UN-run radio

Box 5.4 UNMIBH's Mandate

ESTABLISHMENT: UNMIBH was established by Security Council Resolution 1035 (December 21, 1995), which created the United Nations International Police Task Force (IPTF) and a UN civilian office in Bosnia and Herzegovina as contemplated in the December 14, 1995, Peace Agreement.[1]

The IPTF's mandate was as follows: "monitoring, observing and inspecting law enforcement activities and facilities, including associated judicial organizations, structures and proceedings; advising law enforcement personnel and forces; training law enforcement personnel; facilitating, within the IPTF mission of assistance, the parties' law enforcement activities; assessing threats to public order and advising on the capability of law enforcement agencies to deal with such threats; advising government authorities in Bosnia and Herzegovina on the organization of effective civilian law enforcement agencies; assisting by accompanying the parties' law enforcement personnel as they carry out their responsibilities, as the Task Force deems appropriate."[2]

CHANGES TO MANDATE: After the Peace Implementation Conference (December 4–5, 1996), UNMIBH's mandate was expanded by Security Council Resolution 1088 (December 12, 1996) to include dealing with investigations of human rights abuses by law enforcement officials.[3] The mandate was also extended until December 21, 1997.

By Resolution 1103 (March 31, 1997) the Security Council endorsed the recommendation in the Secretary-General's March 14, 1997 report regarding international policing of Brcko and authorized an increase of 186 police personnel.[4] Shortly thereafter, the Security Council endorsed the Secretary-General's recommendation that more police experts in specialized fields be included in the mission and added 120 civilian personnel to UNMIBH by Resolution 1107 (May 16, 1997).[5]

Security Council Resolution 1144 (December 19, 1997) extended the mandate until June 21, 1998, and encouraged the Secretary-General to restructure the IPTF in accordance with the recommendations of the Bonn Peace Implementation Conference.[6] This involved: "(a) the creation of specialized IPTF training units to address key public security issues, such as refugee returns; organized crime, drugs, corruption and terrorism; and public security crisis management

continued

Box 5.4 continued

(including crowd control); as well as training in the detection of financial crime and smuggling; and (b) cooperation with the Council of Europe and OSCE, under the coordination of the High Representative, in a programme of judicial and legal reforms, including assessment and monitoring of the courtsystem, development and training of legal professionals and restructuring of institutions within the judicial system."[7]

By Resolution 1168 (May 21, 1998),[8] thirty more civilian police were added to the mission and by Resolution 1184 (7/16/1998) a monitoring program of the court system (later known as the Judicial Assessment Program) was approved.[9]

TERMINATION: UNMIBH's mandate was extended several more times before the final extension mandated in Resolution 1423 (7/12/02).[10] On 12/31/02 UNMIBH's mandate was terminated, in preparation for the handover to the Europe Union Police Mission, which took over on 1/1/03.

[1] S/RES/1035 (1995) *available at* http://ods-dds-ny.un.org/doc/UNDOC/GEN/N95/413/60/PDF/N9541360.pdf

[2] http://www.un.org/Depts/dpko/missions/unmibh/mandate.html

[3] S/RES/1088 (1996) *available at* http://ods-dds-ny.un.org/doc/UNDOC/GEN/N97/026/19/PDF/N9702619.pdf

[4] S/RES/1103 (1997) *available at* http://ods-dds-ny.un.org/doc/UNDOC/GEN/N97/085/71/PDF/N9708571.pdf

[5] S/RES/1107 (1997) *available at* http://ods-dds-ny.un.org/doc/UNDOC/GEN/N97/128/99/PDF/N9712899.pdf

[6] S/RES/1144 (1997) *available at* http://ods-dds-ny.un.org/doc/UNDOC/GEN/N97/375/23/PDF/N9737523.pdf

[7] http://www.un.org/Depts/dpko/missions/unmibh/mandate.html.

[8] S/RES/1168 (1998) *available at* http://ods-dds-ny.un.org/doc/UNDOC/GEN/N98/141/10/PDF/N9814110.pdf

[9] S/RES/1184 (1998) *available at* http://ods-dds-ny.un.org/doc/UNDOC/GEN/N98/207/87/PDF/N9820787.pdf

[10] S/RES/1423 (2002) *available at* http://ods-dds-ny.un.org/doc/UNDOC/GEN/N02/477/85/PDF/N0247785.pdf

---

and UN-sponsored Cambodian public information troupes delivered accurate and unbiased information across the country. Any lasting peace settlement needs to restore a climate of truth.

Peace Piecemeal in Brcko

Some thought that the Republika Srpska would fall into line and acquiesce to the parameters of the Dayton Peace through remote pressure.[25] Serbs in the region regularly remind Americans that we too had our ethnic cleansings in the nineteenth-century West (as if that was reason to applaud their Wounded Knees). Ironically, some of the Western strategy seems to have lingered in U.S. attitudes toward shaping a peace in Bosnia, at least if the views of Meriwether Lewis, writing in the 1800s, of the Lewis and Clark expedition are given weight:[26] " 'If trade between the British and the Sioux were prohibited for a few years,' he wrote, 'the Sioux will be made to feel their dependance [sic] on the will of our government for their supplies of merchandise, and in the course of two or three years, they may most probably be reduced to order without the necessity of bloodshed.' " Merriwether Lewis was anticipating the pacification of the Sioux by cutting them off from overland British trade from Canada. Dayton anticipated the pacification of the Serbs through trade sanctions and peacekeeping, once they were cut off from Serbia. But a degree of peace arrived only when NATO, the Office of the High Representative (OHR) and the UN became much more closely involved in governance, as they did in the small district of Brcko in northern Bosnia.

Brcko's history was indeed special, but the international mandate was even more so. Brcko municipality was a once-productive port of northern Bosnia, on the Sava River, the northern border of Bosnia separating it and Croatia. Its prewar area of 80 square kilometers and its population of 88,000 composed of 44 percent Bosniac (Muslim), 25 percent Croat (Catholic), 21 percent Serb (Orthodox), and 10 percent "other" (including Roma) was not atypical of Yugoslav mixed towns. In May 1992, Jugoslav National Army and Serb paramilitaries took control of the town and killed or drove out the Bosniacs and Croats. Many war crimes occurred in the *grad* (town center) where estimates range from 3,000 to 6,000 deaths, most notoriously at the Luka Port Facilities under the control of Jelisic, the self-proclaimed Serb "Adolf," later convicted by the Hague Tribunal. In the course of the war, 26,000 or so Serb displaced persons (refugees) from Sarajevo or elsewhere settled in the town. Bosniacs and Croats formed separate ethnic municipalities in Federation Brka (Bosniac) and Ravne Brcko (Croat). Today, entire Brcko, including Brka and Ravne Brcko, has a population of 84,000, which is roughly 49 percent Serb, 36 percent Bosniac, and 15 percent Croat.[27]

---

[25] This section benefited from interviews with Supervisor Bill Farrand and Mr. Terry O'Neil, Jesse Bunch, Bill Quayle, Mike Austin, Eamon O'Riordan, Lieutenant Colonel Connor, Ms. Katya Sienkewicz, Mayor Kisic of Brcko, and deputy mayors Ivan Krndelj and Mirsad Islamovic, Mr. Osman Osmanovic and the Brcko police patrols that kindly let Doyle join them, in the summers of 1999 and 2000.

[26] Stephen Ambrose, *Undaunted Courage* (New York: Simon and Schuster, 1996), p. 206.

[27] See Doyle interview with Terry O'Neil, June 22, 2000.

Today, the economy is defined by unemployment, about 60 to 70 percent. Before the war the district had thirty-four publicly owned enterprises, including port facilities, textile, meat, shoe, and car battery industries, all destroyed during the war. Today, they provide employment for only two thousand, where previously fifteen thousand were employed in those enterprises. Agriculture and minerals were also key contributors to the economy before the war and can be so again, once the mines are cleared, equipment is restored, and ethnic tensions abate. The Port of Brcko was once a major facility. In 1984 cargo traffic reached a high of 744,000 tons, but fell afterward due to the decline of the Yugoslav economy and the war, 1991–95. Major items were coal, steel products, and sand and gravel (together 95 percent) and then forest products, fertilizers, and grain equipment. Now the port needs extensive rehabilitation of buildings, track, cranes, and the like.[28]

Just about everywhere but in Brcko, the news from Bosnia in recent years makes sustainable peace seem impossibly remote, more remote than it actually is. The images are indeed bleak. In summer 2000 we saw pictures of busloads of Muslim Bosniac women seeking justice for the massacre of their husbands and sons that took place at Srebrenica five years ago, and we saw the hostile reception they received from the current Serb residents of Srebrenica when the women returned for their ceremony of remembrance. What we tend to overlook is that there is another Bosnia where peace is being built, village by village, despite the many acts of not-so-ancient hatred. Those village islands of peace can be replicated.

In May 1992, Serb paramilitaries "ethnically cleansed" the village of Klanac, a Bosniac suburb of Brcko in northern Bosnia. Repeatedly over the past two years, the Bosniac "displaced persons" (DPs, or internal refugees) have attempted to return in order either to reclaim their intact homes or rebuild the destroyed ones.

As has happened many times elsewhere in Bosnia, each time the hopeful returnees were met with a hail of stones thrown by present residents. Few were surprised by the clashes. The Serbs in Klanac were thought to

[28] The river has not been dredged since 1991 and there is yet no navigation treaty between Serbia and BiH. Major customers were BH Steel in Zenica, KHK Coke in Lukavac (near Tuzla), sand and gravel for local construction, grains and sunflower for processing at BIM Galames (formerly BIMEX, food processing), and BIMAL sunflower oil production. The best base case assumption is BH Steel does not restart production but imports steel from Russia, etc; coke does not restart; but agriculture does make a comeback with BIMAL and BIMEX, etc., which will provide business for the port as a low-cost water shipper. If steel actually recovers and makes its own product in an integrated way, this will reduce the port traffic and reduce the value of the rehabilitation of the port; otherwise with steel imports the port will generate a positive return on investment. This is documented in Parsons Brinckerhoff Int'l, Brcko Port Feasibility Study (March 2000).

Box 5.5 Brcko Arbitration

ESTABLISHMENT: Annex 2, Article V of the Dayton Peace Agreement left the status of Brcko unresolved, pending binding international arbitration. The Arbitration Tribunal was established in 1996, and initially intended to issue its decision on Brcko's status by December 14, 1996.

The Tribunal's first award (issued 2/14/1997) put Brcko under international supervision and authorized the Supervisor to implement the provisions of the Peace Agreement. The Supervisor's mandate was envisioned as follows: "to facilitate the phased and orderly return of refugees and displaced persons to their original homes and assist in the provision of housing to accommodate old and new residents; to enhance democratic government and a multiethnic administration in the town of Brcko; to ensure freedom of movement and the establishment of normal democratic policing functions; to work with international customs monitors towards the establishment of efficient customs procedures and controls; and to promote economic revitalization."[1]

CHANGES TO MANDATE: The Tribunal's March 15, 1998, Supplemental Award asked the Supervisor to work toward reintegrating economically with the surrounding regions, by: "creating in the Brcko area a duty-free or special economic zone to stimulate the region's economy; for the same purpose of establishing a program of privatization of state-owned and socially owned enterprises in the area; and looking toward the reopening of the Sava River port in Brcko, to activate the Bosnia and Herzegovina Transportation Corporation and facilitate international support for the port program."[2] The Supplemental Award also required the leaders of the Republika Srpska to "show significant new achievements in terms of returns of former Brcko residents, unfettered freedom of movement, strong support for the multi-ethnic governmental institutions including the multi-ethnic police force, and full cooperation with the Supervisor and the authorities responsible for conducting fair and democratic elections in September 1998."[3]

TERMINATION: By its Final Award of March 3, 1999 (and Annex of August 18, 1999), the Tribunal established a self-governing district

continued

Box 5.5 continued

> under sovereignty of Bosnia-Herzegovina, the territory belonging to
> both the Republika Srpska and the Federation.
>
> [1] "History and Mandate of the OHR North/Brcko" at http://www.ohr.int/
> print/?content_id=5531.
> [2] History and Mandate of the OHR North/Brcko.
> [3] History and Mandate of the OHR North/Brcko.

be the most hardline opponents of reintegration. But the Serbs were also
victimized refugees, another displaced community who feared being displaced once again.

But in mid-May, less than a month after the latest clash, sixty Bosniac
families began work on their houses in the neighborhood. Serbs and
Bosniacs formed a neighborhood committee, and Serbs expressed a willingness to vacate the houses they were occupying.[29] Soon Serbs were
helping over seven hundred Bosniacs return.

What happened? Part of the credit belongs to the international community. The new Brcko District of northern Bosnia is special, but its key
features can be replicated. The sticking point at the Dayton negotiations
is that Brcko is both the strategic corridor linking the two halves of the
Serb Republic "entity" and the northern access route from the Bosniac-
Croat Federation "entity" to Croatia and Europe.

Irresolvable at Dayton, the problem was handed over to international
arbitration. In a Solomonic decision, the international arbitrator, U.S. attorney Roberts Owen, made it an autonomous district of Bosnia, owned
by both entities but by neither exclusively. Earlier he had given nearly
limitless authority to implement the arbitration to Ambassador R. William
Farrand, the international supervisor of Brcko. Relying on this authority,
the backing of nearby Stabilization Force (SFOR) troops and the assistance of the UN police monitors, Farrand established the only functioning multiethnic administration and police in Bosnia. The district gave the
displaced Serbs a sense that they could find a new home and be safe and
not be forced back into the Federation. It was the multiethnic local police that quelled the last Klanac riot.

The other part of the credit belonged to the courage and common sense
of the Klanac residents, both Bosniac original and Serb current. Manipulated for years by their hardline DP organizations and the ethnic political
parties that relied on them for cheap votes, both groups of DPs stood up

---

[29] "Election Campaign in the Village of Klanac," *Reporter*, November 15, 2000 (Bosnia
local paper).

for themselves and stretched a hand across the ethnic divide when they saw a way to live together safely. Taking advantage of an offer from Supervisor Farrand, the Serbs agreed to vacate the Bosniac houses they occupied in return for free and secure land plots elsewhere in the district. When the DP leadership organizations balked at this sensible compromise and the new local District Assembly hesitated to pass enabling legislation, the current Serb and prospective Bosniac residents threatened to organize a multiethnic demonstration. (This surely would have been Bosnia's first.) The Assembly voted wisely, and Klanac made peace.

The struggle for a sustainable peace in Bosnia was far from over. Even in Brcko, unemployment stood at 60 percent, organized smuggling was rampant, ethnic tensions still simmered and sometimes boiled over, and thousands more sought a return to their homes. But Klanac was an important step.

The strategic importance of Brcko has been clear to all. It was the link between the two halves of the Republika Srpska (RS), sitting in the middle of the Posavina Corridor and the northward link of the Federation to Croatia and European markets. Its ownership could not be resolved at Dayton and it was thus left to international arbitration by a three-person arbitral tribunal chaired by U.S. attorney Roberts Owen.

The supervisory mandate has had large positive effects that include especially:

1. Multiethnic Administration was established early and embodied in a District Government and Assembly, both of which went much further than anywhere else in Bosnia and Herzegovina (BiH). Following the completion of the arbitral process, a District Government and District Assembly were appointed (March 8, 2000) as interim bodies for a transition to local elections (unlike elsewhere in Bosnia, postponed until the district is ready, in 2002 or later).

2. A Multiethnic Police was established early for the grad, then for the district, again much further than anywhere else in the BiH. They had their own uniforms different from those of the Federation and RS, were highly paid compared to other professions, but suffered from the temporary character of their contracts and thus uncertainty. Overall, the ME Police seemed to work well in that the police treated each other respectfully and professionally and seemed to have cordial and respectful relations with the neighborhoods they patroled.[30]

How can we account for the success of the supervision? Why was Brcko so far ahead of the rest of BiH? Partly, we can attribute the success to pressure for compliance by the entities, each of whom sought to prove to the arbitral panel that it was best fitted to assume full control of the district

---

[30] Doyle interview and patrol with Brcko Grad ME police officers.

(despite their reluctance to weaken ethnic monopolies). Also, cooperation among the internationals seemed to have been better here, partly because the UN and OHR had the same special mandate. Brcko was also seen as an international test bed for progress, in part due to the dedication and leadership of the supervisor, U.S. Ambassador R. William Farrand. A significant comparison was another divided city, Mostar, where the factions have barely combined to form a single administration, four years lagging on Brcko—and where otherwise integration was absent.

The unusually intensive presence of IFOR/SFOR also has been important. At first, through 1999, a reinforced battalion was assigned to cover the small area around Brcko. Beginning in 2000, the Second Battalion of the Third Armored Cavalry was assigned to cover a considerably larger area. But compared to the coverage elsewhere in Bosnia (and the significance of the U.S. presence), SFOR still signaled a distinct U.S. commitment to the Brcko arbitration.

The military fulfilled many roles. Patrolling provided "information"— meaning control. Cavalry unit doctrine was geared to "patrolling" for information, but information was the functional route to influence. By knowing what might happen and by communicating a clear sense of the Dayton obligations to which all were to be held responsible and by demonstrating SFOR commitment to those Dayton principles and the capabilities that the battalion could exercise, SFOR exercised a palpable influence. It could also single out potential troublemakers and identify them with video or digital camera still photos displayed, if needed, in the neighborhood. No one was anonymous as a potential violator, which significantly deterred violations.[31]

The "district management team" played an equally important role in developing influence through assisting local governance. Its presence and expertise allowed influence to be actual, implemented in positive practice that contributed to the provision of basic public services, such as water, electricity, tax collection, budgeting, and education. The team both advised and (with the authority of the supervisor) directed, not completely unlike the role of colonial officials or U.S. officials in Vietnam and their "counterparting" of South Vietnamese officials.

The International Police Task Force in Brcko played an equivalent role with their intensive investment in support of the local police. IPTF's numbers started at 300 plus before April 1999. For comparison: Tuzla, with a much bigger area and population, had 150 IPTF monitors). Bosnia as a whole had 2,035 IPTF in March 1999 and 1,752 in April, 2000, for 5 million population, or 2,457 persons per IPTF in 1999 and 2,864 in 2000. At the same time, Brcko had 280 people per IPTF and 626 in 2000.

---

[31] Doyle interviews with Lieutenant Colonels Connor and Hickey.

The Brcko Multiethnic Police amounted to 320, for a population of 84,000, or 263 persons per officer. Bosnia as a whole will have 20,000 for a population of 5 million (a roughly equal 250 per cop). Thus, as with IFOR/SFOR, the significant number was the unusually heavy international investment in the supervision of the local police in Brcko.[32]

Not every aspect of the mandate progressed as hoped. Although Brcko has achieved more minority returns than elsewhere and much earlier than anywhere else in Bosnia, problems remain. The Brcko international authorities early on resolved to "throw no one [Serb occupiers] in the street." Consequently, returns of Bosniacs to Brcko have been limited by restrictions on returns in BiH, as well as by discouragement of two-way returns by Serb leaders seeking to hold on to their dependent voters and the popular reluctance to leave safe Serb communities.

One striking case of failed supervisory authority is telling as an indication of its limits. The Serb Displaced Persons (DPs) who resided in the district built an Orthodox church in Meraje on the site of a destroyed mosque. The act was provocative in two respects: building on the site of a destroyed mosque and conveying the appearance that the DPs planned to be in continuous occupation and thus would need a parish church—that is, they planned not to return the houses and land plots of the Bosniacs. The supervisor ordered construction to stop in Supervisory Order number 20 of 1997. It had no effect; construction continued. The dilemma was: could one arrest church members building a church by hand? Authority in these circumstances is shaped *conventionally* and dynamically. It is constructed by social practice, and prevalent norms define limits to influence.[33] Even supervisors cannot do what everyone thinks should not be done. Moreover, Serbs are advantaged simply because they are the local, immediate, and present constituency. They can riot on the supervisor's doorstep. Bosniacs and Croats are remote, and distance defines a declining power gradient.[34]

A different limit arose in "penthouse" construction. The local leadership (Serb and Bosniac together) saw profit in meeting the housing shortage by licensing (privately it appears) permits to construct penthouses on top of existing apartments. They also saw themselves as addressing a historic Yugoslav fault, placing Communist flat roofs in place of what "should" have been Balkan red-tiled peaked roofs. Stealth and the status quo made for successful defiance. Once the preexisting roofs were removed and construction underway, the construction was too costly to

[32] See the Bezrouchenko, Nielsen, and Rumin interviews by Doyle.

[33] See George Orwell's classic essay, "Shooting an Elephant," to see how popular expectations can shape official action, http://www.online-literature.com/Orwell/887/.

[34] Boulding 1964, pp. 70–87.

stop. For principals to control local agents, information is vital. But here it was missing, and agents became their own principals.

Information also played a role in the blocking of the supervisor's finance order of April 13, 2000. The supervisor bit off too much, trying to implement reform from the top. But he lacked an understanding of exactly how the Yugoslav Payment Bureaus (which were in the hand of Republika Srpska politicians) worked, and he lacked the organizational capacity to control or replace their functions. The Serb officials replied with a classic "close the Washington Monument" strategy: who would audit the new district accounts? Who would set electricity prices? Who would manage the hospitals and pensions? Moreover, the last two did not have sufficient scale in the district to make them efficient as pension insurance or health schemes (for who will pay tertiary care for so small a population?). Still, the order could have been implemented by contracting for tertiary care and serving as an electricity purchaser, not producer. Doing so might have served as another test bed for national-level standards and laws. But under pressure from OHR and the resistance of the entities, the supervisor revised the order on June 21, 2000. Why? OHR was subsidizing the entities, so any loss of entity revenue meant further OHR subsidies. OHR-Sarajevo and OHR-North (Brcko) had backed themselves into a serious rivalry for personal and institutional control in which Farrand had moved too far ahead of his nominal superiors in OHR.[35] Successes and failures in the exercise of authority interacted. Each failure hurt the credibility of the supervisor's authority and thus spilled over.

Another limit lay in international coordination and was evident in the most famous problem, the Arizona Market, haven for international prostitution ("white slavery") and smuggling and widespread customs evasion—and the most profitable and dynamic free enterprise cluster in all northern Bosnia (not to speak of the source of most of the district's private-sector jobs). The problem here was, "Who will bell the cat?" If the market were closed and moved elsewhere, regulated from the ground up, then SFOR had to take on the large, dangerous task. Doing so would lose jobs in the short run, but perhaps it would be more stable and legal in the longer run. If, on the other hand, it were regulated in place, then

[35] Further complications were that the revised order cut back on claims to control electric distribution, pensions, health care and revenues from the Payments Bureaus attached to them. The District keeps the former revenues that were sent to the local municipalities. But the new plan envisaged a district with much wider functions than former municipalities (including education and police, for example, that were formally state level functions). How to pay for the new functions without rewriting the tax laws? Brcko had an additional 2 million KM per month from the customs authority, but that was not enough. A key issue for OHR then was: Is Brcko allowed to move ahead of the rest of BiH? If the district kept these functions, then how would it pay for it other than through central funding on the 1/3–2/3 formula?

the local Multiethnic Police, backed by the UN, would do the job and face the strain of conflict and corruption. This preserved jobs for the district, but risked further deterioration of the rule of law. The IPTF preferred the first (having SFOR do it); SFOR and OHR, the second.

Other challenges were in economic development planning where there was a need to write the laws for property, commercial transactions, investments, and taxation; none then were stable and reliable. No property was securely owned or salable. Taxation discouraged investment; taxes on labor were 87 percent, 92 percent, and 94 percent in each ethnic area of the district. Medical and other benefits posed another task: the district could not provide tertiary medical care. In the past, funds came from the entities, but hospital directors confiscated them (80 percent of the beds were non-occupyable due to funding limitations). None of these challenges could overcome quickly, and new ones arose over multiethnic schooling. But the striking feature of Brcko was movement; problems of governance in a deeply divided multiethnic society were being addressed, step by step.

How many potential Brckos did Bosnia have? Until recently, very very few. But with the use of international authority, a continued SFOR presence, active efforts to enlist moderate Bosnian leaders in the construction of multiethnic institutions, the economic resources to design expanding-pie solutions, and the courage and imagination of ordinary villagers, many hoped perhaps someday there would soon be many more.

East Timor

The major peacebuiding initiative in East Timor offers a good context for an application of our model. The East Timor case is just outside the period coverage for our data, so it is not included in the statistical analysis. But we can apply the model to obtain predictions of peacebuilding success and analyze the progress of the peacebuilding mission as we have done for the other cases in this chapter.

A Portuguese colony since the seventeenth century, the island of Timor came under Dutch rule in 1859, when it came to be divided between the Portuguese-ruled Catholic East Timor and Dutch-controlled West Timor. Indonesia, including West Timor, gained independence from the Dutch in 1949. The "carnation revolution" of Social Democrats in Portugal in April 1974 loosened the Portuguese grip on East Timor, and political parties began to spring up. The Timorese Democratic Union (UDT), a party generally associated with elites in the region who had benefited from the Portuguese presence, supported continued association with Portugal within the context of a new federal association, while Fretilin

(Revolutionary Front for an Independent East Timor) supported outright independence.[36] In the wake of a coup by the UDT in August 1975, Portuguese officials abandoned the island.[37] Hostilities broke out between the UDT and Fretilin. Fretilin and its hastily organized military branch known as Falintil (Armed Forces of the National Liberation of East Timor) quickly defeated the UDT, which fled to the western part of Timor.

For three months, the new Fretilin government sought and failed to gain international or UN recognition. As cross-border attacks by former UDT supporters, allied with forces in Indonesia, intensified, Fretilin leaders declared the independence of East Timor on November 28. The Indonesian government, expressing concern about the prospect of a potentially Marxist state in East Timor, invaded with the tacit approval of the United States. Although both the UN General Assembly and Security Council passed subsequent resolutions reaffirming the right of East Timor to self-determination, the territory was formally annexed by Indonesia in July 1976.[38]

Falintil engaged in spirited resistance against the Indonesian Army for several years. Gradually, however, the Indonesian army eliminated the Falintil threat, reducing it from 27,000 to 5,000 by 1978 and then, by 1987, to some 100 guerillas hiding in the mountains.[39] Most estimates place the total direct and indirect deaths attributable to Indonesian counterinsurgency measures at approximately 200,000, with perhaps as many as 60,000 occurring in the first month after the invasion alone (see table 5.4).[40] The total is staggering considering in a population of less than a million.[41]

Indonesian authorities initiated significant public works and invested in infrastructure, education, and health. Although East Timor remained Indonesia's poorest province, the decrease in illiteracy rates from more than 90 percent in 1974 to approximately 46 percent in 1999 reveals an improvement in the standard of living as compared to the period under

---

[36] Jonathan Steele, "Nation Building in East Timor," *World Policy Journal* 19 (Summer 2002): 76.

[37] Smith and Dee (2003: 38) suggest that the UDT coup was motivated by the desire to stave off Indonesian invasion as well as preempt an anticipated coup by Fretilin. See Michael Smith and Moreen Dee, *Peacekeeping in East Timor: The Path to Independence*. International Peace Academy Occasional Paper Series (Boulder, CO: Lynne Rienner Publishers, 2003).

[38] Australia was the only state to officially recognize the annexation.

[39] Smith and Dee 2003, p. 40.

[40] Erin Trowbridge, "Back Road Reckoning," *Dissent* 49, no. 1 (Winter 2002), p. 103.

[41] Most estimates place East Timor's population as somewhat less than 800,000. The United Nations registered almost the entire population in preparation for the August 1999 elections. The UN registered 737,811 people—although tens of thousands more East Timorese had already fled the country by this point. See "East Timor: Education and Health in Focus," *UN Chronicle*, no. 2 (2002): 34–35.

TABLE 5.4
Indonesia and East Timor

	Indonesia/East Timor (1975–99) INTERFET/UMISET (1999–2002)
Sovereign peace	—
Participatory peace	—
War type	"Ethnic"
Factions	3
UN mandate	Enforcement/Transitional administration
Duration of UN mission (months)	2
Was UN present during the war? If so, for how long?	No
Troop strength of UN mission, if any	9,302
War duration (in months)	286
Real per capita GDP (year before war start; constant $)	892
Real per capita GDP (at end of the war; constant $)	2,304
GDP growth at end of the war (% annual change)	—
People killed during the war	200,000
People displaced during the war	200,000
Outcome of the War	Rebel victory
Was a treaty signed by most parties?	No
Date of the treaty, if any was signed	n/a
Was the treaty implemented?	n/a
Primary commodity exports as % of GDP	27 (for Indonesia, not just East Timor)
Is the country a major oil exporter?	Yes
Ethnolinguistic fractionalization (100 = highest)	76
Ethnic heterogeneity index (1 = highly diverse)	0.766
Population at start of war (in thousands)	132,589
Area (square kilometers)	1,904,570
Effective Development Assistance as % of GDP	279.068

Portuguese rule.[42] However, what Indonesia provided in terms of infra-structure was largely destroyed by local militias and the Indonesian army in 1999.

A low-level insurgency in East Timor had gone mostly unnoticed by the international community until 1991. On November 12, 1991, how-ever, Indonesian troops massacred up to 270 mourners at a church in

[42] Smith and Dee 2003, p. 36; Steele 2002, p. 79.

Santa Cruz in an event that was videotaped and played around the world. From that point on, human rights organizations and other international groups brought increasing pressure on the government of Indonesia, culminating in the awarding of the Nobel Peace Prize in 1996 to José Ramos Horta, spokesman for the resistance, and Carlos Filipe Ximenes Belo, the bishop of Dili.

The path to independence opened in May 1998, when President Suharto was forced to step down and an elected government, led by B. J. Habibie, surprised the world by announcing in January 1999 that there would be a "popular consultation" in East Timor to decide the region's status.[43] The reason behind President Habibie's decision to call a referendum in East Timor is unclear, and his decision was not well received by the Indonesian military. Local militias in East Timor, pro-Indonesian Timorese armed by the military, vented their anger through acts of violence. Between February and April 1999, several dozen people were killed and thousands were displaced after their homes were burned.[44]

The arrangements for the referendum were negotiated under the auspices of the United Nations between Portugal, negotiating on behalf of East Timor, and Indonesia. The May 5 agreement stipulated that East Timor's citizens would be asked to vote to accept or reject a "special autonomy" arrangement with Indonesia. If autonomy was rejected, the UN would oversee a process of transition to independence.

The "fundamentals" of East Timor's peacebuilding ecology—local capacities and hostility levels—could hardly have looked worse (see figure 5.4). After a long separatist insurgency that had killed more than 200,000 people and displaced at least as many, the parties to the conflict were clearly not reconciled to the prospect of East Timor's independence, as evidenced by the surge of violence caused by pro-Indonesian militias. The prospects for peace were dim. This is reflected in our model's prediction of a below-average probability of peacebuilding success for East Timor (0.25).

This probability estimate would have been much lower had the UN's peacemaking efforts not convinced the Indonesian government to hold the referendum. The statistical estimate in this case is also a little misleading because our country-level proxies for local capacities (per capita income, economic growth, electricity consumption) are higher than the corresponding regional averages for East Timor. Since we use country-level proxies,

[43] Insightful first person analyses of how the Security Council reacted to the Timor crisis and how the UN presence operated in the field can be found in Stewart Eldon, "East Timor," in Malone 2004, pp. 551–66; and Ian Martin, "A Field Perspective," in Malone 2004, pp. 567–74.

[44] Geoffrey Robinson, "If You Leave Us, We Will Die," *Dissent* 49, no. 1 (Winter 2002), 101–12.

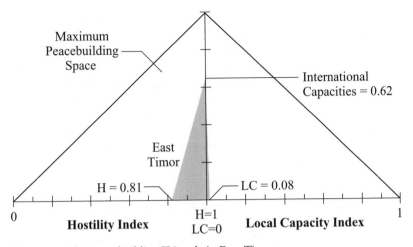

Figure 5.4 The Peacebuilding Triangle in East Timor

our model should overpredict the probability of peacebuilding success in East Timor. Moreover, while our model captures the extensive international involvement in East Timor, it does not do so fully. Very high levels of international economic assistance (see table 5.4) are not reflected in net current transfers at the national level, nor do we capture the substantial technical assistance offered by the World Bank, the UN Development Program, and other international agencies that were very actively involved in East Timor's transition. Additionally, while we code a strong UN mission in East Timor, which has the effect of raising the estimate of peacebuilding success, most of the credible security guarantees in this case came not from UN forces, but rather from Australian troops associated with IN-TERFET (more on this below). But, despite these problems, the basic logic of the peacebuilding triangle seems to fit this case: the international response has measured up to the challenges on the ground and seems able to compensate for high hostility and low levels of local capacities.

The UN Mission in East Timor (UNAMET) had been authorized by UN Security Council Resolution 1246 on June 11, 1999. With a budget of $52.5 million and a staff of 242 civilians, 271 unarmed police advisers, and 50 unarmed military liaisons, UNAMET's chief mission was to conduct the popular consultation (referendum). Through a massive campaign to inform the people about the vote and despite continued reports of scattered murders and intimidation by militias abetted by the Indonesian military, UNAMET registered 451,792 potential voters and established 850 polling stations at two hundred sites around the country. That success was critical in signaling the people's determination to vote and the ineffectiveness of spoiler tactics by militias.

The referendum was held on August 30, 1999. An impressive 98.6 percent of registered voters did vote, 78 percent of them in favor of independence (against special autonomy). Militia violence exploded after the results were announced. Over the ensuing three weeks, Indonesian troops stood by (and sometimes aided) an estimated 18,000 militia troops as they rampaged across the country, destroying anything of value. Catching the United Nations and much of the international community by surprise, the militias destroyed 70 percent of the houses, 77 percent of the health facilities, and 95 percent of the schools in the region. An estimated 1,200 civilians were killed. Over 200,000 refugees fled to West Timor and up to 75 percent of the total population of the region was displaced.[45]

Responding to these events, the Security Council passed resolution 1264 in September 1999 authorizing, with Indonesian consent and also under Chapter VII, a multinational force to "take all necessary means" in order to protect UN personnel, restore peace and security, and protect humanitarian assistance efforts in East Timor. INTERFET troops landed in East Timor on September 20 with Australia at the lead and a maximum strength of 11,000 troops from twenty-two nations.[46] This expansion of the UN mandate in East Timor to include enforcement was a critically important decision, demonstrating flexibility and adaptability on the part of the UN. Australia's participation was crucial in facilitating Indonesian support for the intervention, and the high level of training and intelligence capabilities of the Australian military enabled the operation to proceed smoothly.[47] East Timorese militias offered very light resistance and quickly pulled back, crossing the border into West Timor. In mid-October, the result of the referendum was recognized by the Indonesian People's Consultative Assembly, and by November 1, the last Indonesian security forces had pulled out of the area.

INTERFET's success led to Security Council Resolution 1272 of October 25, establishing the UN Transitional Authority in East Timor (UNTAET). Headed by Sergio Vieira de Mello, UNTAET was designed as a multidimensional peacekeeping operation. With authority much beyond that of the typical peacekeeping operation, but like the sovereign control held by the Brcko arbitration, UNTAET was responsible for all aspects of administration in East Timor until East Timor would become formally independent, on May 20, 2002. Its mission was: "(a) To provide

[45] Trowbridge 2002; see, also, Roland Paris, "The Faulty Assumptions of Post-conflict Peacebuilding," in Crocker, Hampson, and Aal, eds., *Turbulent Peace* (Washington, D.C.: United States Institute of Peace Press, 2001), pp. 773–74; and Simon Chesterman, "East Timor in Transition," *International Peacekeeping* 9, no. 1 (2002): 45–76.

[46] Smith and Dee 2003: 46.

[47] David Dickens, "Can East Timor Be a Blueprint for Burden Sharing?" *Washington Quarterly* 25, no. 3 (Summer 2002): 29–40, 29–30.

Box 5.6 UNTAET's Mandate

ESTABLISHMENT: S/RES/1272 establishes the UN Transitional Administration in East Timor, composed of a "governance and public administration component," a "humanitarian assistance and emergency rehabilitation component," and a "military component." Its mandate was:

(a) to provide security and maintain law and order throughout the territory of East Timor;

(b) to establish an effective administration;

(c) to assist in the development of civil and social services;

(d) to ensure the coordination and delivery of humanitarian assistance, rehabilitation, and development assistance;

(e) to support capacity building for self-government;

(f) to assist in the establishment of conditions for sustainable development.[1]

CHANGES TO MANDATE: Subsequent Security Council Resolutions 1319 and 1338 extended the mandate and urged "further measures to delegate authority to the East Timorese people."[2]

TERMINATION: By resolution 1392, the Council extended the mandate until May 20, 2002, at which point East Timor became an independent nation.

[1] S/RES/1272 (1999) *available at* http://ods-dds-ny.un.org/doc/UNDOC/ GEN/ N99/312/77/PDF/N9931277.pdf
[2] S/RES/1338 (2001) *available at* http://ods-dds-ny.un.org/doc/UNDOC/ GEN/N01/234/39/PDF/N0123439.pdf

---

security and maintain law and order throughout the territory of East Timor; (*b*) To establish an effective administration; (*c*) To assist in the development of civil and social services; (*d*) To ensure the coordination and delivery of humanitarian assistance, rehabilitation and development assistance; (*e*) To support capacity-building for self-government; (*f*) To assist in the establishment of conditions for sustainable development."[48] UNTAET was given full legislative and executive authority, including the "administration of justice" throughout the region. After transfer of peacekeeping duties from INTERFET to UNTAET in February 2000, the UN also formally gained full authority in security matters. Thus, during the initial months, at least, East Timor was governed exclusively by the UN, just as Brcko was by its supervisor.

Aspiring East Timorese leaders were frustrated by UNTAET's heavy-handed mandate. In response, for the next two and a half years, UN-TAET managed its peacekeeping mandate by devolving authority to them in a step-by-step process. Vieira De Mello initially sought input from locals through a fifteen-member National Consultative Council established in December 1999, but East Timorese participants found that this did not give them any political power.[49] The council was replaced in June 2000 with a thirty-three-member council, comprised of a variety of East Timorese regional, political, and civil society leaders. The new council approved the creation of the First Transitional Government in July 2002. The First Transitional Government consisted of an eight-member cabinet—with four departments led by East Timorese and four departments led by UNTAET officials. The evolving NCC and the First Transitional Government provided legitimacy to UN efforts by including many local representatives in the decision-making process, while providing training to locals who had little previous experience in formal governance. UNTAET efforts were also conducted at a grassroots level through civic education program that eventually trained 5,500 community leaders and involved almost 100,000 East Timorese.[50]

The next major step in peacebuilding through devolution occurred in the summer of 2001. During June and July, 38,000 East Timorese took part in UN-sponsored public hearings to consider the future shape of the nation's constitution. On August 30, 2001, elections were held for an eighty-eight-member Constituent Assembly, which was to draft a new constitution and serve as the first postindependence legislature. The elections proceeded without any violence. In September 2001, a Second Transitional Authority, comprised solely of East Timorese representatives, replaced the former joint UNTAET–East Timor Authority. Finally, on April 14, 2002, the UN supervised the region's first presidential election. After another successful and peaceful balloting process, former Falintil leader Xanana Gusmão was elected with 82.7 percent of the vote.

[48] S/RES/1272 (October 25, 1999).

[49] Steele 2002, p. 79; and see Jarat Chopra, "Divided Rule," *World Today* 57, no. 1 (2001): 13–16 who notes that too much of UNTAET's resources were dedicated to centralization and headquarters' staff and too little to building district level UNTAET and local Timorese capacity.

[50] *UN Chronicle*, no. 2 (2002).

Despite all its political success, East Timor joined the United Nations during May 2002 as one of the poorest nations in the world, as is evident by all major socioeconomic indicators. In 1996, the infant mortality rate was 149 per 1,000 live births and life expectancy was equal to fifty-two years. Thirty-eight percent of children were malnourished, 50 percent of the adult population was illiterate, only 19 percent of the population had secondary or higher education, 25 percent of households had access to electricity or safe running water, and about 50 percent of the population lived below the poverty line.[51] The average citizen earned approximately a dollar per day.[52] The violence had devastated the island's limited local capacities: markets collapsed, all agricultural production (except coffee) was disrupted, most power generators and the telephone network were damaged or destroyed, and real GDP declined in 1999 by as much as 40 to 45 percent, while prices increased by 200–500 percent within a few months.[53]

East Timor's economy had to be rebuilt almost from scratch. Initial financial pledges were made at a joint World Bank–UN Conference in Japan on December 17, 1999—the first time such cooperation took place between the UN and the World Bank. Financial planning was based largely upon the World Bank's Joint Assessment Mission study, which estimated that slightly over $300 million was needed for East Timor for the period from 1999 to 2002.[54] Most of the money was channeled through the UN. The East Timorese central authorities' $59.2 million budget for 2000–2001 was dwarfed by UNTAET's $600 million budget. Domestic revenue (projected to rise to $40 million by 2002) amounted to $17 million in 2001, and the budget deficit was covered by

[51] World Bank, Joint Assessment Mission (JAM) Background Report (http://wbln0018. worldbank.org/eap/eap.nsf); and M. Arneberg and J. Pedersen, *Social and Economic Conditions in East Timor* (Columbia University and Fafo Institute of Applied Social Science, 1999.)

[52] Per capita annual income estimates we found ranged from $230–$400: ($230 in 1999 cited in Trowbridge 2002; $500 in 2001, cited in the 2002 CIA World Factbook; and $304 in 1999 cited by a Web site linked to the World Bank, which also records the GDP per capita before the 1999 destruction as $424). http://lnweb18.worldbank.org/eap/eap.nsf/ Attachments/TSS+-+Annex+E.1/$File/Annex+E.1.pdf.)

[53] Helder Da Costa and Hadi Soesastro, "Building East Timor's Economy. Council for Asia-Europe Cooperation conference (2001): http://www.caec-asiaeurope.org/Conference/ Publications/costasoesastro.PDF. They cite as their source the Joint Assessment Mission 1999, and Luis Valdivieso et al., "East Timor: Establishing the Foundations of Strong Macroeconomic Management," IMF Report (2000) [http://imf.org/external/pubs/ft/etimor/ timor.pdf].

[54] The breakdown given in the report was the following: Community Empowerment: $30 million; Education: $57.8 million; Health: $40.2 million; Agriculture: $24.4 million; Infrastructure: $93.1 million; Economic Management: $16.2 million; Civil Service: $42.5 million; Judiciary: $2.9 million. See: http://www.worldbank.org/html/extdr/offrep/eap/etimor/ donorsmtg99/jamsummarytablefinal.pdf

the UNTAET-administered Trust Fund for East Timor. The World Bank provided $150 million in reconstruction aid from 1999 to 2002, administered mostly through a World Bank Trust Fund. Another $360 million was pledged by donor nations in May 2002 to assist in postindependence reconstruction.[55] Development assistance, however, was only a relatively small part of total spending in the region. All told, international donors would contribute $2.2 billion to East Timor over the period 1999–2002—although the majority of this money was paid to UN staff and security forces, rather than directly on reconstruction costs.[56] More than one hundred NGOs were active in East Timor, working in coordination with UNTAET on various areas, including education, health, gender equality, and many others. In order to help sustain long-term development, UNTAET has focused on rebuilding the coffee, rice, and fishery sectors, which were traditionally strong sectors in the local economy. A potentially significant source of future revenue is oil, as oil reserves in the Timor Gap (between East Timor and Australia) are expected to yield up to $300 million in annual revenue.[57]

The UNHCR began operations in East Timor during May 1999 to assist tens of thousands of refugees. In the wake of postreferendum violence, nearly a quarter of the population of East Timor fled to refugee camps in West Timor. UNHCR, in conjunction with the International Organization for Migration and UNTAET, organized the return of almost 200,000 refugees, providing transportation, information, and protection. After a militia killed three UNCHR workers in the border town of Atambua in September 2000, UNCHR halted its operations in West Timor, but continued in East Timor. The Indonesian government's refugee taskforce assumed all refugee operations in West Timor. But, at independence, an estimated 50,000 refugees still remained in West Timor. Intimidation by militias slowed the pace of refugee resettlement after the UNHCR left West Timor, as did fears of retribution against those refugees who took part in the destructive events of 1999.[58] UNHCR operations in East Timor largely ended in January 2003, when the remaining 28,000 East

[55] Top bilateral donors included Portugal, the United States, Japan, the EU, and Australia. See Steele 2002, p. 83.

[56] One source breaks down the year 2000 budget, for instance, as: about $230 million for military personnel; $230 million for administration and salaries; and $130 million for operating costs, http://www.wsws.org/articles/2000/dec2000/timo-d07.shtml.

[57] Trowbridge 2002, p. 105. The Timor Gap Treaty was signed in July 2001, negotiated between Australia and UN officials representing East Timor.

[58] Surprisingly, the UNCHR has not documented even a single revenge killing in East Timor. Multiple sources have noted the surprising lack of reprisals in the region (Steele 2002, p. 79; Smith and Dee 2003, p. 85). See also James Traub, "Inventing East Timor," *Foreign Affairs* 79, no. 4 (2000): 74–89, p. 80. Partly the reason can be found in the strong appeals by Xanana Gusmão for reconciliation, and the legal amnesty granted to former militia members.

Timorese living in West Timor lost their refugee status (most are expected to settle in Indonesia.)

The Australian-led INTERFET multinational force transferred its security responsibilities to the UNTAET-attached peacekeeping force in February 2000. The peacekeeping force was comprised of contingents from twenty-two states—half of which were from Asia/Oceania. Due to the success of INTERFET in pacifying the region, the peacekeeping force did not face a particularly difficult task except for small skirmishes in the summer of 2000.[59] A series of "clearing operations" were conducted in the fall of 2000 in order to root out militia infiltrators. In the wake of these missions (code-named Cobra and Crocodile), the lingering militia presence in western East Timor was virtually eliminated. Nevertheless, through 2003, militia incursions still took place on occasion.

A 3,700-strong (as of December 2002) peacekeeping force remained in East Timor as part of UNMISET (UN Mission of Support In East Timor), a successor mission to UNTAET. UNIMISET's mandate was established by UN Security Council resolution 1410 (2002) of May 17, authorizing the mission to: "provide assistance to core administrative structures critical to the viability and stability of East Timor; provide interim law enforcement and public security and to assist in the development of a new law enforcement agency in East Timor, the East Timor Police Service (ETPS); [and] contribute to the maintenance of the internal and external security of East Timor."[60] UNMISET has been trying to provide both internal and external stability and control and develop a local public security force.

Although mandated to have a maximum strength of 5,000 troops and 1,250 civilian police, only 480 UN-CIVPOL officers had arrived by February 2000 and 641 CIVPOL officers were present in April 2003.[61] One of the few criticisms frequently encountered was the inability of CIVPOL officers to control crime. However, without detention facilities or a functioning judiciary, CIVPOL was hard-pressed to fulfill its mandate during the first part of their mission.[62] An early accomplishment was the establishment of the East Timor Police College in Dili in 2000. Thus far, 1,697 East Timorese have graduated from the college, and it has a target of 2,800 officers to be trained by July 2003.[63] As of May 2002, there were 1,287 UN police officers from thirty-eight countries still serving in

[59] The PKF suffered only two combat-related fatalities during the first twenty-one months of the mission (http://members.optushome.com.au/dvcaa/VLGA/UNTAET_Fact 17.html). These soldiers were killed during the period of militia incursions in separate incidents in July and August 2000.

[60] http://www.un.org/Depts/dpko/missions/unmiset/mandate.html (accessed June 26, 2003).

[61] Smith and Dee 2003, p. 63.

[62] Smith and Dee 2003, p. 83.

[63] UNTAET Press Office, "Law and Order." Fact Sheet 6 (April 2002). (http://www.un .org/peace/etimor/fact/fs6.PDF

Box 5.7 UNMISET's Mandate

ESTABLISHMENT: UNMISET was established by Security Council resolution 1410 (May 17, 2002) and was mandated "[t]o provide assistance to core administrative structures critical to the viability and political stability of East Timor"; "[t]o provide interim law enforcement and public security and to assist in the development of a new law enforcement agency in East Timor, the East Timor Police Service (ETPS)"; and "to contribute to maintenance of the external and internal security of East Timor[.]"[1] In accordance with Section III A 3 of the Secretary-General's April 17, 2002 Report, the Security Council, additionally asked UNMISET to "give full effect to the following three Programmes of the Mandate Implementation Plan . . . Stability, Democracy and Justice; Public Security and Law Enforcement; and External Security and Border Control."[2]

CHANGES TO MANDATE: By its Resolution 1543 (May 14, 2004), the Security Council extended the mandate for six months (envisioning one more extension for a final period ending May 20, 2005), and following the Secretary-General's April 29, 2004 Report, reduced size and revised UNMISET's tasks to consist of: "(i) support for the public administration and justice system of Timor-Leste and for justice in the area of serious crimes; (ii) support to the development of law enforcement in Timor-Leste; (iii) support for the security and stability of Timor-Leste."[3]

TERMINATION: This is an ongoing mission.

[1] S/RES/1410 (2002) *available at* http://ods-dds-ny.un.org/doc/UNDOC/GEN/N02/387/02/PDF/N0238702.pdf
[2] S/RES/1410 (2002)
[3] S/RES/1543 (2004) *available at* http://ods-dds-ny.un.org/doc/UNDOC/GEN/N04/351/38/PDF/N0435138.pdf

---

East Timor (unlike the regular military forces, the UN civilian police force in East Timor has not been drawn down).

The Australian and Portuguese militaries have spearheaded the creation of a new East Timorese Army—officially named the Defense Forces of Timor-Leste.[64] These countries initially committed $26 million dollars

[64] The name East Timor was changed to Timor-Leste when the region gained independence.

toward training a force that is intended to eventually consist of 1,500 active troops and 1,500 reservists. The core of the army (approximately half) will be made of former Falintil troops, which formally agreed to disband in February 2001. The first battalion of 600 troops assumed active duty in mid-2002. East Timorese forces are expected to fully replace UN peacekeepers in 2004.

UN-led efforts to construct a functioning judiciary in East Timor progressed slowly. The largest obstacle was not in codifying a new system of law—Indonesian laws were largely adopted with some modifications emphasizing human rights statues—but rather in building the physical infrastructure and attracting the human capital needed to implement the law.[65] The Dili District court did not begin public proceedings until May 2000, and it was early 2001 before the judicial system for serious crimes began to operate effectively. A UN fact sheet written in April 2002 admits the shortcomings of the judicial development process, highlighting the need to overcome "limited resources and capacity."[66]

A subject of widespread criticism has been the international community's decision not to pursue an international tribunal to punish crimes committed in Indonesia in 1999. However, a Special Panel for the Investigation of Serious Crimes in the Dili District, consisting of two international judges and one East Timorese judge, was established in 2001. Its first verdict indicted ten militia members in December 2001 on numerous charges of violence against the civilian population and property. According to Human Rights Watch, "the Special Panel was believed to have become the first court worldwide to apply laws originally formulated for the International Criminal Court (ICC)."[67] Since that verdict, the Special Panel has filed 39 indictments involving 117 defendants, 8 of them Indonesian nationals, for crimes against humanity committed in East Timor. However, Indonesian cooperation has not been forthcoming in transferring evidence, witnesses, or suspects for prosecution, and the new East Timorese legislature continues to debate a proposed amnesty bill for former militia members.

To sum up, the peacebuilding process in East Timor has been an overall success. The violence that marred the referendum may not have been avoidable, given the unwillingness of the international community to coerce Indonesia even further and risk toppling its civilian government. Insisting that Indonesian troops withdraw from East Timor prior to the referendum might have jeopardized the stability of all of Indonesia at a

[65] Smith and Dee 2003, pp. 82–83.

[66] UNTAET Press Office, Fact Sheet 7, Justice and Serious Crimes http://www.un.org/peace/etimor/fact/fs7.PDF (accessed October 28, 2004).

[67] Human Rights Watch: World Report 2003 Web site: http://www.hrw.org/wr2k3/asia5.html (Accessed October 28, 2004).

time when East Asia's financial crisis had made the entire region a powder keg.[68] Once the Australian-led INTERFET had imposed order, the UN was able to discharge complex peacebuilding functions aimed at slowly rebuilding the country's local capacities. This task was greatly facilitated by the fact that the international community was willing to provide the UN with complete transitional authority over East Timor in a well-resourced Chapter VII mission. In retrospect, the UN probably acquired too much authority, a very rare fault. The independence forces were quite united and enjoyed outstanding political leadership. They lacked institutional capacity and material resources–not political will. But Vieira De Mello wisely reduced the weight of the UN presence by transferring authority to the East Timorese. The "Support Group" that included the United States, United Kingdom, Australia, New Zealand, and Japan offered critically important diplomatic assistance in securing the cooperation of the Indonesian government and pressuring the defense minister, General Wiranto, to reign in Indonesian military support for the militias. Thus, despite the hostility of pro-Indonesian factions in East Timor, despite the heavy human and economic toll of decades of war, the peacebuilding mission proceeded smoothly in preparing the country for independence as a result of concerted and mutually reinforcing peacemaking, peace enforcement, peacekeeping, and peacebuilding missions. This was an example where the right mandates, given in the right order and coupled with sufficient resources, created a space for peace despite the difficulties of East Timor's peacebuilding ecology.

Most civil war countries, however, do not enjoy the kind of proactive peacekeeping and the seemingly unlimited international capacities for peace that we have seen in Brcko, Eastern Slavonia, and East Timor. In many other cases, failures in both the design and the implementation of the mandate contribute to either stagnation or violent escalation. We review two such cases next—Cyprus and Rwanda.

---

[68] Pressure on the Indonesian government was applied by the International Monetary Fund, which linked discussions about the ongoing $12.3 billion bailout of Indonesia (caused by the East Asian economic crisis of 1997) to the situation in East Timor. See Tamrat Samuel, "East Timor: The Path to Self-Determination," in Chandra Lekha Sriram and Karin Wermester, eds., *From Promise to Practice: Strengthening UN Capacities for the Prevention of Violent Conflict* (Boulder, CO: Lynne Rienner, 2003), pp. 197–232.

6

Making Peace: Failures

IT WILL NOT COME as a surprise that it takes much more than an agreement—a truce or a peace treaty—to make a peace. Each of the peace operations we surveyed in the previous chapter, unlike the interventions in Bosnia, Somalia, and the Congo, benefited from an agreement. But so, too, did the peace operations we examine next, the UN's peacekeeping efforts in Cyprus (United Nations Force in Cyprus, UNFICYP) and Rwanda (United Nations Assistance Mission in Rwanda, UNAMIR). These operations, too, deployed military peacekeepers and engaged in some civilian peacebuilding activities. What was missing and made these two operations fail is more subtle: how they were designed and how they were managed. Problems of design, management, and implementation were also partly responsible for the failures in Bosnia and Somalia (see chapter 5).

Failures can have extended consequences. Although a genuine Cyprus peace agreement appeared close at hand in 2003, it too collapsed, and the people of Cyprus have suffered a divided homeland for more than a quarter century. For the people of Rwanda and, particularly, for the 800,000 who succumbed, the consequences were much more severe—the single largest genocide since the Holocaust. Understanding how peace operations can fail is a crucial task for scholars but is not merely an "academic" exercise.

Cyprus

Cyprus, 80 percent Greek and 20 percent Turkish, was a British colony until it became independent in 1960 with a federal government and three "guarantors" of its independence and security—Greece, Turkey, and Britain.[1] Despite these external guarantees, Cyprus descended into civil war soon after independence. Extensive power-sharing arrangements in the 1960 constitution, which provided for a Greek Cypriot (GC) president and a Turkish Cypriot (TC) vice president, failed to resolve intense interethnic antagonism that was fueled by the GCs' desire for *enosis* (union with Greece) and the TCs' desire for *taksim* (partition), and within

---

[1] United Kingdom, *Treaty of Guarantee* (February 19) (London: HMSO, 1959); United Kingdom, *Treaty of Alliance* (February 11) (London: HMSO, 1959).

three years the state was paralyzed. President Makarios proposed thirteen constitutional amendments that would have undermined Turkey's role as a guarantor power and circumscribed the TCs' political rights. Civil war broke out in December 1963. The TCs began to withdraw from ethnically mixed regions and formed self-administered militarized enclaves.[2] Rejecting a proposal for a NATO peacekeeping force to prevent an imminent Turkish invasion of the island, President Makarios asked the Security Council for UN peacekeeping assistance.

UNFICYP was deployed in March 1964. Diplomatic pressure from the UN, the United States, and Britain led the way to intercommunal talks in 1968.[3] The negotiations aimed at a comprehensive solution of both constitutional and territorial problems but, after six years, they were fruitless. The talks were interrupted by a Greek military coup against the GC government in July 1974, followed by a Turkish invasion five days later. The invasion displaced more than 40 percent of the population as Turkey occupied—and continues to occupy—37 percent of the island. In 1977 and 1979, two high-level agreements determined that the Cypriots would negotiate a bicommunal, bizonal federal republic, but all subsequent negotiations have failed to produce an agreement. The de facto partition of the island persists despite the planned European Union membership for Cyprus. As the GC government negotiated its accession to the European Union, the "Turkish Republic of Northern Cyprus (TRNC)" worked toward becoming integrated with Turkey.[4] The reintegration of the island seems improbable, though in recent years that idea was revived in the context of discussions about the integration of Cyprus to the European Union which was decided in April 2003 (more on this later).

The Intercommunal Talks of 1968–73 represented the best—perhaps also the last—opportunity for a formal peace settlement. The talks failed and gave way to a seemingly stable partition, yet the divided sovereignty and continued presence of peacekeepers almost thirty years since their initial deployment does not allow us to speak of a peacebuilding success in Cyprus.

Our model correctly predicts a peacebuilding failure in Cyprus.[5] But, it does not necessarily do so for all the right reasons. The peacebuilding space was narrow, partly as a result of high levels of hostility and partly

[2] United Nations 1996, pp. 149–50

[3] See the Secretary-General's reports in UN Docs. S/8141 and S/8248 on the 1967 crisis. See, also, Nikos Kranidiotis, *Anochyrote Politeia: Kypros, 1960–1974* (Indefensible state: Cyprus, 1960–1974), vols. 1–2 (Athens: Estia, 1985), pp. 464–66). We cite Kranidiotis vol. 1 as (1985a) and vol. 2 as (1985b).

[4] We place the "TRNC" in quotation marks, as it lacks international recognition.

[5] The in-sample prediction of participatory PB success from model A (table 3.3) in chapter 3 is .043 for Cyprus after the 1974 war, as compared to an average probability of .32.

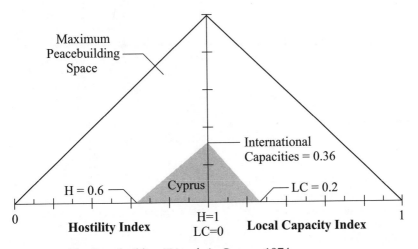

Figure 6.1 The Peacebuilding Triangle in Cyprus, 1974

as a result of insufficient levels of international capacities. We depict this in figure 6.1, where we plot actual values of our three key indices for hostility, international capacities, and local capacities for Cyprus, graphing the peacebuilding triangle that described the peacebuilding ecology in Cyprus in 1974.

The model correctly captures the significant hostility between Greek and Turkish Cypriots, which was intensified by the massive refugee movements after the ethnic war and partition of 1974. Negotiations to reach a settlement were complicated, and it was not possible to reach a treaty, as we will see in more detail below, by the fact that five factions were involved in the peace process, including the governments of Greece and Turkey, which often acted as spoilers. Hostility levels should have been offset at least partially by the relatively high levels of local capacities in Cyprus (see table 6.1). Our proxy of electricity consumption per capita does a good job in capturing the large differential between development levels in Cyprus and other countries in our dataset, but the primary commodity exports proxy is less successful, as it places Cyprus near the average for the universe of cases, while Cyprus did not have a significant dependence on lootable resources such as oil, precious stones, timber, or other resources that have been linked to civil war. Thus, our estimates of the probability of peacebuilding success would have been somewhat higher if we had used a resource-dependence proxy that was better measured for our cases.[6] But, despite high levels of per capita

[6] Sambanis (2004) discusses the implications of poor fit between empirical proxies (including primary commodity exports as a share of GDP) and theoretically significant variables in quantitative studies of civil war. In other cases that we examine in this book (e.g., the Congo), the primary commodity export measure works much better.

TABLE 6.1
Cyprus

	Cyprus (1963–67) UNFICYP (1964–ongoing)	Cyprus (1974) UNFICYP (1964–ongoing)
Sovereign peace	Failure	Failure
Participatory peace	Failure	Failure
War type	"Ethnic"	"Ethnic"
Factions	4	5
UN mandate	Traditional	Traditional
Duration of UN mission (months)	429.5	429.5 (since 1964)
Was UN present during the war? If so, for how long?	Yes; 43 months	Yes; 1 month
Maximum troop strength of UN mission, if any	6,411	4,400
War Duration (in months)	47	1
Real per capita GDP (at start of the war; constant $)	2,437	4,693
Real per capita GDP (at end of the war; constant $)	3,221	3,860
GDP growth at end of the war (% annual change)	5.5	–15.6
People killed during the war	1,000–2,000	5,000
People displaced during the war	60,000	290,000
Outcome of the war	Truce/Stalemate	Truce/Stalemate
Was a treaty signed by most parties?	No	No
Date of the treaty, if any was signed	n/a	n/a
Was the treaty implemented?	n/a	n/a
Primary commodity exports as % of GDP	13.2%	13.2%
Is the country a major oil exporter?	No	No
Ethnolinguistic fractionalization index (100 = highest)	35	35
Ethnic heterogeneity index (1 = highly diverse)	0.36	0.36
Population at start of war (in thousands)	578	610
Area (square kilometers)	9,250	9,250
Effective Development Assistance as % of GDP	—	—

income, income growth was negative immediately after the war, so our model (when we add growth to the equation) captures the declining local capacities after the war.

Looking more closely at this case, we find evidence of what we called microlevel peacekeeping failures, which contributed to a dynamic peacekeeping-peacebuilding relationship that helped institutionalize the conflict. This mechanism, which we described in theory in chapter 2, is illustrated well by the case of Cyprus. Repeated peacekeeping failures undermined the incentives for peace even among moderates and allowed spoilers to dominate the peace process.

It is true that UNFICYP was constrained externally by the UN's financial crisis and major power interests, which explains why a traditional mandate was given to a UN mission that was sent to help resolve a difficult cooperation problem. But UNFICYP had more leverage than it actually used and was responsible for failures that contributed to the conflict's institutionalization over time. The Intercommunal Talks, which we will analyze below in some detail so as to understand better the parties' strategies and their preferences over outcomes, were plagued by spoiler problems. There were extremists on all sides, but the dominant spoiler in Cyprus (after 1971) was EOKA B, a paramilitary organization headed by General George Grivas (Greece and Turkey also acted as spoilers after 1973). Grivas had been the leader of the GC anticolonial struggle during 1955–59 and was fixated on *enosis*, despite the fact that by the mid-1960s most Cypriots preferred independence and *enosis* seemed politically infeasible. Grivas was prepared to start a war with Turkey to achieve *enosis*, despite Turkey's overwhelming military superiority.[7] EOKA B was a destabilizing force that undermined internal GC cohesion through a campaign of terror that culminated in assassination attempts against Makarios.

Consistent with our theoretical arguments about spoiler problems in chapter 2, we argue that UNFICYP should have used all available means to neutralize extremists and EOKA B in particular. Its inability to do so prevented the moderates from acting like peacemakers in the negotiations. This was a peacekeeping failure at the microlevel, which ultimately contributed to a broad peacebuilding failure. UNFICYP had the capacities to do more. Its shortcomings reflected acts of omission more than acts of commission and demonstrate how failed peacekeeping can lead to failed peacemaking.

The discussion in this section focuses on the pre-1975 period, as that was the critical period in Cypriot history. With the de facto partition of the island in 1974 and after the ethnic cleansing and deployment of

---

[7] Interview with a senior member of EOKA B (Limassol, August 1997).

30,000 Turkish troops in the north by 1975, UNFICYP's role was reduced to that of an onlooker. It would be hard to argue that the absence of large-scale violence in Cyprus since 1974–75 was due to the presence of just over 1,000 poorly equipped peacekeepers with a narrow mandate rather than the deterrent effect of Turkey's military superiority over both Cyprus and Greece. Thus, to analyze the effect of UN peacekeeping on UN peacemaking and peacebuilding failures in Cyprus, we have to focus on pre-1974 UNFICYP.

Crawling to the Negotiation Table: The 1968–1974 Intercommunal Talks

The talks were held between GC Speaker of the House Glafcos Clerides and TC leader Rauf Denktash, who was unexpectedly conciliatory, proposing a measure of local autonomy for the TCs in exchange for a GC-dominated central government and acceptance of some of the GCs' constitutional amendments.[8] Makarios opportunistically intervened and demanded the abolition of the TC vice presidency, the abrogation of the 1959 treaties, the creation of a unified voter roll, and a unified regional council appointed by the House with jurisdiction over Greek and Turkish Villages.[9] Interpreting Makarios's proposals as a sign of unwillingness to discuss meaningful TC autonomy, Denktash interrupted the talks on July 18, 1968.[10] When the talks resumed, the military balance on the island had changed (see below) and Denktash retracted his earlier offer.[11] He now asked for a TC regional administration with supreme jurisdiction over regional affairs and focused the talks on the distinction between "administrative and political" local autonomy.[12] Clerides offered administrative autonomy, while Denktash demanded political autonomy.[13] Disagreement over the meaning of "autonomy" ended the

[8] Clerides argues that Denktash's proposals were "well within what is accepted generally as normal local government functions." See Glafkos Clerides, 1989, My Deposition. 4 volumes (Nicosia: Aletheia Press, 1989–92), 2:236–37. Details of the proposals are given in Rauf R. Denktash, The Cyprus Triangle (New York: Office of the Turkish Republic of Northern Cyprus, 1988), p. 54ff.

[9] Michael E. Dekleris, Kypriako, 1972–1974: E teleftea efkeria (Cyprus problem, 1972–1974: The last opportunity) (Athens: Ekdotiki Estia, 1981), p. 48.

[10] See Denktash 1988, p. 56. Clerides (1989, 272–75) believed that the TC enclaves would create a de facto cantonization. To prevent violent conflict, he proposed to recognize the TCs' demands for local self-government in exchange for a reduced TC participation in the central government's executive, but Makarios rejected his proposals.

[11] Kranidiotis 1985a.

[12] Glafcos Clerides, letter to Rauf Denktash, April 24, 1969; Clerides, My Deposition.

[13] Rauf Denktash, letter to G. Clerides, May 20, 1969. See also Polyvios G. Polyviou, Cyprus: Conflict and Negotiation, 1960–1980 (London: Duckworth, 1980), p. 76. The

talks on June 26, 1971. The GCs had not realized how important local autonomy was to the TCs.[14] The Secretary-General broke the deadlock by opening a new round of talks, now including Special Representative Osorio Tafall and two constitutional law experts, Judge Dekleris from Greece and Professor Aldikaçti from Turkey.

The talks resumed on June 8, 1972, on the basis of the Secretary-General's aide-mémoire of October 1971.[15] Local autonomy was again at the forefront, and by the end of 1972 the negotiators seemed to have reached a consensus. This was an electoral period and Makarios decided to proceed with elections before an agreement was reached against the advice of the negotiators, who feared that holding the elections would intensify the GC factional conflict and impede the negotiations.[16] Thus, on December 12, 1972, Clerides asked Makarios to accept the TCs' offer that was then on the table, but Makarios refused to budge. Clerides, in his memoirs, describes this as a missed opportunity: "In 1972, we could have had a solution of our problem based on a much improved constitution than the Zurich one, and on a unitary state, without refugees, missing persons and foreign troops occupying our island. We rejected it because it did not give us the maximum of our aims i.e. Cyprus, a Greek Cypriot island ruled by the Greek Cypriot majority. . . . Today, seventeen years later, if the 1972 solution was possible . . . we would have grasped [it] with both hands."[17]

Makarios was reelected president and Denktash vice president. These results enraged GC paramilitary extremists who launched a guerilla campaign against the government. The National Guard was divided between enosis supporters and Makarios supporters. To avoid a new round of civil war, the negotiators issued a joint statement in June 1973, claiming that they had reached an "agreement in principle." However, in the fall of 1973, regime changes in Greece and Turkey brought to power hardliners who opposed the negotiations. On July 15, 1974, the Greek dictators staged a coup in Cyprus, and five days later Turkey invaded Cyprus, ending six years of negotiations.

TCs argued that "political" autonomy was needed to provide guarantees for their security concerns. See George Ball's memoirs (George W. Ball, *The Past Has Another Pattern: Memoirs* [New York: Norton, 1982]; and Necati M. Ertekun, *The Cyprus Dispute* (Oxford: K. Rustem, 1984): pp. 165–73.

[14] Dekleris 1981, pp. 101–4; 124–38

[15] The Secretary-General's aide-mémoirês outlined the framework and targets of the intercommunal talks. See S/10401, November 30, 1971, and S/10564, Add. 1, 2, March 18, 1972.

[16] Dekleris 1981, 169–80.

[17] Clerides 1990 2:367.

Spoiler Problems in the Cyprus Peace Process

The failure of the Intercommunal Talks was largely the result of spoiler problems. Makarios and Denktash were both opportunistic spoilers and GC paramilitaries consistently acted as if no form of power sharing would be tolerable, undermining the ability of moderates such as Clerides to make peace. EOKA B aggravated Makarios's obstructionism, limited Clerides' room for maneuver, and allowed Denktash to stall, pointing to Makarios's own spoiler behavior in justification of TC noncooperation.

Grivas targeted Makarios-supporters for violence, declaring them traitors. Clerides commented on the constraints that EOKA B had created for the negotiators in a speech at the House of Representatives.[18] According to Clerides, "Makarios and his ministers found it necessary, in order to counter accusations made by Grivas and his supporters that they had betrayed the sacred cause of *enosis*, to deliver patriotic speeches, stressing that *enosis* was a sacred cause and the ultimate goal."[19] Grivas resisted Makarios's efforts at inducement,[20] leaving only coercion as the possible means to control him. Makarios, however, was not lagging far behind in terms of spoiler behavior. He first signaled his extremist preferences in 1964, when he ordered a surprise attack on the TC Mansoura-Kokkina enclave while Dean Acheson was negotiating a peace plan in Athens with representatives from Greece, Turkey, Cyprus, and the GC National Guard.[21] As Turkey responded with air raids and prepared to land troops, the Greek prime minister Papandreou accused Makarios of greed and underhandedness. Papandreou asked the Cypriot ambassador: "Why is Makarios doing these things? We had agreed to maintain the peace. In Geneva, there are at this moment decisive talks concerning the future of Cyprus. Could it be that Makarios' military operations at Mansoura are aimed at undermining these talks? . . . I have been deceived!"[22] Makarios, however, was a rational extremist and, unlike Grivas, was amenable to cooperation if pushed hard enough. But the threat of EOKA B retaliation encouraged him to act like a greedy spoiler.

In contrast to Makarios, Clerides was then—and still was in the negotiations of 2003—a moderate and a peacemaker. Clerides was instrumental in the near agreements of 1968 and 1972–73 and had convinced Makarios to reconcile some of his views with suggestions made by the Athens government. Since 1964, the government of Greece had been trying to

---

[18] Denktash 1988, 62.

[19] Clerides 1990 2:264.

[20] Attempts at inducement were made on several occasions, including at a formal meeting on March 26, 1972. Kranidiotis (1985b, 188ff) gives a detailed account of that meeting.

[21] Kranidiotis 1985b, 240.

[22] Kranidiotis' 1985a, 244 (authors' translation).

destabilize Makarios's authority due to the archbishop's unwillingness to follow Athens' lead.[23] However, after the 1967 crisis, Greece abandoned *enosis* and turned from spoiler to peacemaker. It supported the talks and pressured Makarios to make concessions, such as establishing a constitutional basis for local government and delineating their rights and responsibilities and creating TC police forces for TC villages. The Greek Foreign Affairs minister Palamas believed that "new existing conditions and the real terms in which the whole issue is evolving" necessitated a more compromising GC position.[24] In 1972, after Makarios's unwillingness to follow Clerides' suggestions, the Greek government threatened to intervene against Makarios.[25] However, Greece's peacemaker role was a reluctant one as Greek officials refused to publicly denounce *enosis* unless Makarios did so first. Doing so would have made Makarios the target of ultranationalists in both Cyprus and Greece, so Makarios promised to "cut off his hands" before signing such an agreement, unless Greece did so first.[26] Prisoners of their own nationalist rhetoric, both the Greek leadership and Makarios could not make a peace overture. In November 1973, a coup in Athens brought a more extremist group of officers to power in the Greek junta. Brigadier Ioannides was the new ruler and he now supported EOKA B's hawks, deciding to remove Makarios forcibly.[27] On July 15, 1974, Ioannides staged a coup in Cyprus, opening the door to Turkey's invasion.

Throughout the crisis and until the present, the TC side has been represented by Rauf Denktash. His extremism was kept in check until the GCs rejected his 1968 proposals, which admittedly made him look like a peacemaker. Over time, Denktash realized that secession was a viable option,

[23] Greek governments between 1963 and 1967 had important differences with Makarios. Prime Minister Karamanlis advised Makarios not to try to amend the 1960 constitution. Later, Prime Minister George Papandreou tried to get Makarios to accept the Acheson plan and, when Makarios refused, Papandreou tried to undermine Makarios's government (Clerides 1989, pp. 142–50, 175–91). On Greece's attitude change in 1968, see Kranidiotis (1985a, pp. 521–22), who reproduces Foreign Minister Pipinelis's memorandum of November 27, 1968, accusing Makarios of stalling unnecessarily in the talks. Pipinelis also stressed that the 1967 crisis left no alternative to the Greek side except to support the talks and pressured Makarios to accept Denktash's terms.

[24] Kranidiotis 1985b, 593–600.

[25] See Clerides 1990, vol. 2, app. C for a list of reproduced letters from the Greek government to Makarios, one of which, dated February 1972 from Mr. Panayotakos, a member of the Greek junta, threatened Makarios that "Greece would intervene in the island's affairs if her interests demanded it."

[26] Clerides 1990, 2:270.

[27] Dekleris (1981, 232ff.) writes about Ioannides' links with Grivas. Christopher Hitchens, *Cyprus* (London: Quartet Books, 1984), quotes excerpts from U.S. State Department documents revealing that Ioannides' intentions were to topple the Makarios regime, counting on U.S. support to control Turkey if it tried to intervene.

and he adopted an increasingly uncooperative attitude. In 1970–71, he aggravated the GCs' spoiler problem by demanding that Makarios publicly denounce *enosis* and that he put in writing all of the GCs' concessions.[28] Denktash knew that this would undermine Makarios's position and could have anticipated Makarios's objections. When Makarios refused to publicly and formally announce all his concessions to the TCs, Denktash used this as an excuse to interrupt the talks. His actions since 1971 were consistently those of a greedy spoiler.[29] With Bulent Ecevit's election as prime minister in Turkey in 1973, Denktash acquired a hardline advocate. Denktash now demanded a federation—a solution synonymous to partition for the GCs. This further aggravated GC hardliners, making negotiation even harder for Clerides and Dekleris.

Despite Makarios's and Denktash's obstructionism and opportunism, a compromise might have been possible if the GCs traded constitutional concessions for territorial ones from the TCs. On the basis of interviews and historical and survey research in Cyprus, we have determined that both parties valued constitutional issues more than territorial adjustment, but the TCs wanted territorial adjustment more than the GCs.[30] A welfare-increasing bargain was possible if the parties' relative valuation of constitutional and territorial concessions changed, but this was not possible due to intense pressure by radical extremists on both sides. Moderates such as Clerides were concerned that compromise might cause an internal GC civil war. The important question is if and how UNFICYP might have been able to help control these spoiler problems.

The Need for Proactive Peacekeeping and UNFICYP's Sins of Omission

UNFICYP has been both a blessing and a curse for the United Nations. On the one hand, UN proponents can claim the absence of war in Cyprus since 1974 as a peacekeeping success. Ralph Bunche once remarked that

---

[28] Dekleris 1981, 140–41.

[29] See former Secretary-General Waldheim's memoirs (Kurt Waldheim, *In the Eye of a Storm: A Memoir* [London: Adler and Adler, 1985]). In his memoirs, Javier Perez de Cuellar, *Pilgrimage for Peace: A Secretary-General's Memoir* (New York: St. Martin's Press, 1997), pp. 231–34, described Denktash's tactics as "intolerable" and argued that as long as Denktash was the leader of the TCs, there could not be a settlement.

[30] We used an elite survey and structured interviews conducted by Sambanis during the summer of 1997 to obtain information on policy-maker preferences. We interviewed most Foreign Service officers working on the Cyprus problem, party leaders, and approximately 30 percent of the members of the House of Representatives. TC policy makers did not make themselves available for interviews, with the exception of five interviews over two years with senior TC diplomats representing the "TRNC" in the United States.

if the United Nations "were as good at making peace as UNFICYP [was] at keeping it, then ... [the UN] would have few problems."[31] On the other hand, the lack of a political settlement after more than thirty years of UN peacekeeping suggests to some that UNFICYP may have become part of the problem, a "fixture" that has reduced the parties' incentives to negotiate a settlement.[32] While these two views disagree on the consequences of UNFICYP's success, they agree that UNFICYP has been a peacekeeping success. By reviewing this case and applying the framework for the evaluation of peacekeeping operations that we outlined in chapter 2 (i.e., by distinguishing between macrolevel and microlevel peacekeeping failure), we debunk the myth of UNFICYP's success. We agree with authors who point to UNFICYP's negative effects on peacemaking, but we argue that this was not a perverse consequence of its peacekeeping success, but rather a direct result of its peacekeeping failures.

Security Council Resolution 186 (March 4, 1964) mandated UNFICYP "In the interest of international peace and security, to use its best efforts to prevent a recurrence of fighting and, as necessary, to contribute to the maintenance and restoration of law and order and a return to normal conditions." According to the Secretary-General, UNFICYP was "given a very heavy responsibility without a precise definition of its general mandate to guide it so that it might know exactly what it is entitled to do and how far it may go, particularly in the use of force."[33] As the Council's mandate for UNFICYP was hopelessly vague, the Secretary-General clarified UNFICYP's mandate by outlining a number of concrete objectives for the force.

These objectives make it clear that UNFICYP had an important deterrence and enforcement function. It was also given peacebuilding assignments that resembled mandates given to multidimensional peace

---

[31] Ralph Bunche, addressing UNFICYP officers in 1966, cited in Michael Harbottle, "Cyprus: An Analysis of the UN's Third Party Role in a Small War," in Paschalis Kitromilides and Peter Worsley, eds., *Small States in the Modern World: The Conditions for Survival* (Nicosia: New Cyprus Association, 1979), p. 213.

[32] James H. Wolfe, "The United Nations and the Cyprus Question," in Norma Salem, ed., *Cyprus: A Regional Conflict and Its Resolution* (New York: St. Martin's Press, 1992), pp. 227–41; A.J.R. Groom, "The Process of Negotiation, 1974–1993," in C. H. Dodd, ed., *The Political, Social and Economic Development of Northern Cyprus* (Huntingdon, England: Eothen Press, 1993); James H. Allan, *Peacekeeping: Outspoken Observations by a Field Officer* (Westport, CT: Praeger, 1996); Durch 1996 White 1990; James Stegenga, "UN Peace-Keeping: The Cyprus Venture," *Journal of Peace Research* 7 no. 1 (1970): 1–17, p. 11; Paul F. Diehl, *International Peacekeeping* (Baltimore: Johns Hopkins University Press, 1993); Harbottle 1979, p. 213. (Michael Harbottle was a former UNFICYP commander.)

[33] S/5950, September 10, 1964, para. 215.

Box 6.1 UNFICYP's Mandate

ESTABLISHMENT: The mandate, clarified by the Secretary-General, called for:

- Achievement of freedom of movement on all roads in Cyprus, including the Kyrenia road;

- Achievement of freedom of movement for all communities within the whole town of Nicosia and other cities under conditions of security;

- Progressive evacuation and removal of all fortified positions held by Greek and Turkish Cypriots, with priority given to Nicosia;

- Examination of the problem arising from the division that has taken place in the Cyprus police between the Turkish Cypriots and the Greek Cypriot members and the negotiation of necessary measures for their progressive reintegration;

- The progressive disarming of all civilians other than the regular police "gendarmerie" and the Cyprus army by the Cypriot government and the Turkish community.

- UNFICYP, if requested, would assist in facilitating and verifying the disarming and the storage of arms under conditions of security;

- The control of extremists on both sides;

- The formulation of appropriate general amnesty arrangements;

- The arrangement of security measures and other necessary conditions to facilitate return to normal conditions and particularly normal economic activity;

- The facilitation of the return of Turkish Cypriot civil servants and Government officials to their duties, including the public services, such as postal, telecommunications, public works, etc.

- The normal functioning of the judiciary.[1]

continued

Box 6.1 continued

CHANGES TO MANDATE: Following hostilities between the two sides in 1974, and the cease-fire of August 16, 1974, UNFICYP acquired additional responsibilities, including: inspection of "the deployment of military forces on both sides" following the cease-fire; maintenance of "the status quo" in the buffer zone between the forward lines of the two forces; monitoring of the cease-fire lines; provision of good offices in facilitating activities across the cease-fire lines; humanitarian assistance through delivery of supplies to portions of the island; liaison with the Cyprus police and the Turkish Cypriot police; cooperation with UNHCR and UNDP.[2]

TERMINATION: UNFICYP is an ongoing UN mission.

[1] S/5671, April 29, 1964.
[2] *Blue Helmets*, 164–65.

operations in the 1990s.[34] UNFICYP was not, however, given the resources (e.g., civilian personnel) to discharge these ambitious peace-building functions. UNFICYP did not have the manpower required to disarm civilians; it did not have the technical expertise to reintegrate the Cyprus police and formulate amnesty arrangements; it did not have the fire power to guarantee the safe return of all displaced persons or the return of TC civil servants to their positions; and it did not have the civilian staff required to restore the normal functioning of the judiciary. Thus, these should not be considered as instances of UNFICYP's peacekeeping failure; they are, rather, examples of the Council's failure to match the mandate with appropriate resources. Instead, to properly evaluate UNFICYP's performance, we should assess how well it implemented those aspects of its mandate that it could realistically have achieved given its external constraints, and then assess its impact on the peace process.

Despite shortcomings in manpower and technical specialization, UNFICYP had important successes in nonmilitary activities: it helped improve the TCs' living conditions in the enclaves; worked to restore the operation of public services throughout Cyprus; facilitated the resumption of

[34] UNFICYP had even been asked to monitor elections. Document S/8446, March 9, 1968, para. 97, notes this request from the TC vice president Kutchuk. UNFICYP was ready to assist, but there was no balloting, so it was not necessary for UNFICYP to become involved.

harvest; protected workers in factories in the buffer zone; and worked closely with the International Committee of the Red Cross and later the UNCHR to help refugees and internally displaced persons after 1974.[35] It was also engaged in police work, economic reporting and advising, building construction, schoolteaching, and technical assistance. In the post-1974 period, UNFICYP acquired an expanded humanitarian role.[36] It was responsible for the welfare of GCs residing in the Turkish-occupied northern part of the island and TCs residing in the south. It established liaison arrangements with government agencies and military authorities on both sides and promoted the economic and infrastructure development in the buffer zone;[37] it designed confidence-building measures through bicommunal communication; and it implemented social programs in the last remaining mixed village of Pyla in the buffer zone.[38] All these were considerable achievements primarily in UNFICYP's civilian peacekeeping and peacemaking role.

UNFICYP's nonmilitary activities were complemented by CIVPOL, the civilian police force, which became operational on April 14, 1964. CIVPOL was designed to establish a "liaison with the Cypriot police" and accompany them in their patrols. It was also supposed to man UN police posts in trouble spots throughout the island, conduct searches for missing persons, investigate incidents of violence, and conduct a number of other functions that would be better served by unarmed civilian police officers rather than armed soldiers.[39] CIVPOL's comparative advantage is that its officers are unarmed and not perceived as a threat, so they can be useful in deconfrontation initiatives in the buffer zone.[40] In many regards, CIVPOL is much more directly involved with the people and has greater ability to resolve problems before they escalate into violence.

Despite these unexpected successes with respect to its humanitarian and civil mandate, UNFICYP fared far worse with respect to its military tasks. Importantly, this was also the area where success was relatively easier, as UNFICYP's external constraints were not severe (certainly not in comparison to other cases that we have discussed). In 1964, 6,369 troops were deployed from Austria, Canada, Finland, Ireland, Sweden,

---

[35] Boyd (1966), reports his findings from a review of several UN documents on this issue.

[36] See the Secretary-General's report S/1997/962, December 8, 1997.

[37] UN troops escort workers to plants near enemy lines; provide protection for farmers cultivating land in the buffer zone; work with the GC government on construction projects around roads and highways that pass through the buffer zone; and have helped restore old factories in the buffer zone.

[38] These include, but are not restricted to, forwarding mail across the buffer zone, exchanging currency, and escorting people during visits to the opposite camp.

[39] United Nations 1996, p. 156.

[40] Interview with Barry Carpenter, chief CIVPOL officer, Nicosia, September 1997.

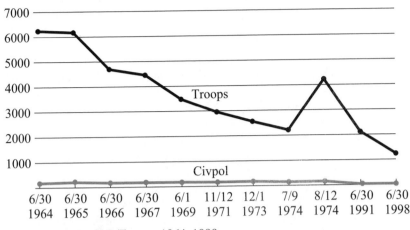

Figure 6.2 UNFICYP Troops, 1964–1998.
Sources: UN Docs S/5764, S/6228, S/7350, S/9233, S/9521, S/10401, S/11137, S/11353

and the United Kingdom, and although UNFICYP's size dwindled over time (see figure 6.2), it still outnumbered the GC National Guard (5,000 troops) and the TC paramilitaries (2,000 fighters).[41] UNFICYP's military superiority vis-à-vis the TCs and the GCs was reinforced when Greece offered to place under UN command its 10,000 soldiers (deployed in Cyprus according to the terms of the Treaty of Guarantee). Moreover, Greece, Turkey, Britain, and the United States were fully supportive of the peace process from 1968 until about 1972, so UNFICYP was not significantly constrained in achieving critical aspects of its mandate: establishing freedom of movement, maintaining the military status quo by preventing the fortification of TC enclaves, and assisting the government in defending itself against extremist violence.

In considering other possible external constraints to UNFICYP's actions, we also find that the force was not constrained by its command structure, the geography of the conflict, or financing.[42] UNFICYP's command structure has been stable since the start of the operation. The Secretary-General is in direct control, appointing the force commander and a special representative, who is the chief of the mission. The island's geography and its small size facilitated troop deployment and communications between components of the force.[43] The establishment of the

[41] S/5764, June 15, 1964, para. 44.

[42] These are factors that in the literature are considered important determinants of peacekeeping success.

[43] A concentrated peacekeeping force is more effective than a widely dispersed force (Diehl 1993, 62).

buffer zone facilitated UNFICYP's work since it limited contact between hostile populations.[44] UNFICYP had financing problems that resulted in the gradual downsizing of the force, but it still maintained considerable strength (relative to the size of the territory and the strength of the parties) and was always a low-cost operation at little risk of being shut down due to financing.[45]

This brief evaluation of UNFICYP's external constraints suggests that we should look at the mission itself (the "microlevel" or "endogenous" aspects of peacekeeping mentioned in chapter 2) to explain its successes and failures in implementing its mandate. Good leadership and a proactive interpretation of the mandate would have allowed UNFICYP to enhance the Cypriots' consent, creating incentives for negotiation. The Secretary-General tried to help UNFICYP be more proactive by interpreting several Council resolutions issued after UNFICYP's deployment as an indirect permission to expand UNFICYP's authority:[46]

> I intend to . . . instruct the Commander of the Force . . . along the following lines:
>
> That in establishing the Force and defining its important function, the Security Council realized that the Force could not discharge that function unless it had complete freedom of movement in Cyprus, which could only mean such unrestricted freedom of movement as may be considered essential by the Force Commander to the implementation of the mandate of the Force. . . .
>
> That the Force, in carrying out its mandate to prevent the recurrence of fighting, is reasonably entitled to remove positions and fortified installations where these endanger the peace, and to take all necessary measures in self-defense if attacked in the performance of this duty. . . .
>
> That in seeking to prevent a recurrence of fighting, it may be demanded by the Commander that the opposing armed forces be separated to reasonable distances in order to create buffer zones in which armed forces would be prohibited.[47]

---

[44] Diehl 1993, 71.

[45] In 1998 UNFICYP cost the UN one-twelfth of ONUMOZ's cost during its first year. Until June 15, 1993, UNFICYP's costs were borne by troop-contributing countries, the Cyprus government, and voluntary contributions. Since UNFICYP's inception, the eight troop-contributing countries have covered 25 percent and NATO countries 88 percent of voluntary contributions, while the Soviet Union did not contribute anything. The cost of the operation in 1998 was U.S. $48 million (gross), close to one-half of which was borne by the governments of Cyprus and Greece. The total cost of the operation since its inception is approximately U.S. $940 million (United Nations 1996; General Assembly A/52/775/Add.1; and authors' calculations).

[46] Alan James, "The UN Force in Cyprus," *International Affairs* 65 (Summer 1989): 481–500, lists as an example UN Doc S/18102, May 31, 1986, para 7. Resolution 383 (1975) was the first of a series of resolutions in the postinvasion years that modified UNFICYP's mandate.

[47] UN Doc S/5950.

These instructions were a green light for UNFICYP to be proactive. Indeed, according to the Secretary-General, field commanders were given wide latitude to interpret their mandate as conservatively or as liberally as they saw fit, and they were allowed to use force if UN troops were coerced to leave their positions or in other circumstances in which the parties "prevent[ed] them from carrying out their responsibilities as ordered by their commanders."[48]

Mandates can be seen either as "ceilings" or "floors." Conservative, risk-averse UN officials or commanders constrained by their home governments will interpret the mandate as a ceiling. By contrast, creative and decisive commanders will take a leadership role by interpreting the mandate as a floor, defining it operationally and using all their capabilities to implement the spirit, not just the word, of the mandate.[49] On several occasions, we found evidence of a conservative interpretation of the mandate that suggested passivity on behalf of UNFICYP. Cypriots frequently overran UNFICYP's posts, manhandled UN troops, and refused to comply with orders issued by UN commanders, undermining UNFICYP's ability to restore law and order. However, UNFICYP was consistently hesitant to use even limited force, when a small amount of force and determination might have gone a long way to restore order. UNFICYP did not restore freedom of movement, control extremists, or defortify the TC enclaves.

More importantly, UNFICYP's shortcomings fueled the conflict. Figure 6.3 shows that despite a drop in violence in the months preceding UNFICYP's deployment, there were two outbreaks of violence, in 1964 and 1967. These incidents were triggered by UNFICYP's inability or unwillingness to restore freedom of movement in two large TC enclaves. On several occasions, UNFICYP had taken action to unman fortified posts if they caused violence that threatened UN officers, so UNFICYP's ability to be forceful was not in question. Indeed, when the UN headquarters came under attack from the Turkish military during the invasion of 1974, UN Force Commander Prem Chand, using the same initiative he had earlier demonstrated in the Congo, showed exceptional resolve and heroism in ordering his troops to stand their ground and fight the invading army. Turkey backed down and Nicosia's International Airport remained under UN control.

In the summer of 1964, just a few months after the force became operational, the GCs were complaining to the Secretary-General that the TCs were unloading arms and troops from Turkey at the port of Kokkina,

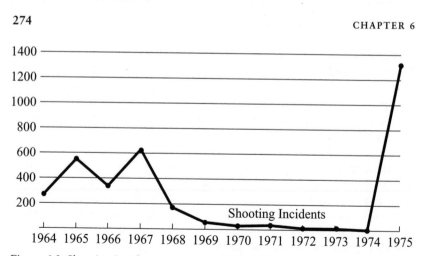

Figure 6.3 Shooting Incidents in Cyprus, 1964–1975.

Sources: UN Docs. S/5593, S/5750, S/5764, S/5950, S/6102, S/6228, S/6426, S/7350, S/8664, S/9233, S/9521, S/9814, S/10005, S/10199, S/10401, S/10664, S/10842, S/10940, S/11294. An entry of zero does not mean that there were no incidents, but rather that there was no report for that trimester. Further, note that the months including the coup and invasion of 1974 have been omitted from the chart (UNFICYP could not have been responsible for controlling these two events, so shooting incidents related to them are not as relevant for our analysis).

which was protected by a fortified TC bridgehead at Mansoura. The GCs' claims were justifiable according to the Secretary-Generals report, so GC "government authorities on more than one occasion had warned UNFICYP to stop this activity in this area or to stand aside and let the Government do it."[50] UNFICYP did not forcibly remove the TCs' fortifications or pressure the TCs to stop their military buildup. This led to a full-blown battle lasting several days between 2,000 GC and Greek soldiers against 500 TCs at Mansoura. Turkey responded by bombing GC military and civilian targets. A Turkish invasion was prevented by U.S. president Johnson's intervention.

On that critical occasion, UNFICYP chose a weak strategy even though the Secretary-General had resolved that UNFICYP should pursue defortification as a necessary strategy for the implementation of its mandate. UNFICYP had the manpower to defortify the enclave and had forcibly removed fortified posts in Nicosia a few weeks prior because they were threatening UN troops.[51] Thus, its choice of strategy reflected a narrow, conservative, and risk-averse interpretation of the mandate— precisely the type of microlevel, or endogenous peacekeeping failure

[50] S/5950, para. 64.
[51] S/5950, paras. 34–36.

described in chapter 2. After the Mansoura fighting, under threat of a Turkish invasion and pressure from the Secretary-General, Greece withdrew 10,000 elite troops that were manning the island's coastal defenses, drastically changing the military status quo in Cyprus.[52] As we saw earlier, that reversal of fortunes emboldened Denktash and made the negotiation of a settlement appreciably more difficult.

UNFICYP proponents claim credit for the decline in shooting incidents starting in 1968 (see figure 6.3). However, that decline coincided with the government's normalization measures implemented in March of 1968. The government unilaterally removed all roadblocks in the areas of Paphos and Limassol, restored freedom of movement for the TCs, and unmanned its fortified posts (except those intended for external defense).[53] The Secretary-General recognized that "there has been no better opportunity in Cyprus for . . . a settlement."[54] The government extended these measures to the whole island, notwithstanding the establishment of the Cyprus Turkish Administration in the enclaves, but insisted that UNFICYP hold the TCs to the same standard. When UNFICYP again used weak strategies and failed to coerce the TCs to restore GC access to the Kophinou enclave, the GCs responded with disproportionate force.

Furthermore, the sharp reduction in shooting incidents from 1967 to 1973 coincided with a decline in UNFICYP's strength (see figure 6.3), so it is hard to argue that UNFICYP was more active or forceful in preventing these incidents. Rather, the main reason for the decline in interethnic violence was the start of Intercommunal Talks, when the attention of the GC government shifted toward the intra-GC factional conflict. When interethnic violence escalated in 1974–75, UNFICYP's inability to control it was evident. In 1975, one year after the establishment of a UN-monitored buffer zone between the two ethnic groups, UNFICYP doubled its strength, but the number of shooting incidents was approximately one hundred times higher than the average for the previous five years.

UNFICYP's sins of commission are overshadowed by its sins of omission, especially its failure to assist the government in its struggle against extremists. UNFICYP feared reprisals and claimed it lacked sufficient

---

[52] Detailed eyewitness accounts of the 1974 fighting by Admiral Skiadopoulos (Greece) reveal that despite the lack of air cover, the National Guard was nearly successful in repelling the Turkish invasion during the first day of fighting. It is clear from these accounts that if the 10,000 Greek troops were still on the island, guaranteeing air cover and naval support from Greece, Turkey's invasion might not have been successful. See Konstantinos Skiadopoulos, *Polemos sten Kypro, Ioulios-Avgoustos 1974* (War in Cyprus; July–August 1974) (Athens: Eleftheri Skepsis, 1989).

[53] S/8286, 8 December 1967, paras. 90–93.

[54] S/8446, 9 March 1968, para. 153.

intelligence to intercept EOKA B members.[55] However, it was possible to control GC spoilers by empowering the GC government. UNFICYP, however, undermined the government's ability to defend itself when, in 1972, it interdicted a large shipment of arms and light artillery. Its mandate never authorized UNFICYP to disarm the parties or inspect imports of arms. Nonetheless, a rapid rate of arms buildup led the Secretary-General to negotiate an informal agreement with the parties to allow UNFICYP to monitor all arms imports that arrived through certain ports.[56] Both parties violated the agreement and Makarios, especially, opposed interference in this area, citing the government's sovereign right to import arms.[57] Despite these constraints, UNFICYP acted decisively to interdict a large arms shipment from Czechoslovakia in 1972. UN intelligence had confirmed that the shipment was intended for Makarios's police and paramilitaries to fight EOKA B.[58] UNFICYP negotiated with the GC government to surrender the arms to UNFICYP personnel.[59] This was an unprecedented action that significantly diminished the GC government's ability to fight terrorists. UNFICYP seems to have been pressured by Greece to prevent Makarios from arming his paramilitaries.[60] However, if UNFICYP did not want to risk peacekeepers' lives in fighting EOKA B, it should have at least allowed the government to defend itself. Moreover, a better armed GC government might have discouraged the coup of 1974.

A second opportunity to control EOKA B presented itself in the fall of 1973 and then again after the death of Grivas in January 1974. Leadership changes present perfect opportunities for spoiler control by providing inducements to new leaders and isolating the extremists.[61] A number of moderates emerged from the ranks of EOKA B wanting to transform the organization into a political party. However, neither UNFICYP nor the UN civilian officers in Cyprus openly supported the moderates, who eventually lost out to hawkish members of EOKA B.[62] Support for moderate leaders during that transition would have been an effective and low-cost strategy for UNFICYP.

---

[55] Interview with UNFICYP's deputy chief of mission, Nicosia, August 1997.

[56] UN Doc S/5828, 23 July 1964 includes telegrams by the UN Secretary General to Cyprus, Greece, and Turkey, urging them to stop the arms buildup in Cyprus.

[57] UN Doc S/5842.

[58] Interview (April 30, 1998) with George Sherry, formerly senior political adviser to UNFICYP.

[59] On the UN's pressure on the GCs to surrender the arms, see Clerides 1990 3:423–24 and UN Doc S/10564, Add. 1, 21 April 1972.

[60] Interview with former UNFICYP official George Sherry (New York, April 1998).

[61] See Stedman 1997 on strategies of spoiler management.

[62] Clerides 1990 2:276–79; Polyviou 1980, p. 125.

After the de facto partition of 1974, UNFICYP's mandate informally adapted to the new conditions. UN troops were redeployed along the cease-fire lines, and their priority was to maintain the new military status quo. UNFICYP's military mandate has been restricted to monitoring, while some of its previous humanitarian, civil, and police activities continue to this day.[63]

Overall, UNFICYP failed to implement its peacekeeping mandate. While actually preventing the 1974 invasion would have been too much to ask of a lightly armed force, we noted several failures at a smaller scale that, over time, allowed the military and political status quo to change and undermined the parties' desire for a negotiated settlement. Failure to defortify the enclaves and restore freedom of movement implied that the TCs could "adaptively" develop stronger preferences for secession—an outcome that was not considered feasible before 1968. As the enclaves grew in size, the TCs developed a political structure and institutions to support independent administration, and the return to a unitary state under GC leadership became less and less likely. The TCs interpreted UNFICYP's passivity as an indication of the legitimacy of their ongoing effort to partition the island.[64] The enclaves were therefore the precursor to the Federated State of Northern Cyprus and later the Turkish Republic of Northern Cyprus.[65] Denktash revealed the significance of experiencing self-administration in the enclaves and in the occupied territories in one of his speeches: *"There has not been a joint State or government embracing both peoples for over a quarter of a century. These two peoples do not have even a single common institution. This reality is of vital importance in defining the starting point of a political association. . . .* Despite the recognition that the Greek Cypriot side enjoys, everyone silently acknowledges that it is nothing but a Greek Cypriot entity and that there is a corresponding Turkish Cypriot entity" (emphasis supplied).[66]

As Turkish foreign minister Ezenbel said years ago, there is "no possibility of turning the clock back" in Cyprus.[67] The conflict has become so institutionalized that it may have passed the "point of no return."[68] As time passed, institutions, norms, and expectations were formed to sustain a different set of possible solutions from the ones that might have

---

[63] A/52/775/Add.1, February 24, 1998, para. 8. Interview with UNFICYP chief of staff, Colonel Ian Talbott (British Army), September 1997. See also Resolution 889 (1993), December 15, 1993; and SC resolution 1000 (1995), June 23, 1995, paras. 4 and 6.

[64] Ertekun 1984, p. 72.

[65] Ertekun 1984.

[66] Rauf Denktash, "Talking Points," February 26, 1990.

[67] See Rossides' letter S/11611, January 31, 1975. Ezenbel's use of these phrases in this context was confirmed in Denktash's letter to the SG, S/11631, February 12, 1975.

[68] UN SRSG Gus Feissel, interview (Nicosia, summer 1997).

been attainable in the first years after 1963. Perhaps the best example of conflict institutionalization in Cyprus is the case of talks on the resettlement of the town of Varosha, a GC town occupied by Turkey after the 1974 invasion. Resolution of the problem of resettling Varosha was given priority in bicommunal negotiations. More than twenty years were spent trying to resolve the Varosha question. In 1977, the UN was pushing for the return of 40,000 GC refugees. Several years later, the return of a smaller number was proposed in exchange for reopening of the Nicosia airport and opening a corridor for tourists to access the TC part of Cyprus through Varosha, giving the TCs annual revenues of up to 20 percent of their GDP. This solution also was rejected by Denktash, and the UN ultimately pushed a plan for the reopening of the town as a location for limited and temporary bicommunal meetings without any rights of refugee return. The GCs' interest in negotiation dwindled as a result of this gradual limitation of their expected gains from a negotiated settlement. Over time and as a result of repeated peacekeeping failures both in the field and at headquarters, the number of feasible bargains became so small that the stalemate was no longer hurting enough to motivate the parties to negotiate.

Cyprus was an example of failed *cyprusization*—the desired effect of traditional peacekeeping of freezing a conflict until a political solution is reached. UN officials sometimes refer to deadlocked conflicts as "cyprusized," suggesting that good peacekeeping may have the perverse effect of discouraging peacemaking and negotiation.[69] Our analysis, however, suggests that the Cyprus conflict was in fact changing over time, partially due to UNFICYP's failure to freeze the military status quo before 1974. Major changes to the status quo included the growth of the enclaves, the establishment of a transitional TC administration, the internal factional conflict on the GC side, the coup and invasion of 1974, the population transfers of 1975 that created ethnically pure regions in a previously demographically mixed country, and the ongoing colonization of Cyprus by Turkish mainlanders as well as the expected EU membership for Cyprus. While in 1968 Denktash seemed eager to negotiate, the failed cyprusization of the conflict changed his incentive structure. Former Secretary-General Perez de Cuellar, who dedicated most of his time in office to the Cyprus problem, summarized the problem's evolution by saying:

> The Turkish Cypriot side, especially its leader, Rauf Denktash, has more to lose than to gain from integration into a reunited Cyprus. . . . For the Greek Cypriots, the attraction of unification is not sufficient to cause them to

---

[69] UN SRSG Gus Feissel, interview (Nicosia, summer 1997).

accept a settlement that would acknowledge a right of the Turkish Cypriots to self-determination. . . . The greatest pressure for a settlement has come from the refugees and displaced persons from the north, who long hoped to regain their property. By the 1980s, however, few actually would have returned. Any [Greek] Cypriot government, no matter what its leadership, is likely to lose politically if it enters into a settlement entailing concessions on the central principles of unified sovereignty and unified identity for the land.[70]

Hugo Gobbi, UN negotiator and former Special Representative in Cyprus, wrote about the 251 meetings held between GC and TC leaders over three years (1980–83) and explained that "the two communities' ideas of a federation are impossible to merge. . . . I would ask the Greek Cypriots who do not live as prisoners of the past, what is better: to own 100% of around three quarters of the Island, or to possess 50% of the whole. Because this is the only present alternative despite optimistic hopes."[71] The GCs, however, have not accepted that the result of the 1974 invasion is final. They are also unable to choose among unappealing alternatives. As a result, another expert on the Cyprus problem suggested that both the GCs and the TCs are "like shoppers who merely come to the store to look around, but are unprepared to make a purchase."[72] Under the political uncertainty of a compromise solution, both parties prefer to live with an inefficient status quo, and this is as true today as it was during the Intercommunal Talks.

Despite the parties' demonstrated lack of interest in compromising their extreme positions in favor of reaching a settlement, the UN has pursued tireless peacemaking initiatives in Cyprus. UNFICYP's peacekeeping role was eclipsed by the Turkish occupation of Northern Cyprus (the Turkish army is the second largest in NATO and Turkey's proximity to Cyprus has had a stabilizing effect, deterring any GC aspirations to reversing the status quo through military action). But in the nearly thirty years since the Turkish invasion, successive UN Special Representatives have tried their best to push the peacemaking process forward.

One of the most impressive efforts was the one launched by Alvaro de Soto's team. Taking advantage of scheduled talks to negotiate the accession of Cyprus to the European Union, the UN drafted a remarkably comprehensive settlement plan known as the Annan plan. The plan followed on the footsteps of previous attempts (such as de Cuellar's Draft

---

[70] De Cuellar 1997, pp. 234–35.
[71] Hugo J. Gobbi, *Rethinking Cyprus* (Tel Aviv: Aurora, 1983), p. 49.
[72] UN SRSG Gus Feissel, interview (Nicosia, summer 1997).

Framework Agreement, or George Vassiliou's Outline Framework for a Settlement) but went further in spelling out the intricate details of the workings of a federal system that would achieve several layers of checks and balances for the TCs. Although intense pressure from the Turkish Cypriot community, which felt that it was missing the train of Cyprus's accession to the EU, was sufficient to push Denktash to the negotiation table, it was not sufficient to make him accept the Annan plan. The United Nations, European Union, United States, and other interested parties pressured Denktash (and political elites in Turkey) to accept the draft, but the talks failed. Ultimately, the GCs also voted against the Annan plan in a referendum. As this book was being completed, Denktash, under extensive domestic pressure, opened the borders of Northern Cyprus and allowed cross-border visits by both GCs and TCs. This move rekindled hopes of integration and revitalized efforts to add the Annan plan as an annex to Cyprus's accession treaty with the EU, so that if and when the Cyprus problem is resolved, the parts of the island and people now controlled by Denktash and Turkey could automatically become part of the EU.

Interestingly, nowhere in these discussions did UNFICYP feature prominently. UNFICYP's poor peacekeeping record and its reputation for weakness and neutrality are hard to forget. Peacekeeping in a new, integrated Cyprus would be provided by an international peacekeeping force with greater credibility than UNFICYP. UNFICYP's contribution to the peace today is more cosmetic or symbolic than substantial. UNFICYP could have helped matters more before 1974, but its passivity prevented a positive contribution. UNFICYP's failure to control extremists is an example of endogenous peacekeeping failure that, over time, helped institutionalize the conflict.

In the late 1960s, George Ball asked Makarios why he was reluctant to agree to a compromise solution. Makarios replied with a question: "[S]hould I be killed by the Turks or the Greeks?" Ball's answer epitomized the scope of international peacebuilding in Cyprus: "Your Beatitude, that's your problem."[73] More recent negotiators such as Kofi Annan and Alvaro de Soto have shown more sensitivity and applied great efforts to achieve an equitable solution in Cyprus. But the legacy of the past is hard to forget.

While many have accused the international community of indifference in Cyprus—even after 30 percent of the population became refugees—this accusation has never been truer than in the case of the peacekeeping and peacebuilding failure in Rwanda. We turn to that case next.

[73] Ball 1982, 346.

Rwanda

> Mandates without the resources needed are
> nothing more than frustrations and a
> guarantee of failure.
> —Major General Romeo Dallaire,
>   force commander, United Nations
>   Assistance Mission for Rwanda[74]

The genocide in Rwanda bears little resemblance to the failed opportunities to achieve a peace in Cyprus. But some of the sources of failure were similar: high levels of hostility, an inadequate mandate (one that did not reflect the responsibilities envisaged in the treaty, which was better focused on the true challenges), and, crucially, meager international capacity that resulted in weak implementation. The peacebuilding space in Rwanda after the war of 1990–93 was narrower than in Cyprus. Like Cyprus, Rwanda had been engaged in an ethnic war that had further polarized an already hostile society dominated by two ethnic groups. Unlike Cyprus, Rwanda had few, if any, local capacities (see figure 6.4). According to our model, Rwanda needed a transformational UN peace operation that combined an extensive multidimensional mandate with an authorization to use force in defense of the mandate so as to deter

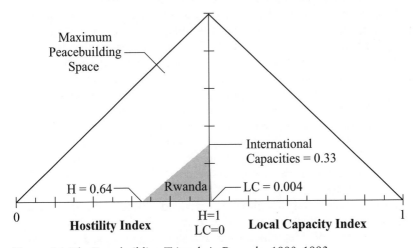

Figure 6.4 The Peacebuilding Triangle in Rwanda, 1990–1993

[74] In "Lessons of Rwanda Unheeded," *Toronto Star*, May 17, 2000.

spoilers. But, as in Cyprus, the mandate was weak and resources relative to the threat were even more meager.

Our model does not perform too badly in this case as it predicts a slightly lower probability of peacebuilding success for Rwanda in 1993 as compared to the average for all other cases.[75] The local capacities measures in this case work as predicted by the model: low levels of development and declining economic growth reduced the economic opportunity costs for violence in Rwanda, making a return to war more likely (see table 6.2). Not all hostility measures work equally well, however, and international capacity measures create a false impression in this case. The numbers of people killed in the war do not adequately reflect the underlying levels of hostility between the factions. There are also fewer factions in this case than in the Cyprus case, but they were even more polarized after decades of ethnic conflict (including prior instances of violence). Polarization, as suggested by our review of the literature on civil war, increases the risk of civil war. The relatively low levels of deaths in the war of 1990–93 fail to capture the extremist aspirations of the Hutu leadership. The large numbers of displacements, by contrast, come closer in measuring the depth of hostility in this case. In the context of such a long history of conflict and intense violence, the mandate that was given to the UN Assistance Mission for Rwanda (UNAMIR) did little to address the conflict or to meet the ambitious tasks that had been envisaged by the Arusha Agreement. The parties took the weak peace operation as an opportunity to regroup and resume the war.

But, the model does not capture the microlevel dimension of failures in peace implementation by the UN. The international capacities index for Rwanda was relatively high, especially if we look at numbers of troops per capita or per square kilometer. And international aid and transfers to the balance of payments were substantial. But the amount of international capacities and the mandate that governed their actions to resolve this conflict were insufficient. The intensity of the parties' preferences for violence would have required a much stronger intervention, but the Security Council was indifferent, and peacekeepers on the ground failed to use all available means at their disposal to constrain the worst spoilers.

After the genocide, a new peace process started and our model here does not fit the case very well as it predicts a low probability of peacebuilding success even though we have coded a peacebuilding success as the outcome of this process. What drives this poor prediction is the legacy of the genocide, which we argue should have raised hostility levels, making peace difficult to take hold. The effects of local capacities are

[75] The in-sample probability estimate of peacebuilding success in Rwanda after the 1990–93 war is 0.23 (the average for all cases in our dataset is about 0.3).

TABLE 6.2
Rwanda

	Rwanda (1963–64)	Rwanda (1990–93) UNAMIR I (1993–94)	Rwanda (1994) UNAMIR II (1994–96)
Sovereign peace	Failure	Failure	Success
Participatory peace	Failure	Failure	Success
War type	"Ethnic"	"Ethnic"	"Ethnic"
Factions	2	3	3
UN mandate	None	Traditional	Monitor
Duration of UN mission (months)	0	9	23
Was UN present during the war? If so, for how long?	No	No	Yes; 4 months
Maximum troop strength of UN mission, if any	0	2,599	5,909
War duration (in months)	3	24	4
Real per capita GDP (year before war start; constant $)	467	730	681
Real per capita GDP (at end of the war; constant $)	368	681	411
GDP growth at end of the war (% annual change)	−4.07	−39.69	30.73
People killed during the war	4,200	2,000	800,000
People displaced during the war	152,000	950,000	2,000,000
Outcome of the War	Gov't victory	Treaty/Settlement	Rebel victory
Was a treaty signed by most parties?	No	Yes	No
Date of the treaty, if any was signed	n/a	March 1993	n/a
Was the treaty implemented?	n/a	No	n/a
Primary commodity exports as % of GDP	7 (imputed)	4.7 (imputed)	3.9 (imputed)
Is the country a major oil exporter?	No	No	No
Ethnolinguistic fractionalization index (100 = highest)	14	14	14
Ethnic heterogeneity index (1 = highly diverse)	0.18	0.18	0.18
Population at start of war (in thousands)	3,007	6,921	6,230
Area (square kilometers)	26,340	26,340	26,340
Effective Development Assistance as % of GDP	—	370.71	1,464.60

less clear in this case: declines in the level of real per capita income were offset by rapidly growing rates of income after the war, and relatively low dependence on natural resources did not introduce incentives to loot by returning to war. Our model would have had a better chance at predicting peacebuilding success if instead of net current transfers we had used our measure of effective development assistance to capture financial inflows to support the peace. Development aid surged after the genocide as the international community tried to assuage its guilt by helping to rebuild Rwanda (see table 6.2). Our estimates are also affected by the difficulty in measuring the UN's involvement in Rwanda after the genocide. We have coded an observer mission on the basis of the activities that UNAMIR was actually able to discharge, even though its mandate was consistent with a multidimensional mission.[76] But the UN was present in other forms—most importantly in the Tribunal for Rwanda, which helped push the national reconciliation process forward.[77] Our coding of the UN's capacities after both Rwandan wars reflects the constraints imposed on the peacekeepers by an apprehensive Council wanting to avoid a repetition of the UN's experience in Somalia.

One key to understanding the tragedy is that the Rwanda genocide was the stepchild of the disaster in Mogadishu. The loss of the eighteen U.S. Rangers and the precipitous U.S. withdrawal left a pall over any ambitions toward the wider enforcement that characterized UNOSOM II's broad peacebuilding mandate. And unlike Bosnia, where the nature of conflict was known and the UN operated within tight peacekeeping limits (despite wider promises), in Rwanda UNAMIR's mandate covered extensive but unfocused peacebuilding responsibilities that never addressed the fear and resentment that underlay Rwandan ethnic politics. UNAMIR reflected the broad responsibilities of Somalia and the constraints of Bosnia. Unfortunately, it was dispatched without a concept of operations that bore a resemblance to the situation on the ground. A woefully underresourced peacebuilding mission premised on the comprehensive consent of the parties was sent to implement a peace that could not have been more flimsy, if it was not illusory from the moment

[76] The coding of the UN mandate in this case is somewhat ambiguous, so this is one of the cases that was recoded in doing robustness tests. Our statistical results from chapter 3 are robust to recoding this case as a multidimensional operation (see supplement).

[77] The picture becomes even more complicated (and the model's predictions become more accurate) if we consider the high levels of violence in border regions of Rwanda and code a peacebuilding failure as a result. This is one of the ambiguous cases that we mentioned in chapter 3. Most of the violence in Rwanda after the mid-1990s is due to rebel incursions from bases across the Rwandan border. We would code a peacebuilding failure if we relax the criterion that rebels must have bases in the country. By coding this case as a failure, the model's fit improves (see results in the supplement).

it was signed. And unlike UNPROFOR, which stuck out a deteriorating situation in an effort to save lives, UNAMIR collapsed soon after ten Belgian soldiers were murdered, leaving the Tutsi and moderate Hutu population in the hands of a genocidal campaign that resulted in the deaths of about 800,000 people and the displacement of 3 million, 2 million of whom became refugees across the borders of Rwanda.[78]

Historical Legacies

The 1994 massacres were not Rwanda's or the region's first, but they were by far its worst. Indeed, as early as 1959 the majority Hutus (85 percent) had risen against the Tutsi minority (14 percent), who had been favored by the Belgian colonialists. Reflecting the regional dimensions of the strife, in Rwanda Hutu slaughtered Tutsi, just as in neighboring Burundi, Tutsi slaughtered Hutu. Tutsi exiles settled in both Burundi to Rwanda's south and Uganda to the north.

The first full-scale civil war in Rwanda, between the government and Tutsi exiles, occurred just one year following independence, in 1963–64, killing nearly 3,000 people in battles and up to 10,000 Tutsi civilians were massacred in retaliation by the government.[79] After the war, Hutus dominated political life and President Gregoire Kayibanda fostered an ideology that emphasized the values of "being Hutu."[80] After state-sponsored massacres of Hutus in Burundi, Kayibanda capitalized on the emotional response in Rwanda to begin implementing a strategy of Hutu "purification" in schools, civil service, and the private sector as a way to increase support for his regime, further polarizing ethnic identities in Rwanda. These "purification" policies were performed by vigilante committees, which served to heighten tensions between northern and southern Hutus[81] and opened the door, in July 1973, to a successful coup by Major General Juvenal Habyarimana of the Rwandese Armed Forces (FAR).[82]

The Tutsi exile movement in Uganda joined with small numbers of Hutu dissidents fleeing Rwanda's dictatorial governments and its oppressive army to form the Rwandan Patriotic Front (RPF), which offered

---

[78] Gerard Prunier, *The Rwanda Crisis: History of a Genocide* (New York: Columbia University Press 1995), p. 265; Alison Des Forges, *Leave None to Tell the Story: Genocide in Rwanda* (New York: Human Rights Watch, 1999); Independent Inquiry into the Actions of the United Nations during the 1994 Genocide in Rwanda. 1999. *Report.* United Nations http://www.un.org/News/ossg/rwanda_report.htm, accessed December 8, 2000, p. 1.

[79] Prunier 1995, p. 56.

[80] Prunier 1995.

[81] Prunier 1995, p. 61.

[82] Alan J. Kuperman, "Rwanda in Retrospect," *Foreign Affairs* 79, no. 1 (2000): 94–118.

significant support for Yowerei Museveni's takeover of Uganda in 1986.[83] In his transition from rebel leader to national political leader, Museveni sought to reduce the role that Rwandans had played in his military forces and assist their repatriation to Rwanda.[84] Supported by Uganda, Fred Rwigyema (formerly a major general in the Ugandan army), Paul Kagame, and several other Ugandan army officers led the RPF in raids across the Uganda border in order to force the Rwandan government to allow the refugees to return.

In 1990–93, the incursions into Rwandan territory culminated in a war between the Hutu-dominated government of Mouvement Republicain National pour la Democratie et le Developpement (MRND), Habyarimana's party, and Tutsi dominated groups of the RPF.[85] The war coincided with escalating political crisis in Rwanda, itself a product of chaotic democratization that resulted from French pressure to democratize in the summer of 1990. The democratization process saw the creation of an active student protest movement and more than ten poorly organized and ineffective opposition parties.[86] Civil society institutions were also growing, especially a number of human rights groups and an active press and radio and television station. However, these institutions were mostly ineffective, and some of them were easily manipulated by the government and extremist groups, fueling ethnic tensions and undermining the spirit of the democratization. Following large-scale protests and an army mutiny in 1992, President Habyarimana was forced to accept a coalition government with the prime ministership assigned to the largest opposition party. But France continued to support President Habyarimana, and he used the disagreement among the parties of the opposition to stall the peace process.[87]

The Rwanda army (FAR), growing in strength from 5,000 troops to about 50,000, successfully repelled the RPF, as France, Belgium, and Zaire sent in troops to advise and indirectly support Habyarimana against an RPF takeover. (France allegedly feared that the RPF, with its Ugandan backing, represented a threat from the "anglo-saxon" camp against a former French-speaking colony.)[88] Paul Kagame took over the RPF's leadership, took refuge back in Uganda, regrouped, and recruited Tutsi

---

[83] Prunier 1995, 70.

[84] Prunier 1995, 74.

[85] About 2,000 people were killed in the war. See Meredith R. Sarkees and David J. Singer, "The Correlates of War Datasets: The Totality of War," paper prepared for the 42nd Annual Convention of the International Studies Association, Chicago, IL (February 20–24, 2001).

[86] Prunier 1995, p. 127.

[87] Human Rights Watch, Annual Report 1994.

[88] Prunier 1995, pp. 103–6.

volunteers driven out of Rwanda by FAR repression. RPF then grew from 12,000 fighters in 1992 to 25,000 in 1994.[89]

Rather than leading to a simple stalemate (hurting or otherwise), the growing democratic opposition to the Habyarimana regime made what Filip Renytjens has called an "objective alliance" with the RPF as it offered the RPF a peace overture and agreed to meet its leaders.[90] The modalities of the process were worked out in Paris, and a peace process mediated by Tanzania and the Organization of African Unity was launched in early June 1992. The RPF declared an end to the armed struggle, a cease-fire was signed, broken, and re-signed, and the war finally "ended" with the signing of the Arusha Accords in August 1993.

Arusha Accords

The Arusha Accords were both made possible and rendered complicated by growing conflict among unstable coalition groups. Habyarimana signed the Arusha Accords under pressure—military pressure from the advancing RPF and financial pressure from bilateral (France) and multilateral (World Bank) lenders, without whom Rwanda's economy would collapse.[91] While the democratic opposition to Habyarimana supported the peace process, the FAR continued to be a stumbling bloc, supporting rioting and ethnic violence and supplying the extremist militias connected to MNRD, the *interhamwe*, with weapons. Colonel Bagosora, widely perceived to be a dangerous extremist, was appointed director of the Defense Ministry and emphatically opposed the accords, as did a large segment of the population.[92] President Habyarimana thus found himself in the middle of a complex game in which his own continuing power required a delicate manipulation of pressures coming from the RPF and the democratic opposition, on the one hand, and the FAR and the extremist forces on the other. The international community was betting that Habyarimana would want to and could effectively preside over a transition that would allow the forces of peaceful reconciliation to emerge in control, marginalizing the extremists.

Signed in August 1993, the Arusha Accords encompassed a wide-ranging and impressive vision of a transformed Rwanda. They focused on a power-sharing agreement that included details on the composition of a Broad Based Transitional Government (BBTG), involving MRND,

[89] Prunier 1995, p. 117.

[90] Reyntjens 1996, p. 234, and Bruce D. Jones, "The Challenges of Strategic Coordination," in Stephen J. Stedman, Donald Rothchild, and Elizabeth M. Cousens, eds., *Ending Civil Wars: The Implementation of Peace Agreements* (Boulder, CO: Lynne Rienner, 2002), pp. 89–115.

[91] Des Forges 1999, p. 124.

[92] Des Forges 1999, pp. 125–26.

RPF, and various democratic opposition parties, a protocol for the repatriation of refugees, and an armed forces integration agreement. Their Achilles' heel was that the accords were a bet that took at face value the elites' effort to strike a power-sharing deal; they did not plan for the retraining or construction of institutions, the mobilization of civil society or even (the often standard measure) the holding of national elections (other than as an eventual but not scheduled outcome). The BBTG was quickly paralyzed by the level of factional conflict that it had internalized, as a coalition of six parties with extremely divergent interests. By the time there was agreement on the refugee repatriation issue, it had been overtaken by events, as the level of physical threat and the number of refugees and internally displaced went beyond the repatriation issue as initially defined by the Tutsi leadership.

The thorniest issue was the creation of an integrated army, and it was here that the level of persistent conflict became apparent. An armed forces integration agreement is a measure that is generally thought to increase the credibility of the government's commitment as it gives the rebels access to the armed forces and makes the political settlement more easily self-enforceable.[93] However, the implementation of these provisions of the agreement was partly to blame for the genocide that followed.[94] The accords failed to disband Hutu militias, and in fact, these militias grew in size and received better training as an indirect result of the accords. The Arusha Accords provided that in the new army, the senior officer appointments would be divided equally between the Forces Armées Rwandaises (FAR) and the RPF insurgents and the enlisted troops would be recruited on a basis of 40 percent RPF and 60 percent government troops.[95] Over 20,000 FAR soldiers were to be demobilized, twice the number for that of the RPF. A plan for a battalion of RPF soldiers to be stationed in Kigali during the transition was perceived by the FAR as a symbol of defeat for the government.

The process of integrating the military was never fully initiated and contributed significantly to the collapse of the agreement in 1994.[96] Through-

---

[93] Walter 2002. Her general point about the importance of security stands and is illustrated by the Rwandan example.

[94] Bruce D. Jones, "Civil War, the Peace Process, and Genocide in Rwanda," in Taisier M. Ali and Robert O. Matthews, eds., *Civil Wars in Africa* (Montreal: McGill–Queen's University Press, 1999), p. 69.

[95] See Conflict Prevention Web site, http://www.caii-dc.com/ghai/toolbox7.htm (accessed May 31, 2002). See also "Peace Agreement between the Government of the Republic of Rwanda and the Rwandese Patriotic Front" in INCORE Data Service, http://www.incore.ulst.ac.uk/cds/agreements/africa.html (accessed January 19, 2002).

[96] Jones 1999, 2002; and see his fuller account in Bruce D. Jones, *Peacemaking in Rwanda: The Dynamics of Failure* (Boulder, CO: Lynne Rienner, 2001).

out 1993 and 1994, hardliners who were opposed to the Arusha Accords increased their efforts to stockpile machetes and began recruiting more militia members. The RPF was never convinced that the accords would be implemented and continued recruiting members after August 1993.[97] This environment suggested that there were strong incentives to renege on the agreements. Strong external enforcement was necessary to reassure the parties that their adversaries would comply with the terms of the accords. The Arusha Accords provided for a broad role for a Neutral International Force (NIF) under UN command to help in the implementation phase.[98] How that role would be defined and implemented would thus be crucial.

UNAMIR

Despite a report by Mr. Ndiaye, special rapporteur of the Commission on Human Rights, describing widespread violations of human rights in the runup to the Arusha Accords, the Security Council mandate (S/Res 872, October 5, 1993) establishing UNAMIR did not reflect an appreciation of the difficult cooperation problem that UNAMIR was sent in to resolve. The mandate, in effect, papered over rather than filled the gaps in the accords.

A reconnaissance mission led by Brigadier General Romeo A. Dallaire was dispatched during the last two weeks of August to study the possible functions of the peacekeeping force. Dallaire presented his estimates of troop strength in three options: the "ideal" 5,500; the "reasonably viable" 2,500; and the number preferred by the United States, France and Russia, 500–1,000.[99] On September 24, 1993, the Secretary-General presented his report (S/26488) to the Council, recommending the establishment of a peacekeeping operation that, on the basis of the report by the reconnaissance mission, should have 2,548 personnel to help establish a secure area in Kigali and monitor the cease-fire until the BBTG was established.[100] UNAMIR's mandate was unfocused and weak, better suited to facilitating and monitoring a coordination-type problem. Security Council Resolution 872 weakened the mandate by excising the provision the Secretary-General had recommended concerning the sequestering of arms.[101] That, plus the minimal provision of less-than-top-line troops and the scheduled deployment in phases signaled to many in New York and

---

[97] Des Forges 1999, pp. 129–30.

[98] Independent Inquiry, 1999, p. 3.

[99] Dallaire, 2003, pp. 75–76; Des Forges, 1999, p. 132.

[100] Independent Inquiry 1999, 4. In the wake of Somalia and the crisis in peacekeeping, Dallaire had been told to "design the mission to fit the available resources," not to discover and recommend what resources would be needed to do the job (Dallaire 2003, p. 56).

[101] Independent Inquiry 1999, p. 5.

Box 6.2 UNAMIR's Mandate

ESTABLISHMENT: Security Council Resolution 872 of October 5, 1993, established the United Nations Assistance Mission for Rwanda, integrating UNAMIR into it, with a mandate:

- To contribute to the security of the city of Kigali inter alia within a weapons-secure area established by the parties in and around the city;

- To monitor observance of the cease-fire agreement, which calls for the establishment of cantonment and assembly zones and the demarcation of the new demilitarized zone and other demilitarization procedures;

- To monitor the security situation during the final period of the transitional government's mandate, leading up to the elections;

- To assist with mine clearance, primarily through training programmes;

- To investigate at the request of the parties or on its own initiative instances of alleged noncompliance with the provisions of the Arusha Peace Agreement relating to the integration of the armed forces, and pursue any such instances with the parties responsible and report thereon as appropriate to the Secretary-General;

- To monitor the process of repatriation of Rwandese refugees and resettlement of displaced persons to verify that it is carried out in a safe and orderly manner;

- To assist in the coordination of humanitarian assistance activities in conjunction with relief operations;

- To investigate and report on incidents regarding the activities of the gendarmerie and police (S/RES/872, para.3).

CHANGES TO MANDATE: Security Council Resolution 912 (1994) of April 21, 1994 adjusted UNAMIR's mandate so that the mission was to focus its efforts on obtaining a cease-fire, assisting humanitarian relief "to the extent feasible," and monitoring and reporting

continued

Box 6.2 continued

on the situation in Rwanda, "including the safety and security of the civilians who sought refuge with UNAMIR" (S/RES/912). Several subsequent resolutions clarified the mandate, which included provision of security for the personnel of the International Tribunal for Rwanda and assistance in the establishment and training of a new, integrated, national police force" (S/RES/965, para.3) as well as exercising its good offices to help achieve national reconciliation within the frame of reference of the Arusha Peace Agreement; and helping repatriate refugees.

TERMINATION: UNAMIR withdrew on March 1, 1996.

Kigali (though not to all) that UNAMIR was a stopgap measure and not expected to enforce its mandate. In Dallaire's view, the biggest gap was the absence of a provision to fund the demobilization and the integration of the armed forces, the heart of the thin peacebuilding strategy.[102]

In November 1993, Dallaire requested clarifications on UNAMIR's Rules of Engagement. He asked for approval to use force to prevent crimes against humanity ("ethnically or politically motivated criminal acts . . . [such as] executions, attacks on displaced persons or refugees") but never received an official reply from headquarters.[103] From November onward, the peace process seemed stalled, political assassinations increased, the BBTG was deadlocked, and civilian massacres occurred with increased frequency. On January 11, Dallaire telegrammed the military adviser of the Secretary-General letting him know that a high-ranking government official in Rwanda had revealed to him the government's plan to kill Belgian soldiers so as to induce a withdrawal of the Belgian contingent from Rwanda and to compile lists of all Tutsi in Kigali so as to identify and execute them. Dallaire also mentioned that government paramilitaries were stockpiling weapons and that the informant could take UNAMIR to the sites of those arms caches. Dallaire stated his intention to intervene forcibly within thirty-six hours.[104]

On January 12, Dallaire received a reply from Iqbal Riza, writing on behalf of Kofi Annan, the UN's head of Peacekeeping Operations at the time, stating that UNAMIR's mandate did not permit taking actions

---

[102] Dallaire 2003, p. 74.
[103] Independent Inquiry 1999, p. 5.
[104] Independent Inquiry 1999, p. 7.

against the arms caches.[105] Moreover, Riza replied that Dallaire must "assume that he—Habyarimana—is not aware of these activities" and urged him to share his information with the Rwandan president.[106] This inaccurate appreciation must be seen in the context of the mixed signals arriving in New York. The special representative, Jacques-Roger Booh-Booh, was sending reassuring messages. Even the RPF, while concerned about the threat of renewed violence, anticipated a local clash in Kigali, not what would turn into a genocide.[107] Belgium warned the Secretary-General of the prospect of stalemate and increasing violence, though the U.S. CIA, which did a study that did foresee genocide as the extreme scenario, did not. These repeated failures, unlike the case of UNFICYP, were primarily due to severe external constraints placed upon the UN force by the contributing countries and the Security Council. Unlike the Secretariat in New York, which was responding to the Security Council, some of UNAMIR's leadership in the field were willing to see the mandate as a floor, not a ceiling, but they, too, shared some of the blame, and one can identify failures endogenous to the functioning of UNAMIR that aggravated UNAMIR's exogenous constraints and encouraged extremist behavior by the parties.

UNAMIR actually had the capacity to act more decisively, if it had been authorized to do so.[108] It is notable that a few days later, on January 21–22, UNAMIR discovered a shipment of arms sent from France that violated the terms of the accords and confiscated the shipment without effective resistance by the parties.[109] It is worth considering, therefore, that UNAMIR's relative strength did not prevent it from taking tactical enforcement measures to target the most uncooperative parties and reduce spoiler problems in the peace process. According to the Independent Inquiry (1999), UNAMIR was in a position to use its 2,500 men to credibly deter aggression in some protected areas, but some troops (Dallaire highlights the contingent from Bangladesh) proved unwilling to be proactive. UNAMIR logistics appear to have been chaotic, and the political leadership of the mission and the force commander did not seem to be operating in harmony with each other, with, unsurprisingly, Booh-Booh preferring diplomacy and Dallaire, action. General Dallaire seemed ready to act impartially (within the contours of his mandate) but proactively,

---

[105] Des Forges 1999, p. 152.

[106] Philip Gourevitch, *We Wish to Inform You That Tomorrow We Will Be Killed with Our Families: Stories from Rwanda* (New York: Farrar Strauss and Giroux, 1998), p. 105.

[107] See discussion in Jones 2001, pp. 113–14 and for information problems in peacekeeping, see p. 167.

[108] See Des Forges 1999; Scott Feil, *Preventing Genocide* (New York: Carnegie Corporation, 1998); and Dallaire 2003; but for a contrary view, Kuperman 2000.

[109] Des Forges 1999, p. 156.

but he would have had to violate instructions from the Department of Peacekeeping Operations (DPKO) to have done so. This is a decision serving officers are understandably reluctant to take. UNAMIR was thus constrained by a reluctant Secretariat, a disinterested Council, and a sense that its mission, strained for resources, lacked priority in the minds of the international community.[110]

On April 6, a plane carrying President Juvenal Habyarimana of Rwanda and Cyprien Ntaryamira of neighboring Burundi, both returning from another round of regional peace talks, was shot down, killing both of them and marking the start of the genocide. The assassins were, it is widely alleged, members of the RPF unit stationed in Kigali or the Rwandan presidential guard.

The genocide, highly organized and with a faster rate of killing than the Holocaust, began on April 7. Mobilized by a secret political and military chain of command and broadcasts of hate messages by Radio Milles Collines, the extremists struck. By April 19, the death toll had climbed to 100,000, according to Human Rights Watch. Outraged and alarmed by the deaths of ten Belgian peacekeepers and a spate of contradictory press reports, the Security Council, which had been briefed by Boutros-Ghali on available options for UNAMIR on April 13, decided on April 21 to *reduce* UNAMIR's strength to 270 troops and did not authorize UNAMIR to stop the massacres of civilians (Resolution 912). Boutros-Ghali reported on the April 29 that the death toll was climbing and there were plans for an even greater genocide, requesting a large investment of resources and personnel to stop the genocide, but the Security Council again rejected his proposals to increase the UN presence in Rwanda.

Finally, on May 17, Resolution 918 authorized UNAMIR with a troop strength of up to 5,500 and expanded the mandate to include the protection of civilians, with reluctant support by the United States.[111] By September 13, only 4,000 UN peacekeepers had been deployed, while earlier, in June, Resolution 925 endorsed a French intervention in Rwanda, authorized to use "all necessary means" to achieve its humanitarian objectives. By July 4, RPF forces had taken control of Kigali, and Hutus were fleeing to Zaire at the rate of 12,000 an hour. By July 21, a new government had been installed in Rwanda under President Pasteur Bizimungu.

---

[110] The Bangladeshi peacekeepers were sent to UNAMIR unarmed, and even the Belgians—who had the best trained and well-equipped contingent—lacked adequate materiel. Of twenty-two armed personnel carriers requested, UNAMIR received eight and only five were road-worthy. Most units only had food supplies and fuel to last them 2-3 days (Inquiry 1999, 31–32).

[111] U.S. Committee for Refugees Report.

Responsibility?

The peacebuilding space in Rwanda after the Arusha Accords was relatively narrow (see figure 6.4), due to high levels of hostility, extremely low levels of local capacities, and limited international capacities. When we look beyond the complicated train of daily events, the question of responsibility for peacebuilding failure arises. The first circle of responsibility is centered on the genocidaires themselves—those who carried and those who planned the massacres. But General Romeo Dallaire's troops clearly could have done more to prevent or limit the genocide with the resources and troops available in UNAMIR in Rwanda in 1993 and pre-April 1994. General Dallaire has said as much and a number of expert observers agree.[112] UNAMIR's leadership could also have done more to protect moderate leaders. These leaders constituted the basis for a locally supported peace, and they were systematically killed by extremists. An effective spoiler management strategy in this case would have been to provide protection to political leaders and groups of activists and individuals within safe areas. UNAMIR troops showed no resistance when RGF troops threatened them while trying to attack the moderates. This was partly due to confusion about the rules of engagement, partly to a lack of leadership from UNAMIR's headquarters, and partly because of a conservative interpretation of the mandate by peacekeepers who were unwilling to take risks in implementing their mandate.[113] Despite the fact that that there were numerous acts of heroism that saved the lives of thousands of otherwise victims, the troops also in many instances abandoned their clear duty, and units failed to cooperate.[114] Communication and command seem in fact to have broken down.

Moreover, confusions between New York headquarters and the field on how to interpret the mandate were rife. What was missing in this regard was both the clear support of New York to enforce the mandate and rules of engagement that were robust—and adequate reinforcement as the crisis began to mount in early 1994. The failure then is one of a lack of communication and, as Bruce Jones has argued, a failure to coordinate among the numerous peace efforts under way in the region since the very beginning of international engagement.[115] Dallaire repeatedly tried but failed to obtain clarification on when and how he was authorized to use force or to investigate illegal weapons depots or other clear violations of the mandate (the famous January 11, 1994, telegram). The field operation was not able to persuade New York headquarters that

---

[112] Des Forges 1999; Independent Inquiry 1999.
[113] Independent Inquiry 1999, p. 36.
[114] Independent Inquiry 1999, pp. 29–30.
[115] Jones 2001, pp. 172–75.

more robust action was required. Information from the field was also frequently contradictory. Throughout the period when Dallaire was sending requests for more troops and suggesting tougher action by UNAMIR, Jacques-Roger Booh-Booh, the Secretary-General's special representative in Rwanda and formerly finance minister in Cameroon, was sending optimistic assessments of the situation in Rwanda, as he seemed to think highly of Habyarimana and suggested in his reports that there was no ethnic basis for the civilian massacres that occurred in February 1994.[116] Leaving aside for a moment the reasons for the failure of communication, we can note that such failures of communication between the field and headquarters are endemic in UN (and other) peacekeeping. The lack of speedy deployment also hurt effectiveness. UNAMIR did not reach even its modest force level until January 1994. A successful coalition government needed to rely on a powerful and rapidly deployed international force that would (literally) keep alive the coalition of moderates and RPF in favor of accommodation.[117]

The leadership of the UN Secretariat also shares some of the blame for these compounded failures. It is not clear, for example, why DPKO did not inform the Council of the crucial cable of January 11.[118] The Council was not aware of this cable until it was too late. DPKO should have made every effort to communicate Dallaire's fears with the Secretary-General, who was not briefed about the cable. One plausible reason for this failure in communication might have been the fact that the information presented at the Council was limited due to Rwanda's participation as a rotating member of the Council. One might argue, therefore, that DPKO did not want to publicize the existence of an informant to Habyarimana's representative at the Council. But this suggests another organizational failure that makes it difficult for the Council to discharge its collective security functions when the member being targeted for enforcement action is also a member of the Council. But the blame for failing to follow up on the identity and credibility of the informant must also be shared by the Secretariat, which for reasons poorly understood, decided not to investigate further the identity and credibility of Dallaire's informant.[119]

Accidents also played a role, and they undermined the assumptions of a peace led by the accommodationist coalition. UNAMIR was undermined by the October 1993 coup in Burundi in which the Tutsi military minority killed the democratically elected Hutu president. Tens of thou-

---

[116] Des Forges 1999, 172–73.
[117] Jones 2002, p. 481.
[118] Independent Inquiry 1999, p. 26.
[119] Independent Inquiry 1999, p. 26.

sands died, and large numbers of Hutu fled into southern Rwanda. Hutu moderates in Rwanda suddenly found their faith in a peace coalition with the Tutsi RPF that much harder to sell to other Rwandans.[120] And then President Habyarimana, a problematic leader but still the key architect of the coalition regime, was assassinated on April 6, and the extremists had their spark.

But a deeper and more significant failure shaped subsequent febrility. Compared to other UN operations, the Rwanda mission had an inadequate mandate, resources, and troop levels from the start. It was designed in Dallaire's words to be "small, cheap, short and sweet."[121] It was all but the last. UNAMIR's mandate did not reflect the actual challenge of assisting a peaceful transition in Rwanda, mostly because the planners did not have confidence that the Security Council would authorize the resources that were required for a more effective mission.

The international community was misled partly by the seeming eagerness of the RPF and Habyarimana to make peace in 1993. After negotiating an agreement to share power and merge military forces, on September 15 both urged Secretary-General Boutros Boutros-Ghali to deploy a monitoring force of 4,260 as soon as possible.[122] But the Secretary-General responded that following on the crises in Bosnia and Somalia (two weeks short of the October 3 disaster) no such numbers were available. The UN Secretariat, seeing the operation as a chance to reaffirm traditional peacekeeping in the wake of Somalia and cooperate with the OAU, also failed to question the implicit optimistic analysis underlying the peace agreement. It assumed that two coherent factions were resolved to end their civil war but were in need of international monitoring and assistance to effect power sharing, even though a few weeks earlier the Human Rights Commission had reported on the deep-seated and pervasive violations of the rights of the Tutsi population in Rwanda. Nothing in the peace agreement covered these deep-seated sources of hostility that only an extensive peacebuilding reform of social and political institutions might have addressed.[123] Indeed, the international community seemed focused on establishing and maintaining the cease-fire and ignored that the problem after April was one of decentralized, widespread violence against civilians.

---

[120] Jones 2002, p. 485.

[121] Dallaire 2003, p. 89.

[122] De Forges 1999; Independent Inquiry 1999, p. 4.

[123] Given these weaknesses of the mandate, the inability of the parties to actually begin the formation of even the power-sharing arrangement in January 1994 should have been a decisive signal of impending collapse (Mathew Vaccaro, 1996, "The Politics of Genocide: Peacekeeping and Disaster Relief," in Durch 1996, pp. 367–407, 372; Andrea Talentino, "Rwanda," in Michael Brown and Richard Rosecrance, eds. The Costs of Conflict (Lanham, MD: Rowman and Littlefield, 1999), p. 56).

The Council's responsibilities began with the limited mandate it gave to UNAMIR in resolution 872, ignoring the Secretary-General's requests for a broader mandate and a stronger force. Member countries, with the United States and France at the forefront, share responsibility for shaping this Council-induced constraint on the Secretariat and UNAMIR. Given France's ultimate willingness to deploy Operation Turqoise with a Chapter VII mandate, it is not clear why that force could not have joined UNAMIR and been given a broader mandate to stop the genocide.[124]

The Council seemed both unwilling and unable to adapt to changing circumstances in the field and was complacent in not recognizing that a genocide was happening in Rwanda. Both the Council and the Secretariat should have made clear to the BBTG government coalition members that genocide was a crime punishable by law.[125] A realization that they might be individually prosecuted might have limited their proclivity to commit crimes against humanity. Instead of taking such an approach, the Council and Secretariat threatened to withdraw UNAMIR due to the parties' uncooperative behavior. A threatened withdrawal strategy clearly played into the hands of the extremists and undermined the moderates.[126] UNAMIR and the Council never fully appreciated the need for strict spoiler management in Rwanda. This was the result of intelligence failures as well as another example of the consequences of poor planning and training. The planning process failed to take into account the fact that the Arusha Accords had not resolved the conflict. General Dallaire acknowledged that the reconnaissance mission that he led lacked the political competence to make a correct assessment of the level of conflict underlying the Arusha Accords, and he could not assess the threat of conflict escalation.[127] Thus, relying on the Arusha Accords to design a traditional peacekeeping and monitoring mission in an environment that called for decisive enforcement and extensive peacebuilding suggests a complete failure in the UN's analytical capacity and intelligence-gathering abilities.

Following the downing of the presidents' plane, the crisis unfolded as a reflection of how one would expect a shocked and uncommitted international community to behave. Although Belgium had tried to strengthen forces on the ground, once ten of its soldiers were brutally murdered, it insisted on leaving and sought to persuade the Security Council to close the mission altogether. Undermanned and undermined, UNAMIR failed to halt the genocide and was forced to stand by as the Western powers

---

[124] Independent Inquiry 1999.
[125] Independent Inquiry 1999, 31.
[126] This point is effectively made by Stephen Stedman (1997).
[127] Independent Inquiry 1999.

evacuated their nations from Kigali, the capital. Reluctant to become involved despite increasingly credible reports of a well-organized genocide, the United States and others threw sand in the gears of well-meaning (but not well-designed) efforts to mobilize a UN rescue force, going so far as to refuse to name the massacres a genocide for fear of the affirmative obligations the label would entail (under the Genocide Convention of 1948) to stop the killing. The United States had dragged its feet throughout the peace process and even more so during the massacres. According to Alison des Forges,[128] President Clinton had been made aware of the ongoing genocide in Rwanda just two days after it had begun, but the U.S. administration claimed it only found out two weeks later, trying to justify its inaction. Even when confronted with overwhelming evidence of widespread killing, the United States was reluctant to relax the constraints under which UNAMIR operated in the field. Genocide had been declared a crime under international law, and under the 1948 Convention on the Prevention and Punishment of the Crime of Genocide, to which the United States was a signatory member, all contracting parties had an obligation to forcefully intervene to stop the genocide. In June 1994, the United States still had not acknowledged that there had been a genocide in Rwanda and U.S. government spokespeople preferred to say that "acts of genocide may have occurred" in Rwanda.[129]

The Security Council incomprehensibly continued to include previously elected Rwanda (the genocidaires) as a member of its deliberations, allowing the genocidaires to accurately estimate the weakness of the international response and proceed with the killing that begun in the capital with a sense of impunity.[130] On April 21, General Dallaire cabled that if his force was allowed to engage the Hutu extremists, he could stop the genocide with 5,000 well-equipped troops. The RPF objected to the

---

[128] Alison Des Forges, "Shame: Rationalizing Western Apathy on Rwanda," *Foreign Affairs* 79 (May–June 2000): 141–44.

[129] Christine Shelley, a spokeswoman for the State Department, was asked how many acts of genocide were required for the State Department to certify that there had been a genocide. She replied that she could not specify if genocide had happened in Rwanda because "there is reason for the selection of words that we have made, and I have—perhaps I have—I'm not a lawyer. I don't want to approach this from the international legal and scholarly point of view. We try, best as we can, to accurately reflect a description in particularly addressing that issue. It's—the issue is out there. People have obviously been looking at it." What Shelley appears to have been saying was that the United States did not want to assume the responsibilities that were associated with the term "genocide" under the 1948 Convention. Gourevitch 1998, 152; and see more generally on these issues, Samantha Power, *"A Problem from Hell": America in the Age of Genocide* (New York: Basic Books, 2002).

[130] Des Forges 2000.

proposals for increased UN troop deployments and suggested that only southwestern Rwanda might have been in need of UN protection, as these areas were controlled by RGF—the government forces.[131] That same day, the Security Council cut the force by 90 percent—from roughly 2,500 to 270 monitors.

The decision reflected a general lack of commitment, including from the Clinton administration, whose Presidential Decision Directive 25, released in May 1994, was nearing completion. Reflecting the president's October speech, the document argued that "the U.S. cannot be the world's policeman," and should instead select its crises, cutting its UN costs and ensuring control of its troops under UN command. To further tie down policy, Congress passed a bill in late 1993 requiring fifteen days notice of peacekeeping operations and slashing contributions to UN operations—including, and with great consequence, funding for peacekeeping.

France, itself deeply involved in the arming of the Habyarimana regime, at last intervened ostensibly to halt the genocide (Operation Turquoise), but indirectly to rescue its interests in a Francophone regime threatened by the rapid advance of anglophonic Tutsi forces, pushing into Rwanda to complete their conquest and halt the slaughter of their kin.[132] The French mission—Operation Turquoise—that was eventually dispatched to provide a "secure environment" may have saved up to 10,000 Tutsis but its effort to remain politically impartial also meant that it allowed many of the genocidaires to escape into Zaire along with their weapons.[133] All third party peace operations in Rwanda suffered from the same problem— confusing impartiality with passivity and refusing to take a proactive position with respect to implementing their mandate. National contingents seemed reluctant to take orders from UN command, as indicated by the Belgians' unilateral decision to withdraw. After UNAMIR's withdrawal, the Rwandans who had sought refuge in the Ecoles Techniques Officielles,

[131] Independent Inquiry 1999, 19.

[132] Prunier 1995, chap. 8; Des Forges 2000, 141. One senior White House official (private communication with Doyle, fall 1999) explained that the United States refused to intervene both because another failure would destroy the UN and that the quickest way to end the killing was a rapid victory by the RPF, unobstructed by an international intervention. By late May, after the vast bulk of the Tutsi population had died, this makes some sense, but the roots of the killing as described above were much earlier and could have been addressed much earlier. The selective evacuation of foreign nationals from an ETO (Technical School) was caught on tape in an amateur video of a Belgian peacekeeper who was involved in the evacuation. See *Chronicle of a Genocide Foretold*, a documentary filmed during and after the genocide by Daniele Lacourse and Yvan Patry, produced by First Run/Ikarus Films in 1996.

[133] Gourevitch 1998, 161.

mistakenly thinking that UNAMIR would protect civilians, would be slaughtered by government soldiers and militias.[134]

On July 18, the RPF declared a unilateral cease-fire and in late July 1994, the international community finally stepped in. Ironically, international humanitarian operations in eastern Zaire and Tanzania protected many of the Hutus who fled out of fear or to escape punishment for their role in the genocide. From these refugee camps, Hutu extremists continued their killing, launching murderous raids into Rwanda and provoking the civil war that spilled into Zaire, drawing in all Central Africa.[135] But even in its belated intervention, the international community was trying to cut corners and save dollars in Rwanda. By July 25, UNAMIR still only had 550 troops.[136]

During the period after UNAMIR's withdrawal and after the establishment of the International Criminal Tribunal for Rwanda (ICTR) on November 8, 1994, the level of security in Rwanda improved in urban areas but violence continued in the countryside. In 1995, more than a million refugees were still in the camps in Zaire. UNAMIR had sent 1,500 troops to the camps.[137] Members of the exiled Hutu government and army launched raids into Rwanda beginning in 1995, killing thousands of civilians.[138] The army, in retaliation, killed thousands and maintained civilian militias near the areas of fighting with the rebels.[139] Even

[134] Independent Inquiry 1999, 14, 28. UNAMIR and the international community could not have saved all the lives—certainly not those lost in the first few days—but they, together with a more robust mandate and rapid reinforcement, could have saved the vast majority. According to Kuperman (2000), at most one-fourth of the victims of the genocide might have been saved by a faster international response. He notes that the speed of the genocide meant that approximately half the victims had been killed by the end of the third week and that U.S. president Clinton only received the news two weeks after the genocide had started. Moreover, given the constraints on a strategic airlift to Rwanda and other aspects of U.S. military doctrine, any decisive U.S. intervention would have taken several weeks to reach the ground, by which time most victims had been killed. According to Des Forges, Kuperman exaggerates the speed of the slaughter and his analysis rests on the premise that Clinton learned of the massacres two weeks after their initiation. She argues that a U.S. intervention would have been possible earlier and that even smaller measures—such as jamming the radio frequency of Radio Mille Collines in Kigali and allowing peacekeepers on the ground to use force—would have been effective in stopping at least some of the violence.

[135] For a thorough analysis of the humanitarian consequences for the entire region see Thomas Weiss, *Military-Civilian Interactions: Intervening in Humanitarian Crises* (Lanham, MD: Rowan and Littlefield, 1999) chap. 6.

[136] Independent Inquiry 1999, p. 19.

[137] UNA-USA 1997.

[138] Human Rights Watch, *World Report 1996*; Human Rights Watch, *World Report 2000*.

[139] Human Rights Watch Annual Reports 1999, 2000, 2001, 2002.

after 1999, rebel incursions continued from the Democratic Republic of Congo.[140] According to one source, an estimated 15,000 Hutu rebels of the Army for the Liberation of Rwanda (ALIR) continued to urge the destruction of the Tutsi minority and undertook activities to that end from bases in the Democratic Republic of the Congo.[141] Rwanda's army kept troops in the Congo following Kabila's May 1997 victory and fought ALIR in the Congo throughout 1998–99.

UN peace operations succeed when international mandates are robust enough (with sufficient transitional authority) and have sufficient military and civilian capacities to overcome the factional hostility, lack of coherent organization, poverty, and institutional lack of capacity that characterize the particular country in transition from war to peace. Lightly staffed and lightly armed monitoring missions succeed where the parties are well organized and prepared to reconcile and the country has substantial institutional and infrastructural capacity. Much more is needed to deal with a "failed state" or deeply divided, semi-incoherent, and ethnically based strife, such as characterized Rwanda. By the standard of other and semi-successful UN operations UNAMIR was an "orphan operation."[142] Its overriding failure was one of lack of resources and lack of commitment, compounded by a poor understanding of the conflict and reluctance by peacekeepers on the ground to be proactive and assertively implement their mandate.[143]

All this suggests a cycle of compounded peacekeeping and peacemaking failures in Rwanda. The failures started at the planning stage and revealed severe external constraints, limiting the functions that the peacekeepers could have realistically achieved. But the peacekeepers themselves were responsible for some "endogenous" failures, which reinforced their external constraints, and increased the ability of spoilers to undermine the process, aggravating already noncooperative behavior by the factions. As evidence of noncooperation mounted—that is, as deaths due to genocide increased—the international community further tightened the reigns on UNAMIR and reduced even more the force's capacities. This dynamic evolution of constraints and peacekeeping behavior made peacebuilding failure almost inevitable in Rwanda.

---

[140] Human Rights Watch, *World Report 2000*; Human Rights Watch, *World Report 2001*; and Human Rights Watch, *World Report 2002*.

[141] Karen Parker, Anne Heindel and Adam Branch, "Armed Conflict in the World Today: A Country by Country Review" prepared for Humanitarian Law Project/International Educational Development and Parliamentary Human Rights Group, UK (Spring 2000, http://www.hri.ca/doccentre/docs/cpr/armedconflict2000.shtml# Toc486401419).

[142] See Fen Osler Hampson, *Nurturing Peace* (Washington, DC: United States Institute of Peace, 1996) chapter 7.

[143] Independent Inquiry 1999, p. 23.

Rwanda was a tragedy of "many hands."[144] Each of many actors bore distinct, direct or indirect responsibility for the genocide: the Secretariat in New York, the Security Council and various other states, the UN Assistance Mission in Rwanda—and most of all, and criminally, the Rwandese army and militias and their leadership among the radical Hutu factions of the Rwandese government who directed the genocide. Yet, with the exception of the genocidaires themselves, while each made serious mistakes and some have admitted as much, none of the others is responsible for the act in full. But incomplete responsibility does not erase responsibility for the specific acts or failures to act that when added together produced the outcome so disastrous to the Tutsi minority and the moderate Hutus of Rwanda. Michael Barnett, scholar and former U.S. official managing the Rwanda desk during the crisis at the U.S. mission to the UN, persuasively concluded: "UNAMIR was deployed naive and undernourished, a deadly combination, a gift from member countries who hoped for a quick victory and were willing to take short cuts to get there."[145]

[144] Dennis Thompson, "Moral Responsibility of Public Officials: The Problem of Many Hands," *American Political Science Review* 74, no. 4 (December 1980): 905–16.
[145] Michael Barnett, *Eyewitness to a Genocide* (Ithaca: Cornell University Press, 2002).

7

Transitional Strategies

THE RECORD OF CONTEMPORARY peace operations does offer lessons, but not simple ones. We have argued that achieving a sustainable peace could broadly be conceived as a triangle, matching the right level and kind of international capacities to the degree of material destruction and to the political hostility that the civil war had wrought. The message is one of variety: Just as civil wars differ, so must the kind and amount of international assistance be different in each case.

We have drawn two further distinctions of equivalent importance. UN and other peacekeeping operations tend to succeed or fail based on whether they (1) have the right mandate (matching international capabilities to challenges) and whether (2) that mandate is then well implemented. Poorly designed mandates, lacking authority or capacities, can rarely succeed, but well-designed mandates can still fail, based on whether the local factions choose to cooperate and whether the mission's leadership and the wider international community exercises well the capacities and authority at their disposition. In UN missions a well-designed mandate is the major responsibility of the Security Council, although it will generally be advised by the Secretariat in its formulation. A well-managed mandate, on the other hand, is the responsibility of the peacekeepers in the field and the Secretariat in New York, although the Security Council's responsibility to monitor and, if needed, adjust the implementation of its mandate remains.[1]

In this chapter, we take a more nuanced look at the lessons our cases generate for how to manage a mandate well and then how to design one. We explore the strategies of peace-making, peacekeeping, peacebuilding reconstruction, and (limited) enforcement to discover how they do, or do not, fit together to solve the Peacekeeper's Problem: consent is necessary for legitimacy and long-run sustainabililty, yet coercion will be needed to deal with the factions that resist or defect from the peace agreement. We then take up how to design mandates that will increase the probability that peacekeepers in the field will have the authority and the resources they need to manage well.

---

[1] The Secretary-General and the Security Council outline strategies and responsibilities in Kofi Annan, "No Exit without Strategy" (Secretary-General's Report, April 2001).

The Four Strategies

Peacemaking

In 1994, Saadia Touval summarized a widely held view of the UN as a diplomatic negotiator and peace mediator: "The UN does not serve well as an authoritative channel of communication. It has little real political leverage. Its promises and threats lack credibility. And it is incapable of pursuing coherent, flexible, and dynamic negotiations guided by an effective strategy. These limitations are ingrained and embedded and no amount of upgrading, expansion, or revamping of UN powers can correct those flaws."[2]

Fortunately, the UN has been repeatedly able to overcome the obstacles Touval decried. The question is how, since achieving the peace treaty itself will often require heavy persuasion by outside actors. In Cambodia, the USSR and China are said to have let their respective clients in Phnom Penh and the Khmer Rouge know that ongoing levels of financial and military support would not be forthcoming if they resisted the terms of a peace treaty that their patrons found acceptable. In Cyprus, none of those favoring peace (including in the most recent effort in 2002–3) were able to mobilize a dominant coalition prepared to make a comprehensive settlement. Peace treaties may themselves depend on prior sanctions, threats of sanctions, or loss of aid, imposed by the international community.[3]

The construction of an agreed peace is more than worth the effort. It is the first step toward creating the consent-based legitimacy that implementing (and even coercing) a peace will require. The process of negotiation among the contending factions can discover the acceptable parameters of peace that are particular to the conflict. Going beyond an agreed truce or disarmament, a comprehensive peace treaty addresses grievances and establishes new institutions that test the true willingness of the parties to reconcile. Peace negotiations, furthermore, can mobilize the support of local factions and of the international community in support

[2] Saadia Touval, "Why the UN Fails," *Foreign Affairs* 73, no. 5 (September–October 1994): 45.

[3] The Governor's Island Accord, which produced the first (ineffective) settlement of the Haitian conflict, resulted from economic sanctions on arms and oil imposed by the UN and OAS on Haiti as a whole. Sanctions targeted on the perpetrators (the military elite and their supporters) might have been much more effective (and were later imposed in the summer of 1994). Restrictions on the overseas private bank accounts and air travel of the ruling elite would both have been more just and perhaps more effective than general economic sanctions whose impact was most severe on the most vulnerable and from which the elite may actually have benefited. David Malone's *UN Decision-Making in the Security Council: The Case of Haiti* (Oxford: Clarendon Press) covers these events in depth.

of implementing the peace. And a negotiated peace treaty can establish new entities committed to furthering peacekeeping and peacebuilding.[4]

A peace treaty often reflects a convergence of preferences among factions. The mutually "hurting stalemate," as explained by William Zartman, is the classic instance.[5] Factions will fight until both know that they cannot win and both experience negative utility from the stalemated status quo. Short of these conditions at least one faction will want to continue to fight. The problem in Angola for so many years was a stalemate from which both sides, General Savimbi's UNITA and Prime Minister Neto's MPLA, both profited either from diamonds (UNITA) or oil (MPLA). In El Salvador, the FMLN offensive from the mountains was stopped in San Salvador, short of the coast, and the ARENA/Government offensive was stopped in the foothills, short of the border. When their respective patrons—Cuba and Nicaragua for the FMLN and the United States for the government—announced a cessation of support, the stalemate began to hurt and peace became more attractive.

But peacemaking need not be a passive process. The UN has developed a set of crucially important innovations that help manage the making of peace on a consensual basis. First among them is the diplomatic device that has come to be called the "Friends of the Secretary General." This brings together multinational leverage for UN diplomacy to help make and manage peace. Composed of ad hoc, informal, multilateral diplomatic mechanisms that join together states in support of initiatives of the Secretary-General, it legitimates with the stamp of UN approval the pressures interested states can bring to bear to further the purposes of peace and the UN.

For Cambodia, the "Core Group" in New York and "Extended P5" in Phnom Penh played a "Friends" role in the negotiation and the management of the peace process.[6] Composed of the Security Council Permanent Five—the United States, France, the USSR, China, and the United Kingdom—and "extended" to include Australia, Indonesia, Japan and other concerned states, it took the lead in the construction of the Paris Agreements.[7] It provided key support to UNTAC, both political and

---

[4] For a wide ranging collection of recent experience in UN and other peacemaking see Chester Crocker, Fen Hampson, and Pamela Aall, eds., *Herding Cats: Multiparty Mediation in a Complex World* (Washington: United States Institute of Peace, 1999).

[5] William Zartman, *Ripe for Resolution: Conflict and Intervention in Africa* (Oxford: Oxford University Press, 1985); and William Zartman, *The Elusive Peace* (Washington, DC: Brookings, 1995).

[6] John Sanderson, "The Incalculable Dynamic of Using Force," in Wolfgang Biermann and Martin Vadset, eds., *UN Peacekeeping Trouble: Lessons Learned from the Former Yugoslavia* (Aldershot: Ashgate, 1998), pp. 203–17.

[7] Richard Solomon, *Exiting Indochina* (Washington, United States Institute of Peace, 2000), pp. 40–48.

financial, and led by Japan, it helped organize the International Committee on the Reconstruction of Cambodia, which raised pledges for almost $1 billion, while providing special funds for various projects. But the Extended P5 lacked a fixed composition. It, of course, included the P5 but then included or excluded others on an ad hoc basis, depending on the issue and topic covered and the "message" the group wished to send. For example, Thailand was excluded from certain meetings in order to send a signal of concern about its lack of support for the restrictions imposed on the Khmer Rouge. In Cambodia, moreover, there was not a sovereign government to monitor or support. Much of the Extended P5's diplomacy was therefore directed at UNTAC itself, protecting, for example, the interests of national battalions. It also served as a back channel for the UNTAC special representative to communicate directly with the Security Council.[8]

In El Salvador, the Four Friends of the Secretary-General were Venezuela, Mexico, Spain, and Colombia. Frequently joined by a "Fifth Friend," the United States, they together played a crucial role in negotiating and implementing the peace accords.[9] So too did the Core Group in Mozambique. In the Former Yugoslavia the Contact Group including Russia, the United States, France, Germany, and the United Kingdom played a key role in engineering the process that produced the Dayton Agreement for Bosnia and the Erdut Agreement for Eastern Slavonia. A similar group—the Peace Implementation Council, under NATO auspices—met regularly to actively monitor the implementation of peace in Bosnia. And the Article II Commission under the auspices of the Organization for Security and Cooperation in Europe did the same for Eastern Slavonia. Informal diplomatic support groups have also been active in Haiti, Namibia, Nicaragua, Georgia, Afghanistan, Guatemala, and East Timor.[10] Although coalitions were assembled to endorse the truce in Cyprus and the Arusha Agreement for Rwanda, neither enjoyed a sustained monitoring by committed external sponsors of peace. In Cyprus, Turkey and Greece carry much of the blame for the collapse of the peace talks in the early 1970s, and they have yet to establish a firm and reliable coalition in support of a settlement. In Rwanda, France, Belgium, and the

---

[8] Yasushi Akashi, "UNTAC in Cambodia: Lessons for UN Peace-keeping," Charles Rostow Annual Lecture (Washington, DC; SAIS, October 1993); Richard Solomon, "Bringing Peace to Cambodia," in Crocker, Hampson, and Aal; 1999, pp. 275–323; and Doyle interviews in Phnom Penh, March 1993, and New York, November 1993.

[9] Ian Johnstone and Mark LeVine, "Lessons from El Salvador," *Christian Science Monitor*, August 10, 1993. The examples in these pages from UNTAC and ONUSAL are drawn in part from Doyle, Johnstone and Orr 1997.

[10] The group of "Friends" for Haiti consisted of France, the United States, Canada, and Venezuela.

United States were not fully sharing information or offering security support to the UN mission.

Playing a crucial role in the Secretary-General's peacemaking and preventive diplomacy functions, these groupings serve four key functions. First, the limited influence of the Secretary-General can be leveraged, multiplied, and complemented, by the "Friends." The UN's scarce attention and even scarcer resources can be supplemented by the diplomacy, finances, and clout of powerful, interested actors. The second function is legitimization. The very act of constituting themselves as a group, with the formal support of the Secretary-General, lends legitimacy to the diplomatic activities of interested states that they might not otherwise have.[11] It allows for constructive diplomacy when accusations of special and particular national interest could taint bilateral efforts. The third function is coordination. The Friends mechanism provides transparency among the interested external parties, assuring them that they are all working for the same purposes, and when they are doing so, allowing them to pursue a division of labor that enhances their joint effort. It ensures that diplomats are not working at cross-purposes because they regularly meet and inform each other of their activities and encourage each other to undertake special tasks. And fourth, the Friends mechanism provides a politically balanced approach to the resolution of civil wars through negotiation. It often turns out that one particular "Friend" can associate with one faction just as another associates with a second. In the Cambodian peace process, China backstopped the Khmer Rouge, just as France did Prince Sihanouk and Russia (with Vietnam) did the State of Cambodia. The Friends open more flexible channels of communication than a single UN mediator can provide. They also advise and guide the UN intermediaries in the peacekeeping and peacebuilding discussed below, although the process tends to work best when they support rather than move out in front of the UN. It is worth stressing that as much as the UN needs the support of Friends it can all too easily succumb to a highjacking as Boutros Boutros-Ghali remarked (soon after the United States vetoed his reelection effort): "When the United Nations was allowed to do its job without substantial US involvement, as in Mozambique, the operation succeeded. When the United States felt a political need for the United Nations, as in Haiti, the operation also fulfilled its main objectives. But when the United States wanted to appear actively involved while in reality avoiding hard decisions, as in Bosnia, Somalia,

---

[11] For a good discussion of the UN's and especially the Secretary-General's potential strength as a diplomatic legitimater, see Giandommenico Picco, "The U.N. and the Use of Force," *Foreign Affairs* 73, no. 5 (September–October 1994): 14–18. The "Friends" mechanism seems to answer many of the objections to UN mediation expressed by Touval 1994, pp. 44–57.

and Rwanda, the United Nations was misused, abused, or blamed by the United States, and the operations failed, tragically and horribly."[12]

While valuable, the Friends instrument can thus also disrupt the UN's effort to coordinate a peace process and, in effect, use the UN's multilateral credibility for partisan national purposes. In part this danger is the corresponding cost of the many advantages Friends bring. One way to reduce the tendency toward runaway Friends is to have the UN's special representative chair the Friends meetings in the field and an assistant secretary general from the Department of Politics Affairs do so in New York.

Multidimensional Peacekeeping

A peace treaty is a crucial step, mobilizing consent and establishing new international authorities and capacities. Consent-based operations, whether for international or civil wars, have all the manifest advantages discussed in the previous chapters. But even consent-based peace agreements fall apart. In the circumstances of partisan violence and "failed states," agreements tend to be fluid. In the new civil conflicts, parties cannot force policy on their followers and often lack the capacity or will to maintain a difficult process of reconciliation leading to a reestablishment of national sovereignty.

All of this erodes the principles of traditional peacekeeping. Neutrality, impartiality, consent, and the nonuse of force (as we discussed in the introduction) were clearly a related whole. Impartiality ensured that force would not be part of the mandate, and parties to disputes where traditional peacekeeping was used were generally sovereign governments. In international disputes, cease-fires and separation lines tended to be respected, once agreed upon. Buffer zones truly separated the interests of the parties and the UN could patrol them, ensuring transparent cooperation.

Today, new challenges have arisen that require dynamic, proactive peacekeeping. Peace treaties and their peacekeeping mandates tend to be affected by two sets of contradictory tensions. First, in order to get an agreement, diplomats assume all parties are in good faith. But to implement a peacekeeping and peacebuilding operation, planners must assume the opposite—that the parties will not or cannot fulfill their promises. Moreover, diplomats, who design the treaty, tend to think in legal (authority, precedent) not strategic (power, incentives) categories. Treaties thus describe obligations and tend to be unclear about incentives and capacities.

This militates against clear and implementable mandates. Diplomats

---

[12] Boutros Boutros-Ghali 1999, p. 337. Teresa Whitfield is writing a comprehensive study of the "Friends" strategy.

seek to incorporate in the treaty the most complete peace to which the parties will agree. UN officials seek to clarify the UN's obligations. Knowing that much of what was agreed to in the peace treaty will not be implementable in the field, the officials who write the Secretary-General's report (which outlines the implementation of the agreement) contract or expand the mandate of the peace operation. Confused mandates are an almost inevitable result of this tension.

A second tension also shapes the peacekeeping mandate. The mandate, like a natural resource contract, is an obsolescing bargain. When a country begins a negotiation with an oil company for the exploration of its territory, the company holds all the advantages. The costs of exploration are large, while the possibility of oil is uncertain. The country must therefore cede generous terms. As soon as oil is discovered, the bargain shifts, as discovered oil is easy to pump and any oil company can do it. The old bargain has suddenly obsolesced.[13] So it is with a UN peacekeeping operation: the spirit of agreement is never more exalted than at the moment of the signing of the peace treaty; the authority of the United Nations is never again greater. Then the parties assume that the agreement will be achieved and that all are cooperating in good faith. They depend upon the UN to achieve their various hopes. Although the UN has put some of its diplomatic prestige on the line, it as yet has no investment in material resources. The UN, in short, holds most of the cards. But as soon as the UN begins its investment of money, personnel, and operational prestige, then the bargaining relationship alters its balance. The larger the UN investment—these multidimensional operations represent multibillion-dollar investments—the greater is the independent UN interest in success and the greater the influence of the parties becomes. Since the parties control an essential element in the success of the mandate, their bargaining power rapidly rises. So, in the late spring of 1993 as the crucial elections approached, UNTAC chief Akashi acknowledged, "I cannot afford not to succeed."[14]

This dual tension in designing peacekeeping operations emphasizes that time is critical. The UN should be ready to implement the mandate as soon after the signing of a peace treaty as is practicable. UNTAC suffered a large decrease in authority in early 1992 as time passed and expectations of the factions and the Cambodian people were disappointed.[15]

[13] See Raymond Vernon, "Long-Run Trends in Concession Contracts," Proceedings of the Sixty-first Annual Meeting of the American Society of International Law (Washington, DC, 1967).

[14] Yasushi Akashi, Interview in "Peace in the Killing Fields," pt. 3 of *The Thin Blue Line*, BBC Radio 4, released May 9, 1993.

[15] For valuable surveys of the UNTAC experience see, Trevor Findlay, *Cambodia: The Legacy and Lessons of UNTAC* (New York: Oxford University Press, 1995); Janet

These tensions also explain how the ideal framework (both legal and political) of a treaty can dissolve in days or months, as the Cambodian peace agreements did. The provisions of peace accords become so general, ambiguous, or unworkable that many of the details have to be worked out in the implementation process. To be minimally effective under those circumstances, the UN must innovate.[16]

The UN thus needs to develop what we have called dynamic peacekeeping, a flexible and proactive political management of peacekeeping. It requires a political strategy to win and keep popular support and create (not just enjoy) the support of local forces of order. In a failed state, as was the case in a society subject to colonial rule, what is most often missing is modern organization. This was what colonial metropoles supplied, in their own self-interest, as they mobilized local resources to combat local opposition. Over the longer run, indigenous forces such as the political Zamindars and the King's Own African Rifles and other locally recruited military battalions (not metropolitan troops) were the forces that made imperial rule effective, that preserved a balance of local power in favor of metropolitan influence—and that kept it cheap. Learning from the history of imperial institution building (while avoiding imperial exploitation and coercion), an effective and affordable strategy for UN peace operations faces a greater challenge. It needs to discover ways to generate *voluntary* cooperation from divided local political actors and mobilize existing local resources for *locally legitimate*, collective purposes.[17] And it must do so *rapidly*. The crucial mark of the success of a peace operation is self-sustaining self-determination. The sooner that local forces

---

Heininger, *Peacekeeping Transition: The United Nations in Cambodia* (New York; Twentieth Century Fund, 1994); Carlyle Thayer, "The United Nations Transitional Authority in Cambodia: The Restoration of Sovereignty," in Woodhouse, Bruce, and Dando 1998, pp. 145–65; Beatrice Pouligny, "Promoting Democratic Institutions in Post-conflict Societies," *International Peacekeeping* 7, no. 3 (Autumn 2000): 17–35; Sorpong Peou, *Conflict Neutralization in the Cambodia War* (New York: Oxford University Press, 1997).

[16] On peacekeeping, consent, and the use of force see Berdal 1993; Stedman 1997; and Durch 1996.

[17] It is interesting in this light to note that some key, early UN experts in peacekeeping were eminent decolonization experts, deeply familiar with the politics of colonial rule, as was Ralph Bunche from the UN Trusteeship Division. See Brian Urquhart, *Ralph Bunche, An American Life* (New York: Norton, 1993) chap. 5 and for a discussion of imperial strategy, Michael W. Doyle, *Empires* (Ithaca: Cornell University Press, 1986), chap. 12. But there are key differences. Empires were governed primarily in the interests of the metropole; UN peace operations explicitly promote the interests of the host country. And what made imperial strategy work was the possibility of coercive violence, the over-the-horizon gunboats that could be and often were offshore. That, for good and bad, is what the UN usually lacks, unless it calls in the enforcement capacity of the major powers. Rehabilitation assistance is sometimes an effective carrot, but not the equivalent of the Royal Navy.

can take over transitional international authority, the more successful the operation tends to be.

Recent peacekeeping experience has suggested another peacekeeping innovation: an ad hoc, semisovereign mechanism designed to provide effective transitional authority in order to address those new challenges by dynamically managing a peace process and mobilizing local cooperation. Examples of these ad hoc semisovereign mechanisms include the Supreme National Council (SNC) in Cambodia, the Commission on the Peace (COPAZ) in El Salvador, and the National Consultative Council in East Timor.

It has often been remarked that Chapter VI presents the United Nations with too little authority and Chapter VII offers too much; and that Chapter VI is associated with too little use of force and Chapter VII with too much. The value of these ad hoc, semisovereign artificial bodies is that they provide a potentially powerful political means of encouraging and influencing the shape of consent. Indeed, these semisovereign artificial bodies can help contain the erosion of consent and even manufacture it where it is missing. Created by a peace treaty, they permit the temporary consensus of the parties to be formally incorporated in an institution with regular consultation and even, as in the Cambodian Supreme National Council, a semiautonomous sovereign will. These mechanisms have proved crucial in a number of recent UN missions. These transitional authorities can represent the once-warring parties and act in the name of a preponderance of the "nation" without the continuous or complete consent of all the factions. They can both build political support and adjust—in a legitimate way, with the consent of the parties— the mandate in order to respond to unanticipated changes in local circumstances.

In designing these semisovereign, artificial bodies, the UN should try (to the extent that its freedom of negotiation allows) to "preview" the peace that the parties and the international community seek. This means designing the right authority and providing the necessary capacities to implement the authority granted—these are the two issues to which we return in the second half of this chapter.

In Cyprus, this would have meant greater peacekeeping authority and provision of a stronger civilian component in 1964 to help the moderates mobilize coalitions favoring accommodation. For the Paris Peace Agreements for Cambodia, seeking a "pluralist democracy" should have meant supplementing the Supreme National Council with other bodies, such as one for civil society. It might have included Buddhist monks, nongovernmental organizations, and other representatives of society outside the state. These supplementary bodies need not perform executive or legislative functions. The important point is that civil society participate in the decision-making process, at a minimum through formally recognized consultative channels.

Peacebuilding Reconstruction

Multidimensional, second-generation peacekeeping pierces the shell of national autonomy by bringing international involvement to areas long thought to be the exclusive domain of domestic jurisdiction. If a peacekeeping operation is to leave behind a legitimate and independently viable political sovereign, it must help transform the political landscape by building a new basis for domestic peace. Michael Ignatieff puts the problem well when he says, "[w]here chaos and state collapse is the challenge, the test of a successful intervention strategy is no longer whether it defeats an enemy or stops a human rights abuse, but whether it sets in train the nation-building process that will prevent the area from becoming a security threat again."[18]

Traditional strategies of conflict resolution, when successful, were designed to resolve a dispute between conflicting parties. Conflict is seen as a function of situation (divergent interests); behavior (intention to force opponent to change); and attitudes (hostility, etc.).[19] Sometimes conflict is inherent (deeply structured and inevitable) or contingent and it can be based on objective or subjective factors. Bercovitch and Mitchell contend that conflict can be managed by violence and coercion, bargaining, and third parties. Some conflicts are settled by bargaining (split difference, tolerate outcome peacefully); others are resolved by addressing underlying causes.[20]

Successful resolution could be measured by: (1) the stated reconciliation of the parties; (2) the duration of the reconciliation; and (3) changes in the way parties behaved toward each other.[21] Truly successful contem-

[18] Michael Ignatieff, "State Failure and Nation-Building," in J. L. Holzgrefe and Robert Keohane, eds., *Humanitarian Intervention: Ethical, Legal, and Political Dimensions* (Cambridge: Cambridge University Press, 2003), p. 306.

[19] C. R. Mitchell, *The Structure of International Conflict* (London: Macmillan, 1981), pp. 19–34; and see Harry Eckstein, "Theoretical Approaches to Explaining Collective Political Violence," in Ted Robert Gurr, ed., The *Handbook of Political Conflict: Theory and Research* (New York: Free Press, 1980).

[20] Mitchell 1981; and J. Bercovitch, "International Mediation," *Cooperation and Conflict* 21, no. 3 (1986): 155and John Burton, *Resolving Deep-Rooted Conflict: A Handbook* (Lanham, MD: University Press of America, 1987).

[21] For a good account of traditional views of reconciliation see A. B. Fetherston, "Putting the Peace Back into Peacekeeping: Theory Must Inform Practice," *International Peacekeeping* 1, no. 2 (Spring 1994). For an approach stressing in various ways the strife involved in strategic political management illustrated above see I. William Zartman, "The Unfinished Agenda: Negotiating Internal Conflicts," in Roy Licklider, *Stopping the Killing: How Civil Wars End* (New York: New York University Press, 1993), pp. 20–34; Chaim Kaufmann, "Possible and Impossible Solutions to Ethnic Civil Wars," *International Security* 20 (Spring

porary peacebuilding changes not merely behavior but, more importantly, it transforms identities and institutional context. More than reforming play in an old game, it changes the game.

This is the grand strategy General Sanderson invoked when he spoke
of forging an alliance with the Cambodian people, bypassing the factions. Reginald Austin, electoral chief of UNTAC, probed the same issue
when he asked what are the "true objectives [of UNTAC]: Is it a political
operation seeking a solution to the immediate problem of an armed conflict by all means possible? Or does it have a wider objective: to implant
democracy, change values and establish a new pattern of governance
based on multi-partism and free and fair elections?"[22]

UNTAC helped create new actors on the Cambodian political scene:
the electors, a fledgling civil society, a free press, a continuing international and transnational presence. The Cambodian voters gave Prince
Ranariddh institutional power, and the Khmer Rouge was transformed
from an internationally recognized claimant on Cambodian sovereignty
to a domestic guerrilla insurgency. The peacebuilding process, particularly the election, became the politically tolerable substitute for the inability of the factions to reconcile their conflicts.

Transitional justice—trials and truth commissions—can help reconcile
parties once law and order is secure. Its success derives not from foundational or universal or continuous principles but from a successful reconstruction, looking backward to past law and norms and forward to the
future, built therefore on compromises of political feasibility and transitional ideas of what is fair and true in changing historical realities.[23] The
process cannot, for example, fully respect foundational legal principles,
such as that of "no crime without previous law," because past laws, as
did Nazi laws, may have justified the crimes committed. Nor can all
guilty be prosecuted; they may be too many or too powerful.[24] Law offers a measured scheme of reform, more bounded and controlled than
purely normative moral reform. It nonetheless can make a large difference in constructing or reconstructing the landscape of civil society.[25]

1996): 136–75; David Lake and Donald Rothchild, "Containing Fear: The Origins and
Management of Ethnic Conflict," *International Security* 21, no. 2 (Fall 1996): 41–75; Stedman 1997; and Hampson 1996.

[22] Dr. Reginald Austin (UNTAC, 1993).

[23] Ruti Teitel, *Transitional Justice* (Oxford: Oxford University Press, 2000), pp. 215–23

[24] Chandra Sriram, "Truth Commissions and the Quest for Justice: Stability and Accountability after Internal Strife." *International Peacekeeping* 7, no. 4 (2000): 91–106.

[25] Judith Shklar (1986) and Michael Walzer (1974) outline these political choices between
reviving (e.g., Weimar legality in 1945) and breaking with the past (Nazi law and during the
French Revolution, the need to break with the past and create equality under the law by executing the king). For a valuable survey of the role of truth commissions see Hayner 1994.

The UN's role, mandated by these complex agreements rather than Chapter VII, includes monitoring, substituting for, renovating, and in some cases helping to build the basic structures of the state. The UN is called in to demobilize and sometimes to restructure and reform once-warring armies; to monitor or to organize national elections; to promote human rights; to supervise public security and help create a new civilian police force; to control civil administration in order to establish a transitional politically neutral environment; to begin the economic rehabilitation of devastated countries; and, as in the case of Cambodia, to address directly the values of the citizens, with a view to promoting democratic education.

The parties to these agreements, in effect, consent to limitation of their sovereignty for the life of the UN-sponsored peace process. They do so because they need the help of the international community to achieve peace. But acceptance of UN involvement in implementing these agreements is less straightforward than, for example, consenting to observance of a cease-fire. Even when genuine consent is achieved, it is impossible to provide for every contingency in complex peace accords. Problems of interpretation arise, unforeseen gaps in the accords materialize, and circumstances change. The original consent, as the Salvadoran peace process suggests, can become open-ended and, in part, a gesture of faith that later problems can be worked out on a consensual basis. As such, and whether the parties are fully aware of this is uncertain, these agreements serve as strategies of precommitment designed to address the likely emergence of differences among the parties that might not be resolvable by continual acts of consent. In the process, the international community, represented by the United Nations, exercises a monitoring pressure to encourage progress on political reconstruction, including measures such as the reform of the judiciary, the expansion of the electoral rolls, and the operation of free press.

But authentic and firm consent in the aftermath of severe civil strife, such as that which Cambodia endured, is rare. The first clear implication is the importance of risk-spreading multidimensionality. The UN should design in as many routes to peace—institutional reform, elections, international monitoring, economic rehabilitation—as the parties will tolerate. Elections, however, could be destabilizing. Democratic transitions can increase the risk of civil war onset or recurrence in countries with no democratic tradition, no civil society, or no political institutions that can mange the newfound freedoms that democracy brings.[26] To reduce the risk of new war onset, effective multidimensional peacekeeping and peacebuilding will have to provide security during the

---

[26] See Snyder 2000 for the formulation of this argument.

transition process and support the design and building of new institutions that make it harder for peace spoilers to hijack the new democratic process.

Second, the international negotiators of a peace treaty and the UN designers of a mandate should, therefore, attempt to include bargaining advantages for the UN authority. Even seemingly extraneous bargaining chips will become useful as the spirit of cooperation erodes under the pressure of misunderstandings and separating interests. In Mozambique, Special Representative Aldo Ajello skillfully deployed a trust fund to assist Renamo's demobilization. In Cambodia, the UN counted upon the financial needs of the Cambodian factions to ensure their cooperation and designed an extensive rehabilitation component to guarantee steady rewards for cooperative behavior.[27] But the Khmer Rouge's access to illicit trade (with the apparent connivance of elements of the Thai military along the western border) eliminated this bargaining chip. And the suspicion of the dominant faction's (SOC, the "State of Cambodia") rivals prevented a full implementation of rehabilitation in the 80 percent of the country it controlled.

Third, the architects of the UN operation should therefore also design into the mandate as much independent implementation as the parties will agree to in the peace treaty. In Cambodia, the electoral component and refugee repatriation seem to have succeeded simply because they did not depend on the steady and continuous positive support of the four factions. Each had an independent sphere of authority and organizational capacity that allowed it to proceed against everything short of the active military opposition the factions. Civil administrative control and the cantonment of the factions failed because they relied on the continuous direct and positive cooperation of each of the factions. Each of the factions, at one time or another, had reason to expect that the balance of advantages was tilting against itself, and so refused to cooperate. A significant source of the success of the election was Radio UNTAC's ability to speak directly to the potential Cambodian voters, bypassing the propaganda of the four factions and invoking a new Cambodian actor, the voting citizen. But voters are only powerful for the five minutes it takes them to vote, if there is not an institutional mechanism to transfer democratic authority to bureaucratic practice. Lacking such a mechanism in

---

[27] This link was drawn explicitly by Deputy Secretary Lawrence Eagleburger at the Conference on the Reconstruction of Cambodia, June 22, 1992, Tokyo, where he proposed that assistance to Cambodia be "through the SNC—to areas controlled by those Cambodian parties cooperating with UNTAC in implementing the peace accords—and only to those parties which are so cooperating" (Press Release USUN-44-92, June 23, 1992). Disbursing the aid through the SNC, however, gave the Khmer Rouge a voice, as a member of the SNC, in the potential disbursement of the aid.

Cambodia, the voters are vulnerable to the armies, police, and corruption that dominate after the votes are tallied.

In these circumstances, the UN should try to create new institutions to assure that votes in UN sponsored elections "count" more. The UN needs to leave behind a larger institutional legacy, drawing, for example, upon the existing personnel of domestic factions, adding to them a portion of authentic independents, and training a new army, a new civil service, a new police force, and a new judiciary. These are the institutions that can be decisive in ensuring that the voice of the people, as represented by their elected representatives, shapes the future.

It was just this kind of campaign of political reconstruction that was missing in Cyprus and Rwanda. Neither peacekeeping operation was prepared to effect the institutional and social changes that were needed to change the structure of the competition by advantaging moderate forces. By contrast in Eastern Slavonia and Brcko, the peace operations created new social agents—the Serbian Croatian civil service in Vukovar and the new property holders (both Bosniac and Serb) around Brcko whose livelihood now relied on the sustainability of an integrated peace. The strategy developed there, and in Cambodia and El Salvador, was to build a coalition favoring a moderate peace.

Peace Enforcing

The UN must avoid the trade-offs between too much force and too little.[28] The dangers of Chapter VII enforcement operations, whether in Somalia or Bosnia, leave many observers to think that it is extremely unlikely that troop-contributing countries will actually sign up for such operations. The risks are far more costly than the member states are willing to bear for humanitarian purposes. But when we look at Chapter VI operations, we see that consent by parties easily dissolves under the difficult processes of peace. UN operations in the midst of civil strife have often been rescued by the *discrete, impartial, but nonneutral use of force or positive sanctions* by the United Nations, as were the operations in the Congo,[29] when Katanga's secession was forcibly halted, and as

---

[28] For an extensive discussion of the law and tradition of UN doctrine on the use of force see, Katherine E. Cox, "Beyond Self-Defense: United Nations Peacekeeping Operations and the Use of Force," *Denver Journal of International Law and Policy* 27 (Spring 1999): 239–73.

[29] The Congo case, ONUC, is one of the UN's most complex. Enforcement was essential for success and there was no overall peace settlement on which to rest, unlike the other cases we review in this section. Careful management kept the force limited, and the costs nearly destroyed the UN. It is the sort of exception that proves the rule that we advance here. For good accounts of the use of force in ONUC see Trevor Findlay and Thomas Mockaitis, in Morrison and Kiras 1997.

was the operation in Namibia, when the South-West Africa People's Organization's (SWAPO's) violation of the peace agreement was countered with the aid of South African forces.[30] Rather than attempting to enforce an external solution on a civil war (making war as in Somalia), "narrow" or "discrete enforcement" seeks to implement, by force, when needed, a key aspect of a comprehensively agreed peace.

Even when done well, discrete enforcement is nonetheless risky. In Mozambique SRSG Aldo Ajello carefully employed a slush fund financed by Italy to facilitate Resistência Nacional Mozambicana's (RENAMO's) transformation from guerrilla army to political party. But rarely is the provision of discrete incentives so smooth, particularly when the use of force comes into play. Both the Congo and the Namibia instances nearly derailed the peace process by eroding local, regional, or global support. Given those options, the semisovereign peacekeeping authorities (noted above) offer the possibility of midcourse adjustments and "nationally" legitimated enforcement (should it be needed).[31] In Cambodia, for example, UNTAC—operating in full accord with the Paris Agreements—appealed to *all* the factions to protect the election. The appeal was impartial and based upon the peace treaty to which all the parties had consented. (This is now called "strategic" as opposed to "tactical" consent in UN circles.) The result was distinctly not neutral among the parties as the armies (most effectively, SOC's army) that were cooperating with the peace plan pushed the Khmer Rouge back from the population centers. This subcontracted use of force permitted a safer vote with a larger—hence more legitimate—turnout in the last week of May 1993.[32] In 1996, in Eastern Slavonia, relying firmly on the consent of both President Milosevic and President Tudjman, UNTAES successfully exercised its "executive author-

[30] William Durch, "The UN Operation in the Congo," in Durch, 1993, *The Evolution of UN Peacekeeping*, chap. 19, pp. 315–52; and John Carlin, "Namibia's Independence Is UN's triumph," *Independent*, March 20, 1990, p. 11; and for a fine overall accounts of UNTAG, Roger Hearn 1999 and Virginia Page Fortna 1995.

[31] China did not want to see the Khmer Rouge destroyed; the USSR did not want to destroy SOC; and France and the United States did not want to destroy FUNCINPEC. Each of the great powers is a permanent member of the Security Council and has a veto on UN activity. Similar diversity applies with regard to the aims of troop-contributing countries. The gamble is as noted above: an impartial intervention will elicit enough support from international actors and from the parties that multilateral assistance will be sufficient to establish a peace, especially when supplemented by impartial use of force as described in the paragraphs above.

[32] Doyle conversation with Lieutenant General John Sanderson (UNTAC force commander) at the Vienna Seminar, March 5, 1995. On May 28, 1993, Doyle observed this in process around the small town of Stoung, which was surrounded by the Khmer Rouge. The Indonesian battalion established an inner perimeter around the town. The CPAF (SOC army) created an outer perimeter and trucked in voters from outlying villages. And see Frieson 1996 and Shawcross 1994.

ity" and employed overwhelming coercive force against the paramilitary gangs controlling the Djeletovici oil fields. In May 2000, in Sierra Leone, force was once again employed to rescue a floundering peace operation as the British Parachute Regiment rushed to Freetown to prevent the cutoff of the UN force and liberate the city from the Revolutionary United Front that had terrorized the country. The British force stayed to train 1,000 members of the Sierra Leonean army, prop up both the UN peace operation and the government of President Ahmed Kabbah, and free the remaining 220 UN peacekeepers being held by RUF forces.[33] Discrete, impartial uses of force in the context of comprehensive peace operation can be effective, and it is often essential to rescue a challenged peace.

Discrete enforcement was just what was so tragically absent in Rwanda, where limited use of force early might have deterred the Interhamwhe, or in Cyprus, where the unwillingness to enforce the mandate signaled that the moderates could be ignored.

Whether in peacemaking, peacekeeping, reconstructive peacebuilding, or discrete enforcement, the UN's multilateralism—so disadvantageous in making war—contributes significantly to its success in fostering self-sustaining peace. Multilateral impartiality, the principles of equality of states and universal human rights embedded not just in the Charter but deeply in the UN's ethos and composition make the quasi-colonial presence that a multidimensional peace operation entails not only tolerable but effective. The UN's mere presence guarantees that partial national interests are not in control. (Its very inefficiencies make fears of empire-mongering seem far-fetched.) At their best, UN peace operations mobilize a diverse and complementary set of national talents and serve by their very multinational character to announce that cross-ethnic and cross-ideological cooperation can work.

Every peacekeeping operation is different, even if it combines similar parts. Much needed even in a well-designed multidimensional operation is clear leadership. This was achieved in El Salvador, Cambodia, and Eastern Slavonia, accounting for considerable success beyond that that many anticipated. Leadership was absent for Bosnia as a whole under the Dayton Agreement with its regular requirements for continual coordination among the "principals" civilian and military, except in one small and quite special district, Brcko.[34]

The key to effective strategy is the *combined portfolio*. Good peacemaking generates the legitimate capacities that allow peacekeeping to work; just as effective peacekeeping organizes the reconstructive peace-

[33] James Clark and Jon Swain, "SAS Rescue Mission Leads Jungle Hostages to Safety," *Financial Times*, July 16, 2000; and James Clark, "Freetown Parades Its British Army," *Sunday Times*, July 23, 2000.

[34] de Lapresle 1998, pp. 137–52, p. 149.

building that creates the new milieu, new institutions, and new actors through which genuine transformation toward peace can take place. Discrete force and bribes are the inducements that stop the gaps in the previous three and prevent a peace operation from becoming hostage to spoilers who are determined to prevent peace under any terms. The four work together, each reinforcing the other.

The diversity of multidimensional peacekeeping also improves the prospect of peace. One element of the peacekeeping/peacebuilding strategy can fail: disarmament, demobilization, elections, judicial reform, police or military reform, economic rehabilitation—can fail. But provided a crucial mix of the others succeeds, peace will continue to progress. So it did in Cambodia when after the failure of the cease-fire, military demobilization, and administrative control, the Cambodian election served to create a legitimate enough sovereign to carry on the peace process.

Strategies work best when the initial parameters are well designed and when the transitional authority is suited to the case, the issue to which we turn next.

Transitional Authority

As we have discussed, transitional strategy interacts with factional capacities and root causes of factional hostility to shape the legs of the triangular peacebuilding "space." Few peacebuilding plans work unless regional neighbors and other significant international actors desist from supporting war and begin supporting peace. The end of Cold War—globalized civil war—competition thus was an important precondition for the bloom of peacebuilding operations of the early 1990s.

To succeed, transitional authority needs to accommodate the particular circumstances of the conflict, its causes, local capacities, and the quality of the arrangement at the time of the peace negotiations that is or is not made between them. International authorization is a key dimension of peace implementation, but adequate authority is not enough to ensure success. Resources, leadership, a dedicated staff, and local cooperation are just as, if not more, important. But international authority grants a license to assist and, if needed, direct. It conveys an implicit strategy for aiding the difficult transition from civil war to self-sustaining peace. Without appropriately designed authority, peace implementation is headless. Authority can be distinguished by its sources and divided into a variety of ecologies.

Sources of Authority

A transitional peace operation usually needs two authorizations; one is international, the other domestic. The two need not be always connected.

An internationally authorized humanitarian intervention could proceed without host state authorization (but it will not succeed unless it wins the support of significant majority of the local population). And a sovereign government can invite foreign forces to assist it without recourse to the UN or a regional organization for authorization. But the two usually are connected. International authority is needed in order to permit the entry of foreign military forces and civilian officials into the domestic jurisdiction of the civil-war-torn state. Domestic authority is needed to specify the bases on which the once-warring points come to cooperate and accept common rules for deciding conflicts of interest. It is worth noting that the forcible interventions in Somalia, Haiti, Kosovo, and East Timor each had prior national authorizations (albeit each under duress and in the Somali case from twenty hostile factions none of whom appeared to take the Addis Ababa Agreement [March 1993] seriously).

From the international point of view, peace operations—which intrude upon the domestic sovereignty of states—come to be established in two ways. First, under Chapter VI of the UN Charter, they are achieved through the negotiated consent of the parties and then through a series of Status of Forces agreements that specify the legal terms for the presence of foreign forces. Or, second, they are established under Chapter VII, which permits the overriding of domestic jurisdiction (Articles 2–7) without consent of the local parties.

From the domestic point of view, a local authority (or authorities) shares temporarily and, usually, conditionally some of its (or their) own legitimacy with the international peace operation. Domestic authority can be examined in the light of the classic types of authorization and "imperative coordination." Max Weber outlined three ideal types of imperative coordination: traditional, charismatic, and rational.[35] The first two types of authority may be rare in civil war transitions. Traditional authority—an established belief in the sanctity of immemorial traditions and of the status of those exercising authority under them—has often broken down. Under the pressures of economic growth and social mobilization, tradition tends to erode and traditional states collapse. Charismatic authority—resting on devotion to the sanctity, heroism, or exemplary character of the individual leader and the order ordained by him or her—is often in excess supply, claimed by each of the faction leaders. Usually, therefore, rational authority—the legality of patterns of normative rules and the right of those elevated under such rules to exercise commands—justifies the work of reconstruction, and often in competition with preexisting

---

[35] Max Weber, *The Theory of Social and Economic Organization*, trans. M. Henderson and Talcott Parsons, ed. Talcott Parsons (Macmillan, 1947), pp. 324–33.

but weakened traditional and charismatic sources of authority. Transitional authority thus must be constructed through painstaking negotiation, implementing widely recognized international human rights norms, and endorsed through negotiated schemes of power-sharing or popular elections.

It is difficult, however, to imagine the success, limited as it is, that Cambodia has achieved without the leadership of Prince and later King Sihanouk. He repeatedly served as a catalyst for difficult decisions and a bridge between competing factions that would only contact each other under his auspices. The charismatic authority enjoyed by Nelson Mandela was an equally vital part of the difficult transition underway in South Africa. Lacking these forms of unifying authority in Somalia, El Salvador, Guatemala, and Bosnia, peace operations had to rely on enforceable or continually renegotiated agreements, which made the quality of international transitional authority a key component of success or failure.

Ecologies of Authority

Effective transitional authority that governs how peacekeeping, peacebuilding, and peace enforcement are exercised must be designed to fit the case if it is going to succeed in establishing a self-sustaining peace. The necessary extent of authority is a function: first, of the local root causes of conflict; second, of the local (primarily economic) capacities for change; and third, of the specific degree of international commitment available to assist change. Effective transitional authority must take into account levels of hostility and factional capacities. Whether it in fact does so depends on strategic design and international commitment. Designs for transitional authority incorporate a mix of legal and bureaucratic capacities that integrate in a variety of ways domestic and international commitments.

Authority operates not upon stable states, but instead on unstable factions. These factions (to simplify) come in three dimensions (table 7.1). Examining a conceptual map of the post–Cold War world, we can categorize factions as either *coherent or incoherent*: that is, they do or do not follow the orders of their leaders. They reflect varying degrees of *reconciliation or hostility*. Having reached a "hurting stalemate," they accept the process of peace; or (having been dragged to the conference table) they do not. And these factions are *few or many*. They also are in conflict in societies that either have very little economic and social capacity (less developed in GDP, education, etc.) or have more (more developed in those capacities). When one examines the mix of these factors, one can think about differing "ecologies" of transitional authority during peacebuilding that represent differing combinations of those three sets of conditions and differing levels of international response to

TABLE 7.1
Ecologies of Transitional Politics

	More Hostile Factions		More Reconciled Factions	
	Few	*Many*	*Few*	*Many*
Coherent	Third: Bosnia I Cyprus Georgia Cambodia Angola W. Sahara		First: El Salvador Namibia Tajikistan	
Incoherent	Fourth: East Slavonia Brcko Rwanda	Fifth: Bosnia II Somalia DRC Congo Liberia S. Leone	Second: Mozambique East Timor Haiti Guatemala	

them.[36] These ecologies are also influenced by levels of local capacity, as indicated in table 7.2.

There's a *"first ecology"* of peacebuilding where the factions are *few, semi-reconciled, and coherent. Local capacities* are not critically important in these cases, if external assistance is offered to help the reconciled parties implement a peace. And with the usual caveats, the case of El Salvador (more capacity) and Namibia (less capacity) fall into that pattern.[37] The authority often relies on specific commitments made in the peace treaty by established governments, supplemented by new transitional institutions and an international peace operation. In El Salvador, for example, the government undertook a variety of commitments to engage in judicial, police, military, electoral, and other reforms. The peace agreements also created new transitional institutions, including COPAZ, which was designed to promote dialogue between business, labor, and other elements of civil society. ONUSAL was charged with monitoring and assisting the peace process.

[36] We use ecology as a variety of the "worlds" analogy employed by Robert Jervis in "Cooperation under the Security Dilemma," *World Politics* 30 (January 1978).

[37] Lise M. Howard in "The Attempt That Worked" (Stanford University, CISAC, 1999) discusses the complexities of the Namibian case and makes a good case for its successful transition, noting two free and fair elections, little crime, and a white minority that accepts the current regime. The slow pace of economic development, however, is putting considerable strains on the political regime.

TABLE 7.2
Local Capacities and Ecologies of Transitional Politics

	More Hostile Factions		More Reconciled Factions	
	Few	*Many*	*Few*	*Many*
High LC	Bosnia I Cyprus Georgia East Slavonia Brcko	Bosnia II	El Salvador Namibia Tajikistan	
Low LC	Cambodia Angola W. Sahara Rwanda	Somalia DRC Congo Liberia S. Leone	Mozambique East Timor Haiti Guatemala	

Many scholars, for example, have agreed that the root causes of the Salvadoran civil war were the militarization of the state and the persistent inequality of the distribution of landed wealth. Historically the two supported each other. When the landed oligarchy (the "fourteen families") needed to suppress a peasant uprising, the military was available. The military correspondingly enjoyed a first claim on public revenue.[38]

When the FMLN guerrillas, representing the rural poor, and the ARENA government, speaking as the traditional state, came to a military stalemate in the course of the Salvadoran civil war, they began to explore some of the parameters of a future of peace. Each had to compromise in order to arrive at a viable, mutually acceptable, long-term peace. With the collapse of the Soviet Union, the FMLN was losing Soviet Bloc support, and it grew to realize that it could not achieve through the peace process the social and economic revolution for which it had fought. The ARENA government refused to negotiate a more egalitarian distribution of wealth. But the government also realized that the traditional autocratic status quo was not something that it could maintain, following the end of the Cold War and the consequent reduction in U.S. support. Both, therefore, compromised on reforming the militarization of the state, one of the two root causes of civil war. The FMLN took the larger gamble, reflecting its weaker position. It gambled that if military and police impunity could be ended, the judiciary made fair and law abiding, and a free and fair election organized, then they could win their long-term goals through electoral, democratic means. The government,

[38] Edelberto Torres Rivas, "Civil War and Insurrection in El Salvador," in Doyle, Johnstone, and Orr 1997; and Montgomery 1994.

on the other hand, realized that it no longer needed the military. This was partly because the old system of military protection for landed wealth simply was no longer politically viable given the FMLN's resistance, but it was also because ARENA had come to realize that it was no longer necessary. The Salvadoran economy had shifted to an economy based on commerce and small industry. Commerce and small industry could survive very well through legal means in a democratic El Salvador. In short, the more powerful ARENA precluded an effort to address the root causes that were more important to the weaker FMLN. But addressing militarization through democratization and reform of the justice system was a compromise both could accept.[39]

Transitional authority, light as it is, still has a vital role to play in peacebuilding in those circumstances. First, it can create and needs to create transparency. The factions may be reconciled but they don't fully trust each other. The international peacebuilding role consists of monitoring and investigating in order to increase trust so that the parties can believe that the piece of paper they signed has operational significance. In El Salvador, ONUSAL helped to increase trust and transparency through the Ad Hoc Commission, which supervised demobilization, and through the Truth Commission, which investigated human rights violations and recommended reforms. Second, in these circumstances, the international peacebuilders can also offer capacity building. They can bring in the technical assistance that the parties either lack or don't quite trust one another to provide, such as electoral assistance or police training. And thirdly, and perhaps most importantly, the peacebuilders provide insurance of continuing coordination. No matter how well designed the peace treaty happens to have been and despite whatever reconciliation of the parties may have occurred, the parties know that circumstances will arise that were not anticipated in the treaty. Those circumstances will need to be dealt with if the peacebuilding process is to be kept on track.[40]

In the *second ecology* factions are *few* and *reconciled*, but they are *incoherent*. If local capacities are also lower (see table 7.2), more extensive international involvement will be needed. In Guatemala, exhaustion and

---

[39] Doyle Interview with President Cristiani, San Salvador, March 1994; and see Stanley 1996; and Wood 2000.

[40] When it was discovered that one of the factions of the FMLN had a weapons cache, ONUSAL impartially investigated and then dismantled the cache. When it was discovered in November of 1993 that the death squads seemed to be reemerging, many asked: Was the government behind them? The UN was able to investigate; enjoying the trust of the FMLN that it would do as thorough a job as could be done. See Ian Johnstone, *Rights and Reconciliation in El Salvador* (Boulder, CO: Lynne Rienner, 1995); and Charles Call, "Assessing El Salvador's Transition," in Stedman, Rothchild, and Cousens 2002.

international pressure brought the government and the indigenous communities to the peace table, but soon thereafter the indigenous communities lapsed into their many local components, the thousands of communities from which war had mobilized them.[41] In Haiti and East Timor war and intervention radically reduced the influence of the opposition, as General Cedras's forces fled Haiti and the Indonesian militias left East Timor. This left one massive "faction," destitute and lacking in coherent organization. Here factions may be incapable of fulfilling their commitments, even if willing. In Mozambique, ONUMOZ appears to have stepped in to play an active, quasi-sovereign, implementing role through a variety of commissions for disarmament, elections, and humanitarian activities.[42] ONUMOZ actually helped to organize a political party as well as to employ demobilized soldiers in building roads: a true capacity infrastructure-building effort. Proactive peace management oriented toward capacity building was important in both respects, employing the former soldiers and building a transportation grid.

There is also a *third ecology* of peacebuilding where the factions are *few, hostile, and coherent*. When local capacities are low (as in Cambodia), the chances of peacebuilding success are very low in this ecology, so extensive international capacities must be employed. Both Cambodia and Angola fit this space, where the factions were and still are hostile and the country is poor; in Angola, the level of international capacities was decidedly lower than in Cambodia, and the results (failure) were consistent with our expectations. Bosnia is also a part of this ecology, where the parties remain very hostile in a country that has greater social and economic capacity. (In Bosnia, Muslim-Croat relations resemble Cambodia's SOC-FUNCINPEC relations; Federation-Serb relations resemble SOC-FUNCINPEC relations with the Khmer Rouge or Angola I or II—which collapsed.) In this third ecology the peacebuilding role includes all the functions that were exercised in that first happier world of UN peacebuilding—the Salvadoran case, where transparency, coordinating insurance, and capacity building are the keys. But over and above that, because the factions are less than reconciled (the most mild way of describing the Cambodian experience), the peace process needs to embody more substantial transitional authority if it is going to have a chance of success.

In Cambodia, the root causes of civil strife were so deep and the local actors so weak that, by 1990, each entered the peace as a near equal,

[41] William Stanley and David Holiday in "From Fragmentation to a National Project? Peace Implementation in Guatemala" (Stanford University, CISAC, 1999) note both the remarkable and contradictory emergence of both Mayan participation in the political process and the lack of substantive improvement in civic governance.

[42] Richard Synge, *Mozambique: UN Peacekeeping in Action, 1992–1994* (United States Institute of Peace Press, 1997).

each having its own form of monopoly power; and so each had to accommodate each other. For much of its recent postwar history Cambodia found itself in a dangerous neighborhood. Bombed by the United States during the Vietnam War, which radicalized the intellectuals and peasantry, it fell prey to the Khmer Rouge in 1975, the worst fanatics in the second half of the twentieth century. Cambodia was rescued in 1978, but only by its historic enemy, Vietnam; and then it was occupied by Vietnam for a decade. As a result, Cambodia lacked the space in which to address the key challenges of modern development. It has faced crisis after crisis, and each before it had time to adjust to or resolve the previous one.

Cambodia was simultaneously trying to recover from a combination of trials.[43] Cambodia is still seeking to overcome the legacies of colonialism. Indeed, the first generation of postcolonial leadership is still in place. King Sihanouk was first enthroned by the French in 1941. Huge inequalities between city and countryside persist, inequalities typical of export-oriented, metropolitan-based, colonial economic development. Before these inequalities and dependencies had been overcome, the 1978 Vietnamese invasion imposed a new kind of colonialism, as the State of Cambodia (SOC) regime ruled from out of the "knapsack" of Vietnam in 1979 and Vietnam continued to govern from behind the scenes until 1989.[44] Second, Cambodia is still recovering from the destruction inflicted by wars, beginning with the U.S. bombing and Khmer Rouge devastations and continuing into the civil wars of the 1990s. All left deep rehabilitation needs, not unlike the needs of countries such as Vietnam and Eritrea. Third, Cambodia, too, suffers from a postholocaust syndrome. The Khmer Rouge massacres left a desperate need for social reconstruction. Only a handful of monks, intellectuals, medical doctors, and trained lawyers survived the Khmer Rouge massacres. A massive social capital deficit resulted, and many survivors face deep psychological burdens that discourage reconstruction. Fourth, Cambodia is also a post–civil war survivor from the pitched battles of 1979–91 between the SOC and the unified resistance on the Thai border. Like Mozambique and Angola, the reconciliation and reintegration of 370,000 refugees challenges all the country's efforts to rebuild. And, fifth, like the economies of Eastern Europe, Cambodia is undergoing a postcommunist transition to a market economy, begun by the SOC in 1991.

[43] Sorpong Peou, "UNTAC: Implementing the Paris Agreement in Cambodia, Problems and a Prescription" (Stanford University, CISAC, 1999) offers a perspective sympathetic to each of the four major factions.

[44] For a thoughtful discussion of Cambodia's political legacy, see Aun Porn Moniroth, *Democracy in Cambodia: Theories and Realities*, translated by Mrs. Khieu Mealy (Phnom Penh: CICP, 1995).

Any one of these challenges would have been sufficient for one of the poorest countries of the world. Cambodia is unique in facing them all at once. As a result, each of the Cambodian factions—the State of Cambodia imposed by Vietnam in 1978, the Khmer Rouge, and the Royalist faction following Prince Sihanouk—lacked either power or wide legitimacy. In 1990, the royalist FUNCINPEC had traditional legitimacy and the support of the West (but no effective army). The Khmer Rouge had discipline and guns and the support of China (but, as the worst perpetrators of genocide since World War Two, no legitimacy beyond the cadres it controlled). The SOC had an effective bureaucracy and a solid army and the support of Vietnam and the moribund USSR (but it was tainted with its knapsack origins).

Each faction had to accommodate each other. The peace recognized each other's core vulnerabilities. The Khmer Rouge genocide was termed "unfortunate practices of the past." The factions could not agree on the terms of conjoint rule at the First Paris Peace Conference in 1989. They therefore called in the UN to serve as a transitional authority. In 1991, the great powers pressured the factions into signing a contradictory peace at the Second Paris Peace Conference. The peace consequently continued to reflect each faction's strategies of victory. The Khmer Rouge hoped the UN control over the SOC bureaucracy would destroy it. The SOC hoped UN demobilization of the 70 percent of the armed forces would destroy the Khmer Rouge. Rather than accommodation, the UN transitional authority was designed to hold the factions together long enough to allow the people of Cambodia to construct a new state through a UN-run national election. But the peace failed to attend to the deeper social and economic contexts of inequality and devastation that fed the factional rivalry. Indeed, the measures of rehabilitation that were included in the peace were stymied by continuing factional strife as the Khmer Rouge soon defected when it realized that the SOC would not fall and the SOC refused to cooperate in key aspects of the peace when it realized that the Khmer Rouge would not be tamed and that FUNCINPEC would seriously challenge its authority in the election. The "war" continued in political form, with violence increasing as the election approached. The electoral victory of FUNCINPEC did not change the balance of power; FUNCINPEC had to accommodate the SOC's bureaucratic and military capacities and form a coalition government in June 1993.

No faction trusted the established government; alternatively put, the established government is nothing more than another faction, as was the "State of Cambodia." Peacebuilding design may thus call for transitional sovereignty institutions, as in the Supreme National Council of Cambodia, to which the sovereignty of Cambodia was temporarily entrusted.

The SNC represented each of the factions, with Prince Sihanouk in a trustee, titular head-of-state role.

International commitment, nonetheless, is likely to be needed to glue the transitional institutions together and provide economic assistance. When the factions were deadlocked and Prince Sihanouk did not act, the United Nations Transitional Authority in Cambodia (UNTAC), through its Special Representative Yasushi Akashi, was given the authority to decide. UNTAC also received the authority to "control" the administrative activities of the factions (most relevantly the SOC, which alone had substantial administrative capacity) in five areas of sovereign activity (finance, foreign affairs, etc). Carrots and sticks may be needed to supplement legal capacities. In the Paris Peace Agreement economic rehabilitation assistance was designed for, and only for, those factions that would cooperate within the peace process. Given that their former patrons had cut the factions off from financing, it was thought that this would be a very powerful constraint on defection and an incentive to cooperate in the peace process. Unfortunately, one and then another of the factions discovered alternate sources of financing through illegal sales of gems and logs and other means that removed this particularly important carrot and stick from the peace process.

In addition, in this less happy third ecology, the international community may have a very important role in direct implementation. The residual hostility of the factions means that they will not trust each other to implement any crucial element of the peace process. In Cambodia, it was absolutely vital that the UN itself had the authority to organize from the ground up the electoral process.[45] An election run by one of the factions and only monitored by the UN (as in El Salvador) would have been prone to severe exploitation or manipulation. Instead it was the UN, the international community, that organized and ran that election giving more parties authentic access and guaranteeing a much fairer count of the vote. Despite this substantial authority, there is a growing impression that not enough peacebuilding occurred.[46] Significantly, UNAVEM lacked this kind of authority in Angola, and failed.

In the early stages of the Dayton peace process ("Bosnia I"), as Elizabeth Cousens illustrates, the transitional authority available to move the parties to the commitments made at Dayton was far from adequate.

[45] Michael Doyle, *The UN in Cambodia: UNTAC's Civil Mandate* (Boulder, CO: Lynne Rienner, 1995). For a discussion of UNTAC by an experienced international peacekeeper, see Reginald Austin, "New Forms of International Intervention: The United Nations Military-Civilian Intervention in Cambodia," in Mary Kaldor and Basker Vashee, eds., *Restructuring the Global Military Sector, New Wars* (New York: Pinter 1997–98), 1: 231–57.

[46] For a recent assessment, see International Crisis Group, *Cambodia: The Elusive Peace Dividend*, ICG Asia Report No. 8 (Phnom Penh/Brussels: August 11, 2000).

Levels of hostility remained high after the signing of the accords: "having been brought to the table by varying forms and degrees of coercion, the parties had little more than a tactical commitment to settle, making any resulting accord dependent on more than the will of the parties for its implementation."[47] In this strategic situation both formal and effective authority, including the will to use them, are needed. In the military sphere both formal authority and an effective presence on the ground were much in evidence, and the successful separation of forces resulted. However, the narrow interpretation of what constituted security, the weak coordinating authority and "interpretive" authority given the high representative, and the lack of coordination between the civilian and military pillars of the Dayton process had debilitating effects on "civilian" implementation. Refugee return to areas in which they would be a minority was stymied, and the forces that had led the campaigns of exclusion and violence during the civil war stayed in power. International civilian authority, moreover, was both unclear and divided. While the Office of the High Representative coordinated many organizations, its authority vis-à-vis the parties and those other implementing organizations was underspecified. OHR and OSCE and others were empowered to make determinations of compliance and lack of compliance with the Dayton agreements but lacked quasi-sovereign authority to make determinations of policy when the parties disagreed.[48] The mandate in the first phase was interpreted more in lines suited to the degree of genuine reconciliation evidenced in the Salvadoran or Namibian peace operations, rather than to the hostility that characterized the Bosnian factions. Only with the Bonn Summit of the Peace Implementation Council of December 1997 ("Bosnia II"), did the OHR begin to acquire the internationally recognized authority to take decisions against the will of the parties. As the factions themselves began to splinter, raising the need for authoritative coordination, OHR began to make efforts to manage the most blatant spoilers. It instituted neutral license plates, closed hostile media transmitters, targeted the more violent cantonal police forces, and more actively supported minority refugee returns.

In the "*fourth ecology*," where the factions are *few, incoherent, and hostile*, the prospects of sustainable peace are extraordinarily difficult. Only exceptional multilateral and international commitment might succeed in overcoming incentives for resumed armed conflict, though the

[47] Elizabeth Cousens, "From Missed Opportunities to Overcompensation," in Stedman, Rothchild, and Cousens 2002, pp. 538–39.

[48] Nonetheless, as in Cambodia, there were narrow areas of policy in which the international community possessed effective transitional authority. The IMF, for example, had tie-breaking authority on the governing board of the central bank, and the Council of Europe appointed a majority of the members of the Human Rights Chamber.

process was helped by the region's relatively higher local capacities. In Eastern Slavonia, the UN acquired "executive authority" through the Erdut Agreement that gave the transitional administrator, Jacques Klein, the authority to implement the agreement without consent of the Croatian government or the Krajina Serb entities. Interesting disputes arose over whether that authority was constrained or not, and if so by what. On the one hand, Zagreb argued that that Croatian law constrained and UNTAES was "executing" it. On the other hand, certain UNTAES lawyers argued that executive authority was constrained only by international human rights and humanitarian law.[49] Equally noteworthy in the UNTAES operation, however, was the substantial military force at its disposal both locally (in UNTAES) and on call (from IFOR/SFOR). Ongoing operational consent, too, may have played a more significant role than legal mandates might have suggested. UNTAES officials stress the occasional cooperation they have received from Presidents Franjo Tudjman (Croatia) and Slobodan Milosevic (Serbia) as well as from various local actors, both official and unofficial.

At the extreme, as a potentially superior solution to hostile factions with either coherent or incoherent leadership, the international community has established "supervisory authority," i.e., fully sovereign rule, limited so far to the East Timor peace operation and to Bosnia. In the municipality of Brcko in northern Bosnia, U.S. ambassador William Farrand ruled according to the Arbitral Order authorized by the Dayton Agreement, exercising with the assistance of SFOR troops fully sovereign authority. In 2001, Brcko was the only municipality with significant minority returns and the beginnings of a functioning multiethnic police, judiciary, and town council.[50] Following the final arbitral award, in 1999, Brcko was established as an autonomous district, separate from both the Republika Serpska and the Federation, in effect a third entity. To its international administrators, Brcko is an experiment in whether concentrated international authority and substantial international capacity can begin to build self-sustaining, multiethnic peace.

The way peace came to the small village of Klanac illustrated the role that effective international authority can play. As we saw, part of the credit belongs to the international community. Its autonomous character, owned by both entities but by neither exclusively, and working with nearly limitless "supervisory" authority made all the difference. Relying on this authority, the backing of nearby SFOR troops and the assistance

[49] Doyle, Interviews in Vukovar, July 1997 especially Jacques Klein and Jaque Grinberg, July 17, and Gary Collins, July 7 and 16, 1997.

[50] Doyle, Interviews in Brcko, June 1999 and June 2000, especially William Farrand, Julian Harston, and Ralph Johnson.

of the UN police monitors, William Farrand established the only functioning multiethnic administration and police in Bosnia. The District
gave the displaced Serbs a sense that they could find a new home and be
safe and not be forced back into the Federation. It was the multiethnic
local police that quelled the last Klanac riot. The other part of the credit
belongs to the DPs who stood up for themselves and stretched a hand
across the ethnic divide when they saw a way to live together safely. Taking advantage of an offer from Supervisor Farrand, the Serbs agreed to
vacate the Bosniac houses they occupied in return for free and secure land
plots elsewhere in the District. When the DP leadership organizations
balked at this sensible compromise and the new local District Assembly
hesitated to pass enabling legislation, the current Serb and prospective
Bosniac residents threatened to organize a multiethnic demonstration. The
Assembly voted wisely, and Klanac is now at peace.[51]

One of the key difficulties faced by the operations in Cyprus and
Rwanda (for all their differences) is that both seemed to assume that the
parties would or could keep their agreements—that hostility was less
than it seemed and coherence was considerably greater. In reality, both
were closer to Bosnia in the hostility and incoherence of the factions, but
both missions were established in the view that Salvadoran (ONUSAL)
style monitoring and facilitation was sufficient.

In the *fifth ecology*, where there are *many, incoherent, and hostile* factions in a desperately poor economy, as in Somalia, the prospects appear
to be even more grim for effective peacebuilding. What may have been
needed was a partition, on the one hand, and, for the remainder of country, a substantial civilian and developmental effort with a long time horizon and trusteeship-like authority. Instead, the international community
offered a military mission with a constant eye for a fast exit.[52]

There thus appears to be a relation between the depth of hostility
and the number and character of the factions, on the one hand, and
the extent of effective authority needed to build peace, on the other.
There is a functional progression from ONUSAL's monitoring/assisting,
to UNTAC's "administrative control," to UNTAES's "executive authority," to a Brcko-style sovereign "supervision." Authority greater than
monitoring/facilitating would have been redundant in El Salvador;

---

[51] Doyle spent a day in June 2000 walking through the village, talking with the villagers
doing the rebuilding and with the multiethnic committee of safety (three Serb and three
Bosniac DPs).

[52] For an outline of "conservatorship," see Gerald Helman and Steven Ratner "Saving
Failed States," *Foreign Policy* (Winter 1992–93); and Menkhaus 1997; and Thomas Weiss,
"Rekindling Hope," in Walter Clarke and Jeffrey Herbst, eds., *Learning From Somalia*
(Boulder, CO: Westview). For later developments in Somalia, see Ameen Jan, "Peacebuild-
ing in Somalia," IPA Policy Briefing Series (July 1996).

TABLE 7.3
Transitional Authority

	Ecology				
	I	II	III	IV	V
Supervisory Authority		UNTAET[1]		UNMIK Brcko Arb.	
Exec. Authority				UNTAES	Bosnia II[2] UNOMIL[3]
Admin. Authority		ONUMOZ	UNTAC Bosnia I[4] MINURSO[5]		UNOSOM II
Monitor/ Facilitation	ONUSAL UNTAG UNMOT[6]	UNMIH[7] MINUGUA	UNAVEM UNOMIG UNFICYP[8]	UNAMIR[9]	UNOSOM I MONUC UNPROFOR UNOMSIL[10]

Key: **bold** = success; ***bold italics*** = failure; normal type face = ongoing; *italics* = ongoing, recently mandated

[1] This is a curious and exceptional case of *excessive* international authority. The Timorese factions were more than ready to cooperate according to a number of accounts, but the UN insisted on full sovereign control. See Jarat Chopra, "The UN's Kingdom of East Timor," *Survival* 42 (3), Autumn 2000: 27–39. But, fortunately, the UNTAET understood its mistake and devolved authority to the Timorese; see account by Sergio Vieira de Mello at the IPA Seminar on transitional authority (February, 2003). For background on the UNAMET operation and UNTAET, see Ian Martin, *Self-Determination in East Timor* (Bouder, CO: Lynne Rienner, 2001).

[2] This refers to the second set of Bosnia missions, following the Bonn Summit.

[3] This UN monitoring operation in Liberia was paired with and monitored an ECOMOG operation with authority to maintain order, which it achieved in a sporadic fashion.

[4] The NATO missions in Bosnia are still ongoing, so the jury is still out. But here we code this case consistent with our analysis in our case studies, which refer to the implementation of the mandate in Bosnia prior to the strengthening of the mandate at the Bonn Summit.

[5] MINURSO is an ongoing mission. In our data analysis of short-term peacebuilding success, we code a failure in the peace process two years after the end of the war, because of ongoing divided sovereignty. In a longer-term analysis of war recurrence (not of peacebuilding success as we define it more broadly), we would not code this case as a failure, since the UN mission is still ongoing and there has not been a resumption of war (see our detailed discussion of coding rules in the appendix of chapter 3).

[6] UNMOT is not coded as a success in our short-term statistical analysis, because the mission had not withdrawn for at least two years before the end of our analysis time in December 1999. However, UNMOT has since departed and peace is lasting in Tajikistan in 2004, so we code it as a success here.

[7] UNMIH failed after the end of our analysis time (in 2004), when a coup ousted President Aristide. So, we code it here as a peacebuilding failure.

[8] UNFICYP is an ongoing mission. In our data analysis of peacebuilding success or failure two years after the end of the civil war, we code a failure in the peace process in Cyprus in 1974, because of war recurrence and ongoing divided sovereignty. Post-1974, UNFICYP has provided useful monitoring and assisted peacemaking efforts and the peace process is technically still ongoing. However, consistent with our coding rules for the analysis of short-term (two-year) peacebuilding outcomes, we code a peacebuilding failure in Cyprus after the 1974 war due to persistent divided sovereignty. Given that the peace process is ongoing, we code UNFICYP as an ongoing operation here.

[9] This refers to the UN mission up to and including the genocide.

[10] This refers to the UN mission up to the end of 1999. The mandate changed, with some success, after the end of the period we cover in our data analysis.

authority less than supervisory and sovereign in Brcko would be insufficient.[53]

We can think of it as a simple relation in which when we place transitional authority conceived of as legal authority and effective international capacity (troops and budget) on a the vertical axis and the various "ecologies" described above on the horizontal axis, a progressive relation holds (table 7.3). Successful operations (those that lead to an indigenously sustainable peace) demonstrate a one-to-one relation: the more challenging the factional conflict, the more transitional authority seems to be required. (Successful operations are in bold; unsuccessful in italics; ongoing in roman type.)

Optimistically, we can note that the international community seems to be learning past lessons: in the recent cases and trying circumstances of Kosovo and East Timor extensive authority has been provided. In the equally if not more trying Congo, modest promises of monitoring as a step toward a negotiated peace are being offered. No one promises nation building or peace enforcement or humanitarian protection, as was done in Somalia and Bosnia without either the authority or the resources to make those commitments effective. This is a wise development. And, while muddling and innovation toward enhanced authority on the Bosnian model is better than stagnation, ideally such authority is written into the peace agreement or imposed by Security Council fiat at the outset of a mission, rather than retrofitted after earlier efforts fail.

There are few takers for the colonialist role in the late-twentieth century. Since all transitional authorities must end, authority and the capacity to make it effective should fit the case in order to increase the prospects for a successful transition toward self-sustaining national self-determination. Unfortunately, there are few viable alternatives to the United Nations when it comes to the peace operations that no country feels that it needs to own—that is the typical late-twentieth- and early-twenty-first-century civil war. This is the topic of the conclusion.

---

[53] For a good comparison of degrees of authority in peace operations ("mandate reach"), see Michele Griffin and Bruce Jones, "Building Peace through Transitional Authority," *International Peacekeeping* 7, no. 4 (Winter 2000): 75–90.

8

Conclusions

EFFECTIVE PEACEBUILDING DEPENDS ON good strategy and the availability of adequate resources. And in the end we need to ask whether peacebuilding delivers value for money and whether there are better alternatives now available.

Strategies, as we have argued, need to fit the broad parameters of the conflicts—the ecologies—that have characterized recent times. Although there is no recipe for success there are regularly reappearing challenges that must be surmounted if sustainable peace is to be achieved. Some of these challenges come in predictable sequences. These set sequences arose in many of the cases we have examined.

The Peacebuilding Record

Any peacebuilding venture must begin by considering the three critical dimensions of what we have called the peacebuilding triangle.

First, are there sources of unity that the UN can tap into and that it can use to build a lasting peace? Are the deaths and displacements that the civil war generated creating such hostility that the factions are looking toward a resumption of war? Are the factions too many, too hostile, and too incoherent to negotiate a peace? Or are the factions amenable to compromise? Is there a singular national identity or is the country completely fractionalized ethnically, religiously, and ideologically? Peace will be harder to build in heavily fractionalized societies. Does the country have previous experience of democratic constitutional rule or is there a single legitimate traditional authority that can provide legitimate order when the peacekeepers leave? Either prior exposure to democratic governance or some other legitimate solution to the problem of governance is necessary to support participatory peace after the peacekeepers leave.

Second, what are the levels of local capacities in the country? Is there an industrial base or other economic activity that can sustain the country without humanitarian assistance or other foreign economic aid? Or is the economy entirely dependent on a monoculture of natural resource extraction? Peace will be easier to build where there exist foundations for economic growth when the peacekeepers leave—human capital, economic infrastructure, and diversification away from natural resource rents.

Third, has the international community invested enough effort to mediate a peace treaty and enough international capacity to make up for what the post–civil war country lacks in unity and capacity? The most important step in international engagement is the negotiation of a comprehensive peace settlement. Going beyond a simple truce, it outlines the terms on which the once-warring parties are prepared to live in peace with each other. Furthering this, it embeds a strategy of peacebuilding change, including (if needed) a role for the international community with the appropriate level of transitional international authority, and it mandates the institutional and other reforms that can establish an effective sovereign government that can resolve the conflicts that are natural to all societies peacefully. Given a well-designed peace, the next question is whether the international community has actually provided the level of assistance, civilian and military, institutional and economic, that can help make the treaty implementable?

Our analysis of all civil wars since 1945 identifies the crucial ways in which those three dimensions of the triangle operate together. The greater the hostility, measured in terms of casualties, refugees, number of factions, type of war, and ethnic divisions, and the less the local capacity, measured in an underdeveloped and undiversified economy, the lower the probability of peacebuilding success, and the greater must international capacities be to increase that probability.

Our empirical analysis of both the data and the cases also supports the conceptual distinction between peacebuilding understood narrowly as the absence of war, or negative peace, and more demanding standards of participatory peace, positive peace. UN missions that are properly matched to the ecology of the conflict (and especially multidimensional PKOs) help foster positive peace and prevent the recurrence of war by building the local institutions—such as national armies, judiciaries, and electoral politics—that can manage future social conflict peacefully.

A key shortcoming of UN interventions is that, good as UN peacebuilding is in expanding political participation, it has not served to jump-start self-sustaining economic growth. This is an important failing because economic growth and higher levels of development are critical in supporting incentives for peace (particularly negative peace, or the absence of war) and sustainable democracy. UN peacebuilding would clearly benefit from an evolution that enhanced the role of economic reform as an essential component of peacebuilding.

We are also able to suggest how the three dimensions interact in more detail:

- Peacebuilding success is much more likely if hostility is low (measured by the number of casualties and displaced persons).
- Ethnically divided societies are much more likely to experience another war, and ethnoreligious wars are much harder to resolve than ideological wars. But at extremely high levels of deaths and displacements, war type matters less and the prospects of successful peacebuilding are limited.
- The presence of substantial local capacities (measured by electricity consumption per capita, rate of growth of per capita income, and low level of dependence on primary commodity exports) make a reconciled peace easier, especially if the two sides have avoided the worst forms of mutual violence.
- The number of factions has a clearly negative effect on the likelihood of peacebuilding success in the short run, particularly the increase from two to about five, beyond which the effects level out.
- The probability of peacebuilding success is remarkably higher if a transformational peacekeeping operation is used. Even at high levels of local capacity, a peacekeeping operation and treaty make a positive difference, but their greatest effect can be seen at low levels of local capacity: a treaty and transformational UN mission substitute for the lack of local capacities.
- In a difficult case, a case of little local capacity, we find that without a treaty or UN mission, even at the lowest level of hostility, there is a very low likelihood of peacebuilding success, much lower than with a transformational UN mission and a treaty. Peacekeeping does make a positive difference and early intervention pays, particularly where economic development is minimal. But at extreme levels of hostility, after massive civilian slaughter, the UN's ability to negotiate and implement a lasting peace declines, although there is still a greater chance of success with a peacekeeping operation and treaty. For example, a substantial multidimensional peacekeeping operation made a positive difference in Cambodia, despite the massive killings and displacements that took place there; an equivalent effort might have been useful in Rwanda.
- But in an easy case, with substantial local capacities, the probability of success is quite high at low levels of hostility even without a UN peace operation (even though it is still slightly higher if a transformational UN mission is deployed on the basis of a treaty among the parties). The major effect of the treaty and the UN occurs at high levels of hostility, where we are also more likely to see a UN mission and where UN missions are crucial in maintaining the probability of peacebuilding success. Without a treaty and transformational UN mission, the likelihood of success drops substantially.

In our statistical analysis, we find that positive, or participatory, peace is more likely after nonethnic wars, in countries with relatively high development levels and when UN peace operations and substantial financial assistance are available. A more differentiated picture emerges with respect to the achievement of negative or sovereign peace, or simply an end to the violence. In the short run, such peace is more dependent on muscular UN intervention and on low hostility levels rather than on the breadth of local capacities (although here, too, a rapidly improving economic situation will help create disincentives for renewed violence). In the long run, hostility indicators matter less and higher rates of economic development matter more, as does the legacy of consent-based UN missions. Thus, over the long run, for both positive, participatory peace and negative, sovereign peace the UN's effects on war prevention are indirect, yet strong, and they emanate from its success in building the institutions of peace rather than on deterring wars.

A Seven-Step Plan

Given these general constraints and opportunities for success, let us explore difficult lessons about how to sequence the management of peacebuilding that emerge from our case studies and data analysis. The lessons of every case are different, but to understand those differences we need systematic comparisons that explore how they differ on comparable dimensions.

We should begin by recalling that successful peacebuilding is a counterrevolutionary or revolutionary event. A civil war revolutionizes the polity, society, economy, and culture. Civil wars, obviously, break up sovereignty and then sometimes create ferocious hierarchies in factions. Warriors, sometimes criminals, replace civil elites. Economies become geared to military production or looting. Hatred shapes interethnic or factional identity.

To create a self-sustaining peace, peacebuilding has to reverse all that. It must either divide a country, recognize a secession, and help establish two legitimate polities or establish a single legitimate polity. If there is no clear winner to the civil war or if international assistance from the West or the UN is going to be called upon, the polity will need to be participatory enough that factions previously at war become political parties that live with each other. Society must make room for civil elites and disempower the warlords. Economies must be reoriented to civilian production and provide jobs for demobilized soldiers, and new terms of respect among diverse ethnic groups must be found. This last can often be done by punishing the perpetrators of the many abuses that civil wars inflict on innocent civilians in order that these communities can remove them from power and isolate the abusers, convincing each other that not

CHAPTER 8

everyone in the other group was/is a war criminal and thereby helping to find the terms on which to live together as neighbors.[1]

This is a revolutionary task that can be begun in two years, but will usually take a decade or more in some cases. The U.S. civil war took ten years—until the Compromise of 1876—to establish a sustainable peace that allowed the end of occupation, but then only on terms that were not sustainable in terms of American principles. We arrived at sustainable terms about a hundred years after the end of the war, with the victory of the civil rights movement. Cambodia has had its 1876 in two years (in 1993) with the UN-supervised elections; Bosnia is only now in "1873," considerably short of an "1876." Given the extent of the challenge of successful peacebuilding, getting the priorities right can make the difference between progress and stagnation. Staying the course is also important, as the sort of economic and political reconstruction that was necessary in Cambodia and Bosnia takes time. Peacebuilding operations with a sufficiently long horizon can help build peace.[2]

The first step is security. A secure environment is the sine qua non of the beginning of peace. It precedes new courts, human rights, property laws, democracy, and so forth. There must be a new sovereign Leviathan, to borrow Thomas Hobbes's famous label for the state's legitimate monopoly of violence, in order to deter future acts of war and looting. If it is unavailable domestically, enforcement must be provided internationally.

In Bosnia, the unwillingness of NATO to police deeply eroded the prospects of long-run peace, as ethnic cleansing continued fragmenting the country. In Cambodia, the Khmer Rouge quickly reestablished themselves in the absence of international authority and later proved to be a headache to root out. Moreover, the worse—the better armed the factions and the "nastier, poorer, shorter" the life of citizens in the war—the bigger the Leviathan will need to be to restore order. The light footprint strategy in Afghanistan meant that in 2005 the civil Leviathan held sway only in Kabul; elsewhere warlords ruled and sustainable peace was remote.

Chairman Karzai seemed well aware of these challenges in January 2002. In a conversation with Sadako Ogata, former head of UNHCR and

[1] Careful assessments of the conditions needed for the successful use of trials as a form of peacebuilding can be found in Gary Bass, *Stay the Hand of Vengeance* (Princeton University Press, 2000), pp. 284–310; and Jack Snyder and Leslie Vinjamuri, "Trials and Errors: Principle and Pragmatism in Strategies of International Justice," *International Security* 28, no. 3 (Winter 2003–4): 5–44.

[2] By contrast, long enforcement or traditional peacekeeping missions are less likely to succeed as they signal an understanding that the conflict is still very much ongoing, yet the international community is unwilling to give the right mandate to the peacekeepers.

then Japan's envoy for Afghan reconstruction, "Karzai emphasized the importance for the Security Council not only to extend but to expand the presence of ISAF [the International Security Assistance Force] throughout Afghanistan." Ogata then recalled: "When I asked Chairman Karzai what he considered his priority needs, he gave me an interesting and frank response. He said that when he was not in government, he had thought that his first priority would be education, followed by road repair and health. Now that he was leading the administration, he said, he realized the absolute need for state-building centered on a functioning government. He had to have money to pay the civil servants, buildings to house ministries, and telephones to communicate."[3] But what he had to do above all else was survive in the midst of the ferocious warlord rivalry that followed the toppling of the Taliban. In Afghanistan, by training and equipping a national army, the international economy may be able assist the Kabul authorities in the step-by-step acquisition of effective sovereignty over Afghanistan. This seems to be the core concept underlying the "light footprint," which also makes it a "slow tread" solution.

Security is what allows people to begin to reconstruct the rest of their lives. It is the first step to building a state. The looting in Iraq immediately after the fall of Saddam Hussein's regime was costly not merely in material terms—it was as if the United States indiscriminately bombed the country—it also signaled to Fundamentalists, Baathists, and others that no one was in charge and that power was still up for grabs. In 2004, there were about 162,000 coalition troops in Iraq (150,000 U.S.). If Iraq had been as occupied (per capita) as Kosovo was, 500,000 would have been there. The gap was large and significant. A heavy entry is the first step to a faster exit.[4]

Second, regional security must complement national security. It really helps if the international neighbors will stop intervening in order to allow the peace to proceed at home. A key achievement of the Cambodian peace was ensuring that China, Russia, Vietnam, the United States, and the Europeans were no longer supporting and financing rival armies. The UN can help, not least by mobilizing support through the "Friends" mechanism and ensuring regional cooperation with the peace process.

Third, quick "wins" will win support and time. Distributing food, medicine, turning the electricity back on, cleaning up the rubble: all send the message that a new order means a better life. It builds temporary support that is needed for longer term changes. But quick military wins need not translate into long political victories. The new polity will need

[3] Sadako Ogata, *The Turbulent Decade* (New York: W. W. Norton, 2005), p. 299.

[4] For a very good discussion of the military elements of humanitarian intervention, see O'Hanlon 1997.

more than security assistance, and enforcement missions alone will be unable to provide the foundations of a lasting peacebuilding success.

Fourth, the rule of law and constitutional consent are the foundations of all that follow. To build a legitimate state and to establish courts and police one needs locally and nationally legitimate delegates to decide the basic framework of rights and duties of citizens. In many respects a constitutional order should be designed to encourage both effective rule and to support moderate coalitions. Well-designed federal distributions of political authority, careful separations of power, judicial review, and parliamentary regimes—when tailored to local particularities—can be productive.[5]

In a post–civil war situation, the consent often comes from a delicately negotiated peace treaty as in El Salvador and Cambodia that discovers the terms on which the factions are prepared to live with each other. In an international intervention, the "treaty" follows the imposed peace. If constitutional reform (or a new constitution) is necessary, it is key that a constituent assembly—a very broad group that can make credible claim to represent the major forces or elements of society—discusses and writes the framework of a constitution. How such delegates to a constitutional convention are selected and by whom is key. While the people (if one can have a "constitutional" agreement before the constitution) are best, an impartial international body is better at this than an international belligerent. A few weeks after the Taliban fell in the war in Afghanistan, the UN Special Representative Brahimi was already assembling the Bonn Conference at which these kinds of arrangements were developed for the political transition.

Fifth, not least among these rights that must be delimited is the right to property. This is a right the poor need even more than the rich. With ownership can come investment. As economists are wont to say "No one washes a rented car." Hernando de Soto has demonstrated that unless property is titled, it cannot be mortgaged and mortgage capital cannot be invested. The poor already have immense potential assets in their homes, businesses, and use of agricultural land. What they lack is a title to those assets that encourages investment and protects from extortion.[6] With such ownership, then the Smithian magic of the market can quickly come into play, and people will begin to earn themselves into sustainable livelihood. And the market can help diversify production beyond the natural resources such as oil and gems and logs that are the fuel of civil wars and corruption. Diversification of production and economic growth

[5] See Adeed I. Dawisha and Karen Dawisha, 2003, "How to Build a Democratic Iraq." *Foreign Affairs* 82, no. 3 (2003): 36–50; and Samuel Issacharoff, "Constitutionalizing Democracy in Fractured Societies" working draft, Columbia Law School (September 2003).

[6] Hernando de Soto, *The Mystery of Capital* (New York: Basic Books, 2000).

are the critical determinants of long-term war avoidance. With such growth in place, the UN's task of rebuilding ailing polities will be easier and much more effective.

Nat Coletta at the World Bank, in a study of wars in the Great Lakes region of Africa, found that former soldiers who lacked either a farm or job were many, many times more likely to commit violent crimes. Disarmed soldiers always keep at least one gun; they will use it to feed themselves and their families if there is no alternative.[7]

Sixth, democracy or wider participation is likely to be essential for longer run peace. Merely suppressing the other factions is difficult. But premature democracy is dangerous, and the transition process also carries new risks of renewed conflict.[8] In the environment of intercommunal hostility that follows a civil war popular representation accurately represents antagonistic hostility. Overly delayed representation, on the other hand, will make the international peacebuilders into colonial oppressors. In Iraq, the U.S.-UK occupation could have been the precursor to an all-Iraqi Intifada, rather than a limited, if violent, insurgency, if the coalition had not effected a transition to an elected Iraqi transitional regime. It is with respect to this difficult but necessary transition that the UN can make a positive impact by marshaling both its legitimacy and its technical capacities and, by putting its lessons of experience to practice, help design the foundations of a stable participatory peace. Obviously a delicate balance is needed. In countries with the deepest political-ideological or ethnic rifts and legacies of very bloody civil wars, constitutional conventions and a legitimate transitional regime will buy time, and a UN mandate of transitional or executive authority may be the only viable option. Local village democracy takes time and is a necessary component of national democracy. The UN must plan for a national election that does not come too quickly. Elections must usually come after the institutional transformations that establish the foundations of the rule of law.

Seventh and last, genuine moral and psychological reconciliation comes after law and order is established, after the economy is again viable, after the trials of war criminals have taken place or the reports of reconciliation commissions been been made, and with the establishment

---

[7] Interview with Nat Coletta: Rebuilidng in the Wake of War," *ADM Online*, May 1, 2000, http://www.cdi.org/adm/1145/Coletta.html.

[8] This may explain why, in the short-term analysis of peacebuilding, we found that UN missions are generally not significant in reducing the recurrence of civil war: the very solutions that the UN is pushing may increase the risk of new violence. But, if the UN is given the resources and mandate necessary to carry through with its mission (as in the few cases of genuinely multidimensional peacebuilding that we examined in previous chapters), then institutional transformation can take hold, which explains why in the long run, UN missions can have a positive, significant effect in reducing the risk of war recurrence.

of an education system in which all the children can be educated. In all countries, war stirs passions, and the more people have been affected (killed, displaced), the worse the postwar enmity and the more difficult will be the implementation of a peace settlement. Indeed, it is usually the next generation, if all goes well, that reconciles and establishes the beginnings of national or civic consciousness. Developing a common educational curriculum is immensely difficult. It still has not been achieved in the eastern part of Croatia or in Bosnia, where the teaching of history stops in 1990 and the pre-1990 history of the countries is being radically and incompatibly rewritten by each community.

The Seven Step plan need not be conducted in lockstep. Sometimes to achieve security factions will need to be assured and sometimes that assurance, as it was in El Salvador, will be promoted by establishing human rights monitoring (even before the war has ended) or starting reconstruction projects that employ demobilized soldiers and support former military commanders (as was done in Eastern Slavonia). But this list of priorities has an underlying logic. Skipping steps is costly, when, for example, due to lack of sovereign security, humanitarian and reconstruction projects merely fuel the rearmament of the factions.

Even when acknowledging that every peacebuilding effort is different, it is difficult in comparing cases to underestimate how difficult some peacebuilding efforts will be—Iraq, Afghanistan, the Democratic Republic of the Congo, Liberia, and Burundi are all very difficult test cases of the international community's resolve and ability to help rebuild countries after civil war.[9] In several of these cases, the lessons we have learned in this book are not implemented well: the UN is apparently moving backward, fielding traditional peacekeeping missions in the Congo and Burundi—two of the toughest peacebuilding ecologies around. Nonetheless, if you consider that Germany and Japan are today the two great pacifist international powers and that the killing fields of Cambodia are being cultivated, that a democratic Croatia is in line to join the EU, and that a Sandinista rebel commandante became the democratically elected mayor of San Salvador, the seemingly impossible can happen. Partly it is a matter of costs and commitment.

The Costs of Staying—and Not Staying—the Course

In El Salvador, the costs of making peace were about $111 million (at $28.9 million per year for three and one half years, 1991–94, including

---

[9] All of these cases, including Iraq and Afghanistan in 2003–4, meet the definitional criteria for civil war.

$35 million in 1993 for personnel).[10] In Cambodia, estimates suggest that at least a $1 billion in additional costs would have been incurred beyond the official budget of $1.5 billion if the plans for economic rehabilitation could have been implemented. The April 1993 NATO estimates of the cost of implementing an agreed peace in Bosnia indicated a requirement for 50,000 soldiers and $10 billion per year, without including the civilian peacebuilding costs.[11] Actual costs of IFOR ran at about $3.5 billion in the first year.

Good peacebuilding tends to be expensive. Considering the dangers of bluffing with inadequate military operations and the costs of effective peacebuilding in the more expensive operations (and the UN's continuously shaky finances), it is reassuring to note a favorable emerging trend and another key strategic consideration. The fortunate trend is that the surge of civil wars that accompanied the waning days of the Cold War and its immediate aftermath appears to be ebbing.[12] If so, there will be less demand for the UN's costly peace services.[13] The other consideration is that successful operations need not be large and expensive. Good leadership economizes on resources. In addition, political and economic circumstances differ. Factions that have arrived at a negotiated comprehensive, acceptable peace; countries less than devastated; nations retaining a sense of identity and even traditionally legitimate rulers: all require a smaller and less expensive international presence. ONUSAL was thus cheaper than Cambodia, which in turn will have been much cheaper than a sustainable peace in Bosnia (once achieved).

Obviously, more is also needed. The UN has not yet developed a model for better cooperation with those agencies of international development and postwar reconstruction that can help achieve postwar growth and secure employment for former combatants as well as victims of the war. Democracy and development usually go together. The

[10] In 1994 dollars, as of December 31, 1994 (PS/DPI/15/Rev.6, March 1995) and *Jane's Defense Weekly*, February 5, 1994.

[11] For Cambodia, these figures include the costs of refugee repatriation and the $800 million pledged by the International Commission on the Reconstruction of Cambodia. Bosnian costs are found in Bair, 1994, p. 349. The Clinton Administration pledged a U.S. contingent of 25,000 soldiers, drawn primarily from the First Armored Division and Third Infantry Division.

[12] Ted Robert Gurr, "Ethnic Warfare on the Wane," *Foreign Affairs* 79, no. 3 (2000): 52–65.

[13] There has been a steady accumulation of country-years at war since 1960, largely because some conflicts were so difficult to resolve and lasted for years, if not decades. There is a less clear trend in the onset of new civil wars. However, there was a reassuring rise since 2000 in the settlement of several long-lasting civil wars (Angola, Sudan, Burundi, Democratic Republic of the Congo). Many of these cases, however, are too recent and the peace process too fragile to be able to know if there is truly a downward trend in the onset of new wars.

UN's task of building stable polities after civil war will be greatly assisted by favorable economic conditions. Yet frequently the wrong economic policies are forced upon fragile postwar states, creating new sources of social tension that can destabilize the peace.[14] Organizational changes in the UN might help improve the way it interacts with those agencies. The need for better strategy coordination when several international agencies intervene in the same conflict is a lesson that is frequently heard in policy circles, but seldom addressed by the responsible agencies. The United Nations currently has a Department of Political Affairs staffed predominantly with diplomats whose major responsibility is "peacemaking," political analysis, and support for mediated peace processes. It has a Department of Peacekeeping Operations that manages the deployment of military forces for peacekeeping. Peacebuilding is assigned to the Department of Political Affairs, but expertise that focuses on the nexus between institution building and economic development is scattered across the UN system in the United Nations Development Program, the Department of Economic and Social Affairs, the World Bank, and (most significantly) among the officials who manage peacebuilding efforts in the field. The UN system lacks a "Department of Peacebuilding"—an effective focal point that can absorb lessons, manage careers, and plan for future responsibilities.[15] But the recent report of the High Level Panel proposes a useful alternative, a "Peacebuilding Commission" that will focus international attention both on states at risk of collapse and at the vital peacebuilding transition from civil war to sustainable peace.[16] Composed of selected states serving on the Security Council, the Economic and Social Council, and with representation from the World Bank and the IMF, the Peacebuilding Commission would serve as forum for mobilizing and coordinating international action. Itself served by a "Peacebuilding Support Office" in the Secretariat, it might succeed in developing the strategy, ensuring the resources, and improving the management that peacebuilding has shown itself again and again to require.

In the end, improvements, even expensive ones, in the efficiency of peacebuilding need to be judged with a better comparative perspective. For every $1,000 spent by member countries on their own military

---

[14] On the risks associated by the application of neoliberal economic policies (e.g., structural adjustment) in countries emerging from civil war, see Roland Paris, "Peacebuilding and the Limits of Liberal Internationalism," *International Security* 22 (Fall 1997): 54–89; and Roland Paris, *At War's End* (Cambridge: Cambridge University Press, 2004).

[15] An effort is currently (2004–5) underway to improve the coordination of peacebuilding through a UN Peacebuilding Commission.

[16] High-Level Panel on Threats, Challenges and Change, *A More Secure World: Our Shared Responsibility* (New York: United Nations, 2004), pp. 83–85.

forces, they spend, on average, $1.40 on the UN peacekeeping budget.[17] In 1994, the United States budgeted $267 billion on the Defense Department, about $28 billion on the intelligence community, and $1 billion for UN peacekeeping (the then current U.S. 30 percent of the $3.2 billion total). Nor is the United States discriminated against in the assessment of UN costs. The 25 percent U.S. assessment to the UN regular budget (and the peacekeeping rate proposed by the Clinton administration) is 0.0076 of a percent of U.S. national income. The Netherlands, Austria, and Sweden pay 135 percent of the U.S. rate relative to their national income. Ministates, like Sao Tome, pay 330 percent of the U.S. rate relative to their income.[18]

The United States and other large contributors will have to ask whether UN peace operations are worth the cost. Today, for example, although no one calls Cambodia or El Salvador models of growth-oriented, stable democracies; nonetheless, both governments were chosen in UN-supervised elections that were the freest and fairest in their histories. Salvador's police were reformed; Cambodia enjoys an effective coalition government that successfully resisted the remaining and dwindling Khmer Rouge guerrillas. When we consider that the U.S. government once thought (very unwisely) that peace, pro-American states, and democratic development in Southeast Asia were worth more than 50,000 US lives and about $179 billion (1990 dollars) and that as late as the 1980s the U.S. government thought that promoting a friendly regime, peace, and democracy were worth $6.01 billion (FY 1981–90, in 1994 dollars) in El Salvador, both the UN's Cambodian and Salvadoran operations look remarkably cheap and genuinely successful, even when measured solely in terms of U.S. national interests.[19]

[17] Shijuro Ogata and Paul Volcker, *Financing an Effective United Nations* (Ford Foundation, 1993). And see Ambassador Madeleine Albright's testimony, Senate Committee on Armed Services, May 12, 1994.

[18] Report of the Commission on Global Governance, *Our Global Neighbourhood* (Oxford: Oxford University Press, 1995), p. 247. Some countries, such as some of the rapidly developing countries, are paying less than their full share because the UN budget is too slow to adjust to rapid changes in GNP. The United States will be able to shrink its share of the peacekeeping budget from 30 percent to 25 percent with little cost to the UN if Japan and Germany join the Security Council as permanent members, paying at the higher rate permanent members have traditionally accepted for their greater privileges and responsibilities in the direction of UN peace operations.

[19] Of course, the circumstances, including Cold War competition, were vastly different. For the figures see James L. Clayton, 'The Military Budget and National Economic Priorities," originally presented in U.S. Congress, Joint Economic Committee, pt. 1, 91st Congress, 1st session. http://www.census.gov/prod/1/gen/95statab/defense.pdf. CIA; *World Factbook, 1993*; and figures from *US Overseas Loans, Grants and Assistance from International Organizations*, Statistical Annex 1, Annual Development Coordination Committee Report to Congress, (Washington, DC: Statistics and Reports Division, Office of Financial

Alternatives?

When the UN cannot negotiate a peace, should the international community abandon the cause? What responses should have been made to acts of overt aggression, such as Iraq's invasion of Kuwait, or to the looming humanitarian disasters in Bosnia and Somalia in 1992 or Rwanda in the spring of 1994?

Delegation to national action has become, as it was in Korea in 1950, the UN's answer to extreme emergencies—international aggression and humanitarian catastrophe. It offers a traditional national solution to the UN's typical command and control problems. Now it is becoming so widespread that it is being designated "fourth generation" peacekeeping. Stimulated by the temporary success of UNITAF and by the delegations to Russia in Georgia, to France in Rwanda, to the United States in Haiti, and to Australia in East Timor, the UN is surmounting contributors' fatigue by assigning mandates to the national states willing to accept and perhaps enforce them. This, indeed, may be the best compromise available in difficult circumstances.[20] In itself, however, it does little to address the longer run problems of leaving behind a stable form of locally legitimate government. Here there remains an important "hands-off" role for the UN. Imposing a scheme of public order should be avoided in favor of mobilizing the peacemaking, peacekeeping, and peacebuilding strategies of enhanced consent that the UN exercises well. The UNITAF to UNOSOM II handoff failed in part because peacemaking stopped short of negotiating a comprehensive, implementable agreement that included both the warlords and civil society. Instead, the UN attempted to impose law and order from New York and Washington, with all the consequences. In these cases, the UN should try to recruit the beginnings of a "Friends" coalition of interested states to assist and help monitor the intervener. These "Friends" will also be needed to help negotiate, fund, and manage a peace on a multilateral basis.

Delegation also raises difficult issues of UN responsibility. Can the Security Council be confident that the mandate it assigns will be implemented in ways that fulfill multilateral principles and serve the interests of the United Nations as a whole? Security Council "licenses" to intervene with preordained but renewable expiration clauses should address

---

Management, Agency for International Development, various years); all in Michael Switow, "Costs of US Interventions," Woodrow Wilson School, Research memorandum (1995).

[20] For a case for an option similar to this, called "benign spheres of influence," see Charles William Maynes, "A Workable Clinton Doctrine," *Foreign Policy* 93 (Winter 1993–94): 93–94.

some of these concerns. But in our dangerous times, will states volunteer in reliably large enough numbers for international public service?

Another alternative centers about a new attention to the possibilities of regional peacekeeping—a multilateral, burden-sharing strategy recommended in the Secretary General's 1995 *Supplement to the "Agenda for Peace"* A regional approach appears designed to elicit a more locally sensitive approach to political disputes. Under the aegis of the OSCE and with UN endorsement, Italy played a constructive role in providing security for the transition in Albania. But the lack of institutional, military, and financial capacity of the regional organizations (with the exception perhaps of NATO) remains a considerable hurdle. The empirical record shows that non-UN peace missions are on average not successful. This is undoubtedly the case because of the vast differences among the capacities and interests of the many regional organizations that have in the past stepped up to provide peace in civil war–torn states. The United States developed an African Crisis Response Initiative and became involved in training African peacekeepers. In a more striking initiative the EU began planning for a 60,000-person force that would be available for peacekeeping.[21] These organizations might be able to respond to crises more effectively than other regional alternatives. The UN must carefully select its regional partners, and regional actors should work as closely as possible with the UN, borrowing from the UN's greater legitimacy and its deep experience with post–civil war peacebuilding.

As yet another alternative, Sir Brian Urquhart has issued an eloquent manifesto in favor of an UN rapid reaction force of 5,000–10,000. Small and centrally controlled, it would be suited for overcoming delays occasioned by the recruiting of peacekeeping forces, enabling the UN to engage in rapid interventions that can sometimes prevent an escalating crisis. In light of our results on the importance of early intervention, this suggestion seems very appealing. Had they been available, these forces might have been decisive in Somalia in early 1992 or Rwanda in April of 1994.[22] Very few countries, however, have expressed a willingness to establish such a force. Current discussions center on a less global but still valuable ready reaction force consisting of designated national units, trained in peacekeeping and available at short notice, and a mobile headquarters unit.

When no state, group of states, or organization will volunteer to intervene, then sometimes the best that can be done is to try to mitigate the

---

[21] Joseph Fitchett "EU Force Takes Shape with Pledge of Troops" *International Herald Tribune,* Monday, November 20, 2000.

[22] Sir Brian Urquhart, "For a UN Volunteer Military Force," *New York Review of Books,* June 10, 1993. See also "Four Views," *New York Review of Books,* June 24, 1993.

consequences of natural disaster or war. Humanitarian assistance from "above"—state efforts to establish "humanitarian corridors" as has been done in the Sudan or protected convoys and even, at the minimum, airdrops as was essayed in Bosnia—can make a valuable difference. Assistance from "below" by nongovernmental organizations, taking all the considerable risks of independent action, can also provide relief, as the voluntary agencies did in Somalia until they were overwhelmed in late 1992.[23] It is remarkable that NGOs and civilians continue to be willing to take risks that governments are not willing to assume for their soldiers. In the UN context, since 1992, more civilian relief workers than military peacekeepers have been killed in the line of duty, a sad but impressive total of 199.[24] In these circumstances, the UN should continue to attempt to recruit coalitions of states—"Friends"—who will dedicate their energies to negotiating and managing a peace.

Failures in Somalia, Rwanda, and Bosnia have made peacekeeping the latest target for many critics of the United Nations. In Somalia, "food for peace" seemed to feed a violent urban quagmire. In Bosnia, the "protection force" never adequately protected. The United States bombed the Serbs to the negotiating table, and the contrasting effectiveness only highlights the UN's perceived failures.

The UN has played a vital legal role in legitimizing collective responses to international aggression. In defense of South Korea (1950) and Kuwait (1991), its stamp of approval constituted a collective condemnation of the aggressors and helped mobilize a collective effort of defense.

Unfortunately, following on the end of the Cold War, some in the UN itself seem to have thought the organization should make war to enforce peace, when it could not. Many Americans, especially members of Congress, seem to think the organization cannot bring about and maintain a peace when, in fact, it very well can. By overestimating the power of the UN after the end of the Cold War, the enthusiasts overstretched the organization. By limiting their judgment to only two operations, most of the skeptics fail to grasp peacekeeping's larger benefits. When they benefited from a negotiated settlement and were rightly sized and granted sufficient authority, UN peace operations have helped build peace. Rather than proving the inadequacies of peacekeeping as a whole, as critics would contend, the UN's recent failures only reflect the difficulties that the organization has had in adjusting to the post–Cold War world.

During the Cold War, peacekeeping operations rested on three pillars: consent, impartiality, and the nonuse of force. These rules fit very well

[23] For a valuable discussion see Stephen Jackson, "Survival of the Cutest," *Irish Reporter*, no. 12, 4th quarter (1993): 5–7.

[24] Barbara Crossette, "9 Aid Workers Held Hostage after Gunfight by Somalis, *New York Times*, March 27, 2001.

limited UN investments in state-to-state conflicts when both parties sought to end a dispute, needed more time to work out their differences, and required an interim monitor of their cease-fire.

With the end of the Cold War, the Security Council was able to bring about operations that East-West tensions had long precluded. Enamored with the peacekeeping solution, the Security Council began more operations between 1988 and 2000 than it had in the previous thirty years of the Cold War. In its rush to solve every conflict across the globe, the Security Council made many mistakes. In Somalia it allowed the United States—acting independently of UN command—to use force to pursue General Aidid, a process that ended in a bloody firefight between peacekeepers and Aidid supporters. In Bosnia the UN began an operation without the lasting consent of all parties, and soon found itself marooned in an ongoing war without the forces to deliver on its promises of protection or even to protect itself.

Post–Cold War conflicts tend to involve factions and civil and ethnic strife rather than disciplined states and rational and material interests. Conflicts tend to be extreme; agreements tend to be hard to reach and when signed, fluid. The factions themselves often change over time, and some of them may even be eliminated in the course of the conflict. In these circumstances, there is often no peace to keep. Attempts at peacekeeping become peace enforcing, which is another name for war. And the UN—a club of 189 states with varied interests, a tiny budget (by national defense standards), and a traditional culture of peaceful resolution—has shown itself to be a very ineffective machine for making war. The UN cannot force sovereign peace—at best, it can keep such peace that exists when the parties are not committed to building the foundations of a broader, participatory peace.

But the failures in Bosnia, Rwanda, and Somalia by no means prove UN peacekeeping to be a bad idea. Recent UN operations have helped bring an end to bloody civil wars in Cambodia, El Salvador, Namibia, Mozambique, Croatia (Eastern Slavonia), and East Timor; all enjoyed free and fair elections and are now on the road to national reconciliation and substantial stability. Other operations have not fared as well. After experiencing difficulties in the handoff from the United States, the UN operation in Haiti assisted an orderly return of democratically elected President Aristide only to find that the failure to deepen peacebuilding into a viable economy, impartial judiciary and police force, and a reconstructed security force made Haiti vulnerable to another cycle of coup and countercoup. The UN's biggest problem with these failing operations is that none of them have received as much attention as the UN's actions in Bosnia and Somalia.

The defining characteristic of all the successful operations is that they each achieved a comprehensive peace agreement—one involving the UN in the entire peace process, from the signing of the first cease-fire to the restoration of the last structures of government. Beyond that, the successful operations coped with the tensions of post–civil wars by innovating within UN capacities and traditions, building upon the Secretary-General's 1992 strategic document, *Agenda for Peace*. First, the Secretary-General developed new strategies to help broker an agreement (*making* the peace) by drawing in the assistance of interested states that lent national clout to UN diplomacy just as the UN legitimized and monitored national interests. Second, the Security Council authorized a peacekeeping operation to build confidence in the agreements (*keeping* the peace) that often included ad hoc semisovereign institutions that encompassed all the previously warring factions. These interim institutions, such as the Supreme National Council in Cambodia, provided forums for consultation and (when necessary) dynamic adjustment of the peace process. And third, the UN as a whole also provided the right tools and assistance to encourage national reconciliation and repair the torn social and economic infrastructure (*building* the peace). By expanding the scope of Cold War peacekeeping operations to include units to organize and monitor elections, investigate human rights abuses, train national police forces, and encourage economic redevelopment, recent operations in Mozambique, Cambodia, and El Salvador have transformed bloody civil wars into democratic elections. Discrete, impartial force sometimes made the difference, but at no point did the peacekeepers rely primarily on force, as they did in both Bosnia and Somalia, to impose outcomes, thereby making war.

Some skeptics may at this point argue that UN peacekeeping is too expensive to justify its continued existence. In reality, peacekeeping is far less costly than most critics imagine. The annual budget for the *entire* United Nations, the largest multinational organization in the world, is $5 billion. While that may at first sound like a large amount, try putting it in this perspective: $5 billion is less than 2 percent of the annual budget for the United States Defense Department. The total cost of *all* UN peacekeeping operations from January 1, 1948, to January 1, 1995, has been only $12.5 billion. Peacekeeping is a relative bargain. Before we decide to go it alone in Colombia (or elsewhere) and pay the entire bill, it is worth remembering that for every dollar the United States spends on UN peacekeeping, the rest of the international community spends three more.

When thinking about the flaws and follies of UN peacekeeping, keep in mind a few simple facts. First, the UN is in many ways no more than the sum of its member states. If nobody wants to send troops to a peacekeeping operation (read: Rwanda) or nobody is willing to provide leadership (read: Bosnia, until the United States stepped in), nothing will happen. Blame for such inaction shouldn't lie with the UN, but rather with the individual nations that had the capacity to act but chose not to. It is in the way in which a mandate is discharged by a UN mission that we should look for evidence of the UN's success or failure. Second, the UN Secretariat is not an independent entity; it doesn't have the right, authority, or power to act on its own. There is no UN army; there are only national battalions wearing blue helmets and driving white tanks with the letters "UN" painted on them. Furthermore, when it comes to peacekeeping operations the Secretary-General and his staff can only act when told to by the Security Council (five veto-wielding permanent members known as the P5—Britain, France, China, the United States, and the Russian Federation—and ten members elected to two-year, nonconsecutive terms). If any one of the P5 does not want the UN to intervene in a conflict, nothing will happen. But the very fact that the UN does intervene in difficult situations to protect international peace and security is at least partially the result of successful diplomacy by the Secretariat, which can help convince the factions to stop fighting and the P5 to intervene. Finally, remember that peacekeeping cannot solve every conflict. It works only when the parties to the conflict are ready to begin the process of reconciliation and are prepared to trust the UN with the job of midwife in the birth of a new and peaceful civil society. But for these vital, messy jobs, no one does it better than the UN.

Neither UN peacemaking nor these alternative strategies will eliminate the formidable challenges of making, keeping, and building peace in the midst of protracted civil wars. Some crises will not find their solution. But today as the United Nations is under attack in the United States and elsewhere, we should not neglect its authentic peacemaking potential. Employing strategies of enhanced consent, the United Nations can play a constructive role in the forging of peace and reconstruction in those areas of the world in need of assistance. Avoiding the dangerous and often counterproductive effects of armed imposition, whether unilateral or multilateral, the UN can be the legitimating broker in the making, keeping, and building of a stable peace that takes the first steps toward the opening of political space for human rights and participatory communal self-expression.

Bibliography

Abadie, Alberto, David Drukker, Jane Leber Herr, and Guido W. Imbens. "Implementing Matching Estimators for Average Treatment Effects in STATA." *Stata Journal* 4, no. 3 (2004): 290–312.

Abadie, Alberto, and Guido W. Imbens. "Simple and Bias-Corrected Matching Estimators," Technical Report, Department of Economics, University of California, Berkeley, 2002. http://emlab.berkeley.edu/users/imbens/.

Abiew, Francis K. *The Evolution of the Doctrine and Practice of Humanitarian Intervention.* The Hague: Kluwer Law International, 1999.

Akashi, Yashushi. Interview in "Peace in the Killing Fields," pt. 3 of *The Thin Blue Line*, BBC Radio 4, 9 May 1993.

———. "UNTAC in Cambodia: Lessons for UN Peace-keeping," Charles Rostow Annual Lecture. Washington, DC: SAIS, October 1993.

Alesina, Alberto, William Easterly, and Reza Baquir. "Public Goods and Ethnic Divisions." Policy Research Working Paper 2108. Washington, DC: World Bank, 1999.

Allan, James H. *Peacekeeping: Outspoken Observations by a Field Officer.* Westport, CT: Praeger, 1996.

Allen, Woody. *Without Feathers.* New York: Warner Books, 1976.

Ambrose, Stephen. *Undaunted Courage.* New York: Simon and Schuster, 1996.

Anderson, Benedict. *Imagined Communities: Reflections on the Origins and Spread of Nationalism.* London: Verso, 1983.

Anderson, Gary. "UNOSOM II: Not Failure, Not Success." In *Beyond Traditional Peacekeeping*, edited by Donald Daniel and Bradd Hayes, 267–82. New York: St. Martin's, 1995.

Annan, Kofi. *The Causes of Conflict and the Promotion of Durable and Sustainable Peace in Africa: Report of the Secretary-General.* New York: United Nations, 1998.

———. "Address to the UN General Assembly." New York: United Nations, September 20, 1999.

———. "Secretary-General's Annual Report to the General Assembly." UN Press Release, September 20, 1999.

———. "Reflections on Intervention." Ditchley Park, UK, June 26, 1998. In *The Question of Intervention.* New York: United Nations, 1999.

———. Report of the Secretary-General pursuant to General Assembly resolution 53/35. (The situation in Bosnia and Herzegovina) The Srebrenica Report. Presented to the General Assembly. A/54/549. New York: United Nations, November 15, 1999.

———. "No Exit without Strategy: Security Council Decision-Making and the Closure or Transaction of United Nations Peacekeeping Operations." Presented to the Security Council, S/2001/394. New York: United Nations, April 20, 2001.

Antonini, Blanca. "El Salvador." In *The UN Security Council*, edited by David Malone, 423–36. Boulder, CO: Lynne Rienner, 2004.

Arendt, Hannah. "What Is Authority." In *Between Past and Future*, 91–141. New York: Viking, 1961.

Arneberg, M., and J. Pedersen. *Social and Economic Conditions in East Timor.* Columbia University and Fafo Institute of Applied Social Science, 1999.

Ashley, D. 1998. "The Failure of Conflict Resolution in Cambodia: Causes and Lessons." In *Cambodia and the International Community: The Quest for Peace, Development, and Democracy*, edited by F. Z. Brown & D. G. Timberman, 49–78. Singapore: Institute for Southeast Asian Studies, 1998.

Atlas, Pierre, and Roy Licklider. "Conflict among Former Allies after Civil War Settlement: Sudan, Zimbabwe, Chad, and Lebanon," *Journal of Peace Research* 36, no. 1 (1999): 35–54.

Austin, Reginald. "Electoral Report." Phnom Penh: UNTAC, 1993.

———. "New Forms of International Intervention: The United Nations Military-Civilian Intervention in Cambodia." In *Restructuring the Global Military Sector: New Wars*, edited by Mary Kaldor and Basker Vashee, 231–57. New York: Pinter, 1997.

Axelrod, Robert, and Robert Keohane. Introduction and Conclusion to *Cooperation under Anarchy*, edited by Kenneth Oye. Princeton: Princeton University Press, 1986.

Azam, Jean Paul. "How to Pay for Peace." *Public Choice* 83, no. 1–2. (1995): 173–84.

Bain, William. *Between Anarchy and Society: Trusteeship and the Obligations of Power*. Oxford: Oxford University Press, 2003.

Bair, Andrew, "Yugoslav Lessons for Future Peacekeepers." *European Security* 3, no. 2 (1994): 340–49.

Ball, George W. *The Past Has Another Pattern: Memoirs*. New York: Norton, 1982.

Barnett, Michael. "The UN Security Council, Indifference, and Genocide in Rwanda." *Cultural Anthropology* 12, no. 4 (1997): 551–78.

———. *Eyewitness to a Genocide: The United Nations and Rwanda*. Ithaca: Cornell University Press, 2002.

Barro, Robert, and David Gordon."Rules, Discretion and Reputation in a Model of Monetary Policy." *Journal of Monetary Economics* 12, no.1 (1983): 101–21.

Bass, Gary. *Stay the Hand of Vengeance*. Princeton: Princeton University Press, 2000.

Bates, Robert H. "Ethnicity, Capital Formation, and Conflict." CID Working Paper no. 27. Cambridge: Harvard University, 1999.

———. *Prosperity and Violence: The Political Economy of Development*. New York: Norton and Norton, 2001.

Becker, Sasha O., and Andrea Ichino. "Estimation of Average Treatment Effects Based on Propensity Scores." *Stata Journal* 2, no.4 (2002): 358–77.

Bednar, Jenna, William N. Eskridge Jr., and John Ferejohn. "A Political Theory of Federalism." In *Constitutional Culture and Democratic Rule*, edited by

J. Ferejohn, J. Riley, and J. N. Rakove. New York: Cambridge University Press, 2001.

Beitz, Charles. "The Reagan Doctrine in Nicaragua." In *Problems of International Justice*, edited by Steven Luper-Foy, 182–95. Boulder, CO: Westview Press, 1988.

Bercovitch, J. "International Mediation: A Study of Incidence, Strategies, and Conditions for Successful Outcomes." *Cooperation and Conflict* 21, no. 3 (1986): 155–69.

Berdal, Mats R. "Whither UN Peacekeeping? An Analysis of the Changing Military Requirements of UN Peacekeeping with Proposals for Its Enhancement." London: Brassey's for the International Institute for Strategic Studies, 1993.

Berdal, M., and D. M. Malone, eds. *Greed and Grievance*. Boulder, CO, and London: Lynne Rienner, 2000.

Biermann, W., and M. Vadset, eds. *UN Peacekeeping in Trouble : Lessons Learned from the Former Yugoslavia; Peacekeepers' Views on the Limits and Possibilities of the United Nations*. Aldershot, UK: Ashgate, 1998.

Blainey, Geoffrey. *The Causes of War*. New York: Free Press, 1973.

Blomberg, Brock, and Gregory Hess. "The Temporal Links between Conflict and Economic Activity." *Journal of Conflict Resolution* 46 (February 2002): 74–90.

Boulding, Kenneth. "Toward a Theory of Peace." In *International Conflict and Behavioral Science*, edited by Roger Fisher, 70–87. New York: Basic Books, 1964.

Boutros-Ghali, Boutros. *An Agenda for Peace*. New York: United Nations, 1992.

———. *Supplement to "An Agenda for Peace": Position Paper of the Secretary-General on the Occasion of the Fiftieth Anniversary of the United Nations*, A/50/60; S/1995/1, January 3, 1995.

———. *An Agenda for Peace*, 2d edition. New York: United Nations, 1995.

———. *Unvanquished*. New York: Random House, 1999.

Bowden, Mark. *Blackhawk Down*. New York: Atlantic Monthly Press, 1999.

Boyce, James K., et al. *Adjustment toward Peace: Economic Policy and Post-war Reconstruction in El Salvador*. San Salvador: UNDP, 1995.

Boyd, James M. "Cyprus: Episode in Peacekeeping." *International Organization* 20, no.1 (1966): 1–17.

Bradbury, Mark. *The Somali Conflict: Prospects for Peace*. Oxford: Oxfam, 1994.

Brahimi, Lakhdar, Brian Atwood, et al. "Report of the Panel on United Nations Peace Operations." Brahimi Report. Presented to the General Assembly and the Security Council, A/55/305—S/2000/809, 2000.

Brass, Paul R. *Ethnic Groups and the State*. London: Croom-Helm, 1985.

———. *Theft of an Idol: Text and Context in the Representation of Collective Violence*. Princeton: Princeton University Press, 1997.

Bratt, Duane. "Explaining Peacekeeping Performance: The UN in Internal Conflicts." *International Peacekeeping* 4, no. 3 (1994): 65–81.

Brito, D., and M. Intriligator. "An Economic Model of Guerrilla Warfare." *International Transactions* 15, no. 3 (1989): 319–29.

Brown, MacAlister, and Joseph Zasloff. *Cambodia Confounds the Peacemakers.* Ithaca: Cornell University Press, 1998.

Brown, Michael E. "The Causes and Regional Dimensions of Internal Conflict." In *International Dimensions of Internal Conflict*, edited by Michael E. Brown, 571–602. Cambridge: MIT Press, 1996.

Brubaker, R. "National Minorities, Nationalizing States, and External National Homelands in the New Europe." *Daedalus* 124 (Spring 1995): 107–32.

Brubaker, Rogers, and David D. Laitin. "Ethnic and Nationalist Violence." *Annual Review of Sociology* 24, no. 1 (1998): 243–52.

Bruk, S. I., and V. S. Apenchenko, eds. *Atlas Narodov Mira.* Moscow: Glavnoe Upravlenie Geodezii I Kartografii Gosudarstvennogo Geologischeskogo komiteta SSSR and Institut etnografii im. H. H. Miklukho-Maklaia, Akademia nauk SSSR, 1964.

Burg, Steven, and Paul Shoup. *The War in Bosnia-Herzegovina.* Armonk, NY: M. E. Sharpe, 1999.

Burton, John. *Resolving Deep-Rooted Conflict: A Handbook.* Lanham, MD: University Press of America, 1987.

Call, Charles. "Assessing El Salvador's Transition from Civil War to Peace." In *Ending Civil Wars*, edited by Stephen Stedman, Donald Rothchild, and Elizabeth Cousens, 383–420. Boulder, CO: Lynne Rienner, 2002.

Carlin, John. "Namibia's Independence Is UN's triumph." *Independent*, March 20, 1990, p. 11.

Chang, Charles C., Eduardo Fernandez-Arias, and Luis Serven. "Measuring Aid Flows: A New Approach." World Bank Working Paper, 1998.

Chesterman, Simon. "East Timor in Transition." *International Peacekeeping* 9, no. 1 (2002): 45–76.

———. *You the People.* Oxford: Oxford University Press, 2004.

Chopra, Jarat. *Peace Maintenance.* London: Routledge, 1999.

———. "The UN's Kingdom of East Timor." *Survival* 42, no. 3 (2000): 27–39.

———. "Divided Rule" *World Today* 57, no. 1 (2001): 13–16.

CIA. 2002. *CIA World Factbook.* Database accessible at: http://www.odci.gov/cia/publications/factbook/index.html (accessed March 25, 2005).

Clark, James. "Freetown Parades Its British Army." *Sunday Times*, July 23, 2000.

Clark, James, and Jon Swain. "SAS Rescue Mission Leads Jungle Hostages to Safety." *Financial Times*, July 16, 2000.

Clark, Jeffrey. "Debacle in Somalia: The Failure of Collective Response." In *Enforcing Restraint*, edited by Lori Damrosch. New York: Council on Foreign Relations, 1993.

Clarke, Walter. "Failed Visions and Uncertain Mandates in Somalia." In *Learning from Somalia*, edited by Walter Clarke and Jeffrey Herbst, 3–19. Boulder, CO: Westview Press, 1997.

Clarke, Walter, and Jeffrey Herbst. "Somalia and the Future of Humanitarian Intervention." In *Learning from Somalia*, edited by Walter Clarke and Jeffrey Herbst, 239–53. Boulder, CO: Westview Press, 1997.

Clausewitz, Carl von. *On War.* Edited and translated by Peter Paret. Princeton: Princeton University Press, 1976.

Clayton, James L. "The Military Budget and National Economic Priorities." Originally presented in U.S. Congress, Joint Economic Committee, pt. 1, 91st Congress, 1st session. http://www.census.gov/prod/1/gen/95statab/defense .pdf.

Clerides, Glafcos. *My Deposition*. 4 vols. Nicosia: Aletheia Press, 1989–92.

Clinton, William. "Remarks by the President to the KFOR Troops," Skopje, June 22, 1999. Washington, DC: Office of the White House Press Secretary.

Coleman, Christopher C. *The Salvadoran Peace Process: A Preliminary Inquiry*, Norwegian Institute of International Affairs, Research Report no. 173. December 1993.

Coletta, Nat. "Rebuilding in the Wake of War," *ADM Online*, May 1, 2000. http://www.cdi.org/adm/1145/Coletta.html.

Collier, P. "Rebellion as a Quasi-Criminal Activity." *Journal of Conflict Resolution* 44 (December 2000): 838–52.

Collier, Paul, Lani Elliott, Håvard Hegre, Anke Hoeffler, Marta Reynal-Querol, and Nicholas Sambanis. *Breaking the Conflict Trap: Civil War and Development Policy*. Oxford and Washington, DC: Oxford University Press and World Bank, 2003.

Collier, Paul, and Anke Hoeffler. "On the Economic Causes of Civil War." *Oxford Economic Papers* 50 (December 1998): 563–73.

———. "Greed and Grievance in Civil War." 2001. http://econ.worldbank .org/programs/conflict/library/doc?id=12205 (accessed July 3, 2002).

———. "Greed and Grievance in Civil War." *Oxford Economic Papers* 56, no. 4 (2004): 563–95.

Collier, Paul, Anke Hoeffler, and Mans Soderbom. 2004. "On the Duration of Civil War." *Journal of Peace Research* 41, no. 3 (2004): 253–74.

Collins, Cindy, and Thomas Weiss. "An Overview and Assessment of 1989–1996 Peace Operations Publications." Thomas J. Watson Institute, Occasional Paper, no. 28 Providence: Watson Institute, 1997.

Commission on Global Governance. *Report of the Commission on Global Governance: Our Global Neighbourhood*. Oxford: Oxford University Press, 1995.

Commission on the Truth for El Salvador. *From Madness to Hope: The 12-Year War in El Salvador; Report of the Commission on the Truth for El Salvador*. United Nations, UN Doc. S/25500/Annex, April 1, 1993.

Connor, Walker. "Beyond Reason: The Nature of the Ethnonational Bond." *Ethnic and Racial Studies* 16 (July 1993): 373–89.

Cousens, Elizabeth. "From Missed Opportunities to Overcompensation." In *Ending Civil Wars*, edited by Stephen Stedman, Donald Rothchild, and Elizabeth Cousens, 538–39. Boulder, CO: Lynne Rienner, 2002.

Cousens, Elizabeth, and Michael W. Doyle. "Dayton Accord's Dangerous Dueling Missions." *Christian Science Monitor*, December 26, 1995, 23.

Cousens, Elizabeth, Chetan Kumar, eds., with Karin Wermester. *Peacebuilding as Politics: Cultivating Peace in Fragile Societies*. Boulder, CO: Lynne Rienner 2001.

Cox, Katherine E. "Beyond Self-Defense: United Nations Peacekeeping Operations and the Use of Force." *Denver Journal of International Law and Policy* 27 (Spring 1999): 239–73.

Crocker, Chester, Fen Hampson, and Pamela Aall, eds. *Herding Cats: Multiparty Mediation in a Complex World*. Washington, DC: United States Institute of Peace, 1999.

Crossette, Barbara. "9 Aid Workers Held Hostage after Gunfight by Somalis," *New York Times*, March 27, 2001.

Curtis, Grant. *Cambodia Reborn? The Transition to Democracy and Development*. Washington, DC: Brookings/UNRISD, 1998.

Da Costa, Helder, and Hadi Soesastro. "Building East Timor's Economy." Council for Asia-Europe Cooperation Conference, 2001. http://www.caec-asiaeurope.org/Conference/Publications/costasoesastro.PDF [Accessed march 25, 2005].

Dallaire, Romeo. *Shake Hands with the Devil: The Failure of Humanity in Rwanda*. Toronto: Random House, 2003.

Damrosch, Lori F., ed. *Enforcing Restraint: Collective Intervention in Internal Conflicts*. New York: Council on Foreign Relations Press, 1993.

Darden, Keith. "The Scholastic Revolution: Explaining Nationalism in the USSR." Unpublished Manuscript, Yale University, 2002.

David, Steven R. "Internal War: Causes and Cures." *World Politics* 49 (July 1997): 552–76.

Dawisha, Adeed I., and Karen Dawisha. " How to Build a Democratic Iraq." *Foreign Affairs* 82, no. 3 (2003): 36–50.

Day, Graham, and Christopher Freeman. 2005. "Operationalizing the Responsibility to Protect—the Policekeeping Approach." *Global Governance* 11(2): 139–46.

De Cuellar, Javier Perez. *Pilgrimage for Peace: A Secretary-General's Memoir*. New York: St. Martin's Press, 1997.

De Figueiredo, Rui, and Barry Weingast."The Rationality of Fear: Political Opportunism and Ethnic Conflict." In *Civil Wars, Insecurity, and Intervention*, edited by Barbara Walter and Jack Snyder. New York: Columbia University Press, 1999.

———. "Propensity Score Matching Methods for Non-experimental Causal Studies." Columbia University, Department of Economics, Discussion Paper 0102-14. 2002.

Dehejia, R. H., and S. Wahba. "Causal Effects in Nonexperimental Studies: Reevaluation of the Evaluation of Training Programs." *Journal of the American Statistical Association* 94 (1999): 1053–62.

Dekleris, Michael E. *Kypriako, 1972–1974: E teleftea efkeria* (Cyprus problem, 1972–1974: The last opportunity). Athens: Ekdotiki Estia, 1981.

De Lapresle, Bertrand. "Principles to be Observed." In *UN Peacekeeping in Trouble: Lessons Learned from the Former Yugoslavia; Peacekeepers' Views on the Limits and Possibilities of the United Nations*, edited by W. Biermann and M. Vadset, 137–52. Aldershot: Ashgate, 1998.

Del Castillo, Graciana."The Arms for Land Deal in El Salvador." In *Keeping the Peace*, edited by M. Doyle, Ian Johnstone, and Robert Orr. Cambridge: Cambridge University Press, 1997, pp. 342–66.

DeNardo, James. *Power in Numbers: The Political Strategy of Protest and Rebellion*. Princeton: Princeton University Press, 1985.

Denktash, Rauf R. *The Cyprus Triangle*. New York: Office of the Turkish Republic of Northern Cyprus, 1988.

Des Forges, Alison. *Leave None to Tell the Story: Genocide in Rwanda*. New York: Human Rights Watch, 1999.

———. "Shame: Rationalizing Western Apathy on Rwanda." *Foreign Affairs* 79 (May–June 2000): 141–44.

DeSoto, Alvaro, and Graciana del Castillo. "Obstacles to Peacebuilding in El Salvador." *Foreign Policy* 94 (Spring 1994): 69–83.

De Soto, Hernando. *The Mystery of Capital*. New York: Basic Books, 2000.

Deutsch, Karl W. *Nationalism and Social Communication: An Inquiry into the Foundations of Nationality*. Cambridge and New York: Published jointly by the Technology Press of the Massachusetts Institute of Technology and Wiley, 1953.

Deutsch, Karl, and J. David Singer. "Multipolar Systems and International Stability." *World Politics* 16 (April 1964): 390–406.

Dickens, David . "Can East Timor Be a Blueprint for Burden Sharing?" *Washington Quarterly* 25 (Summer 2002): 29–40.

Diehl, Paul F. *International Peacekeeping*. Baltimore: Johns Hopkins University Press, 1993.

Diehl, Paul F., Jennifer Reifschneider, and Paul R. Hensel. "United Nations Intervention and Recurring Conflict." *International Organization* 50 (Autumn 1996): 683–700.

Dobbins, James, et al. *America's Role in Nation-Building: From Germany to Iraq*. Santa Monica, CA: RAND, 2003.

———. *The UN's Role in Nation-Building: From the Congo to Iraq*. Santa Monica, CA: RAND, 2005.

Dodd, C. H., ed. *The Political, Social, and Economic Development of Northern Cyprus*. Huntingdon, UK: Eothen Press, 1993.

Doder, Dusko. "Letter from Bosnia." *Nation* 272, no. 6, (February 12, 2001): 14–18.

Doll, William, and Steven Metz. *The Army and Multinational Peace Operations: Problems and Solutions*. Carlisle Barracks, PA: U.S. Army War College, 1993.

Doyle, Michael W. *Empires*. Ithaca: Cornell University Press, 1986.

———. "Liberalism and World Politics." *American Political Science Review* 80, no. 4 (1986): 1151–69.

———. *UN Peacekeeping in Cambodia: UNTAC's Civil Mandate*. Boulder, CO: Lynne Rienner, 1995.

———. *Peacebuilding in Cambodia*, IPA Policy Briefing Series. New York: International Peace Aacademy, December 1996.

———. "Authority and Elections in Cambodia." In *Keeping the Peace*, edited by M. Doyle, Ian Johnstone, and Robert Orr, 134–64. Cambridge: Cambridge University Press, 1997.

———. "UNTAC in Cambodia." In *The United Nations and Regional Security Arrangements: Towards More Effective Task-Sharing and Cooperation*, edited by Winrich Kuhne, 90–98. Berlin: Stiftung Wissenschaft und Politik, 1999.

Doyle, Michael W., and Anne Bayefski. "Sustainable Refugee Return: A Report of a Workshop at Princeton University." Unpublished Paper, Princeton University, February 1998.

Doyle, Michael W., Ian Johnstone, and Robert C. Orr, eds. *Keeping the Peace: Multidimensional UN Operations in Cambodia and El Salvador.* Cambridge: Cambridge University Press, 1997.

Doyle, Michael W., and Jan Mueller.. "Anatomie eines Erfolgs: Die UN-Mission in Ostslawonien" (Anatomy of a Success: The UN Mission in Eastern Slavonia). *Internationale Politik* 53, no. 6 (1998): 34–38.

Doyle, Michael, and Nicholas Sambanis. "International Peacebuilding: A Theoretical and Quantitative Analysis." *American Political Science Review* 94, no. 4 (2000): 778–801.

Drysdale, John. *Whatever Happened to Somalia: A Tale of Tragic Blunders.* London: Haan Associates, 1994.

Dubey, Amitabh. "Domestic Institutions and the Duration of Civil War Settlements." Unpublished paper. 2003.

Durch, William J., ed. *The Evolution of UN Peacekeeping: Case Studies and Comparative Analyses.* New York: St. Martin's Press, 1993.

––––––. "The UN Operation in the Congo." In *The Evolution of UN Peacekeeping: Case Studies and Comparative Analyses,* edited by William J. Durch, 315–52. New York: St. Martin's Press, 1993.

––––––. ed. *UN Peacekeeping, America's Policy, and the Uncivil Wars of the 1990s.* New York: St. Martin's Press, 1996.

Eagleburger, Lawrence. Press Release. June 23, 1992. Cambodia Conference of Reconstruction held on June 22, 1992. USUN-44-92.

Easterly, William, and Ross Levine. "Africa's Growth Tragedy: Policies and Ethnic Divisions." *Quarterly Journal of Economics* 112, no. 4 (1997): 1203–50.

Eckstein, Harry. *Internal War: Problems and Approaches* Glencoe, IL: Free Press, 1964.

––––––. "Theoretical Approaches to Explaining Collective Political Violence." In *The Handbook of Political Conflict Theory and Research,* edited by Ted Gurr, 135–67. New York: Free Press, 1980.

Elbadawi, I., and N. Sambanis. "External Intervention and the Duration of Civil Wars." World Bank Policy Research Working Paper 2433. September 2000.

––––––. "How Much War Will We See? Estimating the Prevalence of Civil War, 1960–1999." *Journal of Conflict Resolution* 46 (June 2002): 307–44.

Eldon, Stewart. "East Timor." In *The UN Security Council,* edited by David Malone, 551–66. Boulder, CO: Lynne Rienner, 2004.

"Election Campaign in the Village of Klanac." *Reporter,* Nov. 15, 2000. (Bosnia local paper).

Ellis, Anthony. "Utilitarianism and International Ethics." In *Traditions of International Ethics,* edited by Terry Nardin and David Mapel, 158–79. Cambridge: Cambridge University Press, 1992.

Epstein, Joshua, John D. Steinbruner, and Miles Parker. "Modeling Civil Violence," Brookings Working Paper no. 20, Washington, DC, 2001.

Ertekun, Necati M. *The Cyprus Dispute.* Oxford: K. Rustem, 1984.

Esty, Daniel C., Jack Goldstone, Ted Robert Gurr, Pamela T. Surko, and Alan N. Unger. *Working Papers: State Failure Task Force Report.* McLean, VA: Science Applications International Corporation, 1995.

Esty, Daniel C., Jack Goldstone, Ted Robert Gurr, Pamela T. Surko, and Alan N. Unger, and R. S. Chen. *The State Failure Task Force Report: Phase II Findings.* McLean, VA: Science Applications International Corporation, 1998.

Evans, Gareth. *Cooperating for Peace.* London: Allen and Unwin, 1993.

Farer, Tom J. "Humanitarian Intervention before and after 9/11: Legality and Legitimacy." In *Humanitarian Intervention: Ethical, Legal, and Political Dilemmas,* edited by J. L. Holzgrefe and Robert Keohane. Cambridge: Cambridge University Press, 2003.

Fearon, James D. "Rationalist Explanations for War." *International Organization* 49 (Summer 1995): 379–414.

———. "Commitment Problems and the Spread of Ethnic Conflict." In *The International Spread of Ethnic Conflict: Fear, Diffusion, and Escalation,* edited by David Lake and Donald Rothchild. Princeton: Princeton University Press, 1998.

———. "Ethnic and Cultural Diversity by Country." *Journal of Economic Growth* 8, no. 2 (2003): 195–222.

Fearon, James D., and David D. Laitin. "Explaining Interethnic Cooperation." *American Political Science Review* 90 (December 1996): 715–35.

———. "Ethnicity, Insurgency and Civil War." *American Political Science Review* 97, no. 1 (2003): 75–90.

Feil, Scott. *Preventing Genocide.* New York: Carnegie Corporation, 1998.

Fetherston, A. B. "Putting the Peace Back into Peacekeeping: Theory Must Inform Practice." *International Peacekeeping* 1, no. 2 (Spring 1994): 3–29.

Findlay, Trevor. *Cambodia: The Legacy and Lessons of UNTAC.* New York: Oxford University Press, 1995.

Findlay, Trevor, and Thomas Mockaitis. "Intervention in Civil Conflict: Peace-Keeping or Enforcement." In *Peacekeeping with Muscle,* edited by Alex Morrison and James Kiras, 31–50. Clementsport, Nova Scotia: Lester Pearson Canadian Peacekeeping Centre, 1997.

Finnemore, Martha, and Kathryn Sikkink. "Taking Stock: The Constructivist Research Program in International Relations and Comparative Politics." *Annual Review of Political Science* 4 (June 2001): 391–416.

Fitchett, Joseph. "EU Force Takes Shape with Pledge of Troops." *International Herald Tribune,* November 20, 2000.

Fortna, Virginia Page. "Success and Failure in Southern Africa: Peacekeeping in Namibia and Angola." In *Beyond Traditional Peacekeeping,* edited by Donald C. F. Daniel and Bradd C. Hayes, 282–301. London: Macmillan, 1995.

———. *Peace Time: Cease-Fire Agreements and the Durability of Peace.* Princeton: Princeton University Press, 2004.

Franck, Thomas. *Fairness in International Law and Institutions.* Oxford: Clarendon Press, 1995.

———. "A Holistic Approach to Peace-building." In *Peacemaking and Peacekeeping for the New Century,* edited by Olara Otunnu and Michael Doyle. Lanham, MD: Rowman and Littlefield, 1998.

———. "Interpretation and Change in the Law of Humanitarian Intervention." In *Humanitarian Intervention: Ethical, Legal, and Political Dilemmas,* edited by J. L. Holzgrefe and Robert O. Keohane. Cambridge: Cambridge University Press, 2003.

Frieson, Kate G. "The Cambodian Elections of 1993: A Case of Power to the People," In *The Politics of Elections in Southeast Asia*, edited by R. H. Taylor, 224–51. Cambridge and New York: Cambridge University Press and Woodrow Wilson Center Press, 1996.

Gandhi, Jennifer, and James Vreeland. "Political Institutions and Civil War: Unpacking Anocracy." Unpublished manuscript, Emory University and Yale University, August 30, 2004 version.

Garrett, Stephen. *Doing Good and Doing Well : An Examination of Humanitarian Intervention.* Westport, CT: Praeger, 1999.

Geertz, Clifford. "The Integrative Revolution: Primordial Sentiments and Civil Politics in the New States." In *Old Societies and New States*, 105–58. New York: Free Press, 1963.

Gellner, Ernest. *Nations and Nationalism.* Ithaca: Cornell University Press, 1983.

Ghobarah, Hazem, P. Huth, and B. Russett. "Civil Wars Kill and Maim People, Long after the Fighting Stops." *American Political Science Review* 97, no. 2 (2003): 189–202.

Gibbs, D. N. "The United Nations, International Peacekeeping and the Question of 'Impartiality': Revisiting the Congo operation of 1960." *Journal of Modern African Studies* 38, no. 3 (2000): 359–82.

Gleditsch, Kristian. "Transnational Dimensions of Civil War." Unpublished paper. University of California, San Diego, January 2003.

Gleditsch, N. P., H. Strand, M. Eriksson, M. Sollenberg, and P. Wallensteen, "Armed Conflict 1945–1999: A New Dataset." Paper prepared for presentation at the Conference "Identifying Wars," Uppsala, Sweden, June 8–9, 2001.

Gleditsch, Nils Petter, Peter Wallensteen, Mikael Eriksson, Margareta Sollenberg, and Håvard Strand. "Armed Conflict, 1946–2001: A New Dataset." *Journal of Peace Research* 39, no. 5 (September 2002.): 615–37.

Glenny, Misha. "Yugoslavia: The Great Fall." *New York Review of Books*, March 23, 1995.

Gobbi, Hugo J. *Rethinking Cyprus.* Tel Aviv: Aurora, 1983.

Goodrich, Leland M., Edvard Hambro, and Anne Simons. *Charter of the United Nations.* New York: Columbia University Press, 1969.

Gordon, Michael. "Pentagon Is Wary of Role in Bosnia." *New York Times*, March 13 1994.

Goulding, Marrack. "The Evolution of United Nations Peacekeeping." *International Affairs* 69, no. 3 (1993): 451–64.

Gourevitch, Philip. *We Wish to Inform You That Tomorrow We Will Be Killed with Our Families: Stories from Rwanda.* New York: Farrar Strauss and Giroux, 1998.

Graham, Gerald. "The Justice of Intervention." *Review of International Studies* 13 (1987): 133–46.

Grieco, Joseph. "Anarchy and the Limits of Cooperation: A Realist Critique of the Newest Liberal Institutionalism." *International Organization* 42, no. 3 (1988): 485–507.

Griffin, Michele, and Bruce Jones. "Building Peace through Transitional Authority: New Directions, Major Challenges." *International Peacekeeping* 7, no. 4 (2000): 75–90.

Groom, A.J.R. "The Process of Negotiation, 1974–1993." In *The Political, Social and Economic Development of Northern Cyprus*, edited by C. H. Dodd. Huntingdon, England: Eothen Press, 1993.

Grossman, Herschel I. "A General Equilibrium Model of Insurrections." *American Economic Review* 81 (September 1991): 912–21.

———. "Insurrections." In *Handbook of Defense Economics*, edited by Keith Hartley and Todd Sandler, 1:191–212. Amsterdam: Elsevier, 1995.

———. "Kleptocracy and Revolutions." *Oxford Economic Papers* 51 (April 1999): 267–83.

Gunderson, Gerald. "The Origins of the American Civil War." *Journal of Economic History* 34, no. 4 (1974): 915–50.

Gurr, Ted Robert. *Why Men Rebel*. Princeton: Princeton University Press, 1970.

———. *Minorities at Risk: A Global View of Ethnopolitical Conflicts*. Washington, DC: United States Institute of Peace, 1993.

———. "Ethnic Warfare on the Wane." *Foreign Affairs* 79, no. 3 (2000): 52–65.

———. *Peoples versus States: Minorities at Risk in the New Century*. Washington, DC: United States Institute of Peace, 2000.

Guttieri, Karen. "Symptom of the Moment: A Juridical Gap for U.S. Occupation Forces." *International Insights* 13, special issue (Fall 1997): 131–55.

Haas, Ernst B. *The United Nations and Collective Management of International Conflict*. New York: UNITAR, 1986.

Haas, Ernst B., Lyle Butterworth, and Joseph Nye. *Conflict Management by International Organization*. Morristown, NJ: General Learning Press, 1972.

Halberstam, David. *War in a Time of Peace: Bush, Clinton, and the Generals*. New York: Scribner's, 2001.

Hampson, Fen Osler. *Nurturing Peace: Why Peace Settlements Succeed or Fail*. Washington, DC: United States Institute of Peace, 1996.

Hanley, Robert. "Ft. Dix Loses Recruits, Customers, Friends." *New York Times*, September 28, 1992.

Harbottle, Michael. "Cyprus: An Analysis of the UN's Third Party Role in a Small War." In *Small States in the Modern World: The Conditions for Survival*, edited by Paschalis Kitromilides and Peter Worsley. Nicosia: New Cyprus Association, 1979.

Hardin, Russell. *One for All: The Logic of Group Conflict*. Princeton: Princeton University Press, 1995.

Harff, Barbara. "No Lessons Learned from the Holocaust? Assessing Risks of Genocide and Political Mass Murder since 1955." *American Political Science Review* 97, no. 1 (2003): 57–73.

Harff, Barbara, and Ted Robert Gurr. "Research Note: Toward Empirical Theory of Genocides and Politicides: Identification and Measurement of Cases since 1945." *International Studies Quarterly* 32, no. 3 (1988): 359–71.

Hassner, Ron. "To Halve and to Hold: Conflicts over Sacred Space and the Problem of Indivisibility." *Security Studies* 12, no. 4 (Summer 2003): 1–33.

Hayner, Priscilla. "Fifteen Truth Commissions: 1974–1994, a Comparative Study." *Human Rights Quarterly* 16, no. 4 (1994): 597–655.

Head, Mike. "Australia and Portuguese to Set up an East Timorese Army." World Socialist Web site (December 7, 2000). http://www.wsws.org/articles/2000/dec2000/timo-d07.shtml (accessed March 25, 2005).

Hearn, Roger. *UN Peacekeeping in Action.* Commarck: Nova Science Press, 1999.

Hechter, Michael. *Internal Colonialism: The Celtic Fringe in British National Development, 1536–1966.* New Brunswick, NJ: Transaction Publishers, 1999.

———. *Containing Nationalism.* Oxford: Oxford University Press, 2001.

Heckman, James J. "Sample Selection Bias as a Specification Error." *Econometrica* 47, no. 1 (1979): 153–61.

Heckman, James J., Hidehiko Ichimura, and Petra Todd. "Matching as an Econometric Evaluation Estimator: Evidence from Evaluating a Job Training Programme." *Review of Economic Studies* 64, no. 4 (1998): 605–54.

Heder, S., and J. Ledgerwood, eds. 1996. *Propaganda, Politics, and Violence in Cambodia: Democratic Transition under United Nations Peace-Keeping.* Armonk, NY, and London: M. E. Sharpe.

Hedges, Chris. "Quarrels of Kurdish Leaders Sour Dreams of a Homeland." *New York Times,* June 18, 1994.

Hegre, Håvard, Tanja Ellingsen, Scott Gates, and Nils Petter Gleditsch. "Toward a Democratic Civil Peace? Democracy, Political Change, and Civil War, 1816–1992." *American Political Science Review* 95, no. 1 (March 2001): 33–48.

Heininger, Janet. *Peacekeeping Transition: The United Nations in Cambodia.* New York: Twentieth Century Fund, 1994.

Heldt, Birger. "Peacekeeping Operations by Regional Actors, 1948–2000," Unpublished paper, Swedish National Defense College, version November 18, 2002.

Helman, Gerald, and Steven Ratner. "Saving Failed States." *Foreign Policy* 89 (Winter 1992–93): 3–20.

Herbst, Jeffrey. "Responding to State Failure in Africa." *International Security* 21(Winter 1996–97): 120–44.

Heston, Alan, Robert Summers, and Bettina Aten. Penn World Table Version 6.1, Center for International Comparisons at the University of Pennsylvania (CICUP), October 2002.

Higgins, Rosalynn. "The New United Nations and the Former Yugoslavia." *International Affairs* 69, no. 3 (1993): 468–70.

High-Level Panel on Threats, Challenges, and Change. *A More Secure World: Our Shared Responsibility.* New York: United Nations, 2004.

Hirsch, John L., and Robert B. Oakley. *Somalia and Operation Restore Hope.* Washington, DC: United States Institute of Peace, 1995.

Hirschleifer, J. "Conflict and Settlement." In *The New Palgrave: A Dictionary of Economics,* edited by J. Eatwell, M. Milgate, and P. Newman. London: Macmillan Press, 1987.

———. "Theorizing about conflict." In *Handbook of Defense Economics,* edited by K. Hartley and T. Sandler, 1:165–192. Amsterdam: Elsevier, 1995.

Hitchens, Christopher. *Cyprus.* London: Quartet Books, 1984.

Hobsbawn, Eric, and Terence Ranger. *The Invention of Tradition*. New York: Cambridge University Press, 1993.

Holbrooke, Richard. *To End a War*. New York: Random House, 1998.

Honig, Jan Willem, and Norbert Both. *Srebrenica: Record of a War Crime*. New York: Penguin, 1997.

Horowitz, Donald L. *Ethnic Groups in Conflict*. Berkeley and Los Angeles: University of California Press, 1985.

———. "Structure and Strategy in Ethnic Conflict." Paper presented at the Annual Bank Conference in Development Economics Washington DC, World Bank, April 20–21, 1998.

Howard, Lise M. "The Attempt That Worked." Stanford University, CISAC, 1999.

Howe, Jonathan T. "The United States and United Nations in Somalia: The Limits of Involvement." *Washington Quarterly* 18, no. 3 (1995): 47.

Hughes, Caroline. *The Political Economy of Cambodia's Transition, 1991–2001*. New York: Routledge Curzon, 2003.

Human Rights Watch. World Report. Various years (1994–2002).

———. World Report 2003. http://www.hrw.org/wr2k3/asia5.html (accessed March 25, 2005).

Humphreys, Macartan. "Natural Resources, Conflict, and Conflict Resolution: Uncovering the Mechanisms." *Journal of Conflict Resolution* (49 (4): 508–537, 2005).

Huntington, Samuel. "The Clash of Civilizations?" *Foreign Affairs* 72 (Summer 1993): 22–49.

Ignatieff, Michael. "State Failure and Nation-Building." In *Humanitarian Intervention: Ethical, Legal, and Political Dimensions*, edited by J. L. Holzgrefe and Robert Keohane. Cambridge: Cambridge University Press, 2003.

Imbens, Guido W. "Simple and Bias-Corrected Matching Estimators for Average Treatment Effects." NBER Technical Working Paper no. 283, October 2002.

———. "Nonparametric Estimation of Average Treatment Effects under Exogeneity: A Review." Unpublished paper, University of California, Berkeley, September 2003.

IMF. *Financial Statistics, 1949–1998*. Washington, DC: International Monetary Fund, 1949–98.

Independent Inquiry into the Actions of the United Nations during the 1994 Genocide in Rwanda. *Report*. New York: United Nations, 1999. http://www.un.org/News/ossg/rwanda_report.htm (accessed Dec. 8, 2000).

International Commission on Intervention and State Sovereignty. *The Responsibility to Protect*. Ottawa: International Development Research Centre, 2001.

International Crisis Group. *Cambodia: The Elusive Peace Dividend*. ICG Asia Report no. 8, Phnom Penh/Brussels, August 11, 2000.

Issacharoff, Samuel. "Constitutionalizing Democracy in Fractured Societies." Working draft, Columbia Law School, September 2003.

Jackson, Stephen. "Survival of the Cutest." *Irish Reporter* 12, no. 4 (1993): 5–7.

James, Alan. "The UN Force in Cyprus." *International Affairs* 65 (Summer 1989): 481–500.

Jan, Ameen. "Peacebuilding in Somalia." IPA Policy Briefing Series, July 1996.

Jervis, Robert. "Cooperation under the Security Dilemma." *World Politics* 30 (January 1978): 167–214.

Johnstone, Ian. "Rights and Reconciliation: UN Strategies in El Salvador." IPA Occasional Paper Series. Boulder: Lynne Rienner, 1995.

———. "Rights and Reconciliation in El Salvador." In *Keeping the Peace*, edited by M. Doyle, Ian Johnstone, and Robert Orr. Cambridge: Cambridge University Press, 1997.

Johnstone, Ian, and Mark LeVine. "Lessons from El Salvador." *Christian Science Monitor*, August 10, 1993, 889.

Jones, Bruce D. "Civil War, the Peace Process, and Genocide in Rwanda." In *Civil Wars in Africa*, edited by Taisier M. Ali and Robert O. Matthews, 52–86. Montreal: McGill–Queen's University Press, 1999.

———. *Peacemaking in Rwanda: The Dynamics of Failure*. Boulder, CO: Lynne Rienner, 2001.

———. "The Challenges of Strategic Coordination." In *Ending Civil Wars: The Implementation of Peace Agreements*, edited by Stephen J. Stedman, Donald Rothchild, and Elizabeth M. Cousens, 89–115. Boulder, CO: Lynne Rienner, 2002.

Kacowicz, Arie. *Peaceful Territorial Change*. Columbia: University of South Carolina Press, 1994.

Kahler, Miles. "Multilateralism with Small and Large Numbers." *International Organization* 46, no. 3 (Summer 1992): 681–708.

Kalyvas, Stathis. "What Is Political Violence? The Ontology of Civil War." *Perspectives on Politics* 1, no. 3 (2003): 475–94.

———. *The Logic of Violence in Civil War*. Cambridge: Cambridge University Press, forthcoming, 2006.

Kant, Immanuel. "Perpetual Peace." In *Kant's Political Writings*, edited by Hans Reiss and translated by H. B. Nisbet, 93–130. Cambridge: Cambridge University Press, 1970.

Karl, Terry Lynne. "El Salvador's Negotiated Revolution." *Foreign Affairs* 71, no. 2 (Spring 1992): 147–64.

Kaufmann, Chaim. "Possible and Impossible Solutions to Ethnic Conflict." *International Security* 20 (Spring 1996): 136–75.

———. "When All Else Fails." *International Security* 23, no. 2 (Fall 1998): 120–56.

Keesing's Archives. http://www.keesings.com/ (accessed March 25, 2005).

Kenney, George. "Bloody Bosnia." *Washington Monthly*, March 1995, 49–52.

Keohane, Robert. *After Hegemony*. Princeton: Princeton University Press, 1984.

Keohane, Robert, and Robert Axelrod. "Achieving Cooperation under Anarchy." In *Cooperation under Anarchy*, edited by Kenneth Oye, 226–45. Princeton: Princeton University Press, 1986.

Kiernan, B. *The Pol Pot Regime: Race, Power and Genocide in Cambodia under the Khmer Rouge, 1975–1979*. New Haven, CT, and London: Yale University Press, 1996.

King, Gary, Michael Tomz, and Jason Wittenberg. "Making the Most of Statistical Analyses: Improving Interpretation and Presentation." *American Journal of Political Science* 44, no. 2 (2000): 347–61.

Kitromilides, Paschalis, and Peter Worsley, eds. *Small States in the Modern World: The Conditions for Survival*. Nicosia: New Cyprus Association, 1979.

Konrad, Kai, and Stergios Skaperdas. "The Market for Protection and the Origin of the State." Working paper, CEPR and University of California, Irvine, 1999.

Kranidiotes, Nikos. *Anochyrote Politeia: Kypros. 1960–1974.* (Indefensible state: Cyprus, 1960–1974). Vol. 1–2. Athens: Estia, 1985.

Kreps, David M. *Game Theory and Economic Modeling*. Oxford: Clarendon Press, 1990.

Kumar, Radha. "The Troubled History of Partition." *Foreign Affairs* 76, no. 1 (1997): 22–35.

Kuperman, Alan J. "Rwanda in Retrospect." *Foreign Affairs* 79, no. 1 (2000): 94–118.

Kydd, Andrew. "Trust, Reassurance, and Cooperation." *International Organization* 54, no. 2 (Spring 2000): 325–57.

Kydland, Finn E., and Edward Prescott. "Rules Rather than Discretion: The Inconsistency of Optimal Plans." *Journal of Political Economy* 85 (June 1977): 473–92.

Laitin, David D., and Said S. Samatar. *Somalia: Nation in Search of a State*. Boulder, CO: Westview Press, 1987.

Lake, Anthony. *6 Nightmares: The Real Threats to American Security*. Boston: Little, Brown, 2000.

Lake, David A., and Donald Rothchild. "Containing Fear: The Origins and Management of Ethnic Conflict." *International Security* 21, no. 2 (Fall 1996): 41–75.

———, eds. *The International Spread of Ethnic Conflict: Fear, Diffusion, and Escalation*. Princeton: Princeton University Press, 1998.

———. "Political Decentralization and Civil War Settlements." In *Governance in a Global Economy: Political Authority in Transition*, edited by Miles Kahler and David Lake. Princeton: Princeton University Press, 2003.

Ledgerwood, J. "Rural Development in Cambodia: The View from the Village." In *Cambodia and the International Community: The Quest for Peace, Development, and Democracy*. Edited by F. Z. Brown and D. G. Timberman, 127–48. Singapore: Asia Society, Institute of Southeast Asian Studies.

Lefever, Ernest W. *Crisis in the Congo: A United Nations Force in Action; Studies of U.S. Policy and the U.N.* Washington, DC: Brookings Institution, 1965.

Lemarchand, Rene. *Political Awakening in the Congo*. Berkeley and Los Angeles: University of California Press, 1964.

Lessons Learned Unit, Department of Peacekeeping Operations *Comprehensive Report on Lessons Learned from United Nations Operation in Somalia, April 1992–March 1995*. Sweden: Life and Peace Institute, December 1995.

Leuven, Edwin, and Barbara Sianesi. "PSMATCH2: Stata Module to Perform Full Mahalanobis and Propensity Score Matching, Common Support Graphing, and Covariate Imbalance Testing." http://ideas.repec.org/c/boc/bocode/s432001.html, version 1.1.3, 5 September 2003.

Lewis, I. M. *Understanding Somalia: Guide to Culture, History, and Social Institutions*. London: Haan Associates, 1993.

———. *A Modern History of Somalia*. Boulder, CO: Westview Press, 1988.

Licklider, Roy. *Stopping the Killing: How Civil Wars End*. New York: New York University Press, 1993.

——. "The Consequences of Negotiated Settlements in Civil Wars, 1945–1993." *American Political Science Review* 89 (September 1995): 681–90.

Liu, F. T. *United Nations Peacekeeping and the Nonuse of Force*. International Peace Academy Occasional Paper Series. Boulder, CO: Lynne Rienner, 1992.

Lloyd, Anthony. "A Very Dirty Little War," Timesonline, May 14, 2002, http::/www.timesonline.co.uk/article/0,7-295526,00.html (accessed March 30, 2005).

Lyons, Terrence, and Ahmed I. Samatar. *Somalia: State Collapse, Multilateral Intervention, and Strategies for Political Reconstruction*. Washington, DC: Brookings Institution, 1995.

Mackinlay, John, and Jarat Chopra. "Second-Generation Multinational Operations." *Washington Quarterly* 25 (Summer 1992): 113–31.

——. *A Draft Concept of Second Generation Operations*. Providence: Watson Institute. Brown University, 1993.

Makinda, Samuel. *Seeking Peace from Chaos: Humanitarian Intervention in Somalia*. Boulder, CO: Lynne Rienner, 1993.

Malone, David. *Decision-Making in the Security Council: The Case of Haiti, 1990–1997*. Oxford: Clarendon Press, 1998.

Mandelbaum, Michael. "The Reluctance to Intervene." *Foreign Policy* 95 (Summer 1994): 3–18.

Mansfield, E. D., and J. Snyder. "Democratization and the Danger of War." *International Security* 20, no. 1 (Summer 1995): 5–38.

Maren, Michael. *The Road to Hell*. New York: Free Press, 1997.

Marks, Stephen P. "The New Cambodian Constitution: From Civil War to a Fragile Democracy." *Columbia Human Rights Law Review* 26 (1994): 45–110.

Marshall, Monty, and Keith Jaggers. Polity IV Project. Codebook and Data Files: www.bsos.umd.edu/cidcm/inscr/polity (accessed March 25, 2005).

Marten, Kimberly. *Enforcing the Peace*. New York: Columbia University Press, 2004.

Martin, Ian. *Self-Determination in East Timor*. Bouder, CO: Lynne Rienner, 2001.

——. "A Field Perspective." In *The UN Security Council*, edited by David Malone, 567–74. Boulder, CO: Lynne Rienner, 2004.

Mason, David, and Patrick Fett. "How Civil Wars End: A Rational Choice Approach." *Journal of Conflict Resolution* 40 no. 4 (December 1996): 546–68.

Mauro, Paolo. "Corruption and Growth." *Quarterly Journal of Economics* 110 (August 1995): 681–711.

Maynes, Charles William. "A Workable Clinton Doctrine." *Foreign Policy* 93 (Winter 1993–94): 3–21.

Melson, Robert, and Howard Wolpe. *Nigeria: Modernization and the Politics of Communalism*. East Lansing: Michigan State University Press, 1976.

Menkhaus, Ken. "International Peacebuilding and the Dynamics of Local and National Reconciliation in Somalia." In *Learning from Somalia*, edited by Walter Clarke and Jeffrey Herbst, 42–63. Boulder, CO: Westview Press, 1997.

Miall, Hugh. *The Peacemakers: Peaceful Settlement of Disputes since 1945.* London: Macmillan, 1992.

Midlarsky, Manus I. "Identity and International conflict." In *Handbook of War Studies II*, edited by M. Midlarsky, 25–58. Ann Arbor: University of Michigan Press, 2000.

Mill, John S. "A Few Words on Nonintervention." In *Essays on Politics and Culture*, edited by Gertrude Himmelfarb, 368–84. Gloucester: Peter Smith, 1973.

Mitchell, C. R. *The Structure of International Conflict.* London: Macmillan, 1981.

Moniroth, Aun Porn. *Democracy in Cambodia: Theories and Realities.* Translated by Mrs. Khieu Mealy. Phnom Penh: CICP, 1995.

Montgomery, Tommie Sue. *Revolution in El Salvador: From Civil Strife to Civil Peace.* 2d ed. Boulder, CO: Westview Press, 1994.

Morrow, James. *Game Theory for Political Scientists.* Princeton: Princeton University Press, 1994.

Mortimer, Edward. "Under What Circumstances Should the UN Intervene Militarily in a 'Domestic' Crisis?" In *Peacemaking and Peacekeeping for the New Century*, edited by Olara Otunnu and Michael Doyle, 111–144. Lanham, MD.: Rowman and Littlefield, 1998.

Murdoch, James C., and Todd Sandler. "Economic Growth, Civil Wars, and Spatial Spillovers." *Journal of Conflict Resolution* 46 (February 2002): 91–110.

Nardin, Terry. *Law, Morality, and the Relations of States.* Princeton: Princeton University Press, 1983.

Natsios, Andrew. "Humanitarian Relief Intervention in Somalia: The Economics of Chaos." In *Learning from Somalia*, edited by Walter Clarke and Jeffrey Herbst. Boulder, CO: Westview Press, 1997.

Ndikumana, Leonce, and Kisangani Emizet. "The Economics of Civil War: The Case of the Democratic Republic of the Congo." Paper prepared for the World Bank Project on Civil Wars, 2003.

Newman, Saul. "Does Modernization Breed Ethnic Conflict?" *World Politics* 43, no. 3 (1991): 451–78.

Oakley, Robert B. "Humanitarian Response: The Consequences of Intervention." Paper presented at the Carnegie Forum, Geneva, Switzerland, February 16–17, 1997.

O'Ballance, Edgar. *The Congo-Zaire Experience, 1960–1998.* New York: Macmillan and St. Martin's Press, 2000.

O'Brien, C. C. *To Katanga and Back.* New York: Universal Library, 1966.

Ogata, Sadako. *The Turbulent Decade.* New York: W. W. Norton, 2005.

Ogata, Shijuro, and Paul Volcker. *Financing an Effective United Nations: A Report of the Independent Advisory Group on UN Financing.* New York: Ford Foundation, 1993.

O'Hanlon, Michael. *Saving Lives with Force: Military Criteria for Humanitarian Intervention.* Washington, DC: Brookings Institution Press, 1997.

Olson, Mancur. "Dictoratorship, Democracy, and Development." *American Political Science Review* 87, no. 3 (1993): 567–76.

Olzak, Susan, and Joane Nagel, eds. *Competitive Ethnic Relations*. New York: Academic Press, 1986.

Orr, Robert, ed. *Winning the Peace: An American Strategy for Post-conflict Reconstruction*. Washington, DC: Center for Strategic and International Studies, 2004.

Orwa, D. K. *The Congo Betrayal: The UN-US and Lumumba*. Nairobi: Kenya Literature, 1985.

Otunnu, Olara, and Michael Doyle, eds. *Peacemaking and Peacekeeping for the New Century*. Lanham, MD: Rowman and Littlefield, 1998.

Owens, John. "The Foreign Imposition of Domestic Institutions." *International Organization* 56, no. 2 (2002): 375–409.

Oye, Kenneth. "Explaining Cooperation under Anarchy." *World Politics* 38, no. 1 (1985): 1–24.

Paris, Roland. "Peacebuilding and the Limits of Liberal Internationalism." *International Security* 22 (Fall 1997): 54–89.

———. "The Faulty Assumptions of Post-conflict Peacebuilding" In *Turbulent Peace: the Challenges of Managing International Conflict*, edited by Chester Crocker, Fen Hampson, and Pamela Aall, 773–74. Washington, DC: United States Institute of Peace Press, 2001.

———. *At War's End*. Cambridge: Cambridge University Press, 2004.

Parker, Karen, Anne Heindel and Adam Branch, "Armed Conflict in the World Today: A Country by Country Review." Prepared for Humanitarian Law Project/International Educational Development and Parliamentary Human Rights Group, United Kingdom, Spring 2000., http://www.hri.ca/doccentre/docs/armedconflict2000.shtml

Parsons Brinckerhoff International. *Brcko Port Feasibility Study*, March 2000.

Pei, Minxin. "Lessons of the Past." *Foreign Policy* 137 (July–August 2003): 52–55.

Peou, Sorpong. *Conflict Neutralization in the Cambodia War*. New York: Oxford University Press, 1997.

———. "UNTAC: Implementing the Paris Agreement in Cambodia: Problems and a Prescription." Stanford University, CISAC, 1999.

———. *Intervention and Change in Cambodia*. New York: St. Martin's, 2000.

Perham, Marjorie. 1946. "The Economics of a Tropical Dependency." In *Studies in Colonial Legislatures*, vol. 1. London: Faber and Faber.

Perlez, Jane. "Somalia Self-Destructs and the World Looks On." *New York Times*, December 29, 1991.

Philpott, Daniel. *Revolutions in Sovereignty*. Princeton: Princeton University Press, 2001.

Picco, Giandommenico. "The U.N. and the Use of Force." *Foreign Affairs* 73, no. 5 (1994): 14–18.

Pirnie, Bruce R., and William E. Simons. *Soldiers for Peace: An Operational Typology*. Santa Monica, CA: RAND, for the Office of the Secretary of Defense, 1996.

Polyviou, Polyvios G. *Cyprus: Conflict and Negotiation, 1960–1980.* London: Duckworth, 1980.

Posen, Barry. "The Security Dilemma and Ethnic Conflict." In *Ethnic Conflict and International Security*, edited by Michael E. Brown, 103–25. Princeton: Princeton University Press, 1993.

Pouligny, Beatrice. "Promoting Democratic Institutions in Post-conflict Societies," *International Peacekeeping* 7, no. 3 (Autumn 2000): 17–35.

———. *Ils nous avaient promis la paix.* Paris: Sciences Po, 2004.

Power, Samantha. *"A Problem from Hell": America and the Age of Genocide.* New York: Basic Books, 2002.

Prunier, Gerard. *The Rwanda Crisis: History of a Genocide.* New York: Columbia University Press, 1995.

Przeworski, Adam, Michael Alvarez, Fernando Limongi, and Jose Cheibub. *Democracy and Development.* Cambridge: Cambridge University Press, 2000.

Raknerud, A., and Hegre, Håvard. "The Hazard of War: Reassessing the Evidence for the Democratic Peace." *Journal of Peace Research* 34, no. 4 (1997): 385–404.

Ramet, Sabrina P. *Nationalism and Federalism in Yugoslavia, 1962–1991.* 2d ed. Bloomington: Indiana University Press, 1992.

———. "War in the Balkans," *Foreign Affairs* 71, no. 4 (1992): 79–99.

Ratner, Steven. "The Cambodia Settlement Agreements." *American Journal of International Law* 87, no. 1 (1993): 1–41.

———. *The New Peacekeeping: Nation-Building after the Cold War and the Cambodia Experience.* Geneva: Institut universitaire de hautes études internationales, 1993.

———. *The New UN Peacekeeping: Building Peace in Lands of Conflict after the Cold War.* New York: St. Martin's Press, 1995.

Regan, Patrick M. "Conditions for Successful Third Party Interventions." *Journal of Conflict Resolution* 40, no. 1 (1996): 336–59.

———. *Civil Wars and Foreign Powers.* Ann Arbor: University of Michigan Press, 2000.

———. "Third Party Interventions and the Duration of Intrastate Conflicts." *Journal of Conflict Resolution* 46 (February 2002): 55–73.

Reuter, A. P. "UN Commander in Bosnia Assails Security Council." *The Montreal Gazette*, December 31, 1993.

Reynal-Querol, Marta. "Ethnicity, Political Systems and Civil Wars." *Journal of Conflict Resolution* 46, no. 1 (2002): 29–54.

Reyntjens, Filip. "Constitution-Making in Extreme Crisis: The Case of Rwanda and Burundi." *Journal of African Law* 40, no. 2 (1996): 234–42.

Rieff, David. *Slaughterhouse: Bosnia and the Failure of the West.* New York: Simon and Schuster, 1995.

Roberts, Adam. "The United Nations and International Security." *Survival* 35, no. 2 (1993): 3–31.

———. *The Crisis in Peacekeeping.* Oslo: Institutt for Forsvarsstudier, 1994.

Robertson, Lord. "The Work Ahead in Bosnia." *New York Times*, Op-Ed, November 25, 2000.

Robinson, Geoffrey. "If You Leave Us, We Will Die." *Dissent* 49 (Winter 2002): 101–12.

Rohde, David. *Endgame*. New York: Farrar, Straus and Giroux, 1997.

Rose, Michael. "Military Aspects of Peacekeeping: Lessons Learned from Bosnia, from a Commander's Perspective." In *UN Peacekeeping in Trouble: Lessons Learned from the Former Yugoslavia; Peacekeepers' Views on the Limits and Possibilities of the United Nations*, edited by W. Biermann and M. Vadset, 153–67. Aldershot: Ashgate, 1998.

Rosenbaum, Paul R., and Donald B. Rubin. "The Central Role of the Propensity Score in Observational Studies for Causal Effects." *Biometrika* 70, no. 1 (1983): 41–55.

Ross, Michael L. 2001. "Does Oil Hinder Democracy?" *World Politics* 53 (April 2001): 325–61.

———. "How Do Natural Resources Influence the Risk of Civil War: Evidence from 13 Case Studies." *International Organization* 58, no. 1 (Winter 2004): 35–67.

Rothchild, Donald. "Implementation and Its Effects on Building and Sustaining Peace: The Effects of Changing Structures of Incentives." Unpublished paper, Center for International Security and Cooperation, Stanford University and University of California, Davis, 2000.

———. "Settlement Terms and Postagreement Stability." In *Ending Civil Wars: The Implementation of Peace Agreements*, edited by Stephen J. Stedman, Donald Rothchild, and Elizabeth M. Cousens, 117–40. Boulder, CO: Lynne Rienner, 2002.

Ruggie, John. "Multilateralism: The Anatomy of an Institution." *International Organization* 46, no. 3 (Summer 1992): 561–98.

———. "The United Nations Stuck in a Fog between Peacekeeping and Peace Enforcement." McNair Paper 25. Washington, DC: National Defense University, 1993.

Sahnoun, Mohamed. *Somalia: The Missed Opportunities*. Washington, DC: United States Institute of Peace, 1994.

Sambanis, Nicholas. "Partition as a Solution to Ethnic War: An Empirical Critique of the Theoretical Literature." *World Politics* 52, no. 4 (2000): 437–83.

———. "Do Ethnic and Non-ethnic Civil Wars Have the Same Causes? A Theoretical and Empirical Inquiry (part 1)." *Journal of Conflict Resolution* 45, no. 3 (2001): 259–82.

Sambanis, Nicholas. "A Review of Recent Advances and Future Directions in the Literature on Civil War." *Defense and Peace Economics* 13, no. 2 (June 2002): 215–43.

———. "Do Ethnic and Non-ethnic Civil Wars Have the Same Causes? Organization and Interests in Ethnic Insurgency." Working paper, Yale University, October 17, 2002.

———. "The Causes of Genocide and Civil War: Are They More Similar Than We Thought?" Unpublished paper, Yale University, 2003.

———. "Expanding Economic Models of Civil War Using Case Studies." *Perspectives on Politics* 2, no. 2 (2004a): 259–80.

————. "What Is Civil War? Conceptual and Empirical Complexities of an Operational Definition." *Journal of Conflict Resolution* 48, no. 6 (2004b): 814–59.

Sambanis, Nicholas, and Branko Milanovic. "Explaining the Demand for Sovereignty." Unpublished manuscript, Yale University, May, 2004.

Samuel, Tamrat. "East Timor: The Path to Self-Determination." In *From Promise to Practice: Strengthening UN Capacities for the Prevention of Violent Conflict*, edited by Chandra Lekha Sriram and Karin Wermester, 197–232. Boulder, CO: Lynne Rienner, 2003.

Sanderson, John. "The Incalculable Dynamic of Using Force." In *UN Peacekeeping Trouble: Lessons Learned from the Former Yugoslavia*, edited by Wolfgang Biermann and Martin Vadset, 203–17. Aldershot: Ashgate, 1998.

Sanderson, Lieutenant General John. "Dabbling in War: The Dilemma of the Use of Force in UN Operations." In *Peacemaking and Peacekeeping for the New Century*, edited by Olara Otunnu and Michael Doyle, 145–68. Lanham, MD: Rowman and Littlefield, 1998.

Sarkees, Meredith R., and David J. Singer. "The Correlates of War Datasets: The Totality of War." Paper prepared for the 42d Annual Convention of the International Studies Association, Chicago, IL, February 20–24, 2001.

Schaeffer, R. *Warpaths: The Politics of Partition*. New York: Hill and Wang, 1990.

Schmitt, Eric. "Somalia's First Lesson for Military Is Caution," *New York Times*, March 5, 1995.

Selten, Reinhard. "A Simple Model of Imperfect Competition: Where 4 are Few and 6 are Many." *International Journal of Game Theory* 2, no. 3 (1973): 141–201.

Shawcross, W. *Cambodia's New Deal*. Washington, DC: Carnegie Endowment for International Peace, 1994.

Shklar, Judith. *Legalism*. New York: Cambridge University Press, 1986.

Silber, Laura, and Allan Little. *The Death of Yugoslavia*. London: Penguin-BBC, 1995.

Singer, J. David, and Melvin Small. "National Material Capabilities Data, 1816–1985." Computer file. Ann Arbor, MI: Inter-university Consortium for Political and Social Research distributor, 1993.

Skaperdas, Stergios. "An Economic Approach to Analyzing Civil Wars." Paper presented at the World Bank Conference "Civil Wars and Post-war Transitions," University of California, Irvine, May 18–20, 2001.

Skiadopoulos, Konstantinos. *Polemos sten Kypro, Ioulios-Avgoustos 1974* (War in Cyprus, July–August 1974). Athens: Eleftheri Skepsis, 1989.

Smith, Anthony D. *National Identity*. Reno: University of Nevada Press, 1991.

————. *Nationalism*. Cambridge: Polity Press, 2001.

Smith, Jeffrey A., and Petra E. Todd. "Reconciling Conflicting Evidence on the Performance of Propensity-Score Matching Methods." *American Economic Review* 91, no. 2 (2001): 112–18.

————. "Does Matching Overcome LaLonde's Critique of Nonexperimental Estimators? (Comments on R. J. Lalonde and R. Dehejia and S. Wahba)." *Journal of Econometrics* 125, no. 1–2 (2005): 305–53.

Smith, Michael, and Moreen Dee. *Peacekeeping in East Timor: The Path to Independence*. International Peace Academy Occasional Paper Series. Boulder, CO: Lynne Rienner, 2003.

Smith, R. Jeffrey. "Proofs of Atrocities Divide Bosnians," *Washington Post*, December 28, 2000, A14.

Smoljan, Jana. "Socio-Economic Aspects of Peacebuilidng: UNTAES and the Organisation of Employment in Eastern Slavonia." *International Peacekeeping* 10, no. 2 (2003): 27–50.

Snyder, Jack. *From Voting to Violence: Democratization and Nationalist Conflict*. New York: Norton Publishers, 2000.

Snyder, Jack, and Leslie Vinjamuri. "Trials and Errors: Principle and Pragmatism in Strategies of International Justice." *International Security* 28, no. 3 (Winter 2003–4): 5–44.

Solomon, Richard H. "Bringing Peace to Cambodia." In *Herding Cats: Multiparty Mediation in a Complex World*, edited by Chester A. Crocker, Fen Osler Hampson, and Pamela Aall, 275–323. Washington, DC: United States Institute of Peace Press, 1999.

Solomon, Richard. *Exiting Indochina: US Leadership of the Cambodia Settlement and Normalization with Vietnam*. Washington, DC: United States Institute of Peace, 2000.

Song, Jin. "The Political Dynamics of the Peacemaking Process in Cambodia." In *Keeping the Peace*, edited by M. Doyle, Ian Johnstone, and Robert Orr. Cambridge: Cambridge University Press, 1997.

Sriram, Chandra. "Truth Commissions and the Quest for Justice: Stability and Accountability after Internal Strife." *International Peacekeeping* 7, no. 4 (2000): 91–106.

———. *Confronting Past Human Rights Violators*. London: Frank Cass, 2004.

Stanley, William. *The Protection Racket State: Elite Politics, Military Extortion, and Civil War in El Salvador*. Philadelphia: Temple University Press, 1996.

Stanley, William, and David Holiday. "From Fragmentation to a National Project? Peace Implementation in Guatemala." Stanford University, Center for International Security and Cooperation, 1999.

Stedman, Stephen J., Donald Rothchild, and Elizabeth M. Cousens, eds. *Ending Civil Wars: The Implementation of Peace Agreements*. Boulder, CO: Lynne Rienner, 2002.

Stedman, Stephen John. "Spoiler Problems in Peace Processes." *International Security* 22 (Fall 1997): 5–53.

Steele, Jonathan. "Nation Building in East Timor." *World Policy Journal* 19 (Summer 2002): 76–87.

Stegenga, James. "UN Peace-Keeping: The Cyprus Venture." *Journal of Peace Research* 7, no. 1 (1970): 1–17.

Stein, Arthur A. *Why Nations Cooperate: Circumstance and Choice in International Relations*. Ithaca: Cornell University Press, 1992.

Steinberg, James B. "International Involvement in the Yugoslav Conflict." In *Enforcing Restraint: Collective Intervention in Internal Conflicts*, edited by Lori Fisler Damrosch. New York: Council on Foreign Relations Press, 1993.

Stevenson, Jonathan. "Hope Restored in Somalia." *Foreign Policy* 91 (Summer 1993): 138–54.

Strohmeyer, Hansjoerg. "Policing the Peace: Post-conflict Judicial System Reform in East Timor." *UNSW Law Journal* 24, no. 1: 171–82.

Switow, Michael. "Costs of US Interventions." Research Memorandum, Woodrow Wilson School, Princeton University, 1995.

Synge, Richard. *Mozambique: UN Peacekeeping in Action, 1992–1994.* Washington, DC: United States Institute of Peace Press, 1997.

Talentino, Andrea. "Rwanda." In *The Costs of Conflict*, edited by Michael Brown and Richard Rosecrance. Lanham, MD: Rowman and Littlefield, 1999.

Teitel, Ruti. *Transitional Justice*. Oxford: Oxford University Press, 2000.

Thakur, Ramesh. "UN Peace Operations and US Unilateralism and Multilateralism." In *Unilateralism and US Foreign Policy*, edited by David Malone and Yuen F. Kong: 153–79. Boulder, CO: Lynne Rienner, 2003.

Tharoor, Shashi. "Should UN Peacekeeping 'Go Back to Basics'?" *Survival* 37, no. 4 (1995–96.): 52–64.

Thayer, Carlyle. "The United Nations Transitional Authority in Cambodia: The Restoration of Sovereignty." In *Peacekeeping and Peacemaking: Towards Effective Intervention in Post–Cold War Conflicts*, edited by Tom Woodhouse, Robert Bruce, and Malcolm Dando, 145–65. New York: St. Martin's Press, 1998.

Thompson, Dennis. "Moral Responsibility of Public Officials: The Problem of Many Hands." *American Political Science Review* 74, no. 4 (1980): 905–16.

Tilly, Charles. *From Mobilization to Revolution*. New York: Random House, 1978.

Toft, Monica. "Indivisibile Territory, Geographic Concentration, and Ethnic War." *Security Studies* 12, no. 2 (2002): 82–119.

———. *The Geography of Ethnic Violence*. Princeton: Princeton University Press, 2003.

Tomz, Michael, Jason Wittenberg, and Gary King. "CLARIFY: Software for Interpreting and Presenting Statistical Results." Version 1.2.1, (June 1, 1999). http://gking.harvard.edu/stats.shtml (accessed January 4, 2000).

Torres Rivas, Edelberto. "Civil War and Insurrection in El Salvador." In *Keeping the Peace*, edited by Michael Doyle, Ian Johnstone, and Robert Orr, 209–26. Cambridge: Cambridge University Press, 1997.

Touval, Saadia. "Why the UN Fails." *Foreign Affairs* 73, no. 5 (1994): 44–57.

Traub, James. "Inventing East Timor." *Foreign Affairs* 79, no. 4 (2000): 74–89.

Trowbridge, Erin. "Back Road Reckoning." *Dissent* 49 (Winter 2002): 101–11.

United Kingdom. *Treaty of Alliance* (February 11) (London: HMSO, 1959).

———. *Treaty of Guarantee* (February 19) (London: HMSO, 1959).

United Nations. *The Blue Helmets: A Review of United Nations Peacekeeping.* 2d edition. New York: United Nations, 1990.

———. *Report of the Commission on the Truth for El Salvador*, "From Madness to Hope: The 12-Year War in /El Salvador," S/25500. April 1, 1993.

———. *Vienna Declaration and Program of Action*. Draft reference number: A/CONF. 157/23. July 12, 1993.

———. *Further Report of the Secretary General Submitted in Pursuance of Para.19 Res. 814 (1993) and para. 5 (Res. 865) of 1993*, S/26738, November 12, 1993.

———. *The Blue Helmets: A Review of United Nations Peacekeeping 3d* edition. New York: United Nations, 1996.

UNA-USA. *Global Agenda 1997–1998*. Lanham, MD: Rowman and Littlefield, 1997.

United Nations. *Agreements on a Comprehensive Political Settlement of the Cambodia Conflict* (Paris, October 23, 1991). New York: United Nations Department of Public Information, 1991.

United Nations Department of Public Information. *The United Nations and El Salvador, 1990-1995*. 1995.

———. "East Timor: Education and Health in Focus." *UN Chronicle*. no. 2 (2002): 34–35.

———. "East Timor: Selected Economic Indicators, 1997-2000." http://lnweb 18.worldbank.org/eap/eap.nsf/Attachments/TSS++Annex+E.1/$File/Annex+E .1.pdf (accessed March 25, 2005).

United Nations Documents: S/8141; S/8248; S/10401, 30 November 1971 and S/10564, Add. 1, 2, March 18, 1972; S/5950, September 10, 1964; S/5671, April 29, 1964; SG's report S/1997/962, December 8, 1997; S/8446, March 9, 1968; S/5764, June 15, 1964; General Assembly A/52/775/Add.1; S/18102, May 31, 1986; Resolution 383 (1975); S/5950; S/8286, December 8, 1967; S/8446, March 9, 1968; S/5828, July 23, 1964; S/10564, Add. 1, April 21, 1972; A/52/775/Add.1, February 24, 1998; Resolution 889 (1993), December 15, 1993; SC resolution 1000 (1995), June 23, 1995; S/11611, January 31, 1975; S/11631, February 12, 1975; S/5764, S/6228, S/7350, S/9233, S/9521, S/10401, S/11137, S/11353; S/5593, S/5750, S/5764, S/5950, S/6102, S/6228, S/6426, S/7350, S/8664, S/9233, S/9521, S/9814, S/10005, S/10199, S/10401, S/10664, S/10842, S/10940, S/11294; S/RES/743 (1992); S/RES/749 (1992); S/RES/762 (1992); S/RES/769(1992); S/RES/776 (1992); S/RES/779 (1992); S/RES/795 (1992); S/RES/693 (1991); S/RES/729 (1992); S/RES/832 (1993); S/RES/836 (1993); S/RES/920 (1994); S/RES/961 (1994); S/RES/991 (1995); S/RES/1035 (1995); S/RES/1037 (1996); S/RES/1079 (1996); S/RES/1088 (1996); S/RES/1120 (1997); S/RES/1145 (1997); S/RES/1103 (1997); S/RES/1107 (1997); S/RES/1144 (1997); S/RES/1168 (1998); S/RES/1184 (1998); S/RES/1423 (2002); S/RES/1272 (October 25, 1999); S/RES/1338 (2001); UNDPI, PS/DPI/15/Rev. March 6, 1995.

United Nations Security Council Resolutions: SC Resolution 814 (March 26, 1993), SC Resolution 837 (June 6, 1993), and SC Resolution 1511 (October 16, 2003).

United States. "Speech by Senator Edward Kennedy." *Congressional Record*, no. 122 Washington, DC, 1976.

United States Senate, Committee on Armed Services. "US Military Operations in Somalia," May 12, 1994.

UNTAET Press Office. "Justice and Serious Crimes," Fact Sheet 7 (April 2002) http://www.un.org/peace/etimor/fact/fs7.PDF (accessed March 25, 2005).

————. "Law and Order." Fact Sheet 6 (April 2002). http://www.un.org/peace/etimor/fact/fs6.PDF (accessed March 25, 2005).

Uphoff-Kato, Elisabeth."Quick Impacts, Slow Rehabilitation in Cambodia." In Keeping the Peace, edited by Michael Doyle, Ian Johnstone, and Robert Orr, 186–206. Cambridge: Cambridge University Press, 1997.

Urquhart, Brian. Hammarskjold. New York: Norton, 1972.

————. A Life in Peace and War. London: Weidenfeld and Nicolson, 1987.

————. Ralph Bunche, An American Life. New York: Norton, 1993.

————. "For a UN Volunteer Military Force." New York Review of Books 40, no. 11 (June 10, 1993): 3–4.

Urquhart, Brian, and Michael W. Doyle. "Peacekeeping Up to Now: Under Fire from Friend and Foe." International Herald Tribune, OpEd, December 16, 1995.

Vaccaro, Mathew. "The Politics of Genocide: Peacekeeping and Disaster Relief." In UN Peacekeeping, American Policy, and the Uncivil Wars of the 1990s, edited by William Durch, 364–407. New York: St. Martin's Press, 1996.

Valdivieso, Luis, et al. "East Timor: Establishing the Foundations of Strong Macroeconomic Management." IMF Report, 2000. http://imf.org/external/pubs/ft/etimor/timor.pdf.

Varshney, Ashutosh. Ethnic Conflict and Civic Life: Hindus and Muslims in India. New Haven: Yale University Press, 2002.

Vernon, Raymond. "Long-Run Trends in Concession Contracts." Proceedings of the Sixty-first Annual Meeting of the American Society of International Law. Washington, DC, 1967.

Vieira de Mello, Sergio. 2003. "Remarks on East Timor." In Sebastian von Einsiedel, rapporteur, You the People, Report of an IPA Seminar on transitional authority. New York: IPA.

Wahlgren, Lars-Eric. "Start and End of Srebenica." In UN Peacekeeping in Trouble : Lessons Learned from the formerYugoslavia : Peacekeepers' Views on the Limits and Possibilities of the United Nations, edited by W. Biermann and M. Vadset, 168–85. Aldershot: Ashgate, 1998.

Waldheim, Kurt. In the Eye of a Storm: A Memoir. London: Adler and Adler, 1985.

Wallensteen, Peter, and Margareta Sollenberg. "Armed Conflicts, Conflict Termination, and Peace Agreements, 1989–1996." Journal of Peace Research 34, no. 3 (1997): 339–58.

Walter, Barbara. "The Critical Barrier to Civil War Settlement." International Organization 51 (Summer 1997): 335–64.

————. Committing to Peace: The Successful Settlement of Civil Wars. Princeton: Princeton University Press, 2002.

————. "Does Conflict Beget Conflict? Explaining Recurring Civil War." Journal of Peace Research 41, no. 3 (2004): 371–88.

Walter, Barbara, and J. Snyder, eds. Civil Wars, Insecurity, and Intervention. New York: Columbia University Press, 1999.

Waltz, Kenneth. The Stability of a Bipolar World. Daedalus 93 (Summer 1964): 881–909.

Walzer, Michael. *Regicide and Revolution. Speehes at the Trial of Louis XVI.* London and New York: Cambridge University Press, 1974.

———. *Just and Unjust Wars.* New York: Basic Books, 1977.

———. "The Politics of Rescue." *Dissent* 49 (Winter 1995): 35–41.

Weber, Max. *The Theory of Social and Economic Organization.* Translated by M. Henderson and Talcott Parsons, edited by Talcott Parsons. Glencoe, IL., Free Press, 1947.

Weiss, Thomas G., ed. *Collective Security in a Changing World.* Boulder, CO: Lynne Rienner, 1993.

———. "Rekindling Hope in UN Humanitarian Intervention." In *Learning From Somalia,* edited by Walter Clarke and Jeffrey Herbst, 207–28. Boulder, CO.: Westview Press, 1997.

———. *Military-Civilian Interactions.* Lanham, MD: Rowman and Littlefield, 1999.

Wendt, Alex. *Social Theory of International Politics.* Cambridge: Cambridge University Press, 1999.

Wheeler, Nicholas. *Saving Strangers.* Oxford: Oxford University Press, 2000.

White, N. D. *The United Nations and the Maintenance of International Peace and Security.* Manchester and New York: Manchester University Press, 1990.

Wilkinson, Steven I. *Votes and Violence: Electoral Competition and Ethnic Riots in India.* Cambridge: Cambridge University Press, 2004.

Williams, Michael C. *Civil-Military Relations and Peacekeeping.* London: Oxford University Press, 1998.

Wines, Michael. "Bush Declares Goal in Somalia to 'Save Thousands.'" *New York Times,* December 5, 1992.

Wintrobe, Ronald. "Some Economics of Ethnic Capital Formation and Conflict." In *Nationalism and Rationality,* edited by A. Breton et al., 43–70. Cambridge: Cambridge University Press, 1995.

Wiseman, Henry. "The United Nations and International Peace." In UNITAR, *The United Nations and the Maintenance of International Peace and Security,* 263–333. Dordecht: Martinus Nijhof, 1987.

Wolfe, James H. "The United Nations and the Cyprus Question." In *Cyprus: A Regional Conflict and Its Resolution,* edited by Norma Salem, 227–43. New York: St. Martin's Press, 1992.

Wood, Elizabeth Jean. *Forging Democracy from Below: Insurgent Transitions in South Africa and El Salvador.* Cambridge: Cambridge University Press, 2000.

———. *Insurgent Collective Action and Civil War in El Salvador.* Cambridge: Cambridge University Press, 2003.

———. "Modeling Robust Settlements to Civil War: Indivisible Stakes and Distributional Compromises." Santa Fe Institue Working Paper no. 03-10-056. 2003.

Woodward, Susan. *Balkan Tragedy: Chaos and Dissolution after the Cold War.* Washington, DC: Brookings Institution, 1995.

Woodwell, Douglas. "Unwelcome Neighbors: Shared Ethnicity and International Conflict during the Cold War." *International Studies Quarterly* 48, no. 1 (2004): 197–223.

World Bank. *World Development Indicators.* Washington, DC: World Bank, 1999.

———. *World Development Indicators*. Washington, DC: World Bank, 2000.

———. *World Development Indicators*. Washington, DC: World Bank, 2001.

———. *World Development Indicators*. Washington, DC: World Bank, 2002.

———. *World Development Indicators*. Washington, DC: World Bank, 2003.

———. Joint Assessment Mission (JAM) Background Report http://wbln0018
.worldbank.org/eap/eap.nsf (accessed October 22, 2004).

———. Joint Assessment Mission (JAM) Study. http://www.worldbank.org/
html/extdr/offrep/eap/etimor/donorsmtg99/jamsummarytablefinal.pdf (accessed
October 22, 2004).

Young, Crawford. *Politics in the Congo*. Princeton: Princeton University Press,
1965.

Young, Crawford, and Thomas Turner. *The Rise and Decline of the Zairian
State*. Madison: University of Wisconsin Press, 1985.

Zartman, I. William. *Ripe for Resolution: Conflict and Intervention in Africa*.
Oxford: Oxford University Press, 1985.

———. "The Unfinished Agenda: Negotiating Internal Conflicts." In *Stopping
the Killing*, edited by Roy Licklider, 20–36. New York: New York University
Press, 1993.

———. *The Elusive Peace*. Washington, DC: Brookings, 1995.

———. "Putting Humpty-Dumpty Together Again." In *The International Spread
of Ethnic Conflict: Fear, Diffusion, and Escalation*, edited by D. Lake and
M. Rothchild, 317–337. Princeton: Princeton University Press, 1998.

Zisk, Kimberly Marten. *Enforcing the Peace*. New York: Columbia University
Press, 2004.

Index

Acheson, Dean, 264

Addis Ababa Agreements, 149, 150, 157, 320

Ad Hoc Commission (El Salvador), 206

Adoula, Cyrille, 178, 183

Afghanistan, 76, 306, 338–39, 340

African Crisis Response Initiative, 347

Aidid, Mohammed Farah, 147, 151, 154, 155, 186, 187, 193, 349

Ajello, Aldo, 315, 317

Akashi, Yashushi, 169, 215, 219, 221, 309, 328

Albania, 347

Albright, Madeleine, 144, 149, 151

Algeria, 76

ALIR. *See* Army for the Liberation of Rwanda

ANC. *See* Armee Nationale Congolaise

Anderson, Gary, 186

Angola, 2, 3, 21, 43, 66, 76, 107, 183, 215, 305, 322, 325, 326, 328

Annan, Kofi, 6, 166, 280, 291

anocracy, 19, 35

APRONUC. *See* l'Autorite Provisoire des Nations Unies en Cambodge

ARENA. *See* Nationalist Republican Alliance party

Argentina, 76

Aristide, Jean-Bertrand, 349

Arizona Market, 242

Armed Forces of the National Liberation of East Timor (Falintil), 244, 250, 255

Armee Nationale Congolaise (ANC), 174, 175, 177, 178, 179

Army for the Liberation of Rwanda (ALIR), 301

Arria, Diego, 167

Arusha Agreement, 282, 287–88, 289, 290, 294, 297, 306

ASEAN. *See* Association of Southeast Asian Nations

Asian Development Bank, 220

Aspin, Les, 156

assistance: and hostility, 110; and motivations for civil war, 30–31; in peacebuilding triangle, 4

assistance, development, 59, 108; to Cambodia, 220, 221, 222; to Congo, 180, 182; to Cyprus, 260; data on, 85–86; to East Timor, 245, 248, 249, 252; and El Salvador, 204; to Rwanda, 284; and UN coordination, 343

assistance, economic: to Cambodia, 220, 221, 328; dual effects of, 69; to East Timor, 247; to El Salvador, 204; and international capacities, 85; and peacebuilding success, 108, 131, 132, 337; and peacekeeping troop level, 112; to Somalia, 155, 159; and success probability, 115, 116; summary statistics on, 140. *See also* economy

assistance, humanitarian: authorization for, 320; to Bosnia, 348; to Cambodia, 216, 221; to Congo, 177; to Cyprus, 270, 277; to East Timor, 248, 249; to former Yugoslavia, 16, 161, 165, 168, 185, 192; and long-term goals, 339; and military enforcement, 155; as mitigating effort, 348; to Rwanda, 286, 290, 293; to Somalia, 148, 151, 154, 155, 156, 158, 160; to Tanzania, 300; in third generation peace operations, 15; and UNOSOM II, 149, 150, 153; to Yugoslavia, 8; to Zaire, 300

assistance, reconstruction: to Cambodia, 215, 222; to former Yugoslavia, 169; and long-term goals, 339. *See also* reconstruction

assistance, technical: to Cyprus, 270; to El Salvador, 206

Association of Southeast Asian Nations (ASEAN), 8, 222

assurance game, 53–54, 58

Austin, Reginald, 219, 313

Australia, 191, 218, 221, 252, 253, 254, 256

Austria, 270

authoritarianism, 41, 73

authority, domestic, 320–21. *See also* government; sovereignty; transitional authority

autocracy, 19, 35

l'Autorite Provisoire des Nations Unies en
    Cambodge (APRONUC), 220
Azerbaijan, 76

Bagosora, Théoneste, 287
Ball, George, 280
Bangladesh, 76, 292
Barnett, Michael, 302
Barre, Mohamed Siad, 146, 147, 152, 158
Belgium, 173, 174, 175, 176, 194, 285,
    286, 291, 293, 297, 306–7
Belo, Carlos Filipe Ximenes, 246
Bercovitch, J., 312
Betts, Richard, 193
Bihac, 167
Bizimungu, Pasteur, 293
Bolivia, 76
Bonn Peace Implementation
    Conference, 233
Bonn Summit of the Peace Implementation
    Council, 329
Booh-Booh, Jacques-Roger, 292, 295
Bosnia, 1, 18, 168, 184, 199; attention to,
    61; authority in, 321; consent in, 349;
    continued problems in, 2, 59; death in,
    162; factions in, 322; failure in, 348,
    349; and Friends of the Secretary-
    General, 306, 307; leadership in, 318;
    and military-civilian coordination, 187;
    NATO in, 85; peacebuilding costs in,
    171, 343; peacebuilding ecology of, 325,
    328–29; peace enforcement in, 16–17,
    18; recognition of, 168; and Rwanda,
    284; safe areas of, 161, 164, 166, 167;
    self-determination in, 163; Serb ethnic
    cleansing in, 164; success in, 184; time-
    table in, 338; transitional authority in,
    328–29, 330, 333; and UNAMIR, 296;
    and UN resolutions, 165. See also Yugo-
    slavia, former
Bosniac-Croat Federation, 238, 239, 330
Bosniacs, in Brcko, 235, 239, 240, 331
Bosnian Muslims, 161, 169, 184
Bosnian Serb republic, 230
Boutros-Ghali, Boutros, 293, 296, 307–8;
    An Agenda for Peace, 10, 15, 144, 198,
    347, 350; and Aidid, 151; and assertive
    multilateralism, 9; and El Salvador, 202;
    on multidimensional peace operations,
    15; and UNITAF mandate, 149; and
    UNPROFOR, 192; and war-making, 185

Brahimi, Lakhdar, 340
Brahimi Report, 189
Brcko, 171, 199, 234–40, 248, 250, 256,
    318, 322, 330–31, 333
Brcko Arbitration, 237–38
Brcko Multiethnic Police, 239, 241, 243
Briquemont, Francois, 185
Broad Based Transitional Government
    (BBTG), 287, 289, 291, 297
buffer zone, 12, 13–14, 109, 308; in
    Cyprus, 269, 270, 272, 275; in former
    Yugoslavia, 164, 231. See also partition
Bunche, Ralph, 187, 266
Burundi, 76, 184, 285, 295
Bush, George H., 144–45
Bush, George H. W., 148, 156

Cambodia, 43, 59, 66, 304, 313, 322; and
    Dayton Agreements, 231; and El Sal-
    vador, 205, 212; and Friends of the
    Secretary-General, 305–6, 307; leader-
    ship in, 318; peacebuilding in, 76, 117,
    209–20, 325, 343, 345; peacebuilding
    success in, 15, 17, 127, 199, 336, 349;
    peacekeeping in, 2, 130, 211, 213, 319;
    Supreme National Council in, 218–19,
    220, 311, 327–28, 350; time-table in,
    338; troop contributions to operations
    in, 17; use of force in, 20
Cambodian People's Party (CPP), 217,
    221–22
Canada, 270
cease-fire. See truce/cease-fire
Cedras, Raul, 191, 325
Central Africa Republic, 76
Chad, 76
Chapultepec Agreement, 202
China: and assertive multilateralism, 9;
    and Cambodia, 218, 304, 305, 307,
    327, 339; and Congo, 178–79; peace-
    building outcomes in, 76, 77; on Secu-
    rity Council, 9
Chinese Chapter Seven, 17
Civilian Police (CIVPOL), 216, 219, 253,
    270, 272
civilians, 4, 214
civil service, 222, 316. See also government
civil society, 15, 22, 50; in Cambodia, 221,
    311, 313; and Dayton Agreements, 231;
    in East Timor, 250; in El Salvador, 322;
    lack of, 314; participation by, 311–12,

313, 351; in Rwanda, 286, 288; in
Somalia, 346
civil war: coding of, 133–36; definition of,
31; and economy, 3; effects of, 3–4; end
of, 82, 83; external support for, 33; inef-
ficiency of, 32–33; international dimension of, 40–42; military victory as better
solution to, 86, 88; motivations for,
28–31; and neoliberalism, 40–41, 42,
51; and neorealism, 40–41, 42, 51; numbers of, 343; opportunity cost of, 83, 84;
opportunity structure for, 32; political-
economic theories of, 31–40; and
rationality, 43, 51; regional dimensions
of, 40, 41–42; theories of, 27–68;
utility of, 43
civil war duration, 43–49; in Cambodia,
210, 211; in Congo, 180; in Croatia,
226; in Cyprus, 260; and death and displacement, 100; and El Salvador, 204; in
former Yugoslavia, 170; and peacebuilding success, 99–100; and peace treaties,
104; in Rwanda, 283; in Somalia, 159
civil war outcome: in Cambodia, 210; in
Congo, 180; in Croatia, 77, 226; in
Cyprus, 260; in East Timor, 245; in El
Salvador, 77, 204; in former Yugoslavia,
81, 170; in Rwanda, 117, 283; in Somalia, 159. See also hostility
civil war recurrence, 43, 74, 87; in Cambodia, 212; in Congo, 183; and economy,
83, 84, 106; and ethnic fractionalization,
37, 40; and ethnicity, 336; in former
Yugoslavia, 227; and institutional development, 132; and local capacities, 40,
118; and military victory, 86, 87, 88;
and multidimensional missions, 110; and
natural resources, 35, 106, 108; and
negotiated settlements, 87, 88; and
partition, 49; and peace treaty, 103; and
postconflict reconstruction, 110; and
real per capita income, 106; in Rwanda,
282, 284; in Somalia, 153; and type of
war, 86; and withdrawal of UN military,
92–93
civil war type: in Cambodia, 210, 211; and
civil war recurrence, 86, 87; in Congo,
180; in Croatia, 226; in Cyprus, 260; in
East Timor, 245; in El Salvador, 204;
and ethnicity, 97, 102; and genocide,
117; and hostility, 75; identification of,

51–53, 56, 57; influence of, 4; and
peacebuilding success, 89, 126, 127; in
Rwanda, 283; in Somalia, 159; and suc-
cess probability, 115, 116; summary sta-
tistics on, 139. See also hostility
Clausewitz, Carl von, 185, 188
Clerides, Glafcos, 262, 263, 264, 265
Clinton, Bill, 191, 298
Clinton administration, 9, 144, 185,
230, 299
Cold War, 1, 7, 22, 85, 86, 183, 319,
343, 348
Coletta, Nat, 341
Collier, Paul, 101
Colombia, 77, 201, 306
colonialism, 5, 7, 145, 153, 172, 174, 193,
195, 243, 310, 318, 325–26
command and control, 60; and Dayton
Agreements, 231, 232; and UN, 189; of
UNFICYP, 271; and UNITAF, 148; and
UNOSOM, 155, 187; and UNTAC, 219,
222–23
Commission on Human Rights, 289, 296
commodity exports: of Cambodia, 210,
211; of Congo, 180; of Croatia, 226; of
Cyprus, 259, 260; of East Timor, 245; of
El Salvador, 200, 204; of former Yugoslavia, 170; as indicator of local capacities, 83; and peacebuilding success, 107,
115, 116, 127; of Rwanda, 283; in Somalia, 159; summary statistics on, 142.
See also local capacities
communication, 52, 53–54, 56–57, 155,
294, 295. See also information; media
Communist Party of El Salvador, 200
conflict: institutionalization of, 58, 278;
resolution of, 312–13; roots of, 48, 321;
transformation of, 56, 59
Congo, 17, 22, 145, 172–83, 186, 194,
316, 317, 322, 333
Congo (Brazzaville), 77
Congo Free State, 174
Congo-Zaire, 77
consent, 7, 348–49; in Bosnia, 349;
Boutros-Ghali on, 144; in Cambodia, 2,
317; and Chapter VI, 320; and Chapter
VII, 320; and coercion, 198; and coordination, 197; and coordination and cooperation problems, 58; definition of, 14;
in Eastern Slavonia, 2; in El Salvador, 2,
314; and impartiality vs. neutrality, 13;

consent (*continued*)
importance of, 2, 340; lack of, 15–16; maintenance of, 60; need for, 303; to peace, 19; and peacebuilding success, 131; and peacekeeping, 50, 56, 144; and peace treaty, 340; problems with, 198, 308; in Rwanda, 284; and sovereignty, 14, 314; strategic vs. tactical, 317; success negotiating, 197; in third generation peace operations, 15–16; in traditional peace operations, 12

constitution: of Bosnia, 231; in Cambodia, 215; in Congo, 173; of Cyprus, 257–58, 263, 265, 266; of East Timor, 250; of El Salvador, 202, 204, 206, 208; importance of, 340; and transitional authority, 341

constructivism, 51

Contadora Group, 201

cooperation, 15, 51, 52, 54–57, 59, 65, 112, 164, 310

coordination, 51, 52, 53–54, 56, 57, 65, 101, 112, 164, 187, 197, 232

corruption, 84, 107

Costa Rica, 77

coup, 2, 117, 212

Cousens, Elizabeth, 328–29

CPP. *See* Cambodian People's Party

Croatia, 225, 226, 227, 330; and Brcko, 239; and command and control, 187; death in, 162; ethnic cleansing by, 169, 171; peacebuilding outcomes in, 77; protected areas in, 164; recognition of, 163, 168; secession of, 163; and Serb Republics, 223; success in, 349; and UN resolutions, 165; and UNTAES, 224. *See also* Eastern Slavonia (Croatia); Yugoslavia, former

Croatian refugees, 223, 225

Croats: and Bosnia as part of Yugoslavia, 169; in Brcko, 235; and Eastern Slavonia (Croatia), 228; and ethnic cleansing, 184; failure to protect, 161; and Ovcara massacre, 225

Cuba, 77, 305

Cyprus, 77, 113, 257–80, 304, 318, 322, 331; and Cold War, 22; conflict institutionalization in, 58, 278; delay vs. resolution of conflict in, 14; and Friends of the Secretary-General, 306; Intercommunal Talks of 1968–1973, 258, 261,

262–63, 275, 279; National Guard, 263, 264, 271; and Rwanda, 282

cyprusization, 278

Dallaire, Romeo A., 289, 291, 292, 294, 295, 297, 298

Dayton Agreement, 2, 24, 130, 166, 171, 199, 306; Arbitral Order, 330; and Brcko, 237, 238, 239, 240; and Croatia, 223, 224, 227; different plans in, 230–31; information in, 232; leadership in, 318

Dayton peace process, 328–29

deaths: in Cambodia, 210, 211, 217; and civil war, 43; and civil war duration, 100; in Congo, 180; in Croatia, 226, 227; in Cyprus, 260; in Eastern Slavonia, 225; in East Timor, 244, 246, 247, 248; in El Salvador, 201, 204; in former Yugoslavia, 161, 162, 168, 169, 170, 184; and hostility, 65, 75, 342; and peacebuilding success, 97–99, 115, 116, 125, 126, 127, 129, 130; in peacebuilding triangle, 4; and peace treaties, 104; in Rwanda, 282, 283, 285, 293, 301; in Somalia, 146, 147, 148, 151, 154, 157, 158, 159, 184; and sovereign peace, 99; summary statistics on, 139. *See also* displacements; hostility

Dekleris, Michael, 263, 266

democracy: in Brcko Arbitration, 237; in Cambodia, 213, 214, 215, 221; and civil war, 35; in Congo, 172, 173; as destabilizing, 314, 315; and economy, 34, 132; effect of UN missions on, 74; in El Salvador, 202, 208, 323, 324; in former Yugoslavia, 163; and impartiality vs. neutrality, 13; institutions for, 315–16; and multidimensional missions, 110; need for, 341; and Organization of American States, 8; and peace, 19, 73; in Rwanda, 287; in Somalia, 146. *See also* elections

Democratic Republic of Congo, 301

Denktash, Rauf, 262, 263, 265, 266, 275, 277, 278, 280

Department of Peacekeeping Operations (DPKO), 188

diplomacy, preventive, 7, 10

displacements, 4; in Brcko, 235, 236, 239; in Cambodia, 210, 211; and civil war,

43; in Congo, 177, 180; in Croatia, 226, 227; in Cyprus, 258, 260, 269, 278; in Eastern Slavonia, 224; in East Timor, 245, 246, 248; in El Salvador, 201, 204; in former Yugoslavia, 161, 169, 170; and hostility, 75, 342; and Klanac, 331; and peacebuilding success, 97–99, 115, 116, 125, 126, 127, 129, 130; in peacebuilding triangle, 4; and peace treaties, 104; in Rwanda, 282, 283, 290; in Somalia, 157, 158, 159; and sovereign peace, 99; summary statistics on, 139; and UNOSOM, 150. See also deaths; hostility
Djeletovici oil fields, 318
Djibouti, 77
Dominican Republic, 77
Duarte, José Napoleon, 200

Eastern Slavonia (Croatia), 2, 15, 17, 20, 171, 199, 223–30, 256, 306, 317–18, 322, 330, 349
East Timor, 2, 59, 191, 199, 243–56, 311, 320, 322, 325, 330, 333, 349; National Consultative Council in, 250, 311
East Timorese Army, 254
East Timor Police College, 253
East Timor Police Service (ETPS), 253, 254
Ecevit, Bulent, 266
Economic Community of West African States Monitoring Group (ECOMOG), 195
economy: of Bosnia, 243, 325; of Brcko, 243; in Brcko Arbitration, 237; of Cambodia, 210, 211, 214, 216, 222, 315, 326, 328; and civil war, 3, 31–40, 46; and civil war recurrence, 106; of Congo, 179; of Cyprus, 270; and democracy, 34, 132; and duration of peace, 111; of Eastern Slavonia, 225; of East Timor, 251; of El Salvador, 200, 204, 206, 209, 323, 324; of former Yugoslavia, 161, 163, 164, 171, 227; and hostility, 105; and institutional reconstruction, 314; and long-term peace, 340–41; and multidimensional peace operations, 15, 199; and natural resource dependence, 106, 107; and peacebuilding, 5, 56; and peacebuilding success, 104–6, 126, 127, 336; in peacebuilding triangle, 4; postwar, 19, 83, 104–5; and property rights,

340, 341; rebuilding of, 5; and reconstruction, 5, 83, 104–5, 132, 314; of Rwanda, 282; of Somalia, 147, 160, 331; and transitional authority, 321; and UN interventions, 335; and war resumption, 83, 84. See also assistance, economic
education, 37, 342
Egypt, 12, 77
Elbadawi, Ibrahim, 35, 44
elections: and Brcko, 239; in Cambodia, 2, 59, 212, 214, 215, 216, 218, 219–20, 223, 232, 313, 315, 316, 317, 319, 327, 328, 338; in Congo, 173; in Cyprus, 262–63; and Dayton Agreements, 232; as destabilizing, 314; in Eastern Slavonia, 224, 229; in El Salvador, 200, 201, 202, 205, 207, 208, 323, 328; and ethnicity, 38; and impartiality vs. neutrality, 13; institutions for, 314, 316; monitoring of, 7, 46–47; and peace operations, 15, 50, 66, 199; reform of, 314; in Rwanda, 288, 290; in Somalia, 154; and transitional authority, 324. See also democracy
electricity consumption: as indicator, 83; summary statistics on, 141, 142. See also local capacities
El Salvador, 2, 59, 77, 305, 318, 321, 331; Ad Hoc Commission in, 206, 324; Agreement on Human Rights, 207; and Cambodia, 205, 212; and Dayton Agreements, 231; death squads in, 201, 209; Forum for Social and Economic Consultation, 209; and Friends of the Secretary-General, 306; and Joint Group, 206; National Civilian Police, 208; National Council for the Defense of Human Rights, 208; peacebuilding in, 15, 17, 199, 200–209, 322–24, 342–43, 345, 349; Supreme Court, 208; Truth Commission in, 202, 206, 324
employment, 154, 163, 171, 239
enosis, 257–58, 261, 264, 265
EOKA B, 261, 264, 265, 276
equidistance, policy of, 181. See also impartiality; neutrality
Erdut Agreement, 306, 330
Eritrea, 326
Esquipulas II Agreement, 201
Ethiopia, 77, 146, 147

ethnic cleansing: in Bosnia, 167, 169, 171,
    185; in Cyprus, 261; prevention of, 184;
    in United States, 235. *See also* genocide;
    war crimes
ethnic fractionalization: and civil war, 36,
    37, 38–39; and civil war recurrence,
    336; and hostility, 82; and intervention,
    44; and peacebuilding success, 94, 101,
    102; summary statistics on, 139
ethnicity, 19, 29; in Brcko, 235, 238, 239;
    in Brcko Arbitration, 237; in Cambodia,
    210, 211; and civil war, 36–40, 82; in
    Congo, 172, 180; and cooperation, 55;
    in Croatia, 226; in Cyprus, 257–58, 259,
    260, 262, 264, 266, 268; in Eastern
    Slavonia, 224; in East Timor, 245; and
    economy, 33; and El Salvador, 203, 204;
    and fear of victimization, 38; in former
    Yugoslavia, 163, 169, 170; and hostility,
    75, 82, 349; and partition, 48–49; and
    peacebuilding success, 101–3, 118; and
    rebel cohesion, 43; in Rwanda, 281,
    282, 283, 284, 285, 286, 295, 301; in
    Somalia, 158, 159; and sovereign peace,
    99; summary statistics on, 139. *See
    also* hostility
ethnoreligious war, 87, 89, 96–97, 127
Europe, 194, 339
European Court of Human Rights, 232
European Union, 8, 171, 187, 258, 278,
    279, 347
extremists: in Cyprus, 261, 262, 264, 265,
    268, 271, 275; in Eastern Slavonia, 229;
    identification of, 57, 58; in Rwanda,
    282, 286, 287, 292, 293, 294, 296, 297,
    298. *See also* factions
Ezenbel, Turkish foreign minister, 277

factions: in Angola, 322; in Bosnia, 322,
    329; in Brcko, 243, 322; in Cambodia,
    210, 211, 212, 213, 214–15, 217–18,
    313, 315, 322, 325–26, 327, 328;
    changes in, 349; and civil war types, 51;
    coherence of, 321, 322, 324, 325, 329,
    331; in Congo, 173, 174, 177, 180, 183,
    194, 322; consent of, 60; in Croatia,
    226, 227; in Cyprus, 260, 262, 265,
    268, 271, 276, 277, 322; in Eastern
    Slavonia, 229, 322; in East Timor, 245,
    246, 247, 322, 325; in El Salvador,
    201, 204, 205, 322, 322; in former

Yugoslavia, 162, 163, 170, 227; in
    Georgia, 322; in Guatemala, 322; in
    Haiti, 322; help in negotiations among,
    48; and hostility, 65–66, 82; identifica-
    tion of, 50, 57, 58; instability of, 198;
    and international capacities, 331; and is-
    sue indivisibility, 50; in Liberia, 322; and
    mandate design, 65; in Mozambique,
    322; in Namibia, 322; and natural re-
    source dependence, 106–7; number of,
    4, 82, 126, 127, 321, 322, 324, 325,
    329, 331, 336; and peacebuilding ecolo-
    gies, 322, 324, 329, 331; and peace-
    building success, 100–101, 126, 127; in
    Rwanda, 1, 282, 283, 285, 286, 287,
    288, 292, 293, 295, 296, 297, 298, 322;
    in Sierra Leone, 322; in Somalia, 146,
    147, 148, 149, 151, 152, 153–54, 155,
    156, 157, 159, 160, 322; and spoiler
    problems, 58; and stalemate, 305; sum-
    mary statistics on, 140; in Tajikistan,
    322; and transitional authority, 321–22;
    and transitional strategy, 63, 319; and
    UNOSOM, 150; in West Sahara, 322.
    See also extremists; hostility; military,
    factional; moderates; spoilers
Falintil. *See* Armed Forces of the
    National Liberation of East
    Timor (Falintil)
Farabundo Martí National Liberation
    Front (FMLN), 200, 202, 205, 206, 207,
    305, 323, 324
Farrand, R. William, 238, 240, 330, 331
Federated State of Northern Cyprus, 277
Federation Brka, 235
FMLN. *See* Farabundo Martí National
    Liberation Front
force: and impartiality vs. neutrality, 13;
    nonuse of, 308, 348–49; in traditional
    peace operations, 12; and UN Charter,
    311. *See also* peace enforcement
France: and Cambodia, 218, 220, 305,
    307, 326; and Congo, 145; and former
    Yugoslavia, 187, 306; and ONUC, 182;
    and Rwanda, 286, 287, 292, 293, 299,
    306–7; on Security Council, 9; and UN-
    AMIR, 289, 297; and UNPROFOR, 192
Fretilin. *See* Revolutionary Front for an In-
    dependent East Timor (Fretilin)
Friends of the Secretary-General, 203,
    305–8, 339, 346

FUNCINPEC. *See* National United Front for an Independent, Neutral, Peaceful, and Co-operative Cambodia

game theory, 51, 100
GDP: in Cambodia, 210, 222; in Congo, 179, 180; in Croatia, 225, 226; in Cyprus, 260; in East Timor, 245, 251; in El Salvador, 204; in former Yugoslavia, 170; and local capacities, 83; and participatory peace, 106; in peacebuilding triangle, 4; in Rwanda, 283; in Somalia, 159; summary statistics on, 142, 143. *See also* local capacities
General Assembly, 12, 60, 177, 182, 244
genocide: and civil war types, 117; in Rwanda, 19, 55, 281, 282, 285, 288, 292, 294, 295, 297, 298, 300, 301. *See also* ethnic cleansing; massacre; war crimes
Genocide Convention, 7, 298
Georgia, 77, 306, 322
Germany, 194, 306
Gizenga, Antoine, 174, 178
Gobbi, Hugo, 279
Golan Heights, 14
Gorazde, 171, 192
government: authorization by, 320; in Brcko, 240; of Cambodia, 214–15, 217, 218–19, 221, 222, 315, 327; of Congo, 172, 173, 175, 176, 177, 178, 179, 180, 181, 183; in Croatia, 225; of Cyprus, 257–58, 262; in East Timor, 246, 248, 249–50, 254; of El Salvador, 200, 201, 202, 208, 322–24; in former Yugoslavia, 163; of Iraq, 341; of Rwanda, 285, 286, 287–88, 291; and self-determination, 194; in Somalia, 146, 147, 151–52, 154–55, 158, 159. *See also* military, government; transitional administration
Greece, 77, 257, 258, 259, 261, 263, 264, 265, 275
Greek Cypriots, 257, 259, 261, 262, 263, 266, 268, 271, 273, 274, 276, 277, 278, 279, 280
Grivas, George, 261, 264, 276
Guatemala, 2, 78, 306, 321, 322, 324–25
Guinea-Bissau, 78
Gulf War, 2, 15
Gurr, Ted Robert, 35
Gusmão, Xana, 250

Habibie, B. J., 246
Habr Gedir, 147
Habyarimana, Juvenal, 285, 286, 287, 292, 293, 295, 296, 297, 299
Haiti, 8, 78, 184, 191, 196, 215, 231, 306, 320, 322, 325, 349
Hammarskjold, Dag, 12, 145, 176, 177, 178, 181, 182, 187
Hegre, Håvard, 35
Herzegovina, 165, 168
Hobbes, Thomas, 18, 29, 30, 338
Hoeffler, Anke, 101
Horowitz, Donald L., 37
Horta, José Ramos, 246
hostility: in Bosnia, 325, 329; in Cambodia, 210, 211, 328; and civil war, 43; in Congo, 179, 180, 181, 182; cooperative vs. competitive interaction of, 70; in Croatia, 225, 226, 227; in Cyprus, 257–58, 259, 260, 272; and deaths, 65, 342; dimensions of, 65–66; and displacements, 342; dual effects of, 69; in East Timor, 245, 246, 247; and economy, 105; elements of, 334; and El Salvador, 203, 204; and ethnicity, 75, 82, 349; and factions, 65–66, 82; in former Yugoslavia, 169, 170; indicators of, 75, 82–83; and international assistance, 110; and international capacities, 67, 131, 331, 335; and motivations for civil war, 29, 30; and observer missions, 112; and peacebuilding ecology, 329, 331; and peacebuilding success, 4, 96–104, 118, 124, 125, 126, 127, 131; in peacebuilding triangle, 4, 64; and peace treaty, 82–83; and refugees, 65; in Rwanda, 98, 99, 281, 282, 283, 294, 296; in Somalia, 156, 157–58, 160; summary statistics on, 139; and transitional authority, 321; and transitional strategy, 63, 319. *See also specific indicators*
Howe, Jonathan, 156
human rights, 318; in Bosnia and Herzegovina, 233; in Cambodia, 214, 216, 218, 221; and Dayton Agreements, 231, 232; in East Timor, 246, 255; in El Salvador, 201, 202, 204, 206, 207, 208, 324; and institutional reconstruction, 314; international protection of, 7; and multidimensional peacekeeping, 199; and peace, 73; promotion of, 17; in

human rights (*continued*)
Rwanda, 289, 291; and self-determination, 194; in Somalia, 158; and UNAMIR, 291
Human Rights Watch, 255, 293
Hun Sen, 211, 217, 219, 221
Hussein, Saddam, 9, 194n
Hutus, 1, 285, 286, 288, 293, 296, 298, 300, 302

ICC. *See* International Criminal Court
ICFY. *See* International Conference on the Former Yugoslavia
ICTR. *See* International Criminal Tribunal for Rwanda
ideology, 28, 29, 33, 37, 211
IFOR. *See* NATO Implementation Force
Ignatieff, Michael, 312
Ileo, Joseph, 175
impartiality, 8, 308, 348–49; and Congo, 182, 194; debate over, 193; definition of, 13; and former Yugoslavia, 169; of France in Rwanda, 299; maintenance of, 60, 61; multilateral, 318; and regional powers, 42; and UNTAC, 317. *See also* neutrality
income, 34; in former Yugoslavia, 163; as indicator of local capacities, 83, 84; and peacebuilding success, 98, 105, 118; and sovereign peace, 117, 118; and war recurrence, 106. *See also* local capacities
India, 38, 78, 187, 194
Indian peacekeepers, 178–79
Indonesia, 78, 218, 221, 244, 245, 252, 255–56, 325
Indonesian military, 244, 245–46, 247, 248
Indonesian People's Consultative Assembly, 248
information: in Cambodia, 216, 221, 223, 232, 234; and Dayton Agreement, 232; flow of, 49; provision of, 52. *See also* communication
infrastructure: in Cyprus, 270; and Dayton Agreements, 231; in East Timor, 244, 245, 251; of former Yugoslavia, 168
institutions, 19; in Cambodia, 313; and civil war recurrence, 132; collapse of, 39; and colonialism, 310; for democracy, 315–16; in El Salvador, 59, 202, 206, 208, 209; failure of, 46; and local

capacities, 67, 84; and natural resource dependence, 107; and peacebuilding, 5, 56, 314; rebuilding of, 46, 312–16; in Somalia, 153, 157, 160; transformation of, 59; trust in, 47
INTERFET. *See* International Force in East Timor
Interhamwe, 287, 318
international capacities, 67; and Angola, 325; and Cambodia, 210, 211; and Congo, 180, 181, 182, 183; cooperative vs. competitive interaction of, 70; and Croatia, 226, 227; and Cyprus, 259, 260; dual effects of, 69; and East Timor, 245, 247; and economic assistance, 85; elements of, 335; and El Salvador, 204; and factions, 331; and former Yugoslavia, 169, 170; and hostility, 67, 131, 331, 335; indicators of, 84–86; and local capacities, 67, 131, 335; and motivations for civil war, 30–31; and peacebuilding ecology, 328; and peacebuilding success, 4, 108–15, 124, 125, 131; in peacebuilding triangle, 4, 64–65; and Rwanda, 282, 283, 294; and Somalia, 159; summary statistics on, 140; and UN presence and mandate, 84–85
International Committee on the Reconstruction of Cambodia, 216, 306
International Committee of the Red Cross, 270
International Conference on the Former Yugoslavia (ICFY), 187
International Criminal Court (ICC), 255
International Criminal Tribunal for the former Yugoslavia, 224, 235
International Criminal Tribunal for Rwanda (ICTR), 284, 291, 300
International Force in East Timor (INTERFET), 247, 248, 250, 253, 256
International Monetary Fund, 163, 220, 344
International Organization for Migration, 252
International Police Task Force, 232, 233, 240
Ioaniddes, Brigadier, 265
Iran, 78, 162
Iraq, 2, 8, 14, 15, 78, 160, 339, 341
Ireland, 270
Israel, 12, 14, 78

issue indivisibility, 47–48, 50
Italy, 146, 347

Janvier, Bernard, 193
Japan, 194, 221, 251, 256, 305, 306
Jelisic, Goran, 235
Jones, Bruce, 294
Jordan, 79
judiciary: in Bosnia and Herzegovina, 234; in Cambodia, 215, 222; cultivation of, 316; in Cyprus, 268, 269; in East Timor, 250, 255; in El Salvador, 202, 205, 208, 323, 324; reform of, 314; in Somalia, 153. *See also* law/law and order
Jugoslav National Army, 235
justice, transitional, 313

Kabila, Laurent, 301
Kagame, Paul, 286
Kalyvas, Stathis, 45
Karzai, Hamid, 338–39
Kasavubu, Joseph, 173, 177, 179, 181
Katanga, 172, 173, 174, 176, 177, 178, 179, 180, 181, 186, 316
Katanga Rule, 17
Kayibanda, Gregoire, 285
Kenya, 79, 151
Khmer People's National Liberation Front (KPLNF), 217, 218
Khmer Rouge, 211, 306, 325; collapse of, 221; and elections, 232, 317; and genocide, 327; as guerrilla insurgency, 313; illicit trade by, 315; legitimacy of, 327; and natural resources, 43, 221; and peace process, 211; resumption of violence by, 2; rise of, 326; support for, 304, 307; and UNTAC operation, 219
Kigali, 288, 289, 290, 293, 298
Klanac, 236, 238, 330–31
Klein, Jacques, 228, 330
Korea, 2, 15, 79, 144, 346
Kosovo, 2, 43, 91, 162, 171, 223, 230, 320, 333
KPNLF. *See* Khmer People's National Liberation Front
Krajina, 169, 171, 330
Kurds, 194n
Kuwait, 14

Lake, D., 41
Laos, 79

Lapresle, Bertrand De, 187
law/law and order: in Bosnia and Herzegovina, 234; in Cambodia, 215, 217; in Cyprus, 267; in Eastern Slavonia, 229; in East Timor, 255; in El Salvador, 202, 209; importance of, 340; and transitional justice, 313; and UNOSOM, 152. *See also* judiciary; police; security
Lebanon, 79, 113
Leviathan, 18, 29, 153, 338
Lewis, Meriwether, 235
Liberia, 79, 107, 322
Liu, F. T., 12
local capacities: in Cambodia, 210, 211, 213, 325; and civil war recurrence, 118; in Congo, 172, 179, 180, 181, 182, 183; cooperative vs. competitive interaction of, 70; in Croatia, 225, 226, 227; in Cyprus, 259, 260; dimensions of, 66–67; dual effects of, 69; in East Timor, 245, 246, 247, 256; elements of, 334–35; and El Salvador, 203, 204; in former Yugoslavia, 169, 170, 227; indicators of, 83–84; and international assistance, 110; and international capacities, 67, 131, 335; and motivations for civil war, 30; and observer missions, 112; and peacebuilding ecology, 325; and peacebuilding success, 104–8, 118, 124, 125, 126, 127, 131, 335, 336, 337; in peacebuilding triangle, 4, 64; and probability of success, 4; in Rwanda, 281, 283, 284, 294; in Somalia, 156, 157, 160; and transitional authority, 321, 322, 324; and war recurrence, 40. *See also specific indicators*
Lumumba, Patrice, 172, 173, 174, 177, 181, 182
Lundula, Victor, 174

Macedonia, 162, 165, 168
Makarios III, 258, 261, 262–65, 266, 276, 280
Malayan insurgency, 192
Malaysia, 218
Mali, 79
mandate: in Bosnia, 329; in Cambodia, 210; and characteristics of factions, 65; coding of, 84–85; confusion in, 308–9; and cooperation, 56; in Croatia, 180, 226; in Cyprus, 260; design of, 20, 21, 22, 315; in East Timor, 245; effectiveness

mandate (*continued*)
  of, 113; in El Salvador, 204; force used
  in defense of, 59; in former Yugoslavia,
  170; and impartiality vs. neutrality, 13;
  implementation of, 59, 60, 303; and implementation delay, 188, 309, 347; and
  international capacities, 84–85; international legitimacy of, 14; and multilateral
  principles, 346; as obsolescing bargain,
  309; operational amendment of, 61,
  62–63; and peace, 20–21; and peacebuilding success, 90, 109, 110; in peacebuilding triangle, 4; and peacekeeping
  troop level, 112–13; in peace operations,
  11; and peace treaty, 111; and resource
  use, 132; robust, 301; in Rwanda, 283;
  in Somalia, 159; and sovereign peace,
  106; and success vs. failure, 62; summary statistics on, 140; and transitional
  authority, 311, 315; and type of conflict,
  57, 112; weak, 112, 113, 115, 228n,
  261. See also specific United Nations
  missions
Mandela, Nelson, 321
Manifesto Group, 147
Mansoura-Kokkina enclave, 264, 274
massacre: in Cambodia, 127; in Congo,
  175, 177; in Eastern Slavonia, 225; in
  East Timor, 245–46; in Rwanda, 185,
  291, 295. See also ethnic cleansing;
  genocide; war crimes
media, 188; in Cambodia, 232, 234,
  315–16; in Congo, 177; and free press,
  314; in Rwanda, 286, 293, 300n; and
  UNTAC, 216, 221, 223, 235, 315–16.
  See also communication
Mexico, 201, 306
Mexico Agreement, 202
Middle East, 106
military, factional, 66; in Bosnia, 329; in
  Brcko, 235, 236, 238; in Cambodia, 54,
  213, 214, 215–16, 219, 220, 315, 327;
  cantonment of, 15, 66, 154, 199, 213,
  214, 215, 216, 219, 220, 290, 315; and
  Congo, 174, 175, 180; in Cyprus, 258,
  261, 263, 268, 271, 274, 276, 278, 279;
  and demilitarization, 206, 224, 229,
  268; demobilization of, 54, 199, 213,
  214, 215–16, 220, 291, 314, 327; in
  Eastern Slavonia, 225, 229; in East
  Timor, 246, 247, 248, 252, 253, 255,

325; in El Salvador, 200, 201, 202, 206,
  207; and former Yugoslavia, 165; and
  institutional reconstruction, 314; in
  multidimensional peace operations, 15;
  political transformation of, 54, 56; in
  Rwanda, 285, 286, 287, 288, 290, 291,
  292, 295, 302; in Somalia, 147, 149,
  150, 152, 153, 154, 158, 160; and
  UNITAF, 154; unsuccessful, 57; and
  UNTAES, 224; weapons of, 48, 149,
  150, 152, 153, 154, 165, 206, 207, 216,
  225, 290, 292, 294. See also factions
military, government: in Cambodia, 222; in
  Congo, 174, 175; in El Salvador, 202,
  204, 206, 208, 323, 324; and former
  Yugoslavia, 165; and peace treaties, 104;
  per capita size of, 86; rebuilding of, 47,
  67; of Rwanda, 285, 286, 288, 295,
  300; of Somalia, 147; training of, 316.
  See also government
military, United Nations: in Bosnia, 329; in
  Brcko, 240; in Cambodia, 211, 215–16,
  219; and Congo, 176, 182; and cooperation, 56; coordination with civilian missions by, 187; in Cyprus, 270–77; and
  Dayton Agreements, 231, 232; in
  Eastern Slavonia, 228; in East Timor,
  249; in El Salvador, 206; force strength
  of, 112–13; and former Yugoslavia, 165;
  geographic deployment of, 60; and
  humanitarian assistance, 155; new interventionism of, 6; in peacebuilding triangle, 4; in Somalia, 148, 150, 151, 152,
  153, 154, 155, 156, 160; in traditional
  peace operations, 12; withdrawal of, 92.
  See also command and control; peace
  enforcement; peacekeeping; specific
  United Nations missions
military victory, 5, 44, 45, 46, 49, 86, 87,
  88, 89, 92, 99, 100, 104, 140, 203. See
  also peace
Milosevic, Slobodan, 171, 227,
  317–18, 330
Ministerial Conference on Rehabilitation
  and Reconstruction of Cambodia, 216
Mission of the United Nations in El Salvador (MINUSAL), 205
Mitchell, C. R., 312
Mladic, Ratko, 167
MNC. See Mouvement National Congolais
  (Congolese National Movement, MNC)

Mobutu, Joseph Desire, 174, 175, 179, 181, 183, 184
moderates: in Brcko, 243; in Cyprus, 261, 262, 276, 311; in Eastern Slavonia, 229; identification of, 50, 57, 58; in Rwanda, 1, 285, 294, 295, 296; and spoiler problems, 58. See also factions
Mogadishu, 147, 151, 153, 154, 284
Moldova, 79
monitoring: in Bosnia and Herzegovina, 233; in Cambodia, 214, 216; and cooperation, 56; and coordination problems, 49; in Cyprus, 277; of elections, 7; in El Salvador, 206, 207, 209, 324; and institutional reconstruction, 314; in multidimensional peace operations, 14, 199; and peacekeeping troop level, 113; in Rwanda, 290, 296, 297; summary statistics on, 141; in traditional peace operations, 12, 14, 144; and transparency, 65–66; and trust, 5; by UNAMIR, 289; and UNOSOM, 150
Montenegro, 165
Montgomery, Thomas, 185
Mouvement National Congolais (Congolese National Movement, MNC), 173, 174
Mouvement republicain national pour la democratie et le developpement (MRND), 286
Movimento Popular de Libertação de Angola (MPLA), 305
Mozambique, 2, 15, 17, 79, 199, 306, 315, 317, 322, 325, 326, 349
MPLA. See Movimento Popular de Libertação de Angola
MRND. See Mouvement republicain national pour la democratie et le developpement
multilateralism: assertive, 9, 144; and Congo operations, 194; and peacebuilding, 3; and strategy, 195; success of, 5, 318; and UN, 5, 189, 195–96, 318; and United States, 9; and UNTAC, 220–21
Multinational Force in Lebanon, 196
Museveni, Yowerei, 286
Muslim-Croat federation, 230
Myanmar/Burma, 79

Namibia, 2, 15, 17, 79, 199, 215, 219, 306, 317, 322, 349

National Commission for the Consolidation of Peace (COPAZ), 202, 311, 322
National Consultative Council, in East Timor, 250, 311
nationalism, 37, 163, 193, 195, 227, 265
Nationalist Republican Alliance party (ARENA), 305, 323–24
National United Front for an Independent, Neutral, Peaceful, and Co-operative Cambodia (FUNCINPEC), 210, 221–22, 325, 327
NATO: and Bosnia, 2, 85, 192; and Brcko, 235; and command and control, 187; and Cyprus, 258; and former Yugoslavia, 168, 169; and peace in Kosovo, 91; and UNTAES, 229
NATO Implementation Force (IFOR), 17, 231, 232, 240, 343
natural resources: and Cambodia, 212; and civil war, 34–35, 43; and civil war recurrence, 35, 106, 108; competition over, 67; and Congo, 174; in Cyprus, 259; and Khmer Rouge, 221; and local capacities, 83, 84; and peacebuilding success, 106–8, 118; in Rwanda, 284; and war recurrence, 35. See also local capacities
Ndiaye, Bacre Waly, 289
neocolonialism, 19–20
neoliberalism, 40–41, 42, 51
neorealism, 40–41, 42, 51
Nepal, 79
Netherlands, 167, 187
Neutral International Force (NIF), 289
neutrality, 12, 13, 154, 193, 308, 316. See also impartiality
New York Agreement, 202
New Zealand, 256
Nicaragua, 79, 215, 305, 306
Nicosia International Airport, 274, 278
Nigeria, 79, 191, 195
nonethnic wars, 87, 89
non-UN operations, 113–14, 141, 347
Norodom Ranariddh, 211, 217, 313
Norodom Sihanouk, 217, 219, 307, 321, 326, 327, 328
North Atlantic Council, 231
Northern Ireland, 43
Ntaryamira, Cyprien, 293

Oakley, Robert B., 155
O'Brien, Conor Cruise, 178, 188

observer mission, 84; in Bosnia and Herzegovina, 233; in Cambodia, 215; and cooperation, 112; and coordination, 112; effectiveness of, 113; in El Salvador, 203; and former Yugoslavia, 165; numbers considered, 88; and peacebuilding success, 109; and peacekeeping troop level, 113; in Rwanda, 284; success of, 112

Office of the High Representative in Bosnia and Herzegovina, 232, 235, 240, 242, 243, 329

Ogaden region, 146

Ogata, Sadako, 338–39

OHR. See Office of the High Representative in Bosnia and Herzegovina

oil exports: and Cambodia, 210; and Congo, 180; in Croatia, 226; in Cyprus, 259, 260; in East Timor, 245; and El Salvador, 204; in former Yugoslavia, 170; and local capacities, 83, 84; and peacebuilding success, 107–8; in Rwanda, 283; in Somalia, 159; summary statistics on, 142. See also local capacities

Oman, 79

ONUMOZ. See United Nations Operations in Mozambique

Operation des Nations Unies en Congo (ONUC), 172, 175–85, 186, 187, 194; mandate of, 176–77, 180, 184

Operation Restore Hope, 148–49

Operation Turquoise, 297, 299

Organization of African Unity (OAU), 8, 287, 296

Organization of American States, 8

Organization for Security and Cooperation in Europe, 306

Organization of Security and Cooperation for Europe (OSCE), 232, 329, 347

OSCE. See Organization of Security and Cooperation for Europe

Ovcara massacre, 225

Owen, David, 163

Owen, Roberts, 238, 239

Pakistan, 79, 152, 153, 155, 187

Palamas, Christos, 265

Panama, 201

Papandreou, George, 264

Papua New Guinea, 79

Paraguay, 80

Paris Peace Agreements, 212, 213, 214, 216, 217, 218, 305, 311, 317, 328

Paris Peace Conferences, 327

partition, 2, 48–49, 171, 262, 266, 277, 331. See also buffer zone

peace: alternatives to, 346–51; in Brcko, 236; comprehensive, 20; consent to, 19; and Dayton Agreements, 230, 231, 232; definition of, 18–19; and democracy, 19; durable, 15; duration of, 111, 122–25; and El Salvador, 203; and factions, 65; and former Yugoslavia, 169; of the grave, 73; imposition of, 20; lenient, 18n, 73; and mandate fulfillment, 20–21; and multidimensional peace operations, 15; negative, 18, 335, 337; participatory, 18–19, 73, 74, 75, 88, 90, 93, 94–95, 96, 103, 106, 107, 110, 112, 117, 124, 136, 137; positive, 18–19, 335; self-sustaining, 14, 19, 56, 59–60, 64–65, 74, 85, 91–92, 112, 192, 321; sovereign, 18, 73, 75, 88, 90, 96, 99, 107, 108, 110, 112, 117–18, 124, 136, 137, 337; success vs. failure in, 62; sustainable, 4, 21, 231, 232, 236; and transitional authority, 321; utility of, 43. See also military victory

peacebuilding: aims of, 22–23; Boutros-Ghali on, 350; in Cambodia, 76, 117, 209–23, 325, 343, 345; and civil war onset vs. duration, 45; in Congo, 180, 183, 194; cost of, 156, 171, 182, 342–45; in Croatia, 226; in Cyprus, 260, 261, 269; dataset for, 72–86; and Dayton Agreements, 231; through devolution, 250; dynamic model of, 59–63; in Eastern Slavonia, 228; in East Timor, 245, 246–56; ecologies of, 322–28, 329–30, 331; and economy, 5, 56; in El Salvador, 200–209, 322–24, 342–43, 345; failure of, 93; in former Yugoslavia, 169, 170; and institutions, 5, 56, 314; and issue indivisibility, 47–48, 50; and mandate type, 90; and military victory, 5, 88, 89; multidimensional, 267, 269, 314; and multidimensional peacekeeping, 199; and multilateralism, 3; participatory, 103; and peacekeeping, 49, 74; and peace operation duration, 92; and peace process, 91; and rationality, 43; regional dimensions of, 42; as revolutionary/counterrevolutionary, 337–38; and risk-spreading, 314; and robustness tests, 116–19; in Rwanda, 80, 282, 283, 284, 296, 297; and security, 5; seven steps for, 337–42; in Somalia, 80, 145–61, 331, 345; sustainable peace through, 4; three generational paradigms of, 11; time needed for, 338; trust in, 308–9; and war type, 89

peacebuilding, failure of: in Cyprus, 261; in Rwanda, 294, 348, 349; in Somalia, 348, 349

peacebuilding, success of, 6, 27; in Cambodia, 15, 17, 127, 199, 211, 336, 349; and civil war type, 89; and Congo, 182–83; in Croatia, 227; in dynamic model of peacekeeping, 59–63; in Eastern Slavonia, 15, 17, 171, 199, 349; in East Timor, 246, 255–56; in El Salvador, 15, 17, 199, 203, 349; and hostility indicators, 96–104, 335, 336; index models of, 123–25; and local capacities, 104–8, 118, 124, 125, 126, 127, 131, 335, 336, 337; logit models of, 94–95; and peacebuilding triangle, 69–75, 334, 335; and peace treaty, 5, 60, 88, 89, 103–4, 116, 118, 126, 129, 130, 131, 336, 349–50; and policy analysis, 125–32; in Rwanda, 98, 99, 127, 282, 336; in short run, 86–93; in Somalia, 17, 184; and transformational peacebuilding, 336; and UN peace operations, 109–16

peacebuilding, transformational: in Cambodia, 210; in Congo, 180; in Croatia, 226; in Cyprus, 260; in East Timor, 245; in El Salvador, 204; in former Yugoslavia, 170; and peacebuilding success, 336; in Rwanda, 283; in Somalia, 158, 159

peacebuilding triangle, 64; and Cambodia, 211, 212; and Congo, 180, 181, 182; and Croatia, 227; and Cyprus, 258–59; and East Timor, 247; elements of, 4–5, 63–68, 69–71, 334–35; and El Salvador, 203, 204; and former Yugoslavia, 169, 171; logistic regressions of, 93; and probability of success, 4–5; and Rwanda, 281–82; and Somalia, 156, 157

peace enforcement: administration of state in, 66; in Cambodia, 317; and Chapter 6 as variable, 84; in combined strategy, 58, 63; in Congo, 182, 183, 316, 317; and cooperation, 52, 55, 58; and coordination, 52, 53, 58; in Cyprus, 267, 318; defined, 10; design of, 316–19; in Eastern Slavonia, 317–18; and elections, 66; failures in, 2; in former Yugoslavia, 162; growth in, 7; and hostility, 66; implementation of, 57; and mandate, 84; in multidimensional peace operations, 15, 199; and multilateralism, 3; in Namibia, 317; numbers considered, 88; and peacebuilding success, 109; and peace duration, 123; and peacekeeping, 50, 109, 109, 349; and police, 66; positive influence of, 109; risk of, 316; in Rwanda, 318; in Somalia, 16, 18, 157, 158, 186, 317; and spoilers, 58; success of, 6, 111; in third generation peace operations, 15–17; and transitional authority, 64. *See also* military, United Nations

peacekeeping: Boutros-Ghali on, 350; budgets for, 6; and civil war theory, 49–50; and civil war types, 56; and combined portfolio, 318–19; in combined strategy, 58, 59, 63; combining multidimensional missions, 109; command structure of, 60; and conflict identification, 51; and Congo, 181, 183; and consent, 50, 56, 144; and cooperation, 52, 54–56; and coordination, 52, 53–54, 188; credibility of, 49; in Cyprus, 266, 267, 270; and cyprusization, 278; as delegated to national action, 346; dynamic model of, 310–12; in East Timor, 253; and elections, 50; in El Salvador, 207; facilitative vs. transformational, 109; financial and logistical support for, 60; first generation, 11, 12–14; in former Yugoslavia, 164, 166, 186; growth in, 7; impartiality of, 61; and impartiality vs. neutrality, 13; and imposed settlement, 46; and information, 49; interstate, 144; and issues in conflict, 50; leadership in, 318; and moderates, 50; Pakistani, 152, 153, 155; and peace agreements, 49–50; and peacebuilding, 49, 74; and peace enforcement, 50, 109, 199, 349; and peacemaking, 61; and peace treaty, 57; and peace violations, 50; and reconstruction, 61; regional, 347; in Rwanda, 113, 301; and security, 49; and self-defense,

peacekeeping (*continued*)
12; and self-sustaining peace, 91; in Somalia, 161, 186; and status quo, 50; success of, 6, 27, 59–63, 74, 266; and transitional authority, 63; trust in, 308–9; by
UNAMIR, 289; UN budget for, 345; and
victimization, 49; and war recurrence,
87; weak, 52, 53, 84, 112, 158, 181,
274, 282
peacekeeping, multidimensional, 14–15,
52, 109, 308–12, 319; in Cambodia,
130, 211, 213, 319; in East Timor,
248–50; effectiveness of, 113; and mandate, 84; numbers considered, 88; and
peacebuilding success, 109; and peace
duration, 123; in Rwanda, 130; and security, 314–15; in Somalia, 157; and
sovereign peace, 117; success in,
198–99, 319; summary statistics on,
141; transformation through, 197
peacekeeping, traditional, 197; in Congo,
145, 180; and coordination problems,
49; and Dayton Agreements, 230–31; elements of, 12–14; and failure of consent,
308; and force strength, 113; and international capacities, 84; and less hostile
circumstances, 65–66; and monitoring,
144; numbers considered, 88; and peacebuilding success, 109; in Rwanda, 297;
success of, 111–12
peacekeeping, transformational: in Congo,
180; and cooperation vs. coordination
conflicts, 53, 54, 56, 59; in East Timor,
245; and economy, 132; in El Salvador,
204; and force strength, 112; and hostility, 128; and institutions, 15, 24, 313; as
multidimensional, 109; and multidimensional operations, 109, 111; and peacebuilding success, 116; and politics, 312;
in Rwanda, 281; as significant variable,
110; and sovereign peace, 106, 117–18;
and success, 115, 116, 127, 336; summary statistics on, 141; and treaty, 131;
and UN force strength, 112–13
peacemaking, 304–8; Boutros-Ghali on,
350; and combined portfolio, 318–19; in
combined strategy, 58, 59, 63; and
Congo, 182; in Cyprus, 267, 270, 278,
279; defined, 10; in El Salvador, 202;
and issues in conflict, 50; and multidimensional peacekeeping, 199; and multi-

lateralism, 318; and peacekeeping, 61; in
Rwanda, 301; success of, 6; and transitional authority, 63; and treaty, 61; UN
success in, 13
peace operations: in Cambodia, 2; and
combined portfolio, 318–19; and Dayton Agreements, 230–31; as designed to
fit case, 5; duration of, 92; facilitative,
115–16; multidimensional, 2, 231, 282;
and peacebuilding success, 109–15; in
Rwanda, 282; second generation, 11,
14–15; and self-sustaining self-
determination, 310–11; and sovereignty,
11; as stimulus to peace, 92; strong, 84;
third generation, 11, 15–17; timing of,
132; troop contributions to, 17; and
withdrawal of UN military, 92
peace process: in combined strategy, 59;
opportunity structures in, 27; and peacebuilding, 91; success of, 27, 91
peace treaty/negotiated settlement, 46, 86,
87; advantages of, 304–5; in Angola, 2;
in Cambodia, 210, 211, 213, 214, 216,
217, 304, 310; in Congo, 172, 180; and
consent, 340; contradictions in, 308–9;
and cooperation, 55; in Croatia, 226; in
Cyprus, 259, 260, 304, 331; design of,
315; in East Timor, 245; in El Salvador,
204; enforcement of, 48; erosion of,
310; and ethnolinguistic fractionalization, 102; and factions, 100–101; in former Yugoslavia, 168, 170; and hostility,
82–83; and impartiality vs. neutrality,
13; importance of, 304–5; lack of, 16;
and mandate, 111; and multidimensional peacekeeping, 199; and negotiated
settlement, 82–83; and partition, 29; and
peacebuilding failures, 257; and peacebuilding success, 5, 60, 88, 89, 103–4,
116, 118, 126, 129, 130, 131, 336,
349–50; and peacekeeping, 49–50; and
peacemaking, 61; as peace stimulus, 92;
in Rwanda, 2, 283, 287, 290, 331; in
Somalia, 150, 154, 157, 159, 160; summary statistics on, 139, 140; in third
generation peace operations, 16; and
transitional authority, 311, 315, 324;
and war recurrence, 87, 88; and war
type, 57. *See also* reconciliation;
truce/cease fire
Pearson, Lester, 12

Pérez de Cuellar, Javier, 203, 278, 279–80
Peru, 8, 80
Philippines, 80
PLO, 162
police: in Bosnia and Herzegovina, 232, 233; and Brcko, 239, 240, 241; in Cambodia, 216, 222; in Cyprus, 268, 269, 270; and Dayton Agreements, 231, 232; in Eastern Slavonia, 224, 229; in East Timor, 253–54; in El Salvador, 205, 208, 323; rebuilding of, 67; in Rwanda, 290; in Somalia, 150, 152, 154; training of, 314, 316; and transitional authority, 324. *See also* law/law and order; security
police, United Nations: in Bosnia and Herzegovina, 232, 233; in Cambodia, 216; in Cyprus, 270, 271, 272, 277; in East Timor, 253, 254; and former Yugoslavia, 165; in multidimensional peace operations, 14; and UNITAF, 153
Port of Brcko, 236
Portugal, 243, 254
Posavina Corridor, 239
Prem Chand, Dewan, 273
Prisoner's Dilemma, 52, 54, 55, 56–57, 58, 66
property rights, 32, 231, 232, 243, 316, 340, 341

Radio Milles Collines, 293
Radio UNTAC, 216, 221, 235, 315–16
Ranariddh. *See* Norodom Ranariddh
Ravne Brcko, 235
reconciliation, 56, 64, 82, 229
reconstruction, 11, 22; and Cambodia, 215, 220, 222; and civil war recurrence, 110; in combined strategy, 58, 59, 63; and economy, 5, 83, 104–5, 132, 314; and force strength, 112; and former Yugoslavia, 169; of institutions, 46, 312–16; and local capacities, 66–67; and long-term goals, 339; and multidimensional missions, 110; and natural resource dependence, 107; and peacekeeping, 61, 112; and peace operation duration, 92; and success, 60; and transitional authority, 64; as transitional strategy, 311–12. *See also* assistance, reconstruction
refugees, 4; in Angola, 326; in Bosnia, 329; in Brcko Arbitration, 237; in Cambodia, 214, 216, 218, 315, 326; Croatian, 223,

225; in Cyprus, 270, 278; and Dayton Agreements, 231, 232; in Eastern Slavonia, 223, 224, 229; in East Timor, 248, 252–53; in former Yugoslavia, 161; and hostility, 65; in Mozambique, 326; in multidimensional peace operations, 15, 199; and peacebuilding success, 97; in Rwanda, 285, 286, 288, 290, 293, 300; in Somalia, 7–8, 146, 158; and UNOSOM, 149, 150
Regan, Patrick, 44
religion, 33, 40, 75, 87, 89, 96–97, 127, 203, 211
RENAMO. *See* Resistência Nacional Mozambicana
Renytjens, Filip, 286
Republika Srpska, 171, 187, 234–35, 237, 238, 239, 242, 330. *See also* Serbs
Resistência Nacional Mozambicana (RENAMO), 315, 317
Revolutionary Front for an Independent East Timor (Fretilin), 243–44
Revolutionary Movement for Democracy and Development (MNRD), 287
Revolutionary United Front (RUF), 318
Reynal-Querol, Marta, 101
Riza, Iqbal, 291
Roberts, Adam, 189
Rothchild, D., 41
Rousseau, Jean-Jacques, 53–54
RUF. *See* Revolutionary United Front
Russia: and Cambodia, 217, 307, 339; and former Yugoslavia, 162; national interests of, 191; peacebuilding outcomes in, 80; on Security Council, 9; and UNAMIR, 289; and UNPROFOR, 192. *See also* USSR
Rwanda, 1, 2, 3, 113, 117, 318, 322, 331; and Friends of the Secretary-General, 306–7; genocide in, 19, 55, 281, 282, 285, 288, 291, 293, 295, 297, 298, 299, 301; as member of Security Council, 295, 298; peacebuilding in, 80, 98, 99, 127, 281–302, 336, 348, 349; peace enforcement in, 318; peacekeeping in, 113, 130, 282, 298, 301; and United States, 184, 191
Rwandan Government Forces (RGF), 294, 299, 300
Rwandan Patriotic Front (RPF), 285, 286, 287, 288, 293, 295, 296, 298, 300

Rwandese Armed Forces (FAR), 285, 286, 287, 288
Rwigyema, Fred, 286

Sahnoun, Mohammed, 149, 153
Sambanis, Nicholas, 35, 41, 44, 101–2
Sanderson, John, 216, 219, 220, 313
San José Agreement on Human Rights, 202
Sarajevo, 16, 187, 192, 235
Savimbi, Jonas, 21, 305
secession, 4, 37, 39, 40, 43, 47
Secretariat: and easy vs. hard cases, 62; election monitoring by, 7; involvement of, 60; resources of, 188; and Rwanda, 293, 297, 302; spending by, 189; and strategy, 61; and UNAMIR, 296
Secretary-General: authorization of, 351; control of forces by, 12; and Cyprus, 263, 267, 275, 276; and Rwanda, 292; in traditional peace operations, 14; and UNAMIR, 289, 297; and UNPROFOR force strength, 166
security: in Afghanistan, 339; in Bosnia and Herzegovina, 233, 338; in Cambodia, 213, 338; in Cyprus, 267, 269; in East Timor, 253; in El Salvador, 209; and institutional reconstruction, 314; need for, 338–39; and peacekeeping, 49; for relief workers in Somalia, 148, 155; in Rwanda, 290, 291. See also judiciary; law/law and order; police
Security Council: authorization of, 9, 12, 351; and Chapter VII, 7; and East Timor, 244; and easy vs. hard cases, 62; and El Salvador, 205; and Esquipulas II Agreement, 201; Extended P5, 221, 305, 306; and former Yugoslavia, 8, 164, 168; and gap between resolutions and means, 185; as global parliament/global jury, 8–9; interventionism of, 1; involvement of, 60; and Iraq, 8; and mandates vs. resources, 188; membership of, 9, 351; and multilateralism, 195; and national interests, 193; and neutrality, 193; new interventionism of, 6; and ONUC, 175, 183; and preventive diplomacy, 7; Resolution 1035 (concerning Bosnia and Herzegovina), 233; Resolution 1088 (concerning Bosnia and Herzegovina), 233; Resolution 1103 (concerning Bosnia and Herzegovina), 233; Resolution 1144 (concerning Bosnia and Herzegovina), 233; Resolution 1168 (concerning Bosnia and Herzegovina), 234; Resolution 143 (concerning Congo), 176; Resolution 145 (concerning Congo), 176; Resolution 146 (concerning Congo), 176–77; Resolution 161 (concerning Congo), 176, 177; Resolution 169 (concerning Congo), 176, 178; Resolution 4387 (concerning Congo), 176–77; Resolution 186 (concerning Cyprus), 267; Resolution 1037 (concerning Eastern Slavonia), 224; Resolution 1079 (concerning Eastern Slavonia), 224; Resolution 1120 (concerning Eastern Slavonia), 224; Resolution 1246 (concerning East Timor), 247; Resolution 1264 (concerning East Timor), 248; Resolution 1272 (concerning East Timor), 249; Resolution 1319 (concerning East Timor), 249; Resolution 1338 (concerning East Timor), 249; Resolution 1392 (concerning East Timor), 249; Resolution 1410 (concerning East Timor), 253, 254; Resolution 1543 (concerning East Timor), 254; Resolution 693 (concerning El Salvador), 207; Resolution 729 (concerning El Salvador), 207; Resolution 832 (concerning El Salvador), 207; Resolution 920 (concerning El Salvador), 207; Resolution 872 (concerning Rwanda), 289, 290, 297; Resolution 912 (concerning Rwanda), 290; Resolution 918 (concerning Rwanda), 293; Resolution 925 (concerning Rwanda), 293; Resolution 794 (concerning Somalia), 148; Resolution 814 (concerning Somalia), 149, 150; Resolution 837 (concerning Somalia), 149; Resolution 897 (concerning Somalia), 149; Resolution 954 (concerning Somalia), 149; Resolution 749 (concerning Yugoslavia), 165; Resolution 758 (concerning Yugoslavia), 165; Resolution 762 (concerning Yugoslavia), 165; Resolution 769 (concerning Yugoslavia), 165; Resolution 776 (concerning Yugoslavia), 165; Resolution 779 (concerning Yugoslavia), 165; Resolution 795 (concerning Yugoslavia), 165; Resolution 819 (concerning

Yugoslavia), 167; Resolution 824 (concerning Yugoslavia), 167; Resolution 836 (concerning Yugoslavia), 167; and Rwanda, 292, 293, 295, 297, 298, 302; and sanctions, 7; and self-sustaining peace, 91; and Somalia, 155, 158; and strategic failures, 188; and strategy, 61; in traditional peace operations, 14; and transitional authority, 333; and UN-AMIR, 296; and UNPROFOR, 167, 168; and war-making, 193
self-determination, 39–40, 194, 244, 249
Senegal, 80
Serbs, 16, 162, 164; Bosnian, 164, 169; in Brcko, 235, 236, 238, 239, 241; and command and control, 187; and Croatia, 227; displaced, 331; and Eastern Slavonia, 223, 228, 229–30; and ethnic cleansing, 164, 184; failure to protect, 161; and federal unity, 168–69; and genocide, 55; and Ovcara massacre, 225; provocation by, 169; separateness of, 91; and UNPROFOR, 192; and UNTAES, 224. See also Republika Srpska
Sierra Leone, 80, 107, 191, 318, 322
Sihanouk. See Norodom Sihanouk
Sinai, 12
Slovenia, 163, 169
SNC. See Supreme National Council
SOC. See State of Cambodia
society: in Cambodia, 214; in Congo, 172; in El Salvador, 201, 202, 205, 206, 209; fractionalized, 118; polarized, 37, 38–39, 49, 100, 101, 102, 281, 282, 285; in Rwanda, 281, 282, 285; in Somalia, 146, 147
Somalia, 1, 7–8, 18, 19, 20, 184, 187, 192, 193, 320, 321, 322, 333; and Bosnia, 164; and Congo, 182; and Dayton Agreements, 231; famine in, 147–48, 151, 152, 153, 158; and former Yugoslavia, 169; and Friends of the Secretary-General, 307; peacebuilding in, 17, 80, 145–61, 184, 331, 345, 348, 349; peace enforcement in, 16, 18, 157–58, 159, 186, 317; peacekeeping in, 157–58, 161, 186, 187; and Rwanda, 284; and UN-AMIR, 296; and United States, 9, 146, 148, 152, 156, 160, 195, 307, 349
Somali army, 147
Somaliland, 146, 147

Somali National Alliance, 193
Somali National Movement (SNM), 147
Somali Salvation Democratic Front (SSDF), 147
Soto, Alvaro de, 201–2, 279, 280
Soto, Hernando de, 340
South Africa, 80, 317
South Mogadishu, 156
South-West Africa People's Organization (SWAPO), 317
sovereignty, 1, 7, 8, 11, 14, 144, 189, 219, 221, 314, 320, 327–28
Spain, 306
Special Panel for the Investigation of Serious Crimes in the Dili District, 255
spoilers, 28, 29, 57–58, 59, 60, 112. See also factions
Srebenica, 167, 171, 184, 187
Sri Lanka, 43, 80
Stabilization Force (SFOR), 238, 240, 242, 330
stalemate, 57, 65, 305; in Angola, 305; in El Salvador, 201, 203, 206, 305, 323; and hostility, 82; and transitional authority, 321
state: consent to limited sovereignty by, 314; decentralized, 39; failed, 7, 15, 22, 158, 160, 301, 308, 310; and Leviathan, 18, 29, 153, 338; protection of individual by, 32; strength vs. weakness of, 33, 34
State of Cambodia (SOC), 211, 217, 219, 220, 307, 315, 317, 325, 326, 327
Stedman, Stephen, 58
Stoltenberg, Thorvald, 163
Sudan, 66, 80, 348
Suharto, Haji Mohamed, 246
Supreme National Council (SNC), 218–19, 220, 311, 327–28, 350
Supreme Revolutionary Council (SRC), 146
SWAPO. See South-West Africa People's Organization
Sweden, 270
Syria, 14, 80

Tajikistan, 80, 322
Taliban, 339, 340
Tanzania, 184, 287, 300
Thailand, 80, 217, 218, 221, 306
third-party interventions, 60, 114, 131

Timorese Democratic Union (UDT), 243
Timor Gap, 252
Tito, Josip Broz, 163
Touval, Saadia, 304
transitional administration, 84, 158, 160,
171, 224, 225, 249; in Brcko, 237, 238,
239; in Cambodia, 213, 214, 218, 315,
328; in East Timor, 248, 249, 254; and
multidimensional peacekeeping, 199;
numbers of considered, 88; and peacebuilding success, 109; and peace enforcement, 66; in Somalia, 157, 158, 160. See
also government
transitional authority, 63–64, 67, 319–33;
appropriate levels of, 335; Boutros-Ghali
on, 350; in Cambodia, 218, 219, 327;
and constitution, 341; design of, 311; in
dynamic peacekeeping, 311; in Eastern
Salvonia, 330; in East Timor, 256; in El
Salvador, 324, 331; and factions,
321–22; need for, 5; and peace agreement implementation, 197; in Somalia,
153, 333
transitional strategy, 63–64, 69, 319
Treaty of Guarantee, 271
truce/cease-fire, 14, 15, 82, 83, 104,
218, 219
trust, 5, 43, 47, 52, 65, 66, 203, 324
Truth Commission (El Salvador), 202,
206, 324
Tshombe, Moise, 173, 178, 181, 186
Tudjman, Franjo, 227, 317–18, 330
Turkey, 80, 257, 258, 259, 261, 262, 263,
264, 266, 271, 273, 278, 279
Turkish Cypriots, 257, 259, 261, 262, 263,
264, 266, 268, 269, 271, 274, 275, 277,
278, 279, 280
Turkish Republic of Northern Cyprus
(TRNC), 258, 277, 279
Tutsis, 1, 285, 286–87, 288, 291, 295,
296, 299, 301, 302

Uganda, 81, 286
UNAMIR. See United Nations Assistance
Mission for Rwanda
UNAVEM. See United Nations Angola
Verification Mission
UNESCO, 232
UNFICYP. See United Nations Force in
Cyprus
Union Miniere du Haut Katanga, 173

Union for the Total Independence of Angola (UNITA), 43, 305
United Kingdom, 12, 81; and Cambodia,
305; and Cyprus, 257, 258, 271; and
East Timor, 256; and former Yugoslavia,
306; and Iraq, 341; and Malayan
insurgency, 192; on Security Council,
9; and Sierra Leone, 318; and
UNPROFOR, 192
United Nations: and command and control, 189; and Congo, 172, 174, 175,
180; and Cyprus, 258, 280; and dataset,
119–22; Department of Economic and
Social Affairs, 344; Department of
Peacekeeping Operations, 295, 344; Department of Political Affairs, 344; and
development agencies, 343; Development Program, 247, 344; in East Timor,
2, 246; and economy, 335; and enforcement coalitions, 2; failures of, 1; and Independent Inquiry into the Actions of
the United Nations during the 1994
Genocide in Rwanda, 292; and institutional reconstruction, 314; legitimacy of,
114; legitimizing role of, 348; limitations
of, 304; member states of, 350–51; and
multilateralism, 5, 189, 195–96, 318;
and national interests, 191; and Neutral
International Force, 289; new interventionism of, 1, 6–10; organization of,
344; Peacebuilding Commission, 344;
peacekeeping budget of, 6, 345, 350;
and peace treaties, 103–4; planning staff
of, 189; rapid reaction force for, 347; in
Rwanda, 283, 284; as scapegoat, 62,
189; in Somalia, 284; strategic failures
of, 184, 185–96; success of, 5, 197; technical capacities of, 114; and temporary
sovereignty, 2; war-making by, 5, 185,
196. See also military, United Nations;
Secretariat; Secretary-General; Security
Council; specific operations
United Nations Angola Verification Mission (UNAVEM), 328, 332
United Nations Assistance Mission in East
Timor (UNAMET), 247
United Nations Assistance Mission for
Rwanda (UNAMIR), 257, 289–302; authority of, 332; force strength of, 282,
289, 292, 295, 297–98, 299, 300; logistics of, 292; mandate of, 282, 284,

289–91, 292, 294, 296, 297, 299; planning of, 297; resources of, 296, 301; rules of engagement of, 291, 294; as undersourced, 284–85

United Nations Charter: Article 2, clause 7, 7; Article 25, 16; Article 42, 16; Article 43, 16; Chapter 6, 84; Chapter 6 and 1/2, 219, 220; Chapter VI, 13, 17, 84, 111, 311, 320; Chapter VII, 1, 7, 10, 11, 15, 17, 151, 160, 167, 248, 297, 311, 314, 316, 320; Chapter VIII, 17; design of, 11

United Nations Emergency Force (UNEF), 12

United Nations Force in Cyprus (UNFICYP), 257, 258, 266–80, 292; and Civilian Police, 270; command structure of, 271; financing problems of, 272; force strength of, 269; mandate of, 261, 262, 267, 268–69, 271, 272–73, 277, 279

United Nations High Commissioner for Refugees (UNHCR), 188, 216, 219, 232, 252–53, 269, 270

United Nations Interim Administration Mission in Kosovo (UNMIK), 190

United Nations International Police Task Force, 232, 233–34

United Nations Mission in Bosnia and Herzegovina (UNMIBH), mandate of, 233–34

United Nations Mission in the Democratic Republic of Congo (MONUC), 190, 332

United Nations Mission in Haiti (UNMIH), 332

United Nations Mission of Observers in Tajikistan (UNMOT), 332

United Nations Mission for the Referendum in Western Sahara (MINURSO), 332

United Nations Mission for Rwanda (UNAMIR), mandate of, 281, 283

United Nations Mission in Sierra Leone (UNAMSIL), 190

United Nations Mission of Support in East Timor (UNMISET), 253, 254; mandate of, 253, 254

United Nations Observer Group in Central America (ONUCA), 17, 201

United Nations Observer Mission in El Salvador (ONUSAL), 209, 322, 324; authority of, 331, 332; force strength of,

203, 204; mandate of, 203, 205, 207–8; success of, 199

United Nations Observer Mission in Georgia (UNOMIG), 332

United Nations Observer Mission in Liberia (UNOMIL), 332

United Nations Observer Mission in Sierra Leone (UNOMSIL), 332

United Nations Operations in Mozambique (ONUMOZ), 199, 325, 332

United Nations Operations in Somalia (UNOSOM), 184, 187, 195

United Nations Operations in Somalia (UNOSOM) I, 153, 155, 156, 332; mandate of, 148, 157–58, 160

United Nations Operations in Somalia (UNOSOM) II, 149–51, 155, 156, 184; authority of, 332; coordination in, 187; force strength of, 154, 185; logistics of, 154; mandate of, 149, 150–51, 153, 154, 158, 160, 284; and UNITAF, 346

United Nations Protection Force (UNPROFOR), 17, 284; accomplishments of, 168, 169, 184; authority of, 332; failures of, 184, 185; force strength of, 166, 169, 170; information problems of, 186; mandate of, 161, 162, 164, 165–67, 169, 191–92; and military-civilian coordination, 187

United Nations Transitional Administration in Eastern Slavonia (UNTAES), 171, 228–29, 317–18; authority of, 330, 331, 332; force strength of, 226; mandate of, 224–25, 226, 227, 228; success of, 199; transitional administrator of, 227, 228–29

United Nations Transitional Administration in East Timor (UNTAET), 251, 252, 253; authority of, 330; mandate of, 248–50; staff of, 190; success of, 199

United Nations Transitional Authority in Cambodia (UNTAC), 2, 204, 212, 213, 215–16; authority of, 328, 331, 332; Civilian Police Component (CIVPOL), 216, 219; delayed implementation of, 309; and elections, 317; failures of, 222; force strength of, 210, 216, 219; and Friends of Secretary General, 305–6; Human Rights Component, 216; Information/Education Division, 216–17,

UNTAC (*continued*)
219; mandate of, 211, 214, 219–20,
222–23, 313; Military Component, 216,
219–20; and multilateralism, 220–21;
Rehabilitation Component, 216; Repa-
triation Component, 216; success of,
199, 211
United Nations Transitions Assistance
Group (UNTAG), 332
United Nations Verification Mission in
Guatemala (MINUGUA), 332
United Somali Congress (USC), 147
United States: and African Crisis Response
Initiative, 347; and Bosnia, 307, 348;
and Cambodia, 217, 218, 220, 221,
305, 326, 339; and Cold War, 22; and
Congo, 175, 178, 179, 181, 194; and
Cyprus, 258, 271, 280; and Dayton
Agreements, 230–31; and Eastern Slavonia, 223, 228; and East Timor, 244, 256;
and El Salvador, 201, 209, 305, 306,
323; ethnic cleansing in, 235; and for-
mer Yugoslavia, 156, 162, 167, 306; and
Friends of the Secretary-General, 307–8;
and Iraq, 341; mission leadership success
of, 195; and multilateralism, 9; national
interests of, 191; need for, 5; power of,
9; and Rwanda, 184, 191, 292, 293,
298, 307, 308; on Security Council, 9;
and Somalia, 9, 146, 148, 152, 156,
160, 195, 307, 349; and UNAMIR,
289, 297; and UN budget, 345; and
UNPROFOR, 192; and USSR, 201; and
Vietnam, 193, 196
United States Central Command (CENT-
COM), 149
United States civil war, 1n, 338
United States Congress, 2
United States Rangers, 187
United Task Force (UNITAF), 17, 150,
151, 152, 153–54, 156, 160, 184, 346;
mandate of, 148–49, 157–58, 160
UNMISET. *See* United Nations Mission of
Support in East Timor
UNTAC. *See* United Nations Transitional
Authority in Cambodia
UNTAES. *See* United Nations Transitional
Authority in Eastern Slavonia
Urquhart, Sir Brian, 144, 187, 347

USSR, 81; and Afghanistan, 193, 196; and
Cambodia, 217, 304, 305, 327; and
Cold War, 22; and Congo, 145, 175,
177, 178, 179, 182, 194; in El Salvador,
323; and Somalia, 146; and United
States, 201. *See also* Russia
U Thant, 178

Vance, Cyrus, 163, 168
Varosha, 278
Vassilou, George, 280
Venezuela, 201, 306
victimization, fear of, 38, 49
Vieira de Mello, Sergio, 248, 250, 256
Vietnam, 81, 213, 215, 217, 307, 326,
327, 339
Vietnam War, 326
violence, 45–46, 74
Vukovar, 224, 229

Wahlgren, Lars-Eric, 167n
war crimes, 56, 66, 341; in Brcko, 235; in
Eastern Slavonia, 229; in Rwanda, 291;
and UNTAES, 224. *See also* ethnic
cleansing; genocide; massacre
Weber, Max, 320
West Pakistan, 98
West Sahara, 79, 322
West Timor, 243, 252, 253
World Bank, 220, 247, 251–52, 287,
341, 344

Yemen, 81
Yemen Arab Republic, 81
Yemen Peoples Republic, 81
Yugoslavia, former, 16, 81, 161–71, 184,
187, 236; arms embargo of, 168; ethnic-
ity in, 38; and Friends of the Secretary-
General, 306; humanitarian assistance
to, 8; local capacities in, 66, 227; peace
enforcement in, 16–17; and United
States, 156. *See also* Bosnia; Brcko;
Croatia; Eastern Slavonia (Croatia); Re-
publika Srpska

Zaire, 179, 184, 286, 299, 300
Zartman, I. William, 30
Zepa, 171
Zimbabwe, 81